Ethnic
Chicago

Ethnic Chicago

REVISED AND EXPANDED

Edited by
**MELVIN G. HOLLI
& PETER d'A. JONES**

Grand Rapids, Michigan
WILLIAM B. EERDMANS PUBLISHING COMPANY

FOR
Flight Sergeant Brian A. Jones
who never got to America

AND

Sylvia Erickson Holli
whose family knew something of
the immigrant epic

Copyright © 1977, 1981, 1984 by Wm. B. Eerdmans Publishing Company
255 Jefferson Ave. S.E., Grand Rapids, MI 49503

Chapters II, VI, VIII, IX, X, and XI originally appeared in The Ethnic
Frontier, *ed. Melvin G. Holli and Peter d'A. Jones (1977). Ethnic Chicago*
was originally published in 1981; this revised and expanded edition
published 1984.

Library of Congress Cataloging in Publication Data
Main entry under title:
Ethnic Chicago.
Includes index.
1. Minorities—Illinois—Chicago—Addresses, essays,
lectures. 2. Chicago (Ill.)—Ethic relations—Addresses,
essays, lectures. 1. Jones, Peter d'Alroy.
II. Holli, Melvin G.
F548.9.A1E85   305.8'009773'11   81-574
ISBN 0-8028-1807-2   AACR2

Contents

THE MELTING POT

List of Illustrations, Maps, and Charts

Introduction

PETER d'A. JONES and MELVIN G. HOLLI
The Ethnic in Chicago

> *America is God's crucible, the great Melting-Pot where all the races of Europe are melting and reforming! . . . Germans and Frenchmen, Irishmen and Englishmen, Jews and Russians—into the Crucible with you all! God is making the American.*
>
> —Israel Zangwill, *The Melting Pot*, 1908

> *The common language of the commonwealth, the language of its great political tradition, is English, but each nationality expresses its emotional and voluntary life in its own language, in its own inevitable aesthetic and intellectual forms.*
>
> —Horace M. Kallen, *"Democracy Versus the Melting Pot,"* 1915

> *Both the Americanization and federation of nationalities theories presume too much to "fix" conditions; the one would make the citizen conform to the nature of a mythical Anglo-Saxon, and the other to harmonize with the soul assumed to reside in the ethnos.*
>
> —Isaac B. Berkson, *Theories of Americanization*, 1920

H ISTORY OFFERS VERY FEW CLEAR, SIM-
ple moral battles. *Ethnic* history is no exception. We have sought to
avoid those simplistic, too easily grasped, polarized scenarios such as
"black" versus "white," "WASP" versus "ethnic," "host" society versus
"immigrant," in favor of a more sophisticated and realistic approach.

What we might term "ethnic democracy" in a multicultural, ideologically egalitarian society such as ours emerges only with painful
slowness over the years—as group after group jockeys for position.
Some true sense of pluralism, or acceptance of many differences,
emerges from struggles both *external* and *internal* to ethnic groups,
and from tensions between and among a great variety of such groups.
The bipolar, adversary model simply does not fit.

Ethnic history is not a mere local argument or dialectic, a battle for
"freedom" and against "prejudice." The richness and variety of ethnic
life is obscured and ignored by such a vision. We seek an ethnic history
for its own sake, a richly detailed and informing portrait, warts and all,
of various ethnic communities, their values, social structures, inner dynamics, and everyday lifestyles. For example, most of us would recognize the indefensibility of a distinction between "host" and
"immigrant" in our society, given the overwhelming number of immigrants and their varying origins over time. But other lessons have
been more difficult to grasp.

Consider the fact that the immigrant almost nowhere faced the
mythical WASP (White Anglo-Saxon Protestant). The mainstream
American culture, which had been forged long before the immigrants
arrived (those of the 1880s, '90s, and 1900s), was a product of English,
Scotch-Irish, Irish, Welsh, Dutch, Swedish, American Indians, blacks,
Germans, and so many more people that it belies the title "Anglo-
Saxon." Present-day writers who complain about the immigrants being
forced to conform to the Anglo-Saxon mold do violence to the historic
truth. The mainstream culture was not the Anglo-Saxon, Puritan culture—but an already *melted* culture. The immigrants found that they
would fit into America, with all its faults (and there were many).

Public education was a cherished institution that they loved. Said
Mary Antin, who came from Russia as a child, "Father himself conducted us to the school. He would not have delegated that mission to

2

the President of the United States." Michael Pupin emigrated to the United States from a Serb village when he was nineteen in 1874. He became a famous inventor and a professor of electromagnetics at Columbia University. He said of his college experience:

> "when American college boys . . . elected for class president the penniless son of a Serbian peasant village, because they admire his mental and physical efforts . . . one can rest assured that the spirit of American democracy was very much alive in those college boys."

Pupin kept alive Serbian attributes—such as language and the Serbian Orthodox Church. He never forgot that he was Serbian.

Other lessons have been difficult to grasp, too: the fact of divisions and tensions *within* ethnic groups (Poles or Jews for instance), or the fact that you cannot speak about "the" black, "the" white, "the" Indian, "the" Jew, or "the" Catholic in American history. The inner complexity of each group is more readily comprehended nowadays. In the present age of ethnic revival and neonationalism the old idea of the Melting Pot, with its assumption (usually unspoken) that the newcomers would melt into an Anglo-Saxon matrix, is an inept metaphor. The immigrants did not "melt" in the expected manner. But "melt" they did, insofar as the American culture was concerned. They all became Americans, while being some other nationality.

So value conflict and adjustment, rejection, alienation, and mediation have been and are the major themes of ethnic history. America has been a cauldron of values.

This volume combines some of the essays of THE ETHNIC FRONTIER (1977) with those of ETHNIC CHICAGO (1981) to make a compact study of ethnic Chicago. A richly detailed and informing portrait, the essays are structured around the continuing national debate over Cultural Pluralism and the Melting Pot. These original essays were commissioned specifically for these books, and are the product of long years of careful and thorough research by seasoned scholars and respected authorities of their various ethnic groups. Frequently revisionist, often evocative, and consistently informative, these selections capture in America's heartland city, Chicago, a microsocial view of the national ethnic processes of adjustment, survival, identity, and even melting into the American Melting Pot.

Cultural Pluralism

In the opening chapter, Michael F. Funchion deals succinctly with the formative years of Irish culture in Chicago and suggests importantly

that the classic "ghetto hypothesis" does not apply. The "Famine" Irish
had come with a love of Ireland, a hatred of England, and their Catholic
religion as their main resources. Beginning as humble canal diggers
and laborers, these sons of the Emerald Isle soon came to dominate the
"Irish trinity" of American urban life: the priesthood, the police, and
(as Paul M. Green shows in another chapter) politics. Every Chicago
bishop from 1847 to 1916 with one exception was Irish; the police force
was disproportionately Irish by the 1890s; and every mayor of Chicago
since 1933 with two exceptions has been of Irish Catholic heritage.
Ironically, some of their success in American life may be attributed to
Anglo oppression, whereby the English had Anglicized the Irish to a
point where they could become the leaders of the newcomers. With
the language of "perfidious Albion" and a goodly store of native wit,
the Irish went on to conquer the American city, introducing and leading
their often less fortunate co-religionists from Europe toward the American mainstream. The Irish had yet another advantage which Funchion
wryly points out: they can get in touch with their roots much easier
than most other third-generation Americans because they speak the
language of their ancestors (and for that the English are responsible).

The first of two Jewish chapters is Edward Mazur's analysis of
Sephardic Jews and the Jews from Eastern Europe. Jews passed through
a period of adjustment when settled (mainly German and Ashkenazic)
Jews found themselves facing mass immigration of Yiddish-speaking,
synagogue-building, religiously conservative—and sometimes politically radical—Jews from Poland, Hungary, Romania, Russia, and elsewhere, the so-called "Orientals." Mazur describes the building of the
first Chicago Jewish community in the pre–Civil War years.

The big challenges, moreover, were still to come, with the arrival
of East European Jews in large numbers beginning in the 1880s. Unlike the German Jews, the newcomers were entering a Chicago which
was by now a fully developed industrial and commercial metropolis,
and they served the machine economy as factory hands and tailors.
They created the ghetto and labor organizations; they brought with
them the Yiddish theater and a street life of their own. Professor Mazur
illustrates the tensions between these *Ostjuden* and the older, settled
Jewish communities in the city, as well as the changing residential
patterns of Jews, before examining the consequences of this division
for politics.

One man managed to straddle the Jewish groups and produce a
more or less unified constituency for himself: Henry Horner, a Chicago-
born lawyer and probate court judge, was governor of Illinois from
1933 until his death in 1940. Horner's ability to fashion a unified constituency and his various political achievements throw light on the

nature of ethnic politics in general, as well as the role of political brokers.

In the second chapter dealing with the Jews, Irving Cutler chronicles with authority and marvelous visual evidence the progress of Chicago's Jews from shtetl to suburb. The mapping and photo documentation add a special dimension to the text. Cutler intertwines into the narrative exemplary ghetto successes—Benny Goodman, Paul Muni, Arthur Goldberg, and Julius Rosenwald. Jews worked hard and within a generation were at the upper reaches of occupational and income achievement. Jewish socialism, once a heady and feisty idea in the ghetto, vanished a victim of the high individual achievements of the group. Jews created their own worldly utopias, not through Karl Marx, but through education, occupation, and high income. Yet it was not all work. As Cutler shows, a colorful street life, an active theater, and even a Chicago version of a "borscht belt" resort grew and flourished. From shtetl to suburb is an important dimension of that urban epic.

Polish Chicago, with the Pope and the troubles in Poland, seems to reflect an age-old problem with an American ethnic group: how to be "American" and still be "Polish." Edward R. Kantowicz, in his insightful and original study of the survival of Chicago's large Polish community, has selected one of the most culturally bonded, in-group peoples to be found anywhere. In Europe, Poles survived as Poles over many decades when there was politically no Polish nation. This deep, tenacious attitude toward national identity the Poles brought with them to America and did not lose in the streets of Chicago or Milwaukee. Thus Kantowicz's theme is "Survival Through Solidarity."

Yet there is a price to pay for a group's singlemindedly internalizing its energies. The Poles of Chicago achieved a greater sense of wholeness than most ethnic groups, no doubt; but, as Professor Kantowicz indicates, the cost was a diminished influence in the wider non-Polish community. Building from within, Polish Americans created a solid Polonia, a nation within a nation, on the basis of their churches, their superb building and loan associations, their parochial schools, and their fraternal associations. Even the major division within the group—between the nationalists and religionists—was milder than splits within comparable groups, such as Lithuanians and Bohemians. (Here, as throughout his chapter, the author makes cross-ethnic comparisons, noting for example that Italians, unlike Poles, were content to use the public school system.) The price Poles paid for commitment to separate treatment within the Catholic Church, and their insistence on Polish priests and parishes, for example, was low general influence in the higher levels of the Church, which lacked Polish leaders. The same was true in the secular realm of city, and for that matter state and national, politics. There are lessons here, as Professor Kantowicz suggests, not only for future Polish-American leaders but for other ethnic groups as well.

For the Greek-Americans, Andrew T. Kopan presents the story of Greek survival through education, an ethnic odyssey that challenges much of the conventional wisdom about ethnics and puts in print for the first time for a larger audience the extraordinary entrepreneurial aspect of this group. Chicago's Hellene immigrants were no "Golden Greeks" with great means, but were humble, rural folk who came to America with neither urban skills nor educations. Yet the drive to succeed was expressed by these extraordinarily enterprising folk, for by 1920 some 10,000 were self-employed, mostly in small businesses in Chicago.

A second important theme underscored by Professor Kopan is that Chicago's Greeks appeared to have reversed the natural process of language deterioration in the second generation. Because of a poor homeland school system Chicago's first-generation Greeks had a relatively high illiteracy rate (27 percent); yet the second generation, through after-school programs and church schools, often developed a more fluent command of the language than their parents. Due to the effective use of private and public education and such an enterprising spirit, the Greeks in our time stand near the very top rungs of the education, occupation, and income ladder. But in spite of these signal successes, as Kopan points out, the Greeks were not swallowed up by the vastness of America; rather, they retained important components of their ethnicity such as their language.

Chicago's Ukrainians are a fascinating people with their own special and often poignant cultural resonances, but they are also a very poorly understood group. Filling in this lacuna in the historical record, Myron B. Kuropas, a former White House Ethnic Adviser to President Gerald Ford, examines the Ukrainian identity crisis and the political struggle here for an independent overseas homeland. Following a time-tested pattern that Poles, Bohemians, and others had employed during World War I, Ukrainians tried to use the United States as an important base for launching an independent state of Ukraine in the Soviet Union. But alas, times had changed and the pendulum of history no longer swung to the tune of self-determination as it had in Woodrow Wilson's time. Utilizing European political models led to disappointment. The Ukrainian nationalist movement in the United States was unfairly tainted and smeared, linked by its detractors to national socialism then rising in Germany in the 1930s. Even so, Ukrainians triumphed over these adversities and realized one of their primary goals: the assertion both in the United States and abroad of a clear title to being a distinctive ethno-cultural people with a strong sense of nationhood. In this effort the Chicago and American host played an important role, for as Kuropas aptly puts it, "For many a Ukrainian emigre the United States was not an ethnic melting pot but rather, a school for his ethno-national development."

Dominic Candeloro's discussion of suburban Italians illustrates the theme that not all of the newcomers were "birds of passage" or trapped in the ghettos of the inner city. In Chicago Heights the sons and grand-sons of Italy created a cozy blue-collar suburb where they realized many of their objectives for emigrating and where they achieved po-litical recognition and some control over the pace at which they wished to enter American life.

A pioneer scholar of Chicano America, Louise Año Nuevo Kerr, has written the study of Mexican Chicago in a period when Chicano assimilation was aborted, during the 1940s. As part of her broader work on the Chicago Chicano community, Kerr offers a special study here of how the assimilation process for Chicanos was aborted during World War II and the immediate postwar years. The large influx of *bracero* workers from Mexico brought by government agreement and induced by industrial and railroad recruiting, the subsequent split between these *braceros* and Chicanos long settled in the city, and the emergence of more overt prejudice against "Mexicans" in general during the war years were the historical forces aborting assimilation. Professor Kerr shows that with the coming of peace, the previously solicitous official attitude toward *braceros* faded and the program was phased out. Even so the number of Chicanos in Chicago continued to grow, as legal immigrants and growing numbers of "illegals" swelled the numbers of early residents and ex-*braceros* who managed to stay. Ethnic tensions in Chicago produced surveys and projects concerning the Chicanos, including the Mexican Social Center, which opened in 1945. Yet, Kerr concludes, after a decade of activity in which Chicanos had looked beyond the limits of their settlements in Chicago toward each other, and outwards toward assimilation with the larger community, the pro-cess faltered and waned.

The argument summarized here has some very interesting impli-cations, and Professor Kerr's essay contains much more: there are com-parisons among Chicanos, Poles, and Italians of income and education in the city, and hints of areas where future research will be needed, such as the recent trend of direct immigration from Mexico and Texas to the suburbs—an idea with striking implications.

That Chicano assimilation was aborted during the 1940s and 1950s is an interesting fact, which takes us to the second of two categories under which we group the essays.

The Melting Pot

The first essay under the Melting Pot heading is Jacqueline Peterson's study of the French-Indian founding fathers of Chicago. Peterson's fluent and evocative portrait of frontier Chicago skillfully describes a microsocial history of the founding families, their homes, occupations, systems of social status, concerns, and lifestyles. This study provides us with a unique picture of an early frontier settlement under the profit-seeking aegis of the American Fur Company. Many sorts of folk were tolerated and accepted: Indians, French, Anglos, *métis*, and other mixed-bloods. For a few brief frontier years, the society was casually multiracial. Then this mixed culture vanished under the impact of an invasion of Americanizing Yankees. The newcomers, with their built-in, inner-directed sense of linear "progress," their capacity for deferred gratification, and their readiness, as Peterson puts it, to "cheat the present," swept everything before them. The clash of values proved too much for a premodern folk, and some of the refugees trekked westward to the Indian reservations. Others fled to remote trapping outposts to insulate themselves from change; and some were absorbed and "melted" into the majority culture.

Our chapters on black Chicagoans are included under the Melting Pot because the historic aspirations of blacks* have been to integrate, assimilate, and enter into the American mainstream. Admittedly, the back-to-Africa movement of the 1920s and the black power and black Muslim movements of the 1960s seem to contradict that goal. Yet those movements involved but a small fraction of blacks, and have less historic force or trajectory behind them than the century-long quest to enter into the mainstream. In politics, blacks wanted to be part of the system. In housing, they wished to integrate. The fact that the barriers of race often impeded such advances does not invalidate their intent. The long-term historic, black direction, then, has not been toward cultural pluralism or separatism, but rather in the opposite direction, to-

---

*We have adopted the lower case "b" for "black" in this book. Nothing is intended by this except convenience (considering the great number of times the word appears) and avoidance of the need to capitalize "white" also. The editors believe people should be called what they want to be called, according to their own spelling; in the matter of capitalization of "black," there seems to be no consensus at present among black Americans.

ward integration and assimilation—steps that lead toward a figurative, if not literal, Melting Pot.

In contrast to the separatism of the Polish community, most black Americans in Chicago, during the years before the Great Migration of World War I and the 1920s, would have chosen as much local and national political influence and integration as they could win—if circumstances and white politics had permitted. Charles Branham describes and explains the nature of black politics and the choices open to would-be leaders in Chicago at this time. From John Jones, the first black American to hold public office in Illinois, down to Edward H. Wilson, politician of the early 1900s, leaders stood—in varying degrees—for accommodationist politics, for working within the system, following party needs and "delivering the goods," particularly at election time. Blacks generally chose to work within the system; but the system paid them less.

Professor Branham's much-needed research on black politics in Chicago between Reconstruction and the Great Migration not only fills a gap in our knowledge of black history for that period, describes the considerable political activity among black Americans, portrays some of their leaders, and indicates the issues with which they were concerned; it also illustrates the abiding faith in America which so many blacks have maintained throughout the worst years of trial and doubt.

The Great Migration of blacks from the deep South brought to Chicago an ethnic conflict for housing which was one of the worst problems that any community had to face. Arnold Hirsch, an imaginative and resourceful young scholar, selects an allegedly "quiescent" period of Chicago history (1940-1960) to illustrate the continuing struggle: the existence during that period of persistent, day-to-day tension and sometimes unrecorded violence over housing. Can we see in these battles over living space a radically transformed—but ancient—peasant land-hunger, the residue of a half-forgotten past that continues to express itself in terms of ethnic and neighborhood solidarity? One is tempted to find atavistic remnants in these struggles, which were begun and carried on by the descendants of European immigrants (WASP names are noticeably absent in the riots). What Hirsch uncovers is a broad community participation in housing "riots"; according to the evidence he marshals, these were not disturbances created or led by "outside agitators" but were communal protests in defense of the neighborhood against undesired "intruders" and would-be settlers.

The unfamiliar role of the press in those days—imposing what sometimes amounted to a virtual news blackout on items of racial violence—was in strong contrast to the media role in the riotous 1960s and later. The well-known riot analyses of the late sixties and the official studies of urban violence always emphasized the role of young unmarried males. Hirsch, in contrast, finds women playing roles during the earlier period, children joining in as aides, and older people fully participating, in what he terms "a grim parody of a community sing," such as the 1949 disturbance at Park Manor. Insofar as whites were successful during the late forties and fifties in excluding blacks from preferred housing, white violence paid: was this a direct lesson for the bigger disturbances of the 1960s?

The Melting Pot has laid claim to a sizable segment of the nation's ethnic population, including one of the largest of our heritage groups, the Catholic Irish. One of the factors that led Chicago's Irish toward greater assimilation was the multi-ethnic road to political machine success, the subject of Paul Michael Green's insightful essay. The give-and-take and compromise of American urban politics is where the Irish excelled, and they often became the teachers of their co-religionists who had fled nondemocratic and authoritarian political cultures and lacked even a rudimentary knowledge of democratic politics. Yet great as they were as teachers of American urban ways, the Chicago Irish also had some lessons to learn, as Green's important revisionist essay establishes. Chicago's Democratic party in the early twentieth century was not unified under strong party discipline as was New York's Tammany, but was instead more like the Boston organization under J. Michael Curley. This fractured political organization was bedeviled by a plethora of mini-machines squabbling for pelf and place. Chicago's Democracy was a loosely knit Balkan treaty organization of Irish fiefdoms, a patchwork quilt of uncoordinated parts fighting fratricidal inside wars for control and boodle until Bohemian-born Anton Cermak appeared on the scene in 1931. As Green so vividly presents it, it required a "Bohunk pushcart" peddler, playing ethnic broker, to bring order out of the chaos and to put together a political machine that pulled the sons of Erin such as Kelly, Nash, Kennelly, and Daley down glory road and to political victory for the next half-century.

War has often forced far-reaching historic change, including more rapid melting into the Melting Pot. We see an example of that in Melvin G. Holli's probing essay into German-Americans, the nation's first great ethnic war victims—but not its last. German-Americans launched one of the best planned, directed, and financially supported propaganda campaigns for an overseas homeland ever registered in the United States until World War I. It was met by a powerful counter surge of Slavic nationalism in Chicago which helped to undo much of German-America's war effort to keep America neutral while the Fatherland punched out victory in Europe. Holli examines in depth the ethnic interaction of Poles, Bohemians, and other belligerent nationals in Chicago and questions the textbook truisms that purport to explain *Deutschtum's* fall. The foreign policy aims and domestic policy interests of Slavic ethnics and Americanizers coincided.

If Americanization is to be seen as a villain, then in Chicago it had Slavic and ethnic accomplices. This critically important *Kulturkampf*, or cultural crisis, has never been completely understood, as it is generally written off by civil libertarians as solely a product of war-time hysteria out of control, which it is not. As Holli's revisionist study shows, *Deutschtum's* fall from its most favored nation status was brought about in part by the bellicose behavior of German-Americans themselves. In the end, it was Kaiser Wilhelm's submarines that sank not only Allied shipping but America's *Deutschtum*. Fittingly, Chicago's best-known German cultural artifact is a captured submarine on display at the Museum of Science and Industry.

Like the Chicago Irish, the Japanese people in Chicago are on the way to assimilation. Like German-Americans, Japanese-Americans also had the misfortune of having an ancestral homeland that waged war against the United States. Japanese-American culture became a war victim, and as Masako Osako relates, World War II caught the Japanese-Americans in an equally unenviable position of being on the wrong side as enemy aliens. In a thoughtful chapter with some comparisons to Chinese-Americans, Osako examines how the pains of the relocation camp experience set the *Nisei* on the road to assimilation. It was through this vale of hardship and tears in the camps that the Japanese redirected their own culture—not toward rejection of America but toward absorption. Many were released during the war and dispersed throughout the nation to small colonies that had few marriage partners and cultural facilities. Having survived this trial, the *Nisei* soon emerged as the "model ethnics" (a phrase many dislike). Japanese-Americans seemingly assuaged the pains of rejection by vaulting up the education, occupation, and income scales with astonishing speed. The social engine behind that progress, according to Osako, is a strong family structure and a stress on hard work, discipline, and achievement. If discrimination depresses occupational success, the *Nisei* case offers little support for such arguments. In a provocative summary, Osako suggests that Japanese-Americans may be the first racial minority to integrate and assimilate biologically into the dominant white stock of America.

Chicago's ethnics, as seen in both *The Ethnic Frontier* and *Ethnic Chicago*, exemplify almost every aspect of the American ethnic experience—those whose cultures persisted in varying degrees such as Poles, Jews, Ukrainians, Greeks, and Mexicans, and in more attenuated form,

Italians; those whose cultures melted or were in the process of doing so—Irish, Germans, and Japanese; and those whose cultures vanished almost without a trace, as with the French-Indian *métis* and the triracial Ben Ishmael tribe.

Entering the Melting Pot by no means deprived ethnics from leaving a lasting impression on the city. The impact of Chicago's Germans on the city's industry and technology endures as does its influence on high culture, exemplified by Chicago's symphony orchestra. The Irish have shaped the character of Chicago's urban politics and the Catholic Church for what appears to be a long term, and the Japanese contribute at the upper levels in the professions. That is what the Melting Pot was all about. It never prescribed total destruction of newcomer culture (as some commentators mistakenly believed).[1]

Israel Zangwill, who did more to popularize the Melting Pot metaphor than anyone, with his 1908 melodrama of that name, turned to music for the source of another metaphor. The young Russian-Jewish hero of his play, David Quixano, yearned to write the "great American symphony." As an amalgamationist (albeit temporarily), Zangwill meant this to imply that the instruments of the orchestra blend together as one voice. It is interesting and ironic that Zangwill's major intellectual opponent, Horace Kallen, champion of "cultural pluralism" and ethnic separatism, also turned to music for his metaphor, speaking of a possible "orchestration of mankind." Presumably, in his orchestration each musical instrument would maintain the integrity of its separate sound and identity.

One image, two opposing lessons: assimilation or fragmentation, melting pot or cultural pluralism. But Americans cannot seek aid in metaphors, however fitting or clever they may be. The Founding Fathers were genuinely confused about America's ethnic future, and though they agreed to admit all and sundry, they had no way of realizing in what great numbers the immigrants would come and how this would transform America. We have still not made up our minds: we fluctuate between separatism and "Americanization," between "desegregation" and "Black Power," between antidiscrimination laws and fears of "affirmative discrimination." The cauldron of American values bubbles on.

Perhaps we should leave the final word in this Introduction to Israel Zangwill. He defended his metaphor in this way in 1914 (when the shadow of the First World War was looming over Europe):

> The process of American amalgamation is not assimilation or simple surrender to the dominant type, as is popularly supposed, but an all-around give-and-take by which the final type may be enriched or impoverished.[2]

CULTURAL PLURALISM

Chapter I

MICHAEL F. FUNCHION

Irish Chicago:
Church, Homeland, Politics, and Class—The Shaping of an Ethnic Group, 1870-1900

*The country has survived the Irish emigration—
the worst with which any other country was ever
afflicted. The Irish fill our prisons, our reform
schools, our hospitals. . . . Scratch a convict or
a pauper and the chances are that you tickle the
skin of an Irish Catholic . . . made a criminal or
a pauper by the priest and politician who have
deceived him and kept him in ignorance, in a
word, a savage, as he was born.*
      —Chicago Evening Post, 1868

*We are a distinctive historic people, and we have
done the Americans a great deal of good by coming to this country.*
      —John Fitzgibbon, *Chicago Irish Businessman*

THE IRISH FIRST CAME TO THE CHIcago region in large numbers in 1836, one year before the incorporation of the city.[1] Lured by promises of good wages and steady employment, scores of Irishmen—some with experience on eastern canals, others fresh off the boat—came to build the Illinois and Michigan Canal, an ambitious project designed to link Lake Michigan with the Illinois River. By the time the canal was completed in 1848, thousands of Irish laborers had left their picks and shovels and had moved to Chicago or to Bridgeport, the northeastern terminus of the canal which at that time was a village separate from Chicago. There, along with other Irish immigrants, they worked mainly as unskilled laborers in meat-packing plants, brickyards, and the like. By 1850, 6,096, or about 20 percent, of Chicago's inhabitants were Irish immigrants. During the next twenty years, as Chicago grew by leaps and bounds and emerged as the transportation, manufacturing, and commercial mecca of the Midwest, thousands more Irish arrived in the city seeking jobs and a better life than they had had back home. By 1870, almost 40,000 Irish natives were living in the city.[2]

During the last three decades of the nineteenth century, the Irishborn population continued to grow, although far more slowly than before. Between 1870 and 1900, the number of Irish immigrants in the city rose from 39,988 to 73,912, or by some 85 percent (see Table I), a substantial increase but not nearly so dramatic as the jump of 556 per-

TABLE I
IRISH-BORN IN CHICAGO, 1870–1900

	Number of Irish-born	Percent of Foreign-born Population	Percent of Total Population
1870	39,988	27.66%	13.37%
1880	44,411	21.68%	8.83%
1890	70,028	15.54%	6.37%
1900	73,912	12.59%	4.35%

Source: U.S., *Ninth Census, 1870,* Vol. I, "Population," pp. 386–391; *Tenth Census, 1880,* "Population," pp. 538–541; *Eleventh Census, 1890,* "Population," Part I, pp. 670–673; *Twelfth Census, 1900,* Vol. I, "Population," Part I, pp. 796–799.

cent that had occurred in the twenty years prior to 1870. The Irishborn, of course, were not the only Irish in Chicago. During the three decades after the Great Fire of 1871, the American-born Irish population expanded rapidly. By 1890, the first year in which the federal census listed the number of Chicagoans of foreign parentage, the Irish population, first and second generations included, totaled 183,844 (see Table II).[3] Of these, only 38 percent were immigrants, and ten years later the Irish-born represented even fewer—31 percent of the 237,478 Irish in the city. Among the adult population, it appears that until sometime during the 1890s, Irish immigrants outnumbered their American-born kinsmen.[4]

TABLE II
FIRST- AND SECOND-GENERATION IRISH IN CHICAGO, 1890–1900

	Number	Percent of Total Population
1890	183,844	16.72%
1900	237,478	13.98%

Source: U.S., *Eleventh Census, 1890*, "Population," Part I, pp. 708, 714, 720, 726, 728; *Twelfth Census, 1900*, Vol. 1, "Population," Part I, pp. 874–875, 882–883, 890–891, 898–899, 902–903.

Nonetheless, from the 1870s on, when a number of them began to reach maturity, the American-born children of immigrants played a significant role in the institutional life of Irish Chicago. Indeed, one of the factors that distinguishes the last three decades of the century from the previous period was the emergence of the second-generation Irish.[5] No statistics are available for the third generation; but considering the years of Irish immigration to the United States, it appears that up until 1900 the overwhelming majority were children. After that date, as a number of these children reached adulthood, Irish Chicago became a community dominated by three instead of two generations.

Compared to that of other cities, the Irish population of Chicago was impressive in size. In 1890, for example, only three American cities—New York, Philadelphia, and Brooklyn—had more Irish than did Chicago.[6] Yet within Chicago the Irish were a minority, and one that was declining relative to the total population (see Tables I and II). Both Germans and Americans of native parentage outnumbered the Irish; toward the end of the century the ratio of Germans to Irish was more than two to one in Chicago. And while other groups—Scandinavians, Poles, Bohemians, and Italians—were less numerous than the Irish, they were increasing at a faster rate.[7]

A minority in the city as a whole, the Irish were also a minority in most of the neighborhoods where they lived. In the decades after the Great Fire, most Irish lived on the South and West sides; except for a small area on the near North Side, they were only sparsely settled in the northern sections of the city. But despite their concentration on the South and West sides, relatively few Irish lived in real ethnic ghettos. The school census of 1884, for example, reveals that out of 303 census canvass districts in the city, the Irish formed a majority of the population in only eleven. Since these eleven districts contained only about 14 percent of the city's Irish, it meant that 86 percent of them lived in areas where they were in a minority.[8] Similarly, a study of the school census of 1898 shows that the Irish were the most dispersed of ten ethnic groups studied.[9] The historian, of course, must be careful not to exaggerate the significance of such dispersal. Geographical proximity to other groups, for example, did not necessarily lead to social interaction with them. This was particularly true when neighboring groups spoke different languages and attended different churches and schools. In fact, one could argue that proximity had the opposite effect: rubbing shoulders with a people of a different national background could often lead to increased resentment.

Though few lived in real ethnic ghettos, the late nineteenth-century Chicago Irish nonetheless formed a highly visible and relatively cohesive ethnic community. Like other immigrants, the Irish derived their sense of unity from a common religious and ethnic heritage, a heritage they preserved through certain key institutions. And like other immigrants, their basic cohesiveness was further strengthened by certain forces and conditions they encountered in Chicago.

Most important in maintaining a separate Irish identity was their Catholicism, which, like the Polish variety, was inextricably intertwined with their national consciousness. Ever since the Protestant Reformation, the ancient Anglo-Irish struggle had been religious as well as national. Even though recent research has shown that the pre-Famine Irish did not practice their religion as devoutly as we have commonly assumed,[10] centuries of religious persecution had ingrained in them a deep attachment to the Church of Rome, an attachment that usually remained strong after their arrival in America. And since the United States was an overwhelmingly Protestant nation, Catholicism was one of the chief factors that distinguished the Irish from other Americans.

Although the first Catholics in the frontier town of Chicago were mainly of French and French-Indian origin, these were overwhelmed in the late 1830s and 1840s by the large influx of Irish as well as German immigrants. Until the 1870s, the Catholic Church remained a predominantly Irish and German institution, with the Irish outnumbering the Germans.[11] Toward the end of the century, as the "new immigrants" arrived from southern and eastern Europe, the church became increasingly multiethnic, though as late as 1900 the Irish still formed the largest bloc of Catholics.

Because of their numerical superiority, and because the American hierarchy looked favorably on English-speaking prelates, the Irish dominated the ecclesiastical administration in Chicago throughout the nineteenth century. From the appointment of the first bishop, William Quarter, in 1844 until the death of Archbishop James Quigley in 1915, all the bishops of Chicago were either Irish-born or of Irish parentage, with the one exception of Bishop James Van De Velde, a Belgian who briefly presided over the diocese from 1849 to 1854. The Germans, the French, and later immigrants naturally resented this Irish domination. They demanded a greater voice in the administration of the diocese, and at times they even demanded the creation of separate dioceses for the various foreign-language groups. And yet, except for a schism among the Poles, the various immigrant groups remained within the Irish fold of Roman Catholicism.

For this the Irish bishops, whatever their shortcomings, deserve some credit. They did much to quell ethnic tensions in the church by permitting the establishment of separate or national parishes for the Germans and other non-English-speaking immigrants. Begun in the 1840s by Bishop Quarter, a native of County Offaly, this practice of creating national parishes was faithfully followed by his successors. By 1870, Chicago had nine national parishes besides the sixteen territorial ones which served English-speaking Catholics. And during the next thirty-odd years, when Bishop Thomas Foley (1870–1879) and Archbishop Patrick Feehan (1880–1902) presided over the diocese, sixty-three national churches, in addition to forty-seven territorial churches, were established. Feehan, an Irish immigrant from County Tipperary and the former bishop of Nashville, strongly emphasized the need for national parishes, believing that they were one of the best means of protecting the faith of non-English-speaking immigrants. The Germans and others obviously agreed with Feehan and praised him for his sensitivity to their needs.[12] One German Catholic editor remarked that "he has proven himself a truly Catholic prelate, guided by principle and zeal, regardless of national consideration."[13] And when he died in 1902, the *Chicago Tribune* lauded him for his "diplomatic handling of the Irish, German, Polish, Bohemian, French and Italian elements in the diocese."[14]

The system of national parishes not only helped to diffuse the po-

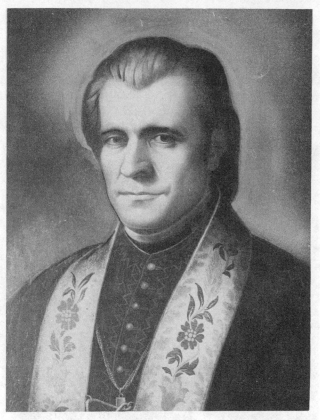

Bishop William J. Quarter, the first bishop of the Chicago Diocese. Beginning with Quarter in 1844 until the death of Archbishop James E. Quigley in 1915, all of the bishops (with one exception) were either Irish born or of Irish parentage. *Courtesy of the Chicago* CATHOLIC.

tential ethnic powderkeg in the church; it also effectively separated the Irish from other Catholics. Although in theory territorial parishes were not necessarily Irish, in practice they were, since virtually all English-speaking Catholics in Chicago were Irish. An Irishman attending mass or a parish function might occasionally meet a non-Irish Catholic, perhaps a convert, but by and large the only people he saw were fellow Irishmen. Thus membership in a universal church did little—at least at this time—to undermine Irish ethnic solidarity.

Just as in Ireland, the local parish played a central role in the lives of the people. Not only did it serve their religious needs, but it also provided a host of other services. Most pastors took a vital interest in the lives of their parishioners. For example, Father Maurice Dorney, pastor of the St. Gabriel parish in the Stockyards District from its es-

Archbishop James E. Quigley and his Irish-American predecessors had eased ethnic tensions in the church by permitting the establishment of separate — or national — parishes for non-English-speaking immigrants. Theoretically, this should have resulted in non-ethnic territorial parishes, but in reality they were predominantly Irish, since virtually all English-speaking Catholics in nineteenth-century Chicago were Irish. *Courtesy of the Chicago* CATHOLIC.

tablishment in 1880 until his death in 1914, was an extremely active figure in his community. He often provided food and fuel to the needy, found jobs for the unemployed, and at times served as an arbitrator in settling strikes and other labor disputes at the stockyards. Keenly aware of the particular evils of alcohol among his Irish flock, he campaigned against its abuse and was, in fact, successful in getting saloons removed from a small area of the Stockyards District.[15] Other priests might not have been as well known or as flamboyant as Dorney, but most shared with him a concern for the material as well as the spiritual welfare of their parishioners.

Affiliated with each parish was a variety of societies designed to meet the spiritual, social, and material needs of the parishioners. Some of these were linked with similar groups in other parishes through central organizations. Among the more common organizations were the St. Vincent de Paul Society, which tried to put the teachings of Christian charity into practice by helping the poor; the Catholic Total Abstinence Union of America, whose members completely abstained from alcohol; and the Catholic Order of Foresters, a mutual aid fraternity which provided assistance to its members in time of need.[16] Most parishes also had various sodalities, youth clubs, and the like; and, of course, there were the inevitable christenings, weddings, and funerals, where old friends could reminisce about the past or gossip about the present. All of these organizations and events helped to lighten the burdens of urban life and to bring the Irish into closer contact with one another.

Of all the institutions attached to a parish, probably the most important was the parochial school. Traditionally, the Catholic Church taught that religious instruction should be an integral part of a general education. To prepare a child for this life and forget about the next was, from the Catholic point of view, morally undesirable, to say the least. Throughout the nineteenth century the Catholic hierarchy in the United States had emphasized the need for Catholic schools. At the Third Plenary Council in Baltimore in 1884, for example, the bishops directed that every Catholic parish have a parochial school and that parents send their children to it.[17]

Yet Catholic educational philosophy was not the only reason behind the decision to build a parochial school system in Chicago. During the decades before 1870 the public schools in Chicago were not simply secular institutions; they were in fact quasi-Protestant schools. Practically all members of the Board of Education were Protestants; Protestants held a virtual monopoly on teaching positions; and the King James Bible was read in the classroom.[18] One Catholic newspaper no doubt typified the view of many Irish parents when it complained that Catholic children "are taught to feel ashamed of the creed of their forefathers."[19]

In the decades after 1870 this situation improved somewhat. Despite a storm of protest, Catholics, liberal Protestants, and others succeeded in getting the King James Bible banned from the classroom in 1875, and by the 1890s more and more Catholics were teaching in the public schools. Yet the schools continued to have a Protestant flavor. Protestants still dominated the Board of Education, and textbooks and other aspects of the curriculum seemed at times to present Catholicism in an unfavorable light.[20]

For these reasons the Irish developed their own parochial school system. By the late nineteenth century most Irish parishes had their own schools, which were attended probably by at least half of the Irish school-age children.[21] Staffed mainly by nuns and—to a lesser extent— brothers of Irish origin, these schools gave their students the standard elementary education, an understanding of the Catholic faith, and perhaps some appreciation for their Irish cultural heritage; and they instilled in them a loyalty toward the United States.

Clearly, the local parish, with its school and various societies, was the most important institution in Irish Chicago. It touched the lives of more Irishmen than did any other institution in the Irish community, for the overwhelming majority of Irish remained practicing Catholics. And while support for the church was an expression of a sincere religious commitment, it was also a manifestation of Irish ethnic identity. Finally, the point bears repeating that while devotion to the church was a legacy of their Irish heritage, it in turn did much to preserve that very heritage; paradoxically, the universal church brought the Irish closer together, by separating them not only from Protestant Chicagoans but from other Catholics as well.

Besides Catholicism, the second major force in the lives of the late nineteenth-century Chicago Irish was Irish nationalism. Like those in other parts of the United States, the Chicago Irish showed a deep and abiding interest in the political future of their homeland. As early as 1842, Chicago had a branch of Daniel O'Connell's Repeal Association, which sought to undo the union between Great Britain and Ireland through nonviolent agitation. After this movement collapsed, the Chicago Irish turned to various revolutionary groups. Of these, the most popular during the years before the Great Fire was the Fenian Brotherhood. Founded in New York in 1858, the Fenians sent money, arms, and men across the sea to the Irish Republican Brotherhood in an effort to help them overthrow British rule in Ireland. Although an uprising did take place in 1867, it ended in a dismal failure. Meanwhile, in

America the Fenians had split into two factions: one group wished to concentrate on military activity in Ireland, while the other advocated an invasion of Canada. The latter faction, known as the "Senate Wing," hoped a Canadian invasion would cause an Anglo-American war, which might possibly lead to the liberation of Ireland. Most Chicago Fenians supported the "Senate Wing," and a number of them, in fact, participated in a series of quixotic raids on Canada. These, like the uprising in Ireland, were total fiascos, and they brought public ridicule upon Chicago's Irish.[22]

Rent by factionalism and failure, Fenian membership quickly dwindled in Chicago, as it did elsewhere. But if as an organization the Fenian Brotherhood was gasping its last breath, its spirit was very much alive. In 1867 a group of disgruntled New York Fenians established the Clan-na-Gael, a secret, oath-bound society which, like the Fenians, was dedicated to "the attainment of the complete and absolute independence of Ireland by the overthrow of English domination" by means of physical force.[23] Irish nationalists in Chicago quickly flocked to this new revolutionary society. In 1869, Chicago's first Clan-na-Gael "camp," as local branches were known, was established in the Bridgeport area.[24] Others soon followed, and for the rest of the century—and indeed beyond it—the Clan was to serve as the nucleus of Irish nationalist activity in Chicago. Led for much of the period by Alexander Sullivan, a crafty lawyer with a rather seamy past, the Clan numbered among its ranks some of the most influential Irishmen in the city. These included, among others: John M. Smyth, a prominent Republican politician and large furniture dealer; Daniel Corkery, a wealthy coal merchant and Democratic leader; John F. Finerty, a one-term congressman and publisher of the *Citizen*, an Irish weekly; and John P. Hopkins, first Irish Catholic mayor of Chicago, from 1893 to 1895.[25]

Although the Clan was never large in numbers, its doctrine of revolutionary republicanism seemed to permeate the Irish community; and it exerted considerable influence over other larger Irish nationalist organizations. Clansmen or individuals sympathetic to their aims dominated the leadership of the Ancient Order of Hibernians and the local branches of the Irish National Land League, the Irish National League, and the Irish National Federation.[26] As affiliates of the Irish Parliamentary party, these latter three groups were ostensibly dedicated to achieving Irish self-government through nonviolent means alone.[27] In practice, however, their members followed the Clan's policy. Although willing to lend moral and monetary support to the Irish Parliamentary party's peaceful efforts on behalf of home rule, they were more than eager, should the opportunity arise, to back a full-scale rebellion to secure an independent Irish Republic.

The Clan also managed to spread its message of revolutionary nationalism to the Irish community at large. Each week Finerty's *Citizen* informed its readers of the latest English misdeeds in Ireland and reminded them of the need for militant action. Furthermore, thousands of Irish Chicagoans, many of whom were probably not members of any nationalist group, attended rallies either sponsored or cosponsored by the Clan-na-Gael. In addition to St. Patrick's Day, major Irish gatherings were held on March 4th, the anniversary of the execution of the patriot Robert Emmet; on August 15th, the Feast of the Assumption; and on November 22, the date three Fenians, known as the Manchester Martyrs, were executed by the British in 1867. Orators at these rallies rekindled the embers of Irish nationalism—if indeed they needed rekindling—among their audiences, recounting the long history of English misrule in Ireland. Though they had kind words for English leaders who were sympathetic to Irish grievances, they often harped on the theme that words alone would never change the hearts of most Englishmen. English deafness to Irish problems, they argued, could only be cured by the bullet and the bomb.[28]

However, if many Irish Chicagoans seemed to support the Clan's revolutionary philosophy, the organization was not without its problems. During the last fifteen years of the century the Clan was plagued by the old Irish nemesis of factionalism. During the mid-1880s a relatively small group of Chicago Clansmen broke with the parent organization run by Sullivan, claiming that he was a thief who used the Irish cause for his own selfish ends. Though small in numbers, the dissidents carried on a vigorous campaign against Sullivan and his cronies. This campaign became intensely bitter after 1889, when one of the dissident leaders, Dr. Patrick Henry Cronin, was murdered by a few of Sullivan's henchmen, an event that brought shock and disgrace to the city's Irish.

While these events undermined some of its popularity, Irish nationalism remained a viable movement in Chicago simply because its underlying causes continued to survive. Concern for the political future of Ireland was a way of reaffirming one's Irishness, a way of keeping in touch with one's roots. Yet there was more behind Irish-American nationalism than the simple need to reinforce a common ethnic bond. Irish-American nationalism was characterized by an intense hatred of England to a much greater degree than was the movement in Ireland itself. After all, the majority of the late nineteenth-century Chicago Irish had either emigrated from Ireland during or in the decade immediately following the Great Famine, or they were the children of such emigrants. Since few returned for any length of time, their memories of Ireland were frozen at a time when British rule was, or at least

Dr. Patrick H. Cronin, a critic of the financial irregularities of Chicago's Clan-na-Gael, was the victim of a ghastly and sensational murder in 1889. The Clan used both violence and non-violence in its efforts to win independence for Ireland, and was an important force in the lives of Chicago's Irish. *Courtesy of the Chicago Historical Society.*

seemed to be, at its worst. They neither could nor would forget the hunger, the evictions, and the poverty, and they took up the cause of Irish nationalism not only in the hope of seeing an independent Ireland but also as an expression of vengeance on England. Indeed, sheer hatred of England does much to explain phenomena like the reckless and futile dynamite campaign that the Clan launched against Britain in the early 1880s. Although it did nothing to bring the dream of an independent Ireland any closer to reality, it served at least to give "Mother England" a few sleepless nights.[29]

Furthermore, as Thomas N. Brown has argued, the fires of Irish-American nationalism were fueled by a need for respect. Coming from a land ruled by authorities who had shown little but contempt for their way of life, and coming to a nation where—at least in the beginning— they had been scorned for their poverty, religion, and culture, the

American Irish had developed a collective sense of inferiority. Perhaps nothing intensified these feelings so much as the fact that their homeland was still in the hands of a foreign power.[30] John Finerty probably typified the sentiments of many Irish Chicagoans when he claimed (forgetting the Jews) that "all other foreign elements in this country, with, perhaps, the exception of the Poles, have strong governments behind them, and they are held in more respect than the Irish who have no government of their own to boast of."[31] Thus, for Ireland to gain self-government would lead to a greater respect for the American Irish.

Finally, Irish-American nationalism helped to meet some of the social and economic needs of the community. Nationalist organizations and rallies provided excellent opportunities for Irish-Americans to mingle with fellow Irishmen. The August 15 picnic in particular was a major social occasion attended by thousands of men, women, and children from various parts of the city. Furthermore, membership in nationalist groups like the Clan-na-Gael often led to economic rewards in the form of jobs. And nationalist connections were particularly useful for advancement in local politics.

The forces sustaining Irish nationalism were much the same in Chicago as elsewhere in Irish-America. Yet Irish nationalist activity in Chicago differed in one respect, and that was in the complete absence of any true constitutional nationalist movement. Chicago did have branches of constitutional organizations like the Irish National League, but behind these there always lurked the shadow of the gunman. In several other cities, however, mainly those in New England and the state of New York, constitutional groups were often what they claimed to be, and a number of their leaders were quick to denounce the revolutionary brand of Irish nationalism.

The differences between the Irish nationalism of Chicago and of the cities in New York and New England can be largely explained, I believe, by the respective attitudes of the church toward nationalism in these areas. The bishops and clergy in New York and New England were for the most part strongly opposed to secret revolutionary organizations. They agreed with traditional Catholic teaching that membership in such groups was sinful because their required oaths conflicted with one's religious and civic obligations and because their revolutionary aims violated the conditions for a just war.[32] As a result, they encouraged their flocks to turn away from revolutionary societies and to support instead the nonviolent nationalism espoused by the Irish Parliamentary party. In fact, a number of priests, such as Father Thomas Conaty of Worcester, Massachusetts and Father Lawrence Walsh of

Waterbury, Connecticut, provided some of the leadership for constitutional Irish-American nationalism during the 1880s and 1890s.[33]

Of all the clerical opponents of revolutionary Irish nationalism, none was so bitter as Archbishop Michael Corrigan of New York and Bishop Bernard McQuaid of Rochester. During the latter eighties and early nineties they did their utmost to have the Clan-na-Gael officially condemned by the Committee of Archbishops, which had ecclesiastical responsibility for such matters. That action, however, was continually blocked by three "liberal" archbishops—James Gibbons of Baltimore, John Ireland of St. Paul, and Feehan of Chicago. These prelates believed it was best to interfere as little as possible in the political activities of the laity, for to do so might needlessly alienate otherwise loyal Catholics.[34] Feehan, who had grown up in one of the more nationalist areas of Ireland, went even further than that.[35] Though never publicly condoning violent methods, he freely associated with Clansmen and was particularly friendly with Alexander Sullivan and his wife, Margaret, a journalist active in Irish affairs. He also contributed to the Clan's nonviolent projects, such as its burial plot at Mount Olivet Cemetery. Obviously, Feehan believed that one could be a good Catholic and still belong to the Clan-na-Gael.[36]

Considering the archbishop's friendly attitude toward the Clan, it is not surprising that most Irish priests in Chicago felt and acted similarly. Father Dorney, the Stockyards priest, was active in the inner circles of the Clan. Other priests often attended Clan demonstrations as honored guests and permitted the Clan as an organization to attend special masses or other church services. While some priests chose sides after the Clan-na-Gael split into factions, criticizing the opposing faction, I have found no Chicago priests who condemned revolutionary activities as such.[37]

The amicable relationship between cleric and Clansman was clearly the major reason Chicago lacked a constitutional nationalist movement. There was no encouragement from the Chicago pulpit to leave the Clan and support nonviolent Irish nationalism as there was in New York and Rochester. There were a few constitutional nationalists like W. P. Rend, a wealthy coal dealer, and William Onahan, a long-time Democratic politician; but without the church pushing people in their direction, they were voices crying in the wilderness. Although Irish Chicago suffered from a certain degree of factionalism, no split ever developed between the church and the Clan, nor did the nationalist movement ever divide along constitutional-extremist lines. In this respect, at least, the Irish in Chicago manifested a level of solidarity absent in cities in New York and New England.

Unlike Catholicism and Irish nationalism, which had their origins in the Irish past, the third important force in Irish Chicago—the local political system—was primarily an American institution. Perhaps because of its rapid growth rate, or perhaps because of a confusing set of overlapping city, county, and township jurisdictions, late nineteenth-century Chicago had a fragmented system of politics. Neither the Republicans, who dominated the city council, nor the Democrats, who occupied the mayor's office more often than the GOP did, were controlled by a centralized political machine like New York's Tammany Hall. Instead, each party was divided into a motley array of factions, or "mini-machines," which were continually involved in making deals with one another. In fact, on the local level at least, deals frequently occurred across party lines: the spoils of office took precedence over party loyalty. Unlike the relatively small group of mainly middle-class Protestant Reformers, who emphasized honest and efficient government, most Chicago politicians looked upon politics as a business designed to bring power and financial rewards to its practitioners. "Boodle" aldermen voted to give contracts and franchises to businessmen willing to pay handsome kickbacks. Local precinct captains and policemen took bribes from owners of gambling and prostitution establishments and in return protected them from the law. But the system also had its positive aspects: machine politicians provided jobs and other needed services to their constituents.[38]

Although their influence was not as extensive as some contemporary newspapers and journals would have us believe, there is little doubt that the Irish played a significant role in Chicago politics. In 1890, for example, when they made up just 17 percent of the city's population, the Irish held at least twenty-three of the sixty-eight seats on the city council. Of these twenty-three councilmen, nineteen were Democrats.[39] The Chicago Irish, like those in other cities, gave the bulk of their support to the Democratic party because it had been traditionally more sympathetic to their needs than had the Republicans. Not only were most Irishmen Democrats, but most Democrats were Irish. In 1885, for instance, the Irish occupied fourteen of the eighteen seats on the Democratic City Central Committee,[40] and in 1890 they accounted for about two-thirds of the Democratic aldermen. Furthermore, most of the major Democratic bosses during the period were Irishmen: Dan O'Hara in the seventies; Mike McDonald and "Chesterfield" Joe Mackin in the eighties; and John Powers, "Bathhouse" John Coughlin, and "Hinky Dink" Kenna in the nineties.[41] A handful of Irishmen, of course, became Republicans, either for practical political reasons or because they felt the national Democratic party had not properly rewarded the Irish for their loyalty. Two of the more prominent of these were John M. Smyth, the furniture dealer, and Martin B. Madden, owner of a large stone company. Smyth and Madden, who both served as aldermen for a time, wielded considerable power in local Republican affairs.[42]

But whether Republicans or Democrats, Irish politicians generally played the game of machine politics. Like others on the city council, most Irish aldermen sold their votes to entrepreneurs seeking municipal franchises and contracts. Irish politicians also successfully mastered the art of election fraud. Several owned saloons where they supplied the party faithful with ample refreshments on election days, encouraging them to vote early and often. Itinerants, illegally naturalized citizens, and even the dead were often duly registered as voters. Frequently, party toughs would pound the heads of opposition voters, or friendly policemen would jail them. And if all else failed, the ballots of a rival faction occasionally landed in the Chicago River.[43]

There is no doubt that the Irish were successful practitioners of urban politics. But why? For one thing, their past experience in Ireland preconditioned them to participate in a political milieu that flaunted the law. The English legal system as practiced in Ireland was anything but just. It often discriminated against Catholics and favored the mighty landlord over the lowly tenant farmer. As a result, the Irish immigrant had developed little respect for the law; instead, he tried to evade it as much as possible and was thus more easily able to adapt himself to a political system that skirted legal refinements.[44] Secondly, the Irish were culturally far more Anglo-Saxon than they liked to admit. An ability to speak English gave them an edge over foreign-speaking immigrants like the Germans, while a familiarity with British election procedures provided them with a better understanding of the workings of American politics. From the 1790s to the 1820s they had watched the landlords organize tenant farmers into effective voting blocs, and in the 1820s they had participated in O'Connell's successful drive to weld the Irish masses into a well-disciplined political force to win Catholic emancipation. The Irish clearly came to the United States well schooled in political organization and electioneering tactics.[45]

If their past experiences in Ireland prepared the Chicago Irish to operate effectively in the political arena, employment opportunities provided the immediate incentive that drew them into it in such large numbers. Several leading Irish politicians, who were also lawyers and businessmen, used their political connections to increase their incomes. Lawyers sometimes served as judges or represented companies with municipal franchises, while building contractors made handsome profits from city contracts. And for many of the party faithful who had neither the education nor financial resources to launch professional or business careers, political patronage jobs on the police force, in the water department, and the like provided them with their only source of livelihood. The federal census of 1900, for example, reported that 43 percent of "watchmen, policemen, firemen, etc." were either Irish immigrants or their children, even though they represented only 14 percent of the city's male labor force.[46] Besides municipal employment, the Irish also held what might be termed indirect patronage jobs, that is, jobs in companies holding city franchises and contracts. In 1900, 58 percent of all gas works employees were first- or second-generation Irish-Americans.[47] And employment was not the only economic service Irish politicians rendered to their constituents; they occasionally helped widows, the unemployed, and the destitute, providing them with modest handouts of food, fuel, and other services.

It was largely for economic reasons that the Clan-na-Gael participated in Chicago politics from the 1870s onward. Though most Irish politicians were probably not Clansmen, virtually all Clansmen—except for the relatively small group of dissidents—were deeply entrenched in machine politics. In fact, with a decentralized political system, the Clan had a golden opportunity to operate as a "mini-machine," wheeling and dealing with various Democratic and Republican factions. Several Clansmen held influential political positions (mainly in the Democratic party) and were able to supply the rank and file with countless patronage jobs. For example, Daniel Corkery was a Democratic leader in Bridgeport during much of the period; Frank Agnew, a building contractor from the near North Side, served for a time as Chairman of the Cook County Democratic Central Committee; and Michael McInerney, owner of a large undertaking establishment, was the Democratic boss of the Stockyards District during the 1880s and 1890s. Besides getting jobs through its own members, the Clan also made deals with other politicians. In the early 1880s, Alexander Sullivan backed Mayor Carter Harrison I for mayor and in return was permitted to name several Clansmen to the police department. He also obtained positions for Clansmen in other city and county offices, so that the Clan-na-Gael could be found everywhere from lofty judicial chambers to the city sewer system.[48]

Politics, then, played an important role in the lives of many Irish Chicagoans.* While the church and Irish nationalism primarily filled their spiritual and emotional needs as Irish Catholics, politics helped to satisfy their practical needs as urban Americans by providing them with jobs and other economic benefits. Since in one way or another these jobs and services were obtained through Irish connections, the

---

*For a detailed, revisionist treatment of Irish politics in Chicago, see Chapter 12, *below*, by Paul Michael Green.

Chicago's police department, symbolized here by the Haymarket Riot statue, was predominately Irish by the 1890s. The policeman, the priest, and the politician formed the trinity of occupations dominated by the Irish in many cities such as Chicago. *Courtesy of the Chicago Police Department.*

political system helped to reinforce rather than lessen their sense of Irishness and thus helped to strengthen community cohesiveness. Undoubtedly, the politician, with jobs and other favors at his disposal, was a leading figure in Irish Chicago. Along with the priest and patriot, he formed part of an important trinity that gave direction and stability to the community.

If the church, Irish nationalism, and politics served to strengthen community ties, so did the fact that most Irish Chicagoans were members of the same general socio-economic class. As Table III shows, from

1870 to 1890 the overwhelming majority of Irish immigrants were manual workers, probably over 85 percent, since it is more than likely that most of those in unclassifiable and unlisted occupations also held blue-collar jobs. (Indeed, in the case of the Irish female labor force in 1890, where over 96 percent could be classified, 88 percent were manual laborers.) Of these blue-collar workers, about half of the men were unskilled laborers, while about three-fourths of the women were domestic servants.[49] In contrast to this, the number of Irish immigrants in the professions or in big business was minuscule.

TABLE III
OCCUPATIONAL DISTRIBUTION OF IRISH-BORN CHICAGOANS, BY PERCENTAGE, 1870–1890

	1870 (Male & Female) (N=22,337)	1880 (Male & Female) (N=23,918)	1890 (Male) (N=32,482)	1890 (Female) (N=8,552)
Professional	0.52	0.97	1.60	0.93
Owners and Officials of Large Businesses	—	—	1.11	—
Owners of Small Businesses	3.98	4.21	1.83	2.89
Other White-Collar Workers	3.67	4.56	7.48	4.71
Manual Workers	76.76	74.08	75.41	88.06
Unclassifiable	8.90	9.48	4.09	1.22
Unlisted	6.17	6.70	8.47	2.19

Source: U.S., *Ninth Census, 1870*, Vol. I, "Population," p. 782; *Tenth Census, 1880*, "Population," p. 870; *Eleventh Census, 1890*, "Population," Part II, pp. 650–651.

The statistics for 1900 (see Table IV), unlike those for 1870 through 1890, include the second-generation Irish; unfortunately, they lump them together with the Irish-born, thus precluding any exact comparison between the two. Yet it seems clear that the American-born Irish had more white-collar workers among their ranks than did the immigrants, because the percentage of nonmanual workers, which had hovered around 10 percent from 1870 to 1890, jumped rather substantially in the 1900 census, when the second generation was included. In 1900, over 25 percent of Irish men and about 60 percent of Irish women were business proprietors, professionals, or in other white-collar jobs. It would seem that, had the second generation been included in the labor statistics prior to 1890, one would have seen a gradual increase in the number of Irish white-collar workers from 1870 onward, as the children of Irish immigrants entered the work force.

TABLE IV
OCCUPATIONAL DISTRIBUTION OF FIRST- AND SECOND-GENERATION IRISH CHICAGOANS, BY PERCENTAGE, 1900

	Male (N=75,695)	Female (N=25,016)
Professional	4.01	8.51
Owners and Officials of Large Businesses	2.19	0.10
Owners of Small Businesses	4.80	3.35
Other White-Collar Workers	16.58	25.19
Manual Workers	69.78	59.90
Unlisted	2.64	2.95

Source: U.S., *Twelfth Census, 1900,* "Special Reports: Occupations," pp. 516–523.

Nonetheless, even at the turn of the century most Irish Chicagoans were still manual workers. Furthermore, one would suspect that the gulf between them and white-collar workers was not too great, since the latter had grown up mainly in working-class environments and probably still had one or more members of their families among the blue-collar ranks. For example, biographical sketches of the leading Irishmen in Chicago in 1897 show that virtually all had come from rather humble backgrounds and that a number had worked as manual laborers before achieving success in business, politics, or the professions. Some, particularly the politicians, continued to live in working-class neighborhoods; and though others were members of the elite Columbus Club, many were also active in religious and nationalist societies made up of individuals from all classes. Relatively few joined the select groups dominated by upper- and upper-middle-class Protestant Americans.[50] Although there were some signs of class differences, particularly during the 1890s, late nineteenth-century Irish Chicago had a predominantly working-class flavor.[51]

In this respect, of course, the Irish were not unique. During the late nineteenth century, blue-collar workers dominated Chicago's work force as a whole. Until the 1890s, when the "new immigration" began to change the composition of the city's labor force, the Irish were on the lower rung of the occupational ladder. As Table V shows, they had a greater percentage of blue-collar workers than did either Americans of native parentage or the British-born; and although they had roughly the same percentage of manual workers as the German-born did and

TABLE V
PERCENTAGE OF MANUAL WORKERS OF SELECTED GROUPS IN THE LABOR FORCE, CHICAGO, 1890*

	Male	Female
Native White of Native Parentage	53.56	55.59
British-born	72.40	71.73
German-born	85.85	90.48
Irish-born	86.24	91.17
Swedish- and Norwegian-born	90.39	95.10
Danish-born	86.02	91.44

*These percentages are based on the total labor force *less* the number in unlisted and unclassifiable occupations. (Compare percentages of Irish manual workers in this table with those in Table III.) The percentage of workers in unlisted and unclassifiable occupations ranged from a high of 19.50 percent for native white males of native parentage to a low of 2.25 percent for Swedish- and Norwegian-born females.

Source: U.S., *Eleventh Census, 1890*, "Population," Part II, pp. 650–651.

a somewhat smaller percentage than the Scandinavian-born did, they had a greater percentage of unskilled workers than did either of these two groups.[52] In the last decade of the century, however, the Irish began to move up the economic ladder (see Table VI). Definitely better off than the "new immigrants," such as the Poles and Italians, they were slightly ahead of the Scandinavians and had narrowed the gap between themselves and the Germans. They still trailed Americans of native parentage and the British.[53]

The economic position of the Irish relative to these last two groups no doubt helped to reinforce their sense of inferiority, for it mirrored the long-standing economic disparity between the Saxon and the Celt. Group inferiority complexes are difficult to quantify, and it is quite conceivable that many Irish, particularly the uneducated and unskilled laborers, never gave the matter much thought. But it certainly bothered the educated middle-class Irish who sought respectability and who often rubbed shoulders with Anglo-Saxons in the workaday world. Much as they liked to talk about the lack of materialism among Celts, they measured success in terms of economic and social mobility; and when they looked at their fellow countrymen, they saw that they fell short of the mark. John Finerty probably expressed the feelings of many of these "respectable" Irish when he advised prospective immigrants to remain in Ireland, claiming that in America the Irishman "is nothing but a poor emigrant, who is left to paddle his own canoe as best he may, and who, however, delicately nurtured at home, must take, at last, to the pick and shovel, perhaps to the recruiting office, or become a

TABLE VI
PERCENTAGE OF MANUAL WORKERS OF SELECTED
GROUPS IN THE LABOR FORCE, CHICAGO, 1900. (Statistics for
ethnic groups include immigrants and their children)*

	Male	Female
Native White of Native Parentage	43.16	39.18
British	56.07	45.53
Germans	69.03	70.03
Irish	71.67	61.72
Scandinavian	78.02	80.54
Poles	90.67	87.66
Italians	83.99	80.03

*These percentages are based on the total labor force *less* the number in unlisted occupations. (Compare percentages of Irish manual workers in this table with those in Table IV.) Unlike the 1890 census all listed occupations could be classified and the percentage of unlisted occupations was less than 5 percent for most groups.
Source: U.S., *Twelfth Census, 1900,* "Special Reports: Occupations," pp. 516-523.

charge upon the country."[54] Such sentiments did not die easily; they lingered on well into the twentieth century, albeit in more subtle ways.

In addition to feeling inferior to Anglo-Americans, the Irish also felt the sting of the anti-Catholic and anti-Irish attitudes of some. Such prejudice was not simply a source of irritation to the Irish, but it also played an important role in reinforcing their sense of group consciousness, for it reminded them that they were a people somewhat apart from the mainstream of American life.

As an infant city, where all groups—native and foreign—were relative newcomers facing the common problems of a semifrontier environment, Chicago did not experience the more rampant anti-Catholic nativism that plagued several eastern cities during the two or three decades before the Civil War. Nonetheless, anti-Irish and, to a lesser extent, anti-German sentiment did exist. Some Americans resented the Irish for their political power, for their support of liberal drinking laws, for their sometimes squalid living conditions, and most of all for their Catholicism, which they felt posed a threat to the very fabric of American life. They often viewed Irish attempts to get public monies for their schools or to ban the King James Bible in the common schools as part of a concerted Roman attack on free American institutions. Only once during the decades before the Civil War, however, did nativism score a major triumph in Chicago. This occurred in 1855, when, after capturing the city council and the mayor's office, the nativist and xenophobic Know-Nothing party passed legislation requiring all applicants for municipal jobs to be native-born Americans. They also increased the cost of beer licenses, which led to the Lager Beer Riots, in which the Germans and Irish teamed up together to battle the nativist authorities. But the Know-Nothing victory, caused as much by a disruption in the two-party system over the slavery issue as by anti-Catholicism, proved to be short-lived. The following year the Know-Nothings were defeated, and their legislation was promptly repealed.[55]

Although the xenophobic occurrences of 1855 were never repeated again, anti-Catholicism continued to survive in Chicago. In the years after the Civil War, certain Protestant ministers repeatedly warned their congregations that the "demon of Romanism" was prowling about, seeking to undermine the democratic institutions of America.[56] Several Protestant newspaper editors and political reformers attacked the Irish for polluting municipal politics. Although most were sincere reformers and not really bigots in the true sense of the word, they often seemed to be more concerned about the number of Irish politicians than about the actual corruption they were responsible for.[57]

During the late 1880s anti-Catholicism, which had been relatively low-keyed and somewhat sporadic since the Know-Nothing period, became more blatant and organized. This new wave of nativism was, of course, a national as well as a local phenomenon. Partially caused by the steady increase in Irish political power—city after city seemed to be electing Irish Catholic mayors—and by the tremendous growth of the Catholic Church and its parochial school system, it also arose from the increasing alienation of middle Americans, or "in-betweeners," as John Higham has described them. Made up mainly of white-collar workers, small businessmen, and non-unionized workers, the "in-betweeners" felt lost in an increasingly industrialized and urbanized America, where giant corporations, labor unions, and political machines rather than individuals seemed to be controlling the nation's destiny. Wishing to return to an earlier and less complex America, they lashed out at the foreign element, which in one way or another seemed to be connected with these new forces.[58] When speaking of the foreign element, they really meant Catholics, not Protestant immigrants. In fact, in many areas foreign-born Protestants actively participated in nativist groups; and in Chicago a number of British and Protestant Irish newcomers were in the forefront of the anti-Catholic crusade.[59]

Of the various anti-Catholic groups active in Chicago during the late 1880s and early 1890s, the most prominent were the United Order of Deputies, founded there in 1886, and the American Protective Association, which opened its first branch in the city in 1888 and eventually made its national headquarters there. Among other demands, these groups advocated immigration restriction, encouraged employers to fire Catholics, campaigned to defeat Catholic political candidates, and supported school laws like the Edwards Law (passed in 1889), which gave local public school boards some control over parochial schools.[60] Besides anti-Catholic organizations, Chicago also had a few short-lived nativist newspapers, including the *Weekly Native Citizen* and *America*, whose editor, Slason Thompson, claimed that "the civilization of Ireland [was] a hissing and a reproach in the ears of history for the past 300 years."[61]

One must be careful not to overemphasize the extent of anti-Irish bigotry in late nineteenth-century Chicago. The more virulent form lasted only a decade, roughly from 1886 to 1896, after which nativists began to ease up on their anti-Irish and anti-German attacks and concentrate their opposition more fully on the large numbers of Catholic and Jewish immigrants arriving from eastern and southern Europe. Even at the height of its popularity, the power of anti-Irish prejudice was far from unlimited, a fact perhaps most forcibly demonstrated by the election of John P. Hopkins as Chicago's first Irish Catholic mayor in 1893. After all, outright bigots formed only a small minority of the city's population. In fact, several Protestant leaders, including a number of ministers, spoke out in defense of the Irish and other Catholics.[62] Nonetheless, anti-Irish sentiment was a fact of life for the Irish in Chicago: it constantly forced them to defend their own traditions, as well as their loyalty to the United States, and, in the process, reinforce their ethnic identity.

In the eyes of anti-Catholic bigots not only, but of most non-Irish Chicagoans, Irish-Americans were a monolithic group. And yet, although they certainly formed a relatively cohesive community, the Chicago Irish were by no means a homogeneous lot. Like any other ethnic group, they exhibited a degree of diversity and disunity. First of all, despite a common Irish Catholic heritage, their geographical backgrounds were far from identical. The most obvious difference, of course, existed between those born in Ireland and those born in America. The former had grown up in a predominantly Catholic, rural, and old-world environment, the latter largely in one that was Protestant, urban, and industrialized. There is no doubt that this resulted in a great many different experiences in their formative years. Since the American-born Irish ranked higher than the immigrants on the occupational ladder, there may also have been certain class differences between the two. Yet the gap between the immigrant and his American-born cousin must not have been as great among the Irish as it was among the non-English-speaking ethnic groups; for both the Irish immigrant and the "narrowback" (a term used for an American-born Irishman) had been exposed to Anglo-Saxon influences in their youth, and both spoke the same language with equal fluency, albeit with different accents. Although there probably was a tendency for immigrants to associate more with other immigrants, and American-born with American-born, I have found that relations between the two were harmonious for the most part. Immigrants and "narrowbacks," for example, seemed to mingle quite well in organizations like the Clan-na-Gael and the Ancient Order of Hibernians.[63] The only major dispute between the two groups occurred in the church, when, at the turn of the century, a band of Irish-born priests tried to block the appointment of the American-born Father Peter Muldoon as an auxiliary bishop of Chicago, claiming that he was prejudiced against native Irish priests. But even this was not a simple generational conflict. The dissident priests had other reasons for opposing Muldoon, and support for and opposition to Muldoon align imperfectly between the two groups: it is noteworthy that the Irish-born Feehan had nominated Muldoon, and that—for a time at least—the disgruntled priests received the support of the American-born bishop of Peoria, John Lancaster Spalding.[64]

If those born in Ireland and the United States came from somewhat different backgrounds but generally got along well together, the same can be said for groups within these two major categories. The native Irish population in Chicago was made up of individuals from every Irish county, though most of them seem to have come from counties in the western provinces of Munster and Connacht. While it is true that in the early days of Chicago, brawls frequently occurred among men from different parts of Ireland, such rampant factionalism had declined by 1870.[65] Immigrants arriving in the years after 1870 came from an Ireland where better communications and a more fully developed national system of education had significantly reduced provincialism. Still, the Chicago Irish were quite aware of county differences. Good-natured rivalries prevailed among men from different counties, and there probably was a tendency for those from the same localities to fraternize more with one another than with other Irishmen.[66]

Far less noticeable than the differences among those of Irish birth were the diverse origins of the American-born Irish. Although the published censuses do not break down the second-generation Irish by state, county, or city of birth, it is apparent that a considerable number of them had spent their formative years in places other than Chicago. Of the 126 American-born Irish Catholics listed in Charles Ffrench's *Biographical History of the American Irish in Chicago*, 69 were born outside the city, and of these the majority arrived there as adults. Most came from the Midwest and the East, some from large and middle-sized cities, others from small towns and farms.[67] It is difficult to know exactly how these individuals differed from the native Chicago Irish, but it seems likely that they tended to blur the distinction between immigrant and "narrowback." They held a sort of intermediary position between those reared in Chicago and those in Ireland, sharing with the former an American upbringing and with the latter the experiences of adjusting to an unfamiliar city.

Chicago's Irish, therefore, came from diverse origins, although it must be emphasized that this diversity rarely led to any serious dissension. Similarly, the class distinctions we have already mentioned never posed any major barriers to community solidarity. However, more research is needed before one can fully grasp the nuances of Irish life in Chicago. Of course, some of the necessary research material is unavailable. No sociological surveys on the Irish of this period exist; virtually all of those who might have been interviewed are dead; and the records of many organizations have been lost forever. Yet an intensive study of the census manuscripts, parish records, and the like may yield some additional insights; interviews with the children of the late nineteenth-century Irish, many of whom are still alive, would also be valuable.

In any event, the sources that are available indicate that differences in background and class caused relatively little friction among the Chicago Irish. The community experienced discord from other quarters. Machine politics, for example, was a perpetual source of trouble. Although Irish "boodle" politicians usually cooperated with one another, no election seemed to pass without dissension on the part of one faction or another. Since political power and patronage jobs were at stake, the struggles were usually bitter and at times led to violence.[68] If Irish machine politicians sometimes fought among themselves, they also had to contend with opposition from a small group of reform-minded Irish. These individuals came from a variety of backgrounds but shared a common feeling that the existing political system was demeaning to the Irish. Rarely successful, they did manage to score a few upsets, most notably in 1882, when the then Independent Democrat John Finerty defeated Henry F. Sheridan, the regular Democratic candidate, in the Second Congressional District race.[69]

The most visible split in Irish Chicago occurred among the ranks of the Irish nationalists. The trouble started shortly after Alexander Sullivan was elected chairman of the national executive committee of the Clan-na-Gael in August 1881. Sullivan and two other members of the committee, who were collectively known as "the Triangle," pursued some rather questionable practices and policies that disgusted a number of Clansmen. They ran the organization in a high-handed and dictatorial manner, launched a futile two-year dynamite campaign in England against the express wishes of the Irish Republican Brotherhood, their affiliate in Ireland and Britain, and apparently pilfered nationalist funds for their own use.

As a result of this, during the winter of 1884-1885 a group of New York Clansmen, led by the former Fenian John Devoy, began a national campaign to oust Sullivan and his cronies from the Clan. Devoy picked up support in Chicago from a small but vocal band of Clansmen, including Patrick Dunne (the father of a future Chicago mayor and governor of Illinois, Edward F. Dunne), who as early as 1882 had publicly complained that Sullivan was using nationalist monies to speculate on the Chicago Board of Trade; William J. Hynes, a local Democratic politician and former congressman from Arkansas; and the ill-fated Dr. Patrick Cronin, who had recently arrived in Chicago from St. Louis.

For fifteen years, up until 1900, when the Clan was finally reunited, the Devoyites waged a relentless crusade against Sullivan and his followers, a crusade that took a tragic turn in May 1889, when a group of Sullivan's followers assassinated Dr. Cronin in a lonely Lake View cottage. Setting up their own Clan-na-Gael and joining the Ancient Order of Hibernians, Board of Erin, which was separate from the Sullivanite-dominated A.O.H., the Devoyites held rival demonstrations on all the major Irish holidays, where they denounced Sullivan and his gang as phony patriots who were using the Irish cause to further their own selfish political ambitions. Since Finerty, a Sullivan supporter since 1885, generally denied them access to the columns of the *Citizen*, they used the pages of the daily press to inform the public about the seamier activities of their enemies. They also joined forces with political reformers in an attempt to undermine Sullivan and the political system in which he was so intimately involved. Yet, as Devoy himself admitted, the anti-Sullivan forces gained the allegiance of only a small minority of Chicago's Irish nationalists. The majority remained loyal to the Sullivanites, for not only did the latter cater to their nationalist aspirations as Irishmen but, by playing the game of machine politics, they also met their economic needs as Chicagoans. If they wondered at times about Sullivan's more dubious activities, the Irish were willing to give him the benefit of the doubt; for he was one of them, one of their own kind, and he had enough detractors in Protestant America. Besides, they probably reasoned, could a man who was the friend of so many priests and of Archbishop Feehan be all that bad?[70]

If the anti-Sullivanites received the support of only a minority of Chicago's Irish, their presence nonetheless points to the fact that the

Irish community had its fissures and cracks. Although such factionalism—whether among nationalists, clerics, or politicians—failed to destroy the essential unity of Irish Chicago, it at least tended to weaken
it, and it certainly belied any claims that the Irish were a monolithic
people. Furthermore, if not a monolith, neither was Irish Chicago cut
off from the rest of the city: every day, in varying ways, the Irish came
into contact with the larger urban community.

One of the major ways the Irish encountered other peoples was
through their jobs. Whether working on construction projects, in the
stockyards, or on street railways, most Irish labored alongside other
Chicagoans. And labor unions like the Knights of Labor had a good
mixture of Irish and non-Irish members.[71] Of particular importance in
bringing the Irish into contact with the outside world were the large
numbers of Irish women who worked as domestic servants in the homes
of upper- and upper-middle-class Americans. No doubt they were influenced to some degree by the manners and customs of their employers, and since many of them later married, their families were also
probably affected by their experiences, although in what way and to
what extent is a matter of speculation.

If contacts made at work helped to break down some of the isolation
between the Irish immigrants and the wider society, so did the fact
that virtually all Irish Chicagoans spoke the English language. Having
English as a mother tongue undoubtedly made their adjustment to
American life much less complicated than it would have been had they
still spoken Irish, the common language of much of Ireland until the
early nineteenth century.[72] English helped to make them feel more
American, more a part of the city and nation in which they lived. And
while it did not put them on the higher rungs of the economic ladder,
knowledge of English gave them an advantage in certain areas, such
as politics. Furthermore, it meant that the ethnic newspaper was far
less important to the Irish than to non-English-speaking immigrants.
Unlike these groups, the Irish never had a daily newspaper of their
own, and their one successful weekly, the *Citizen*, did not begin publication until 1882. Like the Americans and the British, the Irish kept
up on the world around them by reading the regular daily newspapers,
most of which, incidentally, gave rather detailed coverage of Irish events
on both sides of the Atlantic. Reading the English-language dailies, of
course, brought the Irish into more direct contact with the Anglo-
American world, but it did not necessarily lead to better relations with
it, for the local press could often be quite hostile to the Irish, particularly to Irish politicians.

Jobs and a knowledge of the English language were not the only
factors that promoted interaction between the Irish and non-Irish. Each

of the three main institutions in Irish Chicago—the church, the Irish
nationalist movement, and the local political system—helped to link
the Irish with other Chicagoans in varying degrees. Most important
was politics, in which the Irish constantly had to deal with native
Americans, Germans, and Scandinavians, and later on with immigrants
from southern and eastern Europe. True, political factions often divided
along ethnic lines, but there was also a good deal of interethnic cooperation. In the early 1870s, Irish politicians teamed up with Germans
and machine-minded Americans to form the People's party, a coalition
of Democrats and Republicans which defeated the reformist Fire Proof
Ticket in 1873.[73] Throughout the 1880s and 1890s, Irish politicians had
to deal with American politicians like Mayor Carter Harrison I and
Alfred Trude, and with Germans like Washington Hessing and John
Peter Altgeld. And although the "new immigrants" had few influential
political leaders during this period, the Irish had to cater to their needs,
since they supplied an ever-increasing bloc of votes. Alderman Johnny
Powers, for example, kept a hold on the Nineteenth Ward long after
most Irish had left, by providing jobs and other favors to the Italians
who moved in.[74] Powers was typical of most Irish bosses in Chicago.
With a relatively small proportion of the city's population, the Irish
knew that cooperation with other groups was essential to their political
survival. Friction often occurred when other ethnics saw the Irish take
more than their fair share of the prizes. But the Irish usually allowed
their non-Irish political allies enough of the patronage to keep their
allegiance. As a result, they managed to exercise a degree of political
power out of all proportion to their numbers. If in the present century
Chicago politics, to use John Allswang's words, indeed became "a
house for all peoples,"[75] it was one in which the Irish generally seemed
to occupy the best rooms.

Although it failed to bring the Irish into contact with the larger
community to the same extent that politics did, the church served as
a catalyst in linking the Irish with other Catholics in the city. This is
not to deny what was said above: the Irish were indeed separated from
other Catholics by language, customs, and the system of national parishes. Yet running through the motley fabric of Chicago Catholicism
was the single thread of a common faith. A shared religious belief
probably gave the Irish a better understanding of other Catholic groups
than they might otherwise have had. And there is a great deal of truth
in the claim that a common religious background was one of the reasons
Irish politicians were able to deal more effectively with the "new immigrants" than were their American counterparts. While ethnic rivalries often overshadowed the universality of the church, there was a
degree of Catholic solidarity that could become formidable in periods

of anti-Catholic nativism. In the early 1890s, for instance, the Irish supported German Catholics in their campaign to repeal the Edwards Law, which threatened to undermine their parochial schools.[76] Of course, in time, as the non-English-speaking groups lost their native languages and became more Americanized, ethnic differences among Catholics would decrease significantly.

At first glance it may seem that Irish nationalism would have only served to isolate Chicago's Irish from the larger urban community. Yet in certain respects the opposite is true: it tended to make them more tolerant and broad-minded in some matters. Since Irish nationalists played down the Catholic element in Irish identity and emphasized that all Irishmen, be they Catholics, Anglicans, or Presbyterians, were true sons of Erin, and since some of the more notable nationalist leaders like Charles Stewart Parnell were Protestants, the creed of Irish nationalism tended to dilute Irish Catholic prejudice against Protestants. Of course, more often than not, Irish Protestants were the objects of Catholic scorn, since most of them supported the British connection; but it must be emphasized that Catholics generally disliked their Protestant fellow countrymen because they were pro-British, and not because of their religion. Let any Irish Protestant wave the green flag, and he immediately became a hero to Irish Catholics. Arthur Dixon, an Ulster-born Protestant and long-time Republican alderman who supported Irish Home Rule, was revered by Irish nationalists in the city.[77] Two of the most popular out-of-state speakers at Irish meetings in Chicago were George Betts and George Pepper, the former an Episcopalian clergyman from St. Louis, the latter a Methodist minister from Ohio. A correspondent writing to the *Citizen* after hearing Pepper speak at an August 15 rally expressed the feelings of many Irish Catholic Chicagoans when he declared: "It was indeed a happy sight to observe the Rev. Dr. Pepper, a Methodist minister, and the Rev. Father Hayes, a Catholic priest, standing on the same platform. Such a scene augurs well for the future of Ireland."[78]

Secondly, the nationalist tradition helped to give at least some Chicago Irish a sense of empathy for the problems of other peoples. *Citizen* editor Finerty, for example, championed Cuban independence, defended the "new immigration," advocated the teaching of German and other foreign languages in the public schools, and condemned anti-Semitism in the United States and Great Britain.[79] Similarly, Alexander Sullivan professed concern for the plight of American blacks. Though many Irish opposed the antislavery movement, after the death of the New England abolitionist Wendell Phillips, Sullivan recalled that he "was one of the first men whose utterances aroused in my blood hatred of human slavery, and gave my tongue some of its little power to denounce bondage even before I reached manhood."[80] The Irish nationalist experience clearly failed to wipe out Irish prejudice toward other groups, but it probably helped to diminish it. Anyone who spent time condemning English misrule in Ireland must have had some pangs of guilt when he acted in a bigoted manner toward others. Certainly, the frustration of seeing a foreign power control their homeland helps to explain why bishops like Foley and Feehan were willing to grant a certain degree of autonomy in the form of national parishes to the various Catholic ethnic groups.

Finally, and perhaps most important, the Irish were linked to other Chicagoans by a common loyalty to and faith in the United States. Most Irish immigrants came to America to stay, and of these the overwhelming majority became citizens.[81] They were no doubt only too anxious to renounce their legal allegiance to the British crown; but they became citizens more importantly out of a commitment to their adopted country, the country that was to be their home and the home of their children and grandchildren. On meeting with economic hardships or anti-Catholic prejudice they might grow despondent; but by and large they looked on America as a good land, a land that certainly offered them a better future than Ireland had.

Indeed, the Irish identified very closely with the United States. As one Chicago Irishman said some years after the turn of the century, "They're none of them foreigners when they come here, for their hearts and love were in America long before they thought of sailin' for America."[82] Irish-American apologists continually emphasized that the Irish had made significant contributions to the United States. Counting up the number of Irish troops in the Revolutionary War, they claimed that the Irish had played a major role in America's struggle for independence, though they failed to mention that most of these troops were of Ulster Protestant origins. Far more justifiably, they noted the numbers of Irish soldiers who had fought to preserve the Union during the Civil War. Similarly, they recalled that several Irish policemen were wounded (one fatally) in the Haymarket Square Riot of 1886 as they were trying to preserve the American system from the alleged anarchists. And to charges that their commitment to Irish nationalism proved they were Irish first and Americans second, the Irish answered that their concern for Ireland in no way diminished their love for America. After all, they argued, in fighting to overthrow British rule in Ireland, were they not following the example set by America a century before?

Nineteenth-century Irish Chicago, then, was not an isolated enclave cut off from the rest of the city. While they formed a highly self-conscious and relatively cohesive ethnic community, the Irish also came into contact with other Chicagoans. In the present century, of course, the Irish became more totally integrated into the larger urban society. Much of their cohesiveness vanished as the factors that had sustained it changed. The ties that bound third-, fourth-, and fifth-generation Irish-Americans to Ireland were naturally weaker than those that bound the immigrants and their children. The creation of the Irish Free State in 1922 did much to undermine the raison d'être of Irish-American nationalism, though, of course, some Irish Chicagoans continued to show an interest in ousting the British from Northern Ireland. Increased social and economic mobility tended to fragment what had once been a predominantly working-class community. Intermarriage with other ethnic groups (mainly Catholic), the decline of anti-Irish prejudice, and an increasing solidarity with other white groups against a growing black population tied the Irish more closely to other Chicagoans of a European background.

Yet it would be premature to sound the death knell for Irish Chicago. Today there is still a small nucleus of highly ethnic-conscious Irish Chicagoans who support various Irish cultural, athletic, and nationalist organizations in the city. Besides these there are countless others who are aware of their Irish heritage in varying degrees. Indeed, during the past decade or so, in view of the new emphasis on ethnicity, a number of once-marginal Irish have begun to rediscover their Irish past. Young men and women whose grandparents or great-grandparents came from Ireland study Irish history and literature at colleges and universities which once spurned these subjects as too parochial for an institution of higher learning. In recent years increasing numbers of Irish-Americans have visited Ireland, thanks to the fast and relatively cheap transatlantic travel available in this jet age. On the whole, it is probably easier for these Irish-Americans to get back to their roots than it is for the descendants of non-English-speaking immigrants. Unlike them, Irish-Americans speak the language of their immigrant ancestors and the language of present-day Ireland. Ironically, for this, of course, the English are responsible.

Chapter II

EDWARD MAZUR

Jewish Chicago:
From Diversity to Community

> *Upon entering the Yiddish theater, one left America.*
>
> — Ghetto resident (Chicago)

> *I left the Old Country because you couldn't be a Jew over there and still live; but I would rather be dead than be the kind of German Jew that brings the Jewish name into disgrace by being a Goy.*
>
> — Ghetto resident (Chicago)

From A MERE HANDFUL IN 1836, CHI-
cago's Jewish population increased in a century to more than 270,000
persons by 1940. To many outsiders, the Jews of Chicago appeared to
be a monolithic group. Upon closer examination, however, philosophical, economic, religious, geographical, psychological, and linguistic
differences delineate two distinct Jewish communities. Each group, in
varying degrees, re-created in America a somewhat altered version of
its familiar European environment.

The German-speaking Bavarian, Prussian, Bohemian, Polish, and
Austrian Jews who came to America before 1880 found a country that
was warmly receptive to their participation, and avenues for success
appeared limitless. To the two million Eastern European Jews who
came to America between 1880 and 1914, the city's "Little Israels" and
"Jew-towns" were districts bordered by frequently hostile neighbors
and institutions. In addition, the newcomers were regarded by German
Jews as unnecessary public charges, an embarrassment, a backward,
superstitious, the theologically conservative, and Yiddish-speaking
people. Not only did they threaten the German-Jewish position in the
Gentile community, but some observers called for Eastern European
exclusion, declaring that "many of these East European Jews, as reared
in their native land, are not desirable in our American communities;
however much of these may be mixed . . . it would indeed be desirable
if they would stay away altogether."[1]

The German-Jewish movement to this country, prior to the 1830s,
was one in which each individual, for a variety of reasons, had made
his own decision to immigrate. The philosophy of the Enlightenment,
the French Revolution, and the spread of the Napoleonic Empire had
expanded the dimensions of intellectual, political, and economic equality for Western European Jewry, in marked contrast to the previously
familiar lifestyle of recurring massacres, persecution, restricted opportunities, and social ostracism. Following the 1815 Congress of Vienna,
however, Jewish emancipation efforts were thwarted and sabotaged by
general reaction in the post-Napoleonic era, renewed xenophobia, and
increased emphasis on nationality instead of the universality inherent
in the philosophy of the Enlightenment.

47

The failure of emancipation to provide lasting benefits after 1815, the spreading industrial revolution and the economic dislocation of the 1830s, and the political revolutions of 1830 and 1848 provided the impetus to turn the minds of many poor, small-town Jews from the western and southwestern German states toward America. After tasting greater freedom, these Jews could not settle for less. The combination of restrictions and a slump in trade led to the first "mass migration to America." Between 1815 and 1880, the American Jewish population increased from 15,000 to 250,000 and was almost entirely a German-speaking people.[2]

Though the majority of the German-Jewish arrivals settled on the East Coast, some ventured into the Midwest and settled in Chicago. Jacob Gottlieb, the city's first known Jewish resident, was a peddler who arrived in 1838. Within seven years, he was joined by the Benedict Shubarts, the Philip Newburgs, the Isaac Zeiglers, the Henry Horners, and other Jewish families.[3] All but Horner, a Bohemian, were from Bavaria. These families settled near the center of the expanding city in the vicinity of Lake and Wells streets, establishing their residences in one- or two-story frame dwellings near or above their aspiring businesses.[4]

Between 1850 and 1860 the Jewish community grew, as arrivals from Bavaria, Posen, and German Poland swelled the Jewish population from 100 to 1500 and expanded their initial boundaries. Jews settled on Randolph, Clark, and LaSalle streets, and some moved north of the Chicago River. The more prosperous and entrenched members of this community resided on the southern rim of the central business district.

For the first decades of its existence, the community was a tightly integrated entity related by country of origin, religious practice, vocational enterprise, and intermarriage. The tobacco dealer Philip Newburg married Ernestina Shubart, sister of the prosperous merchant tailor and dry goods entrepreneur Benedict Shubart. Business partners Levi Rosenfeld and Jacob Rosenberg married sisters in the Reese family. Of the dozen Lake Street Jewish-owned businesses in 1847, six were clothing stores and the remainder dry goods establishments.[5]

Throughout the nineteenth century the German-Jewish community underwent rapid economic and social achievement and upward mobility. One observer, reminiscing about the evolution of the community, commented that "there were no millionaires among the Jews, but all felt independent." This independence characterized the active involvement of German-Jewish bankers and merchants in the city's financial affairs and the successes of firms such as clothiers Hart, Schaffner, and Marx; B. Kuppenheimer and Company; the Florsheim Shoe Company; and department stores such as Mandel Brothers; Siegel, Cooper, and Company; and Maurice L. Rothschild.[6]

The first communal decision facing the group was the necessity of providing formal religious services and a burial ground. In 1845 the Jewish Burial Ground Society was established and cemetery lots were purchased in what is today Lincoln Park. Later that year two dry goods merchants, Levi Rosenfeld and Jacob Rosenberg, provided facilities for the first formal religious services. Shortly after the Yom Kippur observances in 1846, less than twenty Jews formed Kehilath Anshe Mayriv (Men of the West) Congregation. Fourteen men signed the initial constitution, and the unity of the community continued when the fledgling Jewish Burial Ground Society ceded its property to the new congregation and ceased its independent existence. In 1849, K.A.M. leased a lot on Clark Street between Adams and Quincy Streets and erected a frame house of worship.[7]

Before the Civil War the extrareligious concerns of the community members were also being addressed. Bankers and merchants Moses and Elias Greenebaum, Mayer Klein, Levi Klein, Isaac Wolf, and Moses Rubel founded the Hebrew Benevolent Society in 1851 to provide sick and burial benefits for its members. The group purchased three acres in suburban Lake View for a cemetery and held monthly meetings to discuss the problems of the organization and the greater community. The organization was soon absorbed by the United Hebrew Relief Association (UHRA). This was the first central Jewish relief organization to provide aid for "immediate cases" and maintain a reserve fund to provide for a "hospital in which poor coreligionists shall be attended to when sick and for an asylum to receive Jewish widows and orphans without means."[8]

The UHRA was the result of the unification of the Bavarian and Polish segments of the community into one common organization. The synthesis was facilitated by the development of the first of many B'nai B'rith Lodges, Ramah Number 33 on June 15, 1857. Founded in New York in 1843, B'nai B'rith combined mutual aid functions with purely fraternal features. The charter of the organization promised to "banish from its deliberations all doctrinal and dogmatic discussions . . . and by the practice of moral and benevolent precepts bring about union and harmony" among Jews. The Chicago organizers, led by Henry Greenebaum, optimistically hoped the group would lead to the eradication of "the miserable provincial boundaries existing in Chicago."

In succeeding years other B'nai B'rith chapters, some with distinctly Teutonic names like Germania No. 83 and Teutonia No. 95, were chartered. The use of Germanic names among social, charitable, and fraternal associations was commonplace in the German-Jewish community; and many members identified primarily with the general German population. Morris Gutstein, an historian of the nineteenth-century Jewish community, has written that "the German-speaking Jew considered German his vernacular . . . attended the German theater, preferred German music, read the German newspapers, shaped his social life on the German pattern, sponsored German organizations, and belonged to German clubs."[9]

Perhaps the most important and ambitious undertaking for this community during the nineteenth century was the building of a Jewish hospital. In 1865 the UHRA purchased a site on LaSalle Street between Schiller and Goethe streets for seven thousand dollars. Mass fund-raising meetings were held and pledges made to admit all cases "irrespective of creed or race." Open scarcely a year, the hospital was completely destroyed during the Chicago Fire of 1871. For the next decade the Jewish community was without "their own hospital." In 1881 the new Michael Reese Hospital, located at Twenty-ninth Street and the Lake, began admitting patients. Named after Michael Reese, whose six sisters were pioneer members of the Jewish community, its first officials, staff physicians, and surgeons—with the exception of Dr. Michael Mannheimer—were non-Jews.[10]

The hospital was not the only loss suffered by the Jewish community. The Jewish area in and around the central business district was completely destroyed, rendering over five hundred Jews destitute and homeless. The disaster forced Chicago's Jews to move both north and south of the city's center. Scarcely had the community regained its footing, when another fire raced across the near South Side in 1874, inflicting great damage to the embryonic Russian-Polish settlement located south of the area leveled by the earlier blaze.

Until 1874 there was no definite demarcation between the German-Jewish "Golden Ghetto" of the South and near North Sides and the "West Side Ghetto" of the Russo-Polish Jews. After the second fire a sizable number of East Europeans crossed the Chicago River and relocated on the West Side, thus marking the beginning of Chicago's real ghetto district.[11] The more prosperous members of the German-speaking Jewish community continued drifting south into the Prairie Avenue district, where resided such noteworthy neighbors as the Armours, Fields, Pullmans, and Kimballs, and the Kenwood and Hyde Park areas. By 1900 the area south of 22nd Street attracted the majority of Chicago's German-Jewish population. The near South Side residences were not abandoned because of an "invasion of people of a lower economic status nor the settlement of another racial group. . . ." Rather, the movement of the community's first families and the relocation of community institutions heralded the movement into the Grand Boulevard, Kenwood, and Hyde Park areas.[12]

Despite the apparently ongoing dispersal of Jewish population, the synagogue remained the primary focal point of the Jewish community. It not only provided spiritual sustenance, but also administered the sacrificial slaughter of animals and the baking of matzoth, educated the children, and responded to the needs of the aged and sick. On the Sabbath and other holidays, businesses in both the retail and wholesale district were closed for the day. The windows and doors of every Jewish business house had a placard reading "closed on account of Jewish holiday."[13] However, by the 1850s the successful growth of Jewish business establishments and the desire to become "Americanized" led to public violation of the Sabbath. Many no longer attended religious services, or otherwise arrived late and departed early.

In 1852, Old World distinctions and intragroup differences resulted in the initial division of the community. A group of German-Polish Jews, upset by the clannishness of the Bavarian Jews and their *Bayerische Shul* (KAM), established the B'nai Shalom (Men of Peace) Congregation. The drama of superior and inferior class and caste, of personal, factional, and programmatic differences that resulted in secession and erection of new organizations, would become one of the most familiar characteristics of the Chicago Jewish community.

Declaring that its purpose was "to awaken and cultivate a truer conception of Judaism and a higher realization of Jewish religious life," the *Juedischer Reformverein* society was formed by such notables as real estate inventor Mayer Klein, banker Elias Greenebaum, and schoolteacher Bernard Felsenthal. The introduction of Reform Judaism was concurrent with German-Jewish communal growth and synagogue relocation. Imported from Germany, where Jews of high social status decided to dignify and modernize their religious services, Reform Judaism emphasized the progressive nature of Jewish law and called for the preaching of sermons in the vernacular, the use of organs, and questioning the divinity of the Bible.

Reform Judaism was readily embraced in this country because American Judaism had no overall community leadership or structure. Furthermore, there were so many different synagogues and unaffiliated social, fraternal, and service institutions and organizations concerned with varying aspects of Jewish life. By the 1880s, German-Jewish congregations instituted preaching in both English and German. With the use of the vernacular in the liturgy, the demand for making Sunday the Sabbath increasingly gained momentum. In 1885, Rabbi Emil G. Hirsch of Temple Sinai (formerly the *Juedischer Reformverein* Society) reported that "no services were held on Saturdays for the last four weeks because there was no audience."[14] By the turn of the century German-Jewish temples generally agreed on the substitution of Sunday for the Sabbath. Hirsch's explanation of the change indicates the decline not only of the synagogue as the focus of the community, but of the success of Jewish citizenry within the larger Gentile community and the pressure of the larger community on the minority group. Rabbi Hirsch observed: "It is our opinion that in this hustling and busy country where everyone is compelled to toil six days every week for a living, and where Sunday is a legal day of rest . . . the Jew cannot afford to rest for two days and compete with his neighbors. . . . Speaking for the vast number of Jews here it is safe to say that most of them do not regard Saturday as a holiday. With very rare exception, all Jewish business houses are open. . . . Which would be wiser, to lose all our religion or simply to change our Sabbath day?"[15]

Concerned individuals and religious leaders continually sought to stimulate Jewish intellect and dialogue through the establishment of literary societies, newspapers, journals, and club affiliations. The first literary group, the Clay Literary Society, was established as early as 1859 by Henry Hart: an immigrant from Eppelsheim, Germany who later became a partner in the Hart, Schaffner and Marx clothing firm. He announced that the purpose of the society was to cultivate "literary interests and speaking and debating ability among the Jewish youth of Chicago."[16] Community leaders hoped that the establishment of Jewish publications would facilitate the aims of the group in addition to providing the community with general information, original essays, smatterings of political information, and commentary on Jewish spiritual and religious problems. By 1891 there were at least five publications serving the German-Jewish community. Despite claims of objectivity, the journals became the personal vehicles of editors who were products of Jewish emancipation and advocates of Reform Judaism.

The more prosperous members of the community held their ethnic-oriented meetings and social functions at the *Concordia Club*, located at Dearborn and Monroe streets. The organization was "the rendezvous for leading personalities in Jewish community life." However, by 1869 the membership became bitterly divided over political questions. Sixty-nine Concordians, including the most important members of Chicago's German-Jewish financial and political community, met and established the Standard Club. This event signaled an increasing affluence and security of commercial interests that allowed leisure time for social activities. Several additional social clubs and a country club were added: North Side German-Jewry established the Ideal Club; South Side Jews

Upper-class German Jews at a charity show. *Courtesy of University of Illinois Library at Chicago, Manuscripts Division.*

organized the Lakeside Club; and German-speaking Bohemian Jews who resided on the near West Side founded the West Chicago Club.

When the increasingly affluent German-Jewish community organized the Ravisloe Country Club in south suburban Homewood, Illinois in 1901, it was "the foremost, as it was the first, Jewish organization of its kind in the city." Urbanologist Louis Wirth has written that by 1901 the country club and the Standard Club, "even more than the separate religious institutions that characterized the Jewish community and divided off the various strata from one another . . . was indicative of the great chasm which separated the Bavarians from the . . . latest arrivals, the Russians."[17]

While Chicago's 20,000 German-Jews were undergoing rapid acculturation, showing upward economic, social, and residential mobility, two million Jews from Russia, Romania, Poland, and Austria-Hungary were preparing to come to America. The East European Jews who began to come to America in the 1880s dramatically and indelibly altered the character of the Jewish-American community. They emigrated for a variety of political, religious, social, and economic reasons. During one period, between 1815 and 1914, Russia issued more than one thousand decrees regulating Jewish religious and communal life, economic activities, military service, educational opportunities, and property rights. Between 1882 and 1914 these restrictions culminated in officially sanctioned and frequently ferocious pogroms that resulted in mass emigration. The hardships of Jews from Romania, Austria-Hungary, and Poland differed only in degree from the sufferings of their Russian coreligionists.

Vast numbers of newly arriving immigrants were disappointed in the Chicago that greeted them. Unlike the legends, the streets were not paved with gold—they were not broad and beautiful or even paved at all. Life was not as gay and bright as many had fantasized. They crowded into the near West Side, an area bounded by Canal, Halsted, Polk, and 15th streets. Within a few years the near West Side encompassed both a large and small ghetto. The former was bounded by Polk Street on the north, Blue Island on the west, 15th Street on the south, and Stewart on the east, and had a population of 70,000, of whom 20,000 were Jews. The smaller ghetto, bounded by 12th, Halsted, 15th,

The other Jews: life and trade near Maxwell Street. *Courtesy of Chicago Historical Society.*

and Stewart avenues, had a population of 15,000-16,000 of which 90 percent were Jews. Bohemian Jews were the first to enter the West Side ghetto; in short order they were followed by Russians, Poles, and Hungarians. Though the coreligionists were residentially intermingled, there was a tendency to settle into separate little colonies. Hull House resident Charles Zeublein observed in 1895 that the Russian and Polish Jews clustered between Polk and 12th streets, while the Bohemians resided in the better zone south and west of Halsted and 12th streets.[18]

The near West Side was convenient and commodious to East European Jews because it was close to the train depots, rentals were cheap, and landlords were not finicky about nationality. Furthermore, reminiscences of the European *shtetl* abounded—including bearded males, frock coats, widebrimmed hats, shawled women, and *landsleute* (people from the same town or area). Employment with no Saturday work was frequently available.[19] The ghetto's focal point was the intersection of Halsted and Maxwell streets. Radiating from it was a conglomeration of houses, stores, shops, open stalls, stables, peddlers' carts, kosher butcher shops, dry goods emporiums, matzoh bakeries, synagogues, sweatshops, tailor and seamstress shops, pawnshops, second-hand stores, Hebrew schools, lawyers' and doctors' offices, marriage arrangement bureaus, and approved circumcisers. From early morning to late in the evening the streets were filled with people coming and going to their places of employment, socializing, or seeking everyday necessities.

The tall tenements characteristic of New York's lower East Side were uncommon in Chicago. As the population density of the West Side increased, frame houses and warehouses were converted and partitioned to hold the newcomers. The ghetto-dwelling Jews lived in small, low, one- or two-story wooden shanties built before the streets were elevated and graded, three- or four-story brick tenements, or in buildings erected at the rear of a lot, with no light in front and the ever-present aromas of a squalid alley. Frequently, these accommodations served double duty—as living and working quarters for the sweatshop industry. Single people rented furnished rooms or boarded with already overcrowded Jewish families. Rentals began at one dollar a week and included coffee and tea in the morning. The overcrowding and the poverty taxed even the legendary capabilities of Jewish housekeepers.[20]

Bathtubs were conspicuously absent in the ghetto. One study recorded that almost 97 percent of the people had "no opportunity in their own homes to bathe." The area supported at least six bathing establishments that charged fifteen to twenty-five cents per bath. On the other hand, the area also contained only twenty-four saloons in

1900, the lowest ratio of bars to people of any immigrant quarter in Chicago.

Overcrowding often drove the residents into the streets for relief. At night adults and children slept on the sidewalks and roofs of the ghetto buildings. Disease was a frequent visitor to area residents, and even when preventive measures like the smallpox vaccination became available, many in the Jewish quarter resisted. It was not until the shopowners found their businesses empty during the busy season that they reluctantly consented to vaccination for themselves and their employees. The rapid opening and shuttering of sweatshops inhibited efficient inspection. Smallpox and tuberculosis were concealed because of the fear of financial ruin and the evils—real or imaginary—of the pesthouse.[21]

In contrast to the experience of German-Jews, these East Europeans had entered a Chicago that was in the full bloom of its industrialization. For at least a decade their immediate economic future was to serve that machine economy as a fluid and inexpensive labor supply. Many found employment in the garment trades, not because of any inherent affinity for the needle and thread, but because of the constant demand for cheap labor. The majority were "Columbus tailors" who became wedded to the sewing machine (*Katrinka*) only after they reached America.[22]

Starting in the 1880s, the United Hebrew Charities found jobs for the new arrivals in the burgeoning German-Jewish clothing firms. Critics described the areas on 12th Street between Canal and Jefferson streets as "pools of sweat and blood" where "human lives are sacrificed on the altar of profit." Prior to the workers' organization and unionization, they were lined up "in rows like soldiers seated at their machines. . . . They cannot speak to one another, they cannot sing at their work . . . they must do only what their machine commands. . . . When the workers come home . . . they have not sufficient strength left . . . to think or read . . . and for that reason hundreds of workers . . . are considered slaves. . . ."[23] Employment was seasonal, and wages, low enough during the peak season, became poor or nonexistent in the off-season. Workers received between five and twenty-five dollars per week, but wages varied according to the individual branch of the garment industry and the degree of skill required. Necessity led to the use of child labor in many of the factories and sweatshops. Frequently, fathers had to compete with their own wives and children for survival.[24]

Despite taxing working conditions and inadequate salaries, the clothing trades offered a future; they were part of the "coming business." Shops were often small enterprises run on a shoestring. If a worker could accumulate a few dollars, he was able to enter the circle of bosses. Those who could not find success in the garment industry tried their luck at peddling or trades like tobacco merchandising.

Although small numbers of ghetto residents were employed as store clerks, stockkeepers, office clerks, mail carriers, post-office clerks, government employees, and even as teachers, lawyers, dentists, and physicians, peddling was nonetheless the easiest avenue to entrepreneurial success. The ghetto teemed with a multitude of peddlers. Some rang doorbells, others were customer peddlers who visited a regular clientele. Others owned horses and wagons and collected rags, old bottles, papers, and odds and ends. Some positioned their pushcarts, crammed with wares, at fixed locations, while others plied their carts up and down the streets searching for prospective customers. These pushcarts, boxes, wheelbarrows, and wagons served as mobile department stores, but the peddlers were often the target of well-aimed missiles and physical attacks.[25]

Institutions developed among East European Jews to implement, preserve, and enhance economic, social, and religious practices and traditions. The first permanent Jewish labor organizations appeared after the 1886 Haymarket Riot. Early attempts at unionization were only mildly successful, primarily because of divided ideologies and seemingly utopian demands. The United Hebrew Trades was founded in 1888 by Jewish socialists and labor organizers, and the United German Trades was formed to guide the unionization of Jewish workers and coordinate labor, fraternal, and cultural groups in the Jewish community. At first, the UHT was divorced from the general labor movement, but eventually they sent delegates to conventions of international unions and meetings of central labor federations to protect and enhance "Jewish interests." The UHT became the trade union *modus vivendi* since "there was a need for a separate Jewish trade union movement because of differences in psychology, language, and the general mode of living between Jewish and other workers."[26]

Yiddish *Volkstheaters*, the Metropolitan Hall, Irwin's, and later Glickman's became the dramatic and musical centers of the neighborhood. A resident noted that "upon entering the Yiddish theater, one left America." A similar but unsympathetic sentiment was articulated by a reviewer for the German-Jewish newspaper, *The Occident*, who complained that "the play was decidedly unethical while the culture of the gallery-gods appeared more like cossacklike fiendishness; there was stamping, yelling, whistling, smoking, spitting, and hooting in the manner of the lowest of Arabs."[27]

For those who possessed the inclination and strength, there were night schools dispensing lessons in "American." Social worker Grace

Abbott observed that "they attend night school more regularly than
. . . any other nationality, and in a year they usually make rapid progress
if they are strong enough to keep up the day and evening work." Numerous social and service agencies appeared with increasing rapidity
in the ghetto. The Chicago Hebrew Institute, Maxwell Street Settlement, and Hull House aided the newcomers in adjusting to urban living and offered protection against the multifarious forms of exploitation.
Esther Kohn, a Jewish social worker, commented that "cultural and
recreational needs were met in classes in literature, art, music, and
handicrafts which relieved the monotony of the only jobs offered to
newcomers. They also found appreciation of their worth as human
beings."[28]

For others, the Yiddish newspapers served as classroom and socialization agency. These newspapers enabled both the learned and
the uneducated to follow local, national, and world affairs in a familiar
language while giving the newcomers an elementary education in the
process of Americanization. Between 1877 and 1914 at least twelve
Yiddish newspapers and periodicals were published in Chicago. Unlike the German-Jewish press, the editors of the Yiddish press were
not religious leaders. Rather, they were a varied mixture of printers,
journalists, businessmen, and trade union officials. While the German-
Jewish press concerned itself with ethical and philosophical questions,
the Yiddish press addressed itself more to the problems of adaptation
to and dissemination of information relative to surviving in what was
often a baffling and puzzling America.

In the struggle for existence and advancement the East European
Jew was, however, sustained by his religion. Though religion was assuming a secondary role with the German-Jewish community, it was
growing and strenghtening itself among the newest arrivals. By 1910
more than forty orthodox synagogues were established in the city's East
European Jewish neighborhoods. Some congregations were located in
imposing structures, others in modest and unpretentious surroundings.
For at least one immigrant generation, religious orthodoxy was clearly
interwoven with daily life. Although attendance was not and could not
be compulsory as it had been in the *shtetls*, these synagogues, both
simple and magnificent, were open most of the day and evening. Services began early so that workers could pray before going to work.
Hebrew liturgy was used even though a majority of the congregants
probably could not understand it. Men and women sat separately, and
there were no organs or mixed choirs. Sermons were frequently delivered in Yiddish. Within the confines of the synagogue, Jews of varying
degrees of piety could for a time forget their struggles for existence and
advancement in America.

For those who drifted from Orthodoxy but found Reform Judaism distasteful and foreign, the Conservative movement offered an alternative that claimed to retain "the best of the traditional form and spirit of our heritage, in as thorough an American and modern setting as possible." Nevertheless, the majority of East European Jews clung tenaciously to Orthodox Judaism. They were horrified and dismayed by the lack of religiosity, the desecration of tradition, heterogamy, and lack of knowledge of Yiddish of the German-Jews.

If the assimilated German-Jews were rudely jolted by their Eastern cousins, Russian-Jews often felt as distant from their coreligionists as they did from the Gentile community. One ghetto dweller summed up the general feeling of the community when he proclaimed: "When I first put my feet on the soil of Chicago, I was so disgusted that I wished I had stayed . . . in Russia. I left the Old Country because you couldn't be a Jew over there and still live, but I would rather be dead then be the kind of German Jew that brings the Jewish name into disgrace by being a Goy. That's what hurts: They parade around as Jews, and down deep in their hearts they are worse than Goyim, they are *meshumeds* [apostates]."[29]

Such feelings were reciprocated within the German-Jewish community, resulting in less than harmonious relationships between the coreligionists. Many German-Jews decried the conspicuousness and "antiquarian" religious practices of the Russians, claiming that they were "not a part of the Jewish religion" and placed the immigrants in "a light which is anything but commendable." Ghetto residents were referred to as a "collection of nihilists" who were singled out for praise during one High Holiday season for being peaceable and remaining at home.

Having "arrived" socially and economically, the German-Jews were embarrassed and fearful that association with *Ostjuden* would endanger their marginal acceptance by Gentile society. As 1886 drew to a close, *The Occident* lamented: "Twenty-six thousand Polish Jews in a single year! That is certainly an overdose for our American national economy. . . . Why should we be deceived? These Polish Jews are indigestible for the American stomach as are the Chinese. . . . As they are here, they must be put to some use. . . . It is to be assumed that . . . the first, if not the second generations, may become sufficiently Americanized to be tolerable. . . . It would indeed be desirable if they would stay away altogether. We have enough and sufficient Polish Jews . . . and will thank the powers that be in Europe, to not send us any more."[30]

At times the German-Jewish community urgently sought to exclude East Europeans from the United States by suggesting that they immigrate to South America because Russian-Jews were a "burden upon the well-to-do of their race and religion." One observer falsely claimed that "they are assisted to cross the ocean; but a few are self-sustaining; as a body they are paupers; many are diseased and many are criminals." This German-Jewish observer piously claimed that "this is the judgment of the most intelligent American Jews. . . ."[31]

Lest the East Europeans become embarrassingly visible public charges, German-Jewish organizations somewhat reluctantly voted moneys to aid the Russian refugees. Relief stations providing temporary shelter facilities and hot meals were provided for the needy. The Jewish Training School was established on the near West Side to teach the East Europeans wage-earning skills, while the Society to Aid the Russian Refugees and the Hebrew Immigrant Aid Society attempted to relocate ghetto residents in *rural* areas.

Demands by both the German and East European communities led to the founding of an orphans' home, a residence for aged Jews, and a settlement house. Recognizing that many of the services available to the Jewish communities were overlapping, leaders in the German-Jewish community in 1900 created the Associated Jewish Charities, an umbrella organization responsible for the central collection and distribution of aid and information.

Nevertheless, Russian Jewry believed that the German-Jewish "scientific" approach to charity, complete with documents, inquests, and other forms of "snooping," corrupted the religious obligation of charity—that it be an act of pure loving-kindness. Thus, by 1915 both communities had highly organized charitable groups offering duplicate services. The German-Jews were represented by the Associated Jewish Charities and the East Europeans by the Federated Orthodox Jewish Charities, which supported Maimonides Hospital, the Consumptive Relief Society, the Marks Nathan Orphan Home, and other institutions. The parochialism of Chicago's Jewish communities at the organizational level was at last formally eclipsed in 1922, when the AJC and the FOJC merged to form the Jewish Charities of Chicago.

By 1900 the German-Jewish community, despite the appearance of uniformity, was in reality a diverse amalgam with forebears from Bavaria, Prussia, Western Poland, Bohemia, Austria, and the Netherlands. German Jewry no longer lived "in the bonds of one family circle." Unlike during the founding years, they did not worship "harmoniously in one temple" if they worshipped at all. The sharing of common satisfactions and concerns had become increasingly bothersome, and intracommunity relations were maintained with great effort. Such an evolution had been prophesied as early as 1870 by Dr. Liebman Adler, spiritual leader of KAM. He observed that the Jewish community was composed of "thousands scattered over a space of nearly thirty miles . . . divided by pecuniary, intellectual and social distinctions, provincial jealousies and even religious distinctions and differences." Adler decried the process of acculturation, noting that "we are losing the consciousness of homogeneity and the strength gained for each individual by concerted action."[32]

Early in the first decade of the twentieth century the area south of 22nd Street had increasingly become the residential district for the majority of Chicago's German-Jewish population. By World War I, South Side German-Jewry was located in the Kenwood, Hyde Park, and Grand Boulevard areas. The more affluent and assimilated residents, however, were increasingly attracted to the northern suburbs of Wilmette, Winnetka, and Glencoe. By the middle of that decade the original West Side ghetto of the Eastern Europeans had become a largely non-Jewish area; the Jews had moved to the new "Israels"—Lawndale, Humboldt Park, Columbus Park, Albany Park, Rogers Park, Hyde Park, and South Shore. Those who came earliest were now farthest removed from the original ghetto.

The remaining ghetto residents referred derisively to Lawndale as "Deutschland" and to its residents as "Deitchuks." Those who remained behind viewed the migrations as a desertion of old customs and religious beliefs in an attempt to emulate the non-Jewish ways of the highly assimilated German-Jews. Actually, East European Jews were only demonstrating a new-found socio-economic mobility as they moved westward to areas not yet overcrowded or substandard, but with spacious streets, yards, parks, and substantial duplex apartments. With the Jewish influx, the two-family, two-story buildings were supplanted by large apartment houses with no fewer than ten dwelling units, to accommodate an increased population. By 1930, Lawndale contained a population of 112,000, of whom an estimated 75,000 were Jewish.[33] Once ensconced, the Jews organized a far-flung network of secular and religious institutions throughout Lawndale.

Another secondary area of settlement for East European Jewry was Humboldt Park, located on Chicago's northwest side. In 1906 this area contained approximately one-quarter of Chicago's Jewish population. By the 1930s, Humboldt Park had a Jewish population of almost 25,000, and the area of settlement was expanding. During the 1920s the northside Albany Park community attracted Jewish families striving for rapid secularization and economic advancement. In 1923 an estimated 4,700 Jews resided there; by 1930, Jews made up an estimated 23,000 of the community's population of 55,577.[34]

In the city's far northeast corner, East Rogers Park, two congregations had been established by 1930. Temple Mizpah, founded in 1919 by residents interested in Reform Judaism, had grown to a congregation of 500 families by 1926. The memberships of Mizpah and of B'nai Zion, a nearby Conservative synagogue founded in 1918, were composed primarily of second- or third-generation Jewish-Americans who had moved from the West, Northwest, and South sides.[35] Following World War I, East European Jews began moving into the German-Jewish bastion of Kenwood-Hyde Park. There they joined Reform or Conservative temples and gave up orthodoxy "as they changed their residence." Wirth observes that "even the aristocratic German-Jewish clubs are beginning to open their doors to the more successful and desirable members of the Russian group." In 1930 these areas contained about 12 percent, or 11,000, of Chicago's 270,000 Jews.[36]

By 1930 the Jewish settlements of Chicago included approximately ninety Orthodox synagogues, thirteen Reform temples, and ten Conservative congregations. There were three rabbinical associations, two synagogue federations, a theological seminary, a board of Jewish education, the Jewish People's Institute with an annual total attendance of one million, and a multitude of social, benevolent, fraternal, and charitable organizations.[37] Nonetheless, tangible and intangible boundaries continued to separate and divide the ranks of Chicago Jewry. Tangible differences included location and type of residence, areas and concentrations of employment, religious postures, synagogue and temple affiliations, clubs, lodges, and union or business association memberships. Less discernible to many observers, but of signal importance, were national and ancestral origin, degree of identification with the lifestyles of the larger Anglo-Saxon society, and the expressed political attitudes and voting patterns of Chicago Jews.

The American political milieu acted as a transmitter of economic and psychological succor, individual advancement, and group recognition. Jewish political figures composed a diverse group, including classic boss types who emphasized personalized politics, reformers, and middle-grounders who used machine tactics to achieve beneficial and constructive socio-political ends. Neither the German or East European Jewish communities had a monopoly on any one type. The most successful municipal leaders combined the efficiency and personalization of the machine with the ideology of good government and reform, in order to appeal to the widest possible electorate.

In local affairs the German-Jewish quest for security, status, and acceptability by the larger American community led them to support measures, policies, and candidates advanced by "Protestant Puritans" who found their major supporters in the do-good reformist wing of the Republican party. Increasingly, they called for nonpartisan operation of municipal government as a means of curbing the excesses of urbanization. Favorable Jewish support for Republican commercial and industrial policies, first established in the 1860s, coalesced to forge a strong tradition of voting Republican in state and national contests that remained unchanged until the 1930s.

East European Jews cut their political teeth on issues other than those that attracted the German-Jews to the local and national Republican standards. Faced with the challenge of individual, family, and cultural survival in a strange environment, the East Europeans responded to matters of immediate and pressing concern. These included personal liberty and Sunday closing laws, sensitivity to and recognition of Jewish-Americans, and generous immigration policies. They quickly established a rapport not only with Republican bosses like William Lorimer but also with Democratic chieftains like the Carter Harrisons.[38] Shortly thereafter, individual Jewish political figures like Adolf Kraus, William Loeffler, and Adolph Sabath became trusted lieutenants and confidants of their party leaders. German-Jewish entreaties and blandishments for reform were rejected by the East Europeans in favor of a more comprehensible, traditional, conservative, and trusted approach. However, when reformist policies were advanced by a trusted Democratic leader like a Harrison, Sabath, or Jacob Arvey, they responded positively.

In national and state affairs before World War I, the Eastern European Jewish response was mixed. Regardless of party, they supported those candidates who manifested concern for their socio-economic positions, displayed ethnic sensitivity, and fought to keep a free and open immigration policy. One man, however, was able successfully to unite these diverse propensities and produce a unified "Jewish vote." He was Henry Horner, five-time probate court judge and a favorite of both the German and Eastern European Jewish electorates because he satisfied the ever-present desire for ethnic recognition.

Born in Chicago on November 30, 1878, Henry was the third son of Dilah Horner and Solomon Levy. The relationship of his parents was anything but harmonious, and in 1883 they were divorced. The chidren moved in with Hannah Dernberg Horner, their maternal grandmother, and assumed the family name. Henry grew up in a decidedly political atmosphere. His uncle Isaac was a veteran member of Hinky Dink Kenna's and "Bathhouse" John Coughlin's First Ward forces. As a law student, too young to vote, Henry received his political baptism campaigning for Carter Harrison II in 1897.

In 1899, Horner graduated from Kent College of Law, was admitted to the bar, began specializing in real estate and probate law, and cultivated Harrison leaders and members of the Jewish community. By

1900 he had joined the prestigious German-Jewish Standard Club, where his maternal grandfather, Henry Horner I, had been one of the club's charter members in 1869. Between 1906 and 1912 the enterprising lawyer-politician was serving on the club's board of directors.

In 1902, the Harrison organization slated young Horner as the party's nominee for collector of South Chicago. However, at the same election a referendum was held on the question of abolishing the seven "towns" existing within Chicago. Although Horner defeated his opponent, the elimination of town government also carried; Horner's triumph was meaningless. Significantly, the German-Jewish community began their tradition of rallying to his side. He was, according to the *Reform Advocate,* a "young man, eminently fitted for the responsible position he seeks."[39]

Following the 1902 campaign Horner expanded his law practice, strengthened his political relationships, and furthered his social and business associations with German-Jewish leaders. Between 1907 and 1911, Horner was appointed attorney for the Cook County Board of Assessors. In 1911, Mayor Harrison appointed him delegate to the city charter convention for Chicago. In the succeeding three years he developed an intimate political association with the assistant county treasurer, Jacob Lindheimer. Supported by Lindheimer and Harrison, Horner was elected to the probate court in 1914.

Thereafter—every four years through 1930—he was returned to office by progressively larger margins. In 1926 he had no Democratic primary opposition, and the Republicans encountered difficulty in finding a "strong candidate to oppose him." In 1930 he led the county ticket, a "distinction that carries a great deal of significance among politicians."[40] Judge Horner developed a reputation as one of Cook County's outstanding jurists; he was an efficient and personable judge of impeccable integrity.

Although the jurist belonged to both Sinai and KAM congregations, he was not a devout Jew. He observed the High Holidays but did not practice other Jewish rituals. He enjoyed the social obligations of political life and established working relationships with such Eastern European Jewish political figures as Michael and Moe Rosenberg, Jacob Arvey, Harry Fisher, and Adolph Sabath.[41] Politically, Horner had the ability to relate successfully to Democrats, Republicans, reformers, and organization types. Although friendly with German-Jewish reformers like Emil G. Hirsch and Julius Rosenwald, Horner resisted political involvement with individuals and groups that wanted to function outside the framework of the Democratic and Republican parties, because he believed that it was suicidal to step beyond the working structure of organized politics.

Before a 24th Ward gathering in 1932, Horner paid homage to Mayor Anton Cermak, the Rosenbergs, Alderman Arvey, and other political regulars who were responsible for his gubernatorial candidacy. He realized that political patronage and favors were the mortar that held the organization together. Horner promised to utilize his patronage powers, if he was elected governor, to reward the party faithful.

The 1932 gubernatorial campaign theme declared: "With Horner we'll turn the corner." Horner was depicted as sincerely interested in the welfare of all Illinoisans. The electorate was warned that the 1932 primary contests were of the utmost importance. Precinct workers and newspapers in Jewish areas emphasized the necessity of registering to vote. The Jewish press reported Horner's appearance at any Jewish-oriented event. Voters were reminded that if Horner were victorious, the Democrats would triumph in November at the local and national

The winning Governor Henry Horner, shown with Mayor Anton Cermak, Mrs. Floyd Finley, and Tom Courtney. *Courtesy of Chicago Historical Society.*

levels and a deathblow would be dealt the growing economic depression. The *Daily Jewish Courier* proclaimed that Chicago's Jews had a dual duty: "They must express their appreciation of Judge Horner and confirm the choice of the Democratic party."[42]

Horner's two major opponents in the primary, State Representative Michael Igoe and Democratic State Chairman Bruce Campbell, ran well downstate and succeeded in cancelling each other out. The city's Jewish electorate, regardless of area of residence, degree of assimilation, socioeconomic position, national origin, or religious philosophy, overwhelmingly supported their coreligionst.[43]

With precinct work in the able hands of regulars such as Arvey and the Lindheimer family, Horner was at liberty to stump the state; he emphasized the themes of economic dislocation, the ills of Prohibition, and the influence of corrupt politicians, especially his opponent, former Governor Len Small.

The totals in the November general election mirrored the results of the spring primary. Chicago's Jewish voters provided Horner with handsome majorities. In North Lawndale's 24th Ward, he bested Small by a ten-to-one margin. Nevertheless, so far as the national presidential election was concerned, many already Republican German-Jewish voters also fostered the idea that "with Hoover we'll turn the corner." In Hyde Park's 5th Ward, a "2H Club" for Horner and Hoover was active. Republican precinct captains lamented that the "Jewish vote is not controllable." In one precinct there were only fifteen registered Democrats, but 137 votes were cast for Horner. A distraught captain observed that "this shows that many Jews switched for Horner and then voted a straight Republican ticket." Horner aide and Fifth Ward Committeeman Horace Lindheimer, recognizing the ethnic attraction, indicated that Horner's triumph was more than a "question of turning the ins out and the outs in."[44]

On February, 15, 1933, Mayor Cermak was fatally wounded by an assassin's bullet intended for President Roosevelt, and his death on March 6 germinated the seeds for conflict as well as cooperation. Newly elected Governor Horner bypassed the opportunity to become party leader, perhaps naively believing that fellow Democrats would happily endorse his policies and programs solely on merit. The City Council, authorized to select a new mayor, chose Ed Kelly, party loyalist and chief engineer of the Sanitary District—and a resident of Horner's own 4th Ward.

When Prohibition ended in 1933, Kelly wanted sole control of the licensing and regulation of Chicago's saloons. However, Governor Horner was diametrically opposed to Kelly's plan, believing that the state should have sole control. Mayor Kelly became increasingly agitated over Horner's independence and constantly derided the governor to his associates. By mid-1933 the relationship had deteriorated severely, threatening the unity of the Democratic party. Horner's independent style and executive actions even alienated some of his Jewish allies.

During the 1936 primary campaign, the Democratic organization, led by Mayor Kelly, dedicated itself to prove to Jewish voters that the decision not to endorse Horner's quest for re-election was not based on the issue of religion or ethnicity, but rather was related to the success or failure of the New Deal. Many of the submerged antagonisms between the German and Eastern European Jews surfaced as they became opposing forces.

In the primary, Jewish voters responded to Horner in direct proportion to their degree of assimilation, area of residence, and position on the economic scale. In those areas primarily inhabited by Eastern European Jews, the voter was more likely to be dependent on the favors and gratuities which the regular organization was capable of dispensing. Here these voters gave less weight to ethnic considerations. Horner carried eight Chicago wards, including the 5th, 6th, and 7th. These were South Side districts with large German-Jewish populations. His victories in the 39th, 40th, 48th, and 49th wards in North Side districts can be credited to the large numbers of middle- and upper-class Jewish residents in these areas. The only inner-city ward carried by Horner was Al Horan's 29th. There voters were free to vote their convictions because Committeeman Horan had been the beneficiary of Horner's state bonding patronage and remained loyal to the governor.

West Side Jews were trapped between the practicalities of everyday life and their affection for coreligionist Horner. Although many chose to follow the advice of men like 24th Ward Chief Jacob Arvey, who distributed jobs, obtained aid, and predicted that a Horner victory would threaten Roosevelt's position, they were not happy. "You did a terrible thing to me today. . . ," shouted one elderly man to Arvey. "You made me vote against Henry Horner, our Henry Horner."[45]

Nevertheless, Horner beat Chicago Health Commissioner Herman C. Bundesen, choice of the supposedly invincible machine of Mayor Kelly and county chairman Patrick Nash, and carried every downstate county, amassing a plurality of 317,105 votes outside Cook County.

Preparing for the November election, Horner set about shoring up his ethnic support in Chicago, and the Jewish communities girded up for the general election. On Tuesday, November 4, 1936, Horner was swept to re-election in the great Democratic landslide that engulfed Chicago, Illinois, and the nation. In defeating Republican gubernatorial hopeful C. Wayland Brooks, he received a plurality of 385,176 votes in the state and carried Chicago by a 319,690-vote margin. Jews who were organization Democrats and the Hornerites had ignored past differences, economic and social distinctions, national origins, areas of residence, and religious postures in order to secure the re-election of their coreligionist.[46] Unity reigned throughout the city's Jewish communities as the aspirations of both the Democratic organization and Chicago Jewry were satisfied. The covenant linking "Abraham's descendants" was reaffirmed and made lasting for future generations.

Henry Horner acted as a catalyst, uniting the traditionally Republican German-Jewish community with the Eastern European Jewish masses. Although he suffered a serious stroke following the 1938 elections, and died within twenty-four months, his candidacies and elections represented the apex of the Chicago Jewish electorate's drive for recognition. The bridge formed by Henry Horner and those who slated him for office provided a solid foundation for a lasting rapprochement among the Jewish communities of Chicago.

The ending of mass European immigration and the establishment of national origin quotas in the 1920s accelerated the interweaving of Eastern European and American lifestyles. The Depression, the New Deal, the onset of Nazism, World War II, and, above all, the birth and development of Israel, have dramatically affected and changed not only Chicago's but America's Jewish communities. During the war they knew that the Nazis did not distinguish between areas of origin and national ancestry when they selected victims for the gas chambers and crematoria. Furthermore, intermarriage between members of the Jewish communities and a common concern for the survival of Israel have forged a community consciousness and solidarity that was decidedly absent or ineffectual until relatively recent times.

Chapter III

IRVING CUTLER

The Jews of Chicago:
From Shtetl to Suburb

*The dispersion of the immigrant Jews . . . did not
mean ceasing to be a Jew or . . . ceasing to live
among Jews. It meant, simply, moving away.
Moving away from immigrant neighborhoods in
which Yiddish still prevailed; moving away from
parents whose will to success could unnerve the
most successful sons and daughters; moving to
"another kind" of Jewish neighborhood, more
pleasing in its physical look and allowing a larger
area of personal space; and moving towards new
social arrangements: the calm of a suburb, the
comfort of affluence. . . .*

Irving Howe, *World of Our Fathers*

JEWS CAME TO CHICAGO FROM ALMOST every country in Europe. Like the members of other immigrant groups, they left Europe because of economic, political, and religious difficulties. For Jewish immigrants, however, these difficulties were often compounded by a virulent anti-Semitism and even sporadic massacres. The most affluent and educated members of other immigrant groups often remained in their homelands, where they occupied secure and respected positions; but Jews of all economic strata and educational levels welcomed the opportunity to emigrate from most Central and Eastern European communities. And because of the harsh treatment they suffered, Jews were less interested in returning to Europe than was any other immigrant group. This was true despite the initial difficulties that many Jews experienced in their new American environment.

Most of the European Jewish immigrants to America settled along the East Coast, especially in New York City; but large numbers also made their way westward to the relatively accessible and thriving Chicago area. Although those who came to Chicago were at times limited by covert discrimination on the job, in housing, and in education, especially during the earlier years, the opportunities of a free land enabled them to flourish. Despite their varied homelands and backgrounds, in time Jews overcame periods of internal discord and achieved a degree of unity—a unity based on a common heritage, the problems of being a minority in a Gentile world, and most recently by a common desire for the success of Israel.

The First Wave: The German-Speaking Jews

Unlike the early Jewish settlers of colonial New York, who were mainly Sephardic Jews from the Mediterranean, with their distinct liturgy, religious customs, and pronunciation of the Hebrew language, the Jews who first settled in Chicago were Ashkenazim of Central and Eastern Europe. There were no Sephardim among Chicago's Jewish pioneers, though small numbers of Sephardim came to the city later.

The Ashkenazic Jews of Chicago fell into two relatively distinct groups. The first to arrive were German-speaking Jews from Central Europe—from Bavaria, the Rhenish Palatinate, Prussia, Austria, Bohemia, and the Posen part of Poland that was occupied by the Germans. Many of these Jews had experienced some of the political, intellectual, and economic benefits of the French Revolution during the decades that preceded the Congress of Vienna (1814–1815). They were more secular and urbane and generally more well-to-do than the second group, the Eastern European Jews who came in much larger numbers later. The latter were Yiddish-speaking Jews who came mainly from Russia, Poland, Romania, and Lithuania—areas whose Jews suffered from political and economic handicaps and were often subjected to especially severe persecution. They were a poor, deeply religious people, and most of them lived in small towns and villages (*shtetls*).

Among the earliest settlers in Chicago were small numbers of German Jews, mainly from Bavaria, who began to trickle into the area in the late 1830s and early 1840s. Among those who arrived in 1841 was Henry Horner, a Bohemian Jew who later became an organizer of the Chicago Board of Trade and a founder of a major wholesale grocery company, originally established at the western fringes of settlement at Randolph and Canal streets. His grandson of the same name served as governor of Illinois from 1933 to 1940.

In 1845 the Jews of Chicago held their first religious service on the Day of Atonement. The same year they organized the Jewish Burial Ground Society, and in 1846 they purchased an acre of land for forty-six dollars (in what is now Lincoln Park) for use as a Jewish cemetery. In 1847, above a dry goods store owned by Rosenfeld and Rosenberg on the southwest corner of Lake and Wells, about fifteen men formed Kehilath Anshe Mayriv (Congregation of the People of the West), or K.A.M., Chicago's first Jewish congregation—an Orthodox one. In 1851 the congregation erected a small frame synagogue on Clark Street just south of Adams Street (a site now commemorated by a plaque on the Kluczynski Federal Building).

The *Daily Democrat* of June 14, 1851, reported the dedication of the synagogue as follows:

> The ceremonies at the dedication of the first Jewish synagogue in Illinois, yesterday, were very interesting indeed. An immense number had to go away, from inability to gain admittance. There were persons of all denominations present. We noticed several clergymen of different religious denominations.
>
> The Jewish ladies cannot be beaten in decorating a church. The flowers, leaves and bushes were woven into the most beautiful drapery that Chicago ever saw before. The choir, consisting of a

Founded in 1847, Chicago's first Jewish congregation, Kehilath Anshe Mayriv (Congregation of the People of the West), occupied this building at 33rd and Indiana Avenue from 1891 to 1920 before it moved farther south to the Hyde Park-Kenwood area. Today the building houses the Pilgrim Baptist Church. *Courtesy of Irving Cutler.*

large number of ladies and gentlemen, did honor to the occasion and the denomination. . . .

As for any possible prejudice or anti-Semitism in Chicago, the newspaper went on with considerable enthusiasm:

> No person that has made up his mind to be prejudiced against the Jews ought to hear such a sermon preached. It was very captivating and contained as much real religion as any sermon we ever heard preached. We never could have believed that one of those old Jews we heard denounced so much could have taught so much liberality towards other denominations and earnestly recommended a thorough study of the Old Testament (each one for himself) and entire freedom of opinion and discussion.

The similarity between Judaism of this variety and some Protestant sects, especially Unitarianism/Universalism, was not missed by the Chicago journalist, who commented:

> We would sooner have taken him for one of the independent order of free thinkers, than a Jew. Mr. Isaacs is an Englishman and is settled in New York City. There are Jewish synagogues as far west as Buffalo and Cleveland.

The Jews in our city are not numerous, but are wealthy, very respectable and public spirited.

The Jewish Sabbath is on Saturday, and a very interesting service takes place today. The whole Mosaic law written on parchment (they never have it printed for church services) will be unrolled from a large scroll and read from. Rev. Mr. Isaacs will again preach. The service will commence at 8 A.M. and last until 11 A.M. The earlier part of the service will be the most interesting.

Gentlemen are requested to keep their hats on, and to take seats below. The ladies will take seats upstairs, according to the Jewish custom of separating the sexes.

The defeat of the revolutionary movements that swept Central Europe in 1848 increased Jewish immigration to the United States, and by 1860 there were approximately 1,500 in Chicago. Most of them lived around Lake and Wells streets, the business center, where a few owned clothing and dry goods stores. Such stores were often established by Jews who had started out as virtually penniless backpacking peddlers. The owners usually lived behind or above the stores. Later, large-scale retailers such as Mandel Brothers, Goldblatts, Rothschilds, Maurice B. Sachs, Polk Brothers, Aldens, and Spiegels grew from similarly modest beginnings, as did manufacturers like Hart, Schaffner & Marx, Kuppenheimer, and Florsheim.

By 1870 the Chicago Jewish community, enlarged by further immigration, had spread out somewhat, the largest concentration settling between Van Buren Street (North), Polk Street (South), the Chicago River (West), and Lake Michigan (East). There were by then a number of B'nai Brith fraternal lodges, the United Hebrew Relief Association, literary and dramatic groups, and seven synagogues scattered throughout what is today's central business district. Chicago's second congregation, B'nai Sholom, was founded in 1849 by a K.A.M. splinter group wishing to be more orthodox. B'nai Sholom's first building was on Harrison and Fourth Avenue (Federal Street). Today B'nai Sholom is back with its parent congregation as part of K.A.M. Isaiah Israel in Hyde Park.

The third oldest Jewish congregation in Chicago, Sinai Temple, was first located in a former Christian church on Monroe Street just east of La Salle. It was founded in 1861 as Chicago's first Reform congregation by twenty-six men who seceded from K.A.M. because they considered it too Orthodox. The secessionists wanted a more westernized prayerbook, head coverings to be removed in the temple, and the maintenance of decorum and uniformity in prayer instead of each man being more or less on his own. Developed earlier in the century in Germany, Reform Judaism emphasized the progressive nature of Judaism. Sinai Temple is now in Hyde Park. Other large early congregations that are still in existence include Zion Congregation (today's Oak Park Temple), established in 1864 on Des Plaines between Madison and Washington streets and North Chicago Hebrew Congregation (today's Temple Sholom on north Lake Shore Drive), established at Superior Street near Wells Street in 1867.[1] In time, all these temples adhered to Reform Judaism, though some practiced a more traditional kind of Judaism when they were first founded.

The Great Fire of 1871 and another one on the near South Side in 1874 destroyed most of the homes and businesses of the Chicago Jewish community, as well as most of the synagogues. After these fires the German Jews, who were increasing rapidly in number, moved out of the expanding business area and settled one or more miles south of the downtown area along such streets as Michigan, Wabash, and Indiana. Eventually they moved into the Grand Boulevard, Washington Park, Kenwood-Hyde Park areas and later into South Shore. As they moved they built numerous synagogues and institutions to take care of the needy. After World War I, the South Side Jewish community also included many persons of Eastern European descent.

The southward movement of German Jews can be traced by the relocations of the K.A.M. Congregation. In 1875 it moved from the downtown area to 26th and Indiana Avenue. In 1891 it occupied a beautiful temple at 33rd and Indiana Avenue, built by the renowned architect Dankmar Adler (whose father was a rabbi of K.A.M.). In 1920 it moved to 50th and Drexel Boulevard, and it is now part of K.A.M. Isaiah Israel, located at 1100 Hyde Park Boulevard. This is the congregation's seventh synagogue home in its 135-year history; its average tenure per site has been less than twenty years.

Similarly, Sinai Congregation moved to 21st and Indiana Avenue in 1876, to 46th and King Drive in 1912, and to Hyde Park in 1950. The congregation was headed from 1880 to 1923 by the nationally prominent Rabbi Emil G. Hirsch (1851–1923), who had been born in Luxembourg. Rabbi Hirsch helped to bring about or solidify numerous radical reforms in his congregation, including the controversial and temporary elimination of the traditional ark. In addition, Hebrew reading and prayers were curtailed at the congregation's services, which were held on Sunday instead of Saturday. In forceful sermons and in numerous articles in Reform journals, Rabbi Hirsch strongly defended the evolutionary concept of Judaism. He generally opposed Jewish Zionist-nationalism, and he championed the rights of organized labor and the inauguration of pioneering welfare reforms in Chicago. He edited Jewish Reform periodicals, was one of the original faculty members of the University of Chicago, where he taught rabbinic literature and philosophy, and served as president of the Chicago Public Library Board. More than half a century later, Edward Levi, one of his grandsons, served as president of the University of Chicago and as attorney general in President Gerald Ford's cabinet.

The German Jews were on friendly terms with the non-Jewish Germans of Chicago and identified quite closely with them. German Jews and non-Jews of Chicago spoke the same language, and in many instances they had been forced by common political views to leave Germany after the collapse of the revolutions of 1848. The German Jews read German newspapers, attended German theaters, and belonged to German organizations. Despite their good relations with the German non-Jews, however, they built their own welfare facilities and took care of their own. They founded Michael Reese Hospital on the South Side in 1880, the Chicago Home for the Jewish Aged in 1893, and the Chicago Home for Jewish Orphans in 1899.

During the Civil War some Jews belonged to Army units that were made up predominantly of Germans. Other Jews quickly formed a volunteer company of Jewish troops known as the Concordia Guards, and

Prominent German-Jewish club women at a social-political event in Chicago in 1900. *Courtesy of the University of Illinois Library, Chicago.*

the Jewish community helped finance its expenses. On August 16, 1862, the *Chicago Tribune* published the following tribute to the Jews of Chicago:

> Our Israelite citizens have gone beyond even their most sanguine expectations. Their princely contribution of itself is a record which must ever redound to their patriotism. The rapidity with which the company was enlisted has not its equal in the history of recruiting. In barely thirty-six hours' time they have enlisted a company reaching beyond the maximum, of gallant, strong-armed, stouthearted men, who will make themselves felt in the war. The ladies have set an enduring example by their contributions, their earnest work, and their hearty encouragement of the recruits. In two days, the Israelites have paid in over $11,000; in a day and a half they have raised more than a full company and mustered it in; in one day the ladies have subscribed for and made a beautiful flag. Can any town, city or state in the North show an equally good two days' work? The Concordia Guards have our best wishes for their future and our hopes that victory may always crown their aims.

The Second Wave: The Eastern European Jews of the Maxwell Street Area

In the old country, the world of the *shtetl* Jews of Eastern Europe differed greatly from the more cosmopolitan life of the Jews in Germany; in Chicago, at least initially, the differences between the two groups were probably even greater. When Eastern European Jews began to arrive in large numbers in Chicago during the last quarter of the nineteenth century, the German Jews were for the most part well established and accepted. They mingled quite freely with the general populace, held respected positions in a number of business fields and in the professions, and had even brought their religious practices into closer conformity with those of their Christian neighbors. The hosts of Eastern European Jews who arrived rather suddenly differed markedly from their German brethren in dress, demeanor, economic status, religious beliefs and rituals, and language.

Many of the Jewish immigrants from the small Eastern European villages found it difficult to adjust to the sudden change of living in a large American city. Articles in such Chicago Yiddish newspapers as the *Jewish Daily Courier*, the voice of Orthodox Jewry, reflected these feelings (as reported by S. J. Pomrenze):

> The "hurry up" spirit of the city overwhelmed him at first. The strangeness of the city left him lonely; and the longing to return

"home" increased. "What kind of memories could the immigrant fleeing from a land of persecution have?" asked a *Courier* writer. Why was it that something reminding the immigrant of the old home, like a pouch of tobacco, tea, or a European utensil brought forth a sigh and a tear? How could one compare the little village with the straw-bedecked houses and its crooked streets of dirt with the great American cities where noise, turmoil, hustle and bustle reigned, he quoted older immigrants querying the "greenhorn." Furthermore how could one help but scoff at the longing of the immigrant for his old home when here in a city like Chicago he found himself in the center of a civilization that was prepared to offer him everything with a broad hand? The writer answered these questions in a typical Jewish manner. When one digs a little deeper, he said with a Talmudical flourish of his hand, he will see that there were certain values in the little town that are still lacking in the big city. In a small town everybody was friendly and knew everybody else. In the big city the houses are "cold" inside, no matter how much better built, and how superior in other ways they may be to the little cottages. Moreover, the social recognition given to men of learning and of honorable ancestry was lacking in the city.[2]

In 1880, Eastern European Jews comprised only a small part of Chicago's 10,000 Jews. But when Russia's especially brutal pogroms of 1881 were followed by the repressive May Laws of 1882, expelling many Jews from their homes and towns, a wave of emigration began that lasted for nearly half a century. By 1900, Chicago's Jewish population had reached almost 80,000, of whom an estimated 52,000 were from Eastern Europe, 20,000 were of German descent, and the remaining 8,000 were largely Northwest European and Near Eastern in origin. Although the availability of census data on Jews is often limited, by 1930 the Jews of the Chicago area were estimated at about 275,000, of whom over 80 percent were Eastern European.

The Russian-Polish Jews crowded into the area southwest of the downtown area, a district that had previously been occupied by communities of German, Bohemian, and Irish Gentiles. The Russian-Polish Jews moved south along Canal and Jefferson streets, westward to Halsted Street, and then farther westward as new immigrants increased the congestion. By 1910, Eastern European Jews occupied a ghetto that stretched approximately from Canal Street westward almost to Damen Avenue, and from Polk Street south to the railroad tracks at about 16th Street. Of the estimated 50,000 immigrant Jews who arrived in Chicago during the last two decades of the nineteenth century, most settled in this area. With not much more than their small bundles of belongings, they moved into this railroad area of cheap rents and poor housing. A

Unemployed men marching along 14th Street in the Maxwell Street area en route to City Hall, 1914. *Courtesy of the Chicago Historical Society.*

1901 housing survey noted that almost half of all dwellings there were "dangerous."

The Russian Jewish immigrant Bernard Horwich arrived in Chicago in 1880 as a youth of seventeen. From the railroad station he was directed to the West Side, where the "greenhorns" were to be found. At the time, he had no idea that Jews lived elsewhere in Chicago. He began to earn his living by selling stationery in the streets, and later he became the president of two banks and one of the most prominent leaders in Chicago Jewish charitable, community, and Zionist organizations. In his later years he recalled the hardships of Chicago's Eastern European Jews at the time of his arrival:

> Jews were treated on the streets in a most abhorrent and shameful manner, stones being thrown at them and their beards being pulled by street thugs. Most earned their living peddling from house to house. They carried packs on their backs consisting of notions and

light dry goods, and it was not an unusual sight to see hundreds of them who lived in the Canal Street district, in the early morning, spreading throughout the city. There was hardly a streetcar where there were not to be found some Jewish peddlers with their packs riding to or from their business. Peddling junk and vegetables, and selling various articles on street corners also engaged numbers of our people. Being out on the streets most of the time in these obnoxious occupations, and ignorant of the English language, they were subjected to ridicule, annoyance and attacks of all kinds.[3]

The focal point of the ghetto was around the corner of Halsted and Maxwell. In the blocks around this intersection the population was about 90 percent Jewish. The community in many ways resembled a teeming Eastern European ghetto. It housed kosher meat markets and chicken stores, matzo bakeries, tailor and seamstress shops, bathhouses, and peddlers' stables. Its rich and varied religious and cultural life included synagogues, Hebrew schools, Hebrew- and Yiddish-speaking literary organizations, the offices of the Yiddish newspapers, and a number of Yiddish theaters. At the beginning of the twentieth century a boy named Muni Weisenfreund (1895–1967) performed various roles in his father's playhouse, a Yiddish theater on Roosevelt Road near Halsted Street. Decades later he won an Academy Award as Paul Muni, the stage and screen star.

Dominating the scene were more than forty Orthodox synagogues, for the Orthodox synagogues had to be within walking distance. The synagogues were usually small, with only a few having over a hundred members; and the members of each congregation consisted largely of immigrants from the same community in Europe.[4] In religious matters most of the Eastern European Jews tried to cling to the old traditions, while German Jews espoused new ideas. The Orthodox were devoted to the Torah and its study, daily attendance at the synagogue if possible, and strict observance of the Sabbath, religious holidays, and dietary and other laws prescribed in the *Schulchan Aruch*, the codification of Jewish religious law and practice. Eastern European Jews, with their strict Orthodoxy, did not feel at home in the Reform atmosphere of German Jewish synagogues, and the Germans did not make them feel overly welcome either. Like the German Jews, however, the Eastern Europeans experienced synagogue splits that resulted from personal and ritualistic strife, often based on conflicting local customs. One such split started on a hot summer Sabbath afternoon when a member was ejected from prayer services at Congregation Beth Hamedrosh Hagodol for wearing a straw hat. He was soon followed by his countrymen from the town of Mariampol, Lithuania, and before the year was over they had organized Congregation Ohave Sholom Mariampoller. Most East-

Outdoor market, Maxwell Street area, about 1905. *Courtesy of the Chicago Historical Society.*

ern European Jews found it imperative to belong to a synagogue and to provide religious instruction for their children, as this 1905 description reveals:

> They know that the public school will attend to their secular education, so out of their scant earnings they pay synagogue and Talmud Torah (religious school) dues. The synagogue plays a very important part in the daily life of the Orthodox Russian Jew, for his life and religion are so closely interwoven that public divine worship is to him a duty and a pleasure. The synagogue is the religious and social center around which the activity of the community revolves and it has now become, since the formation of auxiliary loan societies, a distributing agency for its various philanthropies where

"personal service" is not a fad, but has always been recognized in dealing with the unfortunate. Small wonder is it that the Orthodox Russian Jew clings to his synagogue. It is open not only "from early morn till dewy eve," but far into the night, and in some cases the doors are never closed. Daily worship begins early, so that the laboring man can attend services and yet be in time for his work. There are morning, afternoon, and evening services—seldom attended by women. Often the peddler's cart can be seen standing near the entrance while the owner is at prayer within. On Sabbaths and holy days services are always well attended by men and women, the latter occupying a gallery set apart for their use.

For older Jews especially, the synagogue offered intellectual and spiritual sustenance:

> Connected with the synagogue is the beth hamedrash, or house of learning, where students of religious literature are always welcome, and Bible and Talmud are studied and discussed. Many take advantage of the opportunity thus afforded, and form study circles or meet for devotional reading. There is much to attract and hold the older generation, who are continually receiving accessions from abroad, and in their lives the synagogue means much, if not all worth striving for.
>
> The beginning of a congregation is generally a minyan or gathering of at least ten men for divine worship. This is held in rented quarters. As soon as a sufficient number of members are gained they resolve to form an organization and when funds are forthcoming a house of worship is bought or built.

But with the younger generation of East European Jews there were already problems, and the pressures of acculturation were strong:

> Expense is not spared in making the exercises interesting to the older people, but little is done to attract the younger generation. The beautiful Hebrew language, which they do not understand, is used exclusively in the services. And when there is a sermon it is in Yiddish, and rather tedious and uninteresting for young people, who are almost starving for that religious food which would satisfy the heart and mind.[5]

Thus the younger, less religious *Ostjuden* were usually crowded into the neighborhood public schools, and soon such elementary schools as Washburne, Garfield, Smythe, and Foster were more than 80 percent Jewish. For these children, public education became an important vehicle for becoming Americanized and moving upward socially and economically, and often away from the world of their parents.

Jane Addams' Hull House was another agency that helped educate and Americanize the East European Jewish immigrants of the Maxwell

Street area, as it also helped other ethnics, particularly the Greeks. Founded in 1889 at 800 South Halsted Street, this pioneering social settlement complex fought for better conditions for the various peoples of the area and helped them adjust to their new environment. Among the more famous Jewish students at Hull House were Sidney Hillman, Benny Goodman, Studs Terkel, and Arthur Goldberg.

Other major concerns that required the attention of the Jewish immigrants were the disputes arising over *Kashrut* (kosher practices), which eventually came under rabbinical supervision, and also the need to help the large number of newly arriving Jewish immigrants, who were aided especially by the Hebrew Immigrant Aid Society (HIAS) and by the *landsmanshaften*.

Besides synagogues of *landsleit* (fellow townsmen) from the same Eastern European community, Jews organized *landsmanshaften* or *vereins* (as did non-Jewish Germans). These supported the synagogue and its educational functions, but also served as social clubs, loan associations, sick-benefit and cemetery agencies, places to meet old friends and reminisce about the old country, and the means for aiding those who had been left behind. During World War I, Chicago *landsleit* from numerous towns in Russia, Poland, Romania, Lithuania, and Galicia formed relief committees to aid the war victims in the communities of their origin. During World War II there were about 600 Chicago *landsmanshaften*. The Holocaust wiped out virtually all of the Jewish communities of Eastern Europe, and with them millions of the relatives and friends whom the *landsmanshaften* had tried to aid through the years. The *landsmanshaften* then directed their efforts to aiding Israel. In time, however, as the immigrant population began to diminish, the *landsmanshaften* declined rapidly in membership, and one by one they disappeared.

The first branch of the *Arbeiter Ring* (the Workman's Circle) was established in Chicago in 1903. The *Ring* was a Jewish socialist fraternal organization, generally hostile to religion and to Jewish nationalism. At its peak it had many thousands of members in Chicago. It ran secular Yiddish-language schools and camps, and its members read the influential Yiddish daily newspaper *The Forward*, which presented local and world news of Jewish interest while at the same time giving a basic education in Americanization.

Even the dress of the Maxwell Street area was largely that of the Eastern European ghettos. Bearded Jews who wore long black coats and Russian caps and boots were a common sight. The main commercial arteries were Jefferson, Halsted, Roosevelt, and Maxwell streets, the last a crowded, bustling, old-world kind of open-market bazaar. Absent from this area were the many saloons found in other ethnic

קלאוק מאכער דרעס און רעגען קוים מאכער ליידעם טיילערס

דיז יניאן איז אין געפאר!

א מאססען מיטינג פון אלע אינטערנעשאנאל מעמבערס וועט אפגעהאל-
טען ווערען מאנטאג נאוועמבער דעם 15-טען, 1926, 8 אזהר אבענד אין לייבאר
לייסעאום, אגדען קארנער קעדזי עוועניוס.

שוועסטער און ברידער:—

עס איז פון דער גרעסטער וויכטינקייט אז איהר זאלט אנוועזענד זיין ביי דיזען
מאססען פארזאמלונג וואו וויכטיגע פראגען וואס שטעלען אין געפאר דעם עקסיסטמענץ
פון אונזער יוניאן וועלען באשפראכען ווערען.

שוועסטער און ברידער:—

עס האט גענומען לאנגע יאהרען פון שווערע ארבעט ליידען און נויט ביז אונזער
יוניאן איז אויפגעבויטס געווארען צו זיין א זייראקזאמע וואפע גענען די אגדלונגען און
אטאקעס פון די באליבאטים.

ווילט איהר דערלאזען אז אונזער יוניאן זאל צובראכען ווערען?
אויב ניט קומט צום מאססען מיטינג.

מיט גרוס,

וו. דיילי, סעם לעדערמאן, מענדע פיינבערג, דזש. האפמאן
פיליפ דייווידס

דזשאינט באארד דעלענאטען

CLOAK, DRESS, RAIN COAT MAKERS AND LADIES TAILORS

The Union is In Danger!

A MASS MEETING of all International members will be held ON
MONDAY EVENING, NOVEMBER 15th, 1926, 8 P. M. sharp, at the Labor
Lyceum, Ogden and Kedzie Avenues.

Sisters and Brothers, it is of the utmost importance that you be present
at this meeting.

Questions that is now up in our Union and that treatens the existance
of our Union will be discussed.

COME IN MASSES.   PROTECT YOUR UNION.

Brotherly yours.

W. DAYLY, SAM LEDERMAN, MANDY FINEBERG, J. HOFFMAN
and PHILIP DAVIDS

Joint Board Delegates

562

Union poster, in Yiddish and English, announcing a mass meeting at the Workmen's
Circle Labor Lyceum, 1926. *Courtesy of Irving Cutler.*

areas. An account in the *Chicago Tribune* of July 19, 1891, described the ghetto of the near West Side:

> On the West Side, in a district bounded by Sixteenth Street on the south and Polk Street on the north and the Chicago River and Halsted Street on the east and west, one can walk the streets for blocks and see none but Semitic features and hear nothing but the Hebrew patois of Russian Poland. In this restricted boundary, in narrow streets, ill-ventilated tenements and rickety cottages, there is a population of from 15,000 to 16,000 Russian Jews. . . . Every Jew in this quarter who can speak a word of English is engaged in business of some sort. The favorite occupation, probably on account of the small capital required, is fruit and vegetable peddling. Here, also, is the home of the Jewish street merchant, the rag and junk peddler, and the "glass puddin" man. . . . The principal streets in the quarter are lined with stores of every description. Trades with which Jews are not usually associated such as saloonkeeping, shaving and hair cutting, and blacksmithing, have their representatives and Hebrew signs. . . . In a room of a small cottage forty small boys all with hats on sit crowded into a space 10 × 10 feet in size, presided over by a stout middle-aged man with a long, curling, matted beard, who also retains his hat, a battered rusty derby of ancient style. All the old or middle-aged men in the quarter affect this peculiar head gear. . . . The younger generation of men are more progressive and having been born in this country are patriotic and want to be known as Americans and not Russians. . . . Everyone is looking for a bargain and everyone has something to sell. The home life seems to be full of content and easygoing unconcern for what the outside world thinks.

To support themselves, many Jewish immigrants from Eastern Europe worked in the sweatshops of the clothing industry and in cigar-making factories. Others became peddlers, tailors, butchers, bakers, barbers, small merchants, and artisans of every variety. As the immigrants became more Americanized, they organized to fight for better working conditions. In 1886, a day after the Haymarket Riot, thousands of Jews marched from the ghetto toward the downtown area to protest the intolerable conditions of the sweatshop. At the Van Buren Street bridge they were beaten and routed by club-swinging police.

The Jews comprised about 80 percent of the 45,000 workers who participated in the prolonged and successful garment strike of 1910. The strike, largely an action of Jewish workers against a Jewish-owned concern, was led by Sidney Hillman and Bessie Abramowitz (who later became husband and wife). It resulted in the organization of the Amalgamated Clothing Workers of America under Hillman's leadership. In addition, Jews rose to leadership in the other two major needle trade unions—the International Ladies' Garment Workers' Union and the United Hat, Cap and Millinery Workers' Union. All three unions became well known for the progressive benefits they won for their members and for their social democratic philosophy.

The more affluent and established German Jews of the South Side "Golden Ghetto" were embarrassed by the old-world ways and beliefs of the newly arrived Eastern European Jews of Maxwell Street. To the middle-class, Americanized German Jews of the 1880s, the East European immigrants were a frightening apparition. Their poverty was more desperate than German Jewish poverty had ever been, their piety more intense than German Jewish piety, their irreligion more violent than German Jewish irreligion, and their radicalism more extreme than German Jewish radicalism.[6] The Germans did found a number of community facilities to speed the Americanization of their Eastern brethren, the *Ostjuden*. Julius Rosenwald (1862–1932), for example, a German Jew and the president of Sears, Roebuck and Company, was a generous philanthropist who gave great sums for such charities, as well as for other causes, including housing and education for blacks, the University of Chicago, and the great Museum of Science and Industry. Rosenwald helped fund the Chicago Hebrew Institute (later the Jewish People's Institute), the forerunner of today's community centers, which opened in 1908 on the six-acre grounds of a former convent at Taylor and Lyle Streets. The Institute contained classrooms, clubrooms, a library, gymnasiums, assembly halls, and a synagogue. Another of its founders, the attorney Nathan Kaplan, spoke of its purposes as follows:

> The younger generation speaking English and mixing with English-speaking people loses its interest in things Jewish, and the older people speaking nothing but their native language live always in a foreign atmosphere. We hope the Institute will give both an opportunity to meet on common ground and so, while making the Orthodox tolerant and the younger element better fitted to sympathize, preserve all that is best in the race and its faith.

The German Jews were willing to give their Eastern European coreligionists financial and educational assistance, but not social equality. For many years the two Jewish communities lived separately and had separate synagogues, fraternal organizations, and community centers. Having been excluded from the Gentile downtown clubs, German Jews incorporated their own club, the Standard Club, in 1869. Initially it excluded Eastern European Jews. The club became the social center of the Jewish "aristocracy" of Chicago, who lived mainly on the South Side. In 1917 the Eastern European Jews organized their own Covenant Club. Both clubs are now located downtown and serve both social and philanthropic goals. Time has gradually blurred the historic distinctions between the two groups of Jews.

In addition to the Chicago Hebrew Institute, other community service centers in the Maxwell Street area were largely supported by German Jews. These included the Jewish Training School, one of the first vocational training schools in the United States; the Mandel Clinic (one of whose founders was the merchant Leon Mandel), a modern facility which provided free medical care and medicine for the poor immigrants; the Maxwell Street Settlement; and the Chicago Maternity Center, a facility which provided free prenatal and obstetric care. The Chicago Maternity Center was founded and supervised by one of the world's leading obstetricians, the crusading Dr. Joseph De Lee (1869–1942).

The Russian-Polish immigrants sometimes resented the paternalistic attitude of their more worldly German brethren. But they accepted the help extended to them because ghetto life was hard and living conditions were deplorable. The crowded wooden shanties and brick tenements of the area usually had insufficient ventilation and light, few baths, and were usually surrounded by areas of poor drainage and piles

Banquet at the Orthodox Jewish Home for the Aged, Albany Avenue near 18th Street, about 1925. *Courtesy of the Chicago Historical Society.*

of stinking garbage. Recreational facilities were grossly inadequate. Many ghetto families took in lodgers to help defray expenses; sometimes the same bed would be used by a baker during the day and a butcher during the night, which was called the "hot bed" system. The wives and children often had to work. Yet crime was almost nonexistent on Maxwell Street in those days, and the death and disease rate of the Jewish ghetto was lower than that of most immigrant concentrations. Jews of the Maxwell Street neighborhood exhibited a physical and mental vitality that was sustained by a long tradition of hard work and learning. They strove for success, if not for themselves then for their children.

A surprising number of people with roots in the Maxwell Street area became well known.

Joseph Goldberg was one of these immigrants. He came to America from Russia and eventually landed on Maxwell Street. He bought a blind horse, the only horse he could afford. He became a fruit-and-vegetable peddler; his son, Arthur, would serve in President Kennedy's cabinet and become a Supreme Court Justice of the United States.

Samuel Paley became a cigar maker in America, as did Max Guzik. Samuel's son William, born in the back room of the modest family cigar store near Maxwell Street, is founder, president and chairman of the board of the Columbia Broadcasting System. Mr. Guzik's son Jake, known as "Greasy Thumb", became the brains behind the Capone gang. . . .

Eastern European immigrants David Goodman and Abraham Rickover took jobs in Chicago as tailors. Their sons are Benny Goodman and Admiral Hyman G. Rickover.

The father of Barney Ross, onetime world lightweight boxing champion, and the father of Barney Balaban, the late president of Paramount Pictures, each owned a tiny grocery store in the Maxwell Street area.

Paul Muni's father owned a Yiddish theater near Maxwell Street. Jack Ruby's father was a carpenter there.

John Keeshin, once the greatest trucking magnate in America, is the son of a man who owned a chicken store on Maxwell Street, as did the father of Jackie Fields, former welterweight champion of the world. The father of Federal Court Judge Abraham Lincoln Marovitz owned a candy store near Maxwell Street.

Colonel Jacob Arvey, once a nationally prominent political power broker, was the son of a Maxwell Street area peddler.[7]

By 1910 improvements in their economic status, the encroachment of industry and the railroads, and the influx of blacks caused the Jews to start moving out of the Maxwell Street area—first toward the areas

A campaign poster in Yiddish urging the voters to register in order to elect Judge Henry Horner governor. Horner served as governor of Illinois from 1933 to 1940. His grandfather, also named Henry Horner, was one of the first Jewish immigrants to Chicago in 1841, an organizer of the Board of Trade, and owner of a large wholesale grocery company. *Courtesy of Irving Cutler.*

around Ashland and Damen avenues and then to more distant parts. By the 1930s only a small remnant of Jewish businessmen and older Jews remained in the Maxwell Street area. Today the neighborhood is almost wholly black, and the bazaarlike Maxwell Street commercial strip has been reduced to a few short blocks, the result of changing shopping patterns, a changing neighborhood, and the construction of the Dan Ryan Expressway on the eastern fringe and of the University of Illinois, Chicago Circle campus on the north. But on Sundays throngs of curiosity-seekers and shoppers still crowd Maxwell Street looking for bargains and odd merchandise that can range from used toothbrushes, rusty nails, and questionably obtained hubcaps to valuable antiques.

Ironically, in an otherwise solidly Orthodox neighborhood, Temple B'nai Jehoshua, the last surviving synagogue in the area (it closed in 1965) was a Reform congregation. This sole non-Orthodox congregation, at 19th and Ashland Avenue, on the fringe of the Maxwell Street area, was organized by Bohemian Jews who wished to live near their small stores on 18th and 22nd streets in the Gentile Bohemian neighborhood of Pilsen. Like German Jews, Bohemians often favored Reform Judaism. Among the members of B'nai Jehoshua were the Bohemian Jewish immigrants Judge Joseph Sabath (1870–1956), and his brother, the liberal congressman Adolph Sabath (1866–1952), who served in the U.S. House of Representatives for twenty-three consecutive terms, the seond-longest continuous service of any U.S. congressman. Also members were the family that owned the chain of Leader Department Stores, which catered to Eastern European neighborhoods and sold, among other items, thousands of *perinas* (comforters) annually to their largely Bohemian and Polish customers. In 1965, B'nai Jehoshua merged with Congregation Beth Elohim of Glenview. The proceeds from the sale of its building on Ashland Avenue helped pay for the new site of the merged congregations.

The Dispersion

By the 1920s most of the Jews of Maxwell Street had scattered in a number of directions. A small number joined the German Jews in the Golden Ghetto of the South Side. At first some settled in the Grand Boulevard, Washington Park, Englewood, and adjacent community areas, until the region began changing racially. Subsequently, the bulk of the German Jewish community—who by this time had been joined by a minority of Eastern European Jews—became concentrated in the Hyde Park-Kenwood and South Shore areas. Many of them contributed to the success of the nearby University of Chicago, some financially, like Julius Rosenwald and Leon Mandel, and others intellectually, like Nobel Prize winners Albert Abraham Michelson (physics), Milton Friedman (economics), and Saul Bellow (literature).

Bolstered by an influx of refugees from Nazi Germany before and after World War II, each of these two South Side areas had about a dozen synagogues—a mixture of the usually small Orthodox congregations and the generally large Reform and Conservative congregations. The newer Conservative Judaism, like Reform Judaism, was conceived as a developmental religion that was needed to adjust to contemporary conditions, but it adhered more to the traditional practices and spirit of historical Judaism than did Reform Judaism, including the greater use of the Hebrew language and fuller adherence to the time-honored liturgy and religious holidays. However, some modifications or changes from the traditional were allowed, including mixed seating of men and women during worship services, confirmation of girls, and broader interpretation of the Code of Jewish Law. Conservative Judaism was not only a modification of strict Orthodoxy but a reaction against the many major changes instituted by Reform Judaism. Conservative Judaism in time attracted many of the American-born children of Eastern European Jews, who were reconciling their attachments to the traditions of their youth and their acculturation in America. Many of Chicago's Conservative synagogues started out in the Orthodox fold.

The Jewish population and the number of synagogues started to decline rapidly in the late 1950s as the racial composition of Hyde Park-Kenwood and South Shore began to change. Because of the more stable racial balance that has been attained in Hyde Park, the community still has a substantial Jewish population, concentrated largely in its eastern section, which is served by three large synagogues. South Shore is now devoid of synagogues, although Agudath Achim Bikur Cholem, on South Houston Avenue in adjacent South Chicago, still occupies the city's oldest continuously used synagogue building (since 1902).

A small number of Jews moved north into the lakefront communities of Lakeview, Uptown, and Rogers Park. One of Chicago's most beloved rabbis was the Russian-born Solomon Goldman (1893–1953), who served the Lakeview area's Conservative Anshe Emet Synagogue from 1929 to the time of his death. Goldman was a gifted speaker, a prolific writer and scholar, and an ardent Zionist. He was the first president of the Zionist Organization of America who did not come from the eastern United States. His synagogue, like other large lakefront-area congregations such as Temple Sholom and Emanuel Congrega-

One of Chicago's most beloved rabbis was Solomon Goldman, noted scholar and speaker, president of the Zionist Organization of America, and Conservative rabbi of Anshe Emet Synagogue for almost a quarter of a century. He is seated here with Zionist leader Rabbi Stephen S. Wise of New York (left) and Albert Einstein (right). *Courtesy of Irving Cutler.*

tion, was founded in the last century just north of the Loop and was located at its present site after a series of northward moves that followed the Jewish population. Some other early Jewish facilities were also located north of the Loop. In addition to the first Jewish cemetery, located in what is now Lincoln Park, there was also the first Jewish hospital, built in 1867 on La Salle Street near Schiller Avenue (1400 north) and destroyed by the Chicago Fire of 1871.

A large number of Jews moved to the Northwest Side. There the nucleus of a Jewish community had been established in the late 1800s in the West Town area of Milwaukee Avenue and along Division Street. The first synagogues in the West Town area were built in the 1890s, and eventually about twenty served a Jewish community that in time spread to the western side of Humboldt Park. And there were a number of Hebrew schools, including the large *Jabneh*, sponsored by four Orthodox synagogues of the area. Many of the local Jews were inclined to emphasize Yiddish culture and somewhat radical philosophies rather than the religious Orthodoxy of the near West Side. Ideologically, the area was split among adherents of socialism, secularism, Zionism, and Orthodoxy. But these differences declined markedly among their more Americanized children.

On Division Street, the principal commercial artery of the West

Town-Humboldt Park area, were numerous Jewish stores and the Deborah Boys Club. Although Jews were a minority in the West Town area, which included large numbers of Poles, Ukrainians, and Russians, this was the childhood home of such well-known Jews as comedian Jackie Leonard (Fats Levitsky), movie impresario Michael Todd, columnist Sydney J. Harris, and novelist Saul Bellow. The last two, both of whom were alumni of Tuley High School, were part of a distinguished group of Chicago writers of Jewish descent (though Bellow was born in Canada of Russian-Jewish parents and initially brought up in the slums of Montreal), which included Edna Ferber, Ben Hecht, Herman Kogan, Albert Halper, Maxwell Bodenheim, Meyer Levin, Isaac Rosenfeld, Leo Rosten, Studs Terkel, and Louis Zara.

Some Jews moved beyond the West Town-Humboldt Park neighborhood farther northwest into Logan Square and Albany Park; but the vast majority of the Jews who left Maxwell Street leapfrogged over the railroad and industrial area and settled some three miles to the west in the Lawndale-Douglas Park-Garfield Park area. This district was dubbed "Deutschland" by those Jews who chose to remain in the more old-world atmosphere of Maxwell Street, and it now became the largest and most developed Jewish community that ever existed in Chicago. At its peak in 1930 this Greater Lawndale area contained an estimated 110,000 Jews of the city's total Jewish population of about 275,000. Other areas with significant Jewish populations in 1930 included the Lakeview-Uptown-Rogers Park area (27,000), West Town-Humboldt Park-Logan Square (35,000), Albany Park-North Park (27,000), and on the South Side the Kenwood-Hyde Park-Woodlawn-South Shore area (28,000). The Jews of the South Side had the highest economic status, followed by those of the North Side and the Northwest Side. Small Jewish communities were situated in Austin (7,000), Englewood-Greater Grand Crossing (4,000), and Chatham-Avalon Park-South Chicago (3,000). Small numbers of Jews also lived on the near North Side, the Southwest Side, and in other communities of the Northwest Side.

Geographic dispersal and German-East European differences were not the only divisions among the Jews. The Eastern European group included Jews from Lithuania, Poland, the Ukraine, Bessarabia, Galicia, Latvia, and other regions. There were religious divisions along the lines of Orthodox, Conservative, Reform, and secular Jews. There were Zionists and anti-Zionists, radicals and conservatives, and employees and employers.

The Jews continued to be successful in business, and after World War I they moved increasingly into such professions as law, medicine, teaching, writing, accounting, music, and art. However, Jews often had to overcome restrictive provisions and quotas to move ahead. Not only were they barred from higher positions in many industries, but they were also often excluded even from lower-level positions, such as secretarial jobs. Some institutions of higher learning limited the enrollment of Jews by quotas, and until recent decades most North Shore and other suburban realtors severely restricted the sale of homes to Jews.

GREATER LAWNDALE

About 1910, Jews began moving out of the crowded near West Side ghetto to the Chicago community of North Lawndale and—to a lesser extent somewhat later—into the adjacent communities to the north, East Garfield Park and West Garfield Park (the combined communities forming the Greater Lawndale area). This was a quieter residential area whose comparatively spacious streets, yards, and parks were largely encircled by the belt railroads. The German and Irish residents initially tried to stem the influx of Jews by refusing to rent to them. But many Jews then bought the one- and two-family brick homes of the area and also built numerous three-story apartment houses there. By 1920 the neighborhood had become largely Jewish.

The population of the Greater Lawndale area more than doubled between 1910 and 1930, to become one of the most densely populated communities in the city. In 1930 its proportion of foreign-born inhabitants—mainly from Russia and Poland—was higher than that of any other community in Chicago (about 45 percent). The area at its broadest delineation stretched approximately from California Avenue west to Tripp Street (4232 west) and from Washington Boulevard south to 18th Street.[8] The greatest Jewish concentration in this area was in North Lawndale, south of Arthington Avenue, the street along which Sears Roebuck's huge mail-order and headquarters complex was aligned for more than half a mile. There was also a small spin-off to the west into the Columbus Park-Austin area, which contained about 8,000 Jews in 1946. In the central core of the area, south of Roosevelt Road, the Herzl, Penn, Howland, Bryant, and Lawson public schools each averaged about 2,000 Jewish students by 1933. This was probably more than 90 percent of each school's enrollment. The students from these elementary schools went mainly to Marshall and Manley high schools, which were located slightly north of North Lawndale.

The heart of the area was the L-shaped Douglas Boulevard (1400 south) and Independence Boulevard (3800 west), parkways whose wide central grass malls separated one-way roads. These boulevards were about a mile long and were flanked by Douglas Park on the east end and by Garfield Park on the north. Both parks were beautifully land-

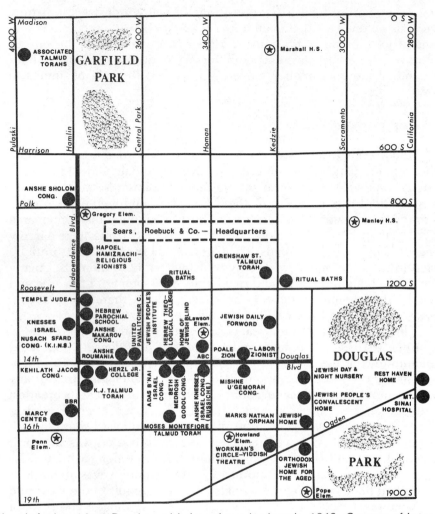

Jewish facilities along Douglas and Independence boulevards, 1948. *Courtesy of Irving Cutler.*

scaped, with flower beds, lagoons, and woodlands. Many of the major Jewish institutions of the community were built along Douglas and Independence, including about a dozen synagogues, many of imposing classical architecture, all but one of which were Orthodox; a huge community center, the Jewish People's Institute; the Hebrew Theological College, whose students came from all over the world; a home for the Jewish blind; and a number of other religious and cultural organizations.

Theodore Herzl Junior College, which had large enrollments of Jewish students, was located on Douglas Boulevard near its junction

In the Lawndale area the Jewish People's Institute (left), on Douglas Boulevard and St. Louis Avenue, was a major social, cultural, and recreational center of Chicago Jewry from 1926 to 1955. The Hebrew Theological College (right) was located here from 1922 to 1956. It now occupies a 16-acre site in Skokie, to which it attracts students from all over the world. These two buildings are now the Julius Hess Elementary School. *Courtesy of Irving Cutler.*

with Independence at Independence Square. Just to its west was the beautiful Kehilath Jacob Synagogue, which maintained the largest *Talmud Torah* (Hebrew School) in the area. There were a number of other Hebrew schools on the two boulevards and more on the side streets, including the large Grenshaw Street Talmud Torah near Kedzie Avenue and the Moses Montefiore Talmud Torah on St. Louis (3500 west) south of 15th Street. This area created a Jewish cultural life that was perhaps without parallel except for that on the East Side of New York.

Among the earliest (1913) larger synagogues on Douglas Boulevard was Congregation Anshe Kneseth Israel, known as the "Russishe shul." It had a seating capacity of 3,500, and some of the most prominent Eastern European Jewish families were members—among them Balabans and the Katzes, the Keeshins, the Lavins, and the Fischers. Some of the best cantors in the world were invited from Europe to conduct its services. The synagogue remained open almost twenty-four hours a day so that scholars, often supported by the congregation, could continue their Hebrew studies. For almost half a century the rabbi of Anshe Kneseth Israel was Ephraim Epstein (1876–1960), a renowned Talmudic scholar who furthered the cause of Jewish education and helped rescue many Jews from Europe during the Nazi period. Another large synagogue on Douglas Boulevard was the First Romanian Congregation. In 1926 its members gave Queen Marie of Romania a royal welcome when she visited the synagogue on her tour of the United States—though many of them had fled her country because they could not tolerate her country's policy regarding Jews.

On the Jewish High Holy Days, Douglas and Independence boulevards were thronged with people in holiday dress. Almost everyone went to the synagogue on these days, and local automobile traffic virtually ceased. On the side streets were about four dozen more synagogues, all Orthodox, many of which bore the names of the communities in Russia, Poland, Lithuania, or Romania from which their founders had come. Some synagogues were organized by occupational groups and consequently were referred to as the laundryman's synagogue or the carpenter's synagogue; one on Spaulding Avenue was even known as the politician's synagogue. As late as 1944 about one-half of the synagogues of Chicago were located in Greater Lawndale. Friday night was very special among the Orthodox Jews, with the synagogue services, the lighting of the Sabbath candles, and the festive Sabbath meal, which was usually followed by singing and religious discussions. Jewish teenagers exchanged "Good Sabbath" greetings on Douglas Boulevard and often gathered at Independence Square to dance the *hora* late into the night.

On Kedzie at Ogden Avenue was the large Labor Lyceum building, which contained the educational and administrative facilities of the Workmen's Circle. The building also housed Chicago's last Yiddish theater (1938–1951). Farther north on Kedzie Avenue was the building of a Jewish daily newspaper, the *Forward*. On both sides of Douglas Park, on California Avenue and Albany Avenue (3100 west), were aligned an imposing array of social service institutions supported by the Jewish community. These included a rehabilitation hospital, a convalescent home, a day-and-night nursery, a large orphanage, a home for the Orthodox Jewish aged, and Mount Sinai Hospital. The hospital was established for a number of reasons, including the need to serve the new growing Jewish community and because Michael Reese Hospital served no kosher meals and originally discriminated against Jewish doctors of Eastern European origin.

The main commercial street bisecting Greater Lawndale was Roosevelt Road, to which Jews would come from all over the city to shop. In the mile stretch from about Kedzie Avenue to Crawford (Pulaski) Avenue were a half-dozen movie houses (where such performers as Sophie Tucker, the Marx Brothers, and Benny Goodman appeared in vaudeville acts), Jewish bookstores, funeral chapels, restaurants, delicatessens, Best's and Lazar's kosher sausage establishments, groceries, fish stores (with elderly horseradish grinders and their machines on the sidewalk outside), meeting halls, and political organizations.

The 24th Ward was the top Democratic stronghold in Chicago. In the 1936 presidential election Roosevelt received 29,000 votes to Landon's 700, and FDR called that ward "the number one ward in the

Democratic Party." In addition to politics, Roosevelt Road was also known for such well-remembered and homely institutions as "Zookie" the Bookie's and Davy Miller's pool hall-boxing gym-gambling-restaurant complex, which had originated on Maxwell Street. Jewish youths who hung around Davy Miller's establishment on Roosevelt near Kedzie served a community function of a special sort: they took on the Gentile youth gangs that harassed Yeshiva students and stuck gum in the beards of elderly Jews. In the 1920s the Miller boys also fought the young Gentiles of Uptown for the territorial right of Jews to make free use of newly created Clarendon Beach, just as in earlier days they had fought for the right of Jews to use Humboldt Park and Douglas Park. In later years such Jewish youths battled members of the Nazi *Bund.*

The Greater Lawndale community was alive with outdoor activity, especially in the warmer months. Through the alleys came a constant procession of peddlers in horse-drawn wagons, hawking their fruits and vegetables in singsong fashion. Mingled among them were the milk-men and the icemen. Occasionally fiddlers would play Jewish melodies in the yards, and the housewives would throw them a few coins wrapped in paper. The area was also traversed by the "old rags and iron" col-lector, the knife sharpener, the umbrella man, and the organ grinder with his monkey. Soul-hunting Christian missionaries canvassed the area often, going from house to house, but they made very few converts.

In the evenings most people would sit on their front porches con-versing with their families and neighbors as a procession of ice cream, candy, and waffle vendors passed. People would go to the parks in the evening. There they would rent rowboats, attend occasional free band concerts, and sometimes sleep all night during the most stifling summer weather. Various groups met in special sections of the parks where they sang to mandolin music or danced the *hora.* Some of the intellectuals congregated outside Silverstein's restaurant on Roosevelt and St. Louis (3500 west) to debate the issues of the day with the soapbox orators— communists, socialists, anarchists, atheists, Zionists, and so on.

Many of the boys of Greater Lawndale participated in the activities, mainly athletic, of three youth centers in the area: ABC (American Boys' Commonwealth), BBR (Boys' Brotherhood Republic), and the Marcy Center. All three had been originally founded in Maxwell Street. While the ABC and BBR were Jewish-sponsored youth centers, Marcy Center was engaged in Christian missionary work and was not wel-comed by the Jews it hoped to convert. Although it had a well-equipped dispensary, people injured nearby usually refused to be taken to the Marcy Center clinic for treatment.

Other Jewish youths, including the future judge Abraham Lincoln Marovitz, Stuart Brent, Barney Ross, and Maurice Goldblatt joined in the athletic, educational, and social activities of the Jewish People's Institute on Douglas Boulevard (declared a national landmark in 1979). They could eat there at the Blintzes Inn, vote for delegates to Jewish congresses, dance under the stars on the roof garden on Sunday evenings, attend lectures, listen to the institute's own orchestra, see Jewish museum exhibitions, see plays by Chekhov and Turgenev in English or Yiddish, attend Herziliah Hebrew School or Central Hebrew High School, and study at the library. Here Leo Rosten taught English to immigrants, an experience that inspired his book *The Education of H*Y*M*A*N K*A*P*L*A*N*. Its hero was an indomitable Russian Jewish night school student who insisted that the Atlantic's opposite ocean was the "Specific," that the fourth president of the United States was James "Medicine," that the Civil War president was Abram Lincohen, that "laktric" lights "short soicused," and that the three pilgrims who followed the star to Bethlehem were the "Tree Vise Guys."

In the summer those Jewish families who could afford it rented cottages in the Indiana Dunes or in the Union Pier and South Haven areas of Michigan, to which the husband of the family would usually commute on weekends. The largest Jewish resort area was South Haven, situated on the eastern shore of Lake Michigan and accessible by boat, train, bus, and auto. It contained summer camps, cottages, and especially resort hotels, most of them kosher and some with entertainment. The South Haven area was a miniature Catskills *borscht* belt—without the mountains.

Whereas the Jews of the Maxwell Street area had been almost a direct transplant of the poor, isolated European ghetto Jews, the Jews of Greater Lawndale were people who lived in pleasant physical surroundings and were working hard to achieve middle-class status. Despite the universally severe hardships caused by the Great Depression of the 1930s, upward mobility continued among the Jews, and old-world cultural patterns were slowly modified by the "American way." This was especially true among younger Jews, who often preferred baseball to Hebrew school, basement social and athletic club "hangouts" to synagogue, and careers in the professions to careers in merchandising. Despite the prejudice that restricted opportunities in certain spheres, more opportunities existed for Jewish youth in Chicago during the thirties than ever before.

Almost as rapidly as Greater Lawndale had changed from Gentile to Jewish earlier in the century, it changed from Jewish to black during the late 1940s and early 1950s. Other choice areas in Chicago and its suburbs had begun to open up for the Jews, and they leapfrogged over intervening zones to reach them. The Jews started to leave this area of their second settlement even though Greater Lawndale had not dete-

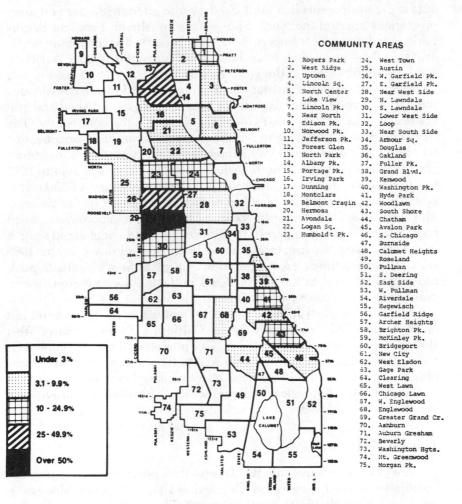

COMMUNITY AREAS

1.	Rogers Park	24.	West Town
2.	West Ridge	25.	Austin
3.	Uptown	26.	W. Garfield Pk.
4.	Lincoln Sq.	27.	E. Garfield Pk.
5.	North Center	28.	Near West Side
6.	Lake View	29.	N. Lawndale
7.	Lincoln Pk.	30.	S. Lawndale
8.	Near North	31.	Lower West Side
9.	Edison Pk.	32.	Loop
10.	Norwood Pk.	33.	Near South Side
11.	Jefferson Pk.	34.	Armour Sq.
12.	Forest Glen	35.	Douglas
13.	North Park	36.	Oakland
14.	Albany Pk.	37.	Fuller Pk.
15.	Portage Pk.	38.	Grand Blvd.
16.	Irving Park	39.	Kenwood
17.	Dunning	40.	Washington Pk.
18.	Montclare	41.	Hyde Park
19.	Belmont Cragin	42.	Woodlawn
20.	Hermosa	43.	South Shore
21.	Avondale	44.	Chatham
22.	Logan Sq.	45.	Avalon Park
23.	Humboldt Pk.	46.	S. Chicago
		47.	Burnside
		48.	Calumet Heights
		49.	Roseland
		50.	Pullman
		51.	S. Deering
		52.	East Side
		53.	W. Pullman
		54.	Riverdale
		55.	Hegewisch
		56.	Garfield Ridge
		57.	Archer Heights
		58.	Brighton Pk.
		59.	McKinley Pk.
		60.	Bridgeport
		61.	New City
		62.	West Elsdon
		63.	Gage Park
		64.	Clearing
		65.	West Lawn
		66.	Chicago Lawn
		67.	W. Englewood
		68.	Englewood
		69.	Greater Grand Cr.
		70.	Ashburn
		71.	Auburn Gresham
		72.	Beverly
		73.	Washington Hgts.
		74.	Mt. Greenwood
		75.	Morgan Pk.

Under 3%

3.1 - 9.9%

10 - 24.9%

25 - 49.9%

Over 50%

Jewish population of Chicago, 1931. *Courtesy of the Jewish Charities of Chicago.*

riorated physically, despite its very dense population. They left because of few opportunities for home ownership, relatively high income which allowed them to move readily from the changing neighborhood, the desire to own homes in areas with more amenities and higher status, and because of the improved mobility provided by the automobile. Jews had been on the move for 2,000 years, and even in Greater Lawndale they had frequently moved from one apartment to another. Relatively few members of the new generation of Jewish adults were interested in clinging to the great institutional structures that their parents and grandparents had built. So they moved to the better and more prestigious areas of the North Side—some to Albany Park and Rogers Park, but more to West Rogers Park (West Ridge) and parts of the northern suburbs—areas that were being built up after World War II. A smaller number went to the western suburbs.

Most of the Jewish institutions that once dotted the Lawndale area were transferred to other uses, though some were demolished and others abandoned. Mount Sinai Hospital still serves the community. The ABC and BBR facilities were turned over to a community organization for use by the new youths of the area. Most of the former synagogues are now black churches. The Jewish People's Institute was sold in 1955 to the Chicago Board of Education for a token payment of $300; it is now a public elementary school, as is the former Herzl Junior College. Most of the facilities formerly occupied by Hebrew schools have been torn down. The eastern part of the Roosevelt Road commercial strip is completely bare, its structures having been burned down in the 1968 riots. This vacantness exposes to view the giant Sears Roebuck mail-order complex just to the north. It has outlasted the numerous immigrant groups that have passed through the area.

Many of the Jewish institutions of Greater Lawndale were rebuilt on the North Side, especially in the California Avenue area of West Rogers Park. Some synagogues of Lawndale liquidated completely, usually donating a portion of their assets to a congregation in a new neighborhood that would perpetuate their name, and another portion to the Hebrew Theological College, which had moved from Douglas Boulevard to Skokie.

THE NORTH SIDE

Jews began to move into the Albany Park area a few years after the completion of the Ravenswood Elevated in 1907 to its terminal at Lawrence and Kimball (3400 west) avenues. The first Albany Park synagogue was the Reform Temple Beth Israel, founded in 1917. One of its members, Shimon Agranat, later became one of the chief justices of Israel. By 1930, Albany Park contained about 23,000 Jews, almost half of the total population of the community. Many came from the older and less affluent Jewish areas of the West and Northwest sides. For them Albany Park represented a movement upward into a more Americanized community as well as a transitional middle ground between the Orthodoxy of the West Side and the Reform Judaism of the South Side. The area developed Orthodox, Conservative, and Reform synagogues and other Jewish institutional facilities, including a Hebrew day school, a rabbinical college, a boys' club, a Yiddish school, and a home for the Jewish blind. A strong concentration of Jewish institutions clustered around Kimball Avenue, on which the two major public high schools, Roosevelt and Von Steuben, were also situated. Lawrence Avenue, the main business street, was somewhat similar in character to Lawndale's Roosevelt Road, from which some of its stores had been transplanted.

During the post–World War II exodus from Lawndale, many Jewish families, including numerous Orthodox ones, settled in Albany Park and adjacent North Park, and at the same time some of the more affluent earlier Jewish settlers of Albany Park moved still farther north. The Jewish movement out of Albany Park accelerated during the 1960s, and by 1975 only an estimated 5,000 Jews remained, most of them elderly and of limited means. The Ark, with its more than 200 professional and lay volunteers, and other organizations, ministered to their needs.

Until the extension of the elevated line to Howard Street in 1907, Chicago's northeastern community, Rogers Park, was largely an area of single-family frame houses. With the improvement of transportation, numerous large apartment buildings and apartment hotels were built in Rogers Park, especially in the eastern portion adjacent to Sheridan Road and Lake Michigan. Jews started to move into this area after 1910, and by 1930 about 10,000 lived there. After World War II the area contained about 20,000 Jews, and they constituted about one-third of the population. Thereafter, the Jewish population in the area gradually declined to an estimated 13,000 by 1979. Most of the Jews who now live in Rogers Park are elderly—retirees, widows, and widowers. Some are residents of the numerous nursing homes along Sheridan Road. There are very few Jewish children; the average age of the Jewish population of Rogers Park is about sixty.

Since World War II, the big intracity movement of Jews who have left their former communities on the South, West, and Northwest sides has been into the area of West Ridge. This neighborhood, generally coinciding with what is popularly referred to as West Rogers Park, lies between Rogers Park and the Albany Park-North Park area. Its approximate boundaries are Ravenswood Avenue (1800 west) on the east, the North Shore Channel (3300 west) on the west, Bryn Mawr Avenue (5600 north) on the south, and Howard Street (7600 north) and the Evanston border on the north.

There were fewer than 2,000 Jews in the area in 1930; by 1950 the number had reached about 11,000. In the 1950s the Jewish population of West Rogers Park quadrupled, and in 1963 it reached an estimated 48,000, or about three-fourths of the total population of the community. Most of the Jews of West Rogers Park were of Russian-Polish descent.

They came from Lawndale and Albany Park, and they purchased single-family homes in the northern part of West Rogers Park. Many Jews also moved into the new Winston Towers condominium complex south of Touhy Avenue.

Today West Rogers Park is the largest Jewish community within the city of Chicago. A number of its synagogues were founded almost a century ago in the Maxwell Street area and reached West Rogers Park via Lawndale. Most of its approximately twenty synagogues are Orthodox. Many are aligned along California Avenue, between Peterson and Touhy avenues, in a way that is reminiscent of Douglas Boulevard in Lawndale. On or near California Avenue are a religiously oriented high school, a large Jewish community center, a home for the Jewish aged, a Jewish convalescent home, and the offices of various Jewish organizations. Devon Avenue is the main business street of West Rogers Park; many of its merchants were previously located on Roosevelt Road or Lawrence Avenue.

The Jewish population of West Rogers Park is older and has a higher median income and a higher median educational level than the rest of Chicago's population. But like the population of the city as a whole, it has been declining in numbers—to about 35,000 Jewish residents at present. Young Jewish Orthodox families continue to maintain their strength and institutions in West Rogers Park, while the Conservative and Reform Jewish population is declining. But increasingly, Greeks, Orientals, Slavs, and others have been moving into the community. Devon Avenue has become a street of many nations.

The Exodus to the Suburbs

The major Jewish population movement in recent years has been out of Chicago into the northern and northwestern suburbs. Small numbers of Jews, mainly descendants of the early German immigrants, moved into North Shore suburbs such as Glencoe and Highland Park shortly after World War I. The first synagogue in the North Shore area was the "branch" of the Sinai Congregation (Reform) of the South Side of Chicago, established in Glencoe in 1920. It soon became the independent North Shore Congregation Israel. But as late as 1950 only about 5 percent of the Chicago area's Jews were living in the suburbs. The 1950s saw a rapid general movement to the suburbs by many groups of people for a variety of reasons, such as changes in city neighborhoods, greater affluence, the desire for suburban amenities and status, improved transportation, and increases in the number and size of young families.

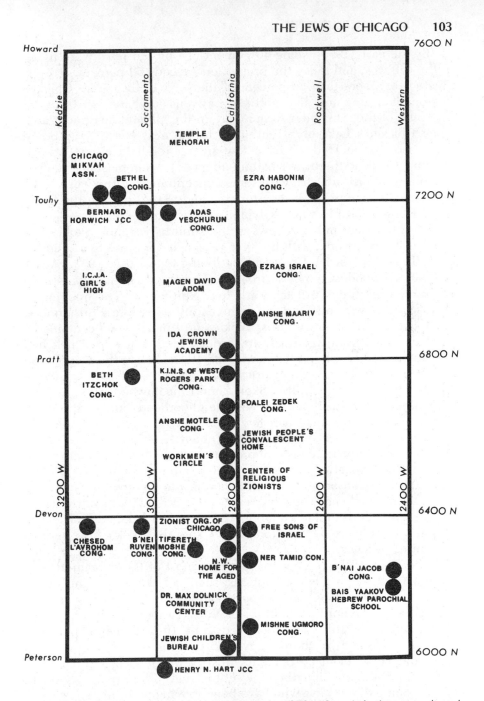

Jewish facilities in the heart of West Rogers Park, 1979: 18 such facilities are aligned along a two-mile stretch of California Avenue. West Rogers Park has Chicago's greatest concentration of Jews today. *Courtesy of Irving Cutler.*

By the early 1960s, some 40 percent of Chicago Jews were living in the suburbs, and today the proportion exceeds 50 percent. It is estimated that more than 80 percent of the Jews of the entire Chicago metropolitan area now live north of Lawrence Avenue (4800 north). The bulk of the remainder form an arc in the affluent apartment area along Chicago's Lakeshore southward to the near North Side. Some Jews also live in Hyde Park; a few are scattered in other Chicago communities; and there are small numbers of Jews in most of the western and southern suburbs, with some concentration to the west in the Oak Park-River Forest-Westchester area and to the south in the Glenwood-Homewood-Flossmoor-Olympia Fields-Park Forest area.

The first major move of Jews to the suburbs was into Skokie and adjacent Lincolnwood, with the first synagogue of these two suburbs, Niles Township Jewish Congregation, being founded in 1952. Skokie and Lincolnwood were not far from the Jewish concentrations in Rogers Park, West Ridge, Albany Park, and North Park. The opening of Edens Expressway in 1951 made them readily accessible. Furthermore, unlike the North Shore suburbs, Skokie and Lincolnwood contained a good deal of vacant, relatively low-priced land, some of which had been prematurely subdivided during the 1920s, before the Depression and World War II halted construction. Thousands of mainly single-family dwellings were built in Skokie and Lincolnwood, often by Jewish builders who advertised in Jewish neighborhoods, and by the 1960s these suburbs were about half Jewish. In 1975 the Jewish Federation of Metropolitan Chicago estimated that about 40,000 of Skokie's almost 70,000 residents were Jewish. At present the two suburbs contain about a dozen congregations, most of which adhere to the Orthodox-Traditional or Conservative ritual, in contrast to the greater concentration of Orthodox synagogues in West Rogers Park, with its much larger numbers of elderly and foreign-born, and the preponderance of Reform temples in the more distant North Shore suburbs. Skokie also has two rabbinical colleges.

After World War II, Jews moved into most of the other northern, outer suburbs, with a few exceptions, such as Lake Forest and Kenilworth, which had long been almost completely closed to Jews. The population of the northern suburbs of Niles, Evanston, Wilmette, Winnetka, and Deerfield is now believed to be 10-25 percent Jewish; of Morton Grove and Northbrook, over 25 percent; and of Glencoe and Highland Park, about 50 percent. Most of the Jewish population of these suburbs moved into the new subdivisions developed after World War II. Some of the Jews who have been moving there in recent years come from Chicago. However, there has also been *intersuburban* movement among Jews, especially from Skokie, whose Jewish population has declined some 15 percent in the last dozen years, partly because its post–World War II children have grown up and moved out. The Jewish population of Northbrook and Deerfield has increased especially rapidly in recent years.

The latest Jewish settlement pattern has been for young Jewish families to move into the still further outlying suburbs to the northwest, where there is vacant land and more reasonably priced housing. Serving these newer Jewish communities are synagogues in Hanover Park, Schaumburg, Hoffman Estates, Des Plaines, Buffalo Grove, and Vernon Hills. Buffalo Grove, some thirty miles northwest of the Loop, now has 4,000 Jews and three synagogues—one Traditional, one Conservative, and one Reform.

Chicago Area Jewry Today: Problems of Identity and Dispersal

The Jewish population of the Chicago metropolitan area has declined in recent years, to an estimated 253,000 in 1975, or about 4 percent of the total population.[9] The decline has been due mainly to a low birthrate, movement to the sunbelt states, assimilation due to intermarriage, lack of Jewish identity and alienation among some youth, and the elimination of most immigration—though some European Jewish refugees after World War II, and more recently several thousand Russian Jewish refugees, have come to the area.

Like American society as a whole, the Jews of the suburbs increasingly are faced with problems dealing with their youth, family relationships, and changing values, though the residual effects of their culture and immigrant experience have helped to soften some of the effects of these problems. Irving Howe takes a long-range and on the whole optimistic view of the future survival of Jewish culture. He believes "cultures are slow to die," and "sometimes they survive long after their more self-conscious members suppose them to have vanished," a view that certainly seems to fit many of America's ethnic groups besides Jews. On the general suburbanization of his own people, Howe comments:

A great many suburban Jews no longer spoke Yiddish, a growing number did not understand it, some failed to appreciate the magnitude of their loss; but their deepest inclinations of conduct, bias, manner, style, intonation, all bore heavy signs of immigrant shaping. What Jewish suburbanites took to be "a good life," the kinds of vocations to which they hoped to lead their children, their sense of appropriate conduct within a family, the ideas capable of winning their respect, the moral appeals to which they remained open,

their modes of argument, their fondness for pacific conduct, their
view of respectability and delinquency—all showed the strains of
immigrant Yiddish culture, usually blurred, sometimes buried, but
still at work. Like their parents, many were still enamored of that
mystery called "education," still awestruck by the goods of
culture. . . .[10]

And suburban Jews are no different in many respects from those who
stay in the American city environment:

. . . the suburban Jews remained a crucial segment of the cultural
audience in America: the operagoers, the ballet supporters, the
book buyers. If Jewish socialism had almost vanished, it took on a
second, less impassioned life in the liberalism prevailing among
suburban Jews. And the tradition of *tsedaka*—charity, in the larger
sense of communal responsibility—remained powerful, lashing the
suburban (and urban) Jews to feats of self-taxation that could not
be matched in any other American community.

Today, the Chicago area Jewish community no longer has the tri-
partite division within the city of North, South, and West Side neighborhoods. Jews are increasingly concentrated in the high-status northern
suburbs and are moving out from there over a wide geographical area.
This broader dispersal reflects economic success, of course, and the
decreasing dependence of Jews on totally Jewish institutions and support systems. However, in many cases the abandoned communal insti-
tuitions of the city have been replaced by new ones, scattered mainly
in the northern fringes of the city and suburbs. Eight city and suburban
Jewish community centers operate under the aegis of the Jewish Federation of Metropolitan Chicago. This model umbrellalike community
organization supports dozens of community, social welfare, cultural,
religious, and educational services and organizations, mainly from funds
raised through contributions by many thousands to the Jewish United
Fund. The Jews have traditionally "taken care of their own" with zeal
and dedication.

The long-established afternoon Hebrew schools, most of which are
synagogue sponsored, have experienced enrollment losses because of
the decline in the Jewish school-age population. However, there has
been a growth of all-day Jewish elementary schools and high schools,
both Orthodox and non-Orthodox, many of them newly organized, as
some parents try to upgrade their children's secular education as well
as instill in them their cultural heritage. Jewish study courses for adults
have also been experiencing a recent resurgence that stems from a
renaissance of interest among many Jews in their heritage and from
their concern about Israel's future.

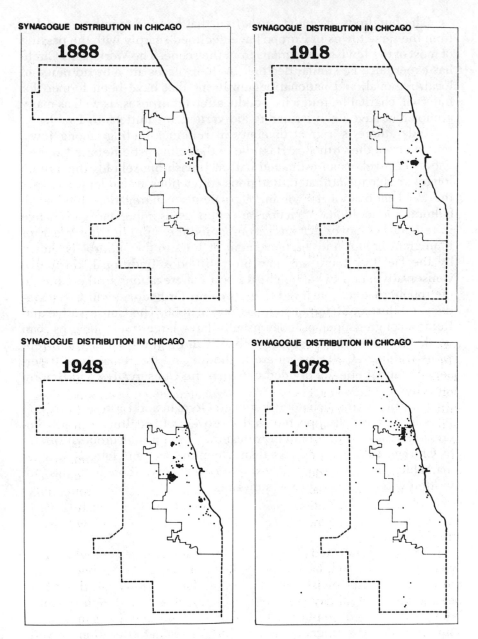

The changing pattern of synagogue distribution in the Chicago area, by 30-year periods, reflects the changing residential locations of the Jews in the area. *Courtesy of Irving Cutler.*

The hundreds of *landsmanshaften* that banded together *landsleit* from the same towns in Europe have declined sharply with the passing of most of the Jewish immigrants from the scene. The Workman's Circle has experienced a similar decline. In their places are a broad range of local, regional, and national organizations that have been formed for fraternal, charitable, religious, or educational purposes, as well as many groups that have been formed to aid various institutions in Israel.

Today there is a great diversity in religious feeling among Jews, ranging from the Orthodox Hassidic to the humanistic Reform Congregations, as well as an estimated half of Jewish households that are no longer synagogue affiliated. Religious convictions are no longer always the chief motivation for joining a particular congregation: the social, cultural, and locational attractions are often just as important. The change in religious behavior that has accompanied the rapid decline of earlier immigrant groups and the movement of Jews to the suburbs is shown by the fact that there are now fifty Orthodox-Traditional, thirty-five Conservative, and twenty-eight Reform congregations in the Chicago metropolitan area, compared to eighty-four Orthodox, eight Conservative, and thirteen Reform congregations in 1930. The Conservative and Reform congregations of today usually have larger memberships than do the Orthodox. It is estimated that of those Jews who remain religiously affiliated, 30 percent are Orthodox and the remaining 70 percent are about equally divided between the Conservative and Reform movements.

The once-sharp dichotomy between German and Eastern European Jews has largely disappeared as the process of acculturation has progressed rapidly. The overall historical transition from European *shtetls* to Chicago suburbs took less than a century to complete. It is a remarkable American—and Jewish—success story, though it was not written without hardship and suffering.

Chapter IV

ANDREW T. KOPAN

Greek Survival in Chicago:
The Role of Ethnic Education, 1890-1980

> The Greek school will train children to be Greeks
> so that they will not be digested in the vastness
> of America.
> — Peter Lambros, editor of the Greek Star

> Πατρός τε καὶ μητρός, καὶ τῶν ἄλλων
> προγόνων τιμιώτερόν ἐστι καὶ ἁγιώτερον
> ἡ πατρίς.
>
> One's country is more honorable and more sa-
> cred than one's parents and ancestors.
> — Socrates (469-399 B.C.)

THE STORY OF THE GREEKS IN CHICAGO
stands today as an example of the survival of a people and the perpetuation of a culture through education. It is the story of an ethnic group
busily going through the process of adjustment in an alien city, grasping
every opportunity to build a better way of life upon the hoped-for
return to the homeland, and retaining tenaciously a profound consciousness of its identity and heritage. But preservation of the Greek
cultural ethos was not achieved without conflict and divisiveness, nor
without the modifying and acculturative impact of the American milieu,
and in time it led to the emergence of a new Greek-American subculture in Chicago.

Every ethnic group must be seen against the background of the
social order of which it is a part. To get the proper perspective, then,
one must see the early Greek immigrants in Chicago as descendants
of Hellas (as the Greeks call their country) and as Hellenes (Greeks)
the proud inheritors of their nation's long and illustrious history. This
"Hellenism" was reflected in the nearly 3,000 years of Greek achievement in the arts, in science, philosophy, politics, and governance, in
education and religion, the bedrock of Western civilization.

Historically, they came from a small country in southeastern Europe, a poor nation about the size of Illinois with less than one-fifth of
its land arable, yet basically an agricultural nation. The mountainous
terrain of Greece, with its 3,000-mile rugged seacoast and its proximity
to the sea, has made the Greeks a nation of emigrants from time immemorial. It was the constant seeking for better conditions, coupled
with political exigencies of the times, that led to the Greeks' emigration
from their country to many parts of the world and later to the United
States. A continuous pattern of emigration has been responsible for the
spread of Greek immigrant culture from ancient times to the modern
period.

This same topography determined the early political development
of Greece into small city-states ruled by kings and tyrants. And even
though Greece's documented history does not begin until 776 B.C., the
year of the first Olympic games, a wealth of mythological literature had
already been created during the eight previous centuries, illustrated
most conspicuously by Homer's epics *The Iliad* and *The Odyssey*.

110

Gradually, democracy evolved with the development of constitutions, social laws, equal rights in court, and the privilege of being tried by jury. The fifth century B.C. was called the Golden Age of Pericles, Socrates, Plato, and Aristotle.

In 336 B.C., Alexander the Great united the Greek city-states and went on to conquer Persia, Phoenicia, Palestine, Egypt, and practically the rest of the known world, ushering in the Hellenistic Age, which saw the spread of Greek culture to the entire civilized world. However, in 46 B.C. Greece was conquered by Rome and became a Roman province. But it in turn Hellenized the Romans. In A.D. 330, Greece became a part of the Byzantine Empire, which became saturated with Greek ideas and became the center of civilization for over 1,000 years. During this period Greece was a buffer state which protected Western Europe from the Eastern hordes.

With the fall of Constantinople in 1453, Greece was conquered by the Turks. This began Hellenism's dark ages of nearly 400 years of misrule, repressive taxation, atrocities, massacres, and the conscription of children to be raised as Mohammedan soldiers. Bands of Greeks known as *klephts* (brigands) maintained a semi-independent existence by hiding in mountains and raiding Turkish territory. And as Turkish severity became unbearable, the Greeks revolted on various occasions. With the aid of the Great Powers, the Greeks succeeded in their 1821 War of Independence, and Greece emerged once again as an independent nation—but with only one-third of the territory it claimed and one-fifth of its people. This led to a series of wars with Turkey down to the present day (for example, on Cyprus), in an effort to redeem Greek lands. These wars—especially the ill-fated Asia Minor campaign of 1922, which resulted in the forcible expulsion of 1,800,000 Greeks from their ancestral lands in Turkey—have encouraged the immigration of Greeks to America. Of prime importance was the grinding poverty that Greek peasants faced in their newly independent country, which had been systematically devastated by the wars for liberation.

Immigration to the United States

The Greek presence in America begins with the first voyage of Columbus, who had a number of Greek crew members.[1] The accounts of Spanish explorers from Cortez to Pizarro and Coronado contains numerous names with "greco" or "griego" affixed to them. These were men without a country—adventurers, merchants, seafarers. Webster defines "gringo" as a corruption of the Spanish "griego," which was used disparagingly by Spaniards for the numerous Greeks in Spanish expeditions to the New World (it has come to be used by the indigenous population to designate any "foreigner"). Greeks were also known to live in the American colonies. The largest colonization attempt took place in 1767, when some 500 Greeks, along with Italians and Minorcans, landed along Florida's Atlantic coast. They had been recruited as indentured laborers by a Scottish entrepreneur who had secured a British land grant. This first episode of Hellenism in America was abandoned ten years later after they encountered enormous difficulties.[2]

The Greek War of Independence (1821–1828) provided another episode of Hellenism in America, a wave of "philhellenism" that swept the United States in support of the Greek cause.[3] Scores of Greek orphaned boys, whose parents had been massacred by the Turks, were brought to the United States by Americans who had gone to Greece to participate in the struggle and by American missionary societies. Most of these orphans, who were adopted by American parents, went on to become prominent professionals in their adopted country. One of them, Lucas Miltiades Miller, was elected to Congress, and another, George Musalas Colvocoressis, became a captain in the Civil War, while his son attained the rank of admiral in the U.S. Navy during the Spanish-American War.[4] Meanwhile, during the nineteenth century another group of Greeks appeared on the American scene. These were merchants who were establishing their import-export businesses in American port cities. It was these merchants who in 1864 established the first Greek Orthodox church in the United States in New Orleans.

But neither the Greek merchants nor the orphans composed a sufficiently large group to establish permanent Greek-American institutions in the New World.[5] This remained to be accomplished by the poor and illiterate but energetic and resourceful immigrants who began a mass exodus from the villages of Greece to the United States near the end of the nineteenth century. The world of the Greek peasant was one of desperate poverty. Crop failures, poor soil conditions, floods, earthquakes, oppressive taxation, family debts, political turmoil, and political harassment—especially for those still living in the unredeemed parts under Turkish control—forced many to look elsewhere for the land of opportunity. This was especially the case in the Peloponnese during the 1890s, when the price of currants, the main money crop, dropped drastically, forcing a massive departure of young and middle-aged males from the villages of this area and leaving them bereft.

America was a beckoning symbol, the land of "gold in the streets," where money could be made quickly, which would enable Greek emigrants to return home with sufficient capital to pay off the family debt, provide dowries for sisters, and live in comfort. Thus, at that time nine out of every ten Greeks immigrating to the United States were male. It has also been estimated that at least one-third of those who immigrated to the United States returned to Greece. Greek immigration became largely a male phenomenon, with one of the highest rates of repatriation.[6]

According to the United States Census, over 15,000 Greeks immigrated to the United States during the 1890s. But during the next two decades, 1900 to 1920, the greatest number of Greek immigrants arrived—some 400,000. Then the figures are drastically reduced because of the passage of the Immigration Quota Act of 1924, the Depression, and World War II; but they increased following the war, especially as a result of the reformed Immigration Act of 1967. The total number of Greeks immigrating to the United States from the time immigration records were begun in 1820 to the present time, is said to be 675,158 (Table 1). Of course, these are only official figures; they do not reflect Greeks who emigrated from Turkey, Cyprus, Rumania, Egypt, and other parts of the Mediterranean world.

For those early immigrants who arrived prior to World War I, a settlement pattern can be discerned. Many moved to the Southwest and West to work on railroads and mines; others went to the milltowns of New England and the Atlantic seaboard, where they worked in textile and shoe factories. Most, however, came to the large cities of the North, where, after a brief so-called apprenticeship, they established their own businesses, especially in the service trades such as restaurants, confectionery or sweet shops, retail and wholesale produce, floral shops, and shoeshine parlors. Chicago was the one city that attracted the largest number, and it remained until after World War II the largest community of Greeks in the United States—containing approximately 10 percent of the Greek population in the United States. The 1890 census shows only 245 Greeks in Chicago, but by 1900 this figure had increased to 1,493, by which time the organized Greek community of Chicago had come into existence.[7]

The Greek population of Chicago never reached more than 75,000 persons, considerably less than the 125,000 to 250,000 usually claimed by the Greek press and community leaders. But from its initial stages until the present it has been one of the most viable Greek communities in the United States and the first to respond to the need for ethnic survival and educational adjustment.

Origin of the Greek Community of Chicago

Historically, it all began in the 1840s with the arrival of a few pioneer Greek traders in Fort Dearborn from New Orleans by way of

TABLE I
IMMIGRATION FROM GREECE BY DECADES,
1821–1980

Decade	Number
1821 – 1830	20
1831 – 1840	49
1841 – 1850	16
1851 – 1860	31
1861 – 1870	72
1871 – 1880	210
1881 – 1890	2,038
1891 – 1900	15,979
1901 – 1910	167,579
1911 – 1920	184,201
1921 – 1930	51,084
1931 – 1940	9,119
1941 – 1950	8,973
1951 – 1960	47,708
1961 – 1970	85,969
1971 – 1980	102,000*
U.S. total for 160 years:	675,158

*Immigration figures for 1977–1980 estimated at 9,000 annually.

Source: Immigration and Naturalization Service, *1965 Annual Reports* (U.S. Government Printing Office), pp. 47–49; Department of Commerce, Bureau of the Census, *Statistical Abstract of the United States, 1972* (U.S. Government Printing Office), p. 92; and Immigration and Naturalization Service, *1976 Annual Reports* (U.S. Government Printing Office), pp. 87–88.

the Mississippi and Chicago rivers. Some returned to their homeland with glowing tales of the Midwest and came back with relatives. One of these was Captain Nicholas Peppas, who arrived in 1857 and lived in Kinzie Street for more than fifty years. Another early pioneer was Constantine Mitchell, who, while a Confederate soldier, was taken prisoner by the Union armies during the Civil War and brought to Chicago. At the end of the war he settled in Chicago permanently. During the same period, "Uncle" Thomas Combiths moved to Chicago, and in 1869 his son Frank became the first child of a Greek father to be born in the city. Frank Combiths' mother was not of Greek descent, nor were there any Greek women in Chicago until many years later.

It was not until after the Great Fire of 1871 that Greek immigration to Chicago accelerated. One of those who settled there after the fire was Christ Chakonas, who became known as the "Columbus of Sparta" for his successful efforts in encouraging Greeks to settle in Chicago. When he first arrived in 1872, Chakonas saw the opportunities the growing city offered and returned to his native city of Sparta to urge his friends to immigrate to Chicago. Many of these early Greek settlers worked on construction jobs, rebuilding the city after the fire. Others became fruit peddlers or merchants along Lake Street, then the city's main business center. News of their "success" reached the homeland, and a new wave of Greeks arrived to seek their fortunes. This time people from the neighboring villages in the province of Laconia and the adjoining province of Arcadia joined the immigration movement, and by 1882 the Greek community was a settlement of several hundred people who resided in the vicinity of Clark and Kinzie streets on the near North Side. Chicago soon became the major terminal point for Greek immigrants to the United States, making the city the largest Greek settlement in the country, with a distinctive Peloponnesian composition—mostly of men from Laconia and Arcadia.

The first Greek *woman* in Chicago is said to be Mrs. Peter Pooley, who came with her sea-captain husband from the Greek island of Corfu in 1885. Mrs. Pooley became active in the minuscule community, organizing a benevolent society together with the Slavic Orthodox community for the purpose of forming a common house of worship. In 1887 the first purely Greek benevolent society, *Therapnon*, was organized, followed in 1891 by a second society, *Lycurgus*, organized by immigrants from Laconia.[8] By 1892 the Greek community acquired its first resident pastor, Rev. Peter Phiambolis, who officiated at the first Greek Orthodox church in a rented upper-level warehouse on the northeast corner of Randolph and Union streets, near the produce market where most Greeks worked.[9] On March 25, 1893, the church was consecrated by the first Greek Orthodox hierarch to visit the United States, Bishop Dionysius Lattas of Zante, who had come to represent the Church of Greece at the Columbian Exposition. Later, the Annunciation Church (as it was named) in cooperation with the Lycurgus Society relocated the church in more appropriate quarters at 60 East Kinzie Street. The contemporary American press described religious services in this early church as follows:

> Greek service is said at a church on the second floor of an unpretentious building in Kinzie near Clark Street. Here come regularly 3,000 members of the Greek colony of Chicago to hear bearded Father Phiambolis clad in canonical robes. The mass is said in the Greek tongue like it has been sung in Greece for nearly 2,000 years. It is, for the time being, a part of ancient Greece, transplanted and set down in the heart of a busy, bustling community, where the rattle of wagon wheels and the clang of street car bells break in

Mr. and Mrs. Peter Pooley (Panagiotis Poulis), the first Greek family known to settle in Chicago, shown shortly after their arrival from Corfu, Greece, in 1885. Mr. Pooley was a sea captain who had visited Chicago several times. Impressed with the city, he returned to his native island of Corfu, married Georgia Bitzi, and brought her to the Windy City. A well-educated and aggressive woman, Mrs. Pooley organized the Greco-Slavonic Brotherhood — the first Greek voluntary association in Chicago. Mr. Pooley died in 1914 and his wife in 1945. They had seven children, all born in Chicago. *Courtesy of Andrew T. Kopan.*

with striking rudeness on the holy intonation of the priest. To the casual visitor who knows the Greeks in a business way and is conversant with their quickness in adapting themselves to American methods and manners, the impression thus given is a forceful one.[10]

The newly relocated church became a source of tension and discord. One account claims that a few influential Spartans of the Lycurgus Society wanted to place a tax on "certain Halsted Street Greeks," namely the Arcadians, who were beginning to settle there in greater numbers. The feud brought about a split in the organized community, forcing the Arcadians to organize their own association, *Tegea*, followed by a parish of their own. This was accomplished in 1897 when they purchased a former Episcopal church at 1101 South Johnson Street (later renamed Peoria Street) and obtained an Arcadian priest. The new parish, Holy Trinity Church, became the focal point of a new "Greektown" on the near West Side.

A profile of Greek population dispersion before 1900 indicates that in the early 1890s the first Greek shops were found at Clark and Kinzie streets, just north of the Loop. It was here, as we have seen, that the city's first "Greektown" was located with the first organized church community. By 1895, newer Greek immigrants, predominantly from the province of Arcadia, began to move to the new West Side. A newspaper account observes:

> The better class of Greeks is to be found on South Water Street, while the poorer class is sandwiched in the settlements of Italians, Syrians and Slavonians [sic] on the West Side. West Polk Street from the river to Blue Island Avenue is thickly populated with Greeks.[11]

A later newspaper account indicates three areas of Greek concentration: Fifth Avenue (Wells) and Sherman Street between Van Buren and 12th Street; the North Side at Kingsbury, Kinzie, and Illinois streets; and the "vicinity of Tilden Avenue, Taylor Street and Center Avenue on the West Side."[12]

The Greek population of Chicago grew rapidly at the beginning of this century. In 1904 there were reportedly 7,500 Greeks, and by 1909 about 15,000, of whom 12,000 came and went according to their work in the city or on the railroad lines in states further west. As the Greeks became more numerous on the West Side, they invaded the Italian section, gradually displacing Italians from the area. The district surrounded by Halsted, Harrison, Blue Island, and Polk streets was known as the "Delta" and was just north and west of the famed Hull House and the present location of the University of Illinois, Chicago Circle campus. It became Chicago's famous "Greektown"—the oldest, largest, and most important settlement of Greeks in the United States. By 1930 the area had a foreign and native-born population of 12,000 to 18,000 Greeks.

The first permanent Greek community consisting of a church and a school was organized in the Delta. In this transplanted part of Greece emerged the first Greek-language newspapers, offices of benevolent, fraternal, and social organizations, and new businesses which soon sur-

Typical of the growing stream of Greek immigrants to the United States during the early part of the twentieth century was this group of 13 young men who emigrated from a small village near Olympia (site of the ancient Olympic games) in 1910. Arriving in New York, they boarded a train and took it to the end of the line—Chicago, where they posed for this photograph to send back to their relatives in the village. *Courtesy of Andrew T. Kopan.*

passed those on Lake Street. According to Fairchild, an early writer on Greek immigration to the United States, the district became more typically Greek than some sections of Athens.

> Practically all stores bear signs in both Greek and English, coffee houses flourish on every corner, in the dark little grocery stores one sees black olives, dried ink-fish, tomato paste, and all the queer, nameless roots and condiments which are so familiar in Greece. On every hand one hears the Greek language, and the boys in the streets and on the vacant lots play, with equal zest, Greek games and baseball. It is a self-sufficient colony, and provision is made to supply all the wants of the Greek immigrant in as near as possible the Greek way. Restaurants, coffee-houses, barber-shops, grocery stores and saloons are all patterned after the Greek type, and Greek doctors, lawyers, editors, and every variety of agent are to be found in abundance.[13]

While the Delta was to remain the largest concentration of Greek immigrants in Chicago, a second concentration of Greek newcomers developed on the South Side. After 1904, Greek shops and stores appeared in the Woodlawn district, mainly along 63rd Street between

Westworth and Cottage Grove Avenue. Subsequently, a second church community was organized with the assistance of a dissident group from the original Delta community. It became known as the Church of Saints Constantine and Helen, and a building was erected in 1909 at 61st and Michigan Avenue, followed by a parochial day school in 1910.

Similarly, Greek immigrants began moving to the North Side, some coming from the first area of settlement at Clark and Kinzie. A third church and school community was organized and erected independently at LaSalle and Oak streets in 1910, dedicated to the Annunciation of the Virgin Mary. Gradually, as Greek immigrants dispersed to other parts of the city, fed by increased immigration, additional church communities were organized. By 1930, Greek immigrants had established eleven formal communities in Chicago. Today persons of Greek descent are dispersed throughout the metropolitan area and clustered around twenty-one Greek Orthodox parish churches, thirteen of which are located in the suburbs. Each parish church represents a *koinotis*, or community, named after its patron saint; and the church as the nucleus of such a *koinotis* serves as a multifunctional center for religious, educational, social, and cultural activities.

The Role of the Church

The church is an ecological concept for Greek Orthodox Christians. If asked where he lives, a Greek is most likely to use the name of the church as a place of reference. Generally, church parishes in the central city, which were the original establishments, tend to be oriented to recent immigrants, especially those coming after World War II, while parishes toward the northern and southern outskirts of the city tend to be oriented to first- and second-generation Greek stock. Suburban parishes are all postwar phenomena, representing the movement of second and third generations to the suburbs. Figure 1 shows the location of the original church communities, their subsequent relocation, and the location of the newly organized church communities in the suburbs.

Historically, Christianity was wedded to Hellenism. It did not clash with the ancient culture, nor did it aim to suppress it. The early Greek Christians had made use of pagan thought and myth to help them in their spirituality. The Greek fathers of the early Christian church were important leaders and formulators of early Christian church doctrines, and by A.D. 380 Christianity was adopted as the official religion in Greece. Out of these influences the early church was born as a religion, a worship, and a theology. Christianity in Greece evolved as part of the Eastern church and came under the jurisdiction of the Ecumenical

Holy Trinity Church, 1897, was the first permanent Greek Orthodox parish in Chicago. It was located in the Greek Delta at Halsted and Harrison Streets, the largest Greektown in the United States. *Courtesy of Andrew T. Kopan.*

FIGURE 1.
GREEK ORTHODOX CHURCH COMMUNITIES OF CHICAGO
AND SUBURBS (1890–1980)

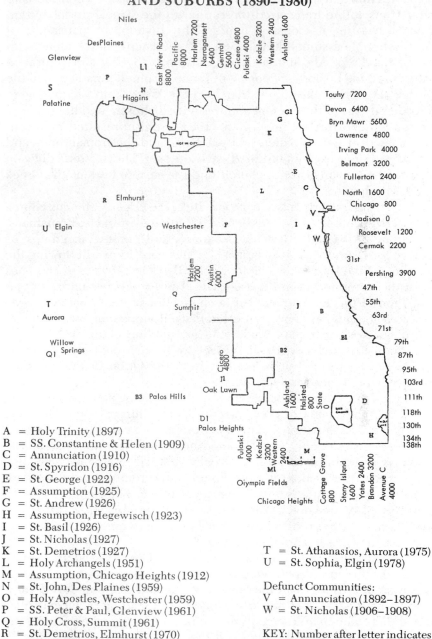

A = Holy Trinity (1897)
B = SS. Constantine & Helen (1909)
C = Annunciation (1910)
D = St. Spyridon (1916)
E = St. George (1922)
F = Assumption (1925)
G = St. Andrew (1926)
H = Assumption, Hegewisch (1923)
I = St. Basil (1926)
J = St. Nicholas (1927)
K = St. Demetrios (1927)
L = Holy Archangels (1951)
M = Assumption, Chicago Heights (1912)
N = St. John, Des Plaines (1959)
O = Holy Apostles, Westchester (1959)
P = SS. Peter & Paul, Glenview (1961)
Q = Holy Cross, Summit (1961)
R = St. Demetrios, Elmhurst (1970)
S = St. Nectarios, Palatine (1972)

T = St. Athanasios, Aurora (1975)
U = St. Sophia, Elgin (1978)

Defunct Communities:
V = Annunciation (1892–1897)
W = St. Nicholas (1906–1908)

KEY: Number after letter indicates
      move to new location.

Patriarch of Constantinople. This was followed by a division of the Christian church into eastern and western sections, which was a result of the administrative separation of the Roman Empire when the Emperor Constantine transferred the capital to the Greek city of Byzantium, renaming it Constantinople. The bishop, or patriarch, of Constantinople assumed jurisdiction of the Eastern church along with the patriarchs of Alexandria (Egypt), Antioch (Syria), and Jerusalem (Palestine); the bishop—or pope—of Rome assumed jurisdiction of the Western church as the sole patriarch in the West. Both sections were considered part of the ancient and undivided church, and both shared the same theological beliefs. In A.D. 1054 a schism resulted from controversies over newer beliefs and practices, and the Roman pope and Greek patriarch excommunicated each other.[14] The western division became the Roman Catholic church, and the eastern became the Greek Orthodox church.

As a result of early missionary activities, the Greek Orthodox church became the church of the Russians, Ukrainians, Serbians, Rumanians, Bulgarians, Albanians, Syrians, Lebanese, and other Arab groups, as well as for some Poles, Hungarians, Czechs, and Finns. Following the conquest of the Byzantine Empire by the Turks in 1453, these churches (with the exception of the Russian and Arab) remained under the jurisdiction of the Ecumenical Patriarchate. But in 1830, when Greece regained its independence, it declared itself autocephalous, meaning it did not wish to remain under the jurisdiction of the Patriarch of Constantinople, who was still subject to Turkish control.[15] As other Balkan nations gained their freedom from the Ottoman Empire, they too established independent churches.

Today the Eastern church consists of fourteen national churches, all sharing the same doctrines, practices, and liturgy, though differing in language. Each national church is independent, self-governing, and administered by a holy synod composed of bishops, the president of whom is called a metropolitan, or patriarch. All groups acknowledge the spiritual jurisdiction of the Ecumenical Patriarchate at Constantinople (Istanbul), analogous to the papacy at Rome. The church of Greece is governed by a synod of bishops, with the archbishop of Athens as president. It is from this church that Greek emigrants began arriving in America at the turn of the century.[16]

The significance of the institution of the Greek Orthodox Church within the structural cohesiveness of the Greek community in Chicago is paramount. Along with the family, it was and is the enduring force in keeping the Greek ethnic group together. A leading theologian once stated that "church and society are one in their essential nature: for the substance of culture is religion and the form of religion is culture."[17]

The prototype of formal organization among the Greek immigrants was, as we have already seen, the *koinotis*, which grew out of the *paroikia*, or "colony." The latter was a term applied to any group of Greek immigrants in a given locality; the former was a specialized term designating a regularly organized community centered on a church organization and usually called "The Orthodox Greek Community."[18] All Greek immigrants were considered members of the *paroikia* (colony), but when the *koinotis*, or "community," was organized, membership was increasingly limited to those who paid dues in support of the community. The purpose of the *koinotis* was to raise enough money to establish and maintain a local Greek Orthodox church. A general assembly of the entire dues-paying membership (consisting only of males) would then be called to elect a *symboulion*, or "board of trustees," which governs the affairs of the community by electing officers headed by a president.

The first task of the *symboulion* was the formal organization of the community by renting or purchasing property for religious services and obtaining a charter of incorporation from the state in which the community was located. The next task was to apply for a priest from either the Patriarchate of Constantinople (Istanbul) or the Church of Greece. Once this had been achieved, the new community would then proceed to establish a school. Thus every community would possess a church and school. The Greek immigrants of Chicago were the first to organize such a community in 1892, followed later in the same year by New York.[19] As noted above, Chicago now has twenty-one such communities.

Greek Orthodox communities in the United States originated from the action of the immigrants themselves and were not instituted by ecclesiastical authorities in Constantinople or Athens. Unlike the hierarchical situation in the old country, priests in America were hired directly by the *koinotis* rather than assigned by bishops. The governance of the church community was in the hands of the *symboulion*, which often served as a barometer of community opinion. The members disputed about priestly qualifications and role expectations, educational concerns, teachers, and board members, political affiliations and rival leaders, use of church funds for projects, community policies, the use of the English language, and kindred concerns.

The early Greek Orthodox churches in America, although independent in all reality, were by canon law under the spiritual aegis of the Ecumenical Patriarchate of Constantinople in Turkey, world headquarters of the Orthodox Catholic Church.[20] However, for practical purposes during this early period of Greek migration, the churches were placed under the spiritual jurisdiction of the Russian Orthodox bishop at San Francisco. The Russians were the first to introduce Orthodoxy into the United States and had the only resident bishop.[21] For the Greeks, however, such dependency meant humiliation; they were proud, nationalistic, and owed allegiance to a state church.[22]

The Patriarchate officially transferred the jurisdiction of its immigrant churches to the Church of Greece in 1908 for composite reasons. Numerous editorials in Greek-language newspapers demanded the establishment of an American diocese, but no action was taken other than special assignments of Greek bishops to visit and return to the homeland. This situation paralleled somewhat that of the colonial Anglican church which, prior to the American Revolution, was forced to fend for itself due to the lack of a resident bishop.

The outbreak of the Russian Bolshevik Revolution and the Venizelist-Royalist dispute, a political issue in Greece, radically altered Greek church development in this country. Deprived of canonical direction between 1917 and 1923, the Russian diocese in America disintegrated. In 1922 the Patriarchate of Constantinople reassumed control of American Orthodox churches to remove them from the political factionalism that had intensified in the communities. Along with this jurisdictional change came the formation of the Archdiocese of North and South America, and Chicago received its first bishop in 1923, when the area was made a diocese. Unfortunately, fierce turmoil persisted within the newly formed archdiocese, with two political factions—Venizelist and Royalist—each establishing its own hierarchy and parishes.[23] Finally, in 1930, with the nomination of Athenagoras as archbishop for the United States, the wounds and the schism gradually healed.

The erratic action of the church community in these years of dramatic political upheaval in Europe created modifications in the statutes: the archdiocese was now called "Hellenic" and was composed of churches using only Greek as the liturgical language. All other Orthodox Christians were formally excluded.[24] This exclusivity and linguistic nationalism is another reminder that Hellenism and Greek Orthodoxy were deeply intertwined: they kept the immigrant attached to the mother country, nourished his patriotic appetite, and helped him to preserve his faith and the language of his parents. The thought of never being able to return home to his ancestral origins and the fear of dying in a strange land caused him for a time to embrace his religion with a fervor unknown in Greece itself.

Thus a compelling aggressiveness characterized the American *koinotis*, with its determined, lay-elected *symboulion*. Many imbroglios resulted, since the *symboulion* managed church finances and paid the priest and teachers.[25] After 1922 the *koinotis* remained singularly autonomous in internal matters, controlling communal property and making parish policy. The hierarchy was left with only spiritual juris-

The interior of Annunciation Cathedral, the seat of the Greek Orthodox Bishop of Chicago, founded in 1910 and still in existence at 1017 North La Salle Street. The elaborate Byzantine decor is typical of the ornamentation in Greek Orthodox churches. *Courtesy of Andrew T. Kopan.*

diction and the task of assigning clergy to the *koinotis*.[26] Membership in the *koinotis* was open to all baptized Orthodox Christians, but only those males who paid dues could vote. Some Greek immigrants could not understand why it was necessary in America to support the church by fees and contributions. The strict separation of church and state in the United States was to them a fresh concept, difficult to grasp at first, because at home in Greece all baptized persons were automatically church members and no dues had to be paid to the state church. They gradually learned this lesson, however, and one other American lesson as well: women were allowed to vote in parish affairs and serve on the parish council after World War II.

The clergy were trained in ecclesiastical colleges in Greece or in territories considered Greek. The early priests sent to Chicago were highly educated and dedicated. They exerted leadership in organizing the parish, the voluntary, philanthropic, and mutual-aid societies, and the parish schools, and they often assumed teaching functions.[27] However, other clergy came without official credentials. As opportunists, they seized the chance to establish rival parishes in order to secure a job. There also came clerics from the Greek districts of the Ottoman Empire who kept their parishioners in a perpetual state of nationalistic excitement by accusing them of being remiss in their patriotic mission.[28]

The role of the priest was not regarded as separate from the community. He was, by special training and ordination, an ambassador of the sacred church, as well as a mortal by nature and existence. The priestly character was thus described:

> As although [the Greeks] may sometimes despise the *man* for his lack of education or his worldly-mindedness, they nevertheless respect the priest and treat him with the proper marks of courtesy, as doffing their hats, or rising when he enters the room.[29]

Because of deep-rooted democratic Greek traditions, the priest had no formal control but had considerable informal influence, if he cared to exercise it. And some exercised it extensively. These "empire builders" led the uphill battle for the promotion of ethnic education. Often they faced direct confrontation with the *koinotis*, which resented control of communal schools by clergy. The *symboulion* leaders were often anticlericals who found such priestly involvement incompatible with the immigrants' former experiences in Greece.

An example of this stance appeared in an editorial at the time the Chicago Greek community was debating the establishment of a communal school.

> With our Greek schools in America springing up like mushrooms beside Greek churches, the Greeks in Chicago and elsewhere are

warned to bear in mind the futile efforts of the church in the past to dominate public instruction. History tells us that the church for many centuries took to itself the role of guardian of the entire education of youth. In Spain, Italy, Austria, Greece, and other countries where the church exercised such influence and its superstitions flourished unchecked, the result was an increase in those dubious theories which are the precursors of sciolism [superficial learning]. This happened simply because the complete education of youth was left in the hands of the church, or rather the church succeeded in dominating the education of youth.

Under so supersitious an education ignorance, antagonism to science, and intolerable nonsense reached such heights that history records no other characteristic products of this theocratic education than religious dogmas, letters of blood, and the resigned submission of the populace.

The real educational system, under which the human mind expands cosmologically, and by which false theories and superstitions are routed, is to be found here in America. And we Greeks of America, for our own interest, the interest of coming generations, the interest of our adopted country, and the interest of the church itself must accept this great American educational system which is free from any ecclesiastical domination. Church is an imperative necessity for a nation, but school is the nation's whole life, and public schools which are free from theocracy are the real bulwarks of the country. Let us profit by the pitfalls into which others have fallen and maintain freedom of education if we wish to produce good, useful, broad-minded citizens whose knowledge and enlightenment will promote and protect the welfare of the church.[30]

A Greek was born into his religion and nationality; it was thus unthinkable to be anything else. Yet some evangelical groups succeeded in making inroads in converting Greeks away from the Orthodox faith.[31] Strong opposition set in, with Greeks blaming the chaotic conditions on quarreling parish councils and partisan clergy failing to minister to the needy and distressed. Others had little sympathy for "traitors" who embraced a strange faith. In their patriotic estimation, a man who renounced the Greek Orthodox church was no Greek.[32]

All of these vexing problems—dissension within church communities, unqualified priests, evangelism—underscored the long-recognized need for a workable central authority. Chicago's Greeks awaited a bishop who could function with a stern hand, but none came because of the difficult political conditions in Greece.[33] So the Greek church communities floundered on their own.

Conditions in Chicago from 1914 to 1917 revealed the low opinion the *koinotis* held of the clergy and local ecclesiastical administrations. The Greek press continued its attack on allegedly greedy, grasping priests who, in league with conscienceless members of parish councils, trampled on the dignity of the church and integrity of the communities. Lengthy court trials, criminal waste, and extravagant use of church funds for litigation and fees became a disgrace.[34] Clerical commercialism was a common journalistic theme. Priests were accused of neglecting pastoral duties in order to officiate at sacramental events for lucrative fees.[35] Additional complaints involved their failure to adjust and relate to new surroundings, furnish relevant educational programs, and meet basic concerns of parishioners.[36]

Frequent pleas were voiced for unifying the parishes of Chicago. In the autumn of 1915 the United Greek Parishes of Chicago announced the formation of a committee designed to bring order out of confusion. It was comprised of local priests, council presidents, and representatives, and called for a thorough auditing of financial records, a public listing of debts, purchase of a communal cemetery, maintenance of a consolidated school, establishment of a high school with dormitories for all Greek students in the United States, creation of special funds for the needy, and the building of a hospital.[37]

This ambitious plan for unification foundered, as usual, on the factionalist feud over the Venizelist-Royalist political issue in Greece. Even the formation of the diocesan structure of 1923 failed to effect a real union of the Greek community. The damage had been done, and they were unable to agree to unite.[38] Greek individualism and divisiveness would remain, despite the attempt to superimpose a formal church structure.[39] The precepts of Hellenism would, however, be taught and transferred to ensuing generations through the ethnic community schools.[40] But down to the 1980s, each community attacked its local concerns independently.

Economic Status

In view of the Greek immigrants' peasant background, it is noteworthy that in America they should have such business skill and resourcefulness. At home few immigrants had ventured beyond their native villages or made contact with other ethnic groups. They arrived in the New World with no liquid capital or experience in the world of work in which they were to become so conspicuous.[41] Unskilled Greeks found work in the textile mills and shoe factories of New England and in diverse industries in New York, Philadelphia, and Chicago. Labor agents persuaded many to take heavy labor on railroad and waterfront construction jobs in Utah, Nevada, Oregon, and Washington. But many

Pan Orthodox Day at the Chicago World's Fair in 1933. Symbolic of the large multi-ethnic Orthodox population in Chicago is this rare gathering of Greek, Russian, Serbian, Ukrainian, and Syrian clergymen who participated in services at the city's 100th birthday celebration—"A Century of Progress" exposition. *Courtesy of Andrew T. Kopan.*

newcomers underwent mental and physical suffering on such jobs and as soon as possible ventured into business on their own.

Business appealed to the Greek immigrants for many reasons in addition to the typically American desire to be "one's own boss." Some, desiring wealth and status so that they could return to their native villages and flaunt their success before their detractors, believed this was the surest way to economic success, and it certainly was preferable to working for others for wages. Wherever one turned in America, the admonition was to work hard, save, invest, succeed, and become independent.[42] In short, the Greeks—unknowingly perhaps—were practicing the "Protestant ethic" of hard work and success, the American Dream ideology.

Marked individualism was obviously one of the innate traits of

Greek immigrants. An early writer commented on the dominant characteristics of the Greek *Zeitgeist*:

> We noted as characteristic of ancient Hellas an extreme individual freedom. The same individualism is as marked today as in ancient times. Jealousy, rivalry, restiveness, factiousness, self-assertion, inherent in the national character.[43]

These traits had a profound impact on Greek business successes and economic failures. They were, for the most part, unable or unwilling to work cooperatively and harmoniously with one another. But in time, through exposure, interaction, and acculturation with the dominant American culture, there appeared some modification of these traits.

In their early years in Chicago many Greek immigrants became peddlers. It was not long before Greek peddlers, fighting for control from the Italians, achieved a large share of the banana and fruit business, and began moving into the wholesale business. The *Chicago Tribune* said:

> . . . the Greeks have almost run the Italians out of the fruit business in Chicago not only in a small retail way, but as wholesalers as well, for the big wholesale fruit houses on South Water Street are nearly all owned by men from the isles of burning Sappho. As a result, there is a bitter feud between these two races, as deeply seated as the emnity that engendered the Graeco-Roman wars.[44]

Two years later the same newspaper described the proclivity of Greek immigrants toward economic independence by saying that the ". . . true Greek will not work at hard manual labor like digging sewers, carrying the hod, or building railways. He is either an artisan or a merchant, generally the latter."[45]

The successful Greek fruit and vegetable peddlers were confronted with numerous problems besides the confrontations with Italians. One was the neighborhood merchant who resented their competition. In 1904 the Grocers' Association accused the peddlers of being the parasites of the trade and asked the city council to prohibit them from selling in alleys and streets, or else to impose a heavy tax. The struggle between established grocers and the peddlers was fierce. In some cases it was a Greek grocer versus a Greek peddler. The peddlers, by insisting that they rendered a public service to the housewives who preferred produce that was cheap and fresh, won a temporary victory and were thus encouraged to organize a fruit and vegetable dealers' association to ward off future attacks from grocers.[46]

The peddlers also suffered from the effects of graft-ridden law enforcement agencies. They were often intimidated and forced to pay small fees to dishonest policemen. Their ignorance of the law, a passive attitude, or a lack of necessary funds to acquire a license often invited unscrupulous police officers to threaten them with prosecution for the violation of municipal ordinances.[47]

Because of such alleged legal violations, Greeks were arrested in large numbers. The Abbott study indicates that in 1908 alone there were 1,157 Greek arrests, of which 891 were for a city ordinance violation. Based on the Greek population in the 1908 school census, it claimed that twenty-seven out of every one hundred Greeks in Chicago had violated the law; for the rest of the city's populace the ratio was only four per hundred. The Abbott study suggests that these figures were further distorted because there were probably three to four times more Greeks in Chicago than revealed by the 1908 census.[48]

In 1909, when the city of Chicago attempted to raise the peddlers' license fee from $25 to $200 a year, the anger of the Greeks and other nationality groups was aroused. The Greeks had special reason to believe that this legislation was aimed at them because of their firm grasp on the peddling business. These legal maneuvers made clear to them the need to become American citizens and reinforce their protests through the power of the vote.[49]

Other ventures undertaken by Greek immigrants met with similar obstacles and discrimination. The restaurant business, which became a major economic enterprise for them, began with their selling "red hots" and "hot tamales" from pushcarts and lunch-wagons throughout the city. Then, under the administration of Mayor Carter H. Harrison II, the city-county, responding to pressure from native restaurateurs who feared Greek competition, passed an ordinance prohibiting the sale of food on the streets.[50] At first, Greek merchants organized to fight the ordinance, but finally they agreed to abandon their street vehicles. All those who could scrape together enough money, often by mortgaging the homestead in the old country, rented stores and opened restaurants. Their apparent success aroused increased resentment from rivals, from Americans who opposed foreigners, and from an unsympathetic press.

Eventually, Greek restaurant owners organized to defend their growing trade against the antiforeign attitudes and measures of native businessmen. They formed the Greek Restaurant Keepers' Association, but typical factionalism among the Greeks made the association almost impotent.[51] Nonetheless, Greek immigrants began to realize that they could compete with Americans, and their restaurants became an important part of the Chicago commercial establishment.

Similarly, Greek merchants entered the shoeshine and shoe repair, florist, confectionery, ice cream, and hotel businesses. Beginning mea-

This meat market was located on Halsted Street in Chicago's Greektown (or "Delta"). By 1920 Chicago's entrepreneurial Greeks operated more than 10,000 stores, meat markets, bakeries, flower shops, confectioneries, restaurants, shoe repair and shine shops, and other small businesses. *Courtesy of the Jane Addams Memorial Collection, University of Illinois, Chicago.*

gerly with small stands, they expanded their respective industries and in some cases became pioneers in the field. In fact, the first soda fountain was established in a Greek ice cream parlor, and the first *sundae* reputedly was invented by Greeks in Chicago.* Fairchild predicted that if immigration from Greece were to continue at the current rate,

---

*The origins of the *sundae* remain obscure, though it seems agreed that the strange spelling derives from "Sunday," and that the ice cream, fruit, and nuts concoction was sold on that day—a response to the sabbatarianism of the Women's Christian Temperance Union, headquartered in Evanston, Illinois, a northern suburb of Chicago.

the candy, soda, and perhaps the fruit businesses of the country would be a Greek monopoly after twenty years.[52]

By the 1920s, in fact, Greek immigrants were among the foremost restaurant owners, ice cream manufacturers, florists, fruit and vegetable operators, and confectionery merchants in Chicago. A metropolitan newspaper declared:

> Chicago Greeks operate more than 10,000 stores—500 of them in the loop—an aggregate monthly rental that exceeds $2,500,000. These stores, it is estimated, do a business of more than $2,000,000 a day.[53]

The attitude of the Greek immigrant community toward their success was expressed in 1907, in an editorial in a Chicago Greek-language newspaper, the *Greek Star*:

> The Greek with his active mind and his American-acquired scope of operations, enhanced by the greatness of the American spirit, has flooded America with confectioneries, restaurants, flower shops, fruit stores, commission houses, shoe repair shops, shoe shine stands, grocery stores and many other businesses. . . . And this handful of Greeks in America have made themselves known to the whole country as a progressive element in the United States, and have made themselves a locomotive power pushing Mother Greece. . . . The phenomenal superiority of the American-Greeks over all Greeks, according to our reasoning, is attributed to the spirit of America which the Greek immigrant to America has accepted, adopted, and injected into his being.[54]

Despite obstacles, many climbed the socioeconomic ladder, and by 1919 it was estimated that 10,000 of the 18,000 men owned their establishments.[55]

Later the Greeks moved into the coffee and fur businesses, real estate, and the entertainment field. They gained holdings in the movie industry and became operators of theater chains and ballrooms, such as the famed Aragon and Trianon. An indication of their economic progress was reflected in the large sums of remittances they sent back to the homeland. As dutiful sons, they lived abstemiously and frugally, usually saving half of the profits. They sent sizable portions back home to pay off mortgages and family debts, buy real estate, and provide dowries for unmarried sisters or relatives. Between 1903 and 1908 these remittances amounted to approximately $5 million annually—an average of $50 per capita. According to American consular officials in Greece, it was the highest average remittance of any ethnic group surveyed.[56] Between 1919 and 1928 they averaged $52 million annually, the peak being $121 million in 1920;[57] not until 1963 was this amount surpassed with a figure of $126 million.[58] These remittances formed one of the chief invisible imports of Greece.

The role of Greek women in the American labor force was another story. For the most part, rigid tradition forbade their entrance into the labor market, especially after marriage. If they worked, it was usually in industries which also employed Polish, Bohemian, Russian, and Italian females. To be a domestic was frowned upon. With some exceptions, domestic work was done by Swedish, Norwegian, Irish, German, Canadian, and Scotch women.[59] Only 5 of 246 Greek women and girls over fifteen years of age were gainfully employed, according to the Abbott investigation. And because the Greek male considered it a disgrace to have a wife or a sister working outside the home, many families suffered financially.[60] This "sacred tradition" was part of the Greek immigrant's cultural baggage inherited from his agrarian background.

That the Greek immigrant had finally achieved status as a successful entrepreneur was revealed in 1952 at the hearings of the Truman Commission on Immigration and Naturalization. The argument in favor of liberalizing the quota for immigrants from Greece claimed that the contemporary professional, commercial, and intellectual prominence of Greeks was "impressive." The Greeks had come to America and "carved successful niches in the business and professional worlds. They were on their way to a new status ... the immigrant of yesteryear had established sobriety, industry, and integrity."[61] This was also underscored by a well-known study in 1959 which found that Greek immigrants and their offspring had the highest achievement motivation in a sample of white Protestant Americans and other ethnic groups in America.[62] This conclusion was supported by United States census data, a further corroboration of the social and economic attainments of Greeks. An anlysis of the 1960 census revealed that second-generation Greek-Americans possessed the highest educational levels of all and were exceeded only by Jews in average income.[63] The same pattern was confirmed in the 1970 census, which showed that among twenty-four second-generation nationality groups, Greeks trailed only Jews in income levels and continued to rank first in educational attainment.[64]

The economic wealth of Greek immigrants helped reinforce their ethnic pride and provided the means for them to give financial assistance to the Greek community for ethnic schooling. Successful businessmen provided leadership by becoming members of church boards of trustees and school boards.

Communal Institutions

Preservation of the Greek cultural ethos was not achieved without conflict and divisiveness, nor without the modifying and acculturative impact of the American milieu; and in time it led to the emergence of a new Greek-American subculture in Chicago. Despite the extreme individualism of Greek immigrants, the urgent need for coping and survival made for a cohesive and highly structured quality of their community life in Chicago. The close connection between Greek religious life and Hellenism was a bond strongly reflected in their educational aspirations in the New World. The Greek way of life, which revolved around its communal institutions, provided a sheltered enclave for aliens in which insecurity could be overcome at the individual's own pace. This was possible since sufficient numbers had immigrated to Chicago, the largest Greek-American community, with approximately 10 percent of the Greek population in the United States at any given time. The Greek "colony" on the near West Side, with its established churches, schools, coffeehouses, voluntary associations, and immigrant press, offered a self-contained communal life, served as a decompression chamber for uprooted immigrants, and enabled them to face some of the stresses and strains of the unknown setting. The social agencies of the family and the church were the most unifying forces in Greek ethnic survival. But given their economic expertise and political orientation, Greeks moved quickly upward into middle-class status and into participation in the economic and political life of the broader community.

Important also, from a structural point of view, were the many voluntary associations, Greek and non-Greek, which financially supported the educational endeavors of the Greek community. In particular, Greek immigrants were closely associated with the famed Hull House of Jane Addams, which tried to preserve their best traditional values and at the same time assist them in adapting to the ways and values of a new culture. Thus all these institutions were part of a highly cohesive structure that made possible the Greek community's efforts for ethnic survival.

In the Greek community, formal organizations appeared as early as did the informal ones like the coffeehouses. Despite their factionalism, the Greeks were quicker than most other immigrants, with the possible exception of the Jews, to develop enterprising community organizations to meet utilitarian needs.[65] The long period of persecution by the Turks had forced them to gain expertise with self-help organizations in the absence of a civil government. The formation of voluntary associations was as much a part of community life as the establishment of churches and Greek-language schools. These helped the immigrants in their educational adjustment and ethnic survival, as illustrated by their wide range of activities: mutual aid, charity, and humanitarianism. These groups came into existence before many members even knew how to speak English.

The first groups formed, such as the Greco-Slavonic Brotherhood in 1885 and the Lycurgus Society in 1892, were concerned with establishing a church to meet the religious needs of the growing Greek community. Once this task had been accomplished, the majority of the newer voluntary groups became mutual aid societies. Others were the *topika somateia* (local "hometown" clubs) consisting of persons who came from the same village or province. These were in turn followed by business organizations, fraternal groups, and professional and literary societies. By 1897 the Greeks of Chicago had six flourishing voluntary associations to serve a variety of purposes.[66] According to a *Greek Guide* published by Canoutas in 1903, they had by that time grown to a hundred societies—benevolent and fraternal groups. Less than half a century later, the Greek immigrants of Chicago had established over two hundred such voluntary associations (Table II).[67] Park and Burgess state: ". . . it is the immigrants who have maintained in this country their simple village religious and mutual aid organizations who have been able to withstand the shock of the new environment."[68]

In 1907 a national organization was formed under the name of the Pan Hellenic Union to further the nationalistic aspirations of a "Greater Greece."[69] Many local societies (*topika somateia*) affiliated with the Pan Hellenic Union focused on building roads, schools, churches, and public works in Greece, along with providing for health care and medical needs of their local members. Their strength was indicated by those large sums of money continually remitted to the home villages, which formed a chief invisible import of the Greek economy, as we have seen, but also reflected the intent of the Greek immigrants to return to their homeland.[70]

Greek immigrants demonstrated a mania for the forming of these local *topika somateia*, and every village and parish in Greece had counterpart "sons" in Chicago. The purpose of the societies was to bring together immigrants who were from a particular part of a province of Greece, to provide assistance for the region, and to perpetuate its cultural traditions. The majority of these organizations, at least in the beginning, were small, composed of fifteen to thirty people and governed by a council of twelve to fifteen. Gold tassels and buttons adorned the officers' uniforms on every public occasion, and banners, flags, and organization seals were essential equipment. Onlookers undoubtedly found it difficult to understand this zeal for societies, especially since

TABLE II
NUMBER AND MEMBERSHIP OF 200 VOLUNTARY ORGANIZATIONS OF THE GREEK COMMUNITY OF CHICAGO BY SEX REQUIREMENT AND 14 TYPES
31 December 1948

	Number of Organizations					Membership				
	All		By Sex Requirement			All		By Sex Requirement		
	Number	Percent	Male	Female	Mixed	Number	Percent	Male	Female	Mixed
AHEPA[1]	28	14.0	19	9	—	3,352	14.8	2,768	594	—
Auxiliaries	12	—	3	9	—	829	—	235	594	—
Main	16	—	16	—	—	2,523	—	2,523	—	—
GAPA[2]	6	3.0	2	4	—	295	1.3	170	125	—
Social	12	6.0	4	5	3	556	2.5	220	160	176
Cultural Affiliated with the Church	24	12.0	—	14	10	2,202	9.7	—	1,171	1,031
Youth Serving	10	—	—	—	10	1,031	—	—	—	1,031
Educational	10	—	—	10	—	850	—	—	850	—
Philoptochos	4	—	—	4	—	321	—	—	321	—
Professional	3	1.5	1	1	1	230	1.0	60	150	20
IWO[3]	2	1.0	1	—	1	200	0.9	180	—	20
Religious	10	5.0	10	—	—	5,377	23.8	5,377	—	—
Beneficiary	87	43.5	54	25	8	8,418	37.2	5,858	1,728	832
Philanthropic for the Native Land	20	10.0	9	6	5	1,492	6.6	710	417	365
Philanthropic for U.S. and Greece	6	3.0	1	6	—	275	1.2	—	275	—
National Liberation	1	0.5	—	—	1	180	0.8	180	—	—
Phalanx of Greek Veterans	1	0.5	—	—	—	50	0.2	—	—	50
American Legion[4]	—	—	—	—	—	—	—	—	—	—
Masons[4]	—	—	—	—	—	—	—	—	—	—
Total	200	100.0	101	70	29	22,627	100.0	15,513	4,620	2,494

SOURCE: Adapted from Yeracaris, p. 13.
[1] AHEPA: American Hellenic Progressive and Educational Association
[2] GAPA: Greek American Progressive Association
[3] IWO: International Workers' Order
[4] Were not included in the tabulation.

the members were poor and had to deny themselves basic comforts to pay dues and raise money to aid their villages. In time they joined other formal Greek organizations to support the educational efforts of the Greek community in perpetuating the ethno-religious heritage among American-born offspring.[71]

Eventually, the *topika somateia* united to form nationwide federations of societies from the same provinces of Greece. In this manner the Pan Arcadian Federation (those from villages in the province of Arcadia), the Pan Laconian, Pan Epirotan, Pan Cretan, Pan Messenian, and other "pan" groups evolved, and Chicago became the national headquarters for many. These federations continued to collect monies for public projects in Greece that benefited the entire province or district rather than individual villages. And while their emphasis remained on providing aid to the homeland, they increasingly became involved in ethnic and language maintenance activities among American-born children.

Following the Great Depression of the 1930s, the *topika somateia* gradually declined. Their activities quickened again after World War II to help the war-ridden areas in Greece. However, they soon became mere vehicles for personal aggrandizement. Native-born Greek children rarely joined the *topika somateia* upon reaching adulthood, despite organized attempts to recruit them. They did not know the village of their parents, nor did they share the nostalgic dream to resettle in Greece. Instead, they preferred to look upon Greece as another cultural entity.[72] Despite the demise of many of these organizations, they contributed much to the ethnic survival of Greek immigrants in Chicago. Their constant campaign to raise funds for projects in Greece, their strong intention of returning to the homeland, the sponsorship of language maintenance programs, and their aid to Greek schools helped keep alive the flames of ethnic survival, even though their organizational activities were viewed by many of the younger American-born generation as chauvinistic.

Hull House

In addition to *topika somateia* organizations, the Chicago Greeks formed a plethora of mutual aid and burial societies, business and trade groups, professional, religious, and educational organizations, athletic, theatrical, and musical associations. Many organized under the protective concern of Hull House and the benevolent influence of Jane Addams, who had an immeasurable impact on their lives. In commenting on these kinds of societies, Park states:

Chicago's great philhellene was Jane Addams, founder and director of Hull House from 1889 until her death in 1935. Hull House served as the "home away from home" and Miss Addams as a "mother" for the thousands of young Greek immigrant boys in Chicago. On the day of her funeral, all Greek-owned businesses were closed in mourning. *Courtesy of Andrew T. Kopan.*

These organizations are not, in fact, pure heritages, but the products of the immigrants' efforts to adapt their heritage to American conditions. The immigrant, therefore, comes to a society of his own people, and this non-native American society is the matrix which gives him his first impression. The character of this society . . . is the primary influence in determining the desire and capacity of the immigrant to participate in American life.[73]

The Hull House Theater, the first of its kind in the nation, was inaugurated in December 1899 with a presentation of the classical Greek tragedy *The Return of Odysseus*. The actors were Greek immigrants and they attracted wide attention in the city, which was the first public recognition for Greek immigrants in Chicago. This play, which was presented again at Studebaker Hall in May 1900, was unique because it was the first time an ancient Greek tragedy was acted out by actual Greeks rather than American college students. Hull House imported a director from Boston expressly to train the Greeks for the occasion. Indicative of the wide attention it received is the sympathetic account written by Lorado Taft:

> The thought which came over and over again into every mind was: These are the real sons of Hellas chanting the songs of their ancestors, enacting the life of thousands of years ago. There is a background for you! How noble it made these fruit merchants for the nonce; what distinction it gave them! They seemed to feel that they had come into their own. They were set right at last in our eyes. . . . The sons of princes, they had known their heritage all the time; it was our ignorance which had belittled them. And they had waited.
> The feeling which these humbly proud fellow-citizens of ours put into the play was at the same time their tribute to a noble ancestry and a plea for respect. Those who saw them on that stage will never think of them again in quite the same way as before. . . .[74]

The success of *The Return of Odysseus* prompted the Greek community to work on another theatrical production. Under the tutelage of Miss Addams, they presented Sophocles' *Ajax* in December 1903 in six performances at the Hull House Auditorium. As in the production four years earlier, it was presented in the original Greek, with all actors and performers in the chorus being young Greek men who had recently immigrated to Chicago, some of whom had performed in the previous production. As stated in a Hull House publication of the period:

> For many reasons "The Ajax of Sophocles" was chosen as suitable to be given by native Greeks on Hull House stage. . . . A large part of the work is that of the chorus, the music for whose laments and rejoicing was written by Mrs. Willys Peck Kent of New York for the special occasion. . . . When invited by Miss Addams to give a Greek tragedy at Hull House, Miss Barrows studied nearly a year in the best libraries of the country, for there was no other source of suggestion, "Ajax" having never been played in this country, and but once on an English stage, in Cambridge many years ago.[75]

Chicago's Hull House as it looked around 1910. This world-famous settlement house was in the midst of Chicago's original Greektown. It became an important institution in the life of the Greek community, providing facilities for educational, social, athletic, and charitable events for Greek immigrants. *Courtesy of the Jane Addams Memorial Collection, University of Illinois, Chicago.*

The special attention given by Jane Addams to Greek immigrants and her espousal of Greek culture which is indicated by these activities and the many others she sponsored quickly endeared her to the Greek community as a patroness of Hellenic arts and ideals. She did much to help solidify ethnic solidarity and pride among the Greek immigrants of Chicago. A regular participant in the activities of Hull House in the early days remembers the philhellenic attitude of Jane Addams, which encouraged Greeks to center around Hull House.[76] The Greeks had more and larger clubs than the other ethnic groups using Hull House.[77] In fact, Greeks began to think of it as their own institution, often trying to keep other ethnic groups from using the facilities.[78]

Numerous clubs for men and women met regularly at Hull House. On Sunday evenings a large male social club attracted an average of 400 people weekly to provide entertainment for lonely men. A Greek-American athletic club had exclusive use of a room for its trophies as well as the use of the gymnasium on Sunday mornings. Many began to engage in amateur wrestling and won national and regional titles for Hull House.[79]

Ironically, in view of Jane Addams' leadership of the pacifist move-ment, the gymnasium was allowed to be used by young Greeks for military training in preparation for the Balkan Wars (as we shall see later), and that matter was cited against Addams before she was awarded the Nobel Peace Prize.[80] Even the boards of trustees of Greek church parishes used the Hull House facilities, and the numerous educational activities of the settlement house served as "springboards" for subse-quent educational designs by the Greeks. They availed themselves of every opportunity to attend night classes to study the English language, learn music, dancing, and handicrafts, and hear lectures on various topics. The staff made a concerted effort to accommodate the Greeks, since they were the most immediate neighbors of the settlement.[81]

Hull House, located on Halsted Street, was in the approximate center of Chicago's great immigrant colonies. Immediately adjoining it to the north was the Greek community; immediately to the south was the Italian colony, followed by the Jewish, German, Polish, Rus-sian, and Bohemian neighborhoods.[82]

The Greeks complained constantly about the hostility and discrim-ination they encountered from the "native" American population. The *Hull House Bulletin* lists the following grievance:

> In the last five years, since Greeks have been coming in large numbers to Chicago, they found that Americans made no distinc-tion between them and other more ignorant immigrants from south-ern Europe. As the modern Greek is devoted to his own country and race, the Greek immigrant bitterly resents the criticism of his manners and habits in America by Americans who, he believes, disregard his historical background and tradition.[83]

Hence Greek leaders arranged with Miss Addams to host a meeting "in which Americans should speak in English of the glorious history of Greece, and the Greek speakers should tell their countrymen in their native tongue some of the duties and requirements of their adopted country."[84] This first of a series of sessions was held on January 3, 1904, to a capacity crowd, which viewed a cultural program, listened to speeches by Jane Addams, Professor Paul Shorey, classicist from the University of Chicago, and Mayor Dunne of Chicago, who received a standing ovation. Miss Addams describes the event as follows:

> As the mayor of Chicago was seated upon the right hand of the dignified senior priest of the Greek Church and they were greeted

alternately in the national hymns of America and Greece, one felt a curious sense of the possibility of transplanting to new and crude Chicago some of the traditions of Athens itself, so deeply cherished in the hearts of this group of citizens.[85]

Due to Jane Addams' ceaseless dedication, Hull House became the spiritual and cultural hearth of the Greek immigrants—their veritable second home. A young arrival who aspired to become a poet wrote:

We had problems and Jane Addams was always there to straighten them out for us. She was like a mother to us; she was our protector and our advisor. It was a great alliance based on nobility and understanding. What's more, Jane Addams admired Greek culture, and felt that the modern Greeks who had come here to make America their home, possessed many of the virtues of their ancestors.

I used to go to Hull House quite often. One day I showed Jane Addams some of my poetry, some verses I had published here and

The first Greek women's organization of Chicago, the Philoptohos Sisterhood, was organized at Hull House in 1909 under the patronage of Jane Addams and Miss Neukon, a resident of Hull House. This group served as the forerunner of all Greek women's organizations in Chicago. *Courtesy of Andrew T. Kopan.*

there. She became interested. She was always ready to give advice and I learned to appreciate her judgment. And when in 1930 my sonnets were about to be published, under the title "Sonnets of An Immigrant," she wrote the foreword to the book. . . .[86]

In 1930, in recognition of Addams' meritorious work on behalf of the Greek immigrants, the Greek Consul of Chicago awarded her a medallion.[87]

The Greek immigrants' apogee at Hull House was reached on February 12, 1911. On that day, while visiting the world-famed settlement, former President Theodore Roosevelt was informed that the young men in the gymnasium were Greeks. Seizing this opportunity, the president addressed the assembled immigrants and stated that they, unlike other ethnic groups who were expected to abandon old-world loyalties and look toward a new life in America, were exempt because of their own illustrious history.[88]

Those who had an intimate association with Hull House, when interviewed, described the settlement house as epitomizing humaneness toward fellowmen—a lone outpost of succor in a bewildering metropolis. The "soul" of Hull House is commemorated in this example:

I remember the red brick Hull House well. My mother used to press three pennies in my hand and send my sister and me two blocks to the House, where we were showered, cleaned, and sent to an "open air" room to dry off. Later, we spent our three pennies for a bowl of lentil soup, a bologna sandwich, and a glass of milk.[89]

It is small wonder that on the death of Jane Addams in 1935, a Chicago Greek newspaper editorialized:

Her death has stirred in us memories that go back . . . to those days when in the buoyancy of our youth we would walk into Hull House as though we walked into our own house, there in absolute freedom to enjoy the House, not in its physical aspects but in that nurturing warmth that animated everything and all . . . there sound in our ears the soft words and sentences of the women of the House, the only soft and kind words we immigrant boys heard in those days . . . for we of foreign birth have lost our best friend and the only one who understood us.[90]

In short, the arrival of Greek immigrants during the 1890s and 1900s coincided with one of the most colorful eras of Chicago's multifaceted history. And it was amid such surroundings that they found their "home-away-from-home" at Hull House and thus were assisted in coping with problems of economic sufficiency, socialization, and educational adjustment.

National Groups

Greek immigrant participation in voluntary ethnic organizations, within and outside Hull House, mediated their cultural adjustment to American life and made their community one of the most structured ethnic groups in the city.

Two of the most viable Greek national organizations were the American Hellenic Educational and Progressive Association (AHEPA), founded in 1922, in Atlanta, Georgia in response to antiforeign agitation of the revived Ku Klux Klan in the South, and the Greek American Progressive Association (GAPA), founded in 1923 at East Pittsburgh, Pennsylvania as a reaction to AHEPA. Soon local chapters formed. In Chicago the first AHEPA unit was Chapter #46, started in 1924, followed by Woodlawn #93 in 1926. The former served the original Greektown and the West and North sides; the latter served the South Side. GAPA chapters organized simultaneously, but they were never as numerous or as potent as those of AHEPA. Nonetheless, GAPA became more instrumental in aiding established Greek-language schools and in maintaining the cultural heritage.[91]

These two organizations perhaps best exemplify conflicting Greek views on "Americanization" during the 1920s and 1930s. The clue to each group's orientation is found in the first word of its official name. AHEPA espoused a doctrine of Americanization, assimilation, and adaptation. GAPA looked upon the assimilative nature of AHEPA as threatening and unwise for the future of the Greek language and church. It became culturally conservative and ethnocentric, giving preference to "Greek" over "American," even though both groups exerted energies to adjust to American society.

AHEPA assumed the trappings of an American structure. For membership, applicants had to be United States citizens or eligible to be so. They had to be Caucasians and believers in the divinity of Christ.[92] After a lengthy furor and perhaps due to the Americanization movement, the English language was adopted for all official matters of the fraternal order. It appears that AHEPA was influenced by the rituals of the Masons and other fraternal orders and formed along their lines, with secret rituals and auxiliaries, such as the Daughters of Penelope for senior women, Sons of Pericles for males under twenty-one, and the Maids of Athens for young women. AHEPA abandoned its super-assimilative role when the auxiliaries organized, and began to try to blend the positive features of Hellenism with Americanism.[93]

Despite the fact that AHEPA undertook the Americanization of Greek immigrants on a national scale and claimed to be an American organization, its raison d'être was decidedly Greek. Its establishment in 1922 illustrates the manner in which self-conscious ethnic group activity was shaped by the situation it had to meet. Amid the alien-baiting following World War I and the Ku Klux Klan activism, AHEPA formed for the specific purpose of establishing Greek prestige in the American community. Its program was to fete every distinguished person from Greece or of Greek origin, being sure to invite press and important persons to get maximum publicity and a sense of dignity. It organized expeditions of bachelors to Greece, saw that the expedition was pictured in the rotogravure section of the *New York Times* and other hometown newspapers, that it was received and feted by the prime minister or king in Greece and reports carried in the American press, and that those who brought back wives from Greece got their pictures in the papers when they returned home. AHEPA made a policy of holding its affairs, wherever possible, in the best hotels; of giving banquets for outstanding political figures; of picking up and answering all references that tended to slur Greeks. In this respect, it was the Greek national image and the attempt to win a favorable consideration for it in America that concerned AHEPA, a situation largely brought about by American conditions and antipathy to foreign groups. This purpose was reflected in the public announcements of early leaders. In speaking of the thinking of the founders of AHEPA, one supreme president of the fraternity stated:

> They realized that the great need of our people was to found an organization not for the purpose of impressing upon them the grandeur of their history and the glory of their language—things which they very well know and appreciate—but for the purpose of impressing upon the American people the worth of the Greeks as constructive and useful citizens of this Republic.
>
> They realized that if Greek prestige was to be elevated, that such elevation must come through an organization which breathes of the atmosphere and speaks the language of the land.
>
> And so, fully realizing these great principles, they founded an American non-sectarian, non-political organization for men of Hellenic extraction, and called it AHEPA.[94]

The Greek men of Chicago who joined the ranks of AHEPA in the 1920s did so because they espoused the organization's belief, and in a short time the Chicago chapter became one of the most active in the order. In 1925 it hosted the association's third national convention. The pride of these AHEPA members is reflected in the following caption taken from a Chicago newspaper:

> The chapter has had the honor of being host to over two hundred delegates from various chapters, who assembled in Chicago for the Third Annual convention of the order. The convention was held at the Drake Hotel and lasted for five days, during which time several public events were given with various prominent citizens from Chicago present. It may be stated that the Hellenes in the United States have been the first and only element that has taken upon itself to teach the true and sound principles of Americanism among its members, instead of waiting for the American government to accomplish the truly great task of educating foreign elements in this country.[95]

During the ensuing years the AHEPA chapters in Chicago implemented their twin program of Americanization and Greek adjustment into American society, despite opposition to its principles by GAPA and other ethnically conservative groups. AHEPA members, at least those in Chicago, were also concerned with the fate of the Greek language and the Hellenic tradition. Therefore, they sponsored parallel activities to Americanize the Chicago Greek immigrant and promote Greek studies and financial assistance for the city's Greek schools. Indeed, the order had to explain its position repeatedly to Greek immigrants, stating that its program of Americanization, the use of the English language, and its assertion of being nonpolitical and nonsectarian should not be construed as heretical but rather as a facility for Greek adjustment and survival in the United States without losing cultural heritage. One local chapter officer commented in 1926 on the compatibility between Hellenism and Americanism this way:

> There are ignorant extremists among us who insist that the immigrant of today, to become a real American, must forget entirely and absolutely, the land of his birth, and must wipe his memory clean of all the cherished recollections that cluster around his native land. Such views cause the more reasonable elements of our society to wonder what would we have in this country today if such had been the case with the earliest to the latest arrivals to America from foreign lands. Certainly, we could not have had the Americanism of today. Americanism is the result not of utter forgetfulness, but of vivid memories. We have become the fortunate heirs of the good things of all the ages. The men and women who left their native lands preserved and brought with them only those things worth preserving. And of those things Americanism was born.[96]

Nonetheless, AHEPA continued to be accused of seeking to eradicate the Greek language and of "downgrading the Greek school." The fact was, however, that while the order insisted on the sole use of the English language in its proceedings and functions, chapters in Chicago gave full support and assistance to the enlargement and maintenance of local Greek schools where the sons and daughters of members learned the Greek language either in day or afternoon schools. The order's auxiliaries continually sponsored programs to raise funds for these schools and, in many instances, gave direct financial support to Greek schools.[97] The official view of AHEPA on this matter was perhaps best expressed by the remarks of its supreme president, George E. Phillies, in 1929:

> Much has been written and said these days concerning our attitude towards the Mother language. Once more, and in the most categorical manner, we are declaring that writings tending to show that we are neglectful or antagonistic to our Mother language, either in practice, fact or form, are completely unfounded. Our avowed policy has been to teach the Greek language to those who need it and the English language to those who need it.[98]

Again in 1932, the association's magazine, *The AHEPA*, emphasized the importance of the Greek language by editorializing:

> If you have any respect for your noble ancestry, any love for your adopted country, you will make it a matter of prime concern to yourselves that the language and history of Ancient Greece be not forgotten.
>   This you may do, first by providing in your parochial schools, as you are now doing, for instruction in Greek. . . . But this is not enough. You are required to encourage the youth of this land, whether of Greek descent or otherwise, to the study of Greek language and literature. . . . Only your persistent efforts can save this, your adopted country, from the loss of that which has proved so beneficial to the great men of the past. . . . If you do not do this, you are not worthy of their name. You should not be permitted to call them your fathers. By neglecting these matters you disinherit yourselves.[99]

The history of AHEPA clearly shows that, despite its detractors, it was concerned with the retention of the Hellenic heritage in the New World. After World War II, when AHEPA's task of Americanizing the Greek immigrant had been achieved, it turned its attention to the need for perpetuating the Hellenic heritage among the native-born offspring of immigrants. A 1948 editorial is indicative of this shift in emphasis:

... AHEPA is undergoing a most striking evolution which almost reverses its entire scope—mainly from that of the Americanization of Greek immigrants, which purpose we can proudly say that AHEPA has successfully fulfilled, to that of the maintenance of a Hellenic cultural and religious conscience among the American-born Hellenes. In other words, from Americanization to Hellenization. Hellenization not by any means in the sense of nationalism or ethnical or racial discrimination, but the maintenance of a heritage of ideals and culture which is a contributing factor to the richness of American culture.[100]

In contrast to AHEPA, the Greek American Progressive Association, or GAPA as it became known, espoused openly and with much fanfare the preservation of the Greek church, language, and traditions. Membership was restricted to those belonging to the Greek Orthodox church, and the Greek language was used in all official functions. Its prime purpose was the support of Greek education, and the Chicago chapters of GAPA took upon themselves the responsibility of providing financial aid to the Greek community schools. Faced with the fact that there was no training institution for Greek teachers in America at the time, GAPA underwrote a program of sending American-born Greek women to Greece for training at teacher colleges.[101]

The GAPA organization objected to what it considered an unintelligent program of conformity preached by AHEPA, one that jeopardized the future of the Greek language and church. The battle was joined by critics who charged AHEPA with downgrading the Greek church and schools as well as with general de-Hellenization.[102] *Ahepans* and *Gapans* formed ranks, and Chicago became a veritable battleground. Despite their conflicting philosophies, though, both organizations provided a valuable support for Greek institutions that was crucial during the 1920s and 1930s. Both were products of Greek-American efforts to adjust to American society. Both provided positive programs of action for the perpetuation of the Hellenic heritage in spite of their avowedly different approach. Both accepted in common the belief that their members were in the United States to remain permanently (in contrast to nonmember Greek immigrants), but they differed over the emphasis that was to be placed on matters Greek. Perhaps the most notable argument in defense of GAPA is that members refused to be placed into the strait jacket of conformity by going along with the trend against foreignism. This courageous group waged a relentless, if ineffective, campaign to retain its cultural heritage at a time when many others were discarding theirs.

Despite its gradual demise, brought about in part by the immigration restrictions of the 1920s and the erosion of Hellenic sentiments during the 1930s, GAPA continued to remain a culturally conservative group. While some native-born Greek-Americans joined its ranks, its membership—at least in Chicago—was comprised of first-generation immigrant Greeks who kept alive the ideals of their legacy. As late as 1966, the association presented the University of Chicago with $100,000 (out of a projected $1 million) for the establishment of scholarships for students of Greek ancestry.[103] And the Chicago contingents did not cease to provide financial emoluments to the Greek schools of the city.[104]

Currently the GAPA organization is enjoying a revival of long-dormant chapters in Chicago.[105] This revitalization is probably due to the influx of new Greek immigrants in Chicago after World War II. Once again, voices are being raised for the preservation of the Greek heritage, not unlike those of the founders of GAPA fifty years ago.

Education and Ethnic Survival

Since the Homeric Age, *aristeia*, or the pursuit of excellence, had been a motivating and deliberate pedagogical ideal in Greece.[106] Homer's influential epics *The Iliad* and *The Odyssey* provided the basic education for Greek youth. The advent of the Golden Age of Greece in the fifth century B.C., the rise of Greek intellectual thought and philosophy as reflected in the works of Greece's great educators—Isocrates, Protagoras, Socrates, Plato, and Aristotle—and the establishment of schooling, gave rise to the highest concept of organized education (*paideia*), which set the historic pattern for the entire Western world.[107]

Greece's conversion to Christianity and the establishment of the Byzantine Empire fused pagan classical education with Christian concepts. A vigorous and selective educational system was available in formal schools for intellectually competent youth. The study of religion was prominent in the curriculum but did not dominate secular schooling. Even the church nurtured pagan learning, a factor that helped keep alive Hellenic consciousness through the long period of Turkish occupation from 1453 to 1821. Because of this nurturing, classical education did not disappear in Greece as it did in the West following the fall of Rome in A.D. 476.

Formal schooling, however, reached a low ebb and practically disappeared in Greece after the fall of Constantinople in 1453. Teaching Greek was forbidden by Turkish authorities, but churches could remain open if proper tribute was paid. Schools fell into neglect because personal survival was a primary concern under the deplorable living conditions.[108] Since Greece ceased to exist as a political entity, the churches and monasteries became the educational centers for the populace. Secret common schools were organized in cellars of churches; there Greek was taught and the embers of freedom kept alive by priests who served as teachers. These clandestine schools became the hope for freedom and confirmed the church's historic role in education. A description of the church during the Turkish period and its initial role in the Revolution of 1821 is described by one writer as follows:

> . . . in spite of subjection to Turkish caprice, contempt, and cruelty, the Greek church showed remarkable tenacity in all internal affairs and gradually recovered a measure of independence as a result of its obstinate conservatism. Its state may be pejoratively described as stagnation; but from another point of view it was resistance to change that safe-guarded its existence in those centuries and enabled a strong national Greek church to emerge at the time of the Revolution both with the respect of the Greek revolutionaries and with an ardent devotion to the cause of national liberty. The "stagnant" Greek church was the champion of "liberty," as was none of the "advanced" churches of Western Christendom. The patriarchs, the metropolitans, the bishops, the monastic orders and the village priests, were the protectors of the oppressed nation while there was none other to protect them. In many cases it was the priest who gave the men the summons to strike for freedom; and at the monastery of Megaspelaion on . . . [25 March] 1821 it was not a philhellene from Western Europe, but Germanos, Archbishop of Patras, who raised the standards of revolt.[109]

After the revolution and the establishment of an independent Greece, a public school system was organized that was modeled after the schools of France. But because of the ravages of the war for independence and the continuing turbulent conditions, along with the lack of funds, the nationwide implementation of universal education in Greece had to wait until 1911, when compulsory education laws were imposed by the state.[110]

This then was the general educational situation in Greece at the turn of the century, when Greeks began immigrating to the United States. The vast majority had no schooling, or at best a minimal amount of schooling. Indeed, according to immigration records, the average Greek illiteracy rate for the period 1900–1908, during the height of Greek immigration to America and particularly to Chicago, was approximately 27 percent, higher than most immigrants (except for southern Italians) who were arriving at the same time. In 1910, 24 percent were unable to read and write; but by 1920 the illiteracy rate had dropped to 3.2 percent. This dramatic change was probably due to the compulsory education laws that were beginning to be enforced in Greece.[111]

Thus Greek immigrants arriving in Chicago had a limited amount of schooling and were mostly of peasant stock. Despite this paucity of formal training, however, Greek immigrants were knowledgeable about their illustrious past and the achievements of their people, possibly because of a long oral tradition in Greece. In this respect, they considered their language a binding force. They valued education and were interested in learning more about their 4,000 years of continuous history and linguistic accomplishments. They recognized the fact that Greek stood as the oldest living spoken language in Europe and that it embodied essential aspects of the Greek way of life. In fact, ethnocentric Greeks feel that the Greek tongue made possible the achievements of their people. Twentieth-century Greeks felt kinship with Homer and Plato and with the Byzantine accomplishment; nor could they forget that the New Testament and the development of the Christian Church were Greek accomplishments. A further link with the past was the church's liturgical language, which had remained unchanged through the centuries.

Perpetuation of the Greek language became a prime concern of the early Greek immigrants, and they demanded that their children learn the language that "gave light to the world." The intensity of this universal feeling manifested itself every time a new Greek community was organized. After the establishing of the church, the Greek school received top priority. Every facet of the community, from voluntary associations to the Greek-language press, was used to promote formal and informal schooling for language preservation. This preoccupation with learning the mother tongue probably accounts for the fact that the vast majority of children born in the United States of immigrant Greek parents knew Greek as their first language until the 1930s. Greek immigrants were among the most successful ethnic groups in transmitting their language and cultural heritage to their progeny.[112] They were conditioned by upbringing and history to regard Greek culture as inferior to none. Much to their surprise and chagrin, they found in coming to the United States that many Americans did not share this view. And in the American public schools the Greek legacy, as well as any other non-American culture, with the exception of the Anglo-Saxon, was not openly appreciated or even readily tolerated. The schools appeared to be "destroyers" of ethnic culture; they attempted to do away with the indigenous culture of the immigrants and replace it with an "instant" American way of life—a difficult if not an impossible task.

The schools' formal attempts to bring about the enforced Americanization of Greek immigrants were demeaning to the newcomers.

They could not understand why learning the English language and American ways required the abandonment of loyalty to their homeland and the betrayal of their ethnic and religious identity. In many instances public school policy had the effect of alienating the Greek child from the immigrant parent culture and contributed to tension among family members, especially in the area of language maintenance.

For most Greek students, however, the public school was crucial to their external adjustment and acculturation to mainstream American society. But nearly all Greek children attending public schools were enrolled in supplementary Greek schools and other private educational arrangements. Public schools in Chicago lacked adequate provisions to accommodate immigrants and their children and naturally judged their performance by American cultural standards and conduct. School records and documents, along with available testimony, indicate that Greek children did actively attend public schools; but their actual number is unknown since the schools did not list pupils according to ethnicity. A comparison of the Chicago school census of 1908 with the survey of the Immigration Commission made in the same year reveals that less than half of the Greek children were known to be enrolled.[113] The majority were either not attending school at all or were gainfully employed.

Most Greeks immigrated to America, as we have seen, to make money in order to pay off family debts, provide dowries for sisters, and return to Greece with a sufficient amount of money to live comfortably. Consequently, working rather than schooling was the top priority of young boys. The reports of the Immigrants' Protective League describe many accounts of young men engaged in diverse occupations and often exploited.[114] Another reason for their nonattendance in Chicago schools was the fact that these boys were alone, without kinship guidance, as Abbott's study indicated.[115] Still, there were a few young men who exerted great effort and sacrifice in order to attend school.

Following World War I, the profile of Greek children attending public schools began to change. As more immigrants arrived and moved into all sections of Chicago, Greek children began to be regularly enrolled in the city's public schools, for a number of reasons: (1) Greek communal schools were not conveniently located in all the neighborhoods into which immigrants settled; (2) tuition fees for Greek schools made attendance prohibitive for some; (3) the erosion of Hellenic sentiment along with the acculturative process had induced many parents to send their children to public schools; and (4) the state's compulsory education law was increasingly being enforced.

Greek children enrolled in the public schools were generally placed in "retarded" classes, as was the custom of the time with children having insufficient knowledge of English. Most were in the primary grades, with heavy attrition after the fifth grade. Very few completed elementary school, and few indeed went on to high school. By the 1930s, however, because of a number of factors, most Greek children were attending public schools. By that time children beginning primary grades had a knowledge of English acquired from older siblings or from the broader community, few were placed in "retarded" classes, most finished elementary school, and a large number entered high schools, many graduating. By the 1940s and 1950s third-generation children (grandchildren of the original immigrants) were part of the general American pattern of public school attendance.

The pattern was entirely different with evening public schools, in which young Greek adults were avid participants. From 1902 to 1922 the Greeks were the seventh largest ethnic group in Chicago enrolled in evening programs. During the 1907–1908 school term, one out of every five Greeks officially residing in Chicago attended evening school—one of the highest ratios of all ethnic groups in Chicago.[116] The large attendance of Greek immigrants at evening school is attributed to their desire to learn English for economic competence and the convenience of evening hours for workers. Most attended school from six to ten months, then dropped out when they felt they had learned enough.

Chicago's Greek immigrants were also heavy patronizers of Americanization classes, the most successful being those organized at Hull House exclusively for Greeks. Others were held in Greek churches and at people's places of employment—the factory, railroad, and other areas. Government statistics reveal that the Greek immigrants' incidence of participation in Americanization or citizenship programs was one of the highest of all ethnic groups. Yet they were reluctant to acquire full American citizenship itself, and in Chicago, both in 1910 and 1920, the majority did not hold citizenship.[117] This unusual attitude is explained by the fact that, according to the mentality of the Greek immigrant, acquiring American naturalization was tantamount to betrayal of the homeland. And Greeks still intended to return home. Attendance at citizenship programs was motivated solely by the desire to acquire greater facility in English for improving job opportunities.

To counteract the alienating influence of the public schools, Greek parents persisted in the transmission of the Hellenic heritage to their offspring by organizing various informal and formal educational agencies, especially communal schools. But education in the home was also intense, as the following excerpt indicates:

When I was very young my father used to read Homer to me. While other kids were getting Mother Goose, I was getting Thucydides.

The Peloponnesian Wars became exceptionally meaningful to me, and I remember how I dreamt of being a Spartan. (Father was from Sparta and came to Chicago in 1893.) I also remember many sleepless nights when I felt a restless spirit and wondered if strange and mythological gods, somehow controlled my destiny. . . . I felt different because I was proud that my forefathers were warriors who helped shape the history of mankind.[118]

The pervasive impact of the home is also seen in the following Chicago testimony:

Father was always telling us about the greatness of Greece and her contribution to world culture and civilization. He ran our home like a school, conducting quizzes at the dinner table, asking us questions from our Greek lessons on the great men and events of Greek history. We enjoyed these sessions as he rewarded us with money. . . . But we were dismayed and hurt by the attitude of our teachers in the public school who kept telling us that we should forget about Greece and become good Americans. . . . We wanted to be good Americans but we were also very proud to be Greeks. I, for one, looked forward to the Greek school which we attended after American school. Here, the teacher was always telling us about the glory of Greece and I enjoyed my Greek textbook. I marvelled that I was reading about the great men of Greece in the Greek language and I dreamed of the day when I would go to Greece to visit the land of Plato, Pericles and Alexander the Great. When I finally did many years later, I felt that I had come home. . . . Hellenic culture has been a lifelong obsession with me and for this I am indebted to my father and the Greek school.[119]

Meanwhile, the Greek community of Chicago began to exert direct pressure on the Chicago Board of Education. This took the form of the establishment of the Hellenic Educational League in 1935 by Greek educational leaders charged with the task of language maintenance. The Greeks had become concerned that, with the passage of the years and the erosion of Hellenic sentiment about the military dictatorship in Greece in 1935, the dream of returning to the ancestral homeland was weakening.[120] They became alarmed at the prospect of their offspring's becoming alienated from the Greek heritage, especially in high school. Hoping to counteract the acculturative influence of high school and to legitimize Greek language and culture in the public sector, the Hellenic Educational League petitioned the Board of Education to introduce the study of Greek into the high school curriculum. The League cited the precedent of the German community's successful petition for the inclusion of German in the city's public schools during the previous century. Furthermore, it contended that Greek had been part of the curriculum of Chicago schools from 1856 until 1883, when it was discontinued.[121] The League also hoped that it could prevail on the Board of Education to restore the study of Greek not only because it was one of the world's greatest historical and literary languages but also because the Greek citizens of Chicago were now demanding it.

Despite some characteristic factionalism within the Greek community concerning the plan, it was accepted by the Board of Education with the stipulation that a minimum of 100 students would have to be enrolled. The Greeks responded enthusiastically, and the first Greek-language course was instituted at Austin High School on the city's West Side in the fall of 1936. Other courses were begun at Amundsen and McKinley high schools on the North Side and at Englewood High School on the South Side. The Hellenic Educational League had established as its ultimate goal the introduction of Greek studies in at least ten Chicago high schools. In appreciation for the support of Superintendent of Schools William Johnson, the league sponsored a testimonial dinner in his honor, which was well attended by Greeks, and the Greek government awarded Johnson a medallion through its consul general in Chicago.[122]

The Greek instructional program lasted for twenty-five years, avidly supported by the community, which saw to it that Greek students of high school age enrolled. Additional Greek instructors were hired by the public schools to staff the growing number of classes, and thousands of Greek youngsters from all parts of the city attended.[123] Part of this success, aside from the concerted thrust of the community, stemmed from the authorized permissive transfer plan adopted by the Board of Education, which allowed students to leave their school districts in order to pursue Greek studies in districts that offered them. The permissive transfer was inaugurated to permit flexibility for those Greek families who lived outside such districts. This plan, however, proved to be the downfall of the Greek instruction program years later. Its initial purpose was gradually supplanted when non-Greek students began enrolling in Greek courses at these high schools in order to avoid attending schools in neighborhoods that were racially changing. Finally, in 1961, despite protests from the Greek community, Superintendent Benjamin Willis decreed the end of permissive transfer, and the program collapsed.

Nevertheless, for the period that the program was in operation, it succeeded well in fostering knowledge of Greek, especially among the American-born generations. In the first place, it helped to reinforce the knowledge of Greek among those coming from homes where Greek was spoken. In the second place, it provided advanced knowledge for those who were products of the Greek communal afternoon schools and introduced those who had not attended Greek schools to the formal study of Greek. Finally, it legitimized and gave status to the study of the Greek language by its very inclusion in the public curriculum.

The second time the Greek community applied formal pressure on the Board of Education was as late as 1971, but for different reasons. An ethnic survey of Chicago public schools revealed that next to Spanish-speaking pupils, the largest ethnic group in the schools whose mother tongue was something other than English were the Greeks.[124] The large number of Greek children with inadequate knowledge of English were enrolled primarily in the public schools of the Ravenswood, Albany Park, and Belmont-Cragin districts of Chicago's North Side. The postwar Greek immigrants had settled in these areas, creating new "Greektowns." Children of these immigrants who were enrolled in local public schools were unable to benefit from instruction due to a lack of knowledge of English.

Interestingly, a generation after the first successful attempt was made to introduce Greek studies in the Chicago public schools by the Hellenic Educational League in the 1930s, a similar attempt developed in the 1970s. However, this time the venture was promoted primarily by second- and third-generation Greek-Americans who perceived it as part of the current ethnic revival movement, and it involved more than simply the teaching of Greek in public schools. On December 10, 1971, educators from public and private schools organized the Hellenic Council on Education in order to promote and coordinate the educational concerns of the Greek community of Chicago in light of the new ethnicity awareness.[125] One of the first projects of this new group was to encourage the assignment of Greek-speaking teachers and administrators in schools with large enrollments of Greek-speaking pupils. Their pressure on the Board of Education succeeded in bringing this about.[126] Later the Hellenic Council encouraged Greek parents in these schools to develop bilingual education proposals for the teaching of Greek. With the help of the council and the assistance of Dr. Michael Bakalis, then state superintendent of public instruction, and Dr. Angeline P. Caruso, then associate superintendent of Chicago public schools, both of whom were children of Greek immigrants and products of Greek communal schools, several bilingual programs were established, funded by federal grants from Title VII—the Bilingual Education Act of 1967.

But like the earlier attempt in the 1930s, this movement had its detractors in the Greek community. Many resented the creation of such bilingual programs as insulting to the Greek community, implying that it was unable to take care of its own and that Greeks were in need of the federal aid associated with low-income groups, something the

Greeks were definitely not. The resulting controversy received national attention in the Greek press as well as in the local metropolitan press.[127] Indeed, the dispute had all the marks of a social class conflict between foreign-born and native-born Greek-Americans. But the programs prevailed and are still part of the educational scene in the Greek community of Chicago.

Similarly, the Hellenic Council on Education embarked on the development of Greek ethnic studies units for inclusion in social studies classes in those public schools with large Greek enrollments. This too was achieved as an attempt to provide ethnic and cultural identity for those pupils in keeping with state legislation (Ethnic Studies Bill, H.B. 19H), which required local school districts to develop materials for acquainting school children with ethnic groups that make up the American population.[128] The Greek material, one of the first of its kind in Chicago, was written by Greek educators in the Greek community with cooperation from the Hellenic Council on Education and was subsequently approved for use in the public schools by the Board of Education.[129] The establishment of this new voluntary association of Greek educators, therefore, represents a new commitment on the part of second- and third-generation Greeks to speed the successful adjustment of recently arrived immigrant children in the city's public schools, and to perpetuate the Greek identity and way of life in the culturally pluralistic society which is America.

However, there is no evidence that those who attended public schools were brought into mainstream culture more quickly than those who attended Greek communal day schools. And while public schools did provide for avenues of acculturation, they did not, in the main, obliterate Greek culture because of the high priority Greek immigrants placed on transmitting that cultural heritage to their children at home, and the strong structural cohesiveness of the Chicago community with its supportive informal and formal educational agencies. Furthermore, revisionist studies of American schooling show that most immigrant groups did not achieve the upward social mobility that Greeks, Japanese-Americans, and Eastern European Jews did.[130] The Greeks achieved this upward mobility not because of their attendance at public schools, but because of the heavy emphasis their ethnic culture placed on personal achievement, and the fact that they were among the first of the so-called new immigrants to achieve middle-class status.[131] This process was perhaps hastened by informal educational adjustments that took place among the Greek inhabitants of Chicago via business endeavors, the factory, the church, the playground, and even their limited participation in politics.

Greek Response to Educational Needs: Communal Schools

The historical content of American private and parochial education is the story of an immigrant people facing complex adjustments in a new land. In organizing schools and teaching their young, they had to decide on the kinds of schools to be established, the role of the ethnic church in the schools, its relationship with the broader community, the nature of the curriculum, the governance of the schools, and the groups who would receive schooling. The Greek immigrants to Chicago, though latecomers to the American scene, are part of this historical framework of responding to the educational concerns of the ethnic group.

Every ethnic group has certain knowledge, skills, folkways, and mores that it regards as indispensable to its survival. In order to regularize the transmission of these forms, it sets some sort of educational system. The informal educational system carried on in the home, church, and voluntary associations is not as easily discernible as a formal school system. With the Greek immigrants of Chicago, the formal ethnic school system did not materialize until the first decade of this century, even though its Chicago community was formally established in 1892. The delay apparently was due to agitation over the kind of school to organize, the paucity of families, and their inability to cooperate toward a collective goal. When early communal attempts to establish ethnic schools proved abortive, family men took matters into their own hands and established the first Greek school in Chicago in 1904. This was organized by the Mutual Benevolent Society of Family Men, which broke away from the Greek Orthodox parish of Holy Trinity over educational concerns, and established the abortive parish of St. Nicholas on State Street south of the Loop.[132] Shortly thereafter, another school was organized by another voluntary association of "family men," named the "School of Hellenism."

The local Greek newspaper promoted the fact that Chicago's Greeks not only founded the first organized Greek community in the United States but also the first Greek school. Peter Lambros, editor of the *Greek Star*, spoke of the school as being "the organ that will save our language, and the means by which Greek letters will be taught along with our glorious history." Accordingly, the "Greek school will train children to be Greeks so that they will not be digested in the vastness of America."[133] The school principal announced that church and school were "the two pillars which support our national aspirations ... and they must become our two anchors if we are to maintain our ethnicity in America and remain Greek and Christian Orthodox. ... We must depend on the church and school."[134]

Much editorializing took place in the Greek press concerning the importance of the church and school in perpetuating ethnic heritage in America. One editorial pointed out that ethnic institutions such as schools, churches, voluntary societies, newspapers, and other similar undertakings were needed on a larger scale to combat the "fanatical efforts of Protestant missionaries" to alienate the Greek from his ancestral patrimony.[135] These first schools were short-lived; they did, however, serve as catalysts for the establishment of the first permanent Greek communal day school by the organized *koinotis* of Chicago. This school, named after the philosopher Socrates, was established in 1908 by the oldest Greek Orthodox parish in the city, Holy Trinity Church, but only after overcoming a serious internal feud.[136] The school is still functioning today. After 1908 a variety of educational institutions catering to different segments and age levels of the Greek populace were formed, most of them ephemeral, but illustrative of the Greek immigrant's commitment to education. Among these was a People's School, formed in 1907 to provide "certain necessary general and practical subjects of value" to young men with little formal education, which evolved as a form of adult education;[137] and the Phoenix Music School, organized in 1906 and subsidized by the businessmen and professionals in the community. This school later established a Greek Philharmonic Orchestra, which performed concerts at social and religious events in the community.[138]

Ethnic Education at Hull House

One of the greatest assets to the Greek community in its task of providing educational facilities was, of course, Hull House. Its services to the nearby Greek community helped organize a number of private educational enterprises to take care of needs in two major areas: adjustment to the urban American milieu for the immigrant and his wife, and the transmission of the cultural heritage to his children. Hull House became the educational center for guidance, fellowship, and adjustment for the many Greek immigrants living in the Delta. All kinds of helpful services were available, from finding employment to tracing lost immigrant girls. So important was the work of the social workers, especially that of Jane Addams herself, that the young immigrants looked upon her as their "mother." When she died, as we have seen, the Greek community mourned, and Greek businesses were closed on the day of her funeral. She was eulogized as the "Saint of Halsted Street."[139]

The People's School was, in fact, one of the enterprises held at

The Executive Council of the League for the Development of Greek Youth in Chicago, 1910. The League was organized at Hull House in 1908 to provide paramilitary and athletic experiences for young Greek men in Chicago. During the Balkan Wars of 1912 and 1913, thousands of young men trained by the League returned to Greece to fight the Turks. *Courtesy of Andrew T. Kopan.*

Hull House. One of the most effective endeavors there was the Greek Educational Association, chartered by the state of Illinois on February 9, 1909. A group of young men organized this association to promote the "educational, spiritual and physical development" of young Greek immigrants, and it was popularly known in Greek as the "Hellenic League for the Molding of Young Men." The organization had hundreds of active members and sponsored scholarships and athletic activities along with military drills, in which young men met regularly at the Hull House gym for strenuous workouts under the direction of former Greek army officers. In her memoirs Jane Addams speaks of this group as follows:

> It was in this connection with a large association of Greek lads that Hull-House finally lifted its long restriction against military drill. If athletic contests are the residuum of warfare first waged against the conqueror without and then against the tyrants within the State, the modern Greek youth is still in the first stage so far as his in-

herited attitude against the Turk is concerned. Each lad believes that at any moment he may be called home to fight this longtime enemy of Greece. With such a genuine motive at hand, it seemed mere affection [sic] to deny the use of our boys' club building and gymnasium for organized drill, although happily it forms but a small part of the activities of the Greek Educational Association.[140]

When Theodore Roosevelt visited Hull House in 1911, he was greeted by young Greek men in full-dress uniform who escorted him through the premises. The following day a Chicago newspaper described the event and quoted Roosevelt as saying he "came to Hull House not to teach, but to learn."[141]

With the approaching Balkan Wars, a quasi-military group, the Greek Volunteers of America, was organized by the Greek Educational Association. Larger quarters were procured to maintain military preparedness, and in 1912, 5,000 Chicago Greeks volunteered to help Greece "liberate her subjugated sons and daughters in Macedonia, Epirus and Thrace."[142] The first contingent of 300 men embarked for war after attending religious ceremonies at Holy Trinity Church and civic ceremonies at Hull House, with an accompaniment of Greek organizations, military band, and unfurling banners, departing triumphantly from Union Station.[143] The civic ceremony was held in Bowen Hall of Hull House, where a Greek priest blessed the band of young men prior to their departure, and was attended by Miss Addams, who was subsequently awarded the Order of the Phoenix by the Greek government for her "help" in training young immigrants for the Greek army. Unfortunately, her receipt of this award hindered her peace efforts during World War I, much to her chagrin, and the incident was raised against her when she was considered for the Nobel Peace Prize.[144] Another 3,000 Greek immigrants left later to participate in the wars; many remained in Greece, but others returned to America with wives.[145] It is estimated that as many as 42,000 Greek immigrants returned to Greece from the United States to fight in the Balkan Wars.[146]

The military phase of the Greek Educational Association was only one aspect of its active program. The nightly gymnastic program was well attended because the young men, bereft of families, found it friendly and educational. Many became amateur and professional fighters who won regional and national championships, achievements which contributed to the Greek ethnocentrism of the immigrant.[147] Others were persuaded to attend the craft shops of Hull House, where useful trades became their life's work. And for many, the efforts of the association served as a catalyst for them to enter the professions and broader American society.[148]

Pacifist and Nobel Peace Prize winner Jane Addams (right) with Mary McDowell (left) not only tolerated but permitted military training at Hull House for Greek-Americans preparing to fight in the Balkan Wars (1912-13). Later, however, she opposed American intervention in World War I against Germany and the Austro-Hungarian Empire. *Courtesy of the Jane Addams Memorial Collection, University of Illinois, Chicago.*

But perhaps the most enduring contribution of the Greek Educational Association to perpetuating ethnic identity was its sponsorship of patriotic programs associated with the ancestral homeland. Numerous such events were held, including the annual observance of Greek Independence Day on March 25th. Others commemorated milestones of Greek history and current affairs, such as the one held at Chicago's Blackstone Theatre on June 27, 1918, which observed Greece's one-year participation in World War I, with utility magnate Samuel Insull serving as chairman. Indeed, celebration of patriotic events became an integral part of Greek community ritual, and when the association ceased to function in the 1920s, the Greek churches collectively assumed the sponsorship of such events. From the 1930s to the 1950s, elaborate festivities observing Greece's Independence Day were held at Chicago's Civic Opera House or Medinah Temple. In the 1960s a city-wide organization representing parishes, schools, and voluntary associations assumed the sponsorship of such events, including the now elaborate annual Greek Independence Day parade on the city's main thoroughfares. These events have grown into expensive enterprises and serve once again to reinforce ethnic pride and identity for the Greeks of Chicago.

Ethnic Education in the Broader Greek Community

With the dispersal of Greek immigrants to all parts of the city and the establishment of new communities or parishes, additional Greek communal schools were organized. Up to World War II, eleven organized communities, or parishes, each with its own type of school, made up the Chicago Greek community. Following the war, the influx of new Greek immigrants and the relocation of second-generation descendants to the suburbs increased the number to twenty-one in the metropolitan Chicago area. (See Figure 1, page 92.) Not all were day schools: the large expense necessary to operate such schools made them prohibitive to many parishes. Only three such schools survived through the years: Socrates, of Holy Trinity Church (1908); Koraes, of Saints Constantine and Helen Church (1910); and Plato, of Assumption Church (1952). As a result, a supplementary school—the afternoon Greek school—evolved, meeting several times a week after public school hours. For the most part these schools, like the day schools, bore the names of eminent ancient Greeks—Solon, Aristotle, Pythagoras, Archimedes—symbolizing the immigrant's dual pride in classical heritage and commitment to Byzantine tradition.

The governance of these communal day and afternoon schools was usually under the control of the parish *symboulion*, or under a special appointed or elected school committee. This body generally determined curriculum, the hiring of teachers, and the setting of fees, since all charged tuition. Because each community or parish was organized independently, each made its own educational arrangements, giving rise to the congregational nature of these religio-ethnic schools.

Another type of ethnic school that evolved was the private Greek school, maintained by voluntary associations, parental groups, and individuals, which also met after public school hours and sometimes on Saturdays; organized by professional teachers, most of these met in rented quarters and were short-lived. The exact number of such schools is not known, but it is estimated that some forty-five private Greek schools have existed in Chicago at one time or another.[149] In addition, many youngsters received their Greek education at home with private tutors, especially in areas where Greek schools were not close at hand. The tutorial services were a common practice and lucrative for the many tutors, who also were teachers in the communal or private ethnic schools. Hundreds of them were known to have existed in Chicago. The custom of private tutoring probably developed from the Greek family practice of having boarders who tutored the children in lieu of paying rent. The tutorial practice has endured because of its flexibility.

Still another form of communal school was the Sunday school, which every parish organized after the 1920s (despite its Protestant origins). Ostensibly religious in nature, it was nonetheless ethnically oriented and was utilized as another vehicle to inculcate youngsters with the Greek Orthodox faith and culture, initially using Greek as the medium of instruction.

For the most part communal Greek schools were patterned after the provincial primary schools of Greece. All ethnic education was at the elementary level; it was not until the 1970s that a private *secondary* Greek school was established in Chicago (Hellenic Lyceum). Initially, Greek was the language of instruction, and it was not until after World War I that English was introduced into the day schools, and not until the 1960s that English began replacing Greek as the language of instruction.

The objective of these schools (and indeed the objective of all ethnic Greek education) was to transmit the Greek language and cultural heritage to children born of Greek parents, while religion had a somewhat secondary role. Unlike in Roman Catholic parochial schools, religion did not permeate the total curriculum but was taught as part of Greek ethnic education. The curriculum itself was closely patterned after the six-grade primary schools of Greece. A core curriculum included the Greek language, with particular emphasis on grammar and syntax, as well as conversational and reading skills, Greek classical and modern literature, ancient, Byzantine, and modern Greek history, geography of modern Greece, church history, and cathechism. These were taught by professional teachers who received their training at pedagogical institutes in Greece. In time, the day schools were "accredited" by the Chicago Board of Education, and their graduates were admitted into the city's high schools.

The multiplicity and variety of Greek educational facilities in Chicago made them accessible to Greeks residing throughout the city, poorly organized for the most part, and often inadequate and ill-

Transmitting ethnic heritage continues today as newer Greek Orthodox parochial schools replace older buildings. Koraes Elementary School of the Saints Constantine and Helen parish in suburban Palos Hills has educated thousands of Greek children since its inception in 1910. Its curriculum provides for instruction in the Greek language and Greek Orthodox faith along with the typical elementary school program. *Courtesy of Andrew T. Kopan.*

equipped though they were. Every child born of immigrant parents was exposed to one or another of these educational arrangements. The Greek immigrant's commitment to education and his insistence that children learn the Greek language and heritage probably account for the fact that the vast majority of second-generation Greek-Americans had a fluent command of Greek (indeed, often better than their immigrant parents), and remained active participants and expositors of the Greek ethos, despite alienation and indifference by some. To a great extent, these educational arrangements served members of the third generation and are now serving those of the fourth. According to one product of the system:

> The Greek Orthodox parish in which I was reared had, since 1910, a bilingual day elementary school, whose graduates went straight into the Chicago public schools. For those parents whose children attended the "American" school, an afternoon Greek language was available. I attended this school on Mondays, Wednesdays, and Fridays from 4:00 P.M. to 6:00 P.M. for six years. I graduated from this school. From native Greek-trained teachers I learned both *katharevousa* and *demotiki* types of Greek. The textbooks were imported school books from Greece. The curricular content was literary, historical, religious, and grammatical. From that experi-

ence in Greek language study and with a couple of courses in classical Greek ... I am now able to converse in modern demotic Greek, read a newspaper, write a letter with the aid of a grammar and dictionary, and read technical materials and *Koine* Greek with a dictionary. At the doctoral level, I passed a reading translation test in modern Greek. . . .

I grew up in the shadow of the Greek Orthodox Church and its schools, the Greek language school, the Sunday school, the several youth groups of the church, and several public service Greek-speaking national groups. It is in this church environment that I still live, albeit in another city and state today.[150]

Greek Ethnic Survival

The meaning of Greek-American ethnicity has been a striving to perpetuate and appreciate the best in the Greek heritage and the American nationality. The Greek immigrants of Chicago attempted to preserve their ethnic identity through the use of educational agencies, both formal and informal. Despite Greek individualism and factionalism, they succeeded in the mission of transmitting the cultural legacy by way of the family, voluntary associations, church, school, and communication media.

Naturally, acculturative influences are apparent in the daily life-styles of Greek-Americans. Nonetheless, the retention and expansion of cultural activities and schooling arrangements today indicate a renewed determination to perpetuate ethnic tradition without necessarily using the Greek language to maintain the classic heritage. New problems, however, are arising for Greek ethnic survival. Greek nationalism is favored by the more recent Greek immigrants, while the American-born generations favor preservation of religious and cultural legacies.[151] Perhaps, like the Greeks of the Byzantine period, they are oppressed by the weight of their own history; the continuity of their culture is too strong for alteration.

In this respect, the Greek experience in Chicago has been a blend of ethnic pride and resourceful participation in American life. In its early years it was the story of immigrants who suffered incredible hardships, but many of whom nevertheless became substantial members of the middle class. It was the story of the children and grandchildren of those immigrants, most of whom enjoy levels of education and income surpassing that of the average American, and a disproportionate number of whom have been extraordinarily successful in the country of their birth.[152] And it is the still-evolving story of the new immigrants from Greece who have been coming to America in large numbers over the past decade and a half. But this Greek experience also has an underside: exploitation of Greek by Greek, old immigrant men whose lives were drained away in poverty and loneliness, fights between contending political and church factions, conflicts between generations, and misunderstanding between the older and newer immigrants.

Thus, using the technical language of Milton Gordon, one can say that the Greek immigrants of Chicago went through a *cultural* assimilation, or acculturation, which involved the process of the immigrant group learning the manners and style of a new society.[153] *Structural* assimilation—or simply assimilation—in which members of immigrant groups related to members of other ethnic groups, particularly on the intimate levels of family formation and friendship without regard to ethnic differences, did not occur. In both instances, formal and informal education played a key role. Through the use of formal and informal education in public schools and business endeavors, Greek immigrants made their adjustment to the American way of life. Likewise, through the use of formal and informal education in communal ethnic schools, church, voluntary associations, and family, Greek immigrants preserved their separate cultural heritage, in a "best of two worlds" adaptation. Chicago's Greeks survived as an ethnic group because they were not "digested in the vastness of America."

Chapter V

MYRON BOHDON KUROPAS
Ukrainian Chicago:
The Making of a Nationality Group in America

> *On August 26, the Orthodox Rusins had a picnic sponsored by the Russian Consul, but it looks as if the Virgin Mary didn't give us luck because it rained all day. It seems Rusins are unlucky everywhere; on earth and in heaven, no one pays any attention to us.*
>
> —Svoboda, *September 5, 1900*

> *The United States is the only country in the world where, when one becomes a citizen, one does not betray his own nation.*
>
> —Sich, *January 1, 1930*

> *For many a Ukrainian emigre, the United States was not an ethnic melting pot but rather, a school for his ethno-national development.*
>
> —Myron B. Kuropas, *1974*

BASIC TO ANY UNDERSTANDING OF THE nature of the Ukrainian experience in Chicago is an appreciation for the persistent need of Ukrainian-Americans, wherever they settle, to maintain their ethno-national integrity. Denied an opportunity to develop their unique heritage in a homeland free of foreign rule, Ukrainian immigrants have created a second homeland in the United States and have nurtured it for over one hundred years. It is here in America that Ukrainian institutions have flourished, and it is here that Ukrainian traditions have survived for four generations. If one were asked, therefore, to summarize the Ukrainian-American experience in a brief statement, that statement would be "the development and preservation of Ukrainianism."

Ukrainianism has two fundamental ideological roots: the first, dating as far back as the tenth century, is Ukrainian Christianity, a unique blend of Byzantine-Slavonic religious beliefs, practices, and symbols common to both Ukrainian Catholics and Ukrainian Orthodox, the two major faiths within Ukraine's religious tradition. The second ideological root of Ukrainianism is of far more recent origin: Ukrainian nationalism. Dating back to the nineteenth century, Ukrainian nationalism first emerged as a literary revival based on national nostalgia. This romantic tradition evolved in time into a "national awakening," a vibrant national assertiveness with supporters among Ukrainians of diverse political persuasions, including socialists, communists, monarchists, and nationalists. Each ideological camp struggled to define Ukrainianism in its own way, and each contributed to the evolution of a Ukrainian national vision in a manner that reflected each group's particular religious and political perspective. The Ukrainianization process began in Ukraine. It was continued—generally along a parallel course—in the United States, soon after the first immigrant from Ukraine set foot on American soil.

Ukrainian Immigration

On the eve of the first Ukrainian mass migration to America, there was no Ukrainian political nation. Ukrainians in Europe were members of an ethno-cultural community, and if they had any political identity at all, it was one associated with Russia, Austria, or Hungary. The geographic region called Ukraine was divided between two vast empires: western Ukraine was part of Austro-Hungary, eastern Ukraine was dominated by Russia.

Ukrainian immigration to America began in the early 1870s, with emigrants from that region of western Ukraine known as Subcarpathian Rus (hereafter referred to as Carpatho-Ukraine) arriving first. Dominated for much of its history by the Hungarians, Carpatho-Ukraine was the least ethno-nationally developed of Ukraine's provinces. The religio-cultural heritage had been preserved; but the national awakening, the Ukrainian revival then sweeping other Ukrainian provinces, had barely touched the region. The masses remained what they had always been: deeply devoted to their Byzantine-Slavonic religious tradition but with little sense of nationality. The clergy, on the other hand, had become largely Hungarian both in sentiment and in pro-Magyar national political orientation.

Late in the 1880s another group of Ukrainian immigrants from western Ukraine began to make their appearance on American shores. They came from eastern Galicia, a province of Ukraine which had once been under Polish rule but which later became a part of Austria as a result of the Polish partitions. Thanks largely to a relatively liberal Hapsburg policy toward Ukrainian ethno-cultural aspirations, eastern Galicia had become, by the late 1800s, the most ethno-nationally advanced region in Ukraine. In contrast to the situation in Carpatho-Ukraine, the national awakening in this province was led by the Catholic clergy.

Both the Carpatho-Ukrainians and the Galician Ukrainians called themselves "Rusins" (a derivative of *Rus*, Ukraine's ancient name) when they first arrived in America; both spoke languages that were more related to each other than to any other Slavic tongue; both were also "Uniate," or Greek Catholics, as a result of the union with Rome which had been negotiated by a segment of the Ukrainian Orthodox Church first in Galicia (1596) and later in Carpatho-Ukraine (1646). Under the terms of that agreement, Rome had agreed to preserve, among other things, "the ceremonies and rites, including the administration of the holy sacraments" and the right of the clergy to marry.[1]

Though it is impossible to guess the exact number of Rusins ("Ruthenians") who immigrated to the United States at this time (immigrants were listed according to country of origin, and Ukraine did not legally exist until 1917), a rough approximation can be reached by studying estimates of immigrant writers themselves. Ivan Ardan, editor of *Svoboda*, wrote in *Charities* magazine in 1904 that "even the most conservative estimate cannot place the number of Ruthenians in the United

States much below 350,000."[2] Another source, Julian Bachynsky, who
published his monumental *The Ukrainian Immigration in the United
States* in 1914 estimated that there were 470,000 first- and second-
generation Ukrainians living in America by 1909. It seems likely that
at least 500,000 Ukrainian-Americans were to be found here in 1914.[3]

The first formal Ukrainian religious community was created in
America in 1884, when a group of Rusin immigrants living in Shenandoah, Pennsylvania petitioned Galician Metropolitan (later Cardinal)
Sylvester Sembratovych for a priest because "something is lacking in
us." Sembratovych dispatched Fr. Ivan Volansky, a married priest, who
presented himself to Roman Catholic Archbishop Patrick Ryan in Philadelphia, but was rejected by the Latin-rite Catholic prelate because
he was not a celibate priest. Refusing Ryan's suggestion to go back to
Ukraine, the indignant Volansky continued his pilgrimage to Shenandoah to organize the first Ukrainian parish in the nation.

Fr. Volansky established other parishes in Pennsylvania, as well as
in New Jersey and Minnesota. As other married Ukrainian priests from
Carpatho-Ukraine and Galicia began to arrive, conflict with the American Roman Catholic hierarchy increased. At issue were both the legitimacy of married clergy in a Catholic diocese and control of the
newly established parishes. The first question was resolved—temporarily—in 1907, when Rome agreed to appoint a separate bishop, Soter
Ortynsky, for Rusins in America. The control issue was not settled until
1913, when the Holy See finally granted Ortynsky "full and ordinary
jurisdiction" over all Greek Catholics from Carpatho-Ukraine and
Galicia.[4]

Despite the frustrations, uncertainties, and put-downs, three distinct ethno-national orientations or streams emerged to compete for the
Rusin's national loyalty—Russian, Rusin-Ruthenian, and Ukrainian—
and all three won most of their converts between 1889 and 1914.

The first ethno-national stream to gain ground among the Rusin
emigrants was Russian in orientation and emerged from another clash
with the Irish-dominated American Catholic hierarchy's refusal to accept a separate, non-Latin Catholic rite in the United States. It began
in 1889, when Fr. Alexis Toth, a Catholic priest from Carpatho-Ukraine,
arrived in Minneapolis to take up his duties in a parish recently created
by Fr. Volansky. Fr. Toth presented himself to Bishop Ireland of St.
Paul, who, upon learning that Toth was a widower, refused to recognize
him and forbade all Roman Catholics in his diocese to support the
Rusin parish in any way. Celibacy was again the disrupter. So angered
was Toth by Ireland's cavalier and ecclesiastically illegitimate treatment that he left the church. On February 11, 1891, Fr. Toth converted
to the Russian Orthodox faith and soon became the dynamic leader of

a "Return to Orthodoxy" movement among Rusin-Americans. "If we don't place ourselves under the protection of the Orthodox Church," proclaimed Toth, "the Irish Catholic bishops will soon take our churches from us." With financial help from the czarist government, Toth, who has since come to be known as the "Father of American Russia," proved to be an unusually effective proselytizer in splintering off Greek Catholics for the Russian fold.[5] By 1900 the Russian Orthodox Mission controlled thirteen parishes in America with almost 7,000 faithful. Most were emigrants from either Carpatho-Ukraine or Galicia.[6]

A second ethno-national stream centered around *Sojedineije,* a mutual benefit insurance ("burial") society established by Rusin immigrants in 1892. Dominated by Catholic clergy from Carpatho-Ukraine who called themselves "Uhro-Rusins," *Sojedineije's* initial ethno-national orientation was Hungarian. As time went on, however, and as competition with the Ukrainian-oriented Galician clergy became increasingly intense, *Sojedineije* (which later changed its name to the Greek Catholic Union, or GCU) began to promote a separate, purely Rusin-Ruthenian identity among its membership. Rejecting Ukrainianism entirely, the GCU was instrumental in convincing both President Wilson and the Holy See that Rusins were indeed a separate people. In 1918 the GCU membership, and others associated with the Rusin-Ruthenian camp, voted to have Carpatho-Ukraine incorporated into the newly established Czecho-Slovak Republic as the autonomous province of Ruthenia. That same year, at the behest of Rusin leaders in America, the Vatican agreed to appoint two administrators of the Rusin Catholic Church in America—one for the Rusins and one for the Ukrainians—until a successor to Bishop Ortynsky, who died in 1916, could be found.

The last ethno-national orientation to make its appearance in the Rusin community was the Ukrainian. Associated with the Little Russian National Union, a mutual benefit insurance society organized by another segment of the Rusin community in 1894, the Ukrainian camp really came into its own with the arrival of the so-called "American Circle," a group of Catholic priests from Galicia who, prior to ordination, had decided to dedicate their lives to ethno-national work in America. Immigrating in the early 1900s, the American Circle took over the insurance society (which changed its name to the Ukrainian National Association—UNA—in 1915) and embarked on an ambitious Ukrainianization program that included Ukrainian language publications, the creation of reading rooms for illiterates, and support for Ukrainian cultural enterprises such as choirs, drama groups, and ethnic schools for youth. Reflecting their radical socialist background in Ukraine—they were called "popike radicale" (priestly radicals) by the

GCU—they also became involved with America's nascent labor movement, urging Rusins to become active in union work and to strike if necessary in order to better their lot in life.[7]

At the heart of the Ukrainianization campaign in America was *Svoboda*, the UNA-owned Ukrainian-language newspaper. With the possible exception of the Ukrainian Catholic Church during this period, no other single Ukrainian institution had more of an impact on the Ukrainian Rusin stream than did *Svoboda*. It was, and remains today, the conscience of the Ukrainian community.

Meanwhile, emigration from Ukraine had come to a virtual standstill during World War I. Those Ukrainians who did arrive in America at that time came from countries other than their original homeland—from Argentina primarily, but also from Brazil and Canada. Nor did emigration from Ukraine increase much after the war. Few Ukrainians were allowed to leave the Soviet Union, and the United States itself passed the restrictive and discriminatory immigration laws of the 1920s. The Johnson-Reed Act of 1924 was most restrictive, giving each nation a quota of 2 percent of its immigrants present in the U.S. population in 1890—a poor year for Ukrainians. Thus no more than 40,000 Ukrainians were able to immigrate to the United States between 1920 and 1939. What this second Ukrainian wave lacked in quantity, however, it made up for in ethno-national quality: a higher proportion of the new Ukrainian immigrants, most of whom came from Ukrainian provinces of Poland and Czechoslovakia, were educated, conscious of their ethnicity, and politically astute.

Chicago's First Emigres from Ukraine

The first emigres from Ukraine to settle in Chicago were probably living in the city and environs as early as the 1880s. According to Dr. Volodymyr Simenovych, a physician who settled in Chicago in 1893, there was a Russian Orthodox church already in existence at Madison and Racine when he arrived. Most of the parishoners, Simenovych believed, were from Carpatho-Ukraine,[8] having been converted to Orthodoxy in all probability during Fr. Toth's visit to the city in 1892. Upon learning in 1895 that Bishop Nicholas planned to build a Russian cathedral in the city, *Svoboda* protested against this new "russification":

> During his visit to St. Petersburg, Bishop Nicholas convinced the so-called Synod and the Czar that the time was ripe to energetically develop the area because the "material" here happens to

be more than ample. That "material" happens to be our poor Rusin people from Galicia and Hungarian Rus. Already the poor Rusin nation has far too many unsolicited protectors. In the old country they tried to take away our nationality and to make us Poles, Hungarians, and Slovaks; here in America they wish to take away our faith. Difficult will be the road of our adversaries. We are equal to the struggle and we are confident that our people will not sell their souls to Judas.[9]

Ultimately, the Russian czarist regime allocated $4,000, with a per annum 600 gold rubles as collateral for the building loan.[10] Designed by the famous Chicago architect Louis H. Sullivan, Holy Trinity Russian Orthodox Cathedral was completed at Leavitt and Haddon in 1903. Those Carpatho-Ukrainians who remained with the church were eventually absorbed into the Russian ethno-national stream, but the church remains as a reminder of the non-Russian origins of the Cathedral's founding members.[11]

A second group of Rusins, also from Carpatho-Ukraine, settled on Chicago's South Side. A parish was organized in June of 1903, and in 1905 a church was constructed on the corner of 50th and Seeley with Fr. Victor Kovaliczki as the first pastor. Naming their new edifice "The First Greek Catholic Church of St. Mary's of Chicago," the parishioners steered clear of Russian Orthodoxy and eventually became part of the Rusin-Ruthenian ethno-national stream.[12]

The Ukrainian stream in Chicago began with the arrival of Dr. Simenovych. Once a third-year law student at the University of Lviv, a personal friend of Ivan Franko, Ukraine's leading poet during this period, and an energetic activist in Ukrainian ethno-national organizations in eastern Galicia, Simenovych came to America in 1887 at the request of a priest who was responding to Fr. Volansky's plea to "send me an intelligent young man to assist me with my work in America." Settling in Shenandoah, Pennsylvania, Simenovych was made editor of *Ameryka*, a Ukrainian-language newspaper that Volansky had established in 1886. A man of many and varied talents, Simenovych soon came to manage a Ukrainian cooperative store and to organize a drama troupe, a reading room for illiterates, and an evening school for adults and children. Leaving the co-op following a disagreement with Volansky's successor, Simenovych enrolled in medical school and, with financial assistance from a Lithuanian doctor friend, completed his studies and moved to Chicago, where he practiced medicine until his death in 1932.[13] Chicago's Ukrainian community could not have had a more distinguished and nationally dedicated founder.

Chicago's First Ukrainian Community

Emigrants from Ukraine continued to come to Chicago in ever-increasing numbers, settling for the most part in an area bounded by Division Street on the north, Racine on the west, Roosevelt Road on the south, and Orleans on the east.[14] At a baptismal party in 1905, Fr. Kovaliczki agreed to help immigrants from Carpatho-Ukraine and Galicia to establish a (Rusin) parish on the North Side.[15] Thus a Chicago Ukrainian community came into being on December 31, 1905, when fifty-one Rusins gathered at 939 Robey (now Damen) to establish the St. Nicholas Ruthenian Catholic Church. Learning that a Danish Lutheran Church located at Superior and Bickersdicke was on the market, they purchased it for $8,000, with a 6 percent loan from a bank. A twelve-member board of trustees was elected, with Kovaliczki as chairman and Dr. Simenovych as secretary, and passed a motion to prevent the church from falling into "alien" (Latin-rite or Irish) hands by stipulating:

> . . . all the property of said church which may hereafter be acquired be held in the name of its incorporated name but under no conditions shall said church or its priests or pastors be ever under the jurisdiction of bishop or bishops except those of the same faith and rite.

Some thirty-three individuals pledged $295, while six others promised to loan the parish a total of $350.[16]

The new church had not only a "religious-moral" aspect but also a "national-educational" goal:

> To elevate ourselves through the support of a school, a reading room, political clubs, and whatever else is deemed necessary.

The pastor, of course, was expected to "live up to the religious-moral and national-educational purposes of the parish," and he was to be respected as the "head of the community; he must be consulted in all matters pertaining to the community and he must be obeyed!"[17]

The Strutinskys and the Growth of Ethno-National Consciousness

Fr. Kovaliczki left St. Nicholas parish in the spring of 1907, and he was succeeded by Fr. L. Beseha, who remained for less than six months.[18] By the middle of November, St. Nicholas had a new pastor, one Nicholas Strutinsky, who, at the first church council over which he presided, was able to convince the members to consider deeding all church property to Bishop Ortynsky, the newly arrived Ukrainian prelate, and to pledge 5 percent of all church income to the bishop's office.[19] Given the resistance of other Ukrainian parishes to relinquishing ownership to the bishop—in the minds of many Rusins loss of local ownership meant loss of local control—Strutinsky's early success in this regard was no small accomplishment. But then Strutinsky was no ordinary person. A tall, dynamic, no-nonsense Ukrainian cleric who was not averse to taking an occasional punch at a Polish editor who wrote what Strutinsky believed was an anti-Ukrainian editorial,[20] he remained at St. Nicholas until 1921. It was during his—and his equally energetic wife's—stay in the city that Chicago's Ukrainian community grew, prospered, and became irrevocably Ukrainian in ethno-national thinking, feeling, and action.

Associated with the National Democratic Ukrainian political party in Galicia,[21] Fr. Strutinsky arrived in the United States in 1902 and plunged into the Ukrainian stream with messianic fervor.[22] While a pastor in Olyphant, Pennsylvania, he organized America's first Ukrainian *Sich*[23]—a gymnastic organization for Ukrainian youth patterned after the Czech *Sokol*—and began to write for *Svoboda*. In a series of articles entitled "Understand Rusin, Which Road Is Yours," Strutinsky reported on developments in Ukraine, explaining at the same time why the term "Ukrainian" was being used:

> Most people in the old country belong to the so-called Ukrainian-Rus party. Almost all of the young priests, the majority of the older priests, almost all lawyers, professors, doctors, and students, in short, all the intelligentsia and the enlightened masses call themselves Rus-Ukrainians. . . . They call themselves this name because they realize that even though they are in Galicia, their ancestors came from Ukraine. . . . Galicia, our country, is the child of Ukraine. . . . Just as we came to America, the Rusin-Ukrainians came to Galicia.[24]

After moving to Chicago, Strutinsky joined forces with Simenovych and Stephen Janovych, a lawyer and friend of Simenovych when both were still living in Pennsylvania,[25] to establish in 1906 the Brotherhood of St. Nicholas, the city's first branch of the Ukrainian National Association (UNA). An early achievement of the new organization was the establishment of a reading room in the church basement. In 1908, Fr. Strutinsky helped organize two more UNA branches on Chicago's North Side, the Sisterhood of the Blessed Virgin Mary and the Brotherhood of St. Stephen.[26]

SAINTS PETER AND PAUL CHURCH

On Chicago's South Side, meanwhile, a second Ukrainian community was beginning to coalesce in Burnside. Served initially by a priest from Whiting, Indiana—where *Svoboda* reported a functioning Rusin church as early as 1899[27]—the Burnside community came into its own when Bishop Ortynsky assigned Fr. Volodymyr Petrovsky to the parish in 1909. By the end of the year, a Ukrainian Catholic Church, Saints Peter and Paul, was standing at the corner of 92nd and Avalon.[28]

THE NATIVITY OF THE BVM CHURCH

At about the same time, another Ukrainian community was being organized in the working-class Back of the Yards area. A UNA branch, the Nativity of the Blessed Virgin Mary, was established by Emil Skorodinsky in 1909, and its members became the initiators of Chicago's third Ukrainian parish. Fr. Michael Prodon came to serve the community in 1910, and with seed money from St. Nicholas he established a small chapel in an apartment at 47th and Hermitage.[29] When this facility proved too small, the parish moved temporarily to St. Michael's Roman Catholic Church at 47th and Damen. Finally, in 1912 a church hall was constructed at 49th and Paulina, and the parishioners of the Nativity of the Blessed Virgin Mary had their own Ukrainian house of worship.[30]

THE NEW RUS

Ukrainians on the North Side were also experiencing a substantial population increase, and by 1911 it was obvious that a new, larger church was needed. "Let us move west where much land is still available," urged Dr. Simenovych at a parish meeting in March. "We can build a glorious new church, we can all purchase lots near the church, we can eventually build our homes on these lots and, with God's help, we can have our own, new Rus right here in Chicago."[31]

Simenovych's "new Rus" concept was enthusiastically accepted, and after much discussion during the next few council meetings over possible sites, Fr. Strutinsky announced that twenty lots had been purchased on Rice Street between Oakley and Leavitt for $12,000.[32] The cornerstone of the new church was blessed by Bishop Ortynsky on November 27, 1913, following a construction delay of two years. Finally, after more delays, the magnificent edifice—a Byzantine-Slavonic masterpiece—was completed. On Christmas Day, January 7, 1915, the first divine liturgy was celebrated in what was then, and is still for many today, America's most beautiful Ukrainian church.[33]

Fr. Strutinsky's role in the "making" of Ukrainians in Chicago went far beyond writing articles, normal parish responsibilities, and even building churches. He was one of a dying breed of Ukrainian priests: he was a patriot, a person who, if forced to choose between being a Catholic and being a Ukrainian, would probably have chosen the latter. Few priests then and now could have matched his devotion to his people and to the Ukrainian stream.

RIDNA SHKOLA

An ethnic school for the purpose of "perpetuating the Rusin heritage" was first discussed at a St. Nicholas council meeting as early as 1906,[34] but it was not until the arrival of Fr. Strutinsky that a *Ridna Shkola* (national school) was formally established.[35] By 1909 the parish was willing to pay fifty dollars a month for a *diak-uchytel* (cantor-teacher)[36] who, in addition to his duties as a cantor-respondent during the divine liturgy, was also expected to take responsibility for a variety of cultural activities, such as the organization and direction of a choir, of a drama group, and, most important of all, of an ethnic school for the youth. As might be expected, the approach of the *diak-uchytel* toward American-born youngsters was crucial in determining his effectiveness. If he could establish rapport—a difficult task for some European-born teachers—his efforts to Ukrainianize the younger generation would be generally successful. If, unfortunately, he was like some teachers, for whom, as *Svoboda* once complained, "the only pedagogical tool was the stick," the school often did more harm than good.[37] As the church council minutes point out, St. Nicholas had its share of incompetent educators.[38] Under Strutinsky's firm hand, however, the parish finally assembled a relatively competent teaching staff, and Chicago's *Ridna Shkola* blossomed. In its modest inception in 1907, St. Nicholas had one teacher and ten students who attended Ukrainian school one day per week, Saturday from 10:00 to 12:00 a.m. By 1922 there were four teachers, some 300 students, and a Ukrainianization program that was in operation five days a week—Monday through Friday from 4:00 to 6:00 p.m.[39]

THE UKRAINIAN WOMEN'S ALLIANCE

In 1912 the UNA created the so-called "Board of Education of the Ukrainian National Association of America" (*Prosvita*, or "enlightenment") with Dr. Simenovych as chairman and Emily Strutinsky, the

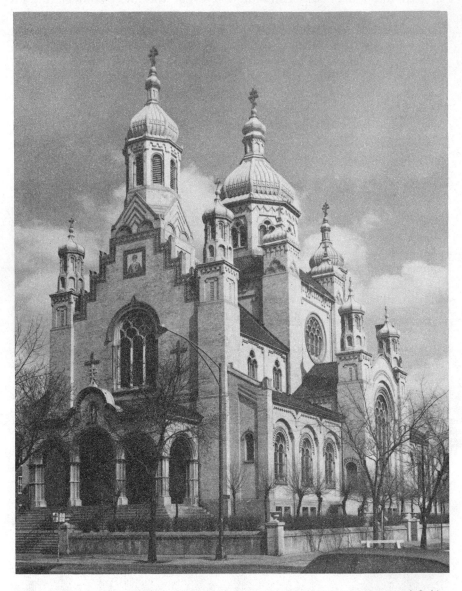

St. Nicholas Ukrainian Catholic Cathedral was constructed in 1913 on Rice and Oakley Streets and is considered by many to be America's most beautiful Ukrainian church. *Courtesy of M. B. Kuropas.*

wife of the St. Nicholas pastor, as secretary.[40] The appointment of these two was evidence of the significant role Chicago's Ukrainians were beginning to play in Ukrainian-American national affairs; but even more important, it was a tribute to Mrs. Strutinsky, who had jumped into Ukrainian affairs with as much vigor as her husband had.

Inspired by the American feminist movement then sweeping the country, as well as by her personal acquaintance with Jane Addams of Hull House, Mrs. Strutinsky helped organize a national congress of Ukrainian women in hopes of forming a national Ukrainian mutual benefit insurance society for women. Held in Chicago in 1917, the congress gave birth to the Ukrainian Women's Alliance of America, an organization with headquarters in the rectory of St. Nicholas Church. A year later the alliance began publishing *Ranna Zorya* (Morning Star), which outlined the purpose of the organization: to help in the hard task of creating a new "free, independent state of ours, Ukraine."[41] Despite the great hope expressed by its founders, the alliance had a short history. It organized classes for illiterates in Chicago and managed to publish a few more issues of *Ranna Zorya*. But in the end, it disappeared

Ukrainian women exhibit cultural objects at the Chicago World's Fair of 1933. *Courtesy of Ukrainian National Museum.*

from the Ukrainian-American scene, to be replaced in 1925 by the Ukrainian National Women's League of America (UNWLA), which has survived until the present day.

THE BIRTH OF UKRAINIAN ORTHODOXY IN AMERICA

Given his forceful and somewhat authoritarian personality—a trait which helped him get things done, but which also served to antagonize some parishioners—it was to be expected that the longer Fr. Strutinsky remained at St. Nicholas, the greater the likelihood that his behavior would lead to a serious rift in the parish. Strutinsky's problems began when it became apparent that he had overestimated the financial resources of the parish while underestimating the cost of constructing the new St. Nicholas. At one point, the contractor had not been paid for as much as five months, and he delayed construction. Some church council members complained. Never one to back away from a fight, Strutinsky took on his critics at every opportunity. As time went on, church council meetings became increasingly acrimonious and difficult to handle.

While church council minutes do not record the exact date, it was during a heated debate at a church council meeting in 1915 that Strutinsky grabbed a wooden cross and hit one of his more vociferous critics over the head.[42] Angered, a group of parishioners led by Jurij Masley, Joseph Kocovsky, and Luka Riza, vice-chairman, treasurer, and curator respectively, left St. Nicholas and formed the so-called Ukrainian National Church. The significance of this event lies in the fact that in the history of the Ukrainian Orthodox Church in America, the newly established Ukrainian parish is considered the first truly *Ukrainian* Orthodox church on these shores. Initially called Holy Trinity, the church was located for many years in the 1900 block of Erie and was referred to be many as "the church on Erie."[43]

Strutinsky weathered the crisis and managed to remain at St. Nicholas until 1921, when certain other financial problems associated with the church surfaced and Strutinsky was given a no-confidence vote by the parish.[44] He left Chicago soon thereafter. Two years later, at a parish meeting held on January 28, 1923, it was unanimously decided to change the name of St. Nicholas Church from Ruthenian Greek Catholic to Ukrainian Greek Catholic.[45] An era had ended.

A Split in the Ukrainian Stream

Unity within the Ukrainian ethno-national stream came to an end at the 1910 Ukrainian National Association convention in Cleveland, when Bishop Ortynsky, chairman of the by-laws committee, pushed through a series of resolutions which, among other things, changed the name of the fraternal society to the Greek Catholic Rusin Association and subordinated the organization to the bishop's office. Despite strong opposition, the resolutions were later accepted by the majority of delegates; but this resulted in the defection of fourteen UNA branches and the formation of a new fraternal society, which became known in time as the Ukrainian Workingmen's Association (UWA).[46]

After the convention ended, however, the UNA leadership was dismayed to learn from legal counsel that the changes had been made in an unconstitutional manner, and that the original name and administrative structure would have to be retained. Unable to control the UNA, Bishop Ortynsky formed his own fraternal benefit society, which in 1912 came to be called the Providence Association of Ruthenian Catholics.[47]

Simenovych and the Ukrainian Independence Movement

Of the three ethno-national streams that prevailed in the Rusin American community prior to 1914, the most radical politically was the Ukrainian. Adopting a posture that was essentially socialist (occasionally anti-capitalistic), the early editors of *Svoboda*, most of whom were members of the American Circle of Galician priests, advocated labor union organization in America and revolutionary activity in Ukraine. "Washington was a revolutionary who mobilized the American people to overthrow the English yoke," wrote *Svoboda* in 1903:

> We must be revolutionaries, agitators on the order of Washington. . . . The Poles and Magyars who agitated against the dictatorship of the emperor now have strength and significance. Today the world is such that only those who have wisdom and strength mean anything. And those who lick the hands and feet of aristocrats will be rewarded with spittle in their soup and a kick by the same aristocrats they venerate.[48]

Throughout 1906, *Svoboda* promoted fund-raising activities for the support of three political parties in Galicia: the National Democrats, the Radicals, and the Socialists.[49] "Take up donations at every opportunity," urged *Svoboda*, "at meetings, concerts, even at weddings and baptisms. . . ."[50]

When the long-anticipated war in Europe finally erupted, *Svoboda*, with guarded optimism, dreamed of an independent Ukrainian state.[51] The cataclysmic train of events during World War I, including the collapse of the Russian Czarist regime; the Bolshevik overthrow of Kerensky's provisional government; Ukraine's declaration of independence (January 22, 1918); President Wilson's promulgation of "The Fourteen Points" underscoring America's commitment to national self-determination; the demise of the Austro-Hungarian empire; the proclamation of a Republic of Western Ukraine (October 1918); and finally, the formal unification of Western and Eastern Ukraine (January 22, 1919)—all these were events that had a profound and electrifying impact on America's Ukrainians especially when the situation in Ukraine seemed to be changing so quickly and dramatically.

During its brief and stormy history, the Ukrainian National Republic had three separate governments: a socialist government headed by Michael Hrushevsky (May 1917 to April 1918); a conservative monarchist government headed by "Hetman" Pavlo Skoropadsky (April 1918 to December 1918);[52] and a coalition government headed by Simon Petlura (December 1918 to November 1920). None of the Allied powers recognized Ukraine because of their hope that Russia would remain in the war and their fear that a dismembered Russia would weaken the war effort. Germany and Austria, on the other hand, needed the grain that Ukraine could provide, and they favored Russia's withdrawal from the war and a weakening of the empire. They recognized Ukraine because it was in their interests, but when the Hrushevsky government could not deliver promised food supplies, it was overthrown by the Germans and replaced by the Skoropadsky regime. Skoropadsky was toppled by Petlura after the war ended and German forces had left Ukraine.

Meanwhile, in 1915, in anticipation of what was about to take place in Europe, the UNA initiated a move to form a national, all-Ukrainian representative body in the United States to represent Ukrainian aspirations overseas.[53] Before anything more could be done, however. Bishop Ortynsky had formed his own all-Rusin representative body of Carpatho-Ukrainians and Galicians. Disappointed but not disheartened, the UNA and other organizations went ahead with their plans, and on October 15 and 16, 1915, the first so-called Diet of Ukrainian-Americans was convened in New York City. During the two days of deliberation a new organization, the "Federation of Ukrainians in America," came into being, with Chicago's Volodymyr Simenovych as chairman.[54] From its inception, the Federation adopted a progressive posture reflective of general political trends then prevalent in the Ukrainian camp.

The UNA, however, was moving away from the socialist fringe it had once occupied and was edging toward the political center. In 1916, in hopes of a rapprochement with the Ukrainian Catholic Church after the death of Bishop Ortynsky (the Holy See had appointed Fr. Peter Poniatyshyn, a UNA sympathizer, as temporary administrator of the eparchy), the UNA and other more moderate elements within the Federation withdrew to form the Ukrainian National Alliance.[55] Following the UNA-led exodus, the Federation came under the ideological control of the Ukrainian Federation of Socialist Parties of America (UFSPA), a left-wing coalition formed in 1915, and the Ukrainian Workingmen's Association (UWA).

In Chicago, meanwhile, the indefatigable Simenovych could now rely on the financial and intellectual support of two recent immigrants to the city, Dr. Stephen Hrynevetsky, also a physician, and Cyril Bilyk, a university student. Born in Ukraine, Hrynevetsky completed his medical studies at the University of Vienna, where, according to one source, he once flirted with the communist political ideology of Nikolai Bukharin, the theorist who later rose to power in Russia and was executed by Stalin in 1938. Hrynevetsky practiced medicine in Austria, spent time as a doctor on a German cruise ship which traveled around the world, met and married Natalie Pidlyashetko, a singer with the Vienna State Opera, immigrated to Chicago sometime between 1903 and 1907, and established a highly successful medical practice here. He and his wife were members of the Erie Street National Church, where Natalie Hrynevetsky eventually organized and directed a choir. Both were elected to the twenty-two-person executive board of the Federation in 1915.[56]

Cyril Bilyk arrived in Chicago as a young man, enrolled at the University of Chicago, and, along with Simenovych and Emily Strutinsky, helped organize the Ukrainian Self-Education Club, an enlightenment society with a socialist flavor. Graduating from Rush Medical College in 1917, Dr. Bilyk became a member of the UWA leadership and in time replaced Simenovych as chairman of the Federation.[57]

Given its somewhat shaky development, the Federation was hardpressed to realize its ambitious program. Undaunted, a delegation consisting of Simenovych, Bilyk, Emily Strutinsky, and the UWA president visited the White House on January 4, 1917, to urge President Wilson to proclaim a national "Ukrainian Day," an effort which also had the support of the rival Ukrainian National Council. With legislative approval in both the House and the Senate, President Wilson responded on March 16 with a proclamation that recognized "the terrible plight" of "at least one million Ruthenians (Ukrainians) in dire need of food, clothing, and shelter," and designated April 21, 1917, "as a day upon which the people of the United States may make such contributions as they feel disposed for the aid of the stricken Ruthenians (Ukrainians) in the belligerent countries.[58] As a result of the proclamation, the Federation and its branches collected a total of $32,217.17 for Ukrainian relief, while the Alliance reported collecting $53,189.32.[59]

On May 19, 1917, Simenovych and Hrynevetsky established *Ukrayina,* Chicago's first Ukrainian-language newspaper, which attempted to accommodate all segments of the Ukrainian community and unite them in a general nationalist effort.[60]

> We are not going to attack any party, sect or individual. Our newspaper is not that of any privileged class in America. . . .
>
> We are publishing *Ukraynia* for Ukrainians in order that Ukrainian nationalism can be elevated to its highest possible level. Our greatest ambition in editing our *Ukrayina* is to acquaint such powerful nations as England, America and France with the Ukrainian question. . . .[61]

The new publication provided a flattering and detailed report on the successful "Ukrainian Day in Chicago," a fund-raiser approved by the city council. The Ukrainian celebration, which raised more than $8,000, had been aided significantly by Chicago's Poles and Lithuanians.[62]

A year later, on May 30, 1918, at the initiative of Simenovych and Hrynevetsky, a mass rally was held at Pulaski Park (Noble and Blackhawk), which attracted some 10,000 persons.[63] The *Ukrayina* reporter recorded his impressions of the event as follows:

> At one o'clock the signal was given at Oakley Blvd. to move forward. The national march began to play and all the lodges moved by fours along Chicago Avenue. . . .
>
> At Hoyne, the independent societies, already waiting in disciplined order, began to fall in, creating one, long unbroken phalanx. They began to flow into one big family, just as the waters of the Dnieper flow into the great depths of the Ukrainian Black Sea. A visible expression of peace and dignity began to appear on the faces of the marchers and in their eyes one could see an unextinguishable flame, a stubborn determination, as if they were answering their brothers who, living across the ocean in the midst of fire and blood, were pleading for their help.
>
> The parade was huge. One had to wait for half an hour until the 30 societies numbering 5,000 people passed in review.
>
> At the head of the parade rode men on two horses and behind them more men bearing thirty or more flags, most of which were American. Only four azure and gold flags were in the parade, belonging to an organization which had captured the true Ukrainian spirit. One yearned for more Ukrainian flags.
>
> After the flags came our women marching proudly in Ukrainian costume. This is our glory and our hope. . . .[64]

The reporter went on to describe numerous floats and placards with proclamations such as "Let Democracy Live" and "Down with the

Kaiser and His Regime." The description of the day's events concluded with comments relating to the manifestation that followed the parade. Held at the Pulaski Park auditorium, where 3,000 people sat and thousands more stood outside listening to the loudspeakers, the gathering was addressed by a number of distinguished guests.

Pulaski Park in 1918 proved to be a high point in the ethno-national development of Chicago's Ukrainian community. No Ukrainian gatherings before and few after have been as successful, both in terms of the number of Ukrainians involved and the unifying spirit that prevailed.

Despite Federation successes in Chicago, its national influence continued to decline, while its rival, the Alliance, became more active. When hostilities in Europe ended, the leadership of the Alliance decided to end its feud with the Federation and make another effort to unite the total Ukrainian community. On November 23, 1918, the Ukrainian National Alliance changed its name to the Ukrainian National Committee and elected a new executive board.[65] It was at about this time that Simenovych and Bilyk agreed to join forces with the Committee.

With President Wilson and the State Department all but ignoring Ukraine's claim to an independent existence, the Committee appealed directly to the nations gathered at Versailles. Dr. Bilyk and Congressman James A. Hamill (D., N.J.), a supporter of Ukrainian causes, arrived in Paris, in March 1919, but they were unable to get the promise of an independent Ukraine from the conference.[66] Hamill returned to the United States within a few months, but Bilyk remained in Europe for over a year, not returning to America until May 27, 1920.[67] Disillusioned and broken-hearted over his inability to convince the peacemakers of the legitimacy of the Ukraine's freedom crusade, Bilyk resumed his medical practice, eventually settling in New York City. Never again active in Ukrainian affairs, Dr. Bilyk died in 1924, as Ukrainian hopes for independence withered.

The Old and New Left

Ukrainian ethno-national aspirations for the permanent establishment of a free and sovereign Ukrainian state after World War I were never realized. With the fall of the Ukrainian National Republic to the Bolshevik Red army, and as a result of agreements reached by the peacemakers, Ukraine was eventually partitioned among four nations and swallowed up. Carpatho-Ukraine, referred to as "Subcarpathian Ruthenia," became a part of the newly created Republic of Czecho-Slovakia (Treaty of St. Germaine-en-laye, 1919).[68] The province of Bukovina was annexed by Rumania (Treaty of St. Germaine-en-laye). Eastern Ukraine came under Russian control (Treaty of Riga, 1921) as the Ukrainian Soviet Socialist Republic (UkSSR); on December 29, 1922, the UkSSR was incorporated into the Union of Soviet Socialist Republics. Western Ukraine became a part of the new Polish state (Decision of the Council of Ambassadors, 1923). Thus, despite a monumental effort and the raising of hundreds of thousands of dollars by the Ukrainian American community between 1914 and 1923, a united and free Ukraine was not to be.

Describing the tragic impact of these events on the morale of the Ukrainian-American community, Fr. Peter Poniatyshyn, administrator of the Ukrainian Catholic Church and an active member of the Ukrainian National Committee, was later to write:

> The Ukrainian defeat at the peace conference at Versallies, that is, the negation by that conference of Ukrainian requests, left the Ukrainian American community throughly disillusioned and in a deep state of depression. In the main, that depression was utilized by "our" Bolsheviks and the Ukrainian National Committee began to lose ground.[69]

Angry and confused by the turn of events in Europe, Ukrainians in America began to search for answers, alternative perspectives, new leaders who could satisfy their recently crystallized and now badly bruised national consciousness. A new era was beginning, a period during which Ukrainian-American awareness would be tempered, hardened as it were, to a new, more sophisticated level of ethno-national assertiveness. Between 1920 and 1939 three new ethno-national political models presented themselves and were accepted by substantial segments of the increasingly pluralistic Ukrainian stream. The first to emerge were the Ukrainian Bolsheviks.

Of the many Ukrainian political ideologies that existed in America during the war, the one that came closest to being called a "party" was socialism. Capitalizing on the radical tradition and left-leaning bias of America's pioneer Ukrainian leaders, the socialists had established the Ukrainian Federation of Socialist Parties of America (UFSPA) in 1915. Within a year the UFSPA leadership had split between the "social patriots," who felt the party's first priority should be national reform in Ukraine, and the Bolsheviks, or as they preferred to be called, the "internationalists," who argued that social reform should be the primary concern.[70]

The Bolsheviks gained ground rapidly, and in 1919, at the third UFSPA convention, they recognized the Third International, a move tantamount to full acceptance of Soviet rule in Ukraine. Ejected from membership in the Socialist Party of America for its action, the UFSPA

joined other expelled socialist groups to give birth that same year to
the Communist Party of America.[71] The UFSPA's journal, *Robitnyk*
(Worker), explained that the organization was, after September 1, 1919,
the Ukrainian Federation of Communist Parties of America.[72] So
sweeping was the enthusiasm of Ukrainian Bolsheviks during this period, and so convinced were they that the victory of the proletariat was
just around the corner—"a few more days, weeks, months and not one
trace of the old order will be found," wrote one *Robitnyk* correspondent—that they viewed all other Ukrainian organizations and American
institutions as anachronistic.[73]

The enthusiasm that prevailed among Ukrainian socialists for the
Bolshevik platform was a reflection of a phenomenon that gripped the
entire socialist movement in America. "For the harassed Left in America," writes Sidney Lens, "Bolshevism was a cool rain after a long dry
spell . . . there was hardly a radical meeting, whether Socialist, anarchist or IWW where the mere mention of Soviet Russia did not bring
deafening applause."[74]

Not all Ukrainian socialists, of course, were taken in by the Bolshevik hysteria. Some, like Myroslav Sichynsky, left the UFSPA and
formed Defense of Ukraine (*Oborony Ukrayiny*) in 1922. By 1923, Defense of Ukraine was publishing its own newspaper and within a few
years had functioning chapters in various Ukrainian communities, including Chicago. Enjoying the support of the UWA, Defense continued
to show promise in the 1920s, but by 1939 it was largely a paper organization kept together by the UWA and a handful of die-hard members scattered throughout the United States.[75] The socialists, the Old
Left, once the guiding ideological light in the Ukrainian stream, were
slowly fading from the political arena.

In 1920 the Ukrainian Communists began publishing *Ukrayinskiy
Shchodynniy Visti* (Ukrainian Daily News)[76]—America's first *daily*
Ukrainian-language newspaper—and by 1923 they felt sufficiently confident of their credibility to appeal to a broad segment of the Ukrainian
community. The vehicle by which they were to promulgate their program was the "Congress of Toilers." In their appeal for new members,
the Communists criticized all of the efforts of the Ukrainian nationalist
camp and attempted to convince the Ukrainian worker that all of his
financial and moral sacrifices during the war years were a waste of time,
a hoax perpetrated by the Ukrainian clergy and the nationalist leadership to keep him in bondage. For many Ukrainians the appeal, coming
as it did on the heels of the Council of Ambassadors' decision to permit
continued Polish rule of eastern Galicia, struck a responsive chord.
Even Dr. Simenovych initially favored the aims of the Congress of
Toilers. In the end, the Congress conveners were able to boast of having delegates from church brotherhoods as well as *Sich* and *Prosvita*

branches, organizations that were usually included on the conservative side of the political ledger.

Held in New York City on April 13-14, 1924, the Congress gave birth to the *Soyuz Ukrayinskikh Robitnyshikh Organizatsiy* (the United Ukrainian Toiler's Organizations, hereafter referred to as SURO).[77] Various branches of SURO were established throughout the United States, and the Chicago branch, which organized lectures, reading rooms, a choir, and a dance group, became one of the most active. By 1928, Ukrainian Communists in Chicago were affluent enough to build a two-story Workers' Home at the corner of Chicago and Campbell.[78]

During the 1930s the Ukrainian Communists established another national organization, an affiliate of the International Workers' Order (IWO) and billed as a "fraternal-benefit insurance society for the laboring class." The first Ukrainian IWO branch (no. 1501) was created in Chicago in January 1932; by 1938 the national Ukrainian IWO membership had grown to over 15,000, of whom 20 percent were children.[79] In Chicago both SURO and the Ukrainian IWO were housed in the Ukrainian Workers' Home. The building was also the home of the Ukrainian Women's Education Society, *Lesya Ukrayinka*, and had a total membership of "between 350 and 400" people. Dramas, choir singing, and Ukrainian dancing were all part of the home's cultural offering.[80]

Ukrainian Communists in Chicago and elsewhere never wavered in their support of Soviet rule in Ukraine. "Sovereignty," they argued in 1939, was guaranteed by the Stalinist Constitution, which makes it possible for all Soviet republics, "of their own free will," to belong to "the brotherly family of Soviet nationalities which exists on the basis of full equality and mutual faith."[81]

Adopting the Popular Front posture in 1936 that the major world struggle was not that of capitalism versus communism but rather of democracy versus fascism, the Communists advanced the notion—accepted at the time by many American liberals—that whatever was "antifascist" was automatically "democratic." Since the Soviet Union was "democratic," only "fascists" could be against it. And included in this latter group were, of course, nationalists of every stripe and hue. Thus the First Congress of the Ukrainian National Front in September 1936 issued a proclamation that declared:

> Let there be unity everywhere under the motto—"Away with Fascism, Fascism is our enemy! . . .
> Away with war, it only hurts the poor. . . .
> Away with the chains of nationalism and socialism.
> We want liberty, bread and peace!"[82]

Hrynevetsky and the Rise of Ukrainian Monarchism in America

The political organization with the greatest strength and influence in the Ukrainian-American nationalist camp all through the 1920s and the early 1930s was the Ukrainian Athletic Association, Sich—later known as the Hetman Sich—the first branch of which was organized by Fr. Strutinsky in 1902. Originally a gymnastic society patterned after the Czech Sokol, Sich gradually evolved into a paramilitary organization which recognized Pavlo Skoropadsky, the former head of the Ukrainian National Republic, as the only legitimate representative of the Ukrainian government-in-exile. As the sole Ukrainian political organization in America that could count on the tacit support of the Ukrainian Catholic Church, Sich was by the early 1930s the most effective political opponent of the Ukrainian Communists.

The metamorphosis of Sich from a nonpartisan athletic society to an ideologically oriented paramilitary organization began in 1918, when Dr. Hrynevetsky, Dr. Simenovych, Fr. Strutinsky, and others managed to convince the U.S. Congress to pass a bill authorizing the creation of a Slavic Legion of "Jugo-Slavs, Czecho-Slovaks, and Ruthenians (Ukrainians) belonging to the oppressed races of the Austro-Hungarian or German empires. . . ."[83] The Ukrainians who supported the legislation were confident that this legion would be the beginning of a Ukrainian liberation army. They were disappointed. Rallies called for the purpose of gaining popular support in the Ukrainian-American community were a failure, resulting in only a handful of recruits, at least one of whom, as Dr. Simenovych once wrote, "was probably trying to get away from his wife." Opposition to the legion came mainly from the Bolsheviks, who at the time had begun to infiltrate the Sich organization. So popular were the Bolsheviks at this time that two Sich branches elected to designate themselves as "Soviet" Siches.

The first Sich branch in Chicago was established in 1917 by Fr. Strutinsky and Dr. Bilyk, and it was here that the dream of a Ukrainian liberation army continued to live.[84] By 1920, Bolshevik influence had been eliminated. That same year the Sich Supreme Executive, headed by "Supreme Ataman" P. Novodvorsky, and the Sich newspaper, *Sichovy Visti*, were moved to Chicago. Reflecting the growing militancy of the organization at this time, Novodvorsky, a veteran of the U.S. army, wrote:

> During the war we honorably and honestly fulfilled our duties toward our American government. . . .
> We gave the American government everything we could to help America win the war. . . .

We spent large sums of money, which we earned by the sweat of our brows, in purchasing American Liberty Bonds. . . .

At the call to the colors by the American government thousands of Ukrainians joined the United States army and shoulder-to-shoulder we fought and shed our blood, helping America to gain victory, glory and power. . . .

The ex-President, Mr. Woodrow Wilson, in the name of the Allies and the American government, solemnly declared that we should go beyond the sea to destroy the aggressive robbers and imperialistic militarists and win independence for all subjugated nations.

Ex-President Wilson, in the name of the American Government, in the name of the American people, solemnly declared before the whole world that we would fight for justice and that all subjugated nations would get their freedom and independence.

We sincerely believed that ex-President Wilson meant what he said and would show himself to be a great and just man. We believed that when he spoke in the name of all of the American people that he would fulfill all promises to the letter.

But President Wilson shamelessly did not keep his promise to us. For our sincere loyalty and our great sacrifices . . . he paid us back with a terrible injustice. . . .

Although President Wilson and the Allies promised justice and independence for all subjugated nations, Mr. Wilson was the first one who ruthlessly stepped upon us and permitted the savage Polish bandits to murder the Ukrainian people and to pillage and plunder our Ukrainian land. . . .

We cannot keep silent! We can no longer plead!

We American Ukrainians have a full right not to ask but to demand that the American government right this wrong![85]

At the IVth Sich convention in Cleveland (May 28–30, 1922) Hrynevetsky was elected to the post of Supreme Ataman of Sich, and a decision was reached to change the title of each Sich branch to *sotnya* (company) and to endow each branch head with the military rank of *sotnik* (captain).[86] Sich assumed an increasingly military character.

Late in 1923, Dr. Osyp Nazaruk arrived in Chicago to become editor of *Sichovi Visty*. A former member of the Western Ukrainian diplomatic mission in Canada, Nazaruk, initially a supporter of Petlura, was one of the few postwar Ukrainian intellectuals to adopt the monarchist ideology. Hrynevetsky welcomed Nazaruk, and as their organizational contacts became more and more frequent the two became close personal friends. It was during this period that Nazaruk convinced Hrynevetsky that the next logical step in the evolution of Sich was for the organization to accept the idea of monarchy—a Ukrainian Hetman. As Nazaruk later admitted, both he and Hrynevetsky were aware that, given the poor reputation of the monarchists in America (monarchism was viewed as antidemocratic among most Ukrainians, as well as among Americans in general), the political transformation would not be an easy task.[87]

At the Vth Sich convention held in Philadelphia on May 30, 1924, despite a long promonarchist speech by Nazaruk, it was evident, on the basis of the poor attention of the delegates and their frequent moving about, that the time had not come to push the monarchist perspective.[88] Hrynevetsky pressed another objective, the consolidation of power in the office of the Supreme Ataman. In this he was successful. The convention passed a series of resolutions which, among other things, gave Hrynevetsky the authority to appoint all company commanders and extended his term of office to three years. Still retaining their political neutrality, the delegates also passed a resolution appealing for support from all segments of the Ukrainian community, except the discredited "Little Russians or Little Poles—who . . . are undependable when the chips are down."[89]

Having consolidated his control, Hrynevetsky returned to Chicago and on November 24, 1924, at an impressive ceremony during which

A group of non-commissioned Sich officers posé for a picture at Chicago's St. Nicholas picnic grove in 1931. *Courtesy of Ukrainian National Museum.*

he received his *bulava* (staff of office used by Kozak commanders), he declared his loyalty to Hetman Pavlo Skoropadsky.[90] This move precipitated a crisis in the Sich organization and the eventual loss of hundreds of members. Many others, such as Peter Zadoretsky, Stephen Musiychuk, and Philip Wasylowsky, were unhappy but remained because no political alternative was available.

Despite the ideological crisis precipitated by the monarchists, the Hetman Sich survived and in the years that followed flourished, especially among that segment of the nationalist Ukrainian-American community that was weary of political bickering, was desperate for a charismatic leader to point the way, and still believed that a future Ukrainian army could be trained in America. So potent was the Sich call for order and discipline that even Dr. Simenovych succumbed. Agreeing to serve as interim editor of its organ, *Sich*, the venerable Ukrainian-American agonized over "the lack of program . . . lack of authority . . . lack of direction . . . lack of goals" and told his conationals that, "in order to emerge from chaos, we must accept a clear idea. . . . There is absolutely nothing left but to support the Hetman monarchist idea." "Democracy and self-rule" will lead Ukrainians nowhere. Simenovych warned, for "first we must get our liberty" and then the people will decide what comes next.[91]

In the years that followed, Simenovych's sentiments were echoed time and again in editorials. *Sich* praised the Poles, Lithuanians, Czechs, and other eastern European groups for their ability to forget some of their individual liberties for the sake of a united effort, and it deplored the excessive factionalism and individualism characterized by the following statement:

> We are individualists at all times and under all circumstances of life. A Ukrainian is his own authority.

The call for unity by Sich promoted the monarchist "one idea" to overcome the cacophony of confusion regarding a "free Ukraine" whereby

> each person who made that cry wanted a different Ukraine. Every editor and every newspaper, every meeting, wanted something different but no one knew what they wanted. . . .
>
> In order to eliminate, once and for all, the fighting among our "leaders" where each believes that only he is capable of being the "head" of the people—condemning and defaming all others—Sich in America . . . has said: "Over all parties and leaders there must be one—the Hetman. . . ."

A rival "Democratic Sich" also came in for its hard knocks, because, according to the monarchists,[92]

Democratic Siches are based on demagoguery . . . and will not help our people because they don't teach the value of work, obedience and respect for leadership.

For many Ukrainian Catholic priests, then under attack from Communists, Socialists, the Orthodox, and a growing number of nationally concerned Catholics, the growth of the Hetman Sich was a welcome development. Fr. Tarnowsky, pastor of St. Nicholas Ukrainian Catholic Church, condemned the "infection of socialism" and praised the need for obedience, authority, and discipline by Chicago Ukrainians.

The Hetman Sich did have a program and it did teach—through an elaborate series of educational directives and teaching aids— Ukrainian history, political economics, Ukrainian culture, and, of course, obedience and respect for authority. For the loyal Sich member, the only important institutions were the Church, "the national ectoderm, the mind and nerves of the Ukrainian nation"; the Sich, "the national mesoderm," the fount of the "people's national consciousness"; the School, "the Ukrainian endoderm . . . that institution which supplies bricks for the building of the Ukrainian nation." The Hetman Sich even prescribed a lifestyle for its members, which included self-control, good citizenship, self-education, respect for law and order, solid family life, regard for the spiritual authority of the church, and behavior that reflected favorably on the "Ukrainian national patriotic community."[93]

The Hetman Sich also realized its dream of a Ukrainian army, at least in part. Soon after the Hetman takeover, great efforts were made to completely militarize the organization, even to the point of wearing uniforms. In addition, separate female Sich companies were organized as Red Cross units and taught first-aid techniques. Initially, only military drills and gymnastics were practiced, but later, as the Sich membership grew, field maneuvers were held in various forest preserves, wooded areas, and farm fields. Speaking at one of the early field maneuvers in Chicago, Dr. Hrynevetsky lauded America,

in which we are permitted to cultivate our national spirit and to even have army exercises with our uniformed Sich soldiers without a special police permit.

The lessons from other ethnics also provided guidance, for here in Chicago,

the Lithuanians organized and now they have their own nation. Here the Czechs organized and now they have their own nation. Here the Poles organized and now they have their own nation. Here we are organizing and we are certain we will have our own nation.

Sich military maneuvers soon became one of the most exciting aspects of being a Sich member, especially for the youth. In time, maneuvers were being held throughout the country, and later still joint maneuvers, involving companies from two or three cities, became a regular part of the Sich summer program. Every able Sich member participated, the men as "combatants," the women as field nurses. A full day's program was usually planned, beginning with a field divine liturgy in the morning, military activities in the afternoon, and a gala outdoor dance and social in the evening.

The activities of the Hetman Sich also won favorable attention from the U.S. government authorities. Hoping to bolster what was then a sagging militia, American military officials suggested that Ukrainians form separate militia units of their own, a proposal that was eagerly seized. Among the first to enlist were a number of Chicago Sich members who formed Company B of the 33d Division of the 132d Infantry.[94] Ecstatic with such good fortune, *Sich* bubbled with excitement:

> The United States is the only country in the world where when one becomes a citizen one does not betray his own nation . . . and that is because the American nation is composed of many nations which have joined together to form a common state. . . . There is no other country in the world where when one becomes a citizen one can continue to be a son of his European Fatherland and actively help and fight for it. . . .
>
> By joining the American militia, we shall realize the main aim. i.e., to be the base and the beginning of the new Ukrainian army.[95]

Later, Sich members joined the militia in Cleveland, where they became part of the 112th Engineers, and in Detroit, where they joined a medical support battalion.[96] With specialized training, U.S. Army uniforms and equipment, and the professional supervision of U.S. military personnel. Sich maneuvers took on a new significance. Future issues of *Sich* carried military critiques of the maneuvers, regular militia news pertaining to Ukrainians, such as promotion sheets, excerpts from U.S. military manuals, and news of Sich participation in U.S. Army-sponsored expositions.[97]

The next step in the development of a Ukrainian fighting force was the creation of a Ukrainian "air corps." During the 1930s the Hetman Sich obtained three airplanes—two biplanes, and a four-passenger, single-wing model—naming them, in order of purchase, "Ukraina," "Lviv," and "Kiev."[98] With the purchase of these planes, Sich "air corps" companies and aviation schools were established in Chicago, Cleveland, and Detroit, where the Hetman movement had its largest membership.[99] At the same time, the Hetman press organ, which in 1934 came

United States military authorities, concerned about the poor state of their forces in the 1930s, encouraged the formation of Sich units. Here (on the top steps) a group of American officers prepare to review a parade of Sich Guards near St. Nicholas church. The picture is matted on "Sitch," the official organ of the Ukrainian American Athletic Association of Chicago. *Courtesy of Ukrainian National Museum.*

to be called *Nash Styakh* (Our Banner), began publishing articles on aviation, such as "Who Can Fly" and "Night Flying," as well as general news items concerning the development of the Hetman "air corps."[100]

Leadership problems, however, continued. Following an ideological dispute in 1930, Hrynevetsky renounced his allegiance to Hetman Skoropadsky (then living in Germany), resigned his position within Sich, and was replaced by Alexander Shapoval as Supreme Ataman. During the 1930s the Hetman Sich changed its name to the United

Hetman Organization (UHO) and came under the helm of four different Supreme Atamans, all from Chicago: Shapoval, Dr. Omelian Tarnawsky (a dentist), Nikolai Hul, and Dr. Myroslaw Siemens, a nephew of Simenovych.

Chicago's Ukrainian community, meanwhile, continued to organize rallies and political protest marches, which in the 1930s condemned Soviet and Polish rule in Ukraine. One such march was held on December 17, 1933, to protest the Soviet-induced famine during which seven million Ukrainians eventually perished. Gathering at St. Nicholas, some 3,000 Ukrainians began to march toward Plumber's Union Hall (1340 W. Washington), where a manifestation was scheduled. Along the way they were attacked by Communists who were throwing rocks and wielding lead pipes and brass knuckles. "100 HURT IN W. SIDE RED RIOT," declared the *Chicago Tribune* headline the next day. The nature of the protest was given full coverage in the headline story, which added: "Mainly with the aid of the Ukrainian siege [*sic*] guards who used clubbed rifles, police within five minutes routed the Reds and quelled the fighting."[101] Allowed to continue, the marchers arrived at their destination and called upon the U.S. President, "in view of the recent recognition of the present Russian government," to use his good offices "to alleviate the unbearable suffering and deliberate starvation now prevailing in Ukraine. . . ."[102]

Despite the best efforts of the new leaders to maintain the viability of the UHO, however, Sich began to decline. The primary reason for the loss of strength in the monarchist camp was the emergence of another nationalist model, a different approach being articulated by the Organization of Ukrainian Nationalists (OUN).

The Organization for the Rebirth of Ukraine (ODWU)

The political group that experienced the most phenomenal growth during the 1930s was the Ukrainian Nationalists, who, despite a relatively late organizational start, were by 1938 the largest Ukrainian political group in the anti-Communist camp and in firm control of the largest Ukrainian fraternal organization, the UNA.

The rise of the Ukrainian Nationalists in America began in 1928 with the arrival of Colonel Evhen Konovalets, a former Ukrainian army commander and head of the Ukrainian Military Organization (UVO). His trip, arranged largely through the efforts of Dr. Luka Myshuha, who was to become the editor of *Svoboda* in 1933, had a twofold purpose: to acquaint Konovalets with the Ukrainian-American community, and to create an effective fund-raising vehicle for UVO activities in

Western Ukraine. Konovalets succeeded in his mission. Before his departure, UVO branches were established in a number of American cities, including Chicago.

In 1929, soon after UVO had been transformed into the Organization of Ukrainian Nationalists (OUN) in Europe, Konovalets returned to America to establish a Ukrainian Nationalist organization with broader community appeal than UVO. It was during his second visit to this country that the idea for a new nationalist society, the Organization for the Rebirth of Ukraine (ODWU), came into being. ODWU branches were soon formed throughout the United States, and by the IVth ODWU convention in 1934, some fifty were in existence.[103]

The extraordinary growth of ODWU and the Ukrainian Nationalist Front in America did not come easily. It was opposed every step of the way by the Ukrainian Communists and their newspaper, *Ukrayinski Schchodenniy Visty*, the Ukrainian Workers' Association (UWA)—then headed by Miroslav Sichynsky—and its organ, *Narodna Volya*, and on the right by the United Hetman Organization and its organ, *Nash Styakh*. Not surprisingly, the most scathing attacks came from the Communists, who openly accused all Ukrainian Nationalists of being Nazis and an integral part of Hitler's subversive network in America. *Narodna Volya*, still under socialist influence, accused OUN and ODWU of subscribing to a totalitarian philosophy and suggested that all denials of association with Fascism were "just a camouflage." The monarchists, on the other hand, dismissed the Nationalists as agitators without a program. Neither OUN nor ODWU, they argued, had developed a succinct, long-range political ideology that could unify the Ukrainian people once an independent Ukrainian state was established.[104]

As a vehicle of Ukrainian ethno-national and socio-political education, ODWU, like its Communist, Socialist, and Hetman-monarchist counterparts, was concerned with influencing the thinking of the broad Ukrainian-American community. The ODWU ideology was similar to that of OUN. Arguing that before one could discuss the future of Ukraine one first had to free her, ODWU placed great emphasis on the need to strengthen Ukrainian self-esteem and pride in the aftermath of the debacle of World War I. What was needed, argued both OUN and ODWU, was an organization that could stabilize the ethno-national readiness of the Ukrainian people, enable them to develop their national instincts, cultivate their spiritual and physical strengths, and provide them with the opportunity to take their rightful place among other nations. Such an organization needed a leadership that was uncompromising, iron-strong, willful, and imbued with a noble and ideal spirit which had as its first premise and final objective "the nation, the nation, and once more the nation."[105] For ODWU, such a leadership was found in the OUN *Provid* (Executive), which in the 1930s lived in Germany.

Not to be outdone by the Hetman Sich, ODWU also made a serious attempt to organize an "army" and an "air corps." ODWU uniforms were designed and purchased, and army surplus rifles were obtained for the fledgling force. Later on, ODWU purchased a biplane, appropriately named "Nationalist," and also made an attempt to establish an aviation school.[106]

In Chicago, the first ODWU branch was established in 1930 by Stephen Musiychuk, a former member of Sich, Michael Belegay, and Stephen Kuropas. The moving force behind the Nationalist surge was Kuropas, a former member of the Ukrainian army in Galicia who arrived in Chicago in 1927. With the help of Harry Semochko, Kuropas organized ODWU branches in Chicago-area suburbs and neighborhoods like Elmwood Park, Hansen Park, Burnside, Back of the Yards, and Pullman. As ODWU began to expand throughout the city, other UHO members such as Philip Wasylowsky, a UHO company commander, left the monarchist fold to become active in the new organization.[107]

With radicalism in America on the increase in the 1930s and with the ideological diatribes of the Left enjoying greater and more favorable exposure in legitimate American political and social journals, the term "nationalist" gradually came to be associated with all that was reactionary, totalitarian, and self-serving in the arena of political progress. For the Communists, and for many of their liberal supporters, nationalism had become synonymous with Fascism.

Ukrainian-American Communists, as well as other left-leaning Ukrainian-American groups, were fond of labeling the Ukrainian Nationalist camp as Fascist-inspired, undemocratic, and even subversive. Given the American climate, these allegations proved to be increasingly threatening, especially during the late 1930s, when the unrelenting Communist barrage first began to have a decided effect on the future development of this segment of the Ukrainian-American community. Especially vulnerable were ODWU and its affiliates, a self-proclaimed Nationalist alliance.

In an attempt to counter Communist allegations and to promulgate their political approach ODWU executives began a concerted effort to reach the American public. Beginning in 1939, ODWU took over the publication and editorship of *The Trident*, an English-language publication begun in Chicago by the Young Ukrainian Nationalists (MUN). At the IXth ODWU convention that same year, the delegates loudly professed their support for democratic freedoms, condemned the Soviet oppression of their kinfolk, and repudiated the "baseless" smear that they engaged in "un-American activities and ideas." Denouncing the "Hetmanci" (monarchists), the "Social Radicals," the "Russian Socialists," and the "Stalinist expositors" as groups that "have recorded themselves in the history of the Ukrainian immigration in the United States as enemies of the Ukrainian Liberation Movement," the delegates also turned their attention to foreign affairs and passed a number of resolutions, including one denying any foreign entanglements and asserting that

> the Ukrainian Independence Movement is based on no foreign ideologies, or international blocs, and especially it has nothing in common with the ideologies which now predominate in Germany and Italy.[108]

Beginning in 1934, Chicago ODWU branches began sponsoring an annual "Nationalist Day," complete with Ukrainian cooking, dancing, choir singing, and the crowning of a Ukrainian queen. One of the more successful of these days was held on May 30, 1937, in Harms Park (4200 W. Western Avenue). According to a *Chicago Herald and Examiner* reporter who covered the event, "nearly 5,000 Chicagoans of Ukrainian descent . . ." were in attendance.[109]

The Dies Committee and Its Aftermath

The unceasing Communist attack on the Nationalists and the UHO finally took its toll when both organizations came under the investigation of a special House Un-American Activities Committee headed by Congressman Martin Dies (D., Tex.). Called to testify concerning Ukrainian-American organizational life was Emil Revyuk, an associate editor of *Svoboda* who confirmed that both the UHO and ODWU were associated with Ukrainian organizations in Germany, wore uniforms, had leaders who once attended a German *Bund* meeting in America, had members who received letters from Germany and had praised Mussolini's Italy in 1933, had airplanes, were once under the national leadership of reserve officers in the U.S. Army—Siemens of the UHO and Gregory Herman of ODWU—had members who worked in munitions plants in the United States, and had publications that occasionally published articles criticizing the "democratic process." After hearing only one witness, and despite numerous attempts to lead the witness, improper translations of OUN communiqués, contradictory testimony, and largely hearsay evidence—most of Revyuk's replies began with "People told me that . . ." or "I believe that . . ." or "He told me that . . ."—Congressman Dies concluded that all of the testimony fit into a neat and tight pattern. At the end of Revyuk's appearance before his committee, Dies declared:

> Here are organizations that have shown to be nothing in the world but agencies of foreign powers. That is all they are under their own admission. They provide an elaborate espionage system in this country. . . .[110]

The Chicago Daily News reported on the testimony with a headline that read: "NAZI GROUPS WOO UKRAINIANS . . . KING ALREADY CHOSEN."[111] And so another era in Chicago's Ukrainian history came to an end.

Unfortunately for the Ukrainian-American community, the political *Zeitgeist* of America had changed considerably during the Roosevelt era. "Saving the world from Fascism" had gradually replaced "self-determination for all nations" as the principal clause in American foreign policy. The Popular Front was calling the Soviet Union a "democracy," and many leading Americans were agreeing. While it had been perfectly "American" for Masaryk and Paderewski to come to the United States during the Wilson era and to agitate on behalf of the dismemberment of the Austro-Hungarian empire, similar agitation for the dismemberment of the Soviet empire by Ukrainian-American political leaders was viewed as "anti-democratic" by some Americans during the Roosevelt era. While it had been perfectly legitimate to raise "liberation armies" in America during the Wilson era, similar efforts during the Roosevelt era were not. In time, the paramilitary activities of UHO and ODWU—as well as association with Ukrainian political leaders who lived in Germany, favorable comments concerning Hitler's adoption of the Wilsonian self-determination model, even correspondence received from Germany—were enough to convince some Americans that a Fascist conspiracy existed in the Ukrainian-American community. Summoned into the national headlines by the House Un-American Activities Committee, then headed by Congressman Martin Dies, Ukrainians stood accused of Fascist ties on the basis of hearsay evidence, and both organizations were subsequently maligned by the American press as subversive. Thus, the Ukrainian-American community's first attempt to actively pursue an objective expressed by the national will ended in political disaster.

Although no Ukrainian was ever arrested, let alone tried for espionage, the negative publicity precipitated by the Dies Committee's investigation damaged the UHO, ODWU, and even the UNA, which had many ODWU members in its Supreme Assembly. In the words of Stephen Kuropas:

It was a very difficult time. We were all confused and disillusioned. The Bolsheviks had tricked us and the Americans. We loved
America and we knew that the American government had always
supported national self-determination. We also loved Ukraine. We
didn't then and we still don't believe that we were doing anything
that was un-American. On the contrary, had America listened to us,
she would not have its present problems with the Soviet Union.[112]

The Religious Response

Political debates were not the only source of friction within the
Ukrainian-American community during this period. A related conflict—
also tied to the preservation of Ukrainianism in America—emerged in
the religious arena when a viable national alternative was offered
Ukrainian Americans in the form of the Ukrainian Orthodox Church.

The establishment of Ukrainian national churches after the founding of the Erie Street Canal proceeded slowly after 1915. By 1919,
there were only six such churches functioning in the United States,
leaving most Ukrainians well within the Catholic fold.

In 1922, Deacon Paul Korsunowsky of the Ukrainian Autocephalous Orthodox Church in Ukraine—an independent church created during the halcyon days of the republic—arrived in America and, in a
series of meetings with the national church leadership, convinced them
to accept Ukraine's newly established church and to petition Kievan
Orthodox Metropolitan Vasyl Lypkiwsky for a bishop. The request was
made and honored and, on February 13, 1924, Bishop John Theodorovich arrived in the United States. Settling in Chicago, Bishop Theodorovich was formally installed as America's first Ukrainian Orthodox
bishop in June. At the time, his diocese consisted of eleven parishes,
8,500 faithful and fourteen priests.[113] Later, as the number of Ukrainian
Orthodox parishes increased, Bishop Theodorovich moved his episcopal seat to Philadelphia.

The Holy See, meanwhile, decided to formalize an earlier decision
to split the late Bishop Ortynsky's eparchy into two jurisdictions—one
for the Carpatho-Ukrainians (who continued to call themselves Rusins)
and one for the Ukrainians—and appointed two bishops to serve Uniate
Catholics in America. On September 1, 1924, Bishop Basil Tkach arrived in the United States to take charge of a Rusin eparchy consisting
of 155 parishes, 129 priests, and 288,290 faithful. He was accompanied
by Bishop Bohachevsky whose Ukrainian eparchy included 144 parishes, 102 priests, and 237,445 faithful.[114]

Within two years after his arrival, Bohachevsky found himself in the center of one of the most prolonged and bitter controversies in the history of the Ukrainian-American community. Believing that the introduction of certain Roman Catholic traditions was essential to the survival of the Ukrainian Catholic Church in America, Bohachevsky decided to enforce a recent Rome-ordained celibacy decree for Uniate Catholic clergy in America and to encourage the adoption of the Gregorian calendar, the stations of the cross, the rosary, May devotions of the Blessed Virgin Mary and other purely Latin rite practices by Ukrainian Catholics throughout America. Angered by what they perceived to be a conscious attempt on the part of their bishop to denationalize their church, a group of lay and clerical leaders came together in Philadelphia and, on December 26, 1926, formed the so-called "Committee for the Defense of the Greek Catholic Church in America."[115] The first resolution passed at the conclave was a demand upon Rome to recall Bohachevsky.[116] Supporting the dissidents was *Svoboda* which praised the Philadelphia congress by writing:

> Ukrainian Catholics demonstrated that they have learned much from the democratic principles they have seen in operation in this country, a land in which they have found not only a piece of bread but knowledge and a new outlook on life and the world as well. The congress demonstrated that no longer can an autocratic church, which recognizes only blind obedience, count on the Ukrainian serf.[117]

Rome, of course, supported Bohachevsky and after all the smoke had cleared, most of the twenty-six priests who had initially resisted Bohachevsky recanted their opposition and reaffirmed their fidelity.[118] A minority group of priests, however, decided to leave the Catholic Church and form a second Ukrainian Orthodox diocese. On April 9, 1929, nine clergy and thirty-four lay representatives met in Allentown, Pennsylvania, to form the "Ukrainian Orthodox Diocese of America" under the leadership of Rev. Joseph Zhuk who became bishop-elect.[119]

Both Orthodox groups grew as a result of Catholic defections during the next few years. By 1939, Bishop Theodorovich's Autocephalous Orthodox Diocese consisted of 24 parishes and 22 priests[120] while the Ukrainian Orthodox Diocese of America that same year claimed 43 parishes and 36 priests.[121]

Chicago, like other Ukrainian-American communities, was deeply affected by the religious turmoil which erupted during the late 1920s. The most serious rift occurred at Sts. Peter and Paul in Burnside, which had a history of dissension dating back to 1917 when some 70 Ukrainian families left to form a fourth Ukrainian Catholic parish in the Chicagoland area—St. Michael's—in West Pullman. In 1928, largely as a result of the Bohachevsky controversy, Sts. Peter and Paul became a

Ukrainian national church and, in time, joined the Ukrainian Orthodox Diocese of America.[122] Another Ukrainian Catholic church, St. Basil's, was eventually established in Burnside by those parishioners who had elected to remain Ukrainian Catholic.

Not all Ukrainian Christians in Chicago became embroiled in the Catholic-Orthodox debate. A small Ukrainian Baptist community was formed in the city in 1915 and remained totally divorced from the religious struggle that erupted in later years.[123]

The American Born

During the 1920s when most American-born Ukrainians were still relatively young, the major vehicle of Ukrainianization was the *Ridna Shkola*. In this regard, St. Nicholas had an outstanding record, especially after the arrival in 1922 of Dmytro Atamanec, a dynamic *diak-uchytel* who was able to increase the ethnic school enrollment to 520 by 1924.[124]

Efforts to build a full-time day school for Ukrainian youth at St. Nicholas were initiated in 1923,[125] and by 1926 *Sich* was able to report that $12,000 had been collected for construction.[126] After more years of fund raising, seriously hampered by the Depression, St. Nicholas Elementary School finally opened its doors in 1935.[127]

In the 1930s, as it became apparent that many of the *Ridna Shkola* graduates and other American-born youth were avoiding involvement in Ukrainian-American community affairs, a certain sense of urgency, even panic, began to emerge among members of the older generation.

The gravity of the youth problem was analyzed by Dr. Simenovych shortly before his death in an article entitled "Why Your Youth Don't Care." Outlining the nature of the problem and its causes, the Chicago pioneer wrote:

> Among our older organizations involved with political work we see very few young people.
>
> In large measure we ourselves are to blame because we still believe that an older person, even without the slightest education, is wiser and more worthy of leadership than a younger person with a higher education.
>
> An older person has more dignity and experience but a young person has more education and views life with wider horizons. Let's bring in our youth, let's give them some of our work, let's give them an opportunity to develop themselves in our midst as Ukrainian patriots; only then will our task be easier and only then will we double our progress. If we do this we will help our cause now and we will keep our youth with us.[128]

Responding to the need for greater youth involvement, every political and religious society embarked on an ambitious program that resulted in the formation of a number of organizations for teenage and older youth. Many were either founded in Chicago or had their national executive located in the city.

Meanwhile, the Communists stepped up their efforts to maintain an influential position in the community by forming youth affiliates with the IWO.[129] In 1931, the Hetman Sich, which had many young people in its ranks in the 1920s, decided to form "Junior Siege" clubs in affiliation with their adult cadres.[130]

That same year Sich began to publish *Siege Youth,* an English-language news magazine.[131] Under the leadership of Fr. John Hundiak, a "Young Ukraine" English-language section was introduced in *Dnipro,* the Autocephalous Orthodox Church organ, and, in 1932, the Ukrainian Orthodox Diocese of America organized the "League of Ukrainian Clubs" for its youth.[132] ODWU created the "Young Ukrainian Nationalists" (MUN) in 1933. The Chicago MUN branch began to publish in 1935 *Trident,* an English-language journal.[133] The UNA decided to publish an English-language supplement to *Svoboda* entitled *The Ukrainian Weekly* in 1932.[134] The editor, Stephen Shumeyko, became the driving force behind America's first Ukrainian Youth Congress in 1933. A total of 85 delegates representing eleven states and four Canadian provinces came to Chicago during the World's Fair and gave birth to the Ukrainian Youth League of North America (UYLNA).[135] Not to be outdone, the Catholic Church chose to organize their own national youth organization in Chicago at the same time. After divine liturgy at St. Nicholas, some 100 delegates retreated to the church basement and established the Ukrainian Catholic Youth League (UCYL).[136] The UCYL began publishing *Ukrainian Youth* in English and Ukrainian in 1934.[137]

All of the youth organizations established during the 1930s managed to attract young people with programs that included choir singing, Ukrainian dancing, and the formation of various athletic teams. The one unfortunate aspect of the effort, however, was that in most instances, youth involvement included the somewhat narrow and often dogmatic approach to Ukrainianism of the parent organization. This seriously reduced the pool of potential marriage partners since Catholics were expected to marry Catholics, Orthodox, Orthodox, and so on. Political loyalties were also a factor in dating as evidenced by an interview conducted by John Zadrozny with a young Communist in Chicago in 1945:

> You know those Ukrainians on Western Avenue—those right-wingers, those fascists—they want the good old days back again. They want the rich land owning class to come back into power in

Ukraine. Everybody knows that they want a reactionary government back in power. . . .

I went to the Ukrainian Civic Center to a "shindig" they had there once. I felt as if I was invading the camp of the enemy—no kidding. I hate 'em. After the dance, I took one of those fascist dames home from there, and we were passing this building, I asked her as if I didn't know,

"By the way, what is this place?"

And she said, "Oh, that's the People's Auditorium; that's where the Bolsheviks hang out."

Boy, I'm telling you, if she had known who she was being walked home by, I'm sure she would have died.[138]

Ukrainian Organized Life

There is an old Ukrainian saying that "when two Ukrainians get together, there are three political parties represented and when three meet, one has the beginnings of a choir." Never reticent to form, as Ukrainians say, "shche udnu organizatsiyu" (one more organization), Chicago's Ukrainians could list a total of 113 separate organizations, societies, and clubs in 1935. When one considers the fact that there were, according to statistical data compiled by Dr. Simenovych in 1930 and updated by Stephen Kuropas in 1935, approximately 41,000 first- and second-generation Ukrainians living in Cook County at that time and that some 57 percent, according to Kuropas, were not members of any Ukrainian organization, then only some 17,630 were what Ukrainians would call "organized."[139]

While many organized Ukrainians in the city were intimately involved with the political and religious life of their community, many more were not. The typical Ukrainian attended the church of his choice and belonged to one of our fraternal societies—the UNA, the UWA, the Providence Association, or the Ukrainian National Aid Association (Narodna Pomich). Concerned about the future of Ukraine and their community in America, they tended nevertheless to remain on the periphery of the turmoil and conflict which many community leaders seemed to relish. The majority of Chicago's Ukrainians preferred to cultivate and express their Ukrainianism in other ways, most often in activities that were culturally oriented.

THE CULTURAL RESPONSE

Ukrainian cultural life developed early in Chicago with two choirs already in existence by 1909 when the Nicholas Lysenko Singing Society and the Ukrainian Singing Society "Sitch" were established. The former was organized by Fr. Strutinsky and Michael Kostiuk and was associated with St. Nicholas Church. The latter was organized by Natalie Hrynevetsky and was affiliated with the Ukrainian National Club, "Sitch."

During the 1920s, Ukrainian cultural life continued to evolve under the leadership of such talented choir directors as Dymtro Atamanec—who also developed drama troupes in his role as *diak-uchytel* at St. Nicholas—and by the 1930s, Chicago's Ukrainian community could boast of numerous choral ensembles, dance groups, drama clubs, bands, and orchestras which enhanced the cultural life of the community. Performing at various *sviatos* (commemorative assemblies) honoring Ukraine's Declaration of Independence (January), the birthday of Taras Shevchenko (March), Western Ukrainian Independence Day (November), as well as at carnivals, balls, picnics, and other festivals, these groups helped sustain the ethno-cultural traditions of Chicago's maturing Ukrainian society.

Ukrainian musicals such as "Kateryna,"[140] "Zaporozhets Za Dunayem,"[141] and "The Fair at Soroschintzi"[142] became annual events along with art exhibits,[143] band concerts under the direction of John Barabash[144] and Stanley Sabor[145] and dance festivals under the leadership of M. Darkowicz[146] and the famed Vasili Avramenko, the "father" of Ukrainian dance in America. Arriving in the United States in 1928, Avramenko dedicated his life to the establishment of dance groups in various Ukrainian-American communities as well as in Canada. His most notable achievement in Chicago was a Ukrainian Festival he helped to organize at the Civic Opera House on November 8, 1932, during which some 200 young dancers, all local talent, performed.[147] Dramas such as "Marusia Bohuslavka,"[148] Gogol's "Inspector General,"[149] and "Verkhouynchi"[150] were also part of the cultural fare offered Chicago's Ukrainians.

A high point of Ukrainian cultural life in Chicago was reached during the early 1930s when the Ukrainian Chorus of Chicago was established. Entering the choral competition associated with the Chicagoland Music Festival, the Ukrainian Chorus won first place three times, twice under the direction of George Benetzky (1930 and 1932) and once under the direction of Leontyn Sorochinsky (1931).[151] The chorus came to be known throughout Chicago, performing at Soldier's Field, the Chicago Stadium, the Studebaker Theater, and Kimball Hall as well as over the national NBC radio network. Reflecting upon one such performance in 1932, *Chicago Daily News* music critic Eugene Stinson wrote:

> The Ukrainian Chorus of Chicago sang once more last night . . . and revived all the favorable recollections centering in its earlier appearances here. In its balance and discipline, as in its tone quality, it is one of the best choruses to be heard in America. . . .

One of the cultural highlights of Chicago's Ukrainian community was the famed Lysenko Chorus, which won first place three times in choral concerts sponsored by the Chicago *Tribune. Courtesy of Katherine Domauchuk-Baran.*

> Mr. Benetzky plans his effects admirably. . . . His chorus sings with abundant contrast and with beautifully shaded expressiveness. It remains a musical instrument. And, therefore, with the charm of its shrewdly selected folk material it combines the precision and authenticity of a formal work of art.
>
> Chicago's music is more than 50 percent dependent upon the foreign born element of its population. Among all the European American groups at work here the Ukrainians, with their chorus, take a very high place.[152]

In praising the Ukrainian Chorus in 1933, Herman Devries, another well-known Chicago music critic, wrote:

> There is nothing but praise to write, nothing but pleasant memories to treasure of the Ukrainian Chorus and its remarkably talented director, George Benetzky.
>
> Hearing it yesterday . . . gave us renewed faith in the musical future of Chicago, for with such resources . . . we need not beg nor insist upon a place among centers of culture.
>
> It is ours by right.[153]

Continuing the Chicago Ukrainian musical tradition was still another group of talented singers under the direction of Sam Czuba. Calling themselves the Young Cossack Chorus, this fine ensemble won second place in the Chicagoland Music Festival in 1933.[154]

The Chicago World's Fair

The zenith of Chicago's pioneer Ukrainian history, however, the one effort which more than any other united all segments of the nationalist community, was the planning and construction of a Ukrainian pavilion at Chicago's World Fair in 1933.

Plans to celebrate Chicago's 100th anniversary with a "Century of Progress" fair and exhibition were greeted by Chicago's Ukrainians as a rare opportunity to better acquaint America with Ukraine and her people. Forming a bi-partisan committee headed by Dr. Myroslaw Siemens, Stephen Kuropas, Taras Shpikula, and Jurij Nebor, Ukrainians in Chicago went to work early in 1932 and on June 25, 1933 opened a pavilion which included a restaurant, an open-air theater, an entrance hall, and two larger halls, one devoted to history, the other to culture.[155] The highlight of the cultural section—divided into folk and modern art—was the exhibition of the world-famous Ukrainian sculptor Alex-

During the period of 1884 to 1939 the Ukrainian people matured from an ethno-cultural group into a politically self-conscious nationality. The Ukrainian Pavilion at the World's Fair in 1933 sharply symbolizes their national self-consciousness. *Courtesy of M. B. Kuropas.*

ander Archipenko.[156] To the delight of the Ukrainian community, the pavilion attracted some 1,800,000 visitors[157]—many of whom, presumably, learned much about a people still waiting for the day when their national will could be realized once and forever.

Summary and Conclusion

The six decades between 1884 and 1940 were years of ethno-national maturation for the Ukrainian people both in Ukraine and in the United States. It was during this crucial period that Ukraine's Rusins were transformed from a religio-cultural people to a politically conscious nationality.

In America, the national metamorphosis occurred in two phases. Prior to World War I, the emphasis was on the preservation of a religio-cultural heritage which was uniquely and irrevocably Ukrainian. This end was achieved when an autonomous Ukrainian Catholic eparchy was established in 1913.

The tempering of the Ukrainian identity took place during the 1920s and 1930s. Three major ideological groups—the Communists, the Monarchists, and the Nationalists—emerged to compete for the political loyalty of Chicago's Ukrainians. Each camp presented its own reasons for the rise and fall of the Ukrainian National Republic and each offered a different plan for the realization of Ukrainian national aspirations.

Having established a new ethno-national identity in America, Ukrainians were determined to preserve it. Perceiving their church to be a symbol of their national identity, they were incensed by the introduction of certain external changes in the Ukrainian Catholic Church during the 1920s which they believed were designed to "Latinize" their faith. A number of Catholic parishes, including Sts. Peter and Paul in Chicago, joined the Ukrainian Orthodox Church in protest.

Following World War II, a third Ukrainian immigration arrived in Chicago and the community experienced a cultural and national revival. The Communists and Monarchists all but disappeared from the Ukrainian political scene and the Nationalists, now divided among three rival factions of the Organization of Ukrainian Nationalists (OUN), became the dominant force.

An increase in Chicago's Ukrainian population resulted in the need for new parishes. In 1956, the indefatigable Fr. Joseph Shary arrived in the city, mobilized a number of second- and third-generation Ukrainian Chicagoans, and established St. Joseph's Ukrainian Catholic parish on the Northwest side. A magnificent new church, which combines traditional and modern trends in current Ukrainian church architecture, was completed in 1977 on Cumberland Road near Lawrence. Meanwhile, within five years after establishing a new parish in the city, Fr. Shary organized the Immaculate Conception parish in Palatine, Illinois, to meet the spiritual needs of the increasing number of Ukrainian families who were purchasing homes in the Northwest suburbs.

In 1961, Chicago's prestige as a center of Ukrainian Catholic life in America was greatly enhanced when the Holy See established an episcopal seat in the city. Msgr. Jaroslaw Gabro, who was born and raised in the city, became the first bishop of the newly created Ukrainian Catholic eparchy.

Religious controversy erupted again when a group of parishioners at St. Nicholas Cathedral objected to the introduction of the Gregorian calendar in their parish. When the change was supported by the bishop, the dissidents, choosing to believe that the change was still another attempt to undermine their ancient religio-cultural heritage, left the parish and in 1974 erected Sts. Volodymyr and Olha, at Oakley and Superior.

Bishop Gabro died in 1980 and was succeeded the following year by Bishop Innocent Lotocky.

Chicago's Ukrainian Orthodox community also experienced a period of growth and expansion following the war. A new church was purchased at Cortez and Oakley in 1946 and rededicated in honor of St. Vladimir. Three new Orthodox parishes—St. Sophia's at 6655 W. Higgins, St. Mary the Protectoress at Iowa and Washtenaw, and Holy Trinity at 1908 N. Humboldt—have been established within recent years along with the first suburban Orthodox parish, St. Andrew's, in Addison, Illinois. In 1969, St. Vladimir's became a cathedral with the creation of a Chicago Ukrainian Orthodox eparchy and the appointment of Fr. Alexander Nowecky as the first bishop. Thus, after a hiatus of almost 50 years, the Ukrainian Orthodox of Chicago once again had a bishop. When Bishop Alexander died, he was succeeded by Bishop Constantine Bagon.

Ukrainian Baptists have prospered as well. Under the leadership of the Rev. Olexa Harbuziuk, Chicago's Ukrainian Baptists—now housed in a church building located on Damen, near Augusta—represent an important segment of Ukrainian religious life in the city.

Today, Chicago's metropolitan area Ukrainian community, now more than 75 years old, is flourishing. With a population of almost 65,000, the resources of the community include two financial institutions (Self-reliance Federal Credit Union and Security Savings and Loan Association), three youth organizations (Plast, ODUM and SUMA), three summer camps for children (two in Wisconsin, one in Illinois), five

Saturday heritage schools for children, a full-time day school at St. Nicholas, the national headquarters of the Ukrainian National Aid Association (*Narodna Pomich*)—a fraternal benefit society which moved from Pittsburgh in 1981—two newspapers—*Nova Zorya* (New Star) and *Ukrayinske Zhittya* (Ukrainian Life)—ten radio programs, three major choirs, three dance groups, two museums (the Ukrainian National Museum and the Ukrainian Museum of Modern Art), and some 96 civic, women's fraternal, professional, and political organizations.

Significantly, religious animosities, once so intense, have subsided. Political clashes, however, are still part of the fiber of Ukrainian-American life.

Ukrainians in Chicago are proud of the vitality of their coummunity, its many achievements, and the fact that the original Ukrainian neighborhood, still centered around Chicago and Oakley, has managed to survive as an urban oasis within Chicago's deteriorating west side. Much has changed since Dr. Simenovych first arrived in the city, but the Ukrainian national spirit is stronger than ever. Like their pioneer predecessors, the Ukrainians of Chicago dearly love the United States but their commitment to the preservation of their ethno-national heritage in America and to the establishment of a free, sovereign, and independent nation-state in Ukraine remains.

Chapter VI

EDWARD R. KANTOWICZ

Polish Chicago:
Survival Through Solidarity

> *A nation . . . is part of nature. A nation is of Divine origin, nor human invention.*
> — Fr. Waclaw Kruszka *(complaining to His Holiness, Pope Pius XI, 1923)*

W HAT PRECISELY IS A POLISH-AMERI-
can? The question is not as thorny as that perpetual puzzler, what is
a Jew? But it occasionally causes confusion. At the first Chicago Con-
sultation on Ethnicity in 1969, a noted urbanologist, expounding on a
series of census maps and tables, concluded that the most heavily Polish neighborhood in Chicago was Rogers Park. But this far north side
neighborhood is populated largely by Polish and other Eastern European *Jews* and is never considered a "Polish neighborhood" by Chicagoans. A meaningful definition of Polish-Americans includes only
Polish Christians.[1]

It is true that the Polish Commonwealth during its heyday in the
late Middle Ages was a multinational state, remarkably tolerant of the
many Jews who fled from persecution in Western Europe. But when,
after the decline and partition of the Polish state, Polish nationalism
arose in the nineteenth century, it was linked very closely with traditional Roman Catholicism. Romantic nationalist writers like Adam
Mickiewicz made a mystic, messianic fusion between God and Nation.

In the United States, Polish-American historians have occasionally
beefed up their filiopietistic lists of great Poles in America with the
names of Polish Jews, like Haym Salomon, a financier of the American
Revolution.[2] But for the most part, though Poles and Polish Jews often
lived close by in American cities, their community histories were separate. No anti-Semitism, simply analytical precision, is intended in excluding Jews from the definition of Polish-Americans.

Counting Polish-Americans is excruciatingly difficult and imprecise. The United States Census Bureau changed its method of enum-
erating immigrants nearly every ten years, sometimes counting only
the foreign-born, at other times including the second generation, "native-born of foreign parentage." No census data includes the third or
subsequent generations of Poles in America. Furthermore, many of the
tables in the 1900 and 1910 censuses, when immigration was at its
peak, contain no listing at all for Poles, counting them instead by their
origin in the partitioning countries of Germany, Austria, and Russia.
Yet by supplementing the federal censuses with other sources, such as
school censuses, it is possible to produce the following population
estimates.

215

TABLE I
POLISH-AMERICANS (1ST AND 2ND GENERATIONS)

	United States	Chicago
1890	250,000	40,000
1910	1,663,808	210,000
1930	3,342,198	401,316

The 400,000 Poles in Chicago in 1930 formed 12 percent of the city's population of 3,376,438. Contemporary guesses for the 1970s place Chicago's Polish population at about 600,000, or roughly 20 percent of Chicagoans. Since at least 1930, Polish-Americans have been Chicago's largest white ethnic group, but they have never approached a majority in the city.

Settlement Patterns: Ethnic Clustering

Polish peasants left the land in the late nineteenth and early twentieth centuries and journeyed to cities in Poland, Germany, and the United States in a search "for bread" (*za chlebem*, in the words of the novelist Sienkiewicz). Their settlement patterns in the United States were largely determined by that search. Most Poles and other turn-of-the-century immigrants settled in the northeastern quarter of the United States, where industry was crying for manpower. But Carol Ann Golab has shown in a survey of fifteen cities from 1870 to 1920 that Polish immigrants, who had only their peasant strength to offer industry, were very selective even within this quadrant. Poles avoided semi-southern cities like Baltimore, Cincinnati, and St. Louis, where large black populations took up the unskilled jobs; they settled sparsely in other cities like Boston and Philadelphia, where light industry demanded mainly skilled labor; but they poured into new, raw cities of heavy industry like Buffalo, Chicago, and the numerous mine and mill towns of Pennsylvania.[4]

Within the city of Chicago, both the search for bread and a desire to find relatively familiar neighbors determined the sites of Polish neighborhoods. By 1890 five large Polish colonies had been settled in Chicago. Each was in an area of heavy industry: Polish Downtown on the northwest side, just west of the Goose Island industrial complex; the Lower West Side, adjacent to many factories along the Burlington Railroad and the ship canal; Bridgeport and Back of the Yards, circling the Union Stock Yards; and South Chicago, hard against the steel mills.

In at least three of these areas the Poles settled among Germans and Bohemians, with whom they were familiar in the old country.[5]

It has been a truism that Poles and other immigrants lived in ethnic clusters or "ghettoes" in American cities; but the term "ghetto" is imprecise and merits a closer look. The Polish settlement pattern was both segregated and decentralized. The segregation can be indicated by a statistical measure, the index of dissimilarity. This index measures the general unevenness of a group's distribution throughout a city. For instance, if Poles were thirty percent of a city's population, a perfectly even distribution would find them forming thirty percent of the population of every ward. This situation would produce an index of zero (0). At the opposite extreme, if all the Poles resided in one ward with no non-Poles present, this situation of perfect segregation would produce an index of 100. The intervening values of the index from 0 to 100, which are the only ones found in reality, give a rough indication of the extent of segregation. In 1898 the Polish index of dissimilarity by wards was fifty-nine; as late as 1930 that index still stood at fifty-five. By way of comparison, the following table gives the index of dissimilarity for most of Chicago's ethnic groups in 1898.

TABLE II
INDEXES OF DISSIMILARITY, BY WARDS, 1898[6]

Russian (Jews)	67	Norwegian	55
Bohemian	64	Danish	43
Italian	61	Swedish	34
"Colored"	60	German	29
Polish	59	Irish	27

Two of the major Polish settlements were overwhelmingly Polish in population. Polish Downtown, near Division and Ashland Avenues, was a classic ghetto. In 1898 eleven precincts in this neighborhood formed a contiguous area, about three-quarters of a mile long and a half mile wide, which was 86.3 percent Polish. One precinct in the heart of this area was 99.9 percent Polish, with only one non-Pole among 2,500 inhabitants. A total of 24,374 Poles—25 percent of all the Poles in the city—lived in just these eleven precincts. Two of the largest Catholic parishes in the world, St. Stanislaw Kostka and Holy Trinity, served the Poles of this neighborhood. Headquarters for three Polish-language daily papers and the two largest Polish fraternal organizations were located here. Polish Downtown was to Chicago Poles what the Lower East Side was to New York's Jews. The Polish area near the steel mills of South Chicago also had a high Polish population dominance: four precincts forming an arc around the gates of the mills were

72.4 percent Polish in 1898. The other three Polish clusters were not as heavily dominated by Poles; each was less than 50 percent Polish.[7]

But if Poles were segregated in clusters, the clusters themselves were decentralized and scattered. Slightly less than half the Poles lived on the northwest side of Chicago; the rest resided in the four other large colonies on the west and south sides, or in several smaller clusters which formed along railroad lines near industries.[8]

Other immigrant groups at the turn of the century showed similar settlement patterns. Each ethnic group settled in at least one classic ghetto and a series of smaller, less dominated clusters. All were highly segregated, but some groups were not as decentralized as the Poles; for instance, 78 percent of the Bohemians lived in a narrow corridor on the west side. The two largest Bohemian neighborhoods, Pilsen and Ceske Kalifornia, were each about 77 percent Bohemian.[9] Three wards of the near west side contained over three-quarters of all Russian Jews in the city in 1898. Four precincts at the heart of the area had a Russian Jewish dominance of nearly 75 percent. The area around Hull House contained about a third of all Italians in the city. An L-shaped area of five contiguous precincts near Hull House had 63 percent Italian dominance.

Poles, then, clearly shared a common experience with other immigrants. Demographic mixing, where it took place, did not generally lead to social mixing. The process of community-building in Polish neighborhoods produced a social and cultural ghetto.[10]

Building a Polish Community

The process of community-building is probably the best-known aspect of Polish-American history, thanks to the monumental sociological work by William I. Thomas and Florian Znaniecki in *The Polish Peasant in Europe and America*. Polish immigrants built a complex of community institutions at the neighborhood level, re-creating in part the milieu of the peasant village they had left behind. The Polish communities in Chicago approached very closely what one sociologist has called "institutional completeness."[11] This meant that the Polish ethnic group supported such a wide range of institutions that it could perform nearly all the services its members required—religious, educational, political, recreational, economic—without recourse to the host society.

The process of community-building generally began, ironically, with thoughts of death. The Polish peasant who was uprooted to Chicago, far from the village churchyard where his ancestors lay, worried about his own final resting-place. The first mutual aid societies formed by Polish immigrants were mainly death-benefit societies. A tiny yearly payment of a dollar or two ensured that when an industrial worker succumbed to disease or occupational hazard, his wife would receive a payment sufficient to bury him properly.

These local mutual-aid societies, often composed of individuals from the same village in Poland, quickly proliferated and took on additional functions. They provided social life for the immigrants, many had religious overtones, and others formed to promote specific activities like community singing or needlework. A particularly important form of mutual aid was provided by the building and loan associations. Land-hunger, a prime motive force in Polish peasant communities, was translated into the urge to buy one's own home in Chicago. While the Bohemians made the most extensive use of building and loan associations, these cooperative institutions were significant in the Polish communities as well. An association member made regular payments of fifty cents or a dollar per week for a number of years to build up a down payment, and the association supplemented this accumulation with a low interest loan when the member actually purchased his home. By 1900, Polish building and loan societies held assets approaching one million dollars.[12]

A local society usually took the next step in the community-building process by founding a Catholic parish. The Catholic Poles worshipped at first in Bohemian or German churches, like St. Wenceslaus on the west wide, or St. Michael's on the north; but before long the Poles organized churches of their own. A society of laymen formed under the patronage of some Polish saint obtained contributions from their countrymen in the neighborhood, purchased a piece of property, and then asked the bishop to help them find a Polish-speaking priest. Thus the first Polish community in Chicago, which had been pioneered by Anton Smarzewski-Schermann in 1851, organized the St. Stanislaw Kostka Society in 1864 under the leadership of Smarzewski-Schermann and Peter Kiolbassa. They formally petitioned the bishop for a priest in 1867, and St. Stanislaw Kostka parish built a small frame church and received a resident pastor in 1869. This process of lay initiative and episcopal approval was repeated in every settlement of Poles; but after this pioneering effort the time lag between the founding of a church-building society and the actual foundation of a parish was generally only a year or two. Eventually, forty-three Polish Catholic churches were founded in the city of Chicago and eighteen more in the suburbs and outlying cities included in the Archdiocese of Chicago.[13]

Local societies were both the cause and effect of the parish-building process. Once a Polish church arose in a neighborhood, some pre-existing societies affiliated with it and numerous others organized.

Community-building: Polish thrift encouraged in bank ads. *Courtesy of the Polish Museum, Chicago.*

Thomas and Znaniecki counted seventy-four parish societies at St. Stanislaw Kostka in 1919, ranging from the Needlework Club of St. Rose of Lima to the Court of Frederic Chopin.

The most important adjunct of a Polish parish was the parochial school. At the Third Plenary Council of Baltimore in 1884, the American bishops had decreed that every church should be accompanied by a school. In Chicago, under Archbishops Feehan, Quigley, and Mundelein, the school was often built first, with church services held in the basement until a more suitable house of worship could be built later. Yet not every parish responded to the Church's call for parochial education. In particular, Italian Catholics saw little reason not to utilize the free public schools. In 1910 only one of the ten Italian parishes in Chicago had a school. But the Poles responded more enthusiastically than most. The Resurrectionist Fathers, who administered St. Stanislaw and several other Polish parishes, not only built large elementary schools but also founded St. Stanislaw College in 1890 as a collegiate preparatory school. By the 1920s every Polish parish in the city and suburbs had its accompanying school. Attendance at Polish parochial schools in 1920 was 36,862, roughly 60 percent of Polish youth between the ages of seven and seventeen. No other Catholic ethnic group in Chicago equaled this percentage of parochial school attendance.[14]

The Polish Catholic Church in Chicago attained a remarkable institutional completeness. Of the estimated 213,000 Poles in Chicago in 1910, 140,000 were members of Polish Catholic churches. The criterion of membership used by the various Polish pastors was generally more than baptism but less than regular Sunday attendance. Probably anyone who at least performed his Easter Duty and made some financial contribution to the parish was counted as a member. Thus about two-thirds of Chicago's Poles were part of the Polish Catholic complex, with the remainder not church members, members of the schismatic Polish National Church, or communicants in non-Polish Catholic parishes. In 1930 the proportion of Chicago Poles attending Polish parishes was still nearly 60 percent.[15] In addition to churches, elementary schools, and St. Stanislaw College, Chicago Poles also supported St. Hedwig's Orphanage and Industrial School, Holy Family Academy for girls, four cemeteries, two day nurseries, an old-age home, and a hospital.

Historians have often noted the tangible evidence of Polish financial support for the Church, particularly the cathedral-like churches in Polish neighborhoods, and have speculated on the sacrifices involved for immigrant laborers earning low wages. Actually though Polish church support was consistent and substantial, it was not as crushing a burden as sometimes supposed. In the year 1908, Polish parishioners in the Chicago area contributed $3.51 per capita to their local churches. For a family of five, this amounted to $17.55 a year. This amount was about one and a half week's wages for an unskilled laborer at that time. Viewed another way, it was equal to two months' rent in a tenement or the amount an ambitious laborer might put away yearly in a savings and loan association.[16]

This level of church support was probably higher, relative to income, than most Chicago Catholics maintain today; but other ethnic groups at the time contributed more. The Immigration Commission in 1911 found that a foreign-born Pole made about one-third less in wages than a foreign-born German.[17] As the following table shows, the territorial (mainly Irish) and German parishes received higher per capita contributions, reflecting the higher economic levels of the Irish and German communities.

TABLE III
CATHOLIC PARISH SUPPORT, 1908

Type of Parish	No. of Parishioners	Total Contributions	Per Capita Contribution
Territorial	208,500	$1,197,400	$5.74
German	69,300	$434,800	$6.27
Slovak	7,300	$28,400	$3.89
Polish	151,400	$532,000	$3.51
Lithuanian	17,800	$55,500	$3.12
Bohemian	32,800	$59,500	$1.81
Italian	39,000	$14,800	.38

The per capita totals fluctuated considerably over the next forty years with the ups and downs of the economic cycle, but the respective positions of the various parish groups stayed largely the same.[18] All in all, it seems that Polish Catholics gave a respectable amount of financial support to their churches, according to their economic means; but they certainly did not drain their family budgets to do so. Yet the evidence of the "Polish cathedrals" is not totally misleading. Both in 1926 and 1947, Polish parish buildings had a higher median valuation than the parish buildings of any other nationality in Chicago. Polish parishes, apparently, channeled more of their resources into bricks and mortar than did others.

After the creation of local societies and parishes, the final step in the building of a mature Polish-American community was the federation of many local societies into a number of national, superterritorial Polish fraternal organizations. National fraternals emerged in the late nineteenth century, such as the Polish Falcons (a gymnastic union on the order of the German Turners), the Polish Alma Mater (which specialized in youth work), and the Alliance of Polish Socialists (not really very socialist, but rather a nationalist organization linked to Pilsudski's party in Poland). But the two most important Polish-American fraternals, both of which had their headquarters in Chicago after 1880, were the Polish National Alliance and the Polish Roman Catholic Union.

An individual immigrant did not belong to one of these fraternals directly but rather as a member of some local society affiliated with it. The key to each society's mass membership was its ability to provide greater insurance benefits through large organization. But in addition to providing practical advantages, both the PNA and the PRCU pursued definite ideological goals. The PNA was a nationalist organization, directed by political *emigrés* from Poland who worked as a sort of Polish "Zionist" force for the liberation of the motherland from the partitioning powers. PNA leaders considered the American-Polish colonies to be a "fourth province of Poland." The Alliance's leaders were laymen, its policies at least mildly anticlerical, and its membership open to Polish Jews, schismatics, and nonbelievers as well as Catholics. The PRCU, as its name implied, was a religious organization, open only to Catholics, dominated by the clergy, and dedicated primarily to the strengthening of Catholicism among the immigrant Poles.

The two organizations were bitter rivals for membership and influence. PNA leaders considered the PRCU insufficiently nationalistic, whereas the PRCU leaders thought the PNA godless. Yet this polarization can be exaggerated. The rank and file members of both organizations were over-whelmingly Catholic; they joined primarily for social and economic benefits, and because they usually belonged to several local societies, they often found themselves affiliated with both PNA and PRCU. The two organizations worked closely together during World War I. Once Poland was liberated, no ideological issue separated the two fraternals.

The national fraternals published Polish-language newspapers and other literature. Each had an association organ that appeared weekly. The PNA's *Zgoda* (Harmony) was started in 1880; the PRCU began publication even earlier, went through several titles, and finally in 1897 settled on *Naród Polski* (Polish Nation) as its main propaganda arm. Both papers are still published in Chicago today. The two organizations later moved into the daily newspaper field in Chicago, the PNA with *Dziennik Zwiazkowy* (Alliance Daily News) in 1908, and the PRCU with *Dziennik Zjednoczenia* (Union Daily News) from 1923 to 1939. The Alliance's *Zwiazkowy* remains today as the last of Chicago's Polish-language dailies.[19]

The PNA-PRCU rivalry reflects an important division in the leadership class of Polish-Americans, a division into two camps which Victor Greene has termed "nationalists" (PNA) and "religionists" (PRCU).[20] Division into two ideological groupings was a common experience for all the East European immigrants. The nationalist-religionist dichotomy that troubled the Polish community actually split the Bohemians into two mutually exclusive groups. Bohemian nationalism harks back to the Protestant followers of Jan Hus in the fifteenth century, who were ruthlessly suppressed by the Catholic Austrian Emperor. When it re-emerged in the nineteenth century, Bohemian nationalism was not only anti-Catholic but secularist. Though Bohemia was a nominally Catholic country, the leading nationalist intellectuals were self-styled atheists and "free-thinkers." In the United States the free-thought movement broadened its base and embraced a large number of uprooted Bohemian peasants and workers as well. Free-thought had all the trappings of a secular church and engaged in its own drive for institutional completeness. The largest Bohemian fraternal organization, the Czech-Slovak Protective Society, identified itself with free-thought; the *Slovenska Lipa* organized as a national cultural center on Chicago's west side; nineteen free-thought schools taught Bohemian language and the principles of free-thought outside regular school hours; and the Bohemian National Cemetery became the final resting-place of those who disdained consecrated ground.

Though Bohemian religionists, led by the Benedictines of St. Procopius Abbey, counter-organized with a full panoply of eleven national parishes, parochial schools, an orphanage, and a Catholic cemetery (shared with Polish Catholics), the free-thinkers greatly outnumbered Bohemian Catholics in Chicago. An estimated seventy percent of the Bohemians in Chicago avoided religion altogether. Compared with this Bohemian split into two completely separate cultural communities, the religionist-nationalist rivalry among Poles was mild. Nationalists and religionists formed two tendencies within one community of Polish-Americans, rather than two separate communities.[21]

Midway between the Bohemian and the Polish experiences was that of the Lithuanians. Though the majority of Lithuanians in Chicago remained Roman Catholics, a vigorous free-thought movement did appeal to some, under the name of Liberalism. During the 1920s and 1930s, an increasing number of Lithuanians chose to be buried in the Lithuanian National Cemetery rather than the Catholic St. Casimir's. Yet in 1934 the burial statistics still ran roughly three to one in favor of the Catholics. Among Slovaks the nationalist-religionist split was complicated by the issue of union with the Czechs in Europe. The free-thinking, secularist element among Slovaks tended to support the Czech-Slovak experiment, but the majority of American Slovaks remained Roman Catholics and Slovak nationalists.[22]

Unlike Bohemian free-thinkers, Lithuanian Liberals, or Slovak Czechophiles, Polish nationalists were not antireligious. The only permanent schism within the Polish-American community produced another religious denomination, the Polish National Church. Most nationalists remained fervent Catholics, and secularism made few inroads. The mutual aid societies, the parishes, the fraternal organizations, and the Polish-language press made Polish Chicago more institutionally complete as a Polish-Catholic community. This interpretation of the community-building process may seem too monolithic to those who lived through the fierce internal quarrels in Polish Chicago. Just how fierce the quarrels were is illustrated in the next section. Yet those divisions remained for the most part within the Polish family, which prayed together and stayed together.

Polish-Catholic Factions

The main theme of Polish-Catholic history in Chicago was the community-building drive for institutional completeness. But as this drive unfolded, three stages of fierce controversy ensued. The first stage, which began as soon as the first Polish parish was organized in 1869 and continued until about 1900, was a struggle for control of the finances and administration of the parishes. The second stage witnessed a campaign, running from about 1900 to 1920, to obtain Polish bishops in America. The final stage was a holding action, to preserve the institutional separateness of Polish Catholics and prevent absorption by the rest of the Church in Chicago. This stage began with the arrival of Cardinal Mundelein in 1916 and still continues today.

The first phase of controversy surrounding the Polish parish dealt not with dogma or belief but rather with church polity, the structure of church government. In the late nineteenth century, Poles, Slovaks, Lithuanians, and other recent Catholic immigrants reopened a fundamental question that had troubled the American Church from the beginning: who held legal title to Catholic Church property? The hierarchy had always maintained that legal title to all parish property must rest with the local bishop. Ultimate authority over parish finance would then be vested in him or in his direct representative, the pastor. But in the early years of the American republic, a more democratic polity, akin to American congregationalism, appealed to many lay leaders. In such a system, repeatedly condemned by the bishops as "lay trusteeism," a board of lay trustees would hold title to parish property, administer the parish finances, and hire and fire the pastor.[23]

The Polish nationalist faction in America revived the demands for lay trustee control, for they viewed the Irish bishops in Chicago and elsewhere as foreigners. Furthermore, the European church custom of *jus patronatus* (right of patronage) seemed to support their position. In Europe a noble patron often founded a local church, retained title to the property, and hired the pastor—all with Vatican approval. Polish lay leaders in America tried to transform this custom into a collective right of patronage by the whole local congregation, expressed through the board of trustees. In order to get a parish founded, the Poles usually surrendered title initially to the bishop; but if a particular pastor's personality or financial management later displeased them, they reasserted demands for lay, nationalist control.[24]

In Chicago the nationalist dissenters were opposed by the Resurrectionist Fathers, and especially by Rev. Wincenty Barzynski, C.R., pastor St. Stanislaw Kostka from 1874 to 1899. In 1871, Bishop Thomas Foley made an agreement with the Resurrectionists whereby legal title to all church property would be vested in the bishop, but the Resurrectionists would exercise administrative supervision over all Polish parishes in Chicago as the bishop's representatives. The nationalists resented the Resurrectionists' "sellout" to the Irish bishop and chafed under their authoritarian control of church affairs. In 1873, when overcrowding at St. Stanislaw necessitated the building of another church, a lay society founded Holy Trinity church three blocks away and tried to retain title and find a pastor more to their liking. The bishop and the Resurrectionists wanted the church to be merely a mission of St. Stanislaw. This Holy Trinity-St. Stanislaw dispute dragged on for twenty years. Several persons were excommunicated, and Holy Trinity was closed by the bishop for long periods of time. Finally, in 1893 a papal representative, Monsignor Francis Satolli, visited Chicago and personally ended the dispute. The dissidents had to yield the formal question of legal title, which was finally ceded to the bishop. But Satolli also ended the special relationship of the Archdiocese of Chicago with the Resurrectionist Order and brought in Rev. Casimir Sztuczko, a Holy Cross Father from South Bend, Indiana and a strong nationalist priest, as pastor of Holy Trinity. This was a compromise solution which worked. Fr. Sztuczko was the pastor at Holy Trinity for the next sixty years.[25]

Controversy broke out again a year later in a new location. A few miles to the northwest of St. Stanislaw, the Resurrectionists had founded a new parish, St. Hedwig. Fr. Wincenty Barzynski unwisely gave ammunition to his opponents by appointing his brother, Joseph Barzynski, to be pastor of St. Hedwig's. When Fr. Anthony Kozlowski came to St. Hedwig as an assistant priest in 1894, he formed an anti-Barzynski faction of parishioners. Noisy disturbances broke out whenever the pastor said mass. On a cold February day in 1895, a mob of dissatisfied parishioners stormed the rectory and had to be driven back by the police. Though the bishop quickly brought in a new pastor, the dissidents would not settle for less than total control. So in June 1895, Fr. Kozlowski and about one thousand families seceded from St. Hedwig and formed a new parish of All Saints.[26]

Over twenty years of nationalist battles with the Resurrectionists and the presence of a willing leader in Fr. Kozlowski had heightened the intensity of the St. Hedwig's conflict. Unlike the Holy Trinity affair, no reconciliation occurred. The dissident parishioners still considered themselves Roman Catholics at first; but when Kozlowski was consecrated a bishop in 1897 by the schismatic Old Catholic Church in Switzerland, and subsequently excommunicated by the Pope, they found themselves outside the Roman Church.[27]

These two church quarrels should not be viewed as freak occurrences, caused only by personality conflicts or the special position of the Resurrectionist Order in Chicago. Trustee quarrels with bishops

St. Stanislaw Kostka, one of the largest Polish parishes in the world. *Courtesy of University of Illinois Library at Chicago, Manuscripts Division.*

Kościół, Hala, Dom Sióstr i Szkoła

and pastors broke out in numerous Polish, Slovak, and Lithuanian communities throughout the United States in the late nineteenth century. Among Poles they resulted in three separate federations of independent, non-Roman parishes, headed by Kozlowski in Chicago, Fr. Stephan Kaminski in Buffalo, and Fr. Francis Hodur in Scranton, Pennsylvania. After Kozlowski's death in 1907 and Kaminski's in 1911, Fr. Hodur obtained Old Catholic consecration as a bishop and consolidated all the schismatic churches into one denomination, the Polish National Church. This church maintains nine parishes in Chicago and embraces an estimated 5 percent of Polish-Americans in the United States.[28]

The first stage of Polish-Catholic controversy had many causes. High-handed pastors, financial mismanagement, the release of pent-up emotions in the free air of America—all contributed to the turbulence; but fundamentally the rebelliousness of the Polish parishioners was rooted in a desire for national autonomy within the American Catholic Church. The majority of Polish Catholics remained within the Roman church, and title to church property was ceded to the Irish bishops; but the struggle for the greatest possible national independence continued at a higher level with the launching of a drive for Polish bishops after the turn of the century.

During the second stage of Polish-Catholic controversy, initiative shifted from laymen to the clergy. This shift has been little noted and never studied in detail, but it is significant. It was part of a general damping down of lay activity in the American Catholic church as bishops and clergy slowly consolidated their administrative control in the twentieth century. What probably happened among the Poles was that the most outspoken lay leaders departed into the Polish National Church, leaving the Roman Catholic clergy in firmer control. It is also significant that at this stage the conflict was purely between Poles and outsiders. Though many Polish priests held aloof from the campaign for Polish bishops, none actually opposed it. Unlike the first stage of controversy, the new campaign united Polish-Americans.

The primary leader in the drive for Polish bishops was Rev. Waclaw Kruszka, a priest of the Milwuakee archdiocese stationed in Ripon, Wisconsin. Fr. Kruszka, one of the first historians of Polish America, was a journalist and publicist of great talent. His brother, Michael Kruszka, edited an influential Polish-Catholic newspaper in Milwaukee. Fr. Kruszka opened the campaign with an article entitled "Polyglot Bishops for Polyglot Dioceses" in the July 1901 issue of the New York *Freeman's Journal.* He carried on the fight at two Polish-Catholic Congresses in 1901 and 1903 and made two trips to Rome. In Chicago he was supported by most of the diocesan Polish clergy, though the Resurrectionists remained aloof.[29]

The watchwords of the new campaign were equality and recognition. The appointment of Polish bishops would recognize both the numerical importance and the special cultural needs of Polish Catholics, which were neglected by the Irish, German, and Anglo-American bishops who ruled virtually all American dioceses in 1900. Ideally, the Polish clergy would have liked a reorganization of the American church completely along ethnic lines. Instead of the existing territorial dioceses, where all Catholics in a given area were subject to one bishop, they desired the creation of purely Polish, Lithuanian, German, and Irish dioceses irrespective of territorial location. Ukrainian Catholics in the United States actually obtained this goal in 1913, over the protests of the American bishops. Since Ukrainians worshiped in a separate rite and utilized Old Slavonic as their liturgical language, Rome removed them completely from the jurisdiction of American bishops and established a separate exarchy, or diocese. But Rome held firm against any jurisdictional separation within the Latin rite.[30]

Failing to obtain separate dioceses, Poles tried to secure the appointment of a fair share of Polish bishops to rule over American dioceses. At the very least, they wanted Rome to appoint Polish auxiliary bishops in dioceses like Chicago, where Poles were numerous. This would give symbolic recognition to Polish Catholics and insure that the ruling bishop had a Polish advisor. The result of the Kruszka campaign was Rome's concession to the minimum demand, the appointment of a Polish auxiliary in Chicago in 1908 and in Milwaukee in 1914. Paul Rhode, the pastor of St. Michael's Polish church in South Chicago, was chosen auxiliary bishop of Chicago by the Polish priests of the archdiocese in a special election called by Archbishop Quigley. When Rome ratified his selection, he became the first bishop of Polish ancestry in the United States.[31]

Bishop Rhode proved a popular, energetic, and diplomatic leader of Chicago's Polish clergy. As Archbishop Quigley's Polish lieutenant, he had more influence than an auxiliary bishop usually does. Besides making the rounds of Polish parishes for confirmations and ordinations, he determined the assignments of Polish priests in the archdiocese. As the only Polish-American bishop until 1914 and an organizer of the Association of Polish Priests in the United States, his influence extended outside Chicago as well. Yet his appointment was essentially outside Chicago as well. Yet his appointment was essentially a form of tokenism. Without jurisdiction over a diocese, an auxiliary bishop's importance is largely symbolic. Rhode was not even a member of the diocesan consultors, the bishop's financial council. But the Polish clergy were satisfied for the moment.[32]

The recognition drive heated up again after Rhode was transferred from Chicago in 1915 to become Bishop of Green Bay, Wisconsin. In a sense this was a promotion, for Rhode now became the first Polish Ordinary, or ruling bishop, of a diocese in America. But Green Bay was a very small see, and the Poles were deprived of their symbolic leader in Chicago. When George Mundelein, a German-American, was appointed Archbishop of Chicago shortly after Rhode's departure and he failed to appoint a Polish auxiliary, the Polish clergy suspected a conspiracy. In the overheated atmosphere of World War I, friction developed between the Poles and their German bishop.

The campaign for Polish bishops climaxed in 1920, when the Polish clergy in the United States joined the newly formed Polish legation of the Vatican in drawing up a thirteen-page memorial. All the Polish nationalist rage against the neglect and insensitivity of "Americanizing" bishops—Archbishop Mundelein in particular—came out in this memorial. Specifically, the Polish priests requested that Bishop Rhode be transferred to a more important see, that Polish auxiliaries be appointed in a number of cities, and that the Poles be allowed a largely separate development of their Catholicism in the United States. The American hierarchy, in their annual meeting of September 1920, formed a three-bishop committee, including Archbishop Mundelein, to draft a strong rebuttal to the Polish memorial. Cardinal Gibbons of Baltimore forwarded the committee's reply to the Vatican, and Rome apparently accepted the American bishops' explanation. No action was taken on the Polish memorial.[33]

Waclaw Kruszka in Wisconsin had still not given up. In 1923 he wrote to Pope Pius XI:

> A nation . . . is part of nature. A nation is of divine origin, not human invention. . . . As a rule, even in the fourth and fifth generation . . . families are purely Polish in America. . . . Parishes of mixed nationalities in America are generally considered a necessary evil. . . . Therefore, as both families and parishes are regularly purely Polish . . . consequently dioceses also should be purely Polish. . . .[34]

Despite the token victories and many defeats of the previous twenty years, Kruszka was reiterating the maximum demand, purely Polish dioceses. But this issue was dead, and even the lesser demands of the Polish recognition drive were ignored. Chicago remained without a Polish auxiliary until 1960; few Polish bishops were appointed elsewhere in the United States.

Previous studies of Polish-Catholic controversies in Chicago have

Paul P. Rhode, the first bishop of Polish ancestry in America. *Courtesy of University of Illinois Library at Chicago, Manuscripts Division.*

not given adequate attention to the third stage of the struggle. Victor Greene ends his book on a note of triumph with Rhode's appointment in 1908; Joseph Parot and Charles Shanabruch end their studies in the early 1920s on a note of defeat for the Poles. Since none of them explores fully the successful holding action of the third stage, they miss much of the significance of the struggles.

By the second decade of the twentieth century, Polish Catholics had suffered notable defeats in their movement for a purely ethnic Catholicism. The right of parish councils to hold church property in their own name had been denied; the desire for purely Polish dioceses had been rejected; and the demand for Polish ordinaries and auxiliaries in existing dioceses had been met with tokenism. Yet Polish Catholics in Chicago retained a remarkably complete complex of churches, schools, and welfare institutions, which, though technically part of the Archdiocese of Chicago, were quite separate. Polish language predominated in the churches and schools, Polish priests served exclusively in their own churches and institutions, and a lively Catholic press was printed in Polish. Furthermore, the existence of an alternative church in the schismatic Polish National denomination gave the Roman Catholic Poles a secret weapon against any Americanizing bishop who might try to break down this institutional complex. If the Polish clergy yelled loud enough, a bishop's hand could be stayed by the fear of further defections. This secret weapon did not prove sufficient to make further gains, such as the appointment of Polish bishops; but it helped the Poles protect what they already had.

The coming of Archbishop George William Mundelein (Cardinal Mundelein after 1924) to Chicago in 1916 made necessary a Polish holding action to preserve their institutional complex. Mundelein ruled the Chicago archdiocese like a Renaissance prince from 1916 to 1939. He was a vigorous centralizer, a consolidating bishop in the mold of Cardinal O'Connell in Boston, Cardinal Dougherty in Philadelphia, and Cardinal Spellman in New York. Furthermore, he prided himself on this third-generation Americanism and was determined to break down the ethnic separatisms within the Church in Chicago. Besides opposing the wishes of Poles, Slovaks, and Lithuanians for auxiliary bishops of their own nationalities, he initiated three policies in the first years of his reign which seemed to threaten the institutional completeness of Polish Catholics: he declared a moratorium on the building of purely national parishes; he initiated a standardization of the curriculum in the parochial schools and a policy of English only for teaching most school subjects; and he began to assign newly ordained priests of Polish and other East European ancestry to Irish or mixed parishes. By vigorous protests and a tacit use of their secret weapon, the Polish clergy deflected the impact of the first two policies and completely defeated the third.[35]

As Polish-Americans and other ethnic groups moved out of their original neighborhoods into more middle-class areas on the southwest and northwest sides, Mundelein was reluctant to establish new national parishes for them, preferring territorial parishes open to all. The revision of canon law in 1918, which required Vatican permission for any new national parishes, supported his position; but he acted largely from his own motives. The expense and inefficiency of building many separate parishes in new areas bothered him; besides, he wished to expose the younger generation of Poles to a more mixed environment. The Poles were numerous and cohesive enough to defeat his purposes. Mundelein founded new parishes that were technically territorial, but in many cases he assigned only Polish priests to them. Parishes like St. Bruno, St. Camillus, and St. Turibius on the southwest side and St. Constance on the north side were just as Polish as any technically national parish.

Mundelein's establishment of the first diocesan school board in 1916, to coordinate the heretofore independent parochial schools, to standardize the curriculum, and to mandate English-language instruction, evoked much favorable comment in the Chicago daily papers and a storm of protest from the Poles, Lithuanians, and even the French-Canadian Catholics. But the centralization implied in this policy extended only to choice of textbooks, and languages other than English were still permitted for the teaching of catechism and reading. In what was perhaps an overreaction to Polish protests, Mundelein made sure that both the school board chairman and one of the two superintendents were always Polish priests throughout the whole of his administration. Through the teaching of the Felician Sisters and other Polish orders of nuns in the elementary schools, and that of the Resurrectionist Fathers, who expanded St. Stanislaw College into two modern high schools, Weber High and Gordon Tech, Polish leaders insured a distinctively Polish education for most of their youth.

Finally, when Mundelein assigned three newly ordained Polish priests to non-Polish parishes in 1917, sixty-eight Polish priests signed a letter of protest against this attempt to denationalize the Polish clergy.[36] Mundelein fumed and wrote testy letters in response. He later fired one of the protest leaders, Fr. Louis Grudzinski, from his post on the board of diocesan consultors, replacing him with one of the few Polish pastors who had not signed the letter, Rev. Thomas Bona. But despite this retaliation, the incident was one of Mundelein's most stinging defeats. Within two years the newly ordained priests in question were back in Polish parishes; and for the rest of his jurisdiction, Mundelein never assigned a single Polish priest to a non-Polish parish, even though he continued to assign priests of other ethnic groups to territorial parishes when the supply of priests permitted. The Polish clergy had succeeded in their holding action against one of the most authoritarian of archbishops.

Despite the losses at the first two stages of Polish-Catholic controversy, the underlying process of community-building and the holding action against Archbishop Mundelein were so successful that the "Polish League" has remained a largely separate component of the Catholic Church in Chicago. Polish pastors acted like feudal barons throughout much of the twentieth century, answerable only to the Polish "boss," Monsignor Thomas Bona, whom Mundelein and his successor left in nearly complete control of Polish clerical affairs. When Mundelein built his new major seminary of St. Mary of the Lake, one of its purposes was to unify the clergy and instill *esprit de corps*. Accordingly, ethnic divisions were slight at the seminary; but after ordination, young Polish priests were assigned to the Polish League, indoctrinated by the pastor, and often forbidden to attend class reunions or to go on vacations with Irish priests. In 1934, Cardinal Mundelein organized a mission band of diocesan priests to preach missions of spiritual renewal in the parishes of the archdiocese; but he had to arrange for a separate Polish mission band since the Polish pastors would not accept the ministrations of outsiders. As late as 1960 students of Polish descent at the minor seminary were required to study the Polish language whereas all other seminarians could choose any modern language.

This victory of the Polish League was a Pyrrhic one in several ways. For the priests themselves, assignment only to Polish parishes meant a longer than average wait to become a pastor. A Polish priest ordained in Chicago in 1926 or 1927 waited an average of twenty-four years until a pastorate in the Polish League opened up, whereas the average waiting time for an Irish priest was sixteen years, and the average for all priests in the diocese was eighteen years.[37]

More important, the Polish commitment to separate Catholic development meant a lack of influence in the affairs of the archdiocese as a whole. Polish priests had influence on the school board, and Monsignor Bona and one other Polish pastor sat on the board of consultors. But none of the newer archdiocesan agencies established by Mundelein and his successors, such as Catholic Charities or the Society for the Propagation of the Faith, had Polish directors. The crucial positions in the chancery office were completely devoid of Polish names. Even today, a glance at the Chicago clergy directory shows very few Polish priests in influential church positions.

Polish Catholics today often decry this lack of influence as discrimination, and discrimination there may have been. But the choice of separate development largely predestined this result. Polish Catholics could not have it both ways—separate development and influence in wider circles. Confined to their own community, Polish priests did not develop the contacts, the political skills, or the diversity of experiences necessary to forge ahead in internal church politics. Cardinal Mundelein offered the Polish clergy a beginning on the road to greater influence in Chicago Catholicism, but the Polish priests chose to stay with the path of separate development. Their choice was thoroughly consistent with the process of community-building that had been going on for half a century in Polish Chicago, but it closed off new options in church politics. Polish leaders made a similar choice in secular politics.

The voting record of Chicago Poles in American politics can be summarized briefly: Poles voted Democratic from the beginning. In eighteen mayoral elections from 1889 to 1935, the identifiably Polish voting precincts gave a majority of their votes to the Democratic candidate in every instance. In thirteen Presidential elections from 1888 to 1936, the Polish precincts produced a Democratic majority in all but two cases. This political allegiance was rooted in a perception of the Democrats as the party of average workingmen and of broad-minded toleration for the Poles' religion and customs. The Republicans, on the other hand, were perceived as puritanical, aloof, and plutocratic. These perceptions and their attendant voting patterns were not a product of Franklin Roosevelt's New Deal, as is sometimes supposed, but of the nineteenth century.[38]

More significant, perhaps, than the voting record is the political strategy pursued by Polish Democratic leaders, a strategy of solidarity politics. Polish politicians organized their bloc vote around in-group concerns, constantly tried to perfect the unity and solidarity of the bloc, and neglected the building of coalitions with other political blocs. The high point of this solidarity strategy came in the 1930s, with the organization of the Polish American Democratic Organization (PADO) as a political service agency and an ethnic lobby within the Democratic party. This strategy parallels the separate development of Poles within the Catholic Church during the same period.

Polish leaders were misled by the fact of their large numbers into thinking that political power would fall to them like a ripe fruit if only they could perfect the solidarity of their group. Since Polish voters never formed a majority of the electorate in Chicago, however, such a strategy was doomed to failure. Despite their large numbers, Polish-Americans never elected a Polish mayor of Chicago and they remained weak in the councils of the Democratic central committee until the late

1970s. With the death of Mayor Richard Daley in the winter of 1976, a special post of vice-mayor was created specifically to represent Poles.

Anton Cermak, the Bohemian political boss, rose to power in Chicago politics in the 1920s by pursuing a different strategy. Through such organizations as the United Societies for Local Self Government, an antiprohibition lobby, Cermak allied a great number of ethnic blocs behind him. Polish leaders, on the other hand, organized around specifically in-group concerns, like having the name of Crawford Avenue changed to Pulaski Road. This won them no allies. At the time of Mayor Cermak's death, the influential *Dziennik Chicagoski* seemed to understand the lesson of his political career:

> A Pole will be mayor of Chicago, only if we continue the politics of the dead mayor Cermak, i.e., if we make alliances with other groups. . . . Unfortunately, the majority among us is now playing at Pan-Slavism and forgetting that Mayor Cermak practiced a different kind of politics. In his organization were found next to the Czechs, Jews; next to the Poles, Irish; next to the Germans, Swedes.[39]

However, neither the *Chicagoski* nor other Polish spokesmen took this advice to heart. As in the Roman Catholic Church so in the Democratic party, Polish leaders continued to nurture separate development and internal solidarity. They did not engage in bridge-building, coalitions, or broker politics.

The Polish In-group

Through their numbers and the success of their community-building process, Poles in Chicago attained a large measure of institutional completeness. Within the Catholic Church and the Democratic party they achieved a cohesive, largely separate existence. This solidarity led to considerable success in preserving a Polish-American sub-culture, in attaining symbolic victories like Paul Rhode's appointment as auxiliary bishop and the renaming of Pulaski Road, and in opposing external threats such as the unfavorable school legislation of the 1890s, the Ku Klux Klan in the 1920s, and Cardinal Mundelein's Americanizing policies. But such success has been purchased at the expense of wider influence in Chicago Catholicism and city politics.

One important area of Polish-American life, economic development, has been left out of consideration. This aspect of the Polish-American experience has not yet received detailed historical treatment, and reliable data is scarce. Such neglect is unfortunate, for the primary goals of Polish immigrants were economic ones. Furthermore, eco-

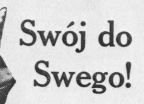

Swój do
Swego!

**Niech nie będzie u nas
Czczem Słowem.**

PIENIĄDZ nasz niech
wspiera nasze polskie składy, nasze pracownie, na-
sze wyroby

Rodacy! — Kto polskie
pieniądze zapracowane
ciężko oddaje obcym fir-
mom, ten krzywdzi swoich
i samego siebie.

Solidarność w pracy jest
podstawą naszej lepszej
przyszłości.

Polecam Wam więc na-
sze dwa olbrzymie składy,
gdzie znajdziecie najlep-
szy wybór i ceny najprzy-
stępniejsze.

Przyjdźcie więc do nas i
niech jeden z pięciu braci
Perłowskich wam usłuży.

**Bracia
Perłowscy**

UNION LIBERTY FURNITURE COMPANY

**1327-29-31-33 MILWAUKEE AVE., Blisko Wood ulicy
4705-09 SO. ASHLAND AVENUE, Blisko 47mej ulicy**

Polish solidarity extends to the business world. *Courtesy of the Polish Museum, Chicago.*

nomic life is the one realm which escaped the institutional complete-ness of community-building. From the very beginning the majority of Poles were salaried workers in large industries not controlled by other Poles. One study counted about 30,000 persons employed in businesses owned by Polish-Americans in the 1920s. But since there were at least 80,000 Polish heads of households in Chicago at that time, the majority of workers still earned their livelihood outside the Polish institutional complex.[40] It is likely, then, that the most significant contact of Polish-Americans with members of other ethnic groups occurred not in the Church or in politics but in factories, trade unions, and businesses.

Yet even in the economic realm it appears, from very fragmentary evidence so far, that Polish-Americans in Chicago were slow to attain prestige or influence. A study by the National Center for Urban Ethnic Affairs revealed a very small number of Polish names on the roster of board members controlling Chicago-based corporations. A National Opinion Research Center study similarly shows few Poles in presti-gious economic positions—though it also indicates that Polish workers make more money than most.[41] This latter finding, if it is solidly based, may provide a clue to the economic history of Poles in Chicago. Polish workers appear to have opted for monetary success in unionized jobs and for economic and psychological security in home-owning rather than for more prestigious occupations in business and the professions. Even though Poles did not achieve separate development in the eco-nomic realm, a process similar to the trend in the Church and politics seems to have been at work. Poles attained one kind of success at the expense of wider influence and prestige.

If Polish immigrants came to Chicago seeking primarily bread and a home, it appears that they got what they wanted. Yet Polish-Ameri-cans of the 1970s seem to be wondering, Is that all there is? Repeatedly Polish leaders now decry their lack of influence in the archdiocese of Chicago, in city politics, and in business and the professions. However, under the banner of the so-called "new ethnicity," these Polish leaders are still often repeating the patterns of the past, calling for progress through ethnic solidarity, quota systems, and group pride. The histor-ical record indicates the limitations of this approach. The present gen-eration of Polish-Americans should notice that many champions of the new ethnicity are spokesmen of the old institutional complex. They may need to look elsewhere if they wish to pursue new goals in politics, religion, and economic life in America.

Chapter VII

DOMINIC CANDELORO

Suburban Italians:
Chicago Heights, 1890-1975

> *The Italians particularly seemed to need accep-*
> *tance. Whereas Germans sometimes settled in*
> *closed communities and fought to maintain their*
> *native language and culture, the Italians were*
> *rarely* chiusi, *or closed, critical, and superior in*
> *attitude. Most felt bound to adopt American val-*
> *ues at least until they had achieved more than*
> *marginal success. Then they could return to their*
> *own ways either in America or in Italy. Their as-*
> *similation, however, was often so complete that*
> *it was impossible to return to the old style of life.*
> —Andrew F. Rolle, *The American Italians*

IT IS COMMON TO THINK OF ITALIANS in America as big-city folk.[1] Yet in the smaller communities and suburbs, richly detailed and continuous information about Italians and other ethnic groups is often most available. The stability of the suburban population, the coverage afforded by local newspapers, and the higher quality of local oral history data can help to provide a relatively complete picture of one part of the Italian-American experience. A comparison of the suburban with the big-city experience of Italian immigrants might also shed new light on the nature of the ethnic frontier and group survival in America.

What is now the suburb of Chicago Heights is an old community. Four Scots-Irish families first settled in the area near the crossing of the Sauk Trail and the Vincennes Trail, thirty miles south of Chicago, in the 1830s. The small community was first known as Thorn Grove. After an influx of German Forty-Eighters, it became Bloom (1849) and finally, in 1892, the village of Chicago Heights; a decade later it was incorporated as a city.

In the early 1890s a syndicate of Chicago businessmen headed by Charles Wacker and Martin Kilgallen formed the Chicago Heights Land Association and aggressively promoted the manufacturing potential of this satellite suburb, which already boasted excellent railroad service by the Chicago and Eastern Illinois, the Elgin, Joliet, and Eastern, the Baltimore and Ohio, the Michigan Central railroads, and a terminal transfer line. Their efforts were rewarded with the decision of Inland Steel, Canedy-Otto (machine tool), and other large manufacturers to locate in the city, eventually making it one of the liveliest industrial centers of its size. The land association, led by Scots-Irish settler William Donovan, set out to sell 25-foot homesites to workers moving into Chicago Heights from rural America and overseas. Donovan went on to build a real estate, insurance, and savings and loan empire, and he claimed he never lost a penny in mortgages extended to Italians.[2]

The city grew rapidly, attaining a population of 20,000 in 1920 and supporting a large downtown shopping district. Encouraged by the boosterism of the local semi-weekly paper, *The Star*, Chicago Heights residents proudly proclaimed their town "the best manufacturing city its size in the country." But the 1920s saw the rise of Prohibition-related crime, lending a shady reputation to the town, a development which *The Star* and civic leaders strongly resented. After limping through the depressed 1930s, the industrial satellite city boomed during the war years and looked forward to great advances thereafter.

The post–World War II period saw the expansion of suburban areas, the development of regional shopping centers, and a decline in community identity. Today, after the proliferation of suburbia, the virtual demise of the once-bustling downtown business district, the decline of the railroads, and the shift away from the glamor of heavy industry, Chicago Heights is no longer a community of rapid growth, and much of the optimism of the turn-of-the-century community boosters is gone. Though it maintains a population of over 40,000, Chicago Heights has experienced what planners call "socioeconomic obsolescence." It is in the bottom fifty of Pierre De Vise's ranking of Chicago's 200 suburbs.[3]

During the period from the 1890s to the present, political and social leadership has also changed. Though there is still some evidence of the Scots-Irish business establishment which dominated the community at the turn of the century, political and business leadership is now largely in the hands of descendants of the ethnic migrants, most notably the Italians.

The 1970 census showed 3,092 of its residents of Italian birth and 8,783 claiming Italian as their mother tongue. If third and fourth generations are included, the number would easily double.[4] Italians are also the best-organized and most powerful political force in the community, dominating the city council, the school board, and the park board. How did Italians achieve this local dominance? Generally, the early migrants from Italy to America were mostly male, and so it was in Chicago Heights. Many—probably most—of these international migrant workers began as "birds of passage," with a sojourner mentality, like the *golondrina* of Argentina and elsewhere. In the period before World War I, there is evidence that few intended to stay permanently; most hoped only to earn enough to purchase a small plot of land back in Italy. Naturalization papers and census records reveal a good deal of internal movement within the United States on the part of the earliest immigrants, but less wandering by the later Italians, who were obviously part of a chain migration.[5]

A study of 1,448 applications for citizenship filed by Italians in Chicago Heights between 1907 and 1954 reveals that the earliest Italians who came to Chicago Heights arrived in the 1890s, but only 3 percent of them came prior to 1900. Most of these migrants moved between 1900 and 1914. After 1900 the pace quickened to almost 100 per year until 1908, when it dipped to 11, presumably in response to the financial panic of that year. Though the national peak for Italian

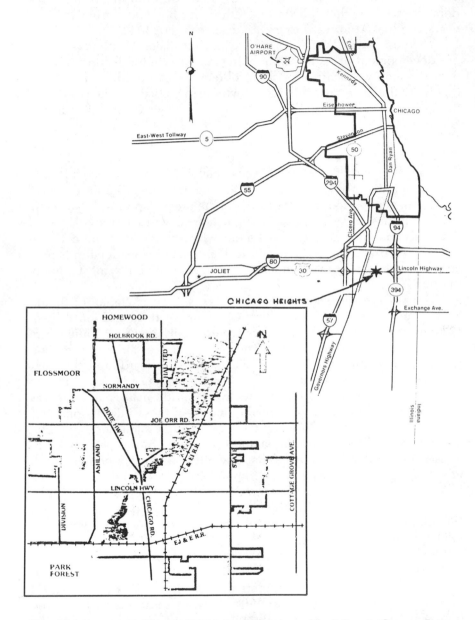

Chicago area map with Chicago Heights inset. *Courtesy of the Italians in Chicago Project, University of Illinois, Chicago. Funded by a grant from the National Endowment for the Humanities.*

immigration was 1907, the Chicago Heights migration peaked in 1913, when 218, or 15 percent, of the people in the sample arrived. Some 74 percent had migrated to the United States by the outbreak of World War I. The war years saw a marked decline, with only one recorded migrant to the city in 1918. However, there was a postwar rush in 1920, when 127 arrived. Some 90 percent of this population had arrived by 1924, the year that quota restrictions went into effect. Thus the impact of the quota on the Chicago Heights Italian community is clear, as shown by the accompanying chart.[6]

The age factor is always significant in defining the nature of a community and in determining many decisions concerning migration. Among the Chicago Heights Italians, 46 percent were born before 1890, 82 percent by 1900. Thus a very high percentage were adults by the

Year of Migration of the 1,448 Italians Who Applied for Citizenship in Chicago Heights, 1889–1954

1889 – 1	1916 – 30	1942 – 0
1891 – 3	1917 – 3	1943 – 0
1892 – 3	1918 – 1	1944 – 0
1893 – 3	1919 – 12	1945 – 0
1894 – 6	1920 – 127	1946 – 1
1895 – 3	1921 – 63	1947 – 1
1896 – 7	1922 – 20	1948 – 1
1897 – 4	1923 – 24	1949 – 1
1898 – 6	1924 – 7	1950 – 3
1899 – 11	1925 – 8	1951 – 2
1900 – 40	1926 – 0	1952 – 0
1901 – 34	1927 – 13	1953 – 0
1902 – 41	1928 – 10	1954 – 0
1903 – 48	1929 – 8	
1904 – 40	1930 – 10	
1905 – 82	1931 – 4	
1906 – 80	1932 – 2	
1907 – 91	1933 – 1	
1908 – 11	1934 – 2	
1909 – 59	1935 – 0	
1910 – 79	1936 – 0	
1911 – 34	1937 – 2	
1912 – 125	1938 – 0	
1913 – 218	1939 – 3	
1914 – 50	1940 – 0	
1915 – 10	1941 – 0	

time World War I began. They produced a large second generation of Italian Americans, who came to adulthood at about the time of World War II. The pattern that emerges from the sample of 1,346 cases for which accurate data is available, holds few surprises.

Age at time of migration
(Chicago Heights Italians, 1907–1954)[7]

Under 12 . . . . 11%
13–21 . . . . 40%
22–31 . . . . 38%
over 31 . . . . 11%

Thus the traditional image of the immigrants as vital young people contributing the best work years of their lives to their new land is borne out in Chicago Heights.

In nearly all the literature concerning Italian-Americans, much is made of the concept of *campanilismo*, the parochialism or sense of place that made an Italian's town or region of birth the most important factor in the relationship among immigrants in this country.[8] The regionalism of Italy, the dialects and different customs, helped to shape the occupational and residential patterns adopted by the newcomers. And town and region of origin continued to shape the attitudes and values of Italians in Chicago Heights for many years after the initial migration. Six major towns in Italy contributed 701 (48%) of the persons who applied for U.S. citizenship: San Benedetto del Tronto, which claimed 216 (15%); Montepradone, a nearby town, which was listed as the birthplace of 143 (10%) of the sample; Amaseno, a sleepy village near Rome, which contributed an even 100 (7%); the Sicilian town of Caccamo near Termini Imerese, which sent 97 of its finest to Chicago Heights; Villetta Barrea, the town of origin of 78 (5%); and Castel del Sangro, which sent 67 (5%). These last two are located in the Abruzzi. Five other towns contributed twenty or more to the survey.

The breakdown by regions is as follows: Marche, 640 (44%); Sicily, 172 (12%); Abruzzi, 159 (11%); Lazio, 147 (10%); and Campagnia, 52 (3%). These five regions contributed 1,170, or 81 percent, of those applying for citizenship. Thus Chicago Heights Italians were strongly Marchegiana, from the San Benedetto area, with an admixture of Sicilians, Abruzzese, and Lazioni. Towns and regions which one might have expected to be strongly represented in Chicago Heights, but which were not, include Naples (6 people) and Calabria (11 people). More surprisingly, few if any came from places in northern Italy, such as Genoa or Venice.

SOURCE TOWNS OF ITALIAN
IMMIGRANTS IN
CHICAGO HEIGHTS

LEGEND
⊛ TOWNS OF ORIGIN
⊛ MAJOR CITIES

Courtesy of the Italians in Chicago Project, University of Illinois, Chicago. Funded by a grant from the National Endowment for the Humanities. Graphics by Joseph Kubal.

Italians moved into several neighborhoods in Chicago Heights, with 53 percent settling on the East Side, a multiethnic and biracial section convenient to the factories and steel mills. Since the 1950s, however, the East Side has lost most of its Italian population and has become heavily black and Chicano. Some 38 percent of the Italians lived in the Hill area, often called "Hungry Hill" because of the one-time poverty of its residents and the steep nature of its terrain.[9] The highest hill in the neighborhood was chosen as the site for the Italian Catholic Church, San Rocco. This area was multiethnic but contained a heavier percentage of Italians than did the East Side, and virtually no blacks. Today the Hill continues to have a heavy Italian population, a strong contingent of Chicanos (who rent from Italian landlords), and a negligible number of blacks.

The East Side is directly north of the Hill, encompassing 11th through 17th streets. South of 17th Street are railroad tracks and factories that separate the East Side from the Hill. The Hill takes up the area from 21st Street through 26th Street, but is considerably smaller in area, population, and density than the East Side. It contained smaller manufacturing establishments and, though less convenient to larger factories than the East Side, was within a half-hour's walk of every factory in town. However, one major factory, the Inland Steel Company, was directly adjacent to the Hill.

Italians in Chicago Heights stuck together according to their towns of origin. Ninety-four of the 100 Amasenese lived in the Hill area, with 88 of them on the western end of the Hill. Only 2 percent of the 97 immigrants from Caccamo lived on the Hill, preferring instead the East Side. The same was true of the former residents of Villetta Barrea, of whom 74 percent chose the East Side; 17 percent of this group of 78 lived on the West Side. Perhaps because they were the most numerous, the progeny of San Benedetto seemed to distribute themselves more evenly than did any of the other groups, with 35 percent on the Hill, 57 percent on the East Side, and 8 percent on the West Side. Curiously, those from Monteprandone, a town quite close to San Benedetto, had a close 89 percent concentration of their members living on the East Side. The contingent that had the highest proportion of its people living among the Scots-Irish and Germans on the West Side at the time of petition was the group from Sulmona. Some 21 percent of their rather modest total of 29 claimed West Side addresses.

Town of birth also seemed to influence or correlate with the rate at which respondents went into business. While former residents of Caccamo accounted for only 10 percent of the sample from the major Italian towns, they represented 36 percent of the saloonkeepers in the sample, 23 percent of the grocers, and 20 percent of the merchants. The San Benedettans were proportionally represented in most occupations, and the Amasenesi were not represented at all among saloonkeepers. The continued influence of *campanilismo* on subsequent generations suggests the strong influence of very localized ethnic, as well as class, factors on the culture of Chicago Heights Italians.[10]

For the most part, early immigrants were listed as "day laborers" in the 1900 U.S. manuscript census. A cluster of Italians in Steger, three miles south of Chicago Heights, worked as furniture finishers in a piano factory. A dozen residents of Hanover Street (East Side), several of whom had come to the United States before 1890, were employed in the Heroy and Marrener Glass Works, apparently at skilled jobs. Many others were railroad workers and steelworkers. A large number, including women and children, worked as field hands in the onion fields of South Holland (five miles to the north), where they were hired by Dutch farmers to plant, weed, and pick the pungent bulb.

The Italian workers reached their workplace by taking the Chicago and Eastern Illinois Railroad train, sharing the cars with white-collar commuters who often turned up their noses at the sight and smells of the transplanted peasant field workers. Only one Italian woman was listed by the 1900 census as employed (a washerwoman), but many more worked hard each day to care for boarders, of whom there were approximately seventy-five in a population of three hundred. Others did needle work for Ederheimer Stein Pants Factory at 12th and Washington, where it was not unusual for a twelve-year-old girl to work as a seamstress and function as an interpreter for the adult Italian female employees.[11] Old-timers also remember Pasquarella, a gutsy widow who worked side by side with the men laying track during World War I.[12]

After 1910, with the establishment of a half-dozen country clubs in the Flossmoor area (two miles north and west), Italian boys and young men had the option of working as caddies at Flossmoor Country Club, Olympia Fields, Idlewild, and others. Idlewild is a Jewish club, and for many years the members had second- and third-generation Italian-American caddies.

The most important employers of Italians in the pre-1920 period were Inland Steel Company, the National Brick Company, and Canedy-Otto Machine Tools. As one observer wrote:

> They worked under brutalizing conditions. Chicago Heights had steel mills, chemical factories, foundries, dye factories, very dusty wood-working factories, etc. Every place was a place of heat, grime, dirt, dust, stench, harsh glares, overtime, piece work, pollution, no safety gadgets, sweat, etc. The workers were, as the Italians called them, "Bestie da Soma," beasts of burden. Emphysema, stomach ailments, heart ailments, booze drinking to make the harsh conditions tolerable were what could be expected from such a context. Many men became morose and intolerant toward their wives. They yelled at them, beat them up at the least provocation and were cruel and indifferent to their children.[13]

By 1900 the few Italian foremen were finding jobs for their friends and relatives at Inland, where the work routine even as late as 1923 was described as follows:

> I started at 6:30 p.m. and quit 6:00 in the morning. I worked on the straightening machines. It was eleven and one half hours of deafening noise. The bars going through the straightening machine, the noise of the machine itself, those huge monstrous shear machines cutting a dozen one-inch bars at a time, the bars falling into the receiving bins, the noisy crane continuously passing overhead carrying bars to be straightened and taking away bundles of bars that had been straightened. One could not hear his partner talk, unless the partner, who was only six feet away, spoke at the top of his voice. We were five men on the machine. Four men worked as one rested. Each man worked two hours and rested a half hour. The machine worked continuously because there were always four men at their place by the machine. I was surprised to see men eat a sandwich, eating it with dirty, greasy, oily hands, I was surprised to see men curled up in a wheel barrow sleeping so restfully as though they were sleeping in a soft downy bed. . . . When I saw the bathroom I was horrified. It took me several years to get courage to use it. They called it by its appropriate name, the Shit House. I usually jumped the fence and went behind the bushes. . . .[14]

Industrial accidents were not uncommon. Oral history sources have no trouble recalling—and accounts in *The Star* confirm—frequent deaths of Italian workers in construction, at the brickyards, and on the railroad.[15]

Of the 300 or so Italians listed in the 1900 census, some half-dozen were saloonkeepers, possibly serving as *padroni* as well. Dominic and Victor Pandolfi, Tony Long, Leo Vellino, and Rocco Castabello (Castabile) had places on 22nd Street, while Peter Cassaza and Mike Rich ran taverns on the East Side's 17th Street. A handful of Italian-born people were listed as barbers. Dominick Napoli of the Marchegiani neighborhood on Hanover Street, reputed to be one of the first Marchegiani immigrants (1894) to the city, owned a grocery store. A Caccamesi, Nick Pagoria, had a similar establishment on Lowe Avenue. Joseph Sinopoli, a Calabrian, began his grocery business in 1900 near Portland Avenue and 16th Street, next door to his residence. He mixed sausage-making with Republican precinct work; both paid off, since he established a sound business (still run today by his descendants) and attained the office of city sealer in 1914. He also taught many young men the art of meat-cutting.[16]

Another early success story was that of Gaetano D'Amico, who arrived in the United States in 1889 from Abbruzzi. After working on the

The Gaetano D'Amico family of Chicago Heights became prosperous spaghetti manufac-
tuers (*Mamma Mia* brand). Their original grocery store of 1902 still stands, operated by
a relative, in a neighborhood that is now Spanish. *Courtesy of the Italians in Chicago
Project, University of Illinois, Chicago. Funded by a grant from the National Endowment
for the Humanities.*

railroad in Missouri, he moved to Chicago in 1892, then to Chicago
Heights in 1895. Seven years later, his family opened up a grocery
store in the heart of the 22nd Street commercial district, while he continued to work at Inland Steel. The success of this business brought
capital, which the family invested in a macaroni business at 17th and
Lowe. "Mamma Mia" brand spaghetti products, bearing the picture of
D'Amico's wife, Giacinta, sold well, and the company expanded into
a larger factory in Steger. Although this side of the business was eventually sold to a large corporation, the original grocery store is still operated by a distant relative in the original location, where it now serves
a mostly Spanish-speaking clientele.[17] Thus the Italian community already had some small and growing businesspeople among its numbers
by 1914.

Oral history sources credit these early immigrants with encouraging
their fellow townspeople to migrate to Chicago Heights. These sources

cannot recall the existence of *padroni* (labor agents) in Chicago Heights. The term itself had a different meaning for them, connoting ownership of a business or a property. They remembered Tom Cellini, the railroad "boss" who hired numerous workers for his crew from among his neighbors in the period during and after World War I. Sources also recalled that grocers and saloonkeepers often helped loyal customers get jobs, but it was not done for a direct cash profit or commission. Another source relates that workers and their wives were often expected to do household favors and chores for their foremen and bosses.[18]

By 1910 the number of Italian people in the city had increased from about 300 to 3,224, more than 20 percent of the town's 15,000 population.[19] This increase set the stage for the development of ethnic social institutions. Most prominent was the founding of San Rocco Church in 1906 under the pastorshop of Pasquale Renzullo. Newspapers credited the land association with helping in the construction of the $15,000 church. Joseph Cercone, then city alderman, is listed as the contractor. Dedication ceremonies included participation by Chicago archdiocesan officials, the Italian band, and several Italian societies—all of which points to a considerable degree of development within the ethnic community.[20]

Renzullo (pastor from 1906 to 1922) had to battle apathy, anticlerical outbursts by Italian socialists, and competition from the Presbyterian Italian mission, the Church of Our Savior. Despite setbacks, however, the pastor succeeded in establishing the Mt. Carmel School in 1912, staffed by the Sisters of St. Joseph, and the Mt. Carmel Social and Athletic Club in 1919, two institutions that played an important role in the community for years to come. The school taught some Italian, and the club taught leadership and discipline, also providing an entree for Italian youth into the very important amateur sports scene in Chicago Heights. The Italian community also looked to Renzullo for solace during World War I, when the Italian army suffered defeat at Capporetto. It was he who led the joyous parade when Austria surrendered to Italy in 1918.[21] He also served as an informal defense attorney for boys who got into trouble with the law. Despite his efforts, Fr. Renzullo was not able to erase the heavy parish debts, and when he was transferred in 1922, Cardinal Mundelein deeded the parish and its debts to the Franciscans. Thus Chicago Heights Italians were ministered to neither by the Scalabrini Fathers (whose special mission it was to serve Italian immigrants) nor the archdiocese.[22]

The San Rocco Church and Mt. Carmel School, however, continued to be important forces in the community. In 1926, Father Pacifico Bonanni, who was to serve there for twenty-five years, was named pastor. Father Pacifico guided the parish through the difficult Depression years, setting up such services as soup kitchens, and in the late 1930s he was successful in getting consistent financial support for the church from Italian businessmen. He was so popular that when he was transferred in the early 1950s, parishioners circulated an unsuccessful petition to keep him on.

Protestantism also played an important role in the Chicago Heights Italian Community. In 1910 the First Presbyterian Church appointed Rev. Eugenio De Luca to make a pitch for support within the Italian community by founding the Church of Our Savior (eventually located at 24th and Wallace in the Hill neighborhood). Under the leadership of Rev. De Luca, the Bible-oriented church used a combination of social services, social functions, and help in finding jobs to pull together a close-knit group of up to 200 Protestant Italian-Americans who participated in a dizzying whirl of Bible readings, choir practices, dramatic performances, youth activities, picnics, parties, and sporting events.[23] Whether these activities were a cause or effect, Protestant Italians in Chicago Heights seemed to Americanize faster and to move into business positions and the professions at a slightly faster rate than did Catholic Italians. A possible explanation of this may be that the church, like the early Puritans, stressed English literacy so that its members could read the Bible. This opportunity to increase their English fluency and the exposure to American culture afforded by church activities speeded up the assimilation process. Although it was accorded a good deal of favorable publicity by *The Star*, however, the Church of Our Savior never represented more than 7 percent of the Italians in the city.

Harsh feelings and name-calling between Catholics and Protestants seemed to characterize the relationship between the two in the early days. Old-timers remember an incident in the early 1920s in which Catholic rowdies led "Svaboda's blind horse" into the sacristy of the little Protestant church.[24] In more recent times feelings have softened considerably. The third generation of the original families is now the mainstay of the Church of Our Savior at its new location on the northern end of Chicago Heights (the original building on the old site has become a Spanish Protestant Church).

Also founded in 1915 by Reverend Eugenio De Luca, pastor of the Church of Our Savior, was the Jones Community Center. Located on the East Side, it was a religiously oriented settlement-house operation aimed at the needs of all the ethnic groups in the neighborhood—Poles, Greeks, Italians, and blacks. Classes in citizenship and literacy, a vacation Bible School, and boys' clubs were part of its program. The center's well-equipped gym was a major draw for generations of East Side youngsters as another avenue for the development of athletic talent, a later key to social mobility. The Jones Center received financial support from the well-established Protestant business community in the city.

However, for most Chicago Heights Italians in the pre-1920 period, the most meaningful social unit remained the family. Sociologist Edward Banfield has proposed the theory that South Italian backwardness can be explained by inability "to act together for their common good or . . . any end transcending the immediate, material interest of the nuclear family."[25] In his 1958 study Banfield criticizes this overemphasis on family to the exclusion of other societal institutions. However, Banfield's "amoral familism" is an exaggeration when applied to Chicago Heights Italians. The churches, mutual benefit societies, *comparaggio* (godparenthood), and the individual immigrant's need to depend on someone other than immediate family in his search for jobs and security in the new land argue against Banfield's concept, as does the rich associative life of Italian-Americans in Chicago Heights.

Yet the fact remains that in Italian and Italian-American culture the family is the strongest social institution. The vast majority of the immigrants were from young families: only 15 percent of the children of citizenship applicants were born in Italy. Eighty-one percent were

A favorite summertime diversion for Italian families was the Sunday picnic in the forest preserve (1930s). *Courtesy of the Italians in Chicago Project, University of Illinois, Chicago. Funded by a grant from the National Endowment for the Humanities.*

born in Chicago Heights, as American-born received citizenship at birth, and were likely to be easily assimilated. Of the 4 percent born elsewhere, only 1.7% were born in Chicago, indicating only a small degree of movement from Chicago to Chicago Heights. The practice of *comparaggio* continued in the new country, thus expanding the biological family. The divorce rate was less than 1% in the Chicago Heights sample, and family size averaged 2.8 children at the time of application for citizenship.[26]

In addition to family and the church, Chicago Heights Italians, like many American ethnics, relied on mutual benefit societies. In the early days, trusted community members went from door to door to collect contributions for people in need. In the years before New Deal social security, unemployment, and disability benefits, these organizations played an important role in softening the impact of hardship in a new land. The Amasenese Society was established in 1906, the Marchegiani Society a few years earlier, and the Unione Siciliana just prior to World War I. They provided visits by a doctor who was on retainer from the society, as well as sick benefits and death benefits. At the wake of a deceased member, the society's standard and badge were displayed. From the money assessed each member at the death of a comrade the societies provided the survivors with funeral expenses, including an Italian band. Wakes were held in people's homes until the 1950s, but Italians also patronized the Gerardi Funeral Home from the mid-1930s. Often the members attended the funeral as a group.

With membership at times of 200-300 people, these mutual benefit organizations spawned women's auxiliaries and sponsored social functions such as dinner dances and picnics. Political candidates appeared at their meetings, typically held once each month on Sunday mornings. One reason for the regional identification of these societies is that membership and benefits were transferable, for instance, between the Amasenese society in Chicago Heights and in Amaseno, Italy, should the widow be a resident of Italy or if the beneficiary returned to live in Italy.[27]

Ethnic societies provided leadership experience and social recognition for their officers, and they reinforced feelings of *companilismo*. Although major offices seem to have been passed around within family clans, mutual benefit societies had little appeal beyond the second generation. Sometimes actuarially unsound, these organizations have dissolved or reorganized in other areas. Currently, the Amaseno Lodge in Chicago Heights is very healthy, benefiting from a sizable post–World War II migration and the institution of the feast of San Lorenzo (August 12th), patron Saint of Amaseno, as a weekend street festival and procession. The smaller Marchegiani Society maintains interest by sponsoring charter trips to Italy. The Sicilian groups seem to have been absorbed by the Italo-American National Union.

Harder to pin down are the Italian radical groups. For example, one small group organized a radical protest in the midst of World War I and had its meeting broken up and four of its leaders arrested by the police for violation of the Espionage Act. *The Star* linked the Italian group and its leader, Dominick Mormile, with the radical-syndicalist Industrial Workers of the World (IWW).[28] The Abruzzesi and the Marchegiani were predominant in this group, which had ties with Chicago radicals and even sponsored a visit during World War I of the Italian philosophical anarchist Carlo Tresca, editor of *Il Martello* (New York).[29] However, strategic placement of a policeman who was taking names near the entrance of the meeting hall ensured a small audience for this dynamic speaker. After World War I, the group seems to have faded out of existence, not even surfacing during the Sacco-Vanzetti controversy, which dragged out until 1927. This lack of involvement was probably the result of pressures by both the authorities and fellow Italian-Americans. Naturalization papers show that several of these radicals, including Mormile, had difficulty obtaining United States citizenship.[30] Surprisingly, oral history sources uniformly testify to the absence of labor radicalism and violence in this rather rough industrial town even in the depressed 1930s.

There is no doubt that Italian immigrants to Chicago Heights suf-

The Devotees of Santa Maria Incoronata bear the statue of the Madonna through the neighborhood streets in the mid-1940s. Note the cash offerings pinned to the streamers flowing from the Madonna's right hand. *Courtesy of the Italians in Chicago Project, University of Illinois, Chicago. Funded by a grant from the National Endowment for the Humanities.*

fered their share of hardships and discrimination, the "uprooting" of earlier immigrants described by Oscar Handlin and other scholars. On the other hand, by 1914 we have some impressive evidence of the ways that Italians were gaining a foothold in business and politics. A 1914 advertising book boosting Chicago Heights listed Rocco Nicosia as the official professional photographer. Italians were listed as owners of five restaurants (possibly saloons) and six groceries. Three ran construction firms, two were in the transport business, and two in the liquor business. Within a few years the Union Co-operative Italiana was founded as a partnership grocery store in a large building on the East Side. Designed to provide lower prices and Italian specialties for its customers, the cooperative also contained a large upstairs meeting hall which became the site of many social and political functions in the years to come.

How did Italians fare in local government in the early years? Orazio Ricchiuto, Michael Costabile, and Vigliotti were members of the police department, but no Italian names appeared on the 1914 roster of the local fire department.[31] Nevertheless, Italians had been represented as

The ethnic store was often an important element in the lives of newcomers. Here they could purchase familiar foods, tobaccos, and condiments, and transplant a part of the Old World into the New. Above is Joe Cipriani (left), in his Chicago Heights store in the 1920s. *Courtesy of Nick Zaranti.*

aldermen in the city since 1904, when Tony Long was elected from the 3rd Ward (Hill). By 1907, three out of ten aldermen were Italian: Sam Zona, Michael Costabile, and Joseph Cercone. Though local government was officially nonpartisan, Italians tended to cooperate with the Republican machine organization of John Mackler and Craig Hood, which actively courted Italians by helping them file for citizenship and by finding them jobs in local industries. The number of wards dropped to seven in 1911, and Italians continued to hold at least one seat, and sometimes two, until the institution of the commission form of government in 1921.[32] For the decade following 1921, no Italian was elected as mayor or as one of the four commissioners.

Newspaper accounts reveal the change from the aldermanic system to the commission form of city government as a progressive effort to eliminate corruption and the influences of liquor and gambling interests. Whether or not this was true in Chicago Heights, the result was a loss of Italian ethnic representation for a lengthy period. In any case, the initiative and apparent success of a number of Italians in business and politics would lend some support to the contention of Humbert Nelli that the history of Italians in Chicago was a history of early social mobility.[33] Their success also illustrates the new opportunities for modest advancement and the middle-class values of the immigrants stressed by John Briggs in *Italian Passage*.[34]

An indigenous organization reflecting the middle-class business orientation of the second generation was the Dante Club. Founded in January 1922 by Pasquale Luongo, Joseph Tintari, Louis Ursitti, Michael Costabile, and John P. Mancini, the club's purposes were to "disseminate American principles . . . to promote the spirit of fraternal life, and to promote social intercourse."[35] Their bimonthly meetings took place in the warehouse of the General Chemical Company on 22nd Street. The Dante Club began with forty-five members but by 1929 had eighty-five, mostly from the Hill neighborhood. In the 1930s the club built its own headquarters on 24th Street. They sponsored patriotic functions, dramatic presentations, and (in the 1930s) spectacular blackface minstrel shows. Proceeds from these events supported the construction of the club building, the paving of the Garfield School grounds, the purchase of stereopticon equipment, the support of a milk program at the school, and other activities. The group also sponsored baseball teams, a boy scout troop, and the distribution of Christmas food baskets. Speakers at Dante Club banquets, held at the Union Cooperative Italiana, included the political and business elite of Chicago Heights, and *The Star* showered this civic organization with good publicity.[36] When the organization made an outright gift of $200 and pledged to buy $35,000 worth of war bonds shortly after Pearl Harbor, *The Star* referred to the club as "in the vanguard of patriots in this community."[37] Such American patriotism, absence of Italian cultural programming, and insistence on the use of the English language at meetings, would seem to characterize the Dante Club as an agent of Americanization rather than as a force for ethnic survival.

Dante Club leadership seemed to rotate among young men whose families were politically active. Infighting among these elements in the late 1930s and early 1940s is said by most observers to have "ruined" the organization. In fact, at the height of the scramble, one faction of the club scheduled a political dinner on the same night as the regular club dinner dance.[38] Nevertheless, the ethnic identification combined with the middle-class aspirations of the Dante Club members is in sharp contrast to the working-class subculture described in Gans's study of Boston Italians.[39] Though not college boys, the Dante Club members seem more like an upwardly mobile Chick Morelli group than the corner boys of Whyte's *Streetcorner Society*.[40]

What was the role of Italians in the Chicago Heights schools? The school system's success at instilling Americanism and perhaps a degree of self-depreciation is illustrated in the following essay by a thirteen-year-old girl at Garfield School in 1925:

> I was born in sunny Italy and came to America when I was nine years old, and I never will go back to Italy again because my father was in America twenty-six years, and after three years he made me come to America. Now he is an American citizen and I thank him very much because he did so many good things for me.
>
> The best thing he did is that he made me learn to read and write American. He said that we should all know the American language.
>
> The first when I came it was in the joyful month of May and he made me go to school to learn. I am so happy that I came to this dear country that I want to be a teacher when I grow up, so I can help other boys and girls learn our language. I am going to be like Miss Peters.[41]

The trend among Italians on the Hill was simply to attend the school nearest them, whether public or Catholic.

Perusal of the 1962 *Mt. Carmel Golden Jubilee Book* suggests that its eighth-grade graduates tended to reside in the eastern portion of the Hill. Convenience, economy, and a male-oriented anticlericalism made for high enrollments at Garfield Public School. When tuition fees for parochial education made Mt. Carmel less attractive to parents, Fr. Renzullo threatened that he would refuse to administer first communion to children not attending Catholic school. Parents sometimes responded by pulling their children out of Mt. Carmel immediately after they had received their communion. Though the Mt. Carmel school staff compromised by offering Sunday morning catechism classes to prepare public school children for the sacraments, antagonism on this subject continued well into the 1950s. As might be expected, this public-Catholic split on the issue of education also served to divide the Italian community from itself.

Governance and control of the public schools remained beyond the grasp of Italians. Until well into the 1930s, few Italian children went beyond the eighth grade; there were no Italian teachers, and no Italians served on the school board. This is in sharp contrast to conditions in the 1950s, when the school board president, most of the board, and many of the teachers were Italian.

How people spend their nonworking hours gives us some picture of their values, lifestyle, and the texture of their existence. Oral history sources stress that in the period before mass media and under circumstances of relatively high population density, ethnic life was filled with the intense and constant interaction of people—relatives, *paesani*, playmates. Chickens, goats, pigs, and horses were also part of the neighborhood scene, as were the corner stores, pharmacies, bakeries, and taverns.

As Albert La Morticella remembered the late teens:

> . . . Chicago Heights was similar to one of the Western towns one sees in the old Western cowboy movies. The streets were unpaved, Twenty-Second Street had twenty-six saloons. Card playing, booze drinking and pool shooting were the only recreation these foreigners would have. Automobiles were very scarce. Everything was horsedrawn. When Twenty-Second Street became paved with cobble stones, the curbs had iron rings imbedded in them to allow horses to be strapped and parked there. The fire engine was drawn by three pairs of horses. It was very thrilling to see the fire engine come thundering down the street to the scene of a fire. The brewery wagons were everyday sights; they were drawn by four horses. Men used to sport around with revolvers in their hip pockets. The ambitious men got special police stars which were pinned to their suspenders. . . .[42]

Families did for themselves: they canned tomatoes for sauce, made wine, beer, and root beer, baked bread, made macaroni, picked *cicoria* in the open fields for both salad and boiled greens, made sausage from the meat of freshly slaughtered pigs, kept goats and made cheese from goat's milk, picked mushrooms, prepared delicacies from burdock stalks, made soap from leftover animal fat, and even prepared natural and "supernatural" cures for broken bones and severe headaches. Old-timers remember "Doctor" Generoso, the herb healer, whose garland

Teenage Italian onion pickers from Chicago Heights pose for a photo in a South Holland onion field, about 1930. Even in the hot summer the girls wore enough clothing to protect themselves from the blowing dust in the fields. *Courtesy of the Italians in Chicago Project, University of Illinois, Chicago. Funded by a grant from the National Endowment for the Humanities.*

of garlic, red peppers, and a magic coin (which supposedly came down from heaven) was used to cure minor ailments. Each neighborhood had a woman who set broken bones. Cicetta Papitto, a midwife, assisted at most births in the Italian community until the mid-1930s, when American-born and -educated Dr. Hugo Long began bringing his patients to St. James Hospital. A Marchegiana woman on the East Side also gained recognition in the community as a fortune-teller.[43]

As members of a self-sufficient community, Italian neighbors freely exchanged food and favors. Family and *campari* visited each other on the slightest pretext, exchanging small money gifts (*buste*) on such occasions as birthdays, baptisms, confirmations, and even the removal of one's tonsils. Close records were kept of these gifts for future reference when the time would come for reciprocation. Weddings, often arranged in the picture-bride mode in the early years, were the highlighted social events in the community. They were often elaborate affairs with a large wedding party and a long list of guests, many of whom received personally hand-carried invitations from the parents of the bride and groom. Because of the importance attached to the proceedings, weddings were often a stressful time: an aunt, a cousin, or an in-law might take umbrage at real or imagined slights or lapses in the demonstration of proper *rispetto* in seating arrangements or the choice of the *compari* (best man) and other members of the wedding party. These events were paid for with the money gifts (*buste*) brought by each family, which sometimes resulted in a valuable nest egg for the couple lucky enough to make a profit on their wedding.

Oral history respondents tell of untutored peasants (first generation) who would regularly make the long trip to Chicago to see the opera and then return home to heated discussion at the barbershops and saloons over the merits of the performance. Further evidence of Italian-American identification with cultural things were the theatrical productions. First- and second-generation young people joined Panteleone Laurino, an East Side (Neopolitan) jeweler, in producing Italian plays and operettas at the Masonic Hall and the Washington Junior High School auditorium in the 1920s and 1930s. In 1925, Laurino's Italian Dramatic Club presented *I Dui Sergenti* and *Romeo and Juliet* (with music).[44] In February 1933 the Eleanora Duse Dramatic Club, under the leadership of Cristoforo Di Sanzo, performed Italian-language radio plays from WJKS (Gary, Indiana) and mounted a production of *I Cieci* at the Washington auditorium on February 3, 1933.[45] During that same month the Dante Club presented its annual lavish blackface minstrel show to a large audience.[46] In April 1933, Attillio Carducci's Italian Presbyterian dramatic group presented *Attorney for the Damned*.[47] A few months later, the Laurino Company presented *La Cieca di Sorrento*, also in Italian.[48] Each production had a sizable cast, and there seems to have been little overlapping of cast members; the audiences were also reportedly large and enthusiastic. This flurry of dramatic presentations reflects elements of cultural retention and assimilation. It also reflects the energetic talent of the young people and (perhaps) the high unemployment rates of the Depression era. But again, it seems inconceivable that Gans's *Urban Villagers* would be engaging in the above activities.[49]

For summer recreation there was the "Tombola," a Sunday evening festival held at Ceroni's Grove or the San Rocco Church grounds, featuring band music and food and climaxed by the "Tombola"—an abbreviated bingo game with ten numbers in two horizontal rows of five. Tickets sold for one dollar each, and these weekly events were sponsored by clubs and the church itself as moneymaking ventures. Prizes of $200 for the first five numbers in a horizontal row (*Cinquina*), $700 for the first full ticket (*Tombola*), and $100 for the second full ticket (*Tombolina*) were standard. Fireworks capped off the evening.

Young men hung around at the gas stations, barber shops, pool halls, and taverns playing *morra*, a finger game, *passatella*, a vicious drinking game, *mozza ferrata*, an Italian version of cricket, and *bocce*. Adjacent open fields and the brickyard swimming hole were the scenes of countless boyhood adventures for generations. Oral history testimony indicates that peer-group influence was strongest among the second-generation cohort, youngsters who entered their teens in the 1920s. The Silver Tavern group and the Dozenettes (both still active) were formed during that era. Later groups appear to have dissipated because of the greater economic and geographic mobility their members experienced.[50]

Second-generation youths also fell prey to the lures of American sports. Many complained that coaches in the 1920s did not give Italian kids a fair break; but impressive percentages of future political and business leaders gained their first community-wide recognition on high school and semiprofessional sports teams. Cases in point are the careers of Hap Bruno and Dominic Pandolfi. Mario "Hap" Bruno moved from the Mt. Carmel teams in the twenties to become manager of the Chicago Heights Athletic Association semipro baseball team in the thirties and one of the first Italians elected to township office in the forties.[51] Young Dominic Pandolfi's stellar performance on the Bloom Township High School basketball team in the 1920s paved the way for his appointment in the early 1930s as the first Italian-American public school teacher in the city.[52] Sonny Talamonte, a race-car driver, was probably the best-known Chicago Heights Italian until his death in the mid-1920s. The success of Chuck Panici as captain of the high school basketball team in the late 1940s and early 1950s laid the groundwork for his successful bid for the mayoralty in 1975.

Italians participated vigorously in another "sport": interethnic conflict. Into the 1950s Italian youths felt alienated from Waspish middle-class West Siders, referring to them as "Mangia Cakes" (cake-eaters or sissies). Gang fights were not infrequent, and in 1925 the conflict became so serious that police moved in and arrested five Italian boys and charged them with harassing the captain of the football team, the son of the fire chief, and other high school athletes. *The Star* reported that the Italian boys protested in court that "everybody had it in for them because of their nationality." The paper advocated a get-tough policy against "gang conceit" and complained about "peanut politicians" making excuses for "poor parents."[53] Nevertheless, delinquency in Chicago Heights was never defined as a serious enough problem to warrant the

A legendary racing car driver of the "Roaring '20s," Sonny Talamonte (Talamont) was the most famous celebrity of the Chicago Heights Italian community. *Courtesy of Nick Zaranti.*

kind of delinquency prevention program that Clifford Shaw and his associates established in Chicago's Taylor Street Italian neighborhood.[54]

The Ku Klux Klan was reportedly strong during the 1920s, and it claimed an attendance of over 3,000 at a 1923 organizational meeting at the Chicago Heights Masonic Lodge. It is quite likely that Italian-Americans were involved in the burning of a "Klantauqua" tent near downtown Chicago Heights in July of 1924.[55] Another incident that possibly indicates interethnic unrest occurred in June of that same year, when a traveling carnival complained to police that "a gang of wops" had plundered their booths.[56]

Community tensions were also reflected in the newspaper, as it felt free to run such anti-immigration material as a cartoon captioned: "This is Not a Dumping Ground—Signed Uncle Sam."[57] The cartoon appeared on the front page of *The Star* in May of 1924. Another insensitive example was the headline "Calabrians Carve" that appeared above a story dealing with Italians involved in an East Side street brawl.[58]

Much of this antagonism on the part of Italian-Americans undoubtedly stemmed from the fact that early Italian political successes under the aldermanic system had been wiped out when Chicago Heights switched to the commission (at large) form of municipal government in 1921. After that, the political commentators repeatedly spoke of the East Side-West Side split. Another gauge of intergroup feelings was job discrimination. Motives are difficult to document, but it was not until 1933 that the school board grudgingly hired Dominic Pandolfi, the first Italian teacher, in a district with 20 percent Italian enrollment. Oral history sources have alleged that the telephone company and other large companies refused to hire people with Italian names for white-collar jobs. Prestigious women's clubs also barred Italian women from their ranks.

Thus—in the 1920s at any rate—there are strong indications of intergroup conflict and the nonpassive reaction of some Italian-Americans to the situation. Yet group identity was never strong enough even to support the establishment of an Italian or Italian-American newspaper.

Probably the matter that irked the Chicago Heights establishment most about the Italian presence was the explosion of Prohibition-related crime in the community during the 1920s and early 1930s. While *The Star* had been apathetic about the murder of "another Italian" before 1920, it was incensed about the negative reputation the city acquired as a result of the activities of Capone-connected bootleggers, which was bad for business. Dozens of gangland murders (including that of former Alderman Tony Sanfilippo), occurring mostly in the East Side neighborhood, shocked the people of metropolitan Chicago.[59] Two major raids—one on the lavish Milano Club in 1925, the other on a variety of booze and slot-machine holdings in 1929—brought national and even international attention to Chicago Heights. In addition, during the late twenties there were sixty-five murders in two years. A federal agent was quoted as saying that Chicago Heights was one huge distillery and that there is nothing in the United States to equal it.[60] Many residents remember Capone's frequent visits to the city, especially his Robin Hood-like performance at a 1931 baptismal reception in the Mt. Carmel School Hall. As "well-wishers" filed past, Capone peeled off one-, five-, ten-, and twenty-dollar bills from random stacks of cash on the front table.[61] Local underworld leaders conducted "Supreme Court" from a bakery on 22nd and Butler—adjudicating everything from domestic squabbles to territorial disputes between "liquor distributors." The bakery was the scene of a spectacular murder in the early 1930s.[62]

One observer has suggested that bootleggers were major employers of runners, sugar buyers, and plumbers (to construct stills), and that the industry brought a measure of prosperity to the community during the Prohibition years.[63] Chicago Heights bootleggers dabbled in both Democratic and Republican politics to protect their illegitimate activities, just as Humbert Nelli has described the phenomenon in Chicago.[64] Oral history narrators suggest that the classic elements for organized crime were all there: an unpopular law, a corrupt municipal government, and a desire for quick economic mobility. Even grandmothers and favorite aunts got into the act, making a little moonshine for a niece's wedding or for a little extra money to pay for piano lesson

The legacy of this plague of lawlessness has been extensive. Former and surviving bootleggers made nest eggs for legitimate businesses or to send their children to college and into the professions. Hundreds of innocent neighborhood people of all ages were terrorized into distorted and cynical attitudes about law and order. Most important has been the criminal image of Italians which non-Italians have held and which non-Sicilians developed of Sicilians within the city. This situation, moreover, added to the burden of young Italians in the Depression era and after in their quest for social mobility and status.

By the mid-1930s there was at least one Italian-American doctor in Chicago Heights, a half-dozen lawyers, a family of successful macaroni manufacturers, the manager of the semiprofessional baseball team, a city commissioner, and a handful of political appointees in mid-level positions. For the majority, however, the 1930s spelled hard times. Along with other groups, Italians appeared on the relief rolls, waiting in line for WPA. Many enrolled in night-school citizenship classes because they feared that noncitizens would be fired from jobs to make room for citizens.[65] Thus applications for naturalization increased in the middle and late thirties. To cope with matters during the difficult winter months, some people resorted to stealing coal from slowly passing railroad hoppers. They formed what the papers called a "moonlight coal company," selling the stolen fuel at bargain prices to friends and neighbors.[66] Others—less creatively but more legally—bartered their work unloading coal cars in return for a small supply for their families.

World War II changed everything. This was no less true for Chicago Heights Italians than it was for other American ethnic groups. War orders brought prosperity to the heavy industries of the city, erasing the ravages of the Depression. The war also brought alien registration and draft registration, and in both categories Chicago Heights Italians were prominent. By March 1942 some 611 people had registered as enemy aliens. While the vast majority were Italians, a considerable number were Germans from the rural periphery of the city.[67] Though there had been thought of relocating Italians, such as was done with the West Coast Japanese, the federal government settled for a photo-identification and registration process. Demographically, second-generation Italian-Americans of Chicago Heights were probably over-represented among draft-age men. The years of birth of the children of citizenship applicants clustered in the late teens and the twenties. An early 1942 monthly draft call included thirteen Italians of the thirty white men called up.[68] A photo of departing inductees in downtown Chicago Heights at about this time also reveals a heavy representation of Italians.

This group of Chicago Heights military inductees in June 1942 includes a large number of Italian-Americans. *Courtesy of Nick Zaranti.*

Toward the end of the War, *The Star* regularly featured Italian-American war heroes, war dead, and even champion war bond buyers.[69] The patriotism of the wartime period, the traveling and education that the war entailed, the Americanization involved in the military service, as well as the GI benefits for postwar education and home purchases, had a strong impact on Italian-Americans as on all Americans. In the post–World War II period, Italian-American GI's went to college and into the professions in significant numbers for the first time, formed new families, and moved during the late forties and early fifties into new housing to the north and west of the old neighborhoods, but housing that was often well within Chicago Heights city limits. The East Side seems to have emptied out the most quickly, partly as a result of the pressures of a new black migration to the neighborhood during the war.

On the other side of the ocean, the war had brought destruction and still greater poverty to southern Italy. This seemed to spark a new exodus from Amaseno of everyone who had any claim whatsoever to American citizenship. They were from a different Italy and were more aggressive, better educated, and better equipped to move ahead than were their predecessors. This was a matter of no little resentment between the old and new immigrants. A new chain of immigrants, including the large Planera family, settled on the western end of the Hill neighborhood, thus preserving it as an ethnic enclave until today—a shot in the arm for Italian retention unparalleled among other ethnic groups in Chicago Heights. There seems to have been no sizable post-war influx from the other major Italian towns which had provided stock earlier to Chicago Heights.

During the post–World War II period, Italians began to come into their own in local elective politics. Though one Italian had been named commissioner in 1927 (one term) and another, Maurino Ricchiuto, in 1935 (he was reelected in 1939), it was not until 1947 that an Italian became mayor. This was Ricchiuto, who had changed his name to Richton. Though Chicago Heights Italians voted Republican on the national and local levels in the 1920s, they joined the Roosevelt coalition in 1932 and stayed in the national Democratic camp through the 1948 presidential election. However, they supported Republican Richton and others on his ticket in the nominally nonpartisan municipal elections in 1935, 1939, and 1947.[70]

A liberal arts graduate of Northwestern University and the son of a Republican grocer, the American-born Richton was drawn into politics in 1935 by an audience's enthusiastic response to his speech in Italian condemning crooked politicians in both parties.[71] His education, youth, and polished speaking style made him the first Italian politician acceptable to West Side voters. However, though he was a hero in the Italian community, Richton did not make much of an effort at a grass-roots organization.[72] He was denied the renomination by the Mackler faction of the Republican party in 1951; but he returned as mayor in 1963 in alliance with Democratic (and Italian) township committeeman John Maloni, who himself was elected commissioner that year. Elected for the third time in 1967, Richton shifted again toward the Republicans. In ethnic terms, the 1967-1971 city commission had three Italian-American commissioners out of five. Further indication that Italians were voting on the basis of ethnicity is the success of Democrat Anthony Scariano, who was returned to the state legislature with consistently heavy majorities from 1958 until the early 1970s. A liberal protégé of Senator Paul Douglas, Scariano was fiercely independent of the pressures of the Richard J. Daley machine in Chicago.

In 1975, Chuck Panici, the son of an Amasenese saloonkeeper on 22nd Street, put together a tightly organized Republican-oriented political machine based on ethnic ties and a reformist desire to make Chicago Heights an "All-American City." Though resisted by The Star, Panici won easily in 1975 and again in 1979. He was, by the beginning of the 1980s, the leader of one of the most successful local Republican organizations in the state. And although his group was often accused of nepotism, Panici pointed out somewhat justly that almost everyone in town (especially among Italians) was related anyway. Politically, Italians in Chicago Heights had arrived. On the other hand, there seemed to be a trend of Italian candidates running against each other, thus negating the ethnic factor.

It had not, however, been a clean sweep. Though Italians dominated the grade school board of education and the park board, in the 1960s and 1970s they were forced to share power in the state legislature, the high school board, and the township board, and they remained underrepresented on the newly created community college board. This last point may be explained by the fact that the district is much larger than the city boundaries. The banks, savings and loan associations, the newspaper, and top management positions in national corporations have thus far resisted heavy Italian penetration. But the professions and small businesses are today very heavily Italian.

The second- and third-generation children of the Italian immigrants have "made it." Their ethnicity, however, is not the ethnicity of their forebears. The Italian language is not spoken much in these later generations. The East Side Italian neighborhood is no more. Bilevel and ranch house dwellers express nostalgia for the cooperative neighborliness of previous generations and for the time when downtown Chicago Heights was alive; but it is only nostalgia. However, interest in San Rocco Church remained high in the post–World War II period. A new school and a refurbished church were financed and paid for within a few years. The parochial school's enrollment remains high, and Italians from all over the city look forward to the church's festival each June, even though the present pastor is not Italian and there are no regular Italian-language masses.

The Marchegiani Society, in cooperation with the city government, has worked out a goodwill, sister-city relationship between Chicago Heights and San Benedetto del Tronto. This has resulted in mutual visits by large delegations in both directions. More the 300 Chicago Heights residents have traveled to Italy to see the birthplace of their parents under the auspices of this sister-city program. Clan-sized family picnics and the Amasenese Society's five-year-old Feast of San Lorenzo celebration are other indications of a continuing but changing ethnic identity in the city.

Thus, the historical movement of Italians into Chicago Heights is one drawn from several Italian regional sources, chain-migration style. In the early part of this century, when the labor needs of the new industrial Chicago Heights coincided with the stagnant economic conditions of a half-dozen Italian towns, a significant transfer of people and culture took place. Though they gained some economic and political success almost from the beginning, the major Italian-American experience was hard work and slow progress. Discrimination and prejudice against the newcomers was heightened by Italian involvement in illicit bootlegging and Prohibition-related activities. The group's quest for economic betterment was interrupted, to say the least, by the Depression but speeded up through the assimilative aspects of sports and their strong participation in World War II. The growth and persistence of the Italian population, as well as the general postwar prosperity, propelled the Italians of Chicago Heights into a dominant role in the community. Their progress is colored, however, by the dynamics of ethnicity, which makes their success story an Italian-American one rather than an Italian one. The culture has shifted from an immigrant one to an ethnic one. And although this culture of Chicago Heights Italians has changed over the past century, theirs remains distinct in many ways from the general American culture. They have moved up in the world without having melted completely.

Moreover, the small-town suburban setting, immune from the harsher forces of change in the urban immigrant experience, has allowed for a higher degree of continuity, group identity, and visible social mobility among Italians than might have been the case in the big city. They were apparently spared the widespread practice of the *padrone* system and the frequent residential changes of Chicago's Italians chronicled by Nelli; but they were not spared the discrimination and the identification with criminal elements that occurred in the big city. Because of continuity and the relatively limited number of Italian cities of their origin, the rich texture of their associative life was probably greater than that of big-city Italians.

Chapter VIII

LOUISE AÑO NUEVO KERR

Mexican Chicago:
Chicano Assimilation Aborted, 1939-1954

> *The Mexican is here and in considerable numbers. He is here to stay. We have welcomed him because he works well and cheaply. We have used him to do the tasks which Anglo-Saxons do not care to do. We have used little or no intelligence in helping him to a decent housing situation. We have given him the back alleys of our cities. We have called him 'greaser' and left him to fight his own way as best he can. We have wondered that he does not show more enthusiasm for becoming Americanized.*
>
> — Hubert Herring *(1931)*

LARGE-SCALE MEXICAN IMMIGRATION to Chicago began in 1916 with the recruitment of 206 railroad track laborers from the Texas-Mexican border. The 1920 census counted 1200 Mexicans in Chicago, most of whom worked for the railroads, the steel plants, and the packing houses. Expanding steadily through the twenties, the Chicano community (Mexican and Mexican-American) reached 20,000 by 1930, establishing Chicago as a major center of Mexican settlement in the United States. Like the European ethnics who preceded them, they gathered in neighborhoods adjacent to the industries which recruited them: the Hull House area of the near West Side (railroads); South Chicago (steel plants); and Back of the Yards (packing houses). As ethnic newcomers they suffered the traditional hardships of limited and unstable employment along with cultural prejudice; as Mexicans they also suffered from racial prejudice. Although family formation was increasing, most of the Mexicans at the end of the decade were still young, male, and unskilled. Hoping to return eventually to their homeland, they remained Mexican rather than "American" in cultural as well as legal nationality.[1]

The Depression years of the thirties markedly reshaped the Chicano community. Immigration halted, back-and-forth journeys to Mexico dwindled, and repatriation—both voluntary and involuntary—reduced the number of Chicago's Mexicans to 16,000 by 1940. Despite Depression rigors, the settlements firmly established their identities, and Mexicans began to play a new—if still limited—role in interethnic union and community activities in all three neighborhoods. While the proportion of Mexican immigrants in the Chicano population decreased, their American-born children grew in number.

By 1940 a relatively large second generation, for the most part born or raised in Chicago, was beginning to reach maturity. On the verge of assuming leadership and defining the direction of community activities, these young people were Americans with little interest in Mexico. Guided by past experience, observers presumed that within a decade, given a normal course of events, Mexicans would find it easier to obtain skilled jobs, move freely throughout the city, and enter the mainstream of life in Chicago. Chicago's 1940 Chicano population showed every sign of becoming Mexican-American instead of Mexican in culture as

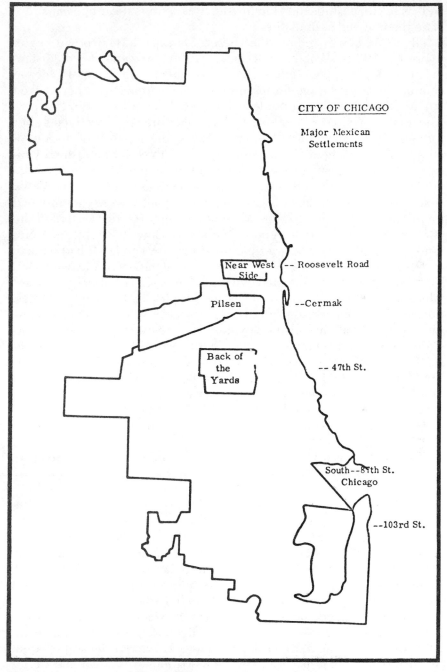

CITY OF CHICAGO

Major Mexican
Settlements

-- Roosevelt Road

Near West
Side

--Cermak

Pilsen

Back of
the
Yards

-- 47th St.

South--87th St.
Chicago

--103rd St.

Major settlement areas of Mexican Chicago, 1945.

well as in citizenship, and of following the traditional European pattern of settlement and assimilation.[2]

By 1940, however, both the United States and Mexico had begun to prepare for war. When war became a reality, two separate and distant events took place. One influenced the nature and direction of Chicano communities in Chicago for more than a generation; the other evoked anti-Mexican-American attitudes which would later be felt in Chicago. The first, the signing of the International Bracero Contract Labor Agreements in 1942 and 1943, precipitated the renewal of both temporary and permanent Mexican immigration, thus re-establishing Chicago as a major destination for Mexican immigrants.[3] The second, the *pachuco* "zoot-suit" riots in Los Angeles in 1943,[4] in which allegedly riotous second-generation Mexican-American youths were carefully and invidiously distinguished from Mexican immigrants, demonstrated the fate awaiting the American-born leaders of Chicago's Chicano community once the pressing wartime need for Mexican labor had passed.

In short, the renewal of permanent in-migration of Mexicans and Mexican-Americans coincided with an increase in antipathy toward Chicanos and other Spanish-speaking peoples in the United States. Suspended during wartime, discrimination against the "Spanish-speaking" in immigration and employment was revived after the war. In Chicago, Mexican-Americans expecting to be assimilated were eventually outnumbered by new immigrants. By the mid-1950s, moreover, the "Spanish-speaking" included Puerto Ricans, Cubans, a variety of South and Central Americans, and Americans of Mexican descent from other parts of the United States. Non-Chicanos—friends as well as enemies—found it difficult to distinguish among the city's "Spanish-speaking." After a promising beginning, Chicanos found their emergence into the life of the larger Chicago community indefinitely delayed.

In 1940, as it became increasingly necessary to prepare for war, the negotiation of labor agreements with Mexico was of strategic importance to the United States. Requiring first the settlement of long-standing disputes, the process of arriving at those agreements was involved and delicate, and no one could have foretold their future ramifications. Relations between the two nations, historically tumultuous, had been particularly strained during the 1920s and 1930s by arguments over expropriated United States industries in Mexico.[5] But Franklin Roosevelt's Good Neighbor Policy had modified the old semicolonial relationship, and as the thirties came to a close, Lazaro Cardenas, president of Mexico from 1934 to 1940, sped negotiations so that an outline for the resolution of outstanding differences had been agreed upon by both nations before the 1940 elections, opening the way for mutual cooperation.

Immediately after the election of Manuel Avila Camacho in the hotly contested Mexican presidential race of 1940, the Western Hemisphere's foreign ministers agreed at Havana on "schemes of political and economic cooperation in the event of war." It was decided that Mexico would supply raw materials while the United States took direct action against the Axis powers. Gradually, following the United States' lead, Mexico began to restrict Nazi activities within her borders and to act as a belligerent neutral. The petroleum expropriation claims finally settled, Mexico shipped increasing amounts of oil to the United States. But not until six months after the United States had declared war did Mexico formally enter the fray, when, in May 1942, two of her tankers were attacked by German submarines and seven of her citizens killed.[6]

For the first time in decades Mexico was a relatively unified nation, the political left pacified by the alliance with Russia and the leaderless right weakened by repressive government action. Mexico agreed to contribute manpower as well as raw materials to the war effort. In fact, one day after the first oil tanker sinking, 3,000 Mexicans were certified by the Immigration and Naturalization Service for temporary entry into the United States to harvest sugar beets.[7] But cognizant of the difficulties which previous immigrants had encountered and fully aware that Mexicans would probably emigrate despite those difficulties, the Mexican government insisted on an international agreement guaranteeing workers decent housing, employment, and health conditions, and freedom from discrimination.[8] For the first and perhaps only time in the history of diplomatic relations between the two countries, Mexico held a competitive bargaining position from which to force the United States to protect the interests of Mexican immigrants, and she took advantage of the opportunity.

Based on recommendations made fifteen years earlier by Manuel Gamio, the first *bracero* ("worker") agreement was designed to alleviate the United States' agricultural labor shortage, especially in the Southwest. The agreement of August 4, 1942, the model for those that came later, guaranteed workers a specified, mutually agreeable contract period (usually six months), prevailing minimum United States wages and hours, paid transportation to and from their homes, and housing during the period of the contract. United States agencies were to supervise the recruitment of workers in Mexican cities, and Mexican government representatives were given inspection and appeal privileges.[9]

While it helped to satisfy the need for agricultural labor in the Southwest, the August 1942 covenant did nothing to stem the growing shortage of unskilled labor in U.S. transportation and industry. Industrial employers looked to Mexico to fill the void.[10] As late as November 1942, the Mexican government opposed any importation of Mexican labor "outside the present labor agreement."[11] Indeed, citing repeated and flagrant violations, Mexican authorities threatened to suspend further recruitment under the August arrangement unless corrective measures were taken.[12]

To convince Mexico of his intention to abide by the labor agreement and to negotiate nonagricultural compacts, President Roosevelt traveled to Mexico on April 20, 1943 to talk with President Avila—only the second time in history that presidents of the neighboring countries had met face to face (the first was when Presidents Taft and Diaz conferred at the border.)[13] Out of this meeting came Avila's commitment to allow the temporary migration of nonagricultural workers under the same terms as agricultural workers. Most of these were destined for track labor on southwestern railroads, but many were recruited directly to the East and Midwest to work in other industries as well as on the railroads.[14]

Chicago's need for additional workers had already been established by the time the negotiations were completed. In the spring of 1943 a government survey of major labor markets reported that without "full use of all minority groups the labor supply [will be] inadequate."[15] In addition, Chicago's industrial diversity proved a handicap to companies dependent on unskilled labor. For as the manpower shortage worsened, the low wages paid for these jobs proved less and less attractive to domestic workers (including blacks). A study of "Unfilled Openings" in the Chicago region predicted that only five percent of track labor jobs would be filled by domestic workers at the prevailing wage of sixty-five cents an hour.[16]

As the headquarters city of the Railroad Retirement Board, the agency charged with supervising the importation of Mexican railroad workers, Chicago had ready access to this new and important source of war manpower. Between May 1, 1943 and September 30,1945, more than 15,000 Mexican railroad workers were brought to Chicago—11 percent of the 135,350 imported to the United States during the war. The number and percentage of workers recruited to Chicago during that period was exceeded only in the San Francisco area. The great majority of workers brought to the Chicago "region"—including Wisconsin and Iowa—were housed in the northern half of Illinois, most of them in the Chicago metropolitan area. Major employers were the Chicago, Burlington, and Quincy; Chicago, Minneapolis, St. Paul, and Pacific; Chicago, Rock Island, and Pacific; Chicago River and Indiana; Chicago and Northwestern; and Chicago's Union Station.[17] These employers alone recruited a total of 15,344 Mexican workers between 1943

Mexican-American camp housing in Rock Island.

and 1945. The Indiana Belt Harbor Railway housed additional workers in Blue Island and Norpaul, two Chicago suburbs which still have Chicano populations.[18]

Of the more than 15,000 workers recruited to Chicago, a substantial but undetermined number renewed their contracts at least once, their average total stay lasting seven and one-half months. In 1944 and 1945, at the peak of labor importation, the Mexican immigrant population in the Chicago area increased by approximately 7,500—the average number of contracts in effect at any given time.[19] Most of these immigrants, of course, had only temporary status. But while the *bracero* agreements provided employers with temporary labor, they offered many workers an opportunity to familiarize themselves with the city in anticipation of returning—legally or illegally. Some workers broke their contracts and attempted to remain permanently. Special instructions were issued by the Immigration and Naturalization Service for the return of "missing workers."[20] Clearly, Chicago was re-established as a major destination for Mexican immigrants.

Although Chicago railroads benefited substantially from the *bracero* program, imported workers were still not adequate to fill labor needs. Even as late as October 1945, when the program was coming to a close, three railroads that had consistently exceeded their quotas of Mexican workers had a combined total of more than one thousand unfilled jobs.[21] This was true of other Chicago industries as well, some of which had also been made eligible for recruitment of Mexican laborers. In order to reduce their manpower shortages further, some employers sought Mexican-American as well as Mexican workers. Mexican-American agricultural workers found industrial wages and working conditions better than those on farms and thus were attracted by the offers of these employers. Northwestern Wire and Steel, needing "861 workers ... to take care of their present needs" in 1945, was unable to provide housing that filled the requirements of the international agreements and was therefore ineligible to obtain immigrant workers. Undaunted, the company decided instead to request "50 or more American born Mexicans ... in the vicinity of Pharr, Victoria, and San Antonio, Texas."[22] For perhaps the same reasons, Sears, Roebuck and Company, in need of "garment markers," asked that a circular be sent to Dallas and Forth Worth, where "the employer feels that persons with these qualifications would probably be available."[23] Thus Mexican-Americans as well as Mexican immigrants came to Chicago as a result of the general labor shortage.

While the wartime need for Mexican laborers continued, and it could be assumed that their stay would be short, the increase in the Mexican population posed little threat to the city or its Chicano settlements. Long-time Chicano residents knew of *braceros* in their neighborhoods but initiated little direct contact with them. While the program lasted, however, Chicanos observed the friendly concern of federal and city officials for the well-being of the temporary workers. For example, when the *braceros* complained about the constant diet of meat and potatoes, demanding beans and tortillas instead, Mexican cooks were hired, if they were available.[24] If they were not, American cooks were given the recipes and foodstuffs necessary for the preparation of Mexican dishes.[25] When the *braceros* objected to filthy and unsanitary bathrooms, federal inspectors made sure that new bathrooms were added and old ones thoroughly cleaned. Wage disputes were submitted to arbitration.[26]

City officials were not less solicitous. English classes were provided for the *braceros*, paid for by the Chicago Board of Education; the Chicago Department of Recreation offered facilities for sports and entertainment; and legal assistance was available in case of arrest. In 1944, 1945, and 1946 the Board of Education added a new social studies unit to the public school curriculum to help familiarize all American students with their nearest good neighbor, Mexico. And public school teachers were encouraged to participate in summer institutes in Mexico to perfect their use of the Spanish language and to increase their understanding of Mexican culture.[27]

After the war, *bracero* recruitment was phased out as the need for

Mexican-Americans learning English in adult education classes during the early forties. *Courtesy of Chicago Historical Society.*

workers diminished. However, the number of Chicanos in the city kept growing. Along with ex-*braceros* who had broken their contracts in order to remain, there were legal and illegal immigrants arriving without the aid of the War Manpower Commission or the Railroad Retirement Board. Faced with a continuous and permanent increase in the Chicano population, city officials gradually became less tolerant. In Chicago, tensions similar to those which had led to the *pachuco* riots in Los Angeles just a few years before were revived, making it clear that the sources of those tensions had only been suspended, not eliminated.

The nature of those tensions had been delineated in Los Angeles in mid-1943, just as an agreement was being negotiated for the importation of nonagricultural Mexican workers for industrial labor in the United States. The California episode began when zoot-suit-clad Mexican-Americans allegedly sought out and beat sailors dating Chicano girls, as a warning to stay out of Chicano neighborhoods. First in Oakland in May 1943, and then in Los Angeles in June, retaliating sailors and other servicemen cruised unmolested through Chicano neighborhoods in taxicabs, seeking zoot-suiters upon whom to vent their anger. These incidents had been preceded by a barrage of incendiary press reports portraying *pachucos* as delinquent, subversive, and socially unredeemable Mexican as well as Mexican-American youths.[28]

The "zoot-suit riots"—and so-called despite the involvement of servicemen—threatened to disrupt friendly relations between the United States and Mexico. After a flurry of correspondence between Mexican consular officials and the State Department, it was reported in the *New York Times* in late June 1943 that there were "no cases where Mexican *citizens* [italics mine] were involved in recent fights in Los Angeles between service men and youths wearing zoot-suits, but the State Department promised speedy action on claims resulting from such cases if there were any. The announcement followed a visit to Secretary Hull yesterday by Francisco Castillo Najero, the Mexican Ambassador, who expressed his government's concern over the disturbance."[29] *Pachuco* youth, whether involved in the incidents or not, were characterized as socially "marginal" *Mexican-Americans* unable to accept either the majority culture or that of their parents (presumably immigrants), and as conscious or unconscious agents of subversion trying to disrupt the war effort.

Under the press of wartime labor needs, a distinction was thus being drawn between the Mexican-Americans who had allegedly participated in the "riots" and the Mexicans who were being exhorted to work—temporarily—in the United States. The actions of the two governments confirmed a belief long held in the Chicano *barrios:* it was better to be an alien protected by the shield of international diplomacy than to be a second-, third-, or fourth-generation American unacceptable to the majority.*

At the time, there were no such disturbances in Chicago, but Chicanos in the settlements were very much aware of and worried by their occurrence in the West. Reaction to the riots, moreover, showed not only awareness but identification with the plight of Chicanos in California—an ethnic identification relatively new in the Chicago neighborhoods. For example, while decrying the "riots," one local Chicano leader called for unified *nation-wide* celebration by all Chicanos of Mexican Independence Day (September 16, 1943), "in honor of the ideal of democracy and of human rights."[30]

The Chicago Area Project, a local social service organization at-

---

*It should be emphasized that the United States-Mexico agreements concerning *braceros* stipulated only that Mexican *nationals* be protected against dicrimination.

tempting to find solutions to the problems of growing juvenile delinquency, was aware of the potential for similar outbreaks in Chicago. In
1942 this predominantly professional and non-Chicano group had req-
uisitioned a "Survey of Resident Latin American Problems" to determine the depths of deprivation and the potential for "subversion" in
Chicago's Latin-American communities. Concluding that there were
severe problems of illiteracy, poverty, and delinquency, the survey
had strongly suggested that the "depressed and downtrodden" were
particularly susceptible to subversive influences.[31]

On the basis of that report, the Chicago Area Project applied for a
$45,000 grant from the Office of Inter-American Affairs, a federal agency
headed during the war by Nelson Rockefeller. The $10,000 eventually
granted was authorized by Rockefeller, perhaps coincidentally, on
April 22, 1943, two days after the meetings between Roosevelt and
Avila.[32] Intended to aid "Latin Americans in Chicago"—inaccurately
described as "first and second generation immigrants from [sic] Chicago"—the grant proposal noted that "it is the conviction of those making this request that the full integration of the Mexicans into *our national
life* [italics mine] depends upon the development of programs which
will build leadership in the Mexican group and the encouragement of
programs of self-help in which the Mexicans themselves can play a
responsible and active part."[33]

The grant's sponsors believed that Chicanos, like any other immigrant group whose immigration flow had ceased, would be easily
assimilated into "our national life." They went ahead with their program for "Latin Americans in Chicago," declining for whatever reasons
to make distinctions between alien and American-born Chicanos and
other "Latin Americans." The program initially met with some success.
A social center, reported by the *Chicago Tribune* to be for "Americans
of Mexican descent," was built on the near West Side.'[34] Community
organizations were formed; an American-born leadership emerged, and
important segments of the Chicano community responded.

By the early 1950s, however, the assimilationist policy enunciated
in the Chicago Area Project program was cast in doubt as the Chicano
population grew and changed in composition. Renewed in-migration,
begun as a temporary measure during the period of wartime tolerance,
drew fire after the war when it turned into permanent, often illegal,
immigration. The antagonisms it fed culminated in 1954 in "Operation
Wetback," the roundup and forcible return of "undocumented" aliens
and their families.[35] Mexican immigrants thus found that, with the need
for their labor ended, they had lost the strong diplomatic support of
their government and were at the mercy of American public opinion.
And the "Americans of Mexican descent" who had been partially suc-

cessful in entering "our national life," though profiting at first from the harsh experience of Mexican-Americans in Los Angeles, soon discovered that the favorable treatment of Chicanos in Chicago had been a temporary expedient. Meanwhile, second-generation Chicano leaders who had developed as spokesmen during the war were being challenged by newly arrived immigrants as well as by those in authority.

Between 1943, when the nonagricultural labor agreements were first implemented, and 1954, when anger against "illegal Mexican immigrants" reached its peak, Chicago's Chicano population grew to include not only the first immigrants and their children, but a new generation of immigrants—legal and illegal—along with a substantial number of Mexican-Americans from elsewhere in the United States. The flow into the Chicago area paralleled the general movement of Chicanos to cities in the 1940s: by 1950, 71 percent of all "Mexican Foreign Stock" recorded in the U.S. Census were living in urban areas; 19 percent were in rural non-farm communities; and only 10 percent were on farms, despite the large-scale recruitment of Chicano agricultural workers during the war.[36] Larger and more widely dispersed than a decade before, the Chicano population of 1950 had undergone other profound demographic changes, the contours of which are only partially revealed by census returns.

We know, for instance, that nationwide there was an extraordinary

Mother and child on the steps of their home in the Hull House neighborhood.

upsurge in the number of illegal immigrants during the late 1940s. A glance at the reports of the Immigration and Naturalization Service shows that between 1946 and 1950, besides the few temporary *braceros* who stayed behind, only 38,000 Mexicans were admitted legally as permanent alien residents. In those same years, however, 1,110,000 undocumented aliens were apprehended by the Immigration and Naturalization Service and returned to Mexico. The agency itself has calculated that, in the absence of extraordinary measures, it has the capacity to "catch" only 20 to 25 percent of the actual illegals in the United States at any given time. In this four-year period, without such measures, by the service's own calculations there were an estimated four million undocumented Mexicans in the United States.[37] As early as 1947 there were reports in the Chicago press of the apprehension of illegal Mexican aliens in the city.[38] Even if INS estimates were reduced by half (that is, to one apprehended illegal for every two in the country), there would still have been an estimated 2,038,000 new immigrants between 1946 and 1950.

In the 1920s, when the first period of Chicano immigration was at its peak, Illinois ranked fourth as the state of intended destination listed by legally admitted Mexican aliens.[39] Though many fewer immigrants journeyed to Illinois than to Texas, California, and Arizona, word-of-mouth news of opportunities in Illinois had been greatly responsible for the rapid increase in its popularity. But for the Depression, the rate of immigration would likely have grown, for since the resumption of immigration in the 1940s, Illinois has maintained its fourth-place position as a state of intended residence. Since 1950, 10 percent or more of all legally admitted Mexican aliens have given Illinois as their destination.[40] Even if only 1 percent of the estimated 2,038,000 illegal Mexican immigrants between 1946 and 1950 (already half the government's estimated figure) had reached Chicago (the only major metropolitan area in Illinois), at least 20,038 new immigrants should have been counted in the city in 1950. It seems surprising, therefore, that the 1950 census showed only 4,200 new Mexican immigrants in the entire Chicago region, half of them in the suburbs rather than in the city. Nor does this figure differentiate among those immigrants who were legally admitted and stated their intended destination, those who were illegal entrants (and may not have been enumerated in any case), and those who migrated to Chicago after living elsewhere in the United States.

Because of clear undercounting of all minorities, occasional miscalculations, and changes in definition over the years, census data must be handled cautiously. Nonetheless, they do give some insight into the nature and extent of the demographic changes that took place among

Chicago's Chicanos between 1940 and 1950. First and most obvious was the growth of the population. Despite undercounting, the number of Chicanos in the city grew from 16,000 to 24,000 (50%), and the number of Chicanos in the metropolitan region grew from 21,000 to 35,000 (66%). Half of the 4,200 new immigrants recorded were living outside the city limits in 1950.[41] While the city's Chicano population expanded by 50 percent, its total population increased by only 6 percent—the smallest proportional increase for any previous decade except that of the Depression. Chicanos arriving in metropolitan Chicago were evidently running counter to the general movement of the entire population, for while their numbers grew by more than 14,000, the region as a whole recorded a net out-migration of more than 18,000. Between 1940 and 1950, the city's officially counted foreign-born Mexican population grew by 21 percent, but was still only a little more than one-third of the total Chicano population.[42]

Those recorded in the 1950 census as "new" or additional immigrants were in all likelihood legal entrants who were eligible to remain permanently. They brought with them greater affluence, better work skills, more education, and more contacts in the United States than had the earlier immigrants. Half of these "new" immigrants settled in the suburbs, making use of their skill advantages in the expanding industries of the metropolitan region. Joining the more than 2,000 immigrants in the suburbs were 2,200 Mexican-Americans; together they formed new Chicano settlements which date their beginnings to the war and postwar periods. Some of these Mexican-Americans may have moved from Chicago, but most were new in-migrants recruited by small suburban factories in Aurora, Bensenville, and Arlington Heights. The emergence of these outlying settlements illustrates a new pattern of migration and settlement which began in the 1940s, one which bypassed Chicago entirely and took the more affluent and skilled from Mexico and Texas directly to the suburbs.[43]

Migrants to the older and more established Chicano settlements in the city included more illegal immigrants ineligible to remain permanently than did those going to the suburbs. Whether Mexican or Mexican-American, moreover, migrants to the city were poorer and less skilled, in search of the same kinds of jobs that had drawn the original immigrants of the 1920s. They became laborers, service workers, and "operatives" (semiskilled industrial workers)—occupational groups which the 1950 census indicated were increasing in number in the city. White-collar and professional positions, also expanding in number, were being filled by better-educated workers who apparently were just beginning to use their higher earnings to leave the city.[44]

The 1950 census made no distinctions between old and new Mexican immigrants, or between Chicago-born and Southwest-born Mexican-Americans, so it is difficult to be precise about their proportions. But the census does show that the average age of the total Chicano population rose more than fifteen years between 1940 and 1950, and that the average age of U.S.-born Chicanos rose more than nineteen years in the same period, certainly indicating a substantial in-migration of older Mexican-Americans. Just as significantly, the average age of the Mexican-born rose hardly at all—from 40.3 years in 1940 to 43.1 in 1950—suggesting that there had been a substantial in-migration of younger Mexican immigrants. Without including either the *braceros* observed by Chicanos in their own neighborhoods, or the undocumented workers complained about by the INS as early as 1947, these figures demonstrate that the recent influx of younger Mexican immigrants and older Mexican-Americans was sufficient to alter the normal aging curve of Chicanos.[45]

Further evidence of major Chicano in-migration was the rising sex ratio, which once again reached the first-generation proportions of the twenties. Reflecting the in-migration of large numbers of young men, the sex ratio for foreign-born over the age of fourteen was 1.926—almost two men for every woman. For the native-born, the ratio was 1.269, lower than that of the foreign-born, yet still higher than in the thirties, when virtually all of the native-born were second-generation children of Chicago's first immigrant Mexican families. For native-born between the ages of fourteen and forty-four, the sex ratio was 1.870, almost as high as that of the immigrants and much higher than a decade earlier.[46]

Of the four groups of Chicanos living in the Chicago settlements in 1950—the first immigrants, their children, new immigrants, and Mexican-Americans from elsewhere—the immigrants, old and new, fared better than the Mexican-Americans, and for the first time compared favorably in average income and education to the European foreign-born with whom they most frequently lived, the Poles and Italians. In fact, foreign-born Mexicans had a higher average education than either the Poles or Italians (probably because of the in-migration of better-educated younger Mexicans from urban Mexico), and they were earning more money than Polish foreign-born immigrants, who were by that time much older than Mexicans.

Midway between what the census calls "whites," whose average income rose from $1100 in 1939 to $3300 in 1951, and "non-whites," whose income rose from an average of $500 in 1939 to $2100 in 1951, all of the foreign-born, including Mexicans, had benefited from the war and postwar prosperity. Though their "real" income had risen very

TABLE I
FOREIGN-BORN INCOME, EDUCATION, AND AGE IN
CHICAGO, 1950

	Income	Years of Education	Age
Mexican	$2,566	5.6	43.1
Italian	$2,630	4.8	
Polish	$2,374	5.5	58.3

U.S. Bureau of the Census, *U.S. Census of Population: 1950*, Vol. IV, *Special Reports*, Part 3, Chapter A, "Nativity and Parentage" (Washington: U.S. Government Printing Office, 1954), pp. 3A-258, 3A-262, 3A-265.

little, their wage increases at least corresponded to those of the general population.[47]

Mexican-Americans, on the other hand, including those from Texas, were receiving lower wages than either the foreign-born or second-generation Italians and Poles, despite the fact that they had more schooling than immigrants and almost as much as other native-born ethnics.

TABLE II
EDUCATION AND INCOME: MEXICAN-AMERICANS,
MEXICAN-BORN, ITALIAN-AMERICAN,
AND POLISH-AMERICAN: CHICAGO, 1950

	Years of Education	Income
Mexican-American	9.0	$2,066
Mexican-born	5.6	$2,566
Italian-American	10.2	$2,610
Polish-American	9.3	$2,701

U.S. Census of Population: 1950, loc. cit.

Mexican-Americans aged fourteen to twenty-four, the group which had received its education most recently, would continue to be at a disadvantage when competing with second-generation European ethnics for jobs because the gap in their years of schooling was growing wider, partly as a result of the in-migration of less-educated Mexican-Americans from Texas (see Table 3).

Despite the apparent and growing disparity in education between native-born Mexican-Americans and other second-generation ethnics in Chicago, Mexican-Americans from Texas and other parts of the Southwest continued to come, in part because they were having an even more difficult time in rural areas and in other urban regions of the United States. In Los Angeles, for example, income was much

TABLE III
EDUCATION: SECOND-GENERATION ETHNICS,
AGES 14 TO 24: CHICAGO, 1950

	Years of Education
Mexican-Americans	9.4
Italian-Americans	11.5
Polish-Americans	11.7

U.S. *Census of Population: 1950, loc. cit.*

lower for both the foreign-born and the native-born, even though their average education was similar to that of Chicanos in Chicago. *Tejanos* (Texas Chicanos) lagged behind in education and income both in cities and rural areas, with rural *Tejanos* earning the least money of all Chicanos and completing the fewest years of school (see Table 4).

TABLE IV
INCOME AND EDUCATION: CHICANOS IN THE U.S., 1950

	Income	Years of Education
Los Angeles		
Mexican-born	$1,931	6.1
Mexican-American	$1,731	9.5
Texas Urban		
Mexican-born	$1,164	3.1
Mexican-American	$1,096	6.0
Texas Rural		
Mexican-born	$ 748	1.4
Mexican-American	$ 803	3.8
Chicago		
Mexican-born	$2,566	5.6
Mexican-American	$2,066	9.0

U.S. *Census of Population: 1950, op. cit.*, pp. 3A-265, 3A-378; U.S. *Census of Population: 1950*, Vol. IV, *Special Reports*, Part 3, Chapter C, "Persons of Spanish Surname," p. 3C-56.

In October 1953, the *Chicago Sun Times* reported that according to the director of the Chicago office of the Immigration and Naturalization Service, there were "nearly 100,000 Mexicans" in the city, including "15,000 wetbacks," even though the census had counted only 24,000 Mexicans three years earlier.[48] Old immigrants, new immigrants, and Mexican-Americans from elsewhere viewed their lives in Chicago through the prism of past experience. The old immigrants, settled into a routine existence, had made great economic strides in the twenty or more years they had been in the city. Nostalgic for a Mexico which no longer existed, they had little in common with recent arrivals except national origin. New immigrants, from a Mexico almost 50 percent urban,[49] came for industrial jobs that were better paying than the agricultural work some of them had done as *braceros*. Mexican-Americans, especially those from Texas, left behind migrant farm work and a depressed rural economy. Economically at least, for all of them—old and new immigrants and Mexican-Americans from the Southwest—life in Chicago was an improvement over what they had known before.

Chicago-born Chicanos, on the other hand, having grown up in the city, realized that the promises of progress made in the thirties and forties had not been fulfilled. At a time of heightened interest in the needs of various "nationality groups" in the city, a time also of official desire to maintain "good Latin American relations" for the sake of the war effort, they had been encouraged to step forward as community leaders and spokesmen. For a brief period, from 1943 to shortly after 1950, these Chicago natives became the articulate representatives of Chicano interests, recognized as the liaison between the settlements and the larger Chicago community. Intent on entering that community and forcing it to take account of Chicano needs, they failed, however, to recognize that in-migration brought with it conflicting needs and, indeed, conflicting interests which they could no longer fully represent. They were supported initially as a counter force to the potential influence of *pachucos*, delinquents, and subversives, only to be outnumbered and eclipsed by the thousands of new migrants who came partly as a result of their success. In the end, their economic status did not improve. For the foreseeable future, in fact, they would continue to fall behind other ethnic groups in the city.

Neither the eruption of intra-ethnic conflict nor the gradual dissipation of utopian promise could have been predicted as the decade of the 1940s opened. The city's need for workers and the fear of subversion enabled Chicanos to gain the attention of civic leaders and their organizations. One such group, the Pan American Council, issued a report in 1942 noting the need for Chicano workers.[50] Speaking on behalf of Mexican immigrants "not accustomed to organize . . . and not vocal about matters which are of deep concern to them," the director of the Immigrants' Protective League observed that United States citizenship was being "forced upon" Mexican immigrant residents working in defense industries and suggested that the pressure be eased if their labor was to be retained.[51] At the same time the *Chicago Tribune*, in February 1942, applauded "loyal" South American allies for severing relations with the Axis powers and acting "to suppress totalitarian influence, bar war materials to the Axis, halt business relations with the same, and outlaw Fifth Column activities."[52] In general, then, the exigencies of war temporarily created a more positive atmosphere for Chicanos as well as for *braceros*.

The Chicago Area Project, led by Clifford Shaw and Henry McKay (associates of Saul Alinsky at the Institute for Juvenile Research), capitalized on the general feeling of good will when it appealed to the Office of Inter-American Affairs for money to develop "Mexican" leaders who could represent their own communities. Shaw and McKay had long ago concluded in *Delinquency Areas* (1929) that "disorganization [juvenile delinquency] is intensified by the influx of foreign national and racial groups whose old cultural and social controls break down in the new cultural and racial situations in the city."[53] Growing out of the research of Shaw and McKay, the Chicago Area Project had been organized in the early 1930s to find ways in which "nationality groups" and low income populations living in deteriorated city neighborhoods could be "incorporated into our culture and through which they could find their place in the physical and social structure of the city."[54] As we have seen, the Project's 1943 grant request in behalf of the "20,000 Latin Americans in Chicago" was based on these assumptions.

The Chicago Area Project, the Immigrants' Protective League, and the Pan American Council had conflicting ideas about who the "Mexicans" were and what they needed. The Pan American Council and the Immigrants' Protective League saw "Mexicans" as immigrants needing help in combating job discrimination—that is, as permanent immigrants. The Chicago Area Project defined "Latin Americans" as Mexican-Americans and Mexican immigrants raised in the United States who required help in developing community leadership. Each of these civic groups, however, was intent on "Americanizing" the foreign-born through naturalization and the United States-born through social programs.

The Immigrants' Protective League, for example, surveyed "Leading Employers of Mexicans in Chicago" in 1944 and found that most Mexicans "still" worked for the railroads, steel mills, and packing houses. In the "tight" wartime labor market "there were no unemployed Mexicans in South Chicago," the railroads had been forced to import "contract laborers from Mexico under international treaty," and the meatpackers were "seeking more contract laborers."[55] Contract workers, protected by the agreement with Mexico, were guaranteed good working conditions and job security. Permanent Mexican aliens, on the other hand, enjoyed no such protection and were subject, as always, to discriminatory hiring practices.

Defense industries were required to screen out undesirable or potentially subversive elements in the work force, and one means of doing so was to require citizenship. Though Mexico was an ally, Mexican alien residents had almost as much difficulty establishing their loyalty as did Italians and Germans, and throughout the war they were continuously pressured to certify their permanence by becoming citizens. On the basis of the survey of "Leading Employers," the Immigrants' Protective League and the Pan American Council, concerned about the rights of resident aliens, spoke out in behalf of Mexicans. Employers and government agents charged with maintaining security eventually agreed to a compromise proposal presented by the Council and the League: aliens registered in citizenship and naturalization programs would be eligible for employment in defense industries.[56]

Adena Miller Rich of the Immigrants' Protective League pointed out, however, that the educational prerequisites for naturalization worked a particular hardship on those who, previously without educational opportunity, found it difficult to attend night classes. There were not enough child-care facilities to allow women to take advantage of English and civics classes. Many communities simply lacked the teachers and social workers necessary to staff adult education programs, though the Board of Education had attempted to provide English instruction for *braceros*. Arguing that "the solidarity of the United States is best promoted by removing old obstacles, not creating new ones, and by making naturalization possible for the great numbers of foreign-born who have cast in their lot with this country and are so eager to call it their own by legal right," Rich urged that the educational requirements for citizenship be modified. Looking beyond domestic "solidarity," moreover, she warned that "the 'shut-out' effect upon the citizenship applications of certain races and peoples at this time, such as Mexicans and Chinese, might easily reverberate abroad and endanger the avowed 'Good Neighbor Policy' of the United States."[57]

Under Rich's leadership, the Immigrants' Protective League took an active part in creating and staffing adult English and civics classes to prepare Mexican aliens for citizenship. These "Americanization" programs were located in railroad work camps, defense plants, and neighborhood schools as well as in the traditional settlement houses. Permanent aliens who were eligible recognized the advantages of acquiring citizenship. Encarnacion Chico, a long-time resident of Back of the Yards, had entered the country legally in the 1920s and worked in the packing houses throughout the Depression. Fluent in English, Chico was able to become a citizen soon after the war began. For him the coming of the *braceros* meant prosperity and job security. "Many braceros," he has recalled, "came to work in the [stockyards] and for the railroads. They lived in their own areas and stayed away from us. Practically all the Mexicans worked in the yards in those days."[58] Chico's language facility and his long experience in the United States enabled him to mediate between the contracted workers and the foremen, and his eligibility for naturalization quickly made him a valuable employee, a candidate for advancement. He became a meat inspector and after the war bought a home in the neighborhood.

On the other hand, a good many long-time residents found it difficult to establish their permanence and to take advantage of their work experience in Chicago. This was especially true for those who had entered the United States before 1924, when registration was first required of entering Mexican aliens, and for those who—knowingly or unknowingly—had continued to cross the border without legal sanction. The Pan American Council pointed out that Mexicans seeking to be naturalized "are now finding that they must apply for a certificate of registry to legalize their unregistered entry. In effect a Mexican who entered the country in a legal manner [that is, before 1924] now finds himself illegally in the country."[59] Illegal aliens, of course, were subject not only to discriminatory hiring practices but to deportation. Many aliens, unsure whether they could prove legal entry, declined to apply for naturalization, thus limiting their participation in wartime prosperity.

The Americanization plan of the Pan American Council and the Immigrants' Protective League was based less on the desire to see Mexicans naturalized than on the realization that there was an intimate connection between the positive public response to "Mexicans" and the war effort, and that this positive response to Mexicans was dependent on the willingness of Mexicans to be Americanized. In fact, while advocating enlightened revision of naturalization requirements and encouraging the creation of programs to benefit Mexicans along with other foreign-born aliens, the League predicted as early as 1942 that xenophobia against non-naturalized Mexicans would surface during postwar demobilization.[60]

In any case, between 1942 and 1945 many older Mexicans were able to take advantage of the wartime labor need and of the help of the Pan American Council and the Immigrants' Protective League. Long-time residents with jobs, especially in the packing houses of Back of the Yards and the steel mills of South Chicago, were better off than younger Mexican-Americans not in the armed services. The latter possessed relatively little work experience, and were less able than their Spanish-speaking elders to mediate between *braceros* and management.

To aid "Americans of Mexican descent," the Chicago Area Project used its $10,000 grant from the Office of Inter-American Affairs to organize the Mexican Civic Committee in 1943. As an ethnically segregated Neighborhood group, the committee was meant to develop political leaders who could articulate and implement social and economic goals for "the community." The organization's English name symbolized its "American" orientation, if not its Mexican-American membership.[61]

Neither the committee nor its leadership generated antagonism during the war. Most permanent residents were too busy working to be concerned about the problems raised by the group. Chicanos, like others in the city, felt unified by their extensive participation in the war. "There is hardly a [Mexican] family," said the *Chicago Tribune,* "that does not have a father, brother or sweetheart in active service."[62] The committee pragmatically cultivated good relations by informing the Chicano community of war news, social news, and current projects through its newsletter, a mimeographed sheet written almost entirely in the American argot of the young.[63] It also capitalized on the general good will fostered by the Pan American Council, the Immigrants' Protective League, and other sympathetic civic organizations by initiating contact with the larger Chicago community.

One of the Mexican Civic Committee's first projects was to launch yet another "Mexican Social Center" on the near West Side. Late in June 1943, days after the outbreak of the *pachuco* riots in Los Angeles, a meeting was held at Hull House to generate backing for the proposed center; in attendance were not only the Mexican Consul and Father Joaquin De Prada, the priest at St. Francis of Assisi Church, but also Mayor Kelly—a demonstration of the Committee's early success in bringing its efforts to the attention of official Chicago. Unfortunately, Father De Prada, speaking after the mayor had departed, ended his expression of support for the project with the words, "Long live Spain, Franco's Spain!" Reflecting the committee's new-found sense of power, Chairman Frank X. Pax did not let the incident pass unnoticed. He complained directly to Cardinal Stritch (with carbon copies to the Mexican Consul, the Chicago Area Project, and the Office of Inter-American Affairs), reporting that members of the priest's congregation had been dismayed at his remarks. "A great majority of the people," Pax informed Cardinal Stritch, "booed Father De Prada's fascist outburst."[64] No doubt one element in the Civic Committee's fledgling display of muscle was its awareness—and perhaps the awareness of the mayor and the Mexican Counsul as well—of what Pax, writing to the local Mexican Patriotic Committee in August 1943, called "unhappy incidents for all the American continent which had taken place recently in Los Angeles"— the *pachuco* riots.[65]

A request for further government funding was denied in 1944,[66] but the Mexican Civic Committee was well enough established by then to continue on its own and to expand its activities, many of which were aimed at overcoming intra-ethnic and neighborhood differences among

"Mexican-Americans" in Chicago. The Mexican Social Center was successfully completed in 1945. Ceremonies dedicating the center to the memory of Manuel Perez, a Chicago-born Congressional Medal of Honor winner who had died in Luzon "en defensa de los ideales libertadores de su patria y de su raza" ("in defense of the liberating ideals of his country and of his race"), received city-wide press coverage.[67] The center's director was paid by the Illinois Department of Welfare and the Chicago Area Project, but its staff was "Mexican."[68] Built for all Chicano residents, in point of fact it served the young, almost all of whom were United States-born.

At war's end the Mexican Civic Committee seemed to have fulfilled two of its major goals: providing a platform for the airing of Chicano grievances and giving leadership training to its members. Part of its success came from its near West Side proximity to the Immigrants' Protective League, the Hull House Association, and the Juvenile Protective Institute, all of which took an interest in Chicano problems. As

Mayor Martin Kennelly honors Toribio Tapia, president of the Latin American Fraternal Society, November 16, 1947. *Courtesy of Calumet Industrial and Railroad Photographs.*

members of the Metropolitan Welfare Council of Chicago, an umbrella organization of social service agencies, these groups were instrumental in aiding the Mexican Civic Committee to find a broader forum. In 1947 the Metropolitan Welfare Council created a subcommittee on Mexican-American intersts. Chaired by Frank Pax, the subcommittee laid the groundwork for a city-wide conference held in May 1949. Composed almost entirely of Mexican-American men and women from all three settlements, most of them long-time residents, the subcommittee agreed on a common set of problems and presented a unified front to the conference, which was convened for the sole purpose of learning about "Mexican Americans in the city."[69]

Representatives of twenty-three organizations listened to the report prepared by Pax and his subcommittee. "Due to the absence of an official survey or study of the Mexican American in Chicago," he noted, "there are no exact figures available on this subject." Beginning with a brief history of the Mexican settlements, Pax went on to acknowledge their contemporary differences. But his major emphasis was on their common achievements and problems. Social life, he said, had changed dramatically since the Depression. Pool halls had given way to *cantinas* as meeting places for men. But ownership of the *cantinas* remained in the hands of "Greeks, Italians, Irishmen, and Poles." Entertainment had expanded in the early forties to include two Spanish-language moviehouses, one of them an abandoned Jewish operahouse, neither of them owned by Mexicans. English-speaking Chicanos freely attended downtown and neighborhood moviehouses where general audience films were shown, without fear of segregation. And there were two weekly radio programs of Chicano news and entertainment.[70]

In the eyes of Pax and the subcommittee, however, these were meager improvements. Despite the wholehearted participation of Chicanos in their churches, unions, settlement houses, jobs, and in the war, they were still isolated from the larger community and subject to conditions outside their control. Pax prodded his audience with the information that the only Spanish-language newspaper in existence in Chicago during the war had opposed the participation of Mexicans and Mexican-Americans because of continued discrimination against them. As proof of Chicano efforts in the war, he cited veterans' groups in all three settlements, most of them composed of "American born or Mexicans raised in the United States since childhood." A state-chartered veterans' group had eighty members, but could claim a "potential of 400." Near West Side veterans organized posts of both the American Legion (named in honor of Manuel Perez) and the Veterans of Foreign Wars. Characteristically, in Back of the Yards, where Chicanos were accustomed to interethnic organization, they joined with other ethnics to form neighborhood veterans' clubs.[71]

Their wartime achievements had presumably confirmed the right of Chicanos to claim the perquisites of "Americanness." But Pax asserted that they were still not accepted by either the churches or the unions. Neither Catholic nor Protestant churches served the communities well, said Pax, because they perceived Chicanos as non-Christians still in need of missionary efforts. And though Mexicans had participated enthusiastically in the unions at first, they were now apathetic—and with good reason. He reported, for example, that although an estimated 6,000 Chicanos worked in Chicago's steel industry, after a decade of unionism there was still "no Mexican American on the staff of the union in the entire Calumet region with the exception of a single office girl in Indiana Harbor."[72] Chicanos were doing somewhat better in the packing house unions, but not as well as in the 1930s, when their support had been important to union survival. Historically ex-

A Spanish-speaking meeting of the United Packing House Workers. *Courtesy of Chicago Historical Society.*

cluded in Chicago as elsewhere, only a small proportion of Mexican railroad workers were unionists.[73] In all these industries, the postwar recession saw many Chicanos lose their jobs to returning veterans.

Even the settlement houses, always more sympathetic to Chicanos than other Chicago institutions, had failed to respond adequately. As of 1948, said Pax, no Mexican had ever served on the Hull House board of directors, and there was only one Chicano staff worker. The Mary McDowell Center (formerly the University of Chicago Settlement House) had never appointed a Mexican to its board, although there were a few in its community advisory group. South Chicago's Bird Memorial Center did have two Chicanos on its board of directors and several staff members as well, but these latter were clerks, semiprofessionals, and janitors.[74]

In sum, Pax's report was a scathing condemnation of the policies and programs carried on by the very organizations he was addressing. Using his experience as past chairman of the Mexican Civic Committee and hoping to capitalize on the general air of receptivity which had prevailed in the 1940s, Pax deliberately made his report stern and unbending in tone.

As a result of the meeting and of Pax's report, the Metropolitan Welfare Council formed another subcommittee, this time on "Special Problems of Mexicans in Chicago," with Pax as coordinator. Citing the lack of Mexican leadership in unions, civic groups, and social service agencies, this new subcommittee recommended that a new and expanded Mexican-American Council be established, along with a citywide umbrella organization of various Mexican-American groups. In the fall of 1949, as a direct result of the Welfare Council's efforts, the Illinois Federation of Mexican Americans (ILFOMA) was born.[75]

Funded initially by government money, staffed by younger Mexican-Americans, and encouraged by receptive Chicago civic leaders, the Mexican Civic Committee must have seemed to have fulfilled its original objectives with relative success in 1949. But already nativistic sentiment against Mexican immigration had begun to rise again. As early as 1948, the number of unwanted illegal aliens in Chicago had increased to such an extent that the Immigration and Naturalization Service included Chicago in its national search for "missing" alien workers.[76]

Still, the attitude toward Mexican immigrants was ambiguous: so long as they did not remain and become a permanent problem, they were acceptable. It was reported, for example, that while illegal immigrants were being deported, approximately 800 contract laborers had been "sited" in Chicago during 1947.[77] That same year, the *Chicago*

Star, according to Frank Pax, had reported a latter-day attempt to use Chicanos as strikebreakers:

> At Inland Steel last week May 1, 1947, the company imported some 250 Mexican workers two days prior to the calling of the strike. They were brought up from Texas for the sole purpose of scabbing, but the company plans back-fired; not only did the Mexicans refuse to scab but they marched into the Inland Steel office in a body to demand the company pay their transportation back home and to add to the company's chagrin, signed up in the union as an indication of their solidarity.[78]

It is not clear whether the "Mexican workers . . . from Texas" were immigrants or Mexican-Americans. In either case, they were used as a weapon against steelworkers in general, especially against long-time Chicano steelworkers who were divided from these "scabs" only by claims of longer residence and employment, and perhaps by citizenship.

On the recommendation of the Metropolitan Welfare Council, the Mexican American Council was formed in 1950. Its stated objective, like that of the Mexican Civic Committee of the 1940s, was to "bring about the integration of the Mexican residents of Chicago into the life of the wider community through education and organization among Mexican Americans."[79] At first the Council had some success in defending Chicanos in the courts: two of its cases received national attention. In October 1951, the *Christian Science Monitor* reported that the Council had proved that a Chicago policeman, Michael Moretti, without provocation or sufficient cause, had fatally shot two Chicanos and wounded another. Moretti was fired, charged with manslaughter, and jailed.[80] In the second case, that of Pedro Romero and his family, the Council reported to the police and the city's Commission on Human Relations that the Romero home in South Chicago had been vandalized, and a sign saying "Get Out! We Don't Want Mexicans!" placed in their front yard. The Council noted that Maynard Wisher, Director of the Civil Rights Division of the Commission on Human Relations, was too busy to investigate the charges. The police, on the other hand, assigned a guard to the family's home, effectively curtailing further harassment.[81]

Notwithstanding these minor successes, a 1953 *Chicago Sun-Times* story demonstrated, graphically and depressingly, that with all the efforts made over the previous decade, there were "in all of Chicago . . . 7 Mexican nurses, 5 teachers, 1 lawyer, 1 dentist, 1 policeman." School enrollment among Chicano children was shrinking even as the population expanded. Between 1951 and 1952, for instance, the number of high school graduates dropped from eighty-three to sity-nine.[82]

Meanwhile, new Mexican immigrants attacked the Mexican American Council's leadership and diluted its effectiveness. Angry at a 1953 press report which referred to Martin Ortiz, the Council's chairman, as a representative spokesman of the "community," Salvador Herrera, president of the newly organized *Comite Patriotico Mexicano,* denounced Ortiz, stating emphatically that the latter did not represent *La Colonia Mexicana* at all, and that if he continued to be so presumptuous as to claim to do so, the *Comite* would consider legal action.[83] The Council and its leadership were similarly criticized by Jose Chapa, Chicago's most popular Mexican radio personality.[84] The Council's loss of support was an ironic blow: Mexican-Americans who had replaced the leadership of an earlier immigrant generation in the forties now found themselves challenged in the early fifties by a new, more outspoken, and more numerous generation of immigrants.

In 1954 the roundup of undocumented workers reached its peak in "Operation Wetback." Virtually everyone in the Chicano settlements was affected in one way or another. Recently arrived illegal immigrants, of course, were vulnerable to apprehension and deportation, as were members of their families, some of them American-born. In addition, older immigrants still without proof of legal entry, and—by virtue of the McCarran-Walters Immigration Acts of 1950 and 1952—naturalized aliens suspected of subversive activities, were also subject to deportation.[85] Mexico, no longer of strategic importance, had lost the diplomatic leverage which had enabled her to support and defend immigrants during the war.

An illustrative if perhaps extreme example of the shifts that had taken place in ethnic identity within the community, in the larger community's response to "Mexicans" in the city, and in the relative position of the two countries, is the case of Ramon Refugio Martinez, a naturalized American citizen who had led Mexican popular front organizations in Chicago during the 1930s and participated in the packinghouse labor controversies of the 1940s. A former president of the Mexican Community Committee, Martinez had been defended during the forties against accusations of subversion and attempted overthrow of the government on the ground that he was a United States citizen whose conviction should be resisted "because the democratic rights of the American people are in danger." In 1953, still accused of unspecified subversive activities and vulnerable to deportation under the McCarran-Walters Act, Martinez was both supported and attacked as a *Mexican* rather than as an American. His defenders wanted to "strike a blow to the oppressive mass-scale deportation of *Mexican* [italics mine] people from the United States."[86]

Despite the official 1950 census count of only 24,000 Chicanos in the city, it was obvious that old residents had been outnumbered. Their claims of permanence and longevity no longer sufficed to distinguish them from newly arrived in-migrants. Mexican-Americans, mindful of the strides made during and after the war, felt ambiguous toward continued Mexican immigration, but resigned themselves to the change which that immigration necessitated. In December 1953, the Mexican American Council took note of the change:

> With the influx of thousands of Puerto Ricans, Mexican nationals and other Spanish-speaking people to the city, particularly during the past five years, the Council has been extending its works and programs to include all Spanish-speaking people. The membership of its board of directors and its city-wide membership list consists of persons from all walks of life and represents many nationalities. ... The Mexican American Council serves as a means to an end by which Spanish-speaking people may have a representative voice in the affairs of the Chicago community.[87]

Mexican-Americans commemorate the 153rd anniversary of Mexico's independence in 1963. *Courtesy of Chicago Historical Society: James M. Hall, photographer.*

But without the ethnic unity that had been encouraged during wartime, Mexican-American leadership receded, representing only a small percentage of the city's Chicanos, and even smaller percentage of the Spanish-speaking. After a decade of vital participation during which Chicanos had looked beyond the settlements toward one another and toward the larger community, they once again turned inward, divided by neighborhood interest and loyalty as in the past, but also by generation and ethnic identity. The assimilationist vision of Mexican-Americans had been overwhelmed by the Mexican ethnicity of postwar immigrants.

THE MELTING POT

Chapter IX

JACQUELINE PETERSON
The Founding Fathers:
The Absorption of
French-Indian
Chicago 1816-1837

> *If we write histories of the way in which hetero-*
> *geneous people arrived on a frontier, come to*
> *form themselves into a community . . . we shall*
> *be writing something complementary to histories*
> *of disintegration. We shall be writing the history*
> *of becoming whole.*
> — Robert Redfield,
>   *The Little Community*

I

Have you built your ship of death, O have you?
O build your ship of death, for you will need it.
And die the death, the long and painful death
that lies between the old self and the new.

— D. H. Lawrence,
"The Ship of Death"

RIDING FROM THE EAST TOWARD CHI-
cago, a visitor today can see, even in bright midday, the hulking steel
mills of Gary burning miles off in the distance. Orange and black clouds
hang heavily in the sky as if to warn of some terrible pestilence. Travelers grimly lock themselves in airtight spaces away from the stench of
sulphur, and hurry by.

Rising with the Chicago Skyway bridge, one wonders what kind of
unheavenly vision William B. Ogden, early nineteenth-century indus-
trialist and railroad maker, could have had. A century after him, the
corroded assemblage of steel girders, rail tracks, foundries, breweries,
and shipping cranes fans out below the bridge like a giant black erector
set devastated in a fiery holocaust. Humans do not easily belong here.

Beyond the curve of the bridge is Wolf Lake. The vision is startling,
for there in the midst of angry waste and decay—and Wolf Lake itself
is an industrial sewage dump—is a scene which has eluded time: the
grassy marshes, frozen in winter, which swell and flood the lowlands
in spring; the shallow lakes and ponds broken only by narrow glacial
or man-made ridges; the stunted scrub oak, poplar, and pines; the reed-
covered banks lying low in the water so that a canoe need only be
pushed up a foot or two to rest on the shore. It is all there, except for
the stillness and the wild rice of the marshes.[1]

This neglected landscape is what Chicago must have looked like
as late as 1833. It was an inhospitable spot. Its sloughs defied the cart
and buggy: "No Bottom" signs marked much of what was later to become a bastion of straight-laced skyscrapers; ladies "calling" in long

301

silk dresses were often seen wading barefoot in the knee-deep mud. Only canoes or hollowed-out skows made their way with ease across the wet grasslands or wound a path through the wild rice blanketing the Chicago River's branches and streams.[2]

The desolation of the unbroken prairie stretching to the south as far as the eye could reach—as far as Springfield—inspired dread and, only occasionally, admiration. The interminable vista reduced people to miniature stature. The gnawing loneliness did not come from a lack of human company; it came rather from the land, a terrain which took nothing in halfway measure.[3]

Old settlers, army scouts, fur trappers, and the Indians before them waited in the silent heat of summer for the brown prairie grasses to burst into flame in the momentary blaze of fusion of sun and horizon. They listened on white winter nights to the thunder of a nor'easter lashing and breaking the frozen piles on the shore and sending the ice-clogged waters of the Chicago River scurrying backward to ravage its tributary banks. Wolves howled at the shore, and weeks without sun or moon made the inhabitants as blindmen whose only guide was the sound of the wind.[4]

It would later occur to easterners that a way to shut out the lonesome vastness was to reshape the landscape. These town builders, less innovative than in need of psychological fortification, laid the imprint of a grid for city streets and in so doing cut through hill, stream, and forest, drained scores of marshes, raised buildings a full story above lake level, and absorbed a population of more than 4,000 within four short years of incorporation (1833-37), whose members filled the more subtle fortresses of judicial, political, religious, and social organization.[5] The master planners had conceived a blueprint for the systematic production of civilization. But it was unnatural; it could have been anywhere.

Its place name was *Checagou*, and that, at least, we owe to its earliest inhabitants. Archaeological diggings at the end of the nineteenth century indicated that prior to the European invasion there were at least twenty-one major Indian villages in Chicago's environs, all located on waterways: the Chicago River and its branches, the Des Plaines, the DuPage, the Calumet, and the lakeshore. In early historic times, the rolling Illinois and Wabash country was held by bands of the Miami and Illinois tribal confederations. The Miami maintained permanent summer residence at Chicago, where native women planted, harvested, and stored maize, squash, and beans. Miami hunters tracked the southern Illinois plains in search of buffalo. In spring and summer whole bands gathered to construct fresh mat-covered houses, to kindle a new fire for the coming year, to attend clan feasts, and to open and bless the sacred medicine bundles. By winter the Miami and the Illinois split into family hunting units to farm the waterways for muskrat and beaver.[6]

The Miami tribe was one of nine major Great Lakes Indian groups which developed, between 1600 and 1760, a distinctive tribal identity and culture. They numbered only 4,000 on the eve of the great white migration, a scant percentage of the approximately 100,000 natives who occupied the region. Living far to the north on the upper shores of Lake Michigan and Lake Superior, the numerically dominant Ojibway (25,000-30,000), adventurers and nomadic hunters, were to become the prototypes for the white fur traders. To the south, along the western shore of Lake Michigan, camped the seminomadic Fox, Sauks, Winnebago, and the Menomini wild rice gatherers. Along the eastern shore lived the farming-hunting Potawatomi and the highly structured urban communities of the Huron and Ottawa farmers. At the bottom bowl of the lake were the Miami and the Illinois tribes.[7]

The wide range of Indian cultural variation that developed in the years 1600-1760 is indicative of a stabilizing geographic and ecological order, although a reverse effect was already in motion by the end of that period.[8] Tribes with a relatively static population, a value system ranking leisure above energy expenditure, and a subsistence economy had little need to wander further out beyond the boundaries marking economic survival, except in years of famine or natural catastrophe. The tribal world, a primarily "spiritual" entity, overlay—in fact, was identical with—the geographic area necessary for subsistence. The tribal world-view was centripetal and cyclical—inward-turning and bent to the symbiotic balance of nature's resources.

Each Great Lakes tribe claimed in seeming perpetuity its own loosely defined territorial domain. No one was foolish enough to think that he might, individually, hold title over the land; but tribes and kin hunting units did, through years of tradition, "own" the lands they occupied. Their boundaries were by and large respected. Warfare was a manifestation of tribal honor or of personal revenge, not of geographical or territorial conquest. There was no cause to obtain more territory.

The arrival of the European fur trade, particularly in its Anglo-Saxon phase, had a profound effect on the Indian conception of time and spatial integrity. All the land, even regions of which the Great Lakes tribes had neither heard nor seen, was said to "belong" to Frenchmen and Englishmen. The natives must have thought them vain, these God-like white men who set their linear-progressive stamp on times and places as yet unknown and who vied with one another for the "protection" of their "primitive" wards. Europeans had no respect for the cyclical stores of nature; nor did they respect the spiritual

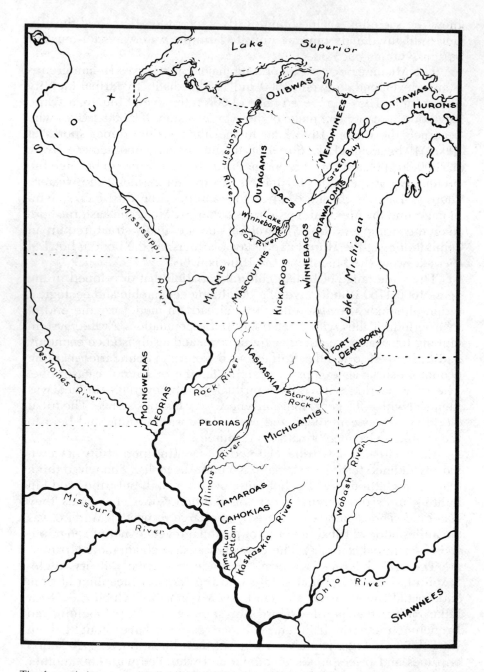

The first inhabitants: Indian tribes of the Great Lakes. *Courtesy of the Illinois State Historical Library.*

knowledge of the "savage." They scoffed at the notion that nature's vicissitudes were personally directed—for good or for evil—toward humans. Natural phenomena were to be understood and then controlled.

Perhaps—although current research signals otherwise—the native momentarily accepted the "superior" notion that a land which had seemed only comfortably to support a population ratio of one per square mile was suddenly limitless in its abundance. Indeed, for the Indian hunter the land was not without limits, and the diminishing herds of elk, caribou, and deer led the natives, already increasingly dependent on European material culture, away from the maize fields into the vast stretches of forest and finally onto the trails of the white fur-trader. These trails, long used by Indian messengers, heavy with wampum and running to announce war, death, birth, or high council, had never been avenues of ingress. They crossed boundaries never surveyed, but which insured the integrity of distinct tribal cultures. With the coming of the fur trade, the ancient roads became highways of destruction.[9]

Competition for hunting grounds and trade routes had by 1800 despoiled most of the diversity and autonomy of the Great Lakes tribes. Early nineteenth-century residents of and visitors to Chicago regarded their Indian neighbors as little more than stray dogs—vermin-infested scavengers. These were, of course, insensitive observers; but a direct result of the fur traffic had indeed been the emergence between 1760 and 1800 of a Pan-Indian culture in the Lakes region, one which mimicked the peripatetic, band-oriented Chippewa social structure and which depended heavily on imported trade goods. The art of pottery-making was lost around 1780. Maize cultivation, once an activity central to the unity of village life, was now carried on primarily for white consumption. Ironically, years of famine brought on by the depletion in game reserves, found Chicago-area Potawatomi buying back at grossly inflated prices corn meal which they had earlier cultivated.[10]

The rapid transition to a fur-trading culture by all of the Great Lakes tribes was propelled by a mistaken supposition that a white-Indian alliance might prove reciprocally enriching. Unfortunately, the disintegration of stable and coexisting tribal structures was the necessary price of the formation of a new social order. Tribal disintegration, even in its earliest stages, had devastating consesquences. The tearing of a social fabric woven by oral tradition left the individual native defenseless in the face of a more sophisticated technology. Indian magic lost face to the gun.

The importation of European goods and foodstuffs destroyed the meaningful division of labor between the sexes. Potters, weavers, basket-makers, stoneworkers, and planters lost their occupations and status rank. Time, once the gentle discipline behind seasons, duties, and rit-

ual, became an albatross. Intricate patterns of consanguineous and af-
fineal recognition and avoidance were destroyed by intermarriage with
whites, who refused to "avoid" certain relatives, tantamount to incest.
Acceptance of "half-blood" chiefs confused, fragmented, and ultimately
defused the potency of clan identification. Above all, the never-ending
search for peltry broke up villages and kin groupings and clouded recognition of tribal boundaries. The result was prolonged intertribal war.[11]

Ancient runners' trails from the north, south, and east crossed at
Chicago. With the establishment of fur-trading centers at St. Louis,
Green Bay, Detroit, Fort Wayne, and Sandusky, the Miami and Illinois
saw their hunting grounds invaded from three sides. From the north
and west came the Sauk, Fox, and Kickapoo, and from the east ma-
rauding Iroquois bands. By the time Fort Dearborn was first built in
1803, the Miami had largely been driven toward the Wabash Valley.[12]

The Potawatomi were already bending under white influence. Earlier habitation near Detroit and Green Bay had exposed their members
to intimate contact with French and British traders. Considerable intermarriage had occurred; dark-skinned daughters of mixed marriages
were often trained and educated in French-Canadian homes, while
sons were encouraged to enter the trade with their fathers. Signs of a
metal age were everywhere: elaborate silver breast plates, crosses, ear-
bobs, and crescent-shaped gorgets; iron spear- and arrowheads; copper
cooking utensils; copper studs ornamenting the avenging end of tribal
war clubs; and finely crafted tomahawks and hatchets.[13]

The influence of educated mixed-bloods within the tribe increased
out of all proportion to their actual numbers. By 1833, on the eve of
Potawatomi removal, a fair number of mixed-blood leaders had assumed, by American appointment, "chiefly" status. Such "chiefs" and
their followers came eventually into the villages to live side by side
with British and French traders, sharing food, equipment, and advice.
They built one- or two-room log and bark huts, and in language, dress,
and material wealth they took on the trappings of European civilization.
Their social movement between white and Indian lifestyles seems to
have been fluid. Their services were at least temporarily needed—as
buffers between antagonistic cultures.[14] The majority of Potawatomi,
meanwhile, still camped in band villages along streams and rivers.
Their mat-covered, dome-shaped wigwams did not impinge on the
landscape but followed its curves and hollows, forming a loose circle
on high, level ground. They retained the language of their ancestors,
traditional religious beliefs, tribal authority, and social structure. However, their lives, like those of their mixed-blood leaders, had been ir-
reparably altered. They had become part of a larger community.[15]

Ancient runners' trails and waterways met at Fort Dearborn (Chicago). *Courtesy of the Illinois State Historical Library.*

No member of the fur-trade world—either white or native—es-caped the anguish dealt by the extinction of the "occupation" and the transition to a highly organized and stratified society launched by the Yankee invasion of the Old Northwest. Most white traders were neither prosperous nor urban in outlook. Rather, they blended into the Pan-Indian culture developing in the Great Lakes region, learning Ojib-way, the *lingua franca* of the trade, as their Indian counterparts learned a French *patois*. They adopted many of the customs and habits of the tribes with whom they wintered. They too were the victims of lavishly financed entrepreneurial ventures emanating from New York and Mon-treal, which culminated in a regionwide monopoly between 1811 and 1834 led by John Jacob Astor's American Fur Company.[16] When Astor's profits dipped sharply between 1828 and 1834, he merely sold his Great Lakes holdings and moved the trade beyond the Mississippi. His white and Indian employees—clerks, traders, *voyageurs,* and *en-gagés*—were left behind to stagger into the new world rising from the East.

Traditionally, the lower Great Lakes fur trade has been divided into pre-Astor entrepreneurial and post-Astor monopoly phases. The division implies that prior to the formation of the American Fur Company access to the trade was open to anyone with gumption, and that profitable competition was carried on by small French-Canadian, British, mixed-blood traders throughout the region. However, this does not appear to have been the case. Few people of little means realized profits from the fur trade; most lived barely above the subsistence level and were perpetually in debt to supply agencies at Detroit, Montreal, or Michilimackinac. In collusion with British investors, Astor's Southwest Fur Company held a virtual monopoly over the Chicago region prior to the War of 1812, which forced his partners to sell their American interests. A reorganized "American" Fur Company was the result.

What actual competition existed prior to the AFC consisted of eastern capitalists who supplied local middlemen traders through their personal agents at Detroit and Michilimackinac. Such high-level competition survived throughout the Astor regime. The Detroit houses of Conant & Mack and William Brewster financed the ventures of two of the most successful traders at Chicago between 1820 and 1828.[17] The local traders themselves were never able to compete successfully. They lacked both capital and the respect of their employers. Despite a wealth of field experience, such men were regularly refused promotion into the inner exeuctive chambers of the great trading houses. Most seriously, prices of pelts and trade goods were fixed in the East and abroad.[18]

The Chicago of 1816-1834 was thus a community of such middlemen traders and their employees—clerks, *voyageurs*, and *engagés* of French, British, American, Indian, and mixed extraction. They existed for the most part under the aegis of the AFC. Their work, social aspirations, and group solidarity revolved around the profit-and-loss ledger kept by Astor's chief assistants at Michilimackinac, Ramsay Crooks and Robert Stuart, and the annual trek to the "great house" on that island. Thus, in the following discussion of early Chicago lifeways, one must not forget the hidden specter of a ruling class looking sternly down Lake Michigan from its storehouse at Mackinac. Entrance to this ruling class was closed to local men. The exclusion of Chicago residents between 1816 and 1834 meant that they were already accustomed to taking orders from outsiders when the eastern speculators arrived. It also meant that the natural instinct of men to acquire status, dignity, and personal gain would exercise itself in other spheres. This was as true for the Potawatomi as for the British, French-Canadian, and "métis" employees of the trade.

The multiracial settlement of the early 1800s at Chicago was no utopian paradise, though exchanges between Indian and white culture had produced perhaps a less sophisticated ordering of financial and social status than that of the eastern newcomers. Slander, theft, moral outrage, extravagant competition, hints of petty squabbling, and even murder marked the social lives of the old settlers. But they were also marked by the security of clan; a tenuous kind of racial harmony; an easy, enveloping spirit that gathered in the entire village; and a peaceful, irreverent disdain for "progress."

II

The earth keeps some vibration going
There in your heart, and that is you.
And if the people find you can fiddle,
Why fiddle you must, for all your life.
— Edgar Lee Masters,
"Fiddler Jones"

Chicago, on the eve of the Fort Dearborn garrison's second coming in 1816, lay fallow, as it had lain for centuries, awaiting the imperceptible retreat of Lake Michigan's glacial waters to dry out its sandy bottom. Riders on horseback, skirting the sand dunes of the lower bowl of the lake, must have been struck, as they took the northward curve, with the notion that they were treading on ground already claimed. Such men were not geologists, but when they saw the blue mist veiling the high hill in the distance, they named it Blue Island. This mound and its less auspicious neighbor, Stony Island, were by some chance of nature built of sturdier bedrock than the surrounding terrain. The mounds had been spared the leveling scrape of the last glacier. And when American soldiers arrived in 1816, the triple arms of the Chicago River still embraced much of the land for six months of the year.[19]

The lifeways of Chicago's early nineteenth-century inhabitants were of necessity waterways. A liquid boundary arc stretched from Wilmette (*Ouillmette*) at the northern lakeshore, down the north branch of the Chicago River to Wolf Point, following the river's south branch to what became 35th Street, and then cutting across to the southern lakeshore. Within this arc were scattered at least fifteen families whose lives were interdependent—united by blood, occupational survival, common values, and the river. As if by instinct, residents set their log and bark cabins and barns on the high bank and let their lives lean to the current. Such houses rarely had more than one or two rooms and fewer windows, but their inhabitants chose, without need of plat, the level ground and placed their doors toward the river road and the yellow sundown prairie.

The human landscape was as careless as the meandering river, but was not without design. A respect for space and the needs of field and stable kept households apart; but there was another meaning to the sprawl. Long before a greedy state legislature—anticipating an Illinois-Michigan Canal—put Chicago on the map, and lots, streets, and ward boundaries were platted, the settlement had its geographic divisions. In addition to the Yankee garrison ensconced on the south bank of the main river branch, four other kin groups or clans had claimed their "turf": the British (Mc)Kinzies and their southern relatives Clybourne and Hall on the north side; the French-Indian Ouillmette, Beaubien, and LaFramboise families on the far north, west, and south sides.

So dispersed was the settlement that it was impossible for the eye to encompass in a single sweeping glance from the fort's blockhouse, which occupied the highest ground. To an outsider accustomed to the comforting spectacle of shelters huddled together, Chicago seemed hardly to exist at all. United States Army Engineer William H. Keating recorded "but a few huts, inhabited by a miserable race of men, scarcely equal to the Indians from whom they are descended . . . [whose] log or bark houses are low, filthy and disgusting." Yet the town probably had a stable population of more than 150 outside the garrison prior to 1831. By its own enduring admission it was a community.[20]

The view to the south of the fort covered a wide grassy plain that stretched for several miles beyond the garrison's orchards and corn fields at the foot of the stockade. A half-mile down the lakeshore lay several scattered shanties used by the fort and the American Fur Company and a commodious, though jerrybuilt house occupied by Jean Baptiste Beaubien, AFC agent, and his mixed-blood family. To the west the plain was interrupted by a thin stand of trees lining the south branch of the river. Hidden among the timber was the establishment called Hardscrabble.[21]

The name Hardscrabble, perhaps derived from limestone outcroppings in the vicinity, is suggestive of a single farm but actually included at least ten cabins, a major house and post, and sleeping quarters for *voyageurs* spread out along the river bank. Title to this establishment, as to almost every other dwelling in the community, was obscure. Located at the entrance to Mud Lake, the spring portage route to the Des Plaines, Illinois, and Mississippi rivers, Hardscrabble rivaled Beaubien's cabin at the lakefront as a trading location. While Beaubien, as well as American Fur Company agents before him, had the advantage of intercepting the first shipments of trade goods from Detroit and

Michilimackinac in late summer, the traders at Hardscrabble were the first to see the *bâteaux* returning heavy with pelts in the spring.

Although Hardscrabble was most consistently occupied by the LaFramboise clan and other mixed-blood traders like Alexander Robinson, it became from time to time the seat of serious competition with the AFC. Prior to being bought out by Astor in 1824, John Crafts, representing Conant & Mack of Detroit, conducted his business there. Afterwards, when Crafts had taken over the lakefront store for the AFC, William H. Wallace of Detroit traded at Hardscrabble until his death in 1827, Antoine Ouillmette, whose home and trading store hugged the lakeshore ten miles north of the principal settlement, also had a connection with the place. Wallace was paying him rent in 1827.[22]

"Improvements" at Chicago lacked the value easterners would later assign to them. Lots and houses were swapped for as little as a cord of wood and a pair of moccasins, or changed hands as the casual winnings off a fast pony or a shrewd card game. Residents almost never registered their property at the early Wayne and Crawford county seats. Their rudely fashioned cabins did not weather the winds or the damp; and the thatched or bark-shingled roofs inevitably invited fire. Like portable wigwams of their Indian neighbors, such houses had little material worth. However, that is not to say that the early residents did not value permanence and stability; rather, their sense of community was not embodied in a tidy row of whitewashed domiciles legally bound and named.[23]

The "Kinzie mansion" was an exception. Although the Kinzie title is still unrecovered, presumably the house on the north bank opposite the fort was the same property which Jean Baptiste Point du Sable registered and sold in 1800 to Jean Lalime, post interpreter and Kinzie's rival. Lalime resided in the house prior to 1804, when the vituperative redbeard Kinzie arrived and immediately took firm possession.[24]

By 1831 the family had abandoned the mansion to a tenant postmaster. Perched on a sandhill, it had seen fifty years of storm and drift and seemed impatient to slide into the river. In its heyday, the house had been an impressive example of the French *habitant* architecture of the Mississippi Valley, the *poteaux en terre*. It had five rooms—a spacious salon with a small room off each corner—and a wide piazza running the length of the river side. Behind were stables, a bakehouse, huts for employees, and, characteristically, a garden and orchard fenced by a palisade. Although it was presumably similar to other dwellings in the vicinity, the Kinzie mansion was certainly the largest, and the only house with a palisade.[25]

Smaller homes of similar construction were indiscriminately lumped with "log cabins" by early travelers. However, the typical American

Typical métis home, *poteaux en terre*, showing the bark-covered upright log structure and French picket fence. *Courtesy of The Newberry Library.*

"log cabin" of Swedish-Finnish origin was formed of logs set horizontally, with a fireplace at one end of the building. Cabins of this style were not unknown at Chicago, but prior to 1820 they were vastly outnumbered by houses of a primitive French-Canadian design, the *pieux en terre*, whose origins probably owe something to the Huron longhouse.[26] Typically, the French-Canadian dwelling was constructed of roughhewn logs set vertically into a trench and chinked with grass and mud mortar. The thatched or shingled roof was peaked high to facilitate runoff; the fireplace sat astride the roof's center. Ordinarily, the logs were covered with bark slabs, but when the timber was clean-shaven and whitewashed, the structure took on the appearance of stone or frame. It is not surprising that Mark Beaubien's "pretentious" two-story, blue-shuttered tavern, the Sauganash, was mistaken for a New England frame house. There is no evidence, however, that the "I" frame, with its central hall, preceded the Yankee influx of 1833.[27]

Fanning out beyond the "mansion," the numerous members of the Kinzie clan populated the wooded sloughs along the north bank and east of the north branch of the Chicago River. The north side was barely habitable: a dense growth of trees, knee-deep in water, choked out the

John Kinzie—"Father of Chicago." *Courtesy of Chicago Historical Society.*

sunlight, and the bogs were unfit for cultivation. When William B. Ogden's brother-in-law purchased the better part of the "Kinzie Addition" on speculation in the early 1830s, he was forced to initiate an extensive drainage program to render it fit for settlement. Yet from the very beginning this gloomy marsh spelled status, as did the Kinzie name.[28]

Viewed variously as the "father of Chicago" and as a common horse thief, Kinzie in fantasy obscures Kinzie in fact. A British subject and native of the Grosse Pointe district, Detroit, John Kinzie entered the fur trade early, after developing a fair skill as a silversmith. Ruthlessly ambitious, he soon wormed his way into the Detroit circle of merchant agents and found a patron for his Sandusky, Maumee, and St. Joseph trading "adventures." He apparently realized the potential value of territory in advance of the line of settlement. In 1795, he, his half-brother Thomas Forsyth, and other Detroit entrepreneurs almost succeeded in a conspiracy to grab title to Indian lands in Michigan and Indiana before General Anthony Wayne could finalize the Treaty of Greenville.[29]

Between 1804 and 1812, Kinzie at Chicago and Forsyth at Peoria together carved out a small empire in northern Illinois. Kinzie was unquestionably the most powerful man at Chicago during this period, outranking even the garrison officers who were humbled monthly by Kinzie currency advanced to cover their overdue military pay. Most of the French-Indian inhabitants—the Mirandeaus, Ouillmettes, La-Framboises, and Robinsons—worked for Kinzie and Forsyth during these years, although it might well be a mistake to label them simply *voyageurs* or *engagés*. At least one mixed-blood, Captain Billy Caldwell, son of an Irish officer and a Mohawk mother, served as clerk, a position of some responsibility.[30] But whatever the aspirations of local residents, guile, intimidation, and the soporific effects of British rum were devices Kinzie used to ensure that renegade trappers thought twice before embarking for Detroit to strike a separate bargain for their beaver pelts. Kinzie's recorded malevolence is limited to the murder of Jean Lalime in 1812, but hints of other threats abound.[31]

Despite Kinzie's local influence, he never escaped the pecuniary grasp of the Detroit merchants. Caught in the vast financial octopus that spread its tentacles to Montreal, London, and as far as Peking, Kinzie owed his livelihood to George McDougall, supply agent at Detroit, who in turn made his commission off trade goods sold by Forsyth and Richardson in Montreal. Imprisoned after the Fort Dearborn Massacre in 1812 for his British sympathies, Kinzie's credit collapsed, and he was forced to sell all his real property. His debt to George McDougall alone was a hefty $22,000.[32]

When the second Fort Dearborn garrison returned to rebuild the post in 1816, an aging Kinzie followed. The wrath of the Potawatomi had been aimed at the Americans; thus the Kinzie place, Hardscrabble, J. B. Beaubien's house on the southern lakeshore, and other assorted cabins stood unchanged. Even the scattered remains of the massacre victims, left to rot on the beach, had settled comfortably into temporary sandy graves. The bleached bones seemed an ominous omen, and the garrison hastily shoved them into wooden coffins and dropped them into higher ground. But for John Kinzie it was a homecoming.

Time had been a visitor. The Kinzie family reclaimed its place on the north bank, but John never recovered his former status. The fort, more self-assured after the recent United States victory, had little need for a quarrelsome old trader whose past allegiances were suspect. Still, from a Yankee perspective, a Britisher was more comely than a Frenchman, and before his death in 1828, Kinzie did manage to wangle brief appointments as interpreter and subagent (the latter a gratuity extended by his Indian agent son-in-law).[33]

The American Fur Company took him more seriously. An established trader, well known among the Potawatomi and mixed-blood *voyageurs*, Kinzie was viewed by Ramsay Crooks at Michilimackinac as the new company's key to the consolidation of the Illinois country. However, Kinzie failed to meet Crooks' expectations. Although reinforced by a second AFC trader, J. B. Beaubien, Kinzie's efforts to overwhelm the competition at Chicago were in vain. In desperation, Astor bought out his competitor's agent, John Crafts, and turned control of the Chicago trade over to him. After Crafts' death in 1825, Kinzie again assumed control, with Beaubien retaining one-third share. The Creole Beaubien, who had an Indian wife, received short shrift at the hands of Ramsay Crooks and Robert Stuart at the big house. Beaubien was treated as a perpetual "second" man, even though his lines of connection with the mixed-blood trappers ran deeper than Kinzie's. When Kinzie died, Astor, plagued by a diminishing return, sold his Illinois interests to Gurdon Hubbard, the American Fur Company agent on the Wabash.[34]

The Chicago settlement in Kinzie's day was dependent to a man on the fur trade. The social hierarchy, therefore, tended to coincide with rank in the occupation, at least in the eyes of the Detroit and Michilimackinac suppliers. The Kinzie family stood at the top of the social pyramid, closely followed by the Beaubiens, and then the mixed-blood families of LaFramboise, Ouillmette, Mirandeau, Billy Caldwell, and Alexander Robinson. The Indian *engagés* and hunters occupied the base. Or so the Kinzies would have said. Whether their version of the community structure was accurate, however, was largely unimportant. The subtle mechanisms that draw human beings together are for the most part unspoken; the sum of individual visions that converge to form a collective consciousness is never large enough to explain the whole. The view from the bottom of the social ladder would no doubt have been considerably different. The Beaubiens and LaFramboises were well-loved by the Potawatomi; and Billy Caldwell and Alexander Robinson carried political weight within the local bands.[35]

With the ebb of the "occupation," the struggle for power and position began anew. The Kinzies would quite naturally choose to align with the fort. The Yankee garrison was the self-styled "bringer of civilization," and the Kinzies had always felt culturally superior to their French Creole and Indian neighbors. They had paid the bad debts of their Indian employees and sheltered numerous children of the Ouillmette and Mirandeau lines, who, while serving as maids and stableboys, were given the opportunity to observe Anglo-Saxon manners and virtues. Still, a turn to the fort was a sharp shift in allegiance; the garrison had always seemed alien, an intrusion upon the measured rhythm of the Chicago community.[36]

At some imperceptible point around 1820, however, the fort merged with the community to become for a brief period its ruling class. Why the inhabitants of Chicago allowed this to happen is unknown. It may have been the unconscious drift of a people who had lost their moorings. Direction had always floated down from Detroit or Mackinac, and when—simultaneously—Ramsay Crooks began to pack his bags and the fur boats came home empty, residents panicked. The paternal symbolism of the fort became, at that point, too obvious to resist.

Union with the fort took two forms. For most of Chicago's inhabitants it was a simple matter of making the best use of the fort's presence. A garrison at the northern mouth of a new state would mean the influx of people, though in numbers more vast than the enterprising Beaubiens ever imagined. Overnight, a number of trading cabins were hastily converted to taverns, hostelries, and food-supply stores.[37]

The Kinzies beat a more direct path. Treating the garrison like a territorial clan, they marched through the front gate and brought home as relatives the highest ranking officials. Kinzie's elder son, John Harris, married Connecticut-born Juliette Magill, niece of the government Indian agent, Alexander Wolcott; his daughters Ellen Marion and Maria Indiana married Alexander Wolcott and Captain (later General) David Hunter, respectively; and his younger son, Robert Allen, married Gwinthlean Whistler, daughter of the commandant of the fort. As added insurance, both John Harris and Robert Allen became Army officers. These were calculated moves to retain status, and they succeeded. The family's prestige had been on the wane between 1816 and 1828, but in the eyes of the first Yankee arrivals in 1832-33, Kinzie was once again the foremost name in Chicago.[38]

Juliette Kinzie was aware of that fact when, on a grey winter night in 1831, she first stood with her new husband on the threshold of Elijah Wentworth's trading store and sometime inn at Wolf Point and looked down the main branch of the river flowing eastward toward Lake Michigan. To her right she could make out the silhouette of the two bastions of Fort Dearborn nestled in the elbow of the river's sharp bend to the south; to her left, directly across the river from the fort, was the old Kinzie home hidden somewhere in the darkness among the sand hills. It was Juliette's initial visit, but she already knew her place.[39]

A few hours earlier, on the last leg of a three-day journey on horseback, she, John Harris, and their company of French-Canadian employees and guides had stumbled up the frozen bank of the Des Plaines River to warm themselves in front of Bernardus Laughton's fireplace. Mrs. Kinzie was shocked to find a stove and carpet in the middle of the Illinois wilderness. However, her hostess, Mrs. Laughton, was not comforted by such accoutrements of civilization. Like so many women— and men—set adrift on the prairie, she waited nervously, with her arms tightly folded, for the westward advance of her "Eastern family" to catch up.[40]

Mrs. Kinzie had more romantic illusions, born in part of her husband's success as an Indian agent at Fort Winnebago and his unusual apprenticeship to Robert Stuart at Michilimackinac, and in part by her own sense of *noblesse oblige*. Although she had never been to Chicago, she understood her rank in the social order. With the old trader Kinzie gone, she and John Harris Kinzie were the acknowledged leaders of the clan. In view of their Anglo-Saxon ancestry, they presumably were the leaders of the community as well.[41]

A new Kinzie kin group began to trickle into the north side as early as 1816: this was a bastard southern line fathered during the American Revolution by the elder John Kinzie; the mother was a young white woman who had been an Indian captive. Juliette Kinzie and other family historians chose to ignore it. However, its importance for early town development was great indeed, and its numbers, even if unacknowledged, served to reinforce the hegemony of the Kinzie name. The anxious adoption of Yankee values by John Kinzie's legitimate second crop of children must be given a fair share of the credit for the testy

Family historian Juliette Kinzie, an easterner with a sense of *noblesse oblige. Courtesy of Chicago Historical Society.*

snubbing, feuding, and inhouse squabbling that marked the relations of the two branches between 1816 and 1833. Unofficial marriages and separations were common enough in unorganized territory, and children of different mothers were usually united without stigma or anguish. When threatened by outside competition or family death, the two sets of Kinzie children could act as a unit, but the alliance was tenuous and easily broken.

In the late 1770s, John Kinzie and a trading companion, Alexander Clark, had either ransomed or been "given" two Giles County, Virginia girls whom Tecumseh's Shawnees had captured in a raid. Margaret and Elizabeth Mackenzie set up housekeeping with John Kinzie and Alexander Clark near Sandusky. Over the next decade John Kinzie had three children: James, William, and Elizabeth. Clark fathered a son, whom he named John Kinzie Clark for his friend.[42]

After the war, the elder Mackenzie, hearing of his daughters' residence at Detroit, rode north to fetch them and their children. For whatever cause—a brutish John Kinzie, a distaste for the northern frontier, or the fear of reprisal due their British husbands—Elizabeth and Margaret fled to Virginia with their children and in short order married Jonas Clybourne and Benjamin Hall, also of Giles County.[43]

As early as 1816, however, a renegade James Kinzie had sought out his natural father and was trading in Chicago. Kinzie apparently took his son in and treated him kindly. His wife Eleanor undoubtedly harbored reservations: as the eldest Kinzie, James threatened the succession rights of John Harris and his younger brother, Robert Allen. Ironically, in terms of native habits and inclinations James was the obvious inheritor of John Kinzie's prairie domain. While Kinzie's daughters were acquiring polish at schools in Detroit and the East, and John and Robert were clerking for the AFC, James and his father worked the trade, chased wolves, raced horses, and got roaring drunk together. Had the rowdy old man lived until 1833, he might well have been a source of embarrassment to his own "refined" children. As it turned out, John Kinzie became a legend; James became the embarrassment.[44]

The southern contingent kept arriving. Word from James of fertile land and a burgeoning Illinois population brought his sister Elizabeth and his mother's and aunt's new families, the Halls and Clybournes. Others who came included John Kinzie Clark (thenceforth known as "Indian Clark"); the Caldwells, relatives of the Halls; and the Virginia-bred Miller brothers, one of whom married Elizabeth Kinzie. By 1829 they were at least twenty strong, too large a population to ignore.[45]

The southerners introduced a diversity of occupations unknown in early Chicago, breaking down the monolithic clutch of the fur trade several years before the easterners brought their crockery and sewing needles. The first attempts were at tavern-keeping, but by 1829 the southern members of the Kinzie clan were also engaged in butchering, tanning, intensive farming, ferrying, and blacksmithing. In addition, it seems clear that the Halls and Clybournes operated a still, Kentucky whiskey having replaced British rum as the liquid staple after 1812. The entire group built their log cabins on the east side of the north branch, running from the forks up to Rolling Meadows, and they settled in, in an uneasy harmony with their northside relatives and neighbors.[46]

The territorial space in which all families met—both occupationally and socially—was Wolf Point, a sort of "free zone." Located on the western, prairie side of the juncture between the two river branches, the Point was about midway between Hardscrabble and Clybourne's cattle yard at Rolling Meadows. A natural intersection, it served for nearly twenty years as the hub of village life—the scene of frolicking, trade, religion, education, and politics.

The Potawatomi were camping there after 1816, and they did not bother to move when stores and cabins were erected. By 1820 the LaFramboise brothers, mixed-blood "chiefs" Alexander Robinson and Billy Caldwell, and James Kinzie were operating out of trading huts at the Point. Shortly thereafter, James Kinzie built the Wolf Tavern and the Green Tree Tavern, which sported a false second-story front and a gallery, because Kinzie said he "wanted a white man's house." By 1828 the itinerant Methodist preachers Jesse Walker and William See were

The territorial space in which all families met, Wolf Point was a sort of "free zone," the hub of village life for twenty years. *Courtesy of The Newberry Library.*

exhorting audiences weekly in a meetinghouse used irregularly as a school for Chicago French-Indian children.[47]

That same year, Mark Beaubien, younger brother of Jean Baptiste Beaubien, was running a tavern which was later expanded into the famed "Sauganash," named for Billy Caldwell, on the bank opposite the Point to the south. Archibald Clybourne and Sam Miller also managed a tavern on the riverbank to the north. A few years later, David Hall and Robert Kinzie erected their own trading stores at the Point; Miller and Hall's tannery operated to the north of Miller's tavern. The Point was, by 1832, a bustling paradise of exotica. Races and accents mingled freely, as if the mere place had momentarily destroyed the compartments in people's minds and the territorial divisions of the town.[48]

Next to survival, "frolicking" was the major preoccupation of the town. No one expected to make a fast buck; that heady prospect had not yet presented itself. Instead, winter and summer, residents spent a part of their day and uncounted evenings at the Point, swapping tales, playing at cards, racing on foot or horseback, trading, dancing, and flying high on corn "likker," rum, and French brandy. Social class and clan affiliation had no bearing here; it was physical prowess, a witty tongue, or a graceful step that brought people into community.

Full-blooded Indian employees of the Kinzies, who were barred from the dinner table, could hold the whole village captive by the gymnastic fluidity of the Discovery Dance at Wolf Point. The French-Indian Beaubien and LaFramboise girls, who had the gayest feet on earth, found admiring partners among the Virginia farmers, who were just as willing as they to dance until dawn. Whiskey was the official solvent. Everyone—even the women—drank, often from the same bottle. It probably was not only the "dissipated" Indians who camped out on the prairie; Virginia boys, too, hitched their ponies and rolled in the long grass to sleep off a night's hilarity. No wonder easterners and ministers were shocked to find a people so ignorant of the healthful, refreshing qualities of water. Liquor was a "problem" all over the state— over the whole region, for that matter.[49]

Perhaps whiskey was seen as a device to break down the barriers between strangers who seemed to have little in common. Or its fantasy-producing properties may have lent a rosier cast to otherwise grey and frightened lives, going nowhere but into the grave. Outwardly, liquor was called a tonic, a body-builder, and a daily necessity for many frontiersmen. That Mark Beaubien's tavern, the Sauganash, was the focal point of the community, therefore, should not seem odd. Its opening in 1826 coincided with several important changes. A declining fur trade threatened the occupational security of many of Chicago's earliest res-

Mark Beaubien "kept tavern like hell." *Courtesy of Chicago Historical Society: Charles D. Mosher, photographer.*

idents, and the population was suddenly growing: the Clybournes, Halls, Galloways, Scotts, Sees, more Mirandeaus, and John K. Clark had already arrived; and the children of the first families—the Kinzies and Beaubiens—were returning fully grown, from school and looking for mates.

There was more to the convergence at Beaubien's place than social need. There were other taverns: Barney Laughton's on the "Aux Plaines," for example, was a favorite resort of the younger Kinzies. Since hospitality was a primary avenue to status, there was always a drinking circle at John Kinzie's, Hardscrabble, and at J. B. Beaubien's house at the lakeshore. But Mark Beaubien, at a pivotal juncture in Chicago's history, offered more: entertainment and a defiant middle finger to the world.[50]

Beaubien joked that he "kept tavern like hell," and he evidently did. From 1826 until 1835, several years after the Yankee flood, when Mark tried a new venture, the Beaubien house was bursting its seams nightly. Mark boarded and slept upwards of twenty or thirty travelers and single townsmen at a time; by 1834 meals and blankets were being served in shifts. No one complained. After his bustling, round wife, the former Monique Nadeau, had cleared the table, Mark commenced the show. He played the fiddle like a madman, and full-blooded Potawatomi, French Creoles, Yankees, and Virginians could not keep from dancing.[51]

Dancing was a principal amusement among French *habitants;* it became, next to drinking, the most significant community-binding ritual at Chicago. Everyone came and everyone danced. Besides the graceful French-Canadian cotillions, residents learned southern reels, the athletic War and Discovery dances, and the sedate social dances of the Potawatomi. There was hardly a man in Chicago in 1832 who did not know how to paint his body, decorate his hair with eagle feathers, leap in frenzied exultation, terrorizing effete easterners. When town dances were formalized and limited by invitation in the 1830s, they were called *wabanos* or Grand Wa-ba-nos, a reference to an Indian medicine society noted for its all-night revelries. The name retained the native flavor. But something had changed: the Potawatomi and most of the mixed-bloods were noticeably absent from the guest lists.[52]

Mark Beaubien liked everyone, and the feeling was mutual. Among the Yankee reminiscences of Chicago's early years, the stories of Mark are the most poignant—filled with memories of handsome Creole charm, mirth, and abundant kindness to Indians and Yankees alike. His first loves were fiddle playing, horse racing at the Point (or later across a rickety bridge erected in front of the Sauganash in 1831, which he was supposed to be "tending" as toll collector), and propagation. The most prolific man in town, he fathered twenty-three children, many of them named after early settlers he esteemed. He gave away to friends valuable lots he had purchased when the first Michigan-Illinois Canal lands were platted and sold; they only land he apparently possessed when Chicago was incorporated as a city in 1837 was a sixty-four-acre tract at the mouth of the Calumet River, which the Indians had given to "their good friend Mark Beaubien" in the 1833 cession.[53]

The Sauganash was more than a watering hole and ballroom; it also saw its share of the meetings of the Chicago Debating Society (J. B. Beaubien presiding in 1831) and of local politics, seen in the chartering of the town. Chicago's incorporation in 1837 was largely a response to outside interest in the Canal and the downstate need for a local county seat. The village had certainly been large enough to incorporate earlier, but it had evidently not occurred to residents to legalize their community status. However, the early settlers were not unmindful of politics and government: when the area was still part of Peoria County between 1825 and 1831, Chicago men, particularly the Virginians, had avidly sought political office.[54]

Prior to 1827, when the Chicago precinct was organized, all offices were appointive. The commissioners at Peoria gave preference to the men of rank in Chicago, but they also appointed men who appeared eager for position. Old John Kinzie and Jean Baptiste Beaubien were made justices of the peace in 1825 (Alexander Wolcott to replace the deceased Kinzie in 1828), and the southern newcomers Archibald Clybourne and John K. Clark received the nod for constable in 1825 and 1827. Local notables also recommended Billy Caldwell's appointment as justice of the peace, and he was installed April 18, 1826.[55] Until 1828, Beaubien, John Kinzie, and Alexander Wolcott, the Indian agent, presided as election judges. James Kinzie later replaced his deceased father in that office. The job of election clerk was in fact that of messenger; the trip to and from Peoria with the voting returns paid $16.00, and that office went to John K. Clark in 1825; Alexander Robinson and

Dancing was a principal amusement among French *habitants;* next to drinking it was the most important community-binding ritual in Chicago. *Courtesy of the Illinois State Historical Library.*

Henley Clybourne for the two years following; and the Reverend Jesse Walker in 1832.[56]

A surprisingly large turnout participated in nine elections between 1825 and 1831. Thirty-five men registered in the first general election in 1826; thirty-three in 1828; and thirty-two in 1830. Nearly all of the available Kinzies (Canadian and southern) participated, as did most of the French Creole and mixed-blood men of the south and west sides. No political preference emerged during these three elections; the most obvious comment that can be made of the returns is that the village voted with the fort.[57]

Beginning in 1828, however, local elections were of a different species. Chicagoans took a provincial view of politics, and when the candidates were familiar a high-spirited campaign ensued. The election in 1830 to replace Wolcott as justice of the peace, for instance, drew fifty-six voters. The southerners clamored for office. In 1828, Henley Clybourne was elected constable, along with David Hunter; together they represented the Kinzie clan and the fort. Archibald Clybourne tried unsuccessfully in 1828 and 1830 to win election as justice of the peace, and in 1832 he ran as an Independent for Congress, losing to the Democratic candidate from Jacksonville. But he did manage to win appointment, along with Samuel Miller, in 1828, as trustee for the school section land sale and as treasurer of the First Court of Cook County Commissioners. James Kinzie was elected first sheriff of Cook County in 1831, but in 1832 he was beaten by Stephen Forbes, a Yankee schoolteacher.[58]

Despite the small trickle of Yankees into Chicago by 1832, Forbes' election was the first clear indication that Chicago's old settlers were about to lose the control they had exerted over their own political destinies. The experiment in political and occupational independence had been too brief to test whether Chicagoans could flourish apace with the rest of the state, under their own leadership. Their confusion and fear of autonomy was still manifest in 1833: when given the opportunity to elect a president of the town trustees, they chose Thomas J. V. Owen, the government Indian agent. A month later, Owen concluded, as United States commissioner, a land cession treaty between the united Potawatomi, Ottawa, and Chippewa nations and the government, which in effect disfranchised half of Chicago's residents. J. B. Beaubien's mixed-blood son Madore was a member of Owen's Board of Town Trustees in 1833, and John H. Kinzie was elected president in 1834. Thereafter, not one old settler held a position of importance in town or city government. Early residents simply could not compete with the horde of Yankees who descended on the prairie village between 1832 and 1836.[59]

The problem was not one of wits. Early Chicago settlers placed a surprisingly high value on education. Despite the historical impression that Yankees brought to a spiritually and educationally impoverished hinterland a fully developed cultural matrix, the cornerstone of which was the school, Chicago residents were already remarkably well educated, though somewhat less than godly.

Perhaps because Chicago was in many ways an extension of urban Detroit (Kinzie and the Beaubien brothers were raised in the same Grosse Pointe district), many of the early settlers were more enlightened than their rural counterparts downstate. However, the southern branch of the Kinzie clan certainly lacked literary and scientific polish. No poets, orators, or physicians rose from their ranks; the most prominent Virginian was the lay Methodist exhorter William See, who flapped his long blacksmith arms like a scarecrow when he preached and ended his delivery with something between a curtsy and a bow. See organized the first church meeting at the Point, but he always became so entangled in the web of his own scattered thoughts that he failed to bring many sinners to Christ.[60]

Bereft of formal religion until 1833, the Catholic French Creoles and mixed-bloods and the Episcopal Kinzies turned to the secular world. They packed their sons and daughters off to Detroit boarding and finishing schools or to Isaac McCoy's Indian mission school at Niles, Michigan. The Kinzie family connection was presumably with Mrs. Pattinson's establishment at Detroit, since John Kinzie, desperately in debt in 1815, had sold his Grosse Pointe farm to Mrs. Pattinson's husband. Kinzie's legal sons both attended school in Detroit, and his daughters went on to college in Middletown, Connecticut.[61] Some of the LaFramboise children studied in Detroit, as did the daughters of the Beaubien brothers. Madore and Charles Henry Beaubien, Jean Baptiste's sons by his first marriage to an Ottawa woman, after a stint at McCoy's Indian school were sent to Hamilton College and Princeton. Captain Billy Caldwell, son of a British army officer, was highly literate, an eloquent speaker, and received a Catholic education at Detroit.[62]

Periodically, the early settlers tried to induce private tutors to come to Chicago. Most of these attempts were ill-fated. Family tutoring was a common means of working one's way west or locating a husband, and most teachers did not last the year. Female teachers paid by the town as late as 1837 still had to be recruited semiannually. The Kinzies and Beaubiens turned to family members: for example, John Harris Kinzie first studied under his father's half brother, Robert Forsyth, and when Charles Henry Beaubien returned from Princeton, he ran a school at home for the Beaubien-LaFramboise children.[63]

The first Yankee schoolteacher arrived unsolicited in 1830. A native of Vermont, Stephen Forbes was received with a mixture of apprehension and curiosity by those who had met his sister, the priggish Mrs. Laughton. Yet there was dire need for his services: the Beaubien and LaFramboise roosts were bursting. Forbes taught in the Beaubien house for a year and then quit to become sheriff. Perhaps he disliked his clientele; the pupils were overwhelmingly of mixed blood. The southerners did not send their offspring to Forbes' school; in fact, there is no indication that children on the north branch received any education at all until the town school districts were formed in 1837.[64]

In 1832, Thomas Watkins taught in the meeting-house at the Point. His pupils, again, were largely French-Indian, although a growing number of Yankee families sent their children. Watkins apparently also agreed to take full-blooded Indian children into the school. Billy Caldwell, convinced that literacy was a key to native survival, offered to pay the tuition of any Potawatomi child who would wear European clothing. None accepted this offer.[65]

The year 1833 was pivotal in the annals of Chicago religion and education, as it was in almost every other sphere. The return of the Fort Dearborn garrison during the Black Hawk War of 1832 brought an eastern Presbyterian minister, the Reverend Jeremiah Porter, and a schoolmarm from Michilimackinac with dreams of a female academy. Chicago's ungodliness scandalized Porter, but he quickly formed a church group around a coterie of eastern arrivals of 1831-32 and members of the garrison. Porter's group was not so much pious or devout as it was conscious of a need for formality. Porter shared the meeting-house at the Point with the Methodists for a brief time, but the congregation pushed for a separate church building. Porter's first communion was embellished with the use of Major Wilcox' silver service. The new six-hundred-dollar church opened its doors six months later. Unfortunately, women filled out the congregation while their men caused "a wanton abuse of the holy day by . . . sin[ning] against clear light and abus[ing] divine compassion and love." On that communion Sunday enterprising Yankee males were busy unloading two vessels in the new harbor.[66]

The Methodists still operated at the Point, reinforced in 1831 and 1833 by the Reverends Stephen Beggs and Jesse Walker, both southerners. By 1834 a revivalistic spirit produced a host of new members, primarily of southern origin, who erected a church on the north side. At the time, it seemed a logical place to build, since most of the Kinzie-Clybourne-Hall clan had settled on the north branch. However, it was not long before the Methodists felt "outclassed" by the wealthy Yankees settling in Ogden's improved "Kinzie's Addition." The congregation bodily moved its church across the river in 1836 to the area just west of the fort, Chicago's new "free zone."[67]

Although Baptists, Catholics, and Episcopalians each established a church in 1833, religion exerted little control over the everyday social and moral lives of most residents. An exception was the devout collection of Episcopalian Methodists who met at the home of Mark Noble on Thursday evenings for prayer and discussion. The group organized the first Sunday School in 1832, which was interdenominational in character.[68] Noble's enthusiastic followers represented in their piety and temperance the only persons in town—with the possible exception of some of Porter's "highfalutin" Presbyterians—who resisted the understandably attractive urge to accommodate themselves to the casual transcultural lifestyle around them. They did not join Beaubien's Debating Society; nor did they frequent the favorite haunts of early residents, the Sauganash and Laughton's Tavern. Instead, they performed charitable acts, nourishing the school system and church attendance, and, though books were scarce, promoting an interest in literature. Mark Noble carried his entire library to the Sunday School wrapped in his pocket handkerchief. Noble's own timber built the Methodists' northside chapel. Arthur Bronson, East Coast financier and

Sauganash Tavern—favorite haunt of Chicago pioneers. *Courtesy of Chicago Historical Society.*

cohort of William B. Ogden, was so impressed with Noble's endeavors that he shipped one hundred free books to the school.[69]

Eighteen thirty-three was a time of ambivalence and guarded optimism. The population had doubled since 1831. There was talk of a canal, of pre-emption, of a land cession, and of the official incorporation of Chicago as a county seat, with all the legal and social trappings. But no one was sure any of this would come about. Lots in the emerging central business district on the south side, formed by the sale of the township's school section, were still going for as little as $200 and were traded away with nonchalance. The Yankee influx had been gradual, so gradual that one easterner's assimilation into the lifeways of the older settlers was accomplished before his next potential ally against the reigning social order arrived.[70]

The Yankee influence was felt in institutional ways: there were churches and classical academies; there were also ordinances for fire, garbage disposal, vagrant cattle, shooting, and horse-racing; and lawyers predominated among the arrivals of 1833. But the more subtle matrix of social habits and relations had not been significantly altered. Hospitality (rather than privacy and exclusivity), essential to the native, French Creole, and southern prestige systems, was still an unspoken requirement. Personal antagonisms that might generate complex patterns of avoidance in private life were inappropriate when the community gathered to act out its wholeness. There were no "private" parties. One's home, more than just a compartment for the family and one's prejudices, displayed the extent of one's generosity. A spacious house, able to fit the whole crowd under its rafters, was a distinct social attribute.[71]

The first Yankees did not build spacious homes; in fact, most rented back rooms or boarded at the Sauganash or at one of James Kinzie's taverns. In a way they became adopted relatives who danced, drank, and caroused until dawn, and sometimes through the following day with the rest. Eastern visitors were startled to see dark-skinned maidens with beaded leggings under their black stroud dresses jigging with army officers, and genteel ladies twirling on the arms of southern hayseeds. All under the merry auspices of Mark Beaubien and his fiddle.[72]

Wolf-hunting, horse-racing, card-sharking, and shooting matches were still in vogue, although mostly removed beyond the town limits. Army officers and later "pillars of the city" met weekly—on Wednesday morning—at the Sauganash for a bracer, before heading out over the wolf-bedeviled prairie with Madore Beaudbien, in brilliant headdress, whooping at the forefront. Jeremiah Porter noticed, to his chagrin, that there were as many Yankees as French-Canadians gambling at cards on the Sabbath (a reputable Sunday pastime for French *habitants*). French *carioles* raced across the ice in winter, and those who lacked a sleigh built their own rude version from timber cut on the north side. Ice-skating by moonlight was a favorite community activity, concluded, as usual, by a rowdy warming at the Sauganash.[73]

Chicago residents did not need holidays to celebrate. However, New Year's Eve warranted something spectacular, particularly for the French-Canadians. In the early years the *Guignolée* and the *Reveillon* enlivened New Year's festivities all over the territory. Around 1833, Madore Beaubien and the "boys" fitted up the garrison's sizable skow with runners and made the rounds of village houses, adding sleigh party revelers at each stop. By the end of the evening the excitement was so out of hand that the group completely broke up a local tavern. The next morning, the "boys" paid $800 in damages without blinking an eye.[74]

There was something frenetic about the village scene. An unhoped-for material prosperity was in the wind, and residents rocked nervously on their heels—waiting. But there was also the scent of death. Black Hawk was defeated. His people, pushed into the turbulent Mississippi, fell like straw before the American scythe. Stragglers on the shore were dying of starvation or at the hands of the Sioux. What were white folks to do? What was anyone to do, in 1833, but wait?[75]

III. EPILOGUE

> . . . If lost to honor and to pride
> Thou wilt become the white man's bride
> Then go within the strong armed wall
> Partake the pomp of brilliant hall
> And wreath above thy maiden brow
> The sparkling gems to which they bow.
> — "The Muse of the Forest"
>   Written for The Chicago Democrat,
>   February 18, 1834

Chicago's future was secured by the tail end of summer 1833. The town received its corporate seal, elected its first set of trustees, and let it be known that the school section was to be auctioned off in order to raise funds for civic improvements, notably a courthouse. Settlers were notified of their pre-emption rights, and there was a dash—at least by some—to register their homesteads. The United Potawatomi, Chippewa, and Ottawa nation ceded all its land east of the Mississippi in exchange for 5,000,000 acres of promised soil west of the Missouri.*[76]

The year 1833 began with a sigh of relief. The Indian war was over, and the cholera that left a hundred army graves on the south bank had spent its malignancy in the winter freeze. General Scott's remaining troops were on their way east to spread the news about a lush green wilderness in Wisconsin and northern Illinois. Food, rationed during the Black Hawk scare, was once more in adequate supply. People got back to the normal business of running their small industries and drinking it up at Beaubien's.[77]

But it was not quite the same. The Yankee stream continued, increasing its breadth and current. The newcomers were primarily young men, single and ambitious, whose main goal in life was not to amass great wealth (although many would change their minds when given the opportunity), but to find a place that suited them and their talents, a place with which to grow. Chicago was not the first stop for many, nor the last for a few. The majority probably agreed, however, that Chicago was an advantageous place to settle during the 1830s. All occupational classes were arriving. Whereas the 1831-32 migration had seen a lopsided preponderance of merchants and a few professionals, 1833 witnessed a flock of lawyers and tradesmen who anticipated a growing urban center.[78]

In small numbers the New Englanders seemed to have been assimilated. Yet one by one they added cement to a structurally different world-view. Linear progress, historians would later call it: the belief that the future was only attainable by cheating the present, by conserving time, currency, energy, and emotion, and by walking a straight line. The Indians did not think people's lives should be bottled up like so much stale spring water. Nor did the French or the southerners (or Old John Kinzie when he lived). The Indians thought rather that the circle was the more natural version of things. The sun was round, the year was round, and if a hill was round, what sense did it make to cut a straight line through it?

Nineteenth-century Yankees, obsessed with their rightness, could not wean the native and his French sympathizer away from such notions. The simultaneous disappearance of the French, the Canadian métis, and the Indian from Illinois indicates a similarity in world-view and survival technique not generally granted significance. The lack of Yankee initiative among *habitants* of the Mississippi valley may be

---

*A surprising number of French-Indians and non-Indian husbands went west with the Potawatomi. Over half of the registered voters between 1828 and 1830 were, or were thought to be, in Indian country during the 1850s.

traced to more than an enslaving land system. The New Englanders had more success with the Kinzies and their southern kinsmen, although the latter had difficulty adjusting to Yankee aloofness and smug moralism as the years passed.[79]

The transition seemed relatively simple in 1833. Many of the town elders were dead: Francis LaFramboise, John Kinzie, Benjamin Hall, and Alexander Wolcott. Young men remained: like their Yankee counterparts, most were under thirty-five, and a fair share of those were under twenty-five. Before the horde of speculators arrived briefly in 1833 for the sale of the school section, and came to stay during the Illinois-Michigan Canal sales of 1835, Chicago was a town of "boys."

There was something innocent, almost naive, about the young men's optimism. Robert Allen, John Kinzie's youngest son, pre-empted 160 acres on the north bank, but rejected an opportunity to register land at the Point because the family would never use all they had acquired. Early in 1833, while on an eastern buying trip for his trading store, the same young man was flabbergasted when he was offered $20,000—by a shrewder judge of land values than he, Mr. Arthur Bronson—for his tract of swamp. In 1835, Bronson sold the acreage to his silent partner, Samuel Butler, for $100,000. In late summer of the same year, William B. Ogden, newly arrived to dispose of his brother-in-law's property, sold one-third of the property for the same amount. Ogden was not impressed at the time. But Robert Allen Kinzie was; his family might have been millionaires had they known.[80]

Mark Beaubien, only thirty-three and one of the "boys" himself, continued to pack travelers into the Sauganash, putting up curtains as sleeping partitions. When they laid out the town in 1831, his tavern sat in the middle of the street. "Didn't expect no town," he said; and the ease with which he continued to give away his lots suggests that he didn't care if it came.[81] Madore Beaubien took a Yankee partner, John Boyer, and married his daughter. The store foundered, but Madore had a high time selling fancy vests, hats, and laces to his Indian friends while the venture lasted. Like his uncle Mark, he sold his lots too early to share in any of the wealth. And he lost his Yankee wife; Madore married, secondly, a Potawatomi woman.[82]

The southerners expanded their cattle raising, butchering, and tanning operation at Rolling Meadows and cashed in on the eastern demand for beef. The newly dredged harbor begun in 1833 turned meatpacking into Chicago's most profitable business in the 1830s, with the exception of plating and selling "paper towns." Archibald Clybourne, the man probably least admired by the old settlers, was easily the most successful in the later city. This negative relationship held true for John H. Kinzie as well, who retained his former prestige as

Mark Beaubien: "Didn't expect no town" — Chicago, 1840. *Courtesy of the Illinois State Historical Library.*

leader of the north side's first family until his death, even though he proved a financial lightweight.[83]

Chicago's French-Indian families and Kinzie's employees appeared to resent his growing air of condescension. Even in the early years, when Kinzie was Indian agent at Fort Winnebago, the habitually sly, joking French-Canadian *engagés* referred to him as "Quinze Nez." Creole *voyageurs* made an art of the French-English double entendre: they called the Judge of Probate, for example, "le juge trope bête." Always sniffing for a way up, Kinzie did not fool his employees. Worse yet was Kinzie's romance-stricken wife, who reveled in her husband's noble attention to the poor "savage."[84]

The route an old settler had to take to rise in the increasingly eastern social milieu, and the amount of selling out that had to occur, is best illustrated by Kinzie's use of his wife's illusions. During the 1830s easterners in Chicago took a fancy to the finer aspects of Indian culture. Yankees were not particularly interested in seeing the display firsthand, but they welcomed Kinzie's tales of the wilderness, his rendition of sacred Potawatomi legend, his war paint, and his mock stag dance. Incredibly, he was so brash as to take an Indain show (in which

he was the principal star) to the 1834-35 state legislature at Jacksonville for the purpose of "delighting" the delegates into passing a bill funding the proposed canal which was to cross land more or less taken from the Indians only a year earlier. Madore Beaubien must have burned down to his toes.[85]

The unmarried Yankee men lived together at the several boarding houses in a manner akin to rival fraternities. They gave in for the most part to the wilder ways of the young early settlers. John Wentworth, one of the "boys" for a time, and later mayor, claimed that he had never seen so much smoking and drinking. He found that the early churches also resembled fraternities, and he urged all of his friends to attend the Baptist services, where the best crowd gathered. The more contemplative Yankees, not so much averse to as timid about the drinking and shouting, were seated nightly in one or the other dry goods store playing checkers. Such games provided a political forum for the numerous young lawyers in town, who immediately swept novice officerholders like James Kinzie, Madore Beaubien, and Samuel Miller off their feet and out of the governmental door.[86]

Aside from politics, there was still in 1833 a healthy rapport among the young men. The Yankees relished a horse race as much as the early residents, and Mark Beaubien's daughters, as well as the dapper gentleman himself, drew the Yankees in as if magnetized. The old territorial divisions of the town were in a state of confusion, and new lines of class and race demarcation had not yet been drawn. Nearly all the Yankees lived on the near south side, the "free zone" which had replaced the Point as the central community meeting place. The boarding houses provided a kind of protective limbo, around which the bewildering array of conflicting values clashed but did not affect the people's lives. They were in the eye of the storm, and Mark Beaubien was Peter Pan. The "boys" were never going to grow up.[87]

The town found its adulthood abruptly and painfully. In early September 1833, the newly elected president of the town board, Robert C.V. Owen, called a grand council of the chiefs and headmen of the United Indian nations to discuss treaty arrangements for their removal west of the Mississippi. Owen, acting in his capacity as United States Government Commissioner, opened the proceedings by explaining to the assembly that he had heard that they wished to sell their lands. This was a blatant untruth; but the Indians unfortunately had no precedent for supposing that they would be allowed to keep their territory, even if they chose to. They deliberated.[88]

The 5,000 men, women, and children took their time, however, spending nearly three weeks at Chicago. They camped along the lakeshore and at the Point and enlarged their already mammoth debts to the local white traders, Robert Allen Kinzie among them. The bulk of the traffic was in liquor—alcohol enough to put them all in a drunken stupor for a week. Tipsy families wept together beside their tents, and in the sober morning there was still the wailing.[89]

On September 26 the treaty was concluded. Under a spacious open shed, specially constructed on the north side of the river for the occasion, the officers and spectators gathered. The chiefs did not arrive until the sun was red in the sky, and again they delayed while two old chiefs, wobbling with whiskey, made incoherent rebuttals. Then they signed. The commissioners sat with the sundown blaze in their faces, appearing, ironically, as brothers of the men they were herding away. Facing east, the Indians huddled in darkness.[90]

The spectacle rocked the inner heart of the town. Yankees were horrified at so pagan and slovenly a group; sympathy gave way to disgust. "Half-breeds" who had been raised as part of the community shunned their previous friends. By order of the court in 1834, Justice of the Peace Beaubien publicly posted a "no trespassing" sign at Hardscrabble. White traders, new and old, hustled the sales while they could and then went home to estimate the amount of indebtedness the tribe had accumulated. The treaty allotted $150,000 to settle past liens, but the final settlement was $175,000. Undoubtedly many traders inflated the sum due; it seems that every white man in Chicago got a slice. The American Fur Company received an outrageous $20,000. The various members of the Kinzie family, including some of the Forsyths, received the next largest payment.[91]

In addition to the land west of the Missouri and the allotment to collectors, the treaty provided for cash payment in lieu of reservations, which was requested by innumerable "mixed-bloods" who wished to remain in Chicago. However, only three applicants' reservations were granted; the rest were given a pittance, ranging downward from $1800. A hungry Kinzie family again received a sizable grant, far exceeding

Hamilton-educated, the mixed-blood Madore Beaubien was one of Chicago's "golden youngsters." *Courtesy of State Historical Society of Wisconsin.*

the sums distributed among the French-Indians. The fourth and fifth
clauses of the treaty provided for a twenty-year annual payment of
$14,000, and $100,000 in goods to be distributed after ratification.[92]
Goods worth $65,000 were presented to the nation on October 4. In
preparation, the traders had ordered vast stores of whiskey; one trader
alone asked for fifteen barrels. Fortunately, a prevailing south wind
hindered ship passage up the river, and the traders were forced to
content themselves with selling the supply on hand, as well as over-
priced trinkets, blankets, knives, and so forth.[93]

It was black Sunday, Worshipers did the only thing respectable
people knew how to do: they hid within their churches from the drunken shouting, wailing, and fleecing. And they prayed. An old Indian
stood playing a "jew" harp at the Reverend Jeremiah Porter's door,
unaware that he was interrupting a religious service. When the payment was concluded, high winds and a driving rain sent the traders
fleeing back into their cabins. The Indians went back to their camp at
the Aux Plaines with $30,000 in silver. Porter thought that someone's
prayer had been answered.[94]

In the months to come, the numerous mixed-blood residents at Chicago
wrenched their hearts over whether to remove with their Potawatomi
kinsmen or stay. Many wanted to remain; the sacred ground in which
their grandfathers were buried meant more to people of native extraction than to the Yankees who were about to gain the territory. But the
breach was irreparable. Indians and mixed-blood settlers willing to
forgive were treated as some ghastly sore, too horrible to look at. The
sore would not heal; it festered because the source of the disease was
inside the Yankee eye. In time the Indian became the real evil in
people's minds.[95]

Typical of the educated "mixed-bloods," Madore Beaubien was no
fool. One of Chicago's "golden youngsters," he had wanted his share
of power. Years later, as he wasted away on a reservation in Kansas, he
explained that he had yearned for recognition in the white world. Denied that, he sought prestige within the tribe. Beaubien and most of
his cohorts joined the local Potawatomi bands in 1835. Painted in the
colors of death, they made their final turn through the streets already
covering the ancient trails and fields, dancing their way out of vision,
their shrieks sticking in the Americans' ears.[96]

In 1835 the land sales—and one of the most incredible heights of
speculative fancy the West had ever seen—began. Chicago was again
a one-horse town; everyone dealt in lots. But the land bore a stigma:

by 1838 the majority of Chicago's newer residents, as well as a few old ones who had managed to keep their heads long enough to see the six-figure totals, were bankrupt.[97]

It would be easy to suggest that William B. Ogden was elected the first mayor of Chicago, incorporated in 1837, because wealth was the measure of power. However, it seems just as likely that residents could not stand to face someone more familiar in their midst. New blood, clean blood, a new family, a new community might root and bloom in the desecrated land and make it whole once more.

Chapter X

CHARLES BRANHAM

Black Chicago:
Accommodationist Politics Before the Great Migration

The Negro vote alone would of course affect but little. It must make combination with the controlling forces in the party . . . Social, intellectual, or other admirable qualities count for nothing if you cannot "deliver the goods."
— Edward E. Wilson
(black leader, 1907)

The growing good of the world is partly dependent on unhistoric acts; and that things are not so ill with you and me as they might have been, is half owing to the number who lived faithfully a hidden life, and rest in unvisited tombs.
— George Eliot,
Middlemarch

NO GOLDEN LADY STANDS ASTRIDE THE
Chicago harbor, bidding welcome to the refugees from Southern tyranny and offering solace to the oppressed. Perhaps it is just as well, for
those black migrants who came to Chicago in the 1890s and the early
1900s found themselves entering a city where the lines of racial restric-
tiveness were being more and more tightly drawn. The idea had preceded the experience; the pattern of ethnic politics, already firmly
entrenched, would draw the energetic and ambitious among them into
the tangled web of organization and personal linkages which would in
time come to characterize black politics in Chicago. Equally important,
the city which came to symbolize the possibilities for black political
advancement in America had already begun to etch out the limits to
those possibilities.

The essential features of black politics in Chicago, then, were clearly
evident before the Great Migration. Most of the leading figures who
were to dominate the politics of Black Metropolis for the first third of
this century had arrived during the 1890s.[1] And while personal and
political fortunes rose and fell, the network of private and public relationships and political obligations between black and white leaders
had been forged before 1900.

According to tradition, the city of Chicago was founded in 1779 by
Jean Baptiste Point du Sable, a French-speaking Negro from Santo
Domingo.[2] Although the city's black population remained small
throughout the 1800s, the relations between the races had been a persistent if not prominent theme in the history of Illinois politics. In 1818,
when Illinois became a state, its constitution was regarded as fairly
liberal. Slavery was forbidden, although provision was made for the
continuance of indentured servitude. Illinois did, however, have a black
code, which required every Negro in the state to post a thousand-dollar
bond and carry a certificate of freedom. A state law passed in 1853
forbade blacks from entering the state. Illinois blacks had no rights
which white men were bound to respect. They could not vote or serve
on juries; they could not serve in the militia; and they could not testify
against a white man in court. Racial intermarriage was expressly forbidden. Although the laws were often ignored, especially after the pas-

Jean Baptiste Point du Sable, a French-speaking Negro from Santo Domingo, who according to tradition founded the city of Chicago. *From Intercollegian* Wonder Book *(Chicago, 1927).*

sage of the Fugitive Slave Law of 1850, black residents were essentially invisible before the law.[3]

Nevertheless, Chicago became a mecca for refugees from Southern bondage—some remaining, others passing through to Canada and points east. Despite the Fugitive Slave Laws of 1793 and 1850, several homes and churches served as "stations" on the Underground Railroad. Planters in the lower Mississippi Valley dubbed Chicago a "nigger-lovin" town, and an editor in southern Illinois contemptuously dismissed Chicago as a "sink hole of abolition"[4]

The city's black population grew quickly in the last half of the nineteenth century. The number of blacks tripled in the 1850s, almost quadrupled in the 1860s, and nearly doubled itself each decade between 1870 and 1900. Yet blacks were only 1.8 percent of the population in 1900. Most were employed in some form of domestic or personal service, the vast majority in white establishments or white households.

Chicago, dubbed "nigger-lovin'," a "sink hole of abolition," became a mecca for refugees from Southern bondage. *From "Negroes in Chicago" (Chicago: Mayor's Committee on Race Relations, 1944).*

By 1900 the black minority were dependent on the white majority for their jobs and their livelihood. The black populace was uncomfortably situated near the lowest rung of the economic ladder in the most menial and unskilled trades.

Although blacks were only 1.3 percent of the population in 1890, they provided 37.7 percent of all the male and 43.3 percent of all the female servants in the city. The servant class claimed 53.7 percent of all Negro workers, 47.3 percent of the males and 77.1 percent of the females.[5] Foreign-born whites still supplied the bulk of the servant population, but black men were viewed as the rightful holders of positions as butlers and coachmen to wealthy whites. "The Negro footman and horseman," writes historian Estelle Hill Scott, "were expected figures around the mansions of the moneyed class."[6] As early as 1878, a contemporary observed, "Negroes were waiters, coachmen and janitors. All the big buildings had colored janitors and a few had colored clerks." Another old resident recalled that all of the fashionable downtown restaurants and hotels employed black waiters and porters, except the Sherman House.[7]

Black Chicagoans were not a significant factor in the city's basic skilled trades before the 1890s. The better jobs in construction, transportation, and industry were already reserved for whites. When blacks did enter local industries in the 1890s, it was as strikebreakers, incurring the hostility of white workers and the enmity of unions. When strikes were settled, whites were usually rehired and blacks fired, leaving the blacks unemployed and facing a legacy of racial hostility. Scant attention was paid to the fact that blacks were merely following in the footsteps of the Poles and Lithuanians, who had often been employed as strikebreakers in the 1880s.[8]

The presence of nonunion black workers at the 39th Street intercepting sewer was the cause of a minor riot in 1899 on the city's South Side. Newspapers spoke of a "reign of terror" which gripped South Side merchants and residents after three hundred and fifty whites struck over a salary dispute. The hostility had been inflamed by white threats to blow up the sewer machinery—and the remaining workers. Tensions within the plant had also resulted from the refusal of two white workers to take orders from "Big Sam," a Negro. The refusal, followed by an exchange of words, led to a fight between several of the black and white workers. When five of the whites took the matter to the work's contractor, he sided with the blacks; the white workers were dismissed. Several blacks were attacked on the way home from the plant and tempers were brought to the flash point when seven dynamite cartridges were found in different parts of the plant machinery used in constructing the sewer.

The actual riot occurred when between 50 and 60 blacks were leaving work and were met by a crowd of 100 to 150 white strikers. A pitched battle took place on 39th Street between Indiana and Michigan Avenues. More than a hundred shots were fired and nine men, including a policeman, were injured; twenty-seven blacks—but no whites— were arrested. The riot received extensive newspaper coverage and, coupled with black strike-breaking activities in the stockyards strike and the 1905 teamster's strike, heightened antiblack feeling in the city. The teamster's strike was especially bitter: hostilities spread far beyond the strikebreakers to threaten the entire black community. The strike, according to one historian, "brought Chicago to the brink of race riot."[9]

Modern black politics emerged during this period of increased racial antipathy in the 1890s. Local businessmen often drew the color line between black and white customers. Numerous community meetings, including the interracial public discussion at the Central Music Hall in February 1890, attested to public concern over the widespread denial of public accommodations in the city. Blacks were often forced to resort to legal action to protest the discriminatory practices of local merchants.[10]

Residential segregation was also beginning to appear after 1890. By 1900 several predominantly Negro enclaves merged to form the beginnings of a South Side Black Belt. Historian Thomas Philpott has argued that the residential segregation of blacks was nearly complete by the turn of the century. By 1900 sixteen wards were 99.5 to 100 percent white. Over half of the city's black population lived in three contiguous South Side wards. While various ethnic groups continued to be identified with specific communities, no single Chicago neighborhood was ever ethnically "pure," and a majority of kinsmen lived outside any one particuar enclave. Immigrants often clustered, but they were rarely segregated. "All groups which had the choice," Philpott points out, "opted for mild clustering and dispersion."[11] On the eve of the twentieth century black Chicagoans had become acutely aware that they no longer had this choice.

For black Americans the last quarter of the nineteenth century was, in Rayford Logan's words, "the nadir, the Dark Ages of Recent American History," when the second-class citizenship and indeed the inherent inferiority of black Americans was accepted by the vast majority of white Americans. Southern blacks had been systematically stripped of the franchise. Jim Crow, the jocular prewar minstrel figure, had come to symbolize institutional white supremacy.[12]

It was an era of social Darwinism and the "white man's burden." In the decades after 1885, Richard Hofstadter points out, the racist myth of Anglo-Saxon superiority "was the dominant abstract rational of American imperialism." It was a period of unprecedented violence directed against blacks. Race riots increased in number and severity. Whites attacked blacks in Wilmington, North Carolina in 1898, in New York City in 1900, in Atlanta in 1906, in Springfield in 1908. The new century offered no respite and little hope for a race at bay: in the first year of the new century more than one hundred blacks were lynched. Before the outbreak of World War I, the number had risen to eleven hundred.[13]

Black leadership—locally and nationally—was divided and unsure of its response to this era of racist dementia. Many counseled accommodation and retrenchment; others accused conservative leaders like Booker T. Washington of acquiescence if not complicity in fostering notions of white supremacy. Edward H. Morris, a prominent Chicago attorney and politician, charged that Washington believed in Negro inferiority and that his statements encouraged racial segregation. The man from Tuskegee, he contended, was "largely responsible for the lynching in this country." Washington encouraged black docility in the face of white violence. Morris argued, and taught "that Negroes are fit only for menial positions. . . . I prefer a radical like Senator Tillman of South Carolina to Booker T. Washington. . . . The colored people think it doesn't matter so much what he says . . . [but they] believe and do what [Washington] tells them. Then they don't insist upon being treated the equals of whites."[14]

Other Chicagoans were not so sure. They admired Washington and encouraged their neighbors to view racial segregation as an opportunity for community uplift and race advancement through group solidarity. They were not happy about increased segregation, they merely accepted its inevitability. Some even held other blacks at least partially responsibile for the unfortunate turn of events. Fannie Barrier Williams, prominent club woman, a member of the pre-Migration black elite and a Washington partisan, blamed the increase of the black population for the social and economic plight of the black middle class. "Prevented from mingling easily and generally with the rest of the city's population, according to their needs and deservings, but with no preparation made for segregation, their life in a great city has been irregular and shifting, with the result that they have been subject to more special ills than any other nationality amongst us." Mrs. Williams was particularly concerned about the "huddling together of the good and bad, compelling the decent element of the colored people to witness the brazen display of vice of all kinds in front of their homes and in the faces of their children." For some, the inconvenience of racial segregation was compounded by the fact that it obscured class distinctions within the black community.[15]

Whatever the divisions among black Chicagoans, the black community that emerged in the last quarter of the nineteenth century was an extremely self-conscious community, aware and increasingly anxious about the emerging pattern of social, economic, and residential proscription. Labor conflict had heightened interracial antipathy. Employment patterns reflected the general dependence of the community on white society. Denials of public accommodation, though illegal, reflected the secondary position of black Americans in the general society. Out of this context came black politics.

* * * * *

The pattern of interracial cooperation that dominated black politics before 1914 had its origins during the Civil War period. In Chicago— as was the case nationally—early black political debate revolved around questions of freedom and enslavement.[16] In the summer of 1862 blacks in Chicago and other Midwestern cities were the victims of violent confrontations with white laborers. In the state constitutional convention of that year, the outnumbered Republicans failed to keep an exclusion article out of the proposed new constitution, and in 1863 the lower house adopted a series of resolutions condemning the Emancipation Proclamation, the "unconstitutional" prosecution of the war, and the transportation of Negroes into the state.*

For Chicago blacks, organized protest activity began as early as 1864 with campaigns to repeal the Illinois Black Code and to challenge the segregationist policies of the city Board of Education. In 1865 the Illinois Black Codes were repealed, and four years later blacks throughout the state met in convention to challenge all racial distinctions in state laws. The Colored Convention, held in 1869, drew up a list of grievances and announced its intention to "devise ways and means whereby a healthy opinion may be created . . . to secure every recognition by the laws of our state and to demand equal school privileges throughout the state." By 1870, Illinois blacks were granted the right to vote, and in 1874 segregation in the public school system was abolished. In 1885 the state passed a comprehensive civil rights law "designed to protect the liberties of Negroes in the less advanced counties of southern Illinois."[18]

The spearhead behind the repeal of the black laws and other antiblack prohibitions was John Jones, the first black man to hold public office in Illinois. Jones was born November 3, 1816 on a plantation in Greene County, North Carolina. His father was a German named Bromfield, his mother a free woman of color. Fearful that his father's relatives might attempt to reduce him to slavery, his mother apprenticed him to a man named Sheppard, who took him to Tennessee, where he was "bound over" to a tailor who taught him the trade. Jones lived as a tailor in Memphis, where he met and married Mary Richardson, the daughter of a blacksmith. He left Memphis for Alton, Illinois and eventually came to Chicago on March 11, 1845, only twelve years after its incorporation.[19]

From the 1850s until his death in 1879, Jones was the unquestioned leader of black Chicago. An ardent abolitionist who frequently played host to such luminaries as John Brown and Frederick Douglass, Jones was active in the state convention of 1856, called by blacks to petition for legal rights in Illinois. Jones was also a member of the prewar Vigilance Committee, and in 1853 was elected vice-president of the Colored National Convention held in Rochester and named a member

---

*By 1861, Illinois and six other Midwestern states barred blacks from suffrage and the state militia. In Illinois no provision was made for black education, and exclusion laws were passed, with severe penalties, to prevent blacks from settling in the state. Indiana and Iowa had similar laws.[17]

John Jones, the first black man to hold public office in Illinois. *Courtesy of Chicago Historical Society.*

of that convention's National Council. Throughout his life he continued to campaign for full and unequivocal manhood rights. "We must have our civil rights; they must not be withheld from us any longer; they are essential to our complete freedom."[20]

Before the war Jones had been instrumental in sending hundreds of fugitives to Canada. In fact, on the day after President Millard Fillmore signed the fugitive slave law, Jones recorded, ten carloads of blacks were sent across state lines to safety. But the "most satisfaction in life" came to Jones from his unremitting "warfare upon Black Laws." In the course of this campaign he had gained some powerful white allies. Joseph Medill, editor of the *Chicago Tribune*, was a former Free Soil newspaper staff writer and an early opponent of the black codes. Many prominent local and state Republican leaders, including Governor Yates and Cook County Senator Francis Eastman, were enlisted in the cause.[21]

From the beginning, the issue of partisan political self-interest intruded. For example, when the Repeal Association sponsored a dance and concert attended by approximately 500 Negroes on November 22, 1864, the pro-Democratic Chicago *Times* suggested that the event had been staged to raise money to buy votes for the Republicans. The entire campaign was marked by partisan as well as sectional self-interest, and when the black laws were finally repealed, the vote was cast along strict party lines.[22]

The repeal campaign highlights the sensitive position in which Illinois blacks found themselves. Jones, in his pamphlet *The Black Laws of Illinois and a Few Reasons Why They Should Be Repealed*, stressed white self-interest as well as humanitarian reasons for the abrogation of the black laws. These laws, he argued, had had a damaging impact on normal interracial business relations. In an open letter to the *Tribune*, dated December 9, 1864, Jones argued that "the great advantage to be gained by the repeal will not only benefit the colored man ... the great benefit will be to the white for reasons that white men employ us and not we them. We hold their property and not they ours. We ask you to repeal these laws and give us the right to testify that you may protect your property."[23]

The repeal campaign set the pattern for early black political activity. Pre-twentieth-century black politics began as an amalgam of the black protest tradition, local and national Republican politics, and the personal, social, and political relationships that had developed among white and black Chicagoans. When Jones was proposed by Republicans—and accepted by Democrats—as one of the fifteen candidates for the county board on the bipartisan "Fire Proof" ticket after the Great Fire of 1871, it was not to secure the votes of the city's approximately 5,000 blacks; most of them were already in the Republican camp. Jones was selected because he had through the repeal controversy established himself as a distinguished member of the larger Chicago community with important and powerful Republican contacts. Jones' election in 1871, then, was not the opening gun for the emergence of black politics in Chicago. Rather, it was part of the legacy of the abolitionist-Republican tradition of the city.[24]

Jones served for one year and was re-elected for a three-year term in 1872; but he was defeated along with other Republicans in 1875. A year later, he and several of his fellow commissioners were indicted for an "alleged conspiracy," but he was acquitted "without difficulty, there being no evidence against him."[25]

After Jones' death no single individual emerged to assume the mantle of leadeship among black Chicagoans. The last few decades of the century presented an increasingly diversified leadership. Civic direction passed to such individuals as Dr. Daniel Hale Williams, the best-known black physician in the country and founder of Provident Hospital; Dr. Williams' colleague at Provident, Dr. Charles E. Bentley, a dentist; lawyer and journalist Ferdinand L. Barnett, who published the city's first black newspaper, and his activist wife, Ida B. Wells-Barnett; and the distinguished attorney and fraternal leader Edward H. Morris. The new elite included men and women who were primarily business people and lawyers, clergymen and journalists—individuals who viewed politics primarily as a sideline, an avocation rather than a basic source of income.

Such men and women were community leaders who saw politics as an extension of their various civic activities. They were important, however, as a bridge between the activist tradition of John Jones and the emerging political professionalism of Ed Wright and Oscar De-Priest. They were the bearers of the heritage of genteel civic protest and of the post-Civil War abolitionist tradition.[26]

The civil rights and protest tradition is central to our understanding of black politics from the mid-1870s to the eve of the Great Migration. In 1876, when the black population was only one percent of the city's total, John W.E. Thomas, a black Republican, was sent to Springfield as a representative from the second senatorial district. His election margin indicated that a large proportion of his supporters was white.[27] Thomas, a native Alabaman, was born in 1847 and came to Chicago at the age of twenty-six. His first enterprise, a grocery business, was destroyed by fire in 1873. He later turned to teaching and opened a private school near the center of the city.

Thomas established the tradition of black representation in the Illinois legislature and is often cited as one of the earliest black politicans of the postwar period. However, he is best remembered as the author of the Civil Rights Bill of 1885. The bill provided for equal access to public accommodations in "inns, restaurants, eating houses, barber shops, public conveyances on land or water, theaters, and all other places," and provided for a fine of between $25 and $500, or a maximum of one year imprisonment, for any person guilty of violating the statute. No other interest or activity of the earliest black legislators was as important as the defense and expansion of the basic provisions of the bill Thomas introduced.[28]

Thomas was not re-elected in 1878, but he served another two terms in 1882 and 1884, and the Civil Rights Bill was passed at the end of his last term. He was succeeded by George F. Ecton, a former Kentuckian, one-time waiter, and later the owner of an all-black baseball

Dr. Daniel Hale Williams, the best-known black physician in the country, and the founder of Provident Hospital. *From* College of Life *(Chicago, ca. 1920).*

team. Ecton's legislative career also reflected black concern for the protection of basic civil liberties. He introduced a bill to fix a penalty for abduction, perhaps in response to black fears of being kidnapped and illegally transported out of the state to stand trial in Southern courts. Ecton also framed a bill fixing greater responsibilities on constables and judges, those who were specifically charged with protecting black prisoners from being kidnapped by white lynch mobs. Ecton was re-elected in 1888, and in 1890 was succeeded by a fellow black Kentuckian, Edward H. Morris.[29]

In the career of Edward H. Morris we can see the fully realized amalgam of civic protest, community leadership, the national black protest tradition, and increasing local political savvy. Born a slave in Fleminsburg, Kentucky in 1858, Morris had been a practicing attorney since 1879 and was regarded as one of the leading black lawyers in the country. He had also gained something of a national reputation as a sharp critic of Booker T. Washington. An uncompromising foe of racial discrimination, Edward Morris was one of the founders and the chairman of the executive committee of the Equal Rights League of Illinois, an organization created to protest the attempt to segregate black school children in the state's public schools.[30]

Dr. Charles E. Bentley, a dentist and Williams' colleague at Provident. *From* College of Life *(Chicago, ca. 1920).*

Morris' first term, however, was legislatively undistinguished, and he was defeated for re-election by James E. Bish, known as Adjutant Bish because of his rank in the Eighth Regiment, an all-black military outfit. Bish alone among pre-twentieth-century black legislators left no record at all of legislative accomplishment, and contemporaries described him as a man of less than sterling character. His election in 1892 was contested, and at least one paper hinted that he won through trickery and corruption.[31]

Morris' second term, in 1902, reflected his main legislative concerns. He introduced an amendment to strengthen the Civil Rights Bill of 1885, and an act to suppress mob violence. He also offered a bill to "investigate the most humane and improved method of carrying into effect the sentence of death" and another to regulate the traffic in "deadly weapons" and to prevent their sale to minors.[32] However, his second term was not without controversy. The *Chicago Tribune* accused him of tampering with an election bill provision that would have allowed a candidate for public office to appear more than once on a ballot. The idea of allowing a candidate's name to appear more than once was seen as an aid to independent and fusion candidates, and Morris was accused of deleting the provision in behalf of vested party

Edward Morris, Illinois legislator and civil rights activist. *From* College of Life *(Chicago, ca. 1920).*

interests. He was also criticized in some quarters of the black community for proposing a bill to legalize some form of gambling in Chicago. Ironically, the measure antagonized not only middle-class black reformers but alienated one of Morris' chief political allies, Robert T. Motts, a black saloon-keeper and South Side gambler who had gradually become a power in Morris' district. Motts had no intention of encouraging legal competition to his illicit but highly successful enterprise, and his defection brought Morris' legislative career to an end.[33]

Probably the most politically active of the pre-twentieth-century black legislators was John C. Buckner, who was elected to the state legislature in 1894. Buckner was a former headwaiter for fashionable parties, and what he lacked in formal education he made up for in

presence and style; he had "the polish of the cultured class."[34] Buckner
was born in Kendall County, Illinois. He entered the catering business
in 1877 and after 1890 held a succession of management jobs with
caterers until 1890, when he was appointed Deputy Collector of Internal Revenue for the First District of Illinois.[35]

Upon his arrival in Springfield, Representative Buckner found himself almost immediately embroiled in controversy with the state leadership. First he quarreled with Democratic Governor John P. Altgeld
"over patronage and preference," and later with Altgeld's Republican
successor, John R. Tanner. After his re-election in 1896, however, Buckner turned his attention to the state Military Affairs Committee, which
he chaired, and to his pet project, the Eighth Regiment.[36]

With John Marshall and B.G. Johnson, Buckner had been a founder
of the all-black Ninth Battalion, a resurrection of the "Old Sixteenth",
a black veterans organization that had ceased to exist because of inadequate aid from the state. With the assistance of his white political
mentor, Martin B. Madden, Buckner maneuvered the passage of a bill
to make room for the Ninth Battalion as a part of the state's National
Guard. He also had himself named the unit's first commanding officer.[37]

Buckner's two terms in the legislature were not completely taken
up by this campaign on behalf of the Eighth Regiment. Like his contemporaries, Buckner's career reveals a concern for welfare legislation and
the protection of black rights. He offered a bill designed to limit the
time young boys and girls could be kept in training and industrial
schools. He also proposed legislation dealing with child abandonment
and the welfare of paupers.[38]

Buckner was widely praised for his activities during the Spring
Valley riots of 1895. When native white miners protested poor working
conditions and a recent cut in pay, the absentee mine owners closed
the mines and brought in Italian, French, and Belgian immigrants.
These new miners learned English, and in 1894 they too struck. This
time the mine owners imported black workers from the South, many
of whom were soon murdered by protesting immigrant strikers in what
came to be known as the "Spring Valley Massacre." Buckner arrived
on the scene and demanded justice on behalf of the beleaguered black
workers. Other blacks joined in to protest police indifference—as did
the Italian consul, who protested the mistreatment of Italian nationals
forced to riot to protect their jobs.[39]

Three years later, John Buckner was succeeded by William L. Martin, a Missouri-born lawyer. Martin was described as a man of "ability
and courage," and his legislative record in Springfield reveals a man
of widely varied reform interests. He introduced bills to suppress mob
violence and to prevent discrimination by life insurance companies

against "persons of color."[40] Martin also pushed legislation to grant tax-paying women the right to vote for presidential electors and for candidates for certain specified offices. He sponsored legislation designed to expand the social service responsibilities of government and to protect the rights of poor and working-class citizens.[41]

One of Martin's measures would have provided attorney's fees for a mechanic, artisan, or laborer who was forced to sue for back wages. Another sought to exempt personal property in certain specified categories from sale due to judgments against debt or rent. Still another would have provided attorney's fees for the defendant in a suit brought for money due or debts incurred for rent, meals, and costs in boardinghouses. Martin also wanted to prohibit exorbitant interest charges on small loans of not more than two hundred dollars.[42]

Martin's successor was John G. "Indignation" Jones, an old settler who made a career of consistently opposing any effort or program designed to segregate or disfranchise black Chicagoans. Jones earned the epithet "Indignation" for his habit of calling "indignation" rallies whenever he felt Negro rights were under attack. He protected both the establishment of an all-black Y.M.C.A. in 1887 and the creation of Provident Hospital in 1891. When Daniel Hale Williams told an interviewer that black Chicagoans were fond of secret societies, Jones called an indignation meeting to protest Williams' "slander" of the Negro race. When a coroner's jury handed down a verdict critical of integrated employment in the city, Jones called another rally and announced that the coroner—and his entire jury—should be tarred and feathered.[43]

Jones, like his predecessor, showed an interest in a wide range of legislative reforms. And, like Martin, Jones' bills often involved the expansion of government to safeguard the rights of the underdog. Following the example of his two predecessors, Jones fought to suppress mob violence in the state as well as to punish law officers if a person in their charge was beaten, struck, or assaulted.[44] He sponsored acts to prohibit false advertisement by doctors; to pay the attorney's fees when a lawyer was appointed by the court of record for indigent clients; to prevent unlicensed lawyers from becoming judges; and to combat vote fraud by having all ballots printed at public expense.[45]

Jones wanted to expand the rights of accused persons in court. One of his bills would require that a grand jury hear witnesses for the defense as well as for the prosecution. Another would protect any person charged with the commission of a crime from making self-incriminating statements by stipulating that no agreement, statement, or confession could be made without the presence of the defendant's lawyer. It was not until sixty years later that the Supreme Court ruled in *Gideon v. Wainwright* (1963) and *Douglas v. California* (1963) that the states were required to guarantee counsel in all criminal trials. And in *Escobedo v. Illinois* (1964) the Court ruled inadmissible a confession extracted through police interrogation during which the accused had been denied the right to consult with an attorney.[46] "Indignation" Jones was thus belatedly vindicated.

These black legislators, from Thomas to Jones, saw themselves as champions of Negro rights and defenders of black civil liberties. Little is known about their political activities and even less about their personal lives; but it is clear from their speeches, legislative records, and contemporary news accounts that they were active in the protection of black rights and in the extension of the social service function of state government. As vigorous—if genteel—opponents of any attempt to curtail black rights or impose segregation by race, they were clearly in the earlier John Jones tradition of black protest. To the extent that they were capable of marshaling community support for their programs, as for the Eighth Regiment, their successes reflect the convergence of civic activity, practical politics, interracial cooperation (and sometimes sponsorship), and the black protest tradition.

What then was the legacy of pre-Great Migration black legislators for black Chicagoans and urban politics in the twentieth century? They are to be praised, if faintly, for their commendable attempts to extend local services and legal protections to disadvantaged citizenry. However, their essential significance lay in another direction: the true legacy of turn-of-the-century black politics was in the extensive and intricate series of personal obligations and practical limitations placed on black politics in the city.

Early black politicians were the often willing—but sometimes petulant—captives of the power fights, patronage deals, petty squabbles, and financial machinations that characterized Chicago politics. Nothing is more obvious in the history of early Chicago politics than the essentially passive and generally subordinate role of black political leadership to white interests. The essential relationship between black and white politicians was a patron-client nexus. Black politics was from its inception inescapably entangled in the web of dominant white political interests.

Ed Morris was elected to his second term with the support of a prominent white politician named Elbridge Hanecy, a "tough South Side judge." Hanecy was himself a protégé of Republican Senator William Lorimer, the "blond boss," a ruthless North Side faction leader who was later unseated by the U.S. Senate in 1912 following two investigations of bribery charges in connection with his election.

Judge Hanecy had been actively building influence with black politicians like Morris and Ed Wright and was a minor force in South Side politics until 1904, when he was forced into premature political retirement after losing a tilt for Republican leadership—and patronage—in the Third Ward with Congressman Martin B. Madden.[47] Madden himself had also been assiduously cultivating young black politicians and indeed maintained himself in the 1920s largely through the support of black politicians and voters.

John Buckner, the "Father of the Eighth Regiment," was Madden's most trusted black lieutenant. Madden had made many contacts with blacks from 1889 to 1897, first as an alderman and later as a congressman for the first congressional district on the near South Side. Buckner was Madden's chief liaison with his black constituents.

Martin Madden had been instrumental in securing Buckner's nomination for the legislature in 1894 and aided him in the creation of the all-black regiment in the National Guard. Buckner, for his part, was particularly effective in organizing the black community. He established the first Negro Bureau of the Republican State Central Committee and was chairman of that bureau during the national campaign of 1898. He held a number of political posts, including membership on the State Central Committee from 1894 to 1896. When Madden sought the Republican nomination for United States Senator in 1897, Buckner got petitions for him from South Side blacks. Buckner also gave Madden his proxy so that Madden could attend the party caucus in Springfield in 1897.[48]

Perhaps Buckner's most significant contribution to Madden's continuing political influence was as a successful recruiter of young political talent in the congressman's behalf. Buckner was an influential "godfather" in the political careers of several young black and white politicians. One of his most successful recruits was Madden's successor, Oscar DePriest, the first black U.S. congressman since Reconstruction, as well as DePriest's secretary, Morris Lewis.[49]

DePriest had begun his political career by going door-to-door in behalf of party candidates. He was so successful as a political organizer that in 1904 the still relatively obscure DePriest was influential enough to demand and receive slating by the Madden organization for the county board. After two terms on the board, DePriest entered into a disastrous alliance with Samuel Ettelson, state senator and later corporation counsel under William Hale Thompson against the Madden forces. Ettelson was defeated, and DePriest was out, forced to wander the political wastelands for five years until he was re-established in Madden's good graces. Paradoxically, Ettelson, a protégé of utilities magnate Samuel Insull, had also been a political client of John Buckner.[50]

It is significant that Buckner's most important accomplishment—and the lone institutional creation of these early black politicians—was the Eighth Regiment. When President McKinley requested 175,000 troops for the Spanish-American War, a group of prominent black civic leaders met with Governor Tanner to ask why no blacks had been included in the call. Black service in the Spanish-American War became a source of signal pride for black Chicagoans, and while the regiment was never a base for black political power, it was viewed as an important symbol of black patriotism and state recognition of the contributions of its black population.[51]

Oscar DePriest, the first black U.S. congressman since Reconstruction. *From* Intercollegian Wonder Book *(Chicago, 1927)*.

Beyond its symbolic significance, the Eighth was an inherently limited avenue for the advancement of group political aspirations. It was far too dependent on white patronage for both personal and military advancement. Buckner himself found that out when he was suspended and finally forced to resign over differences with the governor. While the entire community could rally aound the issue of race heroism in the military and the creation of a black regiment as a proper institutional recognition of Negro military contribution, it would always be little more than a source of status and prestige for men who officered it. Many black politicians combined military prestige and political activism. At least two assistant corporation counsels, six state representatives, one state senator, three aldermen, and one congressmen came out of the Eighth or the all-black Giles Post of the American Legion. But regimental politics was not a significant force in the fuller integration of blacks into state and city politics. A source of prestige and important political contacts, perhaps—but not an avenue to political power.[52]

Fannie Barrier Williams had noted as early as 1905 this general dependence of the black population on white Chicagoans. Certainly, in politics the web of political influence and obligation extended throughout the black middle class. President Grover Cleveland appointed Dr. Daniel Hale Williams surgeon-in-chief of Washington's Freedman's Hospital, though Williams was a prominent Chicago Republican. But such appointments on merit, regardless of political affiliation, were rare. S. Laing Williams, a Booker T. Washington informant in Chicago, struggled diligently in beseeching Washington and prominent white politicians for political appointments. In 1910, President Taft made him the first black assistant district attorney in Chicago.[53]

If they were clever, black politicians could play both sides against each other. This was risky business, but it could work if one had a semi-independent power base such as a black church. Rev. Archibald Carey, a minister and later bishop of the African Methodist Episcopal Church, was a close friend of Boss William Lorimer. In 1900, when William Hale Thompson, scion of a wealthy family, ran for alderman of the Second Ward, Carey was his main black supporter. Carey took the political novice door-to-door and advised him on the liberal but well-placed expenditure of money in black saloons. Thompson credited Carey with his election and rewarded the clergymen by introducing an ordinance for Chicago's first public playground, constructed across the street from Carey's own Institutional Church.[54]

But Carey, who remained a trusted Thompson ally, also aided Democrats when it served his interests. He supported Carter Harrison II for re-election in 1911, and Harrison appointed him to the Motion

Picture Censor Board, where he led the protest against the showing of *Birth of a Nation*. In 1912, Carey successfully supported Edward Dunne, the Democratic candidate for Governor, and Dunne subsequently appointed him to head a committee to celebrate the fiftieth anniversary of the Thirteenth Amendment. It was a lucrative as well as prestigious appointment: the legislature appropriated $25,000 for the event, and Carey's church was selected as the committee's headquarters.[55]

The Reverend E.J. Fisher liked to think that he was above the common political fray. He was not, his son and biographer observed, a "hat-in-hand" profiteering politician, as by inference other religious leaders were. He accepted no "filthy lucre"; there was no "office-seeking": "The jobs sought him".[56] If Fisher was less politically active than Carey, he was also less politically prominent. But he *was* active. Almost immediately after arriving in Chicago in 1903 to serve the Olivet Baptist Church, Fisher began to participate in politics. He supported Republican Charles Deneen for governor in 1904, but also worked for Edward Dunne, then mayor of the city. Deneen appointed him a delegate to the National Negro Education Congress in 1912, and a year later Dunne appointed him a delegate to the celebration of the fiftieth anniversary of the Emancipation Proclamation in Atlantic City. Fisher and Carey may have acted from principle rather than the desire for power and financial reward, but their activities did not go unrewarded. Miles Mark Fisher's biography of his father begins with an "appreciation" from Congressman Martin B. Madden.[57]

The close interrelationship between black institutions and party politics may also be seen in a brief overview of the pre-Migration black press. In a 1973 study, Albert Kreiling uncovered eighty-nine magazines, newspapers, and newsletters published in Chicago between 1878 and 1929. Among the most prominent were the *Chicago Conservator*, Chicago *Appeal*, Illinois *Idea*, and Chicago *Broad Ax*.[58] The Chicago *Appeal* was begun in 1885 in Saint Paul, Minnesota, but by 1888 had become a joint St. Paul-Chicago publication with a sizable black readership throughout the Midwest in the eighties and nineties. Its founders, Cyrus Field Adams and his brother, John Quincy Adams, were both active Republicans and supporters of Booker T. Washington. Cyrus Adams was prominent in the work of the first Negro Bureau in Chicago, a race organization connected with the national Republican campaign; between 1900 and 1912 he also served on various Republican advisory committees duirng presidental campaigns. In 1901, President McKinley appointed Adams assistant registrar of the Treasury, a traditional "Negro" post; and in 1912, President Taft appointed him to

The Reverend Archibald Carey, bishop of the African Methodist Episcopal Church. *From* Intercollegian Wonder Book *(Chicago, 1927).*

a position in New York City "protected"—from the incoming Democratic president—by civil service.[59]

The Illinois *Idea* was a Republican newspaper edited by Sheadrick B. Turner, an active Republican politician who served in the Illinois House of Representatives from 1913 to 1917 and from 1919 to 1927. The *Idea* was used to promote Turner's personal political ambitions and the interests of the Republican party among blacks. It had no national news service of its own, and most out-of-town news was garnered through personal exchanges or "appropriated" from other newspapers. The *Idea* carried a good deal of news of local churches and many personal items (such as deaths, illnesses, and accidents), as well as information on the "race problem"; but much of its revenue came from political advertisements and propaganda during election periods.

White politicians were placed on the *Idea's* mailing list, and advertisements from white firms contributed substantially to the paper's coffers.[60]

Julius F. Taylor's *Broad Ax,* which started in Chicago in 1899, attacked the traditional Republican affiliation of Chicago blacks and supported the candidates of the Democratic party. It was suggested that Taylor's Democratic loyalties were based, at least in part, on political opportunism. Taylor arrived in Chicago during the regime of five-term Democratic mayor Carter H. Harrison, and at least one contemporary contended that Taylor found the "Democratic field for the Negro was a relatively fertile and unexplored field."[61] This charge of political opportunism is bolstered by the fact that the *Broad Ax* in Salt Lake City was conspicuously less political; and Taylor's first Chicago edition fea-

The Olivet Baptist Church. *From* Intercollegian Wonder Book *(Chicago, 1927).*

tured a particularly revealing letter of commendation from Mayor Carter Harrison II:

> To Whom It May Concern:
> Julius F. Taylor, who comes to this city well recommended, has begun the publication of the *Broad Ax,* which I am informed will disseminate Democratic principles and contend for the higher intellectual development of the Afro-American Race and mankind in general. *While he is thus engaged* [italics mine] I bespeak for him the hearty support of all loyal and true friends of the Democracy.
>
> > Respectfully,
> > Carter H. Harrison

The paper also boasted the "endorsement" of the Democratic State Central Committee of Illinois.[62]

Taylor was born in Virginia and migrated to Salt Lake City, where he founded the original *Broad Ax* in about 1895. Four years later he moved the paper to Chicago. He was an anomaly at the turn of the century, a western Democrat when most black Chicagoans were Republican; he was also an admirer of William Jennings Bryan and an economic radical in sharp contrast to the generally conservative ideas of the black community's leadership.

Broad Ax was literally a one-man operation, characterized by a type of personal journalism that often veered toward idiosyncratic interpretations of news stories and blatant character assassination. His enemies were generally characterized as drunks, adulterers, and thieves, and his news stories were often indistinguishable from his editorials.[63]

Among the early black Chicago newspapers, the *Chicago Conservator* alone escaped the fate of becoming a vehicle for clearly partisan, patron-client political interests. Founded in 1878, the city's first black newspaper appeared at a time when blacks were not yet fully integrated into South Side political affairs. Yet even here partisan politics intruded. The paper's founder and first editor was Ferdinand L. Barnett, a member of the Deneen faction within the Republican party and a minor officeholder through the sponsorship of both black and white politicians.[64]

Fisher, Carey, DePriest, Morris, Buckner, and the various black editors—these were all articulate and intelligent men. They were not "Uncle Toms"; indeed they saw themselves as champions of Negro rights. But they chose to define black political advancement within the narrow confines of established urban political orthodoxy. They did not see themselves subordinating black advancement to white political interests. They were simply "playing the game." Influence was garnered through party loyalty, votes delivered, services rendered; they did not seek to create separate and independent political organizations. When Buckner formed voters' groups, they were in the service of his patron Madden, or an adjunct to national or local political campaigns. They tended to be the children of whatever campaign was in process. When the election was over, so were the organizations.

The prominent black lawyer and political leader Edward E. Wilson noted the transience of black political organizations—and of some of their members:

> From campaign to campaign some loiter about county buildings, living heaven knows how. Others seem to hibernate like a bear. When a campaign comes on they are in their glory. They attend political meetings and shout "hear, hear"; they hold forth from corners with pot-eloquent fervor, they show mysterious letters from a senator or representative calling on them to come to his district and help him out. These gentlemen go about rather shabby, having refused, as they will tell you, a job paying a thousand dollars a year. A marked characteristic of this kind of statesman is that he is always armed with a number of newspapers—literally weighted down with them—and refers to them on every occasion to prove his prophetic vision and the infallibility of his stand on this or that question. It is gentry of this kind that have given the Negro a bad name in politics; for not a few of these, though burning with patriotism, have a burning palm also, and are not seldom found refusing to vote without being persuaded thereto by some other than patriotic influences.[65]

Black politics was shaped by the aggressive and often vituperative interparty and internecine struggles for place and power which characterized city politics in general. Black leadership was molded in the crucible of white politics. As early as 1892, a group of Second Ward black Republicans held a caucus at 1823 State Street to organize a vigorous campaign for the Republican ticket. James E. Bish, who was elected to the state legislature that year, was selected president. The club made clear its intention of organizing and incorporating a permanent black political organization that would not evaporate after the fall election. In 1893 the newly formed Second Ward Colored Republican Club announced its unanimous endorsement of Republican Mayor Swift for renomination and "took steps to gain recognition for the colored people in the distribution of patronage by the county board." Specific requests for more patronage were made to the president of the County Board, and Bish himself asked to be made custodian of the County Building.[66]

In 1894, Bish's name was again mentioned, this time as a possible candidate for county commissioner; but another group of newly organized black politicians were sponsoring a prominent black political organizer for the post—Edward H. Wright.[67]

John Jones represented the postwar, postabolitionist tradition of civic protest and civil rights. Black legislators from Thomas to William Martin and "Indignation" Jones reflect the role of the black legislator as a vigilant defender of existing black rights and supporter of the social service role of government. Buckner, Bish, and Morris reveal the relationship between politics and legislation and the importance of white sponsorship in black political careers.

Wright represents something new. In many ways he was the father of twentieth-century black politics in Chicago. This nineteenth-century black legislator was the bridge between civic protest and white clientage politics. Wright illustrated the emergent orientation of black politics toward ward and precinct organization on the city's South Side, and, more important, he pioneered in the establishment of an independent political organization designed to increase black influence in Republican councils and give black politicians a coequal role in the political leadership of the black community.

Edward H. Wright was born in New York City in 1864, attended the city's public schools, and at seventeen graduated from the College of the City of New York. He taught school in New Jersey for three years and came to Chicago in 1884, working his way across the country as a Pullman porter's assistant. Wright held a series of minor posts, but it was politics that landed him a job in the county clerk's office. As a result of his work as delegate to the Republican State Convention in 1888, political service again garnered him a position as bookkeeper and railroad inspection clerk in the secretary of state's office in Springfield, the first clerical position in state government held by a black. When the term of his patron ended, Wright became employed in the city clerk's office in Chicago.[68]

In 1893, Wright emerged as president of a group called the Afro-American League, and a year later he represented one of the two black factions seeking to nominate a "Race Man" to the county board. Since there was no chance that two blacks would be nominated, Wright rose in the county convention and asked that his name be withdrawn from contention. He called on all of his supporters to support the leader of the other faction, Theodore Jones, who was nominated and elected. Jones became the first black member of the county board in almost twenty years. Two years later Wright replaced Jones as the sole black county commissioner.[69]

As county commissioner, Wright was described as "shrewd, forceful

Edward Wright, father of twentieth-century black politics in Chicago. *From* Intercollegian Wonder Book *(Chicago, 1927)*.

and highly race-conscious." "Through sheer ability," wrote the *Chicago Defender*, "he became a power on the county board." Wright and Daniel Healy, a Democrat, led opposing political factions on the board, a feat all the more impressive because Wright was the sole black member.[70]

Perhaps the best example of Wright's political tenacity came in a well-publicized battle with Charles Deneen, later governor and U.S. Senator from Illinois. Deneen had at that time just served a term as a state representative and was seeking the Republican nomination for state's attorney. He made a deal with Wright for the latter's support in the county convention by promising to name a Negro as one of his assistants. Deneen was nominated and elected, but no black assistant state's attorney was nominated. Wright called on Deneen to remind him of their previous agreement and to find out when his nominee, Ferdinand L. Barnett, would be appointed. Deneen said that he would get around to it soon but refused to be committed to a specific date. The nomination "continued to hang fire," and Wright decided to act. When the county board met to appropriate money for various offices, Wright deliberately held up the appropriations for the state's attorney's office.

Deneen inquired among the members of the board about the delay and was told that Commissioner Wright "was sitting on the lid." He called on Wright and is reported to have said: "Ed, what's the idea of you holding up the appropriations for my office?" Wright replied, "You had an understanding with me that in the event of your election you would appoint F.L. Barnett assistant state's attorney and you have failed to keep your word; until that is done I shall continue to prevent the passage of your appropriation." Deneen declared, "I am state's attorney of Cook County and you can't dictate to me!" Wright replied, "Yes, and I am county commissioner." A few days later Barnett became the first black assistant state's attorney for Cook County, and Deneen's appropriations were soon passed.[71]

Wright was re-elected in 1898 and briefly, in 1900, was elected president pro tempore of the county board when the president was away for a short time. Wright accomplished this feat by going around to all the members of the board individually, telling them that he did not expect to be elected but that he would appreciate one or two votes as a sign of recognition for his race. There were two other prominent contenders for the post, but when the votes were counted Wright had received all but two of the fourteen votes cast.[72]

Wright's term as commissioner was not without controversy. This was the era of boodlers, fixed conventions, and frequent utility scandals. In the 1896 Cook County Convention, for example, many of the delegates had criminal records; over one-third of them were saloon-keepers and one-fifth political employees. City and county government were both in the throes of political corruption. Money oiled the wheels of government and soothed discordant political interests.[73]

The problems of local government were exacerbated by the rapid expansion in the city's population. Between 1890 and 1900, Chicago's population grew to 1,698,575—an increase of 595,725, or over 52 percent. Newly annexed territories, many of them villages and expanses of prairies, required large expenditures for normal city improvements and often for the assumption of their former debts. These townships, "vestiges of frontier Chicago," continued to retain their own taxing power and entered, in Ellen Beckman's words, "an era of graft and pillage which frightened the politicians themselves."[74]

Edward Wright's reputation was blemished with more than one charge of corruption. When civic leaders protested the attempts of townships to secure funds for filing fake or padded expense accounts, Wright, acting as attorney for the county board, maintained that the board's president had no legal right to deny funds to the townships. He was also criticized for supporting a measure that granted a blanket franchise without compensation to the Metropolitan Traction Company. The franchise gave the company a monopoly in building street railways over the principal highways outside the Chicago city limits not already occupied by streetcar tracks.[75]

Wright failed to secure nomination in 1900 and for a period moved out of the district that had been his base of political support. He had not been able to work in harmony with Congressman Madden or George F. Harding, Madden's chief lieutenant. Although he was chosen state central committeeman as a reward for his services to Second Ward Committeeman Chauncy Dewey, Wright did not acquire any real political power for another two decades. Dan Jackson, an undertaker and big-time gambler, was slated to replace Wright in 1900. However, Jackson, who ran one of his gambling joints in his funeral home, was defeated when several newspapers, for the first time, drew attention to his color.[76]

In 1904, Oscar DePriest, a Buckner and Madden protégé, was elected to the board. DePriest was born in Florence, Alabama in 1871 and had come to Chicago in 1889 "to grow with the Metropolis of the West."[77] No two men could have been more different—or had more in common. Wright was big (about six-feet-four) and black, an intelligent, intense behind-the-scenes organizer—"the iron master." DePriest was equally tall, but so fair that he successfully passed for white when he first arrived. He was gregarious, sometimes overbearingly so. But he was also an organizer and a skilled politician.

Before the 1904 county convention, DePriest had collected the support of a majority of the black precinct captains. Madden had only just begun his congressional career, and DePriest demanded that he be named to the ticket and that the county convention be held before the state convention. Madden wanted to be sure of united local support, and so he put the still relatively obscure DePriest, seven years Wright's junior at thirty-three, on the ticket. Like Wright, DePriest knew when to be intransigent as well as cooperative.[78]

DePriest was re-elected in 1906. As commissioner he chaired a committee on education and industrial schools and was a member of the committee on outdoor relief. He took part in the planning of the new five-million-dollar courthouse and was praised for his energy in educating blacks to the relief services offered by the county. DePriest benefited from the ambiguous morality of the period. At fifteen De-Priest had been apprenticed to a painter and began his career "carrying a ladder up and down State Street" painting and plastering. He now used his position as commissioner to advance his business. His specialty was salvaging old buildings. He also had a keen sense of the value of a dollar: in 1903, for example, he sued Olivet Baptist Church for an unpaid bill.[79]

By 1905 the *Broad Ax* boasted that DePriest had the "largest painting and decorating contracting business conducted by any member of the Negro race in the Northwest." Between 1903 and 1905 he was awarded contracts for an estimated $25,000 from the Chicago Board of Education. After siding with the losing faction in the Ettelson-Madden tilt, however, DePriest was momentarily consigned to political oblivion. He used the time to invest heavily in real estate. He opened an office on State Street, on the edge of the "black belt," and engaged in "block-busting," buying property, renting it to a black family, and when neighboring whites fled, buying their property and renting it at inflated prices to incoming blacks. Before the Depression, DePriest was reputed to have been a millionaire.[80]

While DePriest made money, Wright was casting about for the appropriate vehicle for black political expression. In 1898, Wright played a leading role in organizing the Sumner Club, designed to hold "much the same position as the Hamilton Club does in the ranks of the white Republican residents."

> While there are social features in the Sumner club, its main object is almost entirely political, and while it neither asked nor received official aid or recognition it has become an influential means for the advancement of Republican politics in Cook County. Being now thoroughly organized and in effective working shape, the members are shaping a program with this end in view.[81]

Wright was also one of the organizers and the first president of the Cook County Bar Association, a black lawyers' organization; but the Sumner Club, and the creation of a viable, independent black political organization were central to Wright's long-range political aspirations. In 1900 the Sumner Club was succeeded by the Appomattox Club, Wright's "one major avocational interest" and a "rendezvous for Negro Republican politicians."[82]

The Appomattox Club, however, never developed into an effective vehicle for the exercise of independent political leadership. From time to time it would be called on to act as the representative spokesman for the Negro community. In 1900, for example, the *Defender,* arguing that "concerted action is better than individual [action]," called on the club "with its representative men" to protest the blatantly racist advertisement that the all-white Hope Cemetery had placed in another paper.[83] But for the most part the Appomattox Club was a place of good comradeship for a group of socially and sometimes politically compatible men.

It is clear from an overview of Edward Wright's entire career that he had sought to create an effective and independent black political organization. In the early 1900s, Wright was wandering in the political wilderness; between 1910 and 1915 he was engaged in a running battle with the white leadership of the Second Ward, in an often bitter campaign to have a black slated as alderman for this increasingly black ward. In 1910, with blacks an estimated 25 percent of the population of the ward, Wright ran as one of four candidates for the post. The *Chicago Defender* made an impassioned plea for racial unity. "We must have a colored alderman not because others were not friendly, but because we should be represented just the same as the Irish, Jews, and Italians." But Wright finished third, capturing only 18 percent of the votes.[84]

Wright tried again in 1912, and the *Defender* again trumpeted race unity and argued that blacks comprised half of the Republican voters in the ward and were entitled to at least one alderman. Again he was defeated, and in 1914 he supported William R. Cowan, a prominent black real estate dealer. Even though he lost, Cowan garnered a very impressive 45 percent of the vote. The White organization was visibly shaken. Madden assured blacks that although he was obligated to support the present white incumbent, as soon as an opening occurred he would support a black candidate.

The chance came the next year when Madden's chief lieutenant was elected to the state senate, thus vacating an aldermanic post. The nomination and subsequent election went to a black, but one who had supported the organization throughout the Wright-Cowan insurgency. Much to Ed Wright's displeasure, the plum went to Oscar DePriest.[85]

Wright was simply unable to mold the Appomattox Club into a strong independent political force. Even Appomattox leaders like Louis B. Anderson, who owed their early political careers to Wright, were unable to withstand the blandishments and ready rewards of the organization. The club's membership was simply too divergent in private ambitions and factional allegiances to coalesce on all but the most basic—and trivial—political concerns.[86]

A brief overview of some of the more prominent members of the Appomattox Club reveals the inherent difficulties of creating a truly independent coalition of black political leaders. Dr. George Cleveland Hall, for example, was an active Republican partisan as well as a widely respected civic leader. In 1895 he had served as treasurer of the Young Colored Men's Republican League of Cook County, but his interests in politics were, for the most part, an adjunct to his civic activities in the NAACP or as president of the Chicago Urban League. Men like Wright, DePriest, and Anderson, by contrast, were earnest if not intense in their quest for political advancement. Anderson, DePriest, and R. R. Jackson, all future South Side aldermen, had become allied with Martin B. Madden and later with William Hale Thompson and Fred Lundin, prominent white politicians and major shapers of black politics in the first third of the twentieth century. Ferdinand L. Barnett and his wife, Ida B. Wells-Barnett, on the other hand, were allied with the opposition camp of Charles E. Deneen, whom they believed had "higher principles than the regular organization."[87]

Beauregard F. Moseley and R. R. Jackson co-founded the *Leland Giants*, the first successful "race" baseball team on the South Side. Moseley was an active Republican and a past president of the Appomattox Club, but in 1912 he supported the Progressive party of Theodore Roosevelt and became president of an organization called the Progressive Negro League.[88]

Dr. Hall tended to ally himself with "good government" organizations and candidates. He was on the "Merriam for Mayor Committee" in 1911 and was a member of the Executive Committee of the Municipal Voters League, a "good government" organization. DePriest, Anderson, and—to a lesser degree—Jackson were routinely criticized by the MVL, which condemned their voting records and opposed their re-election to the city Council.[89]

A critical factor in the early history of the Appomattox Club was the intense rivalry among the members themselves. "It was such a small area," one long-time Chicago resident observed, "that there was always competition among politically inclined Negroes."[90] Equally important, many of the club's leaders and most of its successful politicians had, before 1900, contracted alliances or acquired patrons from one or more of the many factions and subfactions within the city's Republican party. The difficulty of creating a community political consensus amid individual ambitions was evident almost from the organization's inception.

But perhaps the most complex and definitive explanation lay in the inherent limitations of black middle-class politics in Chicago. Pre-Migration black politics was formed from the confluence of post-Civil War black middle-class ideology and black acceptance of established conventions of urban ethnic politics. That the middle class should have effectively maintained political hegemony is not unusual or peculiar to black Chicagoans. The political scientists Heinz Eulau and Kenneth Prewitt have observed:

> To this day, elected legislatures, in the established democracies of the Western world, are overwhelmingly chosen from the middle and upper-middle strata of society. This is the case whether the basic political organization of the society is along vertical or horizontal lines. If politics is vertically organized, as is true where ethnicity, religion, or geography is politically salient, political groups include members of the various social strata in the society, but tend nevertheless to be led by their middle and upper-middle-class members. These leaders provide the pool from which most political officeholders are selected. If politics is horizontally organized, as is true where class is politically salient, the membership of political groups is more homogeneous and the leaders may be of the same social origin as the members. But even under these conditions, the bourgeoisie supplies the large majority of political leaders. . . .[91]

Chicago politics was organized vertically, along ethnic, racial, and—to a lesser extent—geographic and religious lines. Black political leadership, in terms of income, education, social position, and self-perception, was conspicuously middle class. They were conscious of their position as pioneers, and they saw in their own personal advancement the broader advancement of the race.[92]

Several political scientists (but interestingly, no historians) have offered possible explanations for the particular character of black political life in Chicago. Ira Katznelson argues that black politicians had the potential to mobilize the black masses and demand solutions to black problems, but instead they opted for individual rewards for a select few. Black politics, he argues, was inherently and necessarily conservative because any agitation for change that challenged the racial status quo would endanger "structured relationships" with powerful and influential whites and "place the [rewarding] alliance in jeopardy."[93] Black politics was limited, Katznelson strongly implies, because avaricious and status-seeking black politicians entered into narrowly self-serving alliances with corrupt white political machines. Black politics was "co-opted"; black political organizations became "buffers" between the elite and the masses. The "system" offered access only to a "nonrepresentative" black elite while "defusing social conflict" and "leaving the distribution of political power largely intact."[94]

James Q. Wilson's approach is more empirical and less critical. Although his area of concentration is post-World War II and 1950s Chicago politics, his perspective is informing. For Wilson, black politics is dominated by the physical fact of racial segregation. Emerging from this reality is a multi-faceted conflict within black leadership groups over the function of politics. The conflict is between those who believe politics should provide material services to individuals or to the masses—"welfare ends"—and those who seek the less concrete goals of racial integration, civil rights, greater black visibility in public offices—goals generally defined by Wilson as "status ends."[95]

Martin Kilson presents the most clearly defined ideological explanation for the shape of black politics in Chicago. For Kilson, the pattern of "political adaptation" to American cities or political "modernization" begins with clientage or patron-client relationships between black and white politicians, most widespread throughout the period 1900-1920. Clientage, Kilson argues, "was almost exclusively the political method of the Negro middle class," where the black bourgeoisie sought to mask their search for political, social, and economic advantage as "race politics."[96]

In Kilson's conceptual framework, urban black politics advances in stages from clientage politics to interest-group articulation, in which established groups or influential cliques seek to institutionalize black demands. Groups like the NAACP, Urban League, and Marcus Garvey's UNIA took on parapolitical functions, articulating black discontent, making demands on local or national power elites, and exerting pressure or using persuasion on community leaders. The growth of interest-group articulation did not at first replace clientage politics but supplemented it. However, the failure of traditional clientage relations to serve wider segments of the black community and to create its own black political "sub-system" meant that interest-group articulation would eventually "encroach upon" and ultimately supersede clientage politics.[97]

The final stage, the period 1920-1940, showed the rise of black machine politics. In its formative stage whites entered into a "neoclientage" relationship with a hand-picked black "influential," who handed out patronage and was primarily responsible to the "machine." As black machine politics matured, the goal of neutralizing or limiting black political "clout" was replaced by the institutional inclusion of the black sub-machine into "the dominant pattern of machine or boss rule in a given city." Kilson points out that such inclusion was "extremely rare . . . the notable exception being Chicago from 1915 onward."[98]

What these three analysts share is a keen perception of the preeminence of the relationship between black and white politicians in the shaping of black politics in Chicago; of the tendency of black middle-class politics to seek individual or status rewards from politics; and of the generally conservative nature of black politics in the city.

While I have no essential argument with such observations—and am in particular agreement with the Kilson-Katznelson emphasis on the patron-client nature of early Chicago politics—I must add an historian's additional observation about the particular character of pre-Migration black politics. What is missing in these generally admirable observations is the particular historical context of black political development. Morris, Wright, and DePriest did not spring full-blown from the head of Zeus. The generally conservative and essentially individualistic pattern of black politics emerged from a specific tradition of black and Chicago politics.

Returning to John Jones, we can observe two dominant features of the politics of black Chicago: a general faith in the efficacy of American political parties and the essentially defensive nature of black politics. Jones' political ideas had been forged in the anti-black-laws campaign of the 1860s, a campaign which would not have succeeded without powerful white allies and the Republican party. "My colored countrymen," Jones once declared in a speech, "the republican [sic] party has lifted us up from the degradation of slavery and put us upon an equal platform with themselves."[99] Jones' diary contains numerous references to the importance of voting. Jones preserved the full text of a speech entitled "The Importance of a Single Vote," and he counseled the importance of blacks' exercising the franchise. Jones was not unaware of the obstacles that lay ahead of his people, but he seemed genuinely optimistic about the race's future. A quote from Goethe was prominently displayed in his diary: "In imminent danger the faintest hope should be taken into account."[100]

Black Chicagoans clung to Jones' Republican party, the one that offered them protection and some modicum of political advancement. Many black politicians opposed the entire spate of progressive electoral innovations, including the direct primary, initiative, referendum, and recall. When Governor Deneen's administration was considering instituting the direct primary in 1907, Rev. Archibald Carey and other prominent black leaders sent a resolution to each state senator:

> We the undersigned citizens ask in our own behalf and at the special insistence and request of the colored citizens do hereby protest against the passage of the so-called Primary Election Law Bill being House No. 895. We feel that the passage of this bill will completely eliminate from the politics of the state the colored voters and take from them all opportunity of any member of their race being nominated to office and we respectfully ask that you vote against the passage of this bill.[101]

However, the bill was made law. Five years later a *Defender* editorial criticized another set of Progressive reforms.

> The Initiative, Referendum, and Recall is simply a dose of disfranchisement, sugar coated, albeit with high sounding and illusive

verbiage for the consumption of the northern Negro, but nevertheless an emetic which will sooner or later force him to disgorge
every right that he possesses under the law and the constitution.

Out in the broad light of day and in the courts where publicity
obtains, the Negro has a chance for justice, but under the Initiative,
Referendum, and Recall the civil rights of the Negro will be decided in the silence and seclusion of the voting booth, where his
enemies may stab him in the back and none be the wiser; because
they will be swallowed up in the great concrete majority that Roosevelt likes to call "the people."[102]

The *Defender* was magniloquent—but not entirely honest. The "broad
light of day" which they and prominent black politicans sought was
the machine anonymity that would allow blacks to seek city-wide or
county-wide elective office on the Republican ticket and not be "cut"
by regular party voters because of their race. However, their fears were
justified. Before the bill was made law in 1910, several blacks had been
successfully elected to the Cook County Board of Commissioners. After
1910 no black was elected until 1938.[103]

These black machine politicians were not unthinking loyalists.
Carey, DePriest, and Wright would often play faction against faction
and would even abandon particular party nominees when it served
their interests. But they saw in a certain political consistency the quick-
est and safest avenue for their own—and by extension—the race's political advancement.

The era from John Jones to "Indignation" Jones must have seemed
a period of impressive progress. One state representative and a county
commissioner had become the expected reward for black party fealty.
By 1900 there were black policemen, black school teachers, black assistant corporation counsels—all gained through black political influence. Blacks were still economically disadvantaged, and they were still
discriminated against; but from the perspective of middle-class black
politics it was an era of adequate if not exceptional progress for a people
little more than a generation removed from slavery.

The task, then, was to preserve and insure their—and the race's—
advancement amid crumbling race relations. If this was to be achieved,
caution, in the tradition of Booker T. Washington, suggested that it be
done within the established tradition of Chicago ethnic politics. They
were painfully aware of the limits of adventurism. Washington had
implied that Reconstruction and the Populist period had offered a naive
race the illusion of political advancement while robbing them of economic security and the necessary good will of the wealthier classes of
the white South.[104] When Ferdinand Barnett ran for the municipal

court in 1906 on the Republican ticket, blacks were again reminded of their vulnerability. Barnett faced substantial and, apparently to many blacks, surprising white hostility. With one exception, every white newspaper urged that he be defeated, and the Chicago *Chronicle* wrote: "The bench is a position of absolute authority and white people will never willingly submit to receiving the law from a negro." While the rest of the Republican ticket swept to victory, Barnett was defeated, amid charges of election fraud.[105]

What I am suggesting is the convenient convergence of the essentially reactive nature of early black politics and the pre-existent tradition of Chicago ethnic politics that offered certain—if limited—political rewards to a receptive black elite. These rewards were themselves small: financial backing for campaigns, some patronage, a few minor appointive posts, status within their own community, and eventually limited and usually shared power within a narrowly proscribed geographical area with a majority black population. The rewards were perhaps paltry, but they were substantial enough to convince the black political elite, and through them the voters, of the benefits of machine politics and the dangers of political independence.

My reading of the evidence suggests that more than avarice or political cupidity shaped pre-Migration black politics in Chicago. The black political elite was predisposed by the dominant political conservatism of the times toward the relative safety of the ethnic political machine. Booker T. Washington, perhaps the most powerful Republican—black or white—in the South, lunched with President Roosevelt and counseled against radicalism, class antagonism, and political independence. John Jones was certainly radical in his opposition to slavery. But in a speech before a workingman's union, he was careful to delineate his political aims: "We are not demanding what is known as social rights," he said. "The social relations lie entirely outside the domain of legislation and politics. They are simply matters of taste, and thus I leave them."[106]

Jones' rise to wealth and social prominence was the archetypal Horatio Alger story. An ardent advocate of the mid-nineteenth-century capitalist ethic, his vision of the future was entirely conventional and somewhat optimistic. "I expect," he said, "to see the day myself when the colored men of the South will be the cotton lords and bankers of that favored section of the country. We are making rapid strides in acquiring education and wealth. Our children are going to school. We are buying real estate and paying for it, both North and South, and these, my friends, constitute the true road to success." Jones even emulated the upper-class pattern of entertaining, complete with quadrille orchestra to provide "inspiring music" for the "terpsichorean pleasure" of the evening.[107]

DePriest was widely praised throughout his lifetime as a "Race Man," someone firmly committed to black advancement. Yet he was an economic conservative who made a fortune in "block-busting," helped organize the Chicago branch of Booker T. Washington's Negro Business League and later, as a congressman, voted *against* Democratic New Deal relief measures. Carey was critical of the radicalism of labor leader A. Phillip Randolph and was equally conservative: "I believe that the interest of my people lies with the wealth of the nation and with the class of white people who control it. Labor and capital cannot adjust themselves by rival organizations; they must work together."[108]

Perhaps most instructive of the convergence of political and economic conservatism was an incident involving black Chicago postal employees. The Phalanx Forum, a social organization for black postal workers, had been formed in 1911 by members of the Appomattox Club. Black workers in the post office qualified for middle-class status in the early twentieth-century community, and a former postal worker, R. R. Jackson, was the community's state representative in 1912. With the election of Woodrow Wilson, the postal service was segregated and many black workers fired. Instead of joining the National Alliance of Postal Employees, which fought to protect black jobs through trade unionism, the workers opted instead to pursue the more individualistic but safer approach of using the political influence of the Appomattox Club to protect their jobs.[109]

This approach was not unique to black Chicagoans. As Robert Factor makes clear from an overview of the post-Civil War career of Frederick Douglass and black labor organizations in the 1870s, even groups ostensibly formed to deal with the problems of black labor tended to focus attention away from economic and class grievances and toward conventional political demands for equal rights and resolutions of support for the Republican party.[110] Black leaders from Douglass to Washington, from John Jones to Ed Wright, regarded economics as a matter of individual concern, eschewed class antagonism and labor militancy, and entombed black political ideology within the relatively safe and conventional limitations of American partisan orthodoxy.

Black Republicanism, of course, brought with it the heritage of Lincoln and Sumner, with images of abolitionism and emancipation. Negro Democracy, on the other hand, bore the burden of Southern white redemption, the Klan, and lynching. In 1888, when the Cook County Democratic Club opened its headquarters, one old Negro is reported to have wept "to think that Colored men should be Democrats."[111] Yet, whereas suspicion of Democrats was never fully assuaged, many blacks were attracted to Carter Harrison I, the Democratic mayor from 1879 to 1887 and briefly again in 1893 (he was assassinated at the end of the Chicago World's Fair); and his son, Carter II, mayor from 1897 to 1903 and from 1911 to 1915. In 1885, Carter I received an estimated 50 percent of the black vote, and twelve years later his son was elected mayor with 65 percent of the black vote.[112]

The first organized unit of black Democrats is perhaps lost in antiquity, but the Logan Hall Democrats, the Thirteenth Ward Democrats, and the Colored Tammany were among the earliest black Democratic clubs formed in Chicago. By the 1890s the Colored Democratic League, led by Enos Bond, had apparently attained a degree of political permanence unusual for Chicago politics, where most political groups, Republican or Democrat, black or white, tended to be creatures of whatever campaign was at hand.[113]

The most impressive of the early black leaders of the Chicago Democracy was Lawrence Arthur Newby. Newby was born in Pauli, Indiana and spent his early years in Indianapolis, where he served briefly as owner and editor of the black newspaper *Indianapolis Courier*. He came to Chicago in 1895 and became active in the presidential campaign of William Jennings Bryan. In 1898 he was elected president of the Colored Democratic League.[114] While Newby was considered an effective and widely respected political organizer, the nascent Democratic party was racked with petty jealousies and factional discord. Party unity was hampered by the emergence of rival organizations such as the Thomas Jefferson Club. In 1901 the sable Democracy was further splintered with the emergence of the Cook County Colored Democracy under the leadership of Captain H. C. Carter.[115]

For Julius Taylor, the black editor of *Broad Ax*, Captian Carter represented the lowest form of political opportunism. Carter was accused of surrounding himself with the "worst class of Negroes," and failing to recruit new members to the party. *Broad Ax* was also highly critical of Carter's morals. Respectable Democrats, Taylor wrote, "have not forgotten the fact that for years Captain Carter lived with Mrs. Fanny Brown in open violation of all the laws of decency and morality. . . ." Carter responded by having Taylor arrested for libel.[116] Despite Taylor's continued carping, Carter appears to have retained the favor and the financial backing of the Democratic powers.

It is difficult to explain the popularity of the two Carter Harrisons within the black community. They did appoint a few blacks to minor municipal offices, and—equally important—they maintained the pattern of black municipal employment inherited from Republican mayors. Their success, however, seems more a matter of style and personal attractiveness than any general movement of blacks to the Democratic party. With the exception of the Harrisons, *père* and *fils*, black Chicagoans demonstrated an understandable fidelity to the Republican banner. For black Chicagoans, the Harrison periods were glorious exceptions, incongruous eras capped by the election of 1911, when Carter II, running for his last term, carried the black vote against the Republican reformer, Charles E. Merriam, and became the first Democrat to capture the Second Ward. Black Republican loyalty persisted, despite the fact that in twenty mayoralty contests between 1871 and 1915, ten were won by a Carter Harrison.[117]

The failure of the Chicago Democrats to build on the Harrison popularity and to attract a larger black constituency is one of the interesting "might-have-beens" of black history. Traditional Republican loyalty cannot serve as the only answer, for blacks in Boston were attracted to the Democratic machine of Mayor Curley, and certainly the successes of the Harrisons indicated that blacks could be induced to vote for Democratic candidates. Furthermore, many prominent blacks had been critical of Theodore Roosevelt's handling of the Brownsville Incident and of Republican overtures to conservative white Southerners. Prominent black leaders like William Monroe Trotter and W.E.B. DuBois were counseling increased political independence, and Edward E. Wilson argued that Chicago blacks could be induced to support "liberal-leaning" Democrats.

> While the great majority of Chicago Negroes are Republicans there is a respectable and growing element that has allied itself with the Democratic Party. There is but little difference—save in name— between a white Chicago Democrat and a white Chicago Republican. Because of tradition and of the support given it, the Republican party has granted the Negro most of his political recognition, but this party shows manifest restlessness at Negro demands. A Democrat of liberal leanings always commands some Negro votes in city elections and it is a good guess to say that henceforth there will be fewer Negroes of the unalterable Republican faith in local contests.[118]

Wilson failed to recognize the impact of what August Meier has called the migration of the Talented Tenth. Chicago's black population increased by more than 30 percent between 1900 and 1910; already by 1900 over 80 percent of the city's black population had been born outside Illinois, the majority of them coming from the border states and the upper South. As the historian Allan H. Spear has pointed out: "As migration from the South swelled the population of the black belt, it brought with it voters who regarded the Democrats as the natural enemies of the Negro people and whose previous experiences committed them to the Republican Party."[119]

But Wilson's own words reveal an additional element. The Republican party gave the Negro "most of his political recognition." The Chicago Democracy was unable to shake the racial conservatism that dominated that party throughout the first third of the century. They ignored the requests of their few black supporters and never nominated a single black for even the most minor elective office. Blacks were being asked to support a party largely composed of the more overtly antiblack "new immigrants" and identified with working and lower-class whites. It was an unlikely adventure for a largely conservative and essentially cautious black leadership.

* * * * *

The transformation from the civic-protest tradition to organizational politics, the emergence of a small cadre of fulltime black professional politicians, and the conflict between race politics and the patron-client relationships contracted between black and white politicians characterized black politics in Chicago before the Great Migration. The emerging Negro elite attempted, through politics, to translate intracial status into political influence and to manipulate its personal and occupational prestige within the black community into service as a buffer between white leadership and the black masses. The institutional and social circumscription peculiar to the black urban experience, plus the pre-existing tradition of ethnic representation and group politics, combined to aid this new elite in translating credibility with black voters and contacts with white politicians into limited political influence.

Chicago's black politicians recognized their roles as "pioneers" in black political development. They also perceived, perhaps indirectly, the tenuousness of their political leadership roles. They were, to paraphrase Martin Kilson, attempting to assert their eligibility—in concert as an elite or in competition as individuals—to assume a leadership role in the necessary political change that would occur with the introduction of the black voter as a new constituent into the existing political system, an introduction that might well generate friction with existing claimants to political authority.

Thus they were faced with a dual obligation: they had to assure their constituents that their interests were identical with group racial interests, and they had to frame race demands in ways and through channels that would be comprehensible and ultimately resolvable within existing urban political procedures. Those black politicians who chafed under the explicit obligations of Chicago ward politics faced personal (i.e., financial) as well as political punishments for their recalcitrance. Ed Wright and Oscar DePriest were both examples of political self-assertiveness that was rewarded with temporary political banishment.[120]

The period from the mid-1870s to the early 1900s may be seen as a transitional era, in which black leaders were acutely aware of the inherent limitations of their group leadership. Edward E. Wilson, writing in 1907, reflected clearly this perception of the limits of black political possibilities:

> The Negro vote alone would of course affect but little. It must make combination with the controlling forces in the party. He who gets closest to the powers that be is for the time being the biggest leader. Negro political leaders like those among the white rise and fall as their faction is up and down, and he that is so situated as to pass through a desert of official and political obscurity is in the long run the most successful politician. One must necessarily have the ability to bring in delegates to nominating conventions, or greatly influence bringing them in, in order to get any serious consideration from the big leaders or "bosses" as they are sometimes called. In this matter, social, intellectual or other admirable qualities count for nothing if you cannot "deliver the goods."[121]

Black politics was fashioned within the limits of existing Chicago ethnic politics. Black leaders were willing, even eager, to "play by the rules." They were acclimated to the security—and to the rewards—of conventional party loyalty.

A certain consistency pervades this period. Black politicians would continue their vigilance in defense of black civil rights and their opposition to any blatant attempts to segregate or discriminate on the basis of race. Black legislators would remain important political leaders, but by 1910 the thrust was toward building political power bases within the city itself. When hundreds of thousands of blacks migrated to Chicago during and after World War I, their power and their demands for political rewards increased. But black demands, and indeed black aspirations, were limited by a black political tradition molded in pre-Migration experiences.

The politics of Black Metropolis, then, were forged before the ghetto, before the Great Migration, the mayoralty of "Big Bill" Thompson, or the political sub-machines of Ed Wright and Oscar DePriest. This is the legacy—and perhaps the tragedy—of the pre-Migration period.

Chapter XI

ARNOLD HIRSCH
The Black Struggle for Integrated Housing in Chicago

> *Some of those with whom I talked [had] . . . such thick Bohemian, German, Polish or Greek accents that it was not always easy to know what they were saying. . . . It was appalling to see . . . those who were . . . beneficiaries of American opportunity . . . as virulent as any Mississippian in their willingness to deny a place to live to a member of a race which had preceded them to America by many generations.*
>
> — Walter White *(1951)*

T HE WAVE OF RIOTS THAT SWEPT THE
United States in the mid-1960s revolutionized popular perceptions regarding the place and significance of collective violence in the nation's
history. Before the sixties violence was viewed as an idiosyncratic form
of behavior existing outside and apart from the American social structure and political process. Now its occurrence is seen more as a "natural" part and expression of both.[1]

The race riots, however, blinded us even as they opened our eyes.
The fact that much violence was committed by blacks, for example,
played no small part in the whites' sudden interest in the subject. A
grim fascination for the study of black violence, and its prevention,
marked much of the later literature.[2] Furthermore, the explosions of
the 1960s conditioned observers to equate the significance of violence
with its *visibility*. But if, in fact, violence is an expression of our social
order, its judicious and less visible use by those holding power may
have a more lasting impact than its open exploitation, in race riots, by
the essentially powerless.

This chapter deals with a large American city in the pre-1960s,
during what has been seen as a quiescent period. By exposing and
examining a previously hidden though significant pattern of white-ini-
tiated racial violence in Chicago during the years following World War II,
the focus is not on the discovery of a new sensational wave of riots, but
rather on the revelation of a persistent form of day-to-day violence and
what it can tell us about social and ethnic change in the post-war city.
The examination of disorder—its frequency, discernible features, and
historical context—will be used as an analytical tool to lay bare the
structure and workings of society in an era during which many decisions were made which shaped the modern American city.

Despite official attempts to control racial tensions, a competitive struggle for homes and "turf" engulfed portions of Chicago in the 1940s and
1950s. This battle was rooted in shifting demographic realities as the
racial composition of the city underwent drastic change. White population declined while black population rose dramatically, from 8 percent in 1940 to nearly 25 percent by 1960.[3] Prior to World War II, the
area in which this growing black population was compelled to live

From rural slum...to urban slum. *Courtesy of University of Illinois Library at Chicago, Manuscripts Division.*

remained relatively stable; its borders were still largely those drawn during the Great Migration. After World War II, black territorial expansion began anew. Pushing out to the south and west, the growth of the old Black Belt generated violent resistance. The resulting battles for living space were carried on by local residents of contested neighborhoods whose actions, though charged by a strident emotionalism, were generally measured, limited, and purposeful. Even more important was the perception of that purposefulness by the City Council. Embarking on a program to redevelop the city, the Council's reaction to violence was to be instrumental in shaping Chicago's race relations throughout the civil rights era and into the turbulent 1960s.

The extent of postwar racial violence in Chicago, as well as the degree to which it was hidden from public view, is best illustrated by way of contrast. The most widely publicized racial disorder of these years occurred not within the city proper but at its western edge in the working-class suburb of Cicero. There, during the summer of 1951, a mob assaulted a large apartment building which housed a single black family in one of its twenty units. The burning and looting of the building's contents lasted several nights until order was finally restored by the presence of some 450 National Guardsmen and 200 Cicero and Cook County Sheriff's police.[4]

The reaction to this incident was immediate, outraged, and worldwide. Thomas E. Dewey, visiting Singapore, was "shocked" to find the Cicero riot front page news in South East Asia. News of the riot was also carried in the *Pakistan Observer* and apparently reached Africa as well; a resident of Accra wrote to the mayor of Cicero protesting the mob's "savagery" and asking for an "apology to the civilized world. . . ."[5]

At home the Chicago press provided extensive coverage of the riot, complete with editorials denouncing the violence and letters to the editor protesting racial barbarism. However, buried among those letters was one of a slightly different tone written by Homer Jack, a Unitarian minister and co-founder of the Congress of Racial Equality (CORE). The Cicero disorder "contained perhaps more vandalism than recent racial disturbances in Chicago," Jack wrote, "but fortunately there was no persistent attack on the police . . . or violence towards Negroes," as had been the case elsewhere in the city.[6] Jack was referring to two recent Chicago riots, one at the Chicago Housing Authority's (CHA) southside Fernwood Park Homes and another in the southside Englewood community. In each case the issue was the same: the introduction of black residents into previously all-white communities. Yet, though he was minimizing the level of violence seen in Cicero compared with these other disorders, it was only through his role as a social activist

A black tenement on the South Side. *Courtesy of University of Illinois Library at Chicago, Manuscripts Division.*

that Jack was aware of them at all. The Chicago press had virtually ignored these earlier riots and, as a contemporary observer noted, "the man in the street . . . is wholly unaware that a cruel kind of warfare is going on in the no-man's land around Chicago's Black Belt."[7]

The unpublicized Chicago riots dwarfed the better-known Cicero incident by every possible measure. Four or five rioters were found in the streets of Chicago for each one mobilized in Cicero. While a mere building was attacked in Cicero (there was not a black within miles of the area when the rioting started), both Chicago mobs vented their wrath on human victims. In Fernwood blacks were hauled off streetcars in a fashion reminiscent of 1919; in Englewood the crowd attacked not only blacks, but also Jews, University of Chicago students, and anyone else labeled on "outsider." Even in terms of the size of the force needed to quell the violence, the Cicero disorder seemed less dangerous than the Chicago outbursts. One thousand police were needed in Fernwood, and 700 were kept on duty for a full two weeks in the area. At the height of the rioting the police were compelled to quarantine an area of nearly eight square miles in order to contain the incident. In comparison, there were never more than 650 peace officers on duty in Cicero, nor were they obliged to clear more than a single square mile as a precaution.[8]

Not only were the Chicago riots larger and more threatening than Cicero's, but they were only two of many such incidents. The Fernwood riot was the second disorder to erupt at a veterans' housing project; the Airport Homes at 60th and Karlov suffered a riot comparable to that of Cicero in December 1946. Similarly, the block-by-block expansion of the Black Belt was not Englewood's concern alone. To the south of the ghetto, Park Manor endured its worst of several disorders in July 1949 as thousands gathered in the attempt to destroy a black family's newly purchased home. Other Chicago disturbances occurred after the Cicero episode as well. The Trumbull Park Homes, another CHA project on the far South Side, experienced chronic violence for several years in the mid-1950s; beaches and other public facilities became bones of racial contention as the neighborhoods surrounding them changed in these years. The most serious incidents ignited a large portion of the South Side around Calumet Park in the summer of 1957, lasted the better part of a week, and injured at least fifty people.[9]

More than a string of isolated incidents, these events present a pattern which shows that Chicago was undergoing an ordeal by fire in the postwar years as the spatial accommodation of the races underwent adjustment. In the mid-1940s individual attacks—arson, bombings, stonings—against homes sold to blacks in previously all-white areas reached proportions similar to those of the 1917-1921 period, when one

National Guardsman in fighting gear, with bayonet-tipped rifles, form a cordon around the riot center, Cicero, 1951. *Courtesy of Chicago Historical Society.*

racially motivated bombing occurred every twenty days.[10] By the fifties this form of violence was supplemented by another, related to the blacks' consolidation of newly acquired territory. Confrontations over the use of local parks, beaches, and schoolyards followed the increased migration of blacks into previously restricted areas. Large-scale disturbances became less frequent, but those that developed in this context necessarily involved many more assaults on persons than property. The connecting thread, however, was still the battle for living space and the perquisites that went with neighborhood control. The sheer force of numbers was compelling the city to alter its heretofore rigid racial boundaries. It proved to be a painful process.[11]

The question remains: how could all of this be hidden from the public at large? Again the contrast with Cicero is illustrative. When Cicero's fifty-man police force lost control of the situation and Chicago's

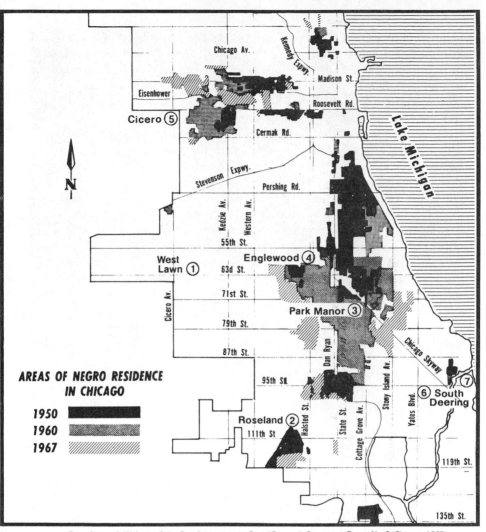

From Chicago's Widening Color Gap, *Interuniversity Social Research Committee: Report No. 2 (Chicago, 1967)*

Locations of the housing disturbances

1 Airport Homes housing project, 1946
2 Fernwood Park housing project, 1947
3 Park Manor (71st and St. Lawrence), 1949
4 Englewood (56th and Peoria), 1949
5 Cicero, 1951
6 Trumbull Park, 1953
7 Calumet Park, 1957

police refused aid, the suburb had no choice but to appeal to the governor to send out the National Guard. On the other hand, Chicago had been able to dispatch as many as 1,200 of its own police to calm far more serious disorders without asking for outside help; thus the city was able to avoid the publicity arising from the presence of bayonet-armed troops. Also of critical importance was the fact that the Cicero riot was the first racial disturbance covered by local television. Most Chicagoans viewed the turmoil in Cicero from the comfort of their living rooms before they read about it in the papers.[12]

This reticence in reporting news of racial violence on the part of the Chicago press kept the earlier riots out of the public eye. The Chicago Commission on Human Relations (CHR) had successfully solicited the cooperation of the city's editors in developing a policy of "circumspection" in reporting news of racial altercations, and the latter voluntarily refrained from running "inflammatory" stories. There was a unanimity born of fear as Chicago's grisly past and uncertain future were contemplated. No one wanted to repeat the mistakes of 1919 or follow the hideous example set by Detroit in 1943. The result was severely truncated treatment of racial conflict, the most extensive accounts being a paragraph or two buried well within the dailies' interior pages. Even if the reader located the stories, he soon found that they bore little semblance to reality: riots were transformed into "demonstrations," the issue of race was never mentioned, and the lists of those arrested provided precious little in the way of explanation.[13]

The primary rationale for this policy was the belief that it kept outsiders away from the scene of disorder. It had long been postulated that "outside agitators" greatly aggravated Chicago's racial tensions. Scholarly analysis seemed to confirm that view. Allen Day Grimshaw, a leading observer of American racial violence, hypothesized in 1959 that the participants in "contested area" riots were not local residents of those areas. Seeking an explanation for the relative absence of violence in residential districts during major upheavals, Grimshaw speculated that those usually operating in contested areas were "outside fanatics" who naturally gravitated towards the "action" in large riots, thus leaving residential neighborhoods alone.[14]

An effective way to test this hypothesis is to compile and analyze *arrest lists* for five of the worst postwar riots.[15] Individually and collectively, such lists demonstrate clearly the opposite of Grimshaw's hypothesis: the participants in "contested area" riots were, with few exceptions, residents of the territory involved. Of the total of 319 persons arrested, 78.7 percent lived within one mile of their respective riot areas, and 87.5 percent lived within one and a half miles; only 22 of the arrestees lived more than three miles away. Most striking in this regard was the Fernwood riot, where only 7 of the 113 arrestees lived more than twelve blocks from the officially designated riot area. Moreover, of the 22 "outsiders" in these five riots, 10 were arrested at the Trumbull Park Homes disorders—the only incident covered by television, given national publicity, and of several months' duration. But even during this disturbance, 7 of every 10 rioters arrested lived either within the project or less than a mere four blocks away; 86.1 percent of those arrested here lived within twelve blocks of the project. Despite the television coverage and the widespread publicity, the participants in the Trumbull Park Homes uprising conformed to the pattern established by the earlier and lesser-known incidents, a pattern which saw nearly 90 percent of all rioters living within twelve blocks of their riot scenes (Table I).

The seeming exceptions to these findings, on closer examination, prove to be no exceptions at all. The Peoria Street incident in Englewood provides the most illuminating case. At first glance it appears that the rioters in this episode came from all over the city; nearly a quarter of the sixty-six arrested lived more than four miles away from the house whose rumored sale precipitated the riot (Table II). A look at the conduct of the police during the riot, however, reveals that for the first two nights of the disorder police officers were sympathetic to the mob and arrested victims as well as attackers. It was only on the third night, after the Commission on Human Relations complained about police actions, that the authorities cracked down on the rioters rather than on their prey.[16] A comparison of arrests made the third night with those made the previous two nights discloses the distribution anticipated if local residents were indeed the rioters. Three out of four arrested on the third night lived within twelve blocks of the riot scene; all sixteen of those living more than four miles away were arrested during the first two nights and probably were victims. Here, as in other riots, local residents fought to prevent racial change in their neighborhood.

The central fact that emerges from this analysis is the prominence of local defenders in each of the rioting communities. Placing these findings in the proper historical context, it appears that while there were widely shared assumptions regarding the undesirability of racial change, the various neighborhoods responded to it independently, reacting only as it actually touched them. Consequently, the housing battles, these struggles over "turf," were localized by nature. Black residence in a particular home or use of a specific park were not issues around which a city of millions could be mobilized; they did, however, have a significant local impact on those who perceived themselves to be immediately threatened by such developments. The fact that a wave of such disorders occurred testified only to the magnitude of the changes

TABLE I
RESIDENTIAL PROXIMITY OF ARRESTEES TO RIOT AREAS BY NUMBER AND PERCENTAGE

Distance	1947 (a) Fernwood Park	1949 (b) Park Manor	1949 (c) Engle-wood	1953-54 (d) Trumbull Park	1957 (e) Calumet Park	Total
0-4 blocks*	89 (78.8)	9 (50.0)	10 (34.5)	76 (70.4)	35 (68.6)	219 (68.7)
5-8 blocks	13 (11.5)	3 (16.6)	3 (10.3)	5 (4.6)	8 (15.7)	32 (10.0)
9-12 blocks	4 (3.5)	2 (11.1)	9 (31.0)	12 (11.1)	1 (2.0)	28 (8.8)
13-16 blocks	0 (0.0)	1 (5.5)	4 (13.8)	3 (2.8)	1 (2.0)	9 (2.8)
17-24 blocks	2 (1.8)	3 (16.6)	2 (6.9)	2 (1.9)	0 (0.0)	9 (2.8)
25-32 blocks	2 (1.8)	0 (0.0)	1 (3.4)	3 (2.8)	1 (2.0)	7 (2.2)
over 32 blocks	3 (2.7)	0 (0.0)	0 (0.0)	7 (6.5)	5 (9.8)	15 (4.7)
Total	113 (100.1)	18 (99.8)	29 (99.9)	108 (100.1)	51 (100.1)	319 (100.0)

*Eight blocks are equal to one mile.

(a)

Though this riot started at the site of the Fernwood Park Homes, it became a more generalized conflict in which blacks throughout the community were attacked. It was thus deemed more appropriate to measure the distance between the addresses of the arrestees and the main riot area rather than the distance between those addresses and the project proper. The riot area, defined by the deployment of police patrols intended to quarantine the violence, stretched from 95th to 130th and from Michigan Avenue to Vincennes and the city limits.

(b)

All addresses were measured from the intersection of 71st and St. Lawrence; the house under attack was located at 7153 St. Lawrence.

(c)

This riot was also generalized throughout the community. The police, however, did not establish a clearly defined riot area as had been the case at Fernwood. Thus, the intersection of 56th and Peoria, the riot's point of origin, was taken as the base from which to measure the distance between the arrestees' addresses and the scene of the riot. This procedure would, obviously, *overestimate* the distance between the arrestees' homes and the locale of the disorder. Those arrested during the first two nights of rioting here were not included as it was impossible to separate rioters from victims on the arrest lists.

(d)

The project site was the base from which the rioters' addresses were measured.

(e)

This riot began at Calumet Park (95th to 102nd on the lakefront) but spread throughout the area and eventually included disorders at the nearby Trumbull Park Homes. Since the Chicago Commission on Human Relations reported numerous related incidents occurring between the park and the CHA project, the area from 95th to 109th and from Lake Michigan and the Indiana state line to Bensley was considered the riot area. All addresses were measured from that base.

TABLE II
RESIDENTIAL PROXIMITY OF ARRESTEES TO RIOT AREA
AT 56TH AND PEORIA (ENGLEWOOD) BY NIGHT OF ARREST

Distance	All 3 Nights	First 2 Nights	Third Night
0-4 blocks	19	9	10
5-8 blocks	6	3	3
9-12 blocks	9	0	9
13-16 blocks	5	1	4
17-24 blocks	8	6	2
25-32 blocks	3	2	1
over 32 blocks	16	16	0
Total	66	37	29

sweeping the city; it was not, apparently, due to a clique of professional race-haters or outside agitators.* The typical Chicago housing riot was thus a "communal riot" in the most literal sense of the term; each community rose up in its own defense, produced its own defenders, and proceeded to fight for its self-defined goals and interests.

The truly communal nature of these scattered uprisings can be demonstrated in a number of ways. First, though arrest lists supply valuable information regarding the most visibly active participants in any disorder, they tend to emphasize the role played by young males, that social segment from which the "soldiers" in any battle are traditionally drawn. Eyewitness accounts of these housing riots, however, bring into clear relief not only the supportive roles played by older males, but also the truly instrumental part played by women. Many housing riots were complex communal endeavors launched by a demographic cross-section of the areas involved. The division of labor which—more or less—naturally appeared during these disturbances simply placed the young males in the greatest danger of arrest. The relative absence of women, children, and older men from such lists cannot be interpreted as evidence of their nonparticipation.[18] Indeed, the whole community, or at least every segment in it, often took part in housing riots. The violent ones who were most often arrested were

---

*Significantly, the one violence-prone racist organization that was active in some of these disorders, the White Circle League, was founded in Park Manor *after* that area's worst disorder. Representatives of the League were present at both Trumbull Park and Cicero during those disturbances, but they followed the outbreak of violence there and were the exploiters rather than the precipitators of those incidents. The CHR was well aware of the League's activities and had, in fact, been keeping watch on founder Joseph Beauharnais for months before the League was formally organized. There is no evidence to suggest they had a hand in starting any disorder.[17]

the community's representatives, not, as was believed by those denouncing the criminality of "hoodlums," its aberrations.

The most destructive mobs, those attacking persons as well as property, had the youngest arrestees. The average age of forty-four persons arrested during the 1957 Calumet Park riot was 22.6 years, and the average age of those arrested on the third night of the Peoria Street disturbance was only 20 years. The Fernwood riot, however, though as violent as any of the others, had rioters who averaged a mature 27.8 years of age. More important, fully 34.3 percent of the 108 arrested rioters for whom information is available were thirty or more years of age. Lending additional weight to the adult-role argument is the fact that 16.6 percent of the Fernwood rioters were over forty and that eight of those (8.3%) were at least fifty years old.

The more typical housing mobs, those that confined themselves largely to harassment and property destruction, had an age distribution similar to that of the Fernwood crowd. The average age of those arrested in the 1949 Park Manor disturbance was 27.1 years; even if one assumes that four unidentified "juveniles" arrested there were all only 16 years old, the average age of the Park Manor rioters is still 25 years. Over one-fifth (22.2%) of the rioters were at least forty, and one-third (33.3%) were over thirty. The same apparently holds true for the Trumbull Park Homes. Although the incomplete sample suggests caution (ages were found for only 29 of 109 rioters), the data reveal an average age of 33.3 years for these arrestees. Moreover, nearly half of the rioters in South Deering (48.3%) were over thirty years of age, and more than a quarter (27.6%) of them were over forty.

Eyewitness accounts of these disorders provide further proof that they were not merely the productions of bored or uncontrollable youths. The people in Park Manor, for example, displayed their neighborhood ingenuity as police developed techniques for keeping the streets and walks clear in front of the homes of unwanted black neighbors. Families threw open their front porches and yards and furnished legal sanctuary for their friends who, in a grim parody of a community sing, hurled racial epithets and verbal abuse—along with the occasional rock or bottle—at the neighborhood's "intruders." In one 1950 Park Manor disorder, CHR observers reported that "about 150 people had gathered on the porches and in the yards" of five homes within shouting distance of a new black resident. From there "shouting and heckling became . . . organized" and cries of "Bring out Bushman," "Get the rope," and "String him up" could be heard. Songs such as "Old Black Joe" and "Carry Me Back to Old Virginny" were sung in derision.[19]

The Cicero and Airport Homes incidents were communal endeavors of a similar sort. An informant for the American Civil Liberties

Union mingled with the Cicero crowd and noted its "jovial mood." Another observer reported that "boys and girls," aged twelve to their "late teens," gathered rocks and broke bricks for the older boys to throw. "There was a great deal of camaraderie and spirit of fun throughout this whole group," the observer wrote, "and it was apparent that all were having a good time." Included within that group were adults who encouraged their children's actions and whose approval often "took on the form of urging and initiating the aggression." The same set of circumstances also seems to have prevailed at the Airport Homes, where, official reports state, the crowd was composed of "men and women, boys and girls of all ages."[20]

The broad community participation characteristic of most of these incidents, however, is best demonstrated by the roles played by women. It was a woman who first alerted the Englewood community to the presence of blacks in the home at 56th and Peoria; and adult women, no less than youngsters, were seen arming Cicero's brick throwers.[21] Women were certainly present, if not prominent, in the yards and porches of Park Manor, though CHR reports failed to identify members of these crowds by sex. It was the Airport Homes and the Trumbull Park disorders, though, that demonstrated that women not only supported but at times supplanted men as the most virulent and violent antiblack protestors.

At the Airport Homes the CHA tried to move in black veterans during daylight hours when most of the community's men were at work. The task of protesting, if not preventing, that development consequently fell to the area's women and older men. Both groups kept up a "constant shouting" as officials tried to escort blacks into the project. One eyewitness felt the crowd was composed of "mostly women" who "booed and hissed recognized civil leaders, talked with newspaper photographers, and made numerous threats" before the fighting broke out. When the violence erupted, it was found that "a great many women were in the front ranks of the mob," and it was they who "began to fight with policemen, kicking and scratching and slapping at them." The police, for reasons unknown, made no arrests but were compelled, the *Tribune* noted with a trace of condescension, to "spank unruly housewives" with their clubs in self-defense. It proved a dangerous task: one lieutenant was struck on the head by a missile "while preventing a woman from taking away his . . . club." Thus, while no female names graced any police blotters, their protest was duly registered, and the next day several appeared at the project, pushing their baby carriages while "carrying sticks and bricks."[22]

Women were equally involved in the Trumbull Park Homes disorders. There, as at the Airport Homes, women carried on alone in the

A woman attempting to throw a brick at the Airport housing project loses her balance as a policeman grabs her arm. *Courtesy of the* Chicago Tribune.

front lines when the community's men were away at work. The women seized and freed neighbors arrested by the police and battled the latter, on occasion hand-to-hand. One police sergeant had to be hospitalized after being kicked in the groin by a female rioter. The most notable incident, however, came in October 1953, when the CHA again attempted a midweek daylight move-in of blacks. It was reported that several local women

> . . . literally hurled themselves, first at a truck loaded with the new-comers' furniture, and later at a new car driven by the head of one Negro family. A gray-haired woman of about 65 fell prostrate in front of the car. . . . When the halted car began to inch ahead, the woman clung to its front bumper. Police seized her, and carried her, kicking and fighting, to a curb.

The men of South Deering were not unmoved by that display. At a later fund-raising dinner, the lawyer for the local improvement association paid homage to the three mothers arrested that day and "in tribute to them sang 'Mother Machree.' " It was an accolade that could well have been given to the community's women as a group. For the first time, police were compelled to arrest women as well as men in significant numbers. Nearly one out of every five persons held by police in connection with these disturbances (21 of 109) was female.[23]

These communal uprisings and their participants were more than demographically representative of their respective communities. They were also expressions of the general feelings of the city's poorer white "ethnics." As native whites and the more mobile descendants of the "old" immigration moved to the city's periphery or to its suburbs, the children and grandchildren of predominantly Catholic Irish and South and East European immigrants were left to face a rapidly growing and territorially starved black population. Unable—or simply unwilling—to leave their old neighborhoods, the "ethnics" were reacting against their involuntary transformation into natural "buffers" between fleeing whites and inner-city blacks. This growing confrontation between "ethnic and black metropolis" is especially evident in the riots occurring during or after 1949; before then the housing shortage was unrelieved, and even those possessing the means and desire to leave the city were left no alternative to racial succession save the active physical "defense" of their homes.[24] Consequently, one of the earliest housing riots included substantial representation from the "old" as well as the "new" immigration. Once new postwar housing construction permitted the possibility of flight, however, those who wished to avail themselves of it did so and thus not only left behind those who could not similarly leave, but also, in some cases, provided the very vacancies into which blacks could move.

Blacks were fully aware of the sources of the most active and violent opposition to their movement. In each of the major riots occurring in the 1950s, black commentators noted repeatedly, and often disparagingly, the ethnic origins of anti-black rioters. Walter White compared the Cicero crowd to Southern lynch mobs, noting that he had never encountered as much "implacable hatred as I found in Cicero." Significantly, he added that "some of those with whom I talked" had "such thick Bohemian, German, Polish, or Greek accents that it was not always easy to know what they were saying. It was appalling," he concluded, "to see and listen to those who were but recently the targets of hate and deprivations, who, beneficiaries of American opportunity, were as virulent as any Mississippian in their willingness to deny a place to live to a member of a race which had preceded them to America by many generations."[25]

Similar conclusions were drawn by blacks regarding the Trumbull Park Homes disorders, the Calumet Park riot, and lesser 1950s disturbances as well. St. Clair Drake reported on the "vicious and poisonous" propaganda circulating in the neighborhood press serving the Calumet Park area. These local newspapers "boast[ed] that it was Southern and Eastern Europeans who really built this country while Negroes were 'swinging in trees,' 'eating each other.' " This, plus an examination of the names of arrested rioters, led him to believe that they were "immigrants and the children of immigrants. . . ."[26] The *Defender* had much the same to say about the Trumbull Park violence and some minor West Side incidents as well. Crowds screaming in "thick foreign-accent[s]" were denounced, as was the "strange paradox" that saw "foreigners, some of them not yet naturalized, who can scarcely speak English," denying freedom and justice to others even as they themselves were seeking these rights. "Evidently the free courses in Americanism which are offered to prospective citizens have failed of their mark," the *Defender* editorialized. "Or perhaps," it concluded even more ominously, "they are taught by people who inject the venom of race prejudice into the bloodstream of the new-comer."[27] The growing sense of frustration and bitterness blacks felt toward these racially aggressive immigrants was epitomized by Chandler Owen, a black social analyst, who urged the adoption of a vigorous deportation campaign as a means of bringing the Trumbull Park violence to an end.[28]

Such impressionistic conclusions about the make-up of the white mobs proved quite accurate. The victims, or their spokesmen, had a fairly clear idea of who their immediate adversaries were. The only real flaw in their identification of antiblack rioters was their omission of Chicago's Irish, who, along with other predominantly Catholic immigrants of later arrival, combined to form the overwhelming majority of nearly every mob.

The ethnicity of the rioters (Table III) was determined by examining the names on the arrest lists for the Fernwood riot of 1947, the Park Manor and Englewood riots of 1949, and the Trumbull Park Homes and Calumet Park disorders of the mid-1950s.[29] Only one of the five mobs studied failed to have a majority of its members drawn from Irish and "new" immigrant stock.* As expected, the earliest riot—Fernwood—had only 30.4 percent of its rioters with such surnames. After the Park Manor upheaval, however, the remaining three incidents dis-

---

*"New" immigrant stock refers to those of Slavic, Polish, or Italian ancestry as well as those of uncertain Southeast European provenance. All subsequent references to the "new" immigration, whether in the text or in tables, will refer to these groups. The descendants of the "old" immigration are considered those of Dutch, Swedish, or German origin; those of apparent "Anglo" ancestry are kept separate throughout this study. All subsequent references to the "old" immigration thus are only to the former three groups.

TABLE III
ETHNICITY OF ARRESTEES BY PERCENTAGE* AND RIOT

Ethnicity	Fernwood Park 1947 (N = 113)**	Park Manor 1949 (N = 18)	Englewood 1949 (N = 29)	Trumbull Park 1953-4 (N = 109)	Calumet Park 1957 (N = 51)	Total (N = 320)
Anglo	22.4	35.3	16.6	13.6	22.4	19.6
Irish	7.7	25.5	51.2	19.6	18.4	18.2
Slav	4.4	0.0	6.0	25.5	14.5	13.0
Italian	6.5	25.5	0.0	12.0	7.9	9.0
Polish	5.3	0.0	0.0	10.7	16.4	8.2
Southeastern Europe***	6.2	0.0	1.2	6.9	4.6	5.5
Dutch	26.3	0.0	0.0	0.0	0.0	9.4
German	14.7	9.8	22.6	5.7	3.3	10.3
Scandinavian	5.6	0.0	0.0	0.3	0.0	2.1
Jewish	0.0	0.0	0.0	0.0	1.3	0.2
Spanish (surnamed)	0.0	3.9	2.4	4.7	10.5	3.7
Other	0.8	0.0	0.0	0.9	0.7	0.7
Total	99.9	100.0	100.0	99.9	100.0	99.9

* The percentages in the table were produced by averaging the findings of the three independent surveys of the arrest lists.

** N represents the number of those arrested.

***Persons of uncertain nationality but with obviously Southern or Eastern European names were included in this category.

played a mob composition in which approximately 60 percent or more of those arrested appear to have been of Irish or "new" immigrant ancestry. Descendants of the "old" immigration represented 41.4 percent of the more than 300 persons for whom ethnicity was determined but only 26 percent of 200 rioters arrested during or after 1949. In contrast, those of Irish or "new" immigrant origins represented 54 percent of all rioters and 67.2 percent of those arrested in the four later riots (Tables IV and V).

None of the riots is characterized by the exclusive confrontation of a single nationality group defending its ethnically homogeneous territory against a black "invader." Only the riot at 56th and Peoria, where 51.2 percent of those arrested were Irish, had even a bare majority of its participants drawn from a single group. In each of the other riots a liberal mixture of white "ethnics" seemed content to live in close proximity to each other, but not in similar proximity to blacks. Aside from persons with Anglo-sounding surnames, those of Irish and Slavic origin dominated the Calumet Park mob, representing 18.4 percent and 14.5 percent of the known rioters. An additional 24.5 percent of the Calumet Park rioters were either Polish or Italian. At Trumbull Park no group could claim more than 25.5 percent of the rioters as its own; yet the Irish, Slavs, Italians, and Poles represented at least 67.8 percent of that incident's known arrestees. Whatever the degree of white interethnic hostility (and it surely did exist: South Deering's Poles were often heard to complain about the "dago" president of the local improvement association), it was subordinated to an overriding mutual concern. The *Defender* was probably characterizing most housing mobs when it said of one crowd that "although there was no unity in the language backgrounds [of the individuals in the shouting mob], they had a common communicative [*sic*] hatred for Negroes."[30]

The components of these ethnic crowds, moreover, did not appear in random fashion. Linked geographically by their proximity to the omnipresent house, apartment, or park that was about to "change" racially, they were nearly as ethnically representative as they were demographically representative of the communities involved. The Irish predominated in Englewood, with the Germans the next most populous foreign-born group. Together these two nationalities supplied 73.8 percent of those taken into custody there. Slavs, Poles, and Italians were the most numerous foreign-born groups in the Calumet Park area in 1960; in 1957 these three groups, or their descendants, provided 47.5 percent of that community's rioters. The same was true of Trumbull Park: Slavs were both the most numerous and the most arrested foreign-born group in the area; Italians and Poles were not far behind in either category. Most signifcant of all perhaps was the fact that the Roseland community, which supplied most of the Fernwood rioters, had been founded by Dutch farmers, who were followed into the community by Scandinavian, German, Italian, and Polish settlers. The Fernwood riot furnished all the Dutch and virtually all the Scandinavians arrested for racial rioting in Chicago; more than one-third of all the Germans arrested also came from this single disturbance. When the Poles and Italians are added to the other founding groups, fully 58.4 percent of Roseland's rioters are accounted for.[31]

Each of the housing mobs was thus broadly representative of the community in which it was located. Participation was not strictly limited by age, sex, or nationality. The social make-up of the crowd, in general, reflected that of the neighborhood in which it operated. Talk of rioting done only by "hoodlums" or "criminals," however politically satisfying it may have been, was factually meaningless in this context. These were homespun affairs and not the machinations of outside hoo-

TABLE IV
ETHNICITY OF RIOTERS BY PERCENTAGE* AND RIOT

Ethnicity	Fern-wood Park 1947 (N = 113)**	Park Manor 1949 (N = 18)	Engle-wood 1949 (N = 29)	Trum-bull Park 1953-4 (N = 109)	Calu-met Park 1957 (N = 51)	Total (N = 320)
Anglo – "Old" Immigration	69.0	45.1	39.3	19.6	25.7	41.5
Irish + "New" Immigration	30.4	51.0	58.3	74.8	61.8	54.0
Spanish (surnamed)	0.0	3.9	2.4	4.7	10.5	3.7
Other	0.6	0.0	0.0	0.9	1.9	0.8
Total	100.0	100.0	100.0	100.0	99.9	100.0

* The percentages in the table were produced by averaging the findings of the three independent surveys of the arrests lists.
**N represents the number of those arrested.

TABLE V
ETHNICITY OF ARRESTEES BY PERCENTAGE* AND TIME OF RIOT

Ethnicity	All Riots 1947-1957 (N = 320)	4 Riots After 1947 (N = 207)	2 Riots After 1950 (N = 160)
Anglo	19.6	18.0	16.4
Irish	18.2	24.1	19.2
"Old" Immigration	21.8	7.9	5.1
"New" Immigration	35.7	43.0	51.4
Spanish (surnamed)	3.7	5.8	6.6
Other	1.0	1.2	1.3
Total	100.0	100.0	100.0

*The percentages in the table were produced by averaging the findings of the three independent surveys of the arrests lists.
**N represents the number of those arrested.

ligans. This becomes clear when one studies the actions of the mobs; they were far more than mere mindless expressions of racial antipathy.

Despite the independent nature of the uprisings, the behavior of the crowds displayed remarkable similarity. Although often spontaneous in origin, the typical Chicago housing mob was purposeful, both in the targets it selected and in the level of violence it employed to achieve its self-defined goals. Moreover, the duration of the rioting often depended more on the mob's achievement or its prospect of success than on the magnitude and effectiveness of the police forces arrayed against it.

The spontaneity of the violence was evident in the vast majority of cases. The city's first two postwar riots, those at the temporary veterans' quarters at the Airport Homes and Fernwood Park, erupted without benefit of prior planning, despite earlier organized protests against the CHA's non-discriminatory policies. At the Airport Homes, crowds gathered in front of the apartments on the day they were scheduled to be occupied. Their protests were merely verbal until a truck carrying furniture and two black veterans tried to enter the project. At that point, attention shifted immediately to the blacks and their truck; the latter came under immediate attack. Debris found on the ground and clumps of dirt—hardly the arsenal of a mob anticipating violence—served as weapons. The attack on the black veterans was solely the result of their untimely appearance in an exceptionally tense situation; it was neither a well-orchestrated nor a previously organized onslaught. The presence of the veterans was simply the proverbial "last straw" which demonstrated to the crowd that their earlier protests had been to no avail.[32]

At the Fernwood Park Homes there was no single, clearly defined precipitating incident as there was at the Airport Homes. Augmented police forces and a minor car accident, which briefly diverted attention away from the project, permitted the handful of blacks assigned to the apartments to enter peacefully. Violence came only on the following night and, according to official reports, appeared as if by spontaneous generation from a protesting crowd gathered outside the project. Several of those supporting the CHA looked on the mysterious origins of the disturbance with suspicious eyes and charged there was a "conspiracy involved to deprive Negroes of [their] rights." An investigative report on the riot commissioned by the American Jewish Congress, however, noted that these charges came from those who became "highly emotional in condemning the Fernwood community" and concluded, after a sober second look, that "nothing ever materialized to substantiate those suspicions of organized planning behind the violence."[33]

Several other riots were even more clearly spontaneous in origin. The Park Manor disorder at 71st and St. Lawrence began after it became evident that the black man moving furniture into a newly purchased home was not a mere laborer, but the new owner. Here there was no time for planning; people simply filled the streets as word passed through the neighborhood. The ensuing rock-throwing attack on the home caught even the usually alert Chicago Commission on Human Relations by surprise. Through its "listening posts" in communities, its police connections, and its associations with local black organizations, the Commission had always had advance warning when blacks were about to move into an all-white area. This time, however, no one had been forewarned. The move-in, which had been conducted without advance publicity and as unobtrusively as possible, was followed almost immediately by rioting.[34]

Similarly, the disorders at 56th and Peoria and in Calumet Park flowed from events so patently fortuitous that any attempts to ascribe them to prescient conspirators would appear ludicrous. In the former incident, a rumor that a home was being "shown" to blacks sparked the violence. Growing out of the mere appearance of blacks in a local home (they were attending a union meeting), the rumor called forth large crowds which registered a violent protest against the presence of blacks, Jews, University of Chicago students, communists, and "outsiders" in general.[35] In Calumet Park, the attacks on blacks were precipitated by their use of a portion of the park that had previously been "reserved" for whites. It was an event to which white residents could react but not one which they could have planned themselves.[36]

Only the Trumbull Park Homes rioting, which evolved into a war of attrition intended to harass and drive out black project tenants, displayed a considerable degree of planning. But even here the origin of the disturbance was spontaneous. The belated discovery that a black woman had "passed" for white in applying for a Trumbull Park apartment prompted the first rock- and bottle-throwing mobs. Only later, after the situation had become a test of wills between the community and the CHA, did the local residents, aided by the South Deering Improvement Association, plan, coordinate, and organize their violent activities.[37]

The absence of prior planning in nearly every case does not mean, however, that the actions of those engaged in them were chaotic or uncontrolled. In terms of target selection, the housing riots were virtual models of limited, purposeful violence. The crowd at the Airport Homes, for example, displayed considerable discrimination in attacking the units occupied by blacks, the trucks moving their furniture, and cars belonging to city officials. The purpose and extreme selectivity of the West Lawn residents is perhaps best shown by the fact that one official's car was overturned and looted even though it was parked several blocks away, and no other property nearby was damaged. The police also came under attack, but this was due to their efforts to protect the blacks and their subsequent position between the crowd and the objects of its anger.[38] The police became a target of the Fernwood crowd under

A gang of whites overturns a car at the Airport Homes project. *Courtesy of the* Chicago Tribune.

similar conditions, and in this later riot, assaults on nearby black motorists were initially conceived as a tactic to get the police away from the project. An eyewitness to the episode described the scene:

> One of the agitators in the mob yelled that if they could stop traffic, the cops would have to straighten it out, at which time the crowd could break through the weakened police lines and rush the project. So the traffic was impeded. Then a boy shouted "Nigger, Nigger." A stone flew, a safety-glass window crunched. And there started a bloody game of "bash their dirty brains in" which continued unchecked for almost 20 minutes. Every Negro driver was attacked. . . .[39]

The Park Manor and Cicero rioters were no less discriminating in their choice of targets. The main objective of the July 1949 Park Manor mob was the first house bought by blacks in the area south of 71st Street—a street that had been considered a tentative boundary in a changing community. Secondary targets included those homes owned by blacks in the already changing area north of 71st Street. In Cicero the crowd's sole target was the building in which the suburb's new black tenants were to move—a building which the landlord, after a dispute with her tenants, had threatened to open to blacks.[40]

Most notable, perhaps, was the generally limited nature of the violence involved. In Park Manor, as at the Airport Homes, the violence was never random, and despite the fact that the southern border of the Black Belt was a mere five blocks away, there were no assaults on black individuals or forays into the district by white gangs.[41] In Cicero, the crowd was content to merely "pull down" the building that threatened the homogeneity of the community. Indeed, the control of the typical housing mob was such that it asserted itself even when the opportunity for greater violence was clearly present. In a Bridgeport incident, crowds gathered outside a home rumored to have been sold to blacks and attacked it, while less than a quarter of a block away blacks strolled by en route to a White Sox ball game at Comiskey Park. Black transients posed no threat to the residents and were ignored; it was their permanent presence in the area, albeit only rumored, that sparked—but also limited—the mob's actions.[42]

Even in the riots where the violence was escalated to include attacks against people as well as property, the fury of the mob seemed the result of circumstances, given the rioters' perspective, which demanded more drastic action. Before the post-1950 confrontations over the use of community facilities, the Fernwood and Peoria Street disturbances were the most serious in terms of human casualties. The distinguishing feature that separated these neighborhoods from those whose defense took the form of property destruction was the fact that the residents of these areas lacked any alternative to racial succession save the most determined violent resistance. There was no possibility of escape as there was for the more well-to-do in Park Manor; the chronic housing shortage precluded the possibility of flight in 1947, and by 1949 only those with considerable means could afford the small number of relatively expensive homes being constructed. It was also important that each of these communities was being surrounded by black enclaves; their actual "invasion" thus had added significance. Both Fernwood and Englewood had a history of hostile and violent reactions to their becoming white islands in a black sea. The threat was deemed far more serious than the presence of a few isolated blacks, as was the case in the militantly all-white communities surrounding the Airport Homes, Trumbull Park, and the ill-fated building in Cicero. The level of violence increased in Fernwood and Englewood because their desperation and fear were proportionately greater and also because the very situation evoking their anxiety provided ample targets at which to lash out.[43]

The mobs perpetrating the worst violence were, additionally, methodical if not meticulous in their actions. In Calumet Park, as dusk fell on the scene of whites attacking cars occupied by blacks, white handkerchiefs began to appear on the antennas of those driven by whites so that, in the diminishing visibility, the rioters would have no problems in selecting their targets. While similar conduct has been viewed as evidence of prior planning, it appears that such actions were more the result of common sense than conspiracy.[44]

This sort of calculation was also present in the Peoria Street incident, the one riot considered most "irrational" by contemporaries. Aroused by the rumor that a house was being sold to blacks, the Englewood residents blamed "outsiders" for their problems and attacked an array of "subversives" along with whatever blacks were in the area. Those strangers in the vicinity not identified as enemies by the color of their skin were asked to produce identification by roaming gangs; only *after* their status as an "outsider" was officially ascertained were they attacked.[45]

Ultimately, the best evidence of the control under which even the most violent mobs operated was the actual cessation of rioting on the part of the participants themselves when they felt their sought-after goals had been achieved. While ineffectual police work accompanied—perhaps permitted—many disorders, it was not always the increased exertion of the "forces of social control" which brought an end to disturbance. In at least two cases the political context of events played an equal, if not more instrumental, role than did the police in ending a disorder.

The Fernwood rioters knew well the success violent protest had enjoyed during the troubles at the Airport Homes less than a year before. Mob gatherings had frightened away the first black who was supposed to move in and had done the same to all but two families in the second group assigned. Though not driven off by the rioting, these two brave families had been compelled to leave when gunshots ripped through their apartments. At the time of the Fernwood rioting, the Airport project was, via the means of coercion and intimidation, all-white.[46] Subsequently, a delegation from the afflicted Roseland community conferred with Mayor Martin Kennelly while the Fernwood riot was in progress and left with the impression "that some plan would be worked out whereby Negro families would be removed from the project and that keeping quiet was the community's part of the bargain." CHR observers in the neighborhood reported that "such was the 'talk' in the community" and felt that this, in conjunction with increased

An embattled couple in Trumbull Park tests the plywood panel that serves as a barrier against bricks and other missiles. *Courtesy of Chicago Historical Society.*

police activity, produced the "sudden calm" that descended on the area after days of bitter fighting.[47]

The ebb and flow of violence at the Trumbull Park Homes was also closely keyed to political developments. After nearly a year of intermittent destructive protests over the presence of blacks in the project, several clashes took place during the summer of 1954 as black groups from outside the community tried to use the athletic facilities within Trumbull Park. Though white residents had failed to have the black families removed from the area, they had been successful in denying free access to public facilities to all blacks—including those from the project. After a serious incident between local residents and blacks who had been using one of the park's baseball fields, community representatives met with city political leaders and returned claiming a "deal" had been struck. The number of black families in the nearly 500-unit project would be limited to twenty, the leaders said, if only the violence would cease. When publicized, city fathers denied making any such "deal," but the next week black demonstraters played ball unmolested in the same park where they had been mobbed just a few days before. Members of the South Deering Improvement Association had made sure that those unwilling to compromise on a minimal black presence in the area stayed away from the park. However much a "deal" might have been denied, it remained a fact that no more than roughly twenty black families lived in Trumbull Park Homes at any one time throughout the decade.[48]

This close interaction between crowds in the street, community representatives, and city fathers reveals that not only were the actions of these homegrown mobs purposeful to the participants themselves, but that they were purposeful in the broader sense of having an impact on the community at large. Insofar as it shaped and altered public policy, the "creative disorder" of the 1940s and 1950s benefited whites rather than blacks.

The clearest indication of this may be seen in the public housing controversies that swirled around the Chicago Housing Authority at this time. Not only was the CHA responsible for providing low-cost homes for those ignored by private builders, but, given the housing shortage, the Authority was the key to the city's redevelopment program. Until the poor were moved off valuable inner-city property and placed in "relocation" housing, no land would be available for the fulfillment of the developer's dreams.[49] Since the poor involved were mostly black, the CHA had to deal directly with the problem of segregation. In the two areas where the issue presented itself most insistently—tenant selection and site selection—the CHA proved responsive to white resistance against changes in the status quo.

At first it did not appear that this would be the case. The emergency veterans' housing program saw the CHA erect temporary shelters all over the city. The fact that most were located in white areas did not prevent the CHA from selecting its tenants on a nondiscriminatory basis.[50] However, this program quickly provoked violent reactions at the Airport Homes and Fernwood Park. It was to be the last significant attempt to implement a public housing program that employed both scattered sites and a policy of nondiscrimination.

The CHA was able to embark on this limited experiment only because of its independence from the Chicago City Council. Legally, it was not responsible to the council for either its site selections or its policies. Politically, it enjoyed the sponsorship of Mayor Edward J. Kelly until the spring of 1947. With the protests at the Airport Homes, though, came the first calls for the curtailment of the Authority's power. Alderman Michael Hogan, representing the people surrounding the Airport site, presented a petition to the city council just days before violence erupted asking that the CHA be brought under the authority of the mayor and the council. Reginald DuBois, the alderman in whose ward the Fernwood project was located, declined to introduce a similar resolution while that riot was in progress only because of an agreement with black alderman Archibald Carey, Jr.; both felt the necessity for public restraint in a tense situation. After a cooling-off period of two months, however, DuBois finally did offer the resolution that led to the subordination of the CHA.[51]

DuBois charged the CHA with inefficiency and mismanagement and called for an official investigation. His main complaint, though, was that the CHA "persist[ed] in theories of housing which are shared

Mayor Martin Kennelly congratulates CHA Chairman Robert R. Taylor (far right) at the Dearborn Homes groundbreaking. Others pictured are Dr. Edward Welters, Chairman of the People's Welfare Organization; Miss Elizabeth Wood, CHA Executive Secretary; and John Sengstacke, publisher of the *Chicago Defender*. *Courtesy of University of Illinois Library at Chicago, Manuscripts Division.*

by no other representative governmental agencies . . . and are not in accord with those of a great majority of citizens." Though couched in such formal language, it was evident to all informed observers that the charges of mismanagement were being used as a "cover" to attack the CHA for its racial policy. The editors of the *Chicago Defender* denounced the "little bund of rabid racists" seeking the investigation, and even the genteel Board of Directors of the reformist Metropolitan Housing Council was informed that those bringing charges against the CHA "really have the Authority race policy in mind."[52] The City Council eventually cleared the CHA in a generally laudatory report; buried within that report, however, was a council policy statement of the greatest significance.

In issuing its findings exonerating the CHA, the council included a request that it be granted veto power over the CHA's site selection process.[53] The state legislature granted the council the powers it sought in 1949, and the CHA became the only housing authority in the state to have its prerogatives so restrained. The CHA commissioners knew at the time the law was passed that it meant "the end of public housing sites in good residential areas." Ex-commissioner Robert R. Taylor was to say later that he knew the battle to distribute public housing throughout the city "was lost" when the Illinois General Assembly acceded to the council's request—a request resulting from the desire to "prevent the influx of Negroes into white neighborhoods" and from the "pressure of public opinion."[54]

The result was predictable. Although the aldermen were compelled to provide some public housing, they granted, in effect, final approval of public housing sites to protesting whites in the outlying neighborhoods. The CHA's attempt to gain sites in accord with "sound planning principles" proved futile; the "Big Boys" in the council dictated the placement of public housing within the current ghetto boundaries, thus fixing and institutionalizing its borders as they had never been before.[55] By the mid-1950s the CHA refused to submit sites they knew would be controversial, knowing the futility of doing so; their later selections merely completed the process which enshrined a racially and economically segregated South State Street in poured steel and concrete.[56]

It was also during these years that the pressure from violent white resistance to neighborhood change made itself felt in the CHA's tenant selection policy. The CHA was on record as favoring nondiscrimination, but it faced a problem with the older Depression-era projects, which had been occupied under the federal "neighborhood composition" guideline; located in white areas, their tenants were white, and now this pattern had the weight of tradition behind it. Four such projects were kept all-white out of deference to local attitudes, and the situation was exposed only after a fair-skinned black was admitted to the Trumbull Park Homes. After that, the CHA still proclaimed its adherence to a policy of nondiscrimination and, of course, could not publicly back down. However, the commissioners spoke privately of integrating the projects only at a rate consistent with the maintenance of "law and order." The chairman of the CHA, Wilfred Sykes, summarized his own stance when he stated that the CHA had to weigh the views of three million whites against those of a half-million blacks. Such considerations proved paramount; the process of integration would take years.[57]

Thus the CHA, the one governmental agency that might have challenged the city's racial status quo, found itself responding directly and favorably to white protestors taking violent action or to those powers acting in their behalf. In terms of the CHA's tenant selection policy, the link between violent reaction and government response was clear and direct: as long as whites were willing to fight to keep blacks out of the projects already established in their areas, the CHA was unwilling to forcibly speed their integration. In terms of the more important site-selection process, the link is less direct but present nonetheless. City Council pressure, which was itself the institutional response to the violent reactions precipitated by the veterans' housing program, produced the state law that enabled the council to substitute its own will for that of the CHA.[58]

The efficacy of violence was made even more explicit during the confrontation between the CHA and the City Council over the first slate of project sites. Alderman John J. Duffy, the reigning power in the council after Kelly's retirement and the engineer of the "deal" which culminated in the CHA's acceptance of ghetto sites, seemed to have a healthy respect for those who fought. In chastising an alderman who opposed him and consequently had some public housing slated for his ward, Duffy said: "The trouble with you Jews is, when you get backed up against the wall you start crying. When we Irish were backed up against the wall . . . we used clubs, we used bricks, we used stones. But what do you Jews do? You don't fight. You start crying. Well, you asked for it and you're going to get it."[59]

It was in this fashion that the violence that was kept so carefully hidden from the general public made its most lasting impression. The parameters of social change were delimited not by those seeking it, but by the violent and purposeful actions of those challenged by it.

By the late 1950s the worst of the violence was over, as neighborhoods that had been cracked open earlier filled with new residents, and as increasing suburban construction provided alternatives for those unwilling to stay in the city. By that time, however, the key decisions shaping race relations in the city for the next generation had been made. In an era that saw the massive expansion of the old Black Belt, no fundamental alteration in the pattern of segregation was permitted; if anything, that pattern was now reinforced by government sanction and public funds. As civil rights forces mobilized in the South, and the *Brown v. Board of Education of Topeka, Kansas* decision of 1954 was hailed as a possible new beginning in American race relations, Chicago moved in the opposite direction by institutionalizing a greatly enlarged black ghetto and admonishing potential newcomers to stay away.

Speaking in 1957, Francis W. McPeek, executive director of the CHR, issued a "friendly warning" to those planning to come to Chicago looking for work. While he did not wish to discourage those with "energy, drive, and initiative" from migrating to Chicago, he emphasized the housing problems for minorities and felt compelled to remind them that "not even Carl Sandburg ever referred to this town as a bed of roses."[60] With the recent rioting in Calumet Park clearly on his mind, he held out a welcome sign which read simply: "Enter at your own risk."

Chapter XII

PAUL MICHAEL GREEN

Irish Chicago:
The Multiethnic Road to Machine Success

*You can never understand the Irish ... other
races mature — the Irish mellow. ... [The Irish-
man] is the prince of politics because he is a
born democrat and thinks midsection with his
heart. Politics favors the mixer and the spender;
the Irishman's sympathy and good fellowship are
perpetual letters of introduction. He wears his
heart on his sleeve and his purse has no puck-
ering-string.*

— Quin O'Brien, 1916[1]

*He finds fault with my name. That's the same
name I've always had ... I wouldn't trade it for
all the mayors' jobs in the world.*

*Of course we couldn't all come over on the
Mayflower — or maybe the boat would have sunk.
But I got here as soon as I could, and I never
wanted to go back, because to me it is a great
privilege to be an American citizen.*

— Anton J. Cermak, 1931
(Bohemian-born mayor-elect)

The Irish in Nineteenth-Century Politics:
A Battle for Acceptance and Legitimacy

Over THREE MILLION IRISH CAME TO the United States in the years between the onset of the potato famine in 1846 and the death of Charles Parnell in 1891.[2] The advanced guard entered Chicago in the 1830s to work on the Illinois-Michigan canal and later on the newly begun railroads. Working on the railroad became the national Irish occupation, and thousands of destitute Irish immigrants found employment with the Illinois Central Railroad. Gangs of Irish laborers, sailors, and squatters settled on the city's borders and set up innumerable shanty villages along the main branches of the river.[3] These ramshackle communities soon became high-crime areas, and "hoodlum Irish" and "shanty Irish" became popular terms for Irishmen arrested constantly for drunkenness and disorderly conduct. The *Chicago Tribune*, a leading anti-Irish newspaper at the time, could ask in 1874, "Why are the instigators and ring leaders of our riots and tumults, in nine cases out of ten, Irishmen?"[4]

By 1850 the Irish made up almost 40 percent of Chicago's foreign-born and over 20 percent of its total population.[5] They were the city's second largest immigrant group and were to remain near the top throughout the century. They did not move quickly into professions or skilled jobs, and as late as 1870 the majority were unskilled laborers or in domestic service.[6] Nevertheless, many Irish climbed the socio-economic ladder by involving themselves in politics and municipal government. In 1853 the Irish constituted 25 percent of Chicago's public officials and had elected political representation scattered through many local offices.[7] They also gravitated toward the many politically related jobs, such as police, fire, and sanitation positions. In 1865 one-third of the Chicago Police Department was Irish; by 1890 they were the dominant element and had six times as many officers on the force as the next highest immigrant group.[8]

The Irish identification with the Democratic party was due mainly to a lack of political alternatives. They arrived during red-hot Democratic days when Andrew Jackson and Martin Van Buren represented the "Common Man" and the party was cloaking itself in the mantle of the anti-English "Apostle of Liberty," Thomas Jefferson. The heavily Protestant Whig, Free Soil, or Abolitionist parties held little reward for Irish participation. Rough and unskilled, having nothing in common with older residents, being of a different religion and background from most fellow newcomers, the Irish searched for political acceptance. Local Democrats, led by William B. Ogden, Chigago's first mayor, gave the Irish a home and in doing so gained the bitter resentment of their political opponents who believed the Irish to be uncivilized.[9]

Mayor Ogden and his followers, however, saw them as a potentially manageable bloc of voters who would follow native Democratic leadership in return for petty favors and an occasional elected office. One year after Chicago's incorporation as a city in 1837, Ogden and others realized how they had misjudged their new friends' political ambitions. A disgruntled and surprised Democrat wrote:

> The elections are over and all the Democrats are elected, Irish and all. I claim to be a Democrat myself but I do not go for electing Irish Democrats all the way from Ireland to legislate and to execute the laws, as though no one among ourselves is fit for such offices. Dr. Murphy for the Legislature and Issac Gavin for Sheriff are both elected, both Irishmen, as Irish as buttermilk and potatoes.[10]

After 1848 the slavery issue dominated Chicago politics, thereby bringing the Irish even closer to the Democratic party. Stephen A. Douglas, the leading Illinois Democrat, became the first political hero of the Irish as he spoke out against both nativism and abolitionism. Douglas, a non-Catholic, was married to a Catholic woman, and his children were raised Catholic, thus further endearing him to the Irish.[11] Local Irish leaders throughout the city, and especially in the predominantly Irish Tenth Ward, fought in vain with votes and fists for Douglas against the emerging antislavery Republican party.[12]

Douglas's defeat in 1860 set a political pattern in Chicago that persisted almost intact into the next century. The Irish influence within the unorganized Democratic party made presidential and state elections especially difficult for their party's candidates. Many Chicagoans voted Republican due to their dislike for or envy of the Irish. Yet others supported popular Irish and non-Irish local Democratic office-seekers but went back to the Republican fold every four years. The character and personality of the Irish, as well as their leaders' political methods and campaign tactics, often became crucial campaign issues. Irish ethnicity developed as an overriding factor in Chicago politics, a factor that created a general absence of party professionalism and prevented local Democrats from solidifying their party under unified leadership.

Besides fighting abolitionism and nativism, early Irish leaders battled with brutal Gaelic intensity against each other to gain political power. Unlike Germans and Swedes, the Irish constantly moved around the city, and many Irish candidates found it easier appealing to voters from their own county in Ireland than to their neighbors in Chicago. Owen McCarthy (County Cork and Province Munster) and Charles O'Malley (County Mayo and Province Connaught), the leading early protagonists, used intimidation and muscle to keep other potential opponents on the political sidelines.[13] In 1856 Chicagoans elected O'Malley justice of the peace on an election day marked by fighting, drinking, stuffed ballot boxes, and unsolved homicides. However, O'Malley's public career as an ethnic leader ended abruptly because of a malfeasance conviction, for which he served six months in the house of correction. Following O'Malley's demise, John Comiskey, a young articulate alderman from the Blue Island area, attempted to unite his fellow Irish. However, the Irish then as now were not politically monolithic, and Comiskey's and other Irish politicians' early unifying efforts met with general failure.

Chicago was not ready for Irish political leadership in the pre-Fire (1871) era. To make a bad pun, the Irish were too "green" to take charge of the city. Native Chicagoans were not impressed with the Irishman's political ability, and what today is considered Irish charm was then characterized as degenerate racial weakness. And ethnic slurs against the Irish appeared frequently in the press. The Irish lacked the economic and social infrastructures to assume city control. Thus, though they were politically active, the Irish did not instantly achieve power but had to work for decades in Chicago's precincts and neighborhoods to climb the political ladder. The political careers of John Comiskey and other pre-Fire Irish leaders reflect the devastating discrimination experienced by Chicago's Irish.

John Comiskey came to Chicago from County Cavan, Ireland via New Haven, Connecticut in 1852. He found a job with the Chicago, Rock Island, and Pacific Railroad and later worked for the Pittsburgh, Fort Wayne, and Chicago Cattleyards (Union Stockyards had not yet been built). Comiskey was personable, handsome, and articulate, and he used these traits to get himself elected Tenth Ward alderman in 1859. Comiskey gained city-wide recognition by signing a petition calling for Irish volunteers to fight in the Civil War. Later, he and many other Irish leaders would be vilified as pro-South when they supported the Copperheads or Peace Democrats in 1864. Comiskey served eleven years in the city council and rose to the position of council president. He also held the offices of clerk of the Cook County Board, deputy county treasurer, and deputy U.S. internal revenue collector. To Irishmen like Comiskey, politics meant more than holding office; it also meant acting as defenders of their people and way of life—especially where the Democratic party was concerned.

The 1860s were trying times for the Irish and the Democrats in Chicago. Most Irish were not overjoyed at the prospect of fighting in a war to free black slaves, whom they feared as potential employment rivals. But even those Irish who did enlist were not immune from criticism, as seen in the *Chicago Tribune's* comment concerning the Irish Brigade's departure from the city to join the war: "Although in material the men are a credit to every section, they are in outfit a disgrace to Chicago as a city, Cook as a county, and Illinois as a state."[14]

In the 1850s, John O'Mahony came to America from Ireland and formed the Fenian Brotherhood to help liberate his native country from British rule ("Fenian" was derived from the Fianna, an ancient Irish military force). Lawrence McCaffrey points out: "Because of its romantic illusions to the Gaelic past, Fenianism became the popular designation for republicanism in Ireland, Britain and America." In Chicago, Fenianism became a catalyst for Irish social activities. However, to many native residents, it became more a powerful auxiliary of the Democratic party and a threat to public safety and good government.

In 1863, Chicago was the site of the first Fenian Brotherhood national convention. This event and other Fenian projects triggered increased ridicule in the daily press, with the organization's leadership being dubbed radical and foreign. Surprisingly, the pro-Democratic *Chicago Times* made the most scathing attack in an 1865 editorial. Local Republicans, hoping to capitalize on this opportunity, began organizing Republican clubs throughout the city. Their efforts peaked in 1868, when two Irish aldermen, Arthur Dixon and J. F. Scanlan, formed a city-wide GOP club to support the Republican national ticket. However, this Republican move to capture the Irish vote was too much for John Comiskey and his Democratic-Fenian allies. In July, Comiskey led an all-out physical assault on a large Republican-Irish meeting. The confrontation saw little debate because both sides resorted to the use of stones, clubs, and slingshots; when it was over, the Irish Democratic clubs had reasserted their preeminence in local politics.

Chicago newspapers were outraged by the July brawl, but their condemnation of Irish political methods, of course, was nothing new. However, later in July 1868, the *Chicago Tribune* escalated its criticism of the Irish. Describing a Democratic picnic in Lakeview, the *Tribune* claimed: "The majority of Irish present, true to the instincts of the lower orders of these people, had filled themselves early in the day with bad whiskey."[15] The *Tribune* concluded with a quote it attributed to a drunken Irish participant: "By Jases, it is dom hot, so it is, and I'm glad I didn't bring Judy or the children for they would be perished, poor crathers and the gin, pon my sowl, is bad and Judy wod be disheartened so she wod."[16]

Later in 1868, the *Chicago Evening Post* outdid the *Tribune* and probably any other newspaper in a scurrilous editorial on the Irish—the ultimate example of what scorn and antiforeign bigotry John Comiskey, other Irish political leaders, and the Irish people as a whole had to overcome in Chicago. According to the *Post*,

> The country has survived the Irish emigration—the worst with which any other country was ever afflicted. The Irish fill our prisons, our reform schools, our hospitals, our eleemosynary [charity] and reformatory institutions of all sorts. Scratch a convict or a pauper and the chances are that you tickle the skin of an Irish Catholic at the same time—an Irish Catholic made a criminal or a pauper by the priest and politician who have deceived him and kept him in ignorance, in a word, a savage, as he was born.[17]

Only after the Great Fire and the subsequent flurry of new immigration from eastern and southern Europe did the anti-Irish news stories wane. Second-generation Chicago Irishmen assumed the role of political buffers between the strange-speaking newcomers and the native, older residents. The Irish, the city's oldest mass migrants, were pushed up the social, economic, and political ladder because these newer and even more frightening groups were streaming into the city. The Irish had become more acceptable to the city's Protestant establishment; by then even the *Tribune* could write: "They are not cured yet, but around the city . . . we have seen them daily advancing in wealth, refinements, and worth. Faction and bigotry should belong only to savage tribes, and civilized beings should scorn to follow a man who represents no principle and who has none within himself."[18]

Both older and new immigrant groups in Chicago marveled at the Irishman's political surge in the last quarter of the nineteenth century. The Bohemian newspaper *Svornost* believed Irish success rested on a strong sense of loyalty. "The Irish," it argued, "have their own political leaders whom they trust fully. The words of their leaders are law."[19] Other nationalities argued that the Irish politician's roughhouse tactics and election-day hooliganism gave him his advantageous position. The *Illinois Staats-Zeitung* followed this reasoning to explain why a city that was one-third German did not have a comparable number of German officeholders: "It cannot be denied that the average German Americans . . . are indifferent towards public affairs, but they may offer as an excuse for their lack of activity . . . the wild doings of the political Irish gang."[20] But all Chicago groups did marvel at the raw natural ability of the Irish in politics. The Swedish newspaper *Svenska-Tribunen Nyheter*, with unguarded envy, compared a Swedish leader to his Irish counterpart. "The political cake," it suggested, "is sliced and dished out without much regard for fairness, and foreign nationalities with the exception of the Irish get crumbs and leftovers. . . . Ordinarily an Irish politician, who can barely sign his own name, has a very decisive preference (over) a Swede, no matter how well educated and trained by experience a Swede might be."[21]

Chicago's foreign-language newspapers, in examining ethnic political performance, gave only a partial explanation of Irish success. Obviously, the Irish had great advantages for their climb up the political ladder. They arrived early and with enormous numbers in Chicago and were able to speak the English language.[22] Nineteenth-century political battles in Chicago, as Mr. Dooley often said, "weren't bean bag," and the Irish were able to use their strength and brawn to settle many contests. But on the other hand, Chicago's Irish suffered from anti-Catholic prejudice and general discrimination. No other European newcomers in Chicago, except the Jews, faced as much continuous and uncompromising prejudice as the Irish did. It took Chicago's Irish four decades before they were able to break through the bigotry barrier and begin to make real political waves in the city. With a chance for full political involvement, the Irish were then able to use their personality traits and customs brought over from Ireland to gain political power.

"The Irish emigrants," writes William Shannon, "came to America with a live political tradition . . . [and] had passed a threshold of political consciousness that later immigrants . . . had not reached."[23] Living under a long-imposed feudal system in Ireland, the Irish became a people who placed great emphasis on unflinching loyalty and uses of political influence. In Ireland, families and clans, not national allegiance, were the unifying elements among the people. Ferocious wars, sometimes involving hundreds of people, were guided by an elected chief who gave steadfast leadership and demanded total support from his followers. Clan fidelity meant everything; even the powerful moral pull of the church did not prevent an Irish peasant from using any means necessary to help a fellow clan member.

The Irishman at home looked to his chief for protection and counsel during difficult times. Since the landlords served as local justices of the peace, the Irish peasant feared English legal procedures. If a matter could not be settled privately, an Irish farmer believed that knowing the judge counted far more than knowing the law. He viewed political influence with the proper authority as insurance against unfairness or discrimination. According to Thomas Brown, " 'I'll have the law on you' is the saying of an Englishman who expects justice, but 'I'll have you up before his honor' is the threat of an Irishman who hopes for partiality."[24]

Nineteenth-century Irish leaders like Daniel O'Connell utilized the extralegal "chief" concept to build political associations for Catholic Emancipation. Regular voluntary offerings, as low as a penny a week, created large political organizations and instilled a new political awareness among the Irish people. O'Connell's Catholic Association taught the Irish that unity in numbers, along with faith in a leader, could produce political results even against the English landlord. The Irish peasant's old beliefs in clan allegiance and chief loyalty remained untouched, but his political involvement shifted from feudal isolation to representative politics. The *Chicago Tribune* noted this very human concept of power and authority: "With the Irish from time immemorial 'clan' and 'chief' have meant more than country and cause. The Irish have never united for any object unless under Hugh O'Neill and Daniel O'Connell."[25]

The Irish ability and desire to organize did not stop at local politics. Not having to face Protestant prejudice within their own religion, the Irish quickly took over the Catholic Church leadership in the city. Soon after their appearance in Chicago, the words "Catholic" and "Irish" became interchangeable. In 1854 there were seven Catholic churches in Chicago, three of which were Irish. By 1865, Chicago had sixteen Catholic churches, ten of which were Irish.[26] Of the ten bishops, archbishops, and auxiliary bishops who ruled over the destinies of Chicago's Catholics from 1844 until 1915, only two were of non-Irish birth or descent.[27] This almost total domination of Chicago's Catholic hierarchy gave the Irish a tremendous moral influence over the ever-increasing Catholic population of the city. Irish political leaders closely allied themselves with their religious counterparts, and many times their separate roles became indistinguishable. Not only did the church become an important part of the Irish politician's control over his own people, but it helped him gain the respect and support of other Catholics. Most of Chicago's non-Irish Catholic newcomers quickly realized that anti-Catholic bigotry was actually anti-Irish bigotry and that their own attainment of religious equality rested squarely in the hands of the Irish.

Just as with their Catholicism, Irish leaders used newly formed Irish-American social organizations as effective political tools to gain and maintain power. The first settlers were homesick and alienated, lost in a large country and missing the closeness of their county and clan. They soon compensated for their lack of social outlets by starting numerous societies and clubs to complement religious and political activities. Besides the Fenians, Chicago's Irish—prior to the Civil War— had many other associations to free Ireland and help protect fellow immigrants. The United Sons of Erin Benevolent Society, founded in

1860 by John Comiskey, had as its goal the aiding of needy Irish in Chicago and Ireland, but in fact it served as a social center for Southwest Side Irish workers.[28] The friendships developed at these gatherings created personal bonds far stronger than any legal agreement or political alliance. Irish politicians, with clannish determination, distributed the spoils of city government—jobs, contracts, and insurance—long before any political organization had set up a city-wide patronage system to reward its members. No other ethnic group remained as steadfast to its own as the Irish; and whereas other newcomers marveled at this loyalty, the Irish merely looked on it as a fact of life.

In combining old-world traditions with new-world democracy, the Irish developed a unique political personality among Chicago's inhabitants. In their efforts to overcome political discrimination and ethnic prejudice, the Irish used muscle, their organizational skills, and their role as ethnic ambassadors to the city's native leadership to gain political leverage inside Chicago. The Irish became the major catalysts within the Chicago Democratic party, and they caused much of the city's early history to center on their own quest for power and respectability. Local native Democratic leaders throughout the nineteenth century had to depend increasingly on Irish voting strength to keep their party viable. This reliance gave the Irish a strong voice in the selection of Democratic candidates as well as added prestige and control within the party's structure. To Chicagoans, every Irish saloonkeeper, undertaker, and laborer seemed to possess political talent, and more important, the Irish were not afraid to use this ability for personal advantage. Summing up a political lifetime of dealing with different nationalities, Mayor Carter H. Harrison II expressed the belief that, "among the Irish every grown-up was a leader, a potential leader or anxious to lead."[29] Harrison's analysis is only half correct; for besides wanting to lead, the Irish were willing to follow, and their loyalty to individuals with whom they identified and supported mattered more than the law or customs of their adopted country.

Turn-of-the-Century Politics: The Irish Choose Various Political Factions to Gain Power

Turn-of-the-century politics in Chicago found numerous political factions fighting for party supremacy. No one group was "ethnically pure," but rather there were nationality group aggregates who based their loyalty on the personality of the local leader, their own self-interest, or the particular faction's political philosophy.

The Irish were well represented in the three major Democratic factions, as well as within the ranks of several Republican groups. But despite some visible GOP affiliation, the Irishman's main stepping stone to political power in Chicago was to be the Democratic party. Unlike in other Eastern and Midwestern cities, the Irish takeover in Chicago was delayed. Splintered Irish loyalties and equally splintered Irish leadership, a legacy of discrimination, strong periodic reform movements, the diverse population make-up of the city, and the political wizardry of Republican Mayor William Hale Thompson all contributed to the lateness of Irish political control. However, the key single obstacle to Irish domination of the local Democratic party and ultimately of the city was the Carter Harrison family phenomenon.

Carter Harrison and his son of the same name fought for political power inside Chicago's Democratic party for close to forty years. Both were five-term mayors, the first Harrison beginning in 1879, and the second Harrison in 1897. Even when out of office, their personal magnetism held their followers loyal. Theirs was the politics of personality. But personality politics did not produce a total Harrison hegemony in Chicago Democratic politics. In the early 1890s a group of businessmen-politicians, led by John Hopkins and Roger Sullivan, challenged the elder Harrison. Unlike the Harrisons, who were independently wealthy and money-honest, Hopkins and Sullivan looked upon politics as a means to get rich. The expanding city gave them their opportunities, and they took them. By the end of World War I, the future of the Democratic party lay with them and their followers.

The ethnic factor was a unique feature of the Hopkins-Sullivan challenge. Both men were Irish, and their major supporters were Irish; but they did not have a lock on prominent Irish leaders in the city. In fact, Chicago did not fit the traditional thesis set forth by J. P. Bocock in his influential 1894 article "Irish Conquest of Our Cities." Bocock believed that most American cities were under Irish rule or close to an Irish takeover. "The theory of government," he argued, "contemplates the rule of the majority and in the cities of the United States a minority has so long ruled that it will require a veritable revolution to shake off, even for a time, the dominion of our Hibernian oligarchy."[30]

Bocock's Chicago evidence in 1894 was based on the recent election of Hopkins as the city's first Irish Catholic mayor and the appointment of an army of Irish workers on the city payroll. However, Bocock missed the two main conditions that separated Chicago from other large cities. First, Hopkins, though Irish, was not an Irish ward leader or one of the boys but rather a suburban businessman. He and Sullivan did not automatically receive the devotion of the various Irish levee and lodginghouse ward leaders or other Irish city workers. Shared ethnicity was no substitute for political sponsorship, nor was it an insurance for guaranteeing one's job. The other major element Bocock missed was the Harrison family's impact on Chicago politics. Hopkins was not personally popular among the inner-city nationalities, nor was he the new hero of the saloonkeeper-politicians, many of whom were Irish. Both of these potent Democratic voting blocs wanted flexible and understanding leadership, but the Hopkins crowd, unlike the Harrisons, were not politically mature enough to fulfill either demand.

Both Carter Harrisons represent a paradox in American urban history. They were well-educated, wealthy gentlemen who should have represented the interests of Chicago's native, social, and political elite; instead, both found their political home and best allies among the city's gamblers, saloonkeepers, and workingmen. Their "live and let live" attitude toward vice and gambling made them attractive candidates to Chicago's sporting men, and their unwillingness to legislate morality by supporting "no Sunday closing of saloons and cafes" made them heroes to the city's ethnic groups—especially the Irish. One Chicago reformer, frustrated by the unique Harrison political personality, said of the elder Harrison: "In his private life Carter Harrison is genial, whole souled, and an honorable gentlemen; but in his political life he is an irrepressible demagogue and deserves to be flayed alive."[31]

Chicago's Irish Democratic politicians represented and reflected various social and economic strata in the city. However, there is no doubt that the Irish saloonkeeper-politician received most of the publicity at the turn of the twentieth century. Many of them were powerful ward bosses who had vast influence in specific inner-city areas; yet none was ever a city-wide boss. Recent writers have vastly exaggerated their overall influence in Chicago and their power relationships with the Harrisons.[32]

Nobody ever dictated local political or governmental strategy to either Carter Harrison. The elder Harrison's association with the notorious Mike McDonald and Oyster Joe Mackin and the younger Carter's friendship with Michael "Hinky Dink" Kenna and "Bathhouse" John Coughlin were based on Harrison leadership. To be sure, Irish saloon bosses used their Harrison alliances for personal gain; but when the political crunch came at election time or at a party convention battle, it was a Harrison directing the Irish saloonkeeper-politicians. Thus the traditional building block of Irish political power in America's cities, the saloonkeeper, was largely controlled in Chicago not by Irish city leaders but by the native-born Harrison family.

The Irish saloonkeeper-politicians who made up such a vital part of the Harrison political army and the Chicago Democratic party were of two general types: the neighborhooders and the levee and lodginghousers. The neighborhooders were men of the streets, like Jimmy

"Hot Stove" Quinn, Johnny Powers, Edward Cullerton, and John F. O'Malley (the latter supporting only the elder Harrison), who became powerful by using their brains and brawn in a time when physical courage was the handmaiden of political success. Reflecting on this latter point late in his life, Jimmy Quinn remarked, "You had to have a fist like a ham in those days . . . no parlor politicians then . . . sometimes they picked your ring before they took the ballot."[33]

These men—or as they have become more affectionately known, "the boys"—were coarse individualists who believed in personal and not party organization politics. Many of them, especially Powers and Cullerton, were veterans of the "gray wolf" or "boodle" era in Chicago politics. "Boodle," a term coined by muckraker Lincoln Steffens, was a word used to describe graft and corruption in Chicago's city council during the 1890s and early 1900s. The manner in which boodle operated fit nicely with the character and political goals of the successful saloonkeeper-politicians. In short, a company wanting a city franchise contacted the leading boodle aldermen, made the necessary financial arrangements, went through the charade of a public hearing, won the contract in an open city council vote, and with great dignity accepted the honor of serving Chicago.

Successful Irish neighborhood saloonkeeper-politicians controlled their own community. Each neighborhooder was his own "ward lord," and the most ferocious political battles occurred in a party primary or party convention when aspiring challengers sought to take over a part of his kingdom. However, it was very difficult to dislodge the neighborhooder even if the community was undergoing an ethnic change or if the saloonkeeper-politician had the misfortune of having to answer to a judge or a grand jury. The neighborhood saloonkeeper-politicians developed ward servicing techniques that became a model for future Chicago politicians. These men identified with their voters, they were accessible and reliable, and most of all, they seemed to care about people's needs.

Michael "Hinky Dink" Kenna, John "Bathhouse" Coughlin, Barney Grogan, and John Brennan were the leading Irish levee and lodginghouse saloonkeeper-politicians. These men were more colorful and more publicized than their neighborhood counterparts. They controlled wards surrounding downtown Chicago: Kenna and Coughlin's First Ward was considered the wealthiest in America, despite the fact that it included the notorious levee; Grogan and Brennan's Eighteenth Ward ranged from homes on north Lake Shore Drive to flophouses on west Madison Street.

The closeness of the levee and lodginghouse saloonkeepers to the Harrisons puzzled many Chicagoans. When Kenna and Coughlin suc-

Two well-known Irish-American ward politicians of the 1890s were Michael "Hinky Dink" Kenna and Alderman Johnny Powers. *Courtesy of the University of Illinois Library, Chicago.*

ceeded McDonald and Mackin in the First Ward, they cemented a deal with young Harrison similar to the one their predecessors had made with his father. Hinky Dink and Bathhouse would deliver the vote for Harrison, and in return the mayor would give them free control over the lucrative vice, gambling, and insurance interests in their ward. Reformers and good government advocates asked how these rogues from cheap saloons could find a champion in the urbane and educated mayor who lived in an Ashland Boulevard mansion. However, on close examination, one can see that the levee-Harrison alliance was not a riddle. Both Harrisons had a benevolent attitude toward personal liberty and regulated vice. They reflected the view of many Chicagoans that vice should be segregated in certain areas of the city, thereby preventing its spread into decent neighborhoods. Thus Chicago would not become a wide-open city, but it would still be a place where its citizens and visitors could have a good time.

However, the Irish saloonkeeper ties with the Harrison family went beyond mere mutual political advantage. There was a real bond between them—especially in the case of Kenna and Coughlin's friendship with the younger Harrison. Carter Harrison II called his First Ward pals his "Rocks of Gibraltar" when they followed his wishes and stood fast against the blatant streetcar franchise boodle efforts of magnate Charles Yerkes. In return, Kenna and Coughlin called the mayor "Our Carter," and even an unavoidable political break during Harrison's last term did not end their personal friendship with the Harrison family. When "Hinky Dink" died in 1944, his safety deposit box contained many $1,000 bonds, various stock certificates, and Christmas cards from his pal Carter Harrison.

The Harrisons had other important Irish allies scattered throughout the city, but in no sense did they monopolize Irish political loyalty. In the 1890s, Irish Democrats living in the increasingly Irish West Side residential neighborhoods found enough city-wide allies to challenge the Harrison faction. Their political fortunes were immeasurably aided when on October 28, 1893, Eugene Prendergast, a disgruntled office seeker, murdered Carter Harrison I in his Ashland Avenue mansion. It took the martyred mayor's supporters and their new leader, Carter Harrison II, three and a half years to regain City Hall. However, by the time young Carter reasserted his family's power over the city and local Democratic party, an anti-Harrison, heavily Irish-led faction was firmly established as an opposition force within the Chicago Democracy.

Two Irishmen, John Hopkins and Roger Sullivan, were leaders of this fledgling faction, and they exemplified the emerging new force in city politics—the "businessman-politician." These political entrepreneurs brought a new practicality to urban politics; consequently, simply ethnic appeals and blind political loyalty would gradually grow less important as promises of wealth, power, prestige, and patronage took their place. Their ultimate goal was not to gain gambling or drinking privileges but to achieve control of the blossoming politically related businesses, like construction, utilities, and transportation. The old-line Democratic "pol" was not by any means passé; but the traditional saloonkeeper-politician was now facing party opponents who were willing to use his own political methods and techniques against him.

Chicago was a prime political arena for the businessman-politician. Starting in 1889, many nearby towns and suburbs agreed to annexation by Chicago because of the city's growing municipal services. By 1893, Chicago had added sixteen separate parcels of land and over 300,000 residents to its borders.[34] It was also during the 1890s that new urban technology had its greatest impact on Chicago life. City dwellers began demanding reliable and efficient transit, gas, electricity, sanitation, and telephone services from their political and industrial leaders. Thus the increased potential of financial reward brought about by Chicago's rapid geographical expansion and technological innovation paved the way for the businessmen-politicians' arrival.

It is not surprising that the Irish would lead the pack of businessmen-politicians within the Chicago Democratic party. They had been in the city longer than any of the other pro-Democratic ethnic groups. Yet, despite their urban longevity, the Irish had still not broken through into the elite banking, real estate, or commercial-financial circles. New immigrants, most of them Democratic-oriented, were flocking to the city and pressing the Irish from all sides. The Republicans were becoming more and more dominated by native-born Americans, English, German, and Scandinavian residents. Their elected city officials by and large represented the middle-class peripheral ward residents who condemned the marriage of business and politics. In a sense, it was almost predestined that Chicago's Irish Democrats would use the politics-business connection as their main ticket up the mobility ladder; there were few other more attractive alternatives.

John Hopkins personified the new businessman-politician. He was a native of Buffalo, New York, who had come to Chicago in 1880 at the age of twenty-two. There was little extraordinary about his early life except that he had met Grover Cleveland in Buffalo when they lived in the same political ward (later both men would use this experience for mutual political advantage). In Chicago, Hopkins worked for the Pullman Palace Car Company, where he rose from timekeeper to head paymaster by the time he resigned in 1888. On leaving Pullman, Hopkins started his own rapid economic rise by opening a chain of retail stores in Chicago's southern suburbs and adjoining towns.

Throughout the 1880s, Hopkins actively participated in Hyde Park politics and gradually gained political power by serving as village treasurer and in several county party posts. In 1889 he became a spokesman of the proannexation forces and received city-wide recognition for his successful leadership in bringing Hyde Park, Lake View, and the town of Lake into the city limits. Building on this new popularity, Hopkins sought the Democratic nomination for sheriff in 1890; but he lost out to a Harrison partisan. However, with Harrison temporarily retired (the elder Harrison was out of office from 1887 to 1893) Hopkins became president of the Cook County Democratic Club and in 1892 was selected campaign chairman for the Cook County ticket. As the 1893 World's Columbian Exposition was getting ready to open in Chicago, John Hopkins was setting his course to challenge the Harrison coalition for control of the Chicago Democratic party.

A Hopkins cohort, Roger C. Sullivan, came to Chicago from Belvidere, Illinois in 1879. He found a job (at $1.25 a day) in a West Side rail shop, but the eighteen-year-old soon realized that local politics presented a better opportunity for economic success. Sullivan was not a gifted public speaker, but he made friends easily and did not object to the tedious tasks of political organization.[35] He and John Hopkins became inseparable, and they both searched out compatible political allies. In 1890, Sullivan was elected to the patronage-laden office of Probate Court Clerk. The *Chicago Times*, the only pro-Harrison paper in Chicago, called Sullivan a "young, bright, energetic [man] whose integrity has never been questioned."[36]

But actual public office was not to be Roger Sullivan's vehicle for economic and political advancement. His unrivaled behind-the-scenes organizational ability would bring him and his friends enormous financial reward and eventual control of the Chicago Democratic party. In the process Sullivan would be maligned as a grafter, pilloried for his political methods, would make bitter enemies, and yet receive from his followers the highest compliment an Irish politician can receive—the title "chief."

Neither Hopkins nor Sullivan fit the stereotypical mold of Irish politicians. They were not glued to their original neighborhoods; in fact, both men were interested in geographical as well as economic mobility, and both were originally outsiders. Sullivan, as his power and wealth grew, moved from Chicago's near West Side to Lake Shore Drive and eventually to the upper-class suburb of Midlothian. Hopkins, never a city ward leader, called himself a businessman and not a politician, and his personal tastes and lifestyle differed little from those of any other successful Hyde Park merchant. No humble Back-of-the-Yards bungalow in Bridgeport housed these social climbers. Sullivan and Hopkins were shrewd organizers and political tacticians but, unlike the Harrisons, were not comfortable dealing with vice and gambling interests or with the new, poor European immigrants.

The remaining major Democratic faction in Chicago was led by another Irishman, Edward F. Dunne. His group represented the reform and progressive wing of the Chicago Democratic party. Dunne and his chief political mentor, fellow Irishman William L. O'Connell, espoused a philosophy of municipal ownership of public utilities. Dunne's political appeal rested mainly with the city's middle class—especially the growing number of "lace curtain" (well-to-do) Irish residents living in the city's better neighborhoods.

Dunne's career represents an aspect of Irish political involvement that differs dramatically from traditional views of past successful Irish politicians. He was born in Connecticut, spent his early life in Peoria, Illinois, but received much of his education in Dublin, Ireland. Dunne moved to Chicago in 1876, practiced law for fifteen years, and was elected to the Cook County Circuit Court bench in 1892.[37] He married Elizabeth Kelley in 1881, and they had thirteen children. Dunne was a long-time participant in various Catholic clubs, and after leaving public life he became a spokesman for Irish independence organizations in Chicago. Dunne was also an accomplished historian and a legal scholar, and he counted among his close friends the eminent attorney Clarence Darrow. Finally, Dunne was elected governor of the state of

Illinois in 1912, and to this day he remains the only Irish Catholic Democrat ever elected to the state's highest office.

Dunne's election as mayor in 1905 was neither a reform nor an Irish political breakthrough. From 1897 to 1915 the rhythm of local Chicago politics shifted among the three leading Democratic factions. The Republicans could capture City Hall only in 1907, when Democratic feuding allowed a German-American, Fred Busse, to defeat Dunne's reelection bid.

State and national Democratic candidates did not do as well in Chicago as their local colleagues did. Republican strength in the massive peripheral wards of the city, the enormous personal popularity of Teddy Roosevelt, and the lack of real interest of local Democratic leaders in politics outside the city usually combined to give the GOP substantial vote margins in Chicago. In fact, the major presidential battle for local Democrats was in the selection of delegates to the party's national convention. Every four years Democratic factions fought ferociously for the honor of representing Chicago at the convention, but this spring political fever cooled once the autumn campaign got underway.

In 1911, Carter Harrison II made a successful comeback effort to match his father's five mayoral terms. Harrison had served four consecutive two-year terms,* 1897–1905, and had voluntarily accepted retirement for a quieter life in California. But after a half-hearted challenge to Dunne's renomination in 1907, Harrison nipped Dunne by 1,500 votes in a three-way 1911 primary. Running third was Andrew Graham, the Sullivan-Hopkins candidate, who received over 26 percent of the primary vote while carrying five of the city's thirty-five wards. This primary and subsequent Harrison mayoral victory over Republican Charles Merriam not only illustrates the growing power of Irish Chicagoans but also reveals the giant inroads made by Sullivan's faction in traditional Harrison Irish bailiwicks.

Nevertheless, Carter Harrison II pulled off his amazing 1911 primary victory despite mass defections from his once impenetrable Irish guard. His Irish support in the South Side stockyards area went over to Dunne under the urging of the Sullivanites, who in the campaign's last days threw their support to the reform Democrat. The days when ward boss Tom Carey and his "Carey Indians" could automatically deliver their Irish vote for Harrison were over. New leaders were emerging in the stockyards, Canaryville, and Bridgeport neighborhoods, and the future belonged to Sullivanites Patrick "P. J." Carr and his young protégé, "Big Joe" McDonough.

---

*In 1907 the mayoral term was lengthened to four years.

The West Side Irish also fought against a return of Carter Harrison. Sullivan and his West Side Irish lieutenants, Patrick Nash, Robert Sweitzer, and George Brennan, either gave their wards to Graham or threw their support to Dunne. Closer to the Loop, Johnny Powers' Nineteenth Ward supported Graham and even John Brennan's levee and lodginghouse Eighteenth Ward went heavily for Sullivan's man. However, Sullivan and his emerging organization were unable to defeat Harrison because of shoddy strategy (which split the anti-Harrison vote), Harrison's strong support in the Bohemian and Jewish communities, and the former mayor's "Rocks of Gibraltar" in the First Ward. Hinky Dink and Bathhouse John's loyalty and love for their Carter was displayed openly and where it counted the most—the ballot box, with a 74 percent vote total for Carter Harrison.

Harrison defeated his Republican opponent, Charles Merriam, a University of Chicago political science professor, in the mayoral general election. The old warhorses, Sullivan and Hopkins, hated Harrison enough to give their tacit support to the young Progressive Republican academic. However, other Sullivan organization Democrats, especially the Irish committeemen from working-class wards, were not about to elect an avowed enemy (Merriam) over a sometime nemesis (Harrison). Carter Harrison's victory was due in part to a growing maturity on the part of Chicago Democrats. A few days before the general election, Harrison sent a letter to many besieged pro-Sullivan aldermanic candidates seeking a mutual exchange of political support.[38] Almost all of these Sullivanites were Irish, and if today's simplistic Irish versus non-Irish view of past Chicago Democratic politics is correct, these politicians would have turned down Harrison's bid. However, successful local Irish (and non-Irish) ward leaders did not allow single-minded ethnic fanaticism to overshadow political reality. They realized that no Chicago Democrat could ever be blatantly anti-Irish and expect to win a city-wide victory; and the Harrison family knew this better than anyone else. The Irish "chief" philosophy was not diminishing, but Chicago's twentieth-century entrepreneurial politics demanded greater sophistication than blind ethnic obedience. The Chicago Democratic party was becoming more centralized and structured as the multitude of "ward lords" chose Harrison or Sullivan as their leader for sound business reasons. In 1911, Sullivan's and Hopkins' irreconcilable hatred of Harrison turned into a personal vendetta, but many of their followers refused to accept this outdated, unprofessional political posture.

Edward Cullerton, John Brennan, John Powers, and Mike McInerney were the leading pro-Sullivan aldermen running for reelection who accepted Harrison's proposition "to forget past differences and unite behind a proven Democrat."[39] They no longer had any love for

Mayor Carter Harrison, II (1897). The Carter Harrisons (father and son) occupied the mayor's chair for 10 terms (1879-1915) and kept their Irish opponents off balance and unable to control either the Democratic party or city politics for a third of a century. *Courtesy of* STORMY YEARS: THE AUTOBIOGRAPHY OF CARTER H. HARRISON.

Harrison, but they had lived through four previous Harrison terms with few problems. Sullivan's orders to "knife" Harrison and back Professor Merriam made little political or economic sense to the aldermen. After all, the Republican candidate was talking about ending graft, abolishing political favors, and improving the civil service system. Harrison's letter was a great political coup, and on election day he received strong support from these Sullivan wards..Looking back at 1911, one participant summed up the feelings of the Irish Sullivan aldermen: "What assurance could they get that four years of Merriamism might not be fatal?"[40]

Except for a physical routing of Sullivanites at the riotous 1912 Cook County convention, Carter Harrison never again defeated his factional foes. Roger Sullivan, aided immeasurably by his crafty lieutenant George Brennan, was taking over the party. Harrison's last remaining Irish allies were Kenna and Coughlin, and in 1914 they too would leave their Carter as the desperate mayor sought to resurrect his power by becoming a reformer. Irish ethnicity, to be sure, played a vital part in the Sullivan party victory. His most trusted allies were Irish: twenty-four of thirty-five Democratic ward committeemen in 1914 were Irish, and of all the leading Democratic groups they were the most scattered throughout the city. George Brennan used this Irish dispersion to take over weak Democratic organizations in strong Republican wards. A striking example of this strategy was Brennan's elevation of his relative, young Joseph Gill, to power in the near North Side Twenty-third Ward. Gill became a party giant and a patron of Richard J. Daley, though his ward consistently voted Republican.

By 1915 the Irish takeover of the Democratic party was nearly complete. However, it must be emphasized once again: single-group ethnicity was weakening as a political determinant in party matters. Leading non-Irish Democratic figures like Bohemians Anton Cermak and Joseph Kostner and Jewish leader Adolph Sabath were untouchable in their West Side wards. These men were Harrisonites, but the mayor's espousal of reform, Roger Sullivan's mellowing as an ethnic leader (exemplified by his brilliant but unsuccessful 1914 U.S. Senate campaign), and the general desire of Democrats to stop the needless factional bloodletting and unify into one organization brought a more professional, consensus approach to party politics. Though intra-Democratic party battles would continue sporadically for decades, they would never again produce the open-field wheeling and maneuvering of the Harrison-Sullivan-Dunne era.

In 1915 Cook County Clerk Robert Sweitzer, a self-identified German-American and the brother-in-law of Roger Sullivan's brother Mark, trounced Harrison in the mayoral primary. The five-time mayor ended his electoral career in Chicago politics by winning only two of 35 wards in his "last hurrah" campaign. The rampaging Sullivanites, led by second-generation Irish politicians, were now ready to elect their first mayor, not one of their own but a German surrogate, in a regular mayoral campaign (Hopkins had won only a special election to fill out the assassinated elder Harrison's term in 1893). The Irish infrastructure previously missing seemed now to be in place, as Irishmen were prominent in Chicago's major business, utilities, and commercial operations. Moreover, Irish ethnicity seemed no longer to be a detriment to high public office, and even the political corruption charges that had marred the early public careers of Sullivan and his allies were on the wane. Yet a Sweitzer victory and the accompanying Irish rise to city power was not yet to be, for stampeding into Chicago's political picture was the cowpuncher-politician, William Hale ("Big Bill") Thompson.

"Big Bill" Thompson was an easygoing hustler, a sometimes adolescent showman, and probably the greatest political campaigner in Chicago history. He was a yachtsman and western sports enthusiast from a prominent South Side family on his mother's side. In 1900 he parlayed his personal connections with black vote appeals to become alderman in the formerly fashionable but then racially changing Second Ward. He served a lackluster one term in the city council and was then elected county commissioner, where he quickly grew bored with doing the public's business.

Thompson's zest for political office diminished for a decade because, though Big Bill loved the combat of a political campaign, he cared little about the day-to-day administration of government. However, following the dramatic 1912 national Republican-Progressive party split, Thompson and his wily mentor Fred Lundin, "the poor Swede," maneuvered for mayoral support with both groups in Chicago. Thompson narrowly defeated Judge Harry Olson in the 1915 GOP mayoral primary with the help of a late campaign leaflet charging that "because Judge Olson's wife was a Catholic he (Olson) would deliberately destroy the public school system."[41] Some Chicagoans were shocked by Thompson's tactics, but Big Bill was merely warming up for the April general election and an unbelievable political career in the city.

Thompson devoured Sweitzer in the 1915 mayoral election and in so doing delayed the Irish-Democratic takeover of the city for sixteen years. Thompson openly reintroduced religious prejudice in Chicago politics by warning Protestant North Side audiences that a Sweitzer victory would mean a Catholic cabal controlling the school board; he stormed around German neighborhoods making anti-English speeches and thus earning the sobriquet "Kaiser Bill"; he courted the newly enfranchised women's vote, promising to place a mother on the school board; he offered straight-out deals to Harrison's Democratic allies; and he wooed the growing but geographically segregated black voter. These whirlwind tactics and charges forced Sweitzer and his followers into a series of campaign blunders, including the famous "dear fatherland letter." However, Big Bill's most nimble and ingenious campaigning took place among the city's Irish voters.

Big Bill passed himself off as a long-time supporter of Irish Home Rule. He spoke emotionally about "English oppression," and he enlisted Michael J. Faherty, leader of the city's Irish Fellowship Club (an organization heavily supported by John Hopkins), as his chief adviser on Irish affairs. Thompson also talked about jobs and contracts to lesser-known West Side Irish politicians not included in Sullivan's inner circle. The Thompson-Lundin strategy revealed that Irish political strength on the West and North sides was susceptible to Republican appeal. Moreover, Thompson's victory once again brought out the electorate's reluctance to accept a full-fledged Irish-led Democratic organization in control of Chicago.

Was Chicago not ready for Irish leadership? Over four generations of Irish had labored in the political vineyards, had worked their way up to political control of a major party, had seen their countrymen involved in most of the city's leading business and social circles, and yet once again Chicago voters had rejected their candidate. Thompson had reopened old political wounds and beaten the Irish at ethnic politics. Sullivan and his Irish cadre needed other nationalities—especially the Bohemians, Poles, and Jews—in leadership positions; but the Irish old guard could not play Harrisonian ethnic politics and put together a winning city-wide coalition.

In April 1920, Roger Sullivan died, leaving George Brennan in command of the organization. Sullivan's death marks a turning point in Irish Democratic politics in Chicago, because with his departure a new breed of Irish politicians under Brennan's leadership began to emerge. These men would be better educated, more discreet, less flamboyant, and better able to play multiethnic politics Chicago style. Moreover, they would be organization-oriented and not ethnic-oriented politicians. Though their Irishness would be a factor, it would count less than loyalty to the organization, which more and more would become the vehicle of political survival and political glory.

It took Sullivan and his original band of Irish followers nearly three decades to gain control of the local Democracy. They overcame the Harrison family, party reformers, an early narrow ethnic base, various scandals, and powerful newspaper opposition. Though the 1920s would find them facing sniping from political guerillas in their own party, the big question was, could they take over the city? It was to be the ultimate irony that the ethnic group credited with the most political savvy in American politics would need a former Bohemian pushcart peddler to achieve their ultimate goal—city control.

Anton Cermak and his Irish Allies Systematize Their Control Over the Democratic Party and City of Chicago: The Democratic Organization's Takeover of Chicago is Legitimized

From 1920 onward, Irish political fortunes in Chicago were almost solely encased within the city's Democratic party—despite the strenuous efforts of Republican Mayor Big Bill Thompson. Irishmen held elective and appointive offices, dominated leadership positions in the police and fire departments, and were now firmly anchored in business and labor circles. Moreover, their economic advancement also meant geographical liberation, as Irish families moved into previously inhospitable and unattainable neighborhoods, like Beverly on the city's far South Side.

Irish dispersion into the city's peripheral wards was further evidence of their assimilation into the American mainstream. In fact, Andrew Greeley's current theory that the American Irish disappeared as an ethnic group into upper-middle-class suburbs may have its Chicago roots in the 1920s.[42] However, many Irish, unable or unwilling to move from the old neighborhoods, still yearned for the ultimate political triumph in Chicago—City Hall.

Two Irish Catholics had been elected mayor of Chicago, but neither man represented the culmination of Irish efforts in city politics. John Hopkins' 1893 mayoral election victory, after the elder Harrison's assassination, was a political accident and not the beginning of a political tradition. The second Irish mayor, Edward Dunne in 1905, was a reformer who, though devoutly pro-Irish and pro-Ireland, acted more like a Union League Club "WASP" attorney than a politician from the neighborhood. Meanwhile, ethnicity in organizational politics was on the wane, as more sophisticated and educated Chicago politicians manipulated and maneuvered the city's growing heterogeneous electorate. Still, countless Irish pols in Chicago waited for a leader to emerge with the charm, the moxie, and the organizational ability to synthesize the city's diverse population into a solid political machine. More than any other Chicago politicians, the Irish craved order, rank, and hierarchy in their politics. If it was impossible to re-create the old sod's clan-and-chief system, perhaps there was enough time to put together a political apparatus featuring party organization and strong leadership. The new breed of Democratic politicians, many of whom were Irish, represented the best and last hope for such a political evolution in Chicago politics.

During the 1920s the coming of new-breed politicians coincided with Prohibition's arrival and the decline and eventual demise of the saloonkeeper-politicians; and the new-breeders replaced the latter as the mainstays of the local Democracy. These new-breed pols shied away from old-style saloon, gambling, bawdy house, and boodle enterprises, and instead involved themselves in construction, real estate, law, banking, and insurance, while making strenuous efforts to professionalize the administration of local government.

George Brennan personified Chicago's new Democratic leadership and the Irish hopes for a united party. Brennan was a protégé of Roger Sullivan and a longtime member of the anti-Harrison faction within the party. Sullivan's death in 1920 gave Brennan party leadership and the opportunity to consolidate the Democratic party. Brennan was born on May 20, 1865, in Port Byron, New York, but his family soon moved to Braidwood, Illinois, a coal-mining town southwest of Chicago. At sixteen he lost his right leg when a coal car ran over his knee in a freak accident. Following this tragedy, Brennan studied to become a teacher, eventually became a principal, and finally was appointed assistant superintendent of schools in Braidwood. He later went to Springfield and served as clerk to Secretary of State Buck Hinrichsen in liberal Governor John Altgeld's administration. In 1897 he moved to Chicago and quickly aligned himself with the Sullivan forces. He managed a couple of successful campaigns and in a few short years became the Democratic leader's confidant and chief advisor.

Brennan was no saloonkeeper-politician. His education, wit, and speaking ability allowed him to mingle comfortably with the city's social and economic elite. His winning personality and whimsical sense of humor led the *Chicago Tribune* to write in 1923, "George Brennan sees politics as sheer comedy." He made his successful political deals with a chuckle, while other politicians failed using sledge hammers. Under Sullivan his role was often that of the party's "no" man, but even in denying favors or patronage he seldom made real enemies. One observer called Brennan a "centripetal force" in the party's history because he prevented rival chieftains from moving too far in separate directions after Sullivan's death.

George Brennan played a vital and often overlooked role in Chicago politics, the development of the local Democratic party, and the coming of age of Chicago's Irish politicians. Unlike Sullivan, the old-fashioned clan warrior, he accurately saw his political role as healer and conciliator within the local Democratic party and keeper of the standard until the right man at the right time could structure the party and run the city. Brennan moved politically aggressive Irishmen like Tom Nash (Nineteenth Ward) and Jimmy Quinn (Fiftieth Ward) into strong GOP peripheral areas and supported their uphill political battles with money and workers. In 1926, Brennan ran for the U.S. Senate (emulating his mentor Sullivan, who unsuccessfully ran for the Senate in 1914), and although he lost, he was able to carry Chicago by more than 75,000 votes. His efforts for multiethnic leadership within the party kept non-Irish new-breed Democrats like Anton Cermak, Joseph Kostner, and Jacob Arvey from factionalizing the party along rigid nationality lines against a stalwart Irish old guard. Brennan's Senate bid was another step up the acceptability ladder for Chicago's Irish politicians, despite the fact that anti-Irish discrimination still persisted among native voters, and ethnic envy still lingered with other ethnic groups.

Patrick (P. J. or Paddy) J. Carr was the top Democrat in the near Southwest Side stockyards area. In the 1920s he controlled the Thirteenth and Fourteenth wards and had vast influence in Bridgeport's Eleventh Ward. Carr was the consummate Irish politician. He was a charming speaker, did not object to drinking with the boys, and received incredible loyalty from his followers. But he was not a saloon-keeper-politician either, but a new-breed Democrat who rose to prominence on a proven public record as well as by personal charisma. Paddy Carr was a local boy, born in Chicago on September 4, 1880. He lived most of his life at 3619 South Lowe, though he eventually moved to 3529 South Western and St. Agnes parish. Young Paddy was a neighborhood paper-boy, went to De La Salle Institute, spent some time as a lumber pusher on the schooners, and eventually went into politics. He was elected alderman, sanitary district trustee, and in 1921 was picked to fill out the term of deceased County Treasurer Harry Gibbons.

Aided by his assistant, Jacob Lindheimer, Carr turned the county treasurer's office into a political gold mine. In his first year in office he turned back to the county over $1,000,000 in interest. Previous treasurers had suffered from sticky fingers or memory loss when it came to dollars gained from interest; but Carr gained widespread publicity from his exceptional performance. Public approval of Carr was shown in 1926, when Paddy ran for county sheriff and walloped his Republican foe by 127,000 votes. Paddy Carr wanted to be mayor of Chicago, and most observers believed he would be the favorite in 1927. However, two weeks after his sheriff's victory, Carr suddenly died. This changed the future procession of Chicago mayors within the Democratic party.

Carr's legacy as a 1920s new-breed Democrat was crucial. He ran on his public record, received rave press notices, charmed reformers and independents, and presented himself to Chicagoans as a hardworking, honest administrator. This is not to say Paddy forgot to play the political game. His main protégé was "Big Joe" McDonough, and few Chicago Democrats produced more political hoopla than Paddy Carr. His "Paddy Carr Night" at Paddy Harmon's Dreamland Ballroom (on Van Buren and Paulina) had famous entertainers contributing their services for charity. He organized boxing and wrestling shows, provided Christmas baskets for the poor, and was a powerful ward committeeman inside the regular organization. However, Paddy Carr's popularity rested most on his public record, and this separated him from the tarnished saloon and gambling bosses of pre-Prohibition days.

John S. Clark was another new-breed Democrat who rose to power in the 1920s. Clark was born in Chicago on January 5, 1891, and following in his father's footsteps, became a West Side political powerhouse. In 1917 he was elected Thirty-fifth Ward alderman, and in 1927 he became chairman of the crucial city council finance committee. He unsuccessfully challenged the Democratic organization in the mayoral scramble following Cermak's death in 1933. However, one year later he became Cook County's first modern tax assessor, a post he held for twenty years. John Clark was a college man: he attended St. Ignatius College and the Illinois College of Law. He owned a lucrative West Side real estate business and was considered an expert on city fiscal matters. Clearly, Clark was not a saloonkeeper-politician but, like the other aspiring new-breed Democrats, he was not averse to building a political organization. His Thirtieth (the number changed in 1921) Ward Democratic organization was one of the city's best.

Patrick A. Nash, born in 1863, was also a native Chicagoan who grew up on the city's West Side. He became a businessman and along with his brothers started a sewer and construction company. Pat Nash lived in the predominantly Irish Fourteenth Ward, next door to Democratic kingpin Roger Sullivan. His friendship with Sullivan boosted his business and political fortunes in the city. By the 1920s Nash was one of the wealthiest men in Chicago and a member of the Democratic party's inner circle.

Nash viewed party structure not as a friends-and-neighbors social club but as a business relationship among investors. Winning and profits went hand in hand, and it was Nash more than any other Democrat who saw the economic opportunities of politics. He held only one elected office (Board of Review, 1918), but his advice and counsel were vital to George Brennan (whom he disliked) and to Anton Cermak (whom he liked very much). Following Cermak's assassination, it was Nash who took command of the party. He selected Edward J. Kelly to be permanent mayor, he consolidated the Democratic organization into the Kelly-Nash machine, and in businesslike fashion he accelerated the conversion of black Chicagoans to the Democratic party. Pat Nash was a political craftsman, but he possessed little of the saloonkeeper-politician's roguish charm. He was not politically lovable, nor did he engender great personal loyalty from his supporters. Instead, Nash

Pat Nash (center), founder of the Kelly-Nash political machine, accepts congratulations from Democratic stalwarts for another victory. Conspicuously eyeing the "boss" and flashing a toothy grin is Northside Alderman Mathias "Paddy" Bauler who is best known for his 1927 truism: "Chicago ain't ready for reform yet." *Courtesy of Holime.*

acted as a corporation board chairman, and in this position he molded an effective and efficient Democratic organization beyond the saloon-keeper's wildest dreams.

Many other Irish Democratic politicians came of age and tried to reach for power during the 1920s in Chicago. Some were new-breed types like the extraordinarily ambitious Michael Igoe, a South Side lawyer who served eight terms in the state legislature and was an unsuccessful candidate for Cook County state's attorney in 1920 and 1924. Igoe also involved himself in party affairs and for two decades attempted to take over the local Democratic party leadership. After countless party brawls, at which he lost more often than he won, Igoe settled for a federal judgeship.

Another new-breeder was William E. Dever, who may be the least-known Chicago mayor elected in this century. Dever, the son of Irish immigrants, was born in Woburn, Massachusetts in 1862. He came to Chicago twenty-five years later and worked as a tanner on Goose Island while studying at the Chicago College of Law. Dever's ensuing law career led him to the city council as Seventeenth Ward alderman, and in 1910 he was elected to be a superior court judge. In 1923, Dever, under the guidance of old Dunne-Harrison supporters led by William L. O'Connell, made a deal with George Brennan to run as blue-ribbon mayoral candidate against the discredited GOP mayor, Big Bill Thompson. Thompson's subsequent refusal to seek reelection gave

Dever an easy win over the lackluster Republican candidate, Arthur Lueder.

Dever became mayor at a time when Chicago was suffering through the savage Prohibition gang wars. His attempts to enforce the unpopular law alienated many powerful local Democrats, who called him "Czar" and the city police "Cossacks." As mayor Dever made no effort to work with Brennan or to use his office to bolster the local organization. After four years in office, Dever reluctantly agreed to run again, since Paddy Carr's death and various Thompson deals left the Democrats without a viable candidate to confront the resurgent Big Bill. Thompson beat Dever by a five to four margin, and the defeated Democrat closed out his political career declaring that his "administration did not have a scandal in four years."[43] Dever could have added to his farewell remarks that once again—for the third time—an Irish mayor had not used the power of Chicago's top office to consolidate party control over the city.

Not all of Chicago's Irish Democrats fighting for power in the 1920s reflected the new breed's more sophisticated view of government administration or recognized that second- and third-generation ethnic city voters now expected more than rough-and-ready saloon politics. Two West Side Irishmen, Timothy J. ("T. J.") Crowe and Martin J. O'Brien (their close and powerful South Side ally James, "Bill Dailey from Archer Avenue," had died in 1924), with the tacit support of Democratic warhorse Robert Sweitzer, were leaders of this potent old guard. The Crowe-O'Brien forces received support from many veterans of Roger Sullivan's old factional army. Some die-hard Sullivanites disagreed with Brennan's moves of opening party leadership posts to former party foes; others were angered at being by-passed by the new-breeders; still others were unwilling or unable to change their methods of political operation and face a new political era in Chicago.

T. J. Crowe was a gruff man who, in the words of a contemporary, "simply lacked couth." Crowe had first gained political recognition working the precincts as an ardent Sullivan supporter in the Thirty-third Ward on the city's West Side. Sullivan rewarded the burly Crowe by making him Democratic ward committeeman and giving him a good job in County Clerk Sweitzer's office. In the tumultuous and fight-filled 1912 Democratic county convention battle between the Sullivan and Harrison factions, Crowe was Sullivan's chief slugger. Crowe's city strength and influence rose, and in 1920 he was the unsuccessful Democratic candidate for Cook County recorder of deeds. However, two years later he was elected trustee of the patronage-laden Metropolitan Sanitary District, of which he soon became president. Inside the local party, Brennan, seeking harmony, placated Crowe and his allies by giving T. J. and O'Brien leadership positions in the Democratic party's managing committee. According to Jacob Arvey, Crowe demonstrated his power by going around to leading local Democrats and asking them loudly, "Do you want anyone on the payroll?"[44]

Martin J. O'Brien, Crowe's political partner, was also a long-time protégé of County Clerk Robert Sweitzer. O'Brien, a quiet and plodding man, was an original member of Sweitzer's West Side "Green Lantern Marching Club." A veteran of the Sullivan-Harrison factional wars, O'Brien had steadily worked his way up through the ranks to the position of Twenty-ninth Ward committeeman. Like Crowe, O'Brien had run for various public offices throughout the period, but except for his election to the state's 1922 constitutional convention, he had been unsuccessful. O'Brien's political power came from his chairmanship of the party's managing committee—a committee that also had T. J. Crowe serving as secretary.

The managing committee of the Cook County Democratic Central Committee was an extralegal unit that was originally set up during the Sullivan-Harrison period. "It came about," wrote the *Chicago Tribune*, ". . . because each faction wanted to have a headquarters represented by a friendly leader in every ward . . . thus it was considered necessary to create an unofficial body that could ignore the unacceptable ward committeemen by replacing them with hand picked leaders."[45] Unlike the party's county central committee (a group made up of fifty elected ward committeemen and thirty elected township committeemen), members of the managing committee were chosen by party leaders. Individuals could serve on both committees, but membership on the managing committee became the sought-after plum, because this was where patronage decisions took place.

Under the direction of Crowe and O'Brien, the managing committee cut heavily into Brennan's party leadership. This party power, coupled with Crowe's sanitary district patronage, made the Crowe-O'Brien tandem politically formidable and dangerous to Irish new-breed Democrats who were eager to modernize the party structure and city government. Moreover, the always eager and adaptable Michael Igoe, who was serving on the job-rich South Park Board,[46] formed a lukewarm alliance with Crowe and O'Brien which added extra potential power to the old guard's political muscle.

The issue was now joined inside the Chicago Democratic party as to its future direction. The Irish, the party's oldest supporting ethnic group, were at yet another political crossroads. Their ethnic group dominated leadership positions in both philosophical wings inside the old triumphant Sullivan faction. On one hand, there were the new-breeders—Brennan, Nash, Carr, Clark, and others—who were anxious for power but, because of personal dislikes and political ambition, were not united in their actions. These men wanted ethnic diversity in the party hierarchy, were anxious to implement new administrative ideas in running city government, and, to put it bluntly, were a high cut above the old saloonkeeper image of Chicago Democratic politicians.

On the other hand, the Crowe-O'Brien crowd seldom spoke of party harmony, and in fact many were Irish isolationists when it came time for supporting other political candidates. Though not all of them fit the bullheaded image of T. J. Crowe, these sanitary district supporters were not active in innovative technological and administrative efforts to upgrade city government. During the 1920s this entrenched Irish old guard, headquartered on the city's heavily populated West Side, seemed unbending to party leaders' calls for a unified political organization capable of running Chicago. Yet the Irish new-breeders found on the same West Side a champion who would successfully challenge the old guard, unify the party, take over City Hall, and implement a political structure Irish Democrats had worked generations trying to construct. This political wizard was no red-headed, silver-tongued son of Erin; rather, he was a stocky, street-smart Bohemian—Anton J. Cermak.

No man in Chicago history, including Richard J. Daley, has had a more controversial and contradictory political career than has Anton J. Cermak. To some people Cermak was a gruff bully who consorted with known mobsters and shady businessmen to further his political and economic interests. Others viewed Tony Cermak as a friend of the poor, a spokesman for personal liberty, and a master public administrator. However, no matter which viewpoint is correct, one fact stands out: Cermak bridged the gap between pre-1920, faction-riddled saloon-keeper politics and post-1920, unifying, new-breed politics better than anybody else inside the Democratic party.

Anton Cermak was born on May 9, 1873, in a Bohemian village fifty miles from Prague. His family were Hussites (followers of the early fifteenth-century Czech Protestant reformer John Huss), but Cermak married a Catholic girl and raised his children as Catholics. Cermak's family immigrated to America in 1874, settling in Chicago at 15th and Canal streets. Later they moved to Braidwood, Illinois, where the elder Cermak became a coal miner, and everyone expected Tony to follow his father into the mines. Young Cermak was a big strapping lad who earned his own living from the age of eleven. He had only an elementary school education, but one of his Braidwood teachers was George Brennan. Their political relationship within the Chicago Democratic party would run hot and cold, but there is little doubt that Brennan's influence gave Cermak a good start in big-city politics.

By the turn of the century Cermak had moved to Chicago's near

West Side Tenth Ward and was active in his community. In 1902, with Brennan's help, he was elected to the state legislature. During the next two decades Cermak was elected to the following offices: state representative, Chicago alderman, chief bailiff of the municipal court, and in 1922, president of the Cook County Board of Commissioners.

Throughout his early political career Cermak was never classified as a saloonkeeper-politician. His political strength and popularity rested on his identification with the large Bohemian population west of the Loop and his advocacy of personal liberty (the right to drink on all days, but especially on Sunday) throughout Chicago. Both of these issues deserve special mention because they allowed Cermak to withstand Prohibition's impact and to move into 1920s new-breed politics. Cermak was Chicago's Bohemian spokesman for the first three decades of the twentieth century. His Twelfth Ward (latter Twenty-second) committeeman's position gave him opportunities to serve his constituents' needs, as well as various private businesses, including his own lucrative Lawndale Building and Loan Company. Cermak shared fully in the Bohemian desire for upward mobility. There are many examples of his influence inside the Bohemian community, but one of the most charming is his personal involvement in a heavyweight championship wrestling match.

Joe Smejkal, a Bohemian hero, was to fight Frank Gotch, the Pole, for the title at the Coliseum on July 4, 1912. Prior to the bout, Cermak solved two problems that threatened to cancel the entire event. First, Smejkal and Gotch decided that only Cermak could referee this controversial ethnic showdown. He was trusted by both groups and, in case Smejkal lost, he could handle the disappointed crowd. Cermak accepted the offer, but on the condition that no betting be allowed because, he said, ". . . should Gotch beat Smejkal many of my countrymen would lose heavily and many who would wager cannot afford to lose."[47] Gotch whipped Smejkal—he never even used his deadly toehold—and all sides praised Anton Cermak as an excellent and impartial referee.

As for Prohibition, in April 1919 the *Chicago Tribune* called Anton Cermak "the wettest man in Chicago." In the general assembly and city council, Cermak sponsored personal liberty legislation, and on the city streets he led pro-wet marchers demanding Sunday drinking. Fletcher Dobyns, a longtime wet opponent, labeled Cermak a lobbyist and a mouthpiece for liquor interests. He and other drys condemned Cermak's United Societies for Local Self-Government as a political front organization for the Bohemian leader. But Cermak never wavered in his advocacy of personal liberty—it was the right issue for him—

and eventually the dry-dominated Municipal Voters League reformers gave Cermak their political approval.

In 1931, Anton Cermak was elected mayor, thus becoming the first new-breed Chicago mayor to occupy City Hall. As an administrator, Cermak was all business, and this public posture characterized the other new-breed Democrats as well. According to Jacob Arvey, "Cermak knew how to ask questions, was able to digest complex material, and dig out the crucial issues, and possessed what his friend Pat Nash called a 6th sense for practical knowledge." John Delaney, a *Chicago-American* reporter, called this "his come to the point attitude." Little in government escaped Cermak's scrutiny. His remarkable memory for small details and employees' names gave him total command of the most involved problems.

Cermak the ethnic leader, Cermak the wet champion, Cermak the administrator—all contributed to his success following Prohibition. However, it was Cermak the politician that put him in the mayor's seat, elevated new-breed Democrats to power, and completed the unification of the local Democratic party. Cermak was a full-time politician who had, in the words of Otto Kerner, Jr., his son-in-law and later governor of Illinois, "a good understanding of people and a good social consciousness." He was ambitious, earthy, and a perpetual listener. Cermak also had many diversified friends, ranging from Mike and Moe

Czech-born Mayor Anton J. Cermak (seated), elected in 1931, shakes hands with Alderman Mathias "Paddy" Bauler, while Alderman Charles Weber looks on. Cermak put together the multi-ethnic political organization that would later be called the Richard J. Daley machine. *Courtesy of the University of Illinois, Chicago.*

Rosenberg (West Side Jews) to Joe McDonough (South Side Irish) to the City Club of Chicago reformers (mainly North Side and South Side Protestant "goo-goos").

Even Cermak's enemies recognized his mastery in organizing local politics. Former Judge and Alderman Ulysses S. Schwartz said, "Cermak kept books on everybody . . . and if you crossed him he would efficiently and energetically get you." Cermak's rise inside the Chicago Democratic party was linked to his ability to embrace diverse interests and create ethnic alliances. A man from the streets, Cermak dealt with bankers and businessmen as well as hoodlums and hustlers in his climb to dominance. However, he knew that lasting political power rested in a precinct army, and no man was better able to energize patronage workers than Cermak. He uplifted their status, built up a political rewards system that still exists, and cajoled workers into action by chanting his motto: "Only lazy captains steal."

Cermak's takeover of the Chicago Democratic party following the death of George Brennan in 1928, and his subsequent 1931 mayoral victory did not go unchallenged. Several authors have written about these events; Alex Gottfried's *Boss Cermak of Chicago: A Study of Political Leadership* is the best and most thorough analysis of the political maneuvers surrounding Cermak's twin triumphs.[48] Common to all the studies of Cermak's efforts to win party control and then become mayor of Chicago is the belief that Cermak had to "get the Irish." Gottfried sums up this view by saying: "Cermak did not wish to drive the Irish out of the party. All he wanted was that they submit."[49]

There is no doubt that Cermak used ethnic appeals in attracting support from Chicago's diverse population. In private and public meetings he may even have made statements against certain Irish politicians and attacked their unwillingness to share power or to expand the party. However, Cermak was the ultimate professional politician who advocated compromise and not confrontation, and thus it is far too simplistic to label his rise to power a revolt against the Irish. Rather, Cermak used his several Irish new-breed allies (and in return they used him) to attack the Irish old guard who opposed a new direction for the Chicago Democratic party. Moreover, Cermak was able to read election returns better than anyone else around, and to paraphrase an old Chicago political axiom, "he knew where the fish were" and went about catching more of them than any of his major rivals for party leadership.

The 1920s were very lucky years for Tony Cermak. He and his fellow West Side Bohemian ward committeemen Adolf Sabath and Joseph Kostner had been strong Harrison supporters during the faction war years. Following Harrison's 1915 defeat, Cermak sought reconciliation with the victorious Sullivanites; but it was not until Sullivan's death in 1920 that he gained full political recognition from his former political foes. In 1922, Cermak became Cook County Board President by first whipping South Sider Dan Ryan in the primary, and later Republican Charles Peterson in the general election. This office gave Cermak a power base from which he could spread his influence beyond his own Twenty-second Ward bastion.

The 1920s also saw Paddy Carr and Joseph Kostner, Cermak's two greatest potential rivals for party control and city leadership, suddenly die. Carr, the South Side Irishman, was far more friendly with Cermak than was Kostner, a fellow West Side Bohemian. Joe Kostner was more of a new-breed Democrat than Cermak was—or probably any other city politician of this period. Kostner came from an old established family (his father had been an early Chicago settler and was a partner in the Scully, Kostner Coal Company) and was a graduate of Northwestern University and the Illinois College of Law.[50] After college, Kostner worked for his father, dabbled in real estate and insurance, but eventually found his true love to be politics. In 1911, Mayor Harrison appointed him city commissioner of public works, a position that gave Kostner enough public recognition for him to run for congressman-at-large in 1916 at the age of thirty-four. His congressional bid was unsuccessful, but one year later he was elected alderman from the West Side's Thirty-fourth Ward.

Kostner was handsome, politically shrewd, very ambitious, and a dynamic speaker. He was a model ward committeeman in the Thirty-fourth Ward, allying himself with various nationality groups.[51] Kostner was the patron of future Jewish leaders Michael Rosenberg, Jacob Arvey, and Harry Fisher; he had a working relationship with Republican State's Attorney Robert Crowe; and he was a close friend of many Irish aldermen, like Dorsey Crowe and John Touhy. According to Jacob Arvey, "Joe Kostner was the one man Anton Cermak feared because Joe could match Cermak in all political skills and at the same time mingle with the city's educated upper crust."[52] Kostner's death in 1925, after he had been reelected to a fifth aldermanic term by a ten to one margin, and Carr's death one year later, left new-breed Democrats short of leaders capable of putting together a winning coalition. Cermak saw his opportunity and stepped into a leadership vacuum, his new-breed Irish allies giving him his crucial edge to cut down the old guard.

Success in politics often depends as much on luck, circumstance, and chance as on planned strategy or clever tactics. Anton Cermak's political moves following Brennan's death in August 1928, up to his own 1931 mayoral victory, were a combination of all these factors. However, included in this drama was a political fact of life that found Irish new-breed politicians linking arms with the West Side Bohemian leader.

The year 1928 gave Cermak an excellent opportunity to show Chicagoans and Irish Democrats his vote-getting appeal throughout the city. Like his predecessors Roger Sullivan (1914) and George Brennan (1926), Cermak made a spectacular but unsuccessful campaign bid for U.S. Senator. Cermak did defeat his Republican senatorial opponent, Otis Glenn, in the city of Chicago by 77,409 votes.[53] But Cermak ran in a presidential year, when middle-class Republican voters living in the city's peripheral wards historically came out in large numbers to support GOP candidates. In 1928 almost 60 percent more people (most increases being in the peripheral wards) voted for U.S. Senator than had cast a ballot for that office two years earlier. Thus, even in losing, Cermak demonstrated his popularity, and in vote margin terms he outdistanced the Democratic presidential candidate, Al Smith, by almost 100,000 votes, while carrying twenty-eight city wards to Smith's twenty-six.

The year 1928 also saw Cermak's chief political foe, T. J. Crowe, defeated in a remarkable sanitary district race. Crowe was running for reelection with fellow Democrats James Whalen and Henry Berger.[54] Berger topped the field in the six-man, three-winner contest, with South Sider Whalen coming in a comfortable second. However, the Republican, Howard Elmore, a protégé of U.S. Senator Charles Deneen, Cermak's closest GOP pal, edged Crowe by less than 30,000 votes, thus knocking the latter out of his sanitary district power base. Some have suggested that Cermak beat his nemesis by chopping up his vote in strong Democratic West Side ethnic wards. However, an analysis of the vote reveals a city-wide disenchantment with the sanitary district president. Crowe ran ahead of his two Democratic running mates and Elmore in only four wards. He ran behind the three winners in nineteen of the city's fifty wards, and he trailed Berger and Whalen in fifteen other wards. Yet the complete returns show no overt trimming of Crowe by Cermak, since the former beat Whalen and barely lost to Berger in Cermak's own Twenty-second Ward. It was the more reform-minded peripheral wards that buried Crowe and his hopes to challenge Cermak for party leadership.

Cermak and his Irish allies accelerated their drive to take over the city following the 1928 election. He was now the logical mayoral candidate to challenge the often-discredited Republican incumbent, Big Bill Thompson, in 1931. The growing dissatisfaction of Chicagoans with Prohibition also boosted his popularity in the city. Cermak was the city's recognized wet leader, and by a series of referendums Chicago voters overwhelmingly supported his positions on the modification of existing liquor laws. Within the Democratic party structure Cermak and his backers escalated their drive to crush Crowe's power in the managing committee. In the spring of 1929 these political efforts were given an enormous lift when Crowe, O'Brien, and six others were indicted in the famous sanitary district's "Whoopee Scandal."

A whole series of charges were leveled at Crowe, O'Brien, and other sanitary district trustees and employees regarding their mismanagement of district funds and their payroll padding. However, the most sensational accusation against the group concerned their recreational activities in 1927 at the Waldorf Astoria Hotel in New York. Eyewitnesses told of wild drinking parties, visits to Harlem black-and-tan clubs, and furniture-tossing melees at a time "when Cook County taxpayers thought Crowe and his party were in Washington (discussing) flood relief."[55] According to the *Chicago Herald-Examiner*, Crowe's behavior was "an astounding picture of political debauchery."[56]

Crowe and O'Brien called the charges political, claiming that Cermak and GOP State's Attorney John Swanson (a Deneen Republican) had conspired to eliminate them from public life. Another indicted district employee reaffirmed this view years later, claiming, "The whole scandal was political . . . it was an effort to get rid of Crowe . . . that is why the case was first assigned to Judge Harry Fisher . . . he was a Cermak crony."[57] Indeed, Sanitary District Trustee Frank Link was the only defendant ever to go to jail; Crowe died while he was appealing his case in the early 1930s, while the others eventually had the case "nole prossed" (prosecution did not initiate any further action, thus in effect dropping the case).[58]

Whether or not they were behind it, Cermak and his allies used the scandal bombshell to move against Crowe. In October 1929, Irish new-breeders replaced the Irish old guard in the management committee hierarchy. Cook County Recorder Clayton Smith, a North Side Irish Cermak ally,[59] succeeded O'Brien as management committee chairman; Eleventh Ward Alderman Joseph McDonough, P. J. Carr's protégé, South Side Irish leader, and longtime Cermak friend, replaced T. J. Crowe as managing committee secretary. Moreover, the new leadership announced that the committee would assume the indebtedness of the old managing committee stemming from the 1927 mayoral race.[60] The capture of the managing committee, along with Cermak's election as chairman of the county central committee, gave him almost total control of the Democratic party structure in Chicago and Cook County.

The key point in Cermak's political takeover was his use of Irish new-breeders. Besides elevating Smith and McDonough to managing committee leadership, Cermak selected Pat Nash to replace himself as county chairman following the 1931 mayoral election. Cermak also gave another Irishman, Joe Gill, the crucial position of county central committee secretary. One could hardly call these political actions anti-

Irish; rather, they reflected Cermak's view that political loyalty, competence, and professionalism mattered more than simple ethnicity. It also showed Cermak's awareness that no successful Democratic leader in Chicago could afford to be anti-Irish. For, in fact, over 60 percent of Chicago's Democratic ward committeemen in 1928 were Irish, and this figure had declined only slightly since 1914.[61]

The Irish new-breed ward committeemen's acceptance of Cermak as party leader reflected their belief in his organizational ability, personal popularity, and record of political trustworthiness. It also reflected the political inevitability of a Cermak triumph based in part on his successful wooing of non-Irish ward committeemen from bulging Democratic wards. A 1930–1932 ward analysis of Democratic voting strength in Chicago revealed that only three of the top ten Democratic wards had an Irish ward committeeman. Two of these wards were controlled by Cermak stalwarts Joe McDonough (Eleventh) and James McDermott (Fourteenth), while the third was Hinky Dink Kenna's First Ward. The big blocs of deliverable Democratic votes were now, in fact, centered in a string of Jewish, Bohemian, and Polish wards on the city's West Side.[62] Thus, just as Cermak could not be anti-Irish and effectively lead the party, neither could new-breed Irish committeemen interested in Democratic victories challenge his ethnic coalition; he was too strong and they were too politically hungry.

Cermak cemented his control over the Democratic organization by leading it to a brilliant victory in the 1930 elections. State and Cook County Democratic candidates won almost every office, with Cermak himself leading the pack in his landslide reelection as county board president. After three years of plotting and organizing, Cermak and his allies were now ready to go after the ultimate prize—the city.

In 1931, Chicago's Republican mayor, William Hale Thompson, was in deep political trouble. He had alienated GOP middle-class voters living in the city's periphery by his mismanagement of city affairs and his close ties to gangster Al Capone. Chicago newspapers, including the die-hard Republican *Chicago Tribune*, attacked his lackadaisical attitude toward political corruption and the shady manner in which he conducted the city's business. Moreover, being a Republican, Thompson was hurt by the Depression sweeping the country, and few knowledgeable Chicagoans believed that he was capable of dealing with the city's growing economic problems. All Thompson had left to fight Cermak's growing organization were his loyal black supporters, his cadre of political appointees, and his own unique and vicious style of political campaigning.

In 1931, Big Bill Thompson outdid his previous mayoral campaign efforts. From the outset he swung from his heels with his special brand of religious and ethnic intolerance. He called Cermak a "Bohunk" and "pushcart Tony" and made fun of his foreign origins. Cermak restrained himself and coolly replied: "Of course, we couldn't all come on the Mayflower—or maybe that boat would have sunk. But I got here as soon as I could." Thompson also attempted to label Cermak an anti-Semite; but his severest attacks were aimed at separating Cermak from Chicago's Irish Democratic voters.

"It's going pretty far," cried Thompson in a campaign speech, "when Tony the Dictator can tell the Irish in Chicago that they can't run for mayor."[63] This campaign theme was reinforced a few days later when Thompson said: "You [Cermak] may have bluffed the Irish in the Democratic party and made them get out of your way because of your power, but there is one man in this community that you cannot bluff and his name is Bill Thompson."[64] Finally, in a speech at the Apollo Theatre, the mayor pulled out all the rhetorical stops, declaring that "for the first time in my life I saw the Irish lay down to a Bohunk . . . something tells me that the Irish [on election day] are going to tell this Bohunk where to get off."[65]

Thompson and his henchmen attempted to make West Side alderman and Thirtieth Ward Democratic committeeman John Clark part of their Cermak anti-Irish campaign. Clark and Cermak were not personal friends, and it was no secret that Clark wanted to be mayor. Thompson, hoping to break open an intra-Democratic split, asserted that "when Alderman John S. Clark was pushed into the background as a candidate for mayor, it was the first time in my life that I saw the Irish lay down."[66]

If modern writers have been taken in by Thompson's use of the Irish issue, new-breed Irish Democrats of the period were not so easily fooled. According to former alderman and United States Appellate Court Judge Roger Kiley, "Many West Side Irish disliked and resented Cermak . . . simply because he wasn't Irish."[67] But new-breed Irish Democratic leaders like John Clark were not about to throw away an opportunity to finally win City Hall and end Thompson's Chicago political career. At a monstrous Cermak rally in the Chicago Stadium (which was preceded by perhaps Chicago's first torchlight automobile parade), Clark answered Thompson's charges by simply saying: "His only reason for bringing in my name was to engender intolerance."[68]

The 1931 mayoral results reflect the lack of any Irish revolt against Cermak. The West Side Democrat trounced Thompson 671,189 to 476,922—the most one-sided victory in Chicago mayoral history. Cermak carried forty-five of fifty wards, with his largest pluralities coming from his West Side ethnic strongholds and from disgruntled middle-class outer-ward residents. Thompson was left with the black belt (Wards

2, 3, 4) and two near West Side wards (20 and 28) which had growing
black populations. Irish wards came through for Cermak, and though
some wards delivered less than expected, other Irish committeemen
showed the folly of Big Bill's anti-Irish campaign. Cermak won big in
strong Democratic wards controlled by Irish committeemen, including
Clark's own Thirtieth Ward, by margins greater than Dever's totals four
years earlier.[69]

Following his election as mayor, Anton Cermak voluntarily gave
up chairmanship of the Cook County Democratic Central Committee;
he selected his old buddy Pat Nash as his successor and gave him day-
to-day control of party affairs. However, the mayor through Nash remained in command of the local Democracy's future direction. Cermak
also supported another longtime Irish pal, Emmet Whealan, to replace
him as Cook County Board President. Whealan had served on the board
since 1919 and had been a South Side ward committeeman since 1912.
Whealan had been unswervingly loyal to Cermak for over a decade,
and the mayor rewarded his old friend with this choice political plum.
Again, whether it was good judgment or a simple covering of his Irish
flank, Cermak showed his political astuteness in naming Whealan. This
and other actions reveal that if Cermak was anti-Irish he was only
"against those Irishmen who were against him."[70]

Issues concerning the city's Depression woes dominated Cermak's
two-year mayoral reign. Money to pay municipal employees, money
for poor relief, money for public schools and their teachers, and discussions concerning local taxes and city budgets took up most of his
time. Mayor Cermak periodically clashed with the council's finance
chairman, John Clark, on potential remedies, but their disagreements
did not spill over into the political arena or have ethnic overtones. Most
new-breed Irish politicians favored Cermak's efforts to institutionalize
the city's political system by consolidating both the party and public
offices under his control.

In 1932 the ever-eager Mike Igoe challenged Cermak's blue-ribbon
candidate, Probate Court Judge Henry Horner, for the party's gubernatorial nomination. Horner, a Jew, had been a judge since 1914 and
had gained an excellent reputation despite his roots in Hinky Dink
Kenna's First Ward. Only two Democrats had occupied the Springfield
mansion since the Civil War, and Igoe's repeated unsuccessful attempts
for public office made him a less likely third occupant than Horner.
Moreover, Igoe would be a constant political threat to the mayor,
whereas Horner had shown little proclivity for internal Democratic
politics. Horner crushed Igoe in the primary, winning Chicago nearly
two to one while carrying forty-three of the city's fifty wards. Again,
Igoe did have some Irish ethnic attraction in several South Side and

West Side wards; but the majority of Irish committeemen and voters backed Horner and the organization. In the primary's aftermath, Cermak dumped Igoe from his national committeeman's post by taking the job for himself. According to the *Tribune*, "it was the logical solution of a problem created when Michael Igoe opposed the organization. . . ."[71]

The 1932 general election was a great Democratic victory in Chicago. Cermak's hand-picked, multiethnic Democratic ticket trounced the GOP rivals in state and Cook County races. Cermak, a Democratic national convention supporter of former New York Governor (and Irishman) Al Smith—and not of the eventual Democratic nominee, Franklin D. Roosevelt—immediately made overtures to the president-elect for a preinaugural meeting. Thus it was that in February 1933, Cermak headed south for a Florida rendezvous with FDR to discuss federal patronage, among other things. On February 15, 1933, at a Bayfront Park rally in Miami, Giuseppe Zangara, an unemployed bricklayer, attempted to kill Roosevelt but fatally shot Mayor Cermak instead.[72]

Cermak died in a Miami hospital on March 6, 1933. His longtime aide, Henry Sonnenschein, surrounded by party members in the mayor's City Hall office, took the final phone call and announced the tragic news: "Gentlemen, Tony is dead."[73] The mayor's death, followed by a brief mourning period, triggered an intensive month-long political drama involving all the forces inside the local Democracy. At the end of this exciting and highly emotional period, Chicagoans saw Irish new-breed Democrats, loyal to Cermak and his memory, take over the party and city leadership without breaking political stride.

Cermak's death did not shatter his carefully constructed Democratic organization in Chicago. Despite the splintering efforts of a few political powerhouses, the Democratic party structure held firm. The new leaders were mainly Irish ward bosses who had been loyal Cermak supporters, and they were now ready to push forward with his political and administrative plans for the city. Organization opponents, many of whom were also Irish, challenged mayoral succession decisions not on the basis of ethnicity but because of personal political ambition. It was a battle of new-breed Democrats fighting for party control, and all tried to cloak themselves in the mantle of the martyred mayor. On March 14, 1933, the Chicago city council came together to select an interim mayor. Legal issues were raised about how the council was to name a temporary successor and whether the aldermen could in fact choose—without a general election—the individual to serve out the rest of Cermak's term. However, the Democrats controlled the council, and under the masterful direction of county chairman Pat Nash they orchestrated the selection of South Side Alderman Frank J. Corr, a political threat to no one, as interim mayor.

Tony Cermak would have been proud of the way his old Irish ally Pat Nash directed the ethnically diverse Democratic leadership during the intense political maneuverings surrounding the temporary mayor selection. According to Jacob Arvey, "Frank Corr did not want the job but was very interested in a judgeship."[74] Nash wanted Corr for that reason, because the South Side alderman would be politically safe in City Hall until Chicago Democrats in Springfield ironed out any problems over the council's desire to pick a permanent successor.

John Clark challenged Nash's choice of Corr for the interim mayor's office. The West Side alderman was, in the words of a participant, unacceptable to party leaders because he was "too smart and too much a threat to Nash and other long time Cermak allies."[75] Clark's only real party supporter was his old West Side colleague, Twenty-fifth Ward Alderman Jimmy Bowler, who had been with Cermak in Miami.[76] Clark and Bowler never had a chance in the council debate over the selection of a temporary mayor. Nash, using his inherited Irish, Jewish, and East European political axis, beat back Clark by a vote of 33 to 16.[77]

Fiftieth Ward Alderman (and Irishman) Jimmy Quinn was named temporary chairman of the council session. Two Jewish aldermen, West Sider Jacob Arvey (Twenty-fourth Ward) and South Sider Barnett Hodes (Seventh Ward), were Corr's spokesmen in the often vitriolic council debate. Behind the scenes, Polish City Treasurer M. S. Szymczak and Bohemian Twenty-third Ward Alderman John Toman cajoled any potential waverers back into line. And in the "backest" back room, County Treasurer Joe McDonough (Irish) and Twenty-second Ward Alderman Henry Sonnenschein (Bohemian Jew) assisted Pat Nash in running the entire operation. Multiethnic coalition politics was in the saddle.

One month after Corr's interim appointment, the Chicago City Council convened to select a full-term mayor. Unlike in the temporary selection process, they did not have to select an individual who was a sitting member of the council. Once again Nash and his lieutenants overwhelmed their opposition, this time with only a whimper rebellion, and former Sanitary District Engineer (and Irishman) Edward J. Kelly was elevated to the mayor's office.

Ed Kelly, the son of an Irish policeman father and a German mother, was a city native. He had grown up in the South Side Brighton Park neighborhood, and at an early age he received his first political job. "During the first part of the 20th century," wrote former Mayor Carter Harrison II, "Alderman Tom Carey [a legendary stockyards area politician] brought to [my] desk a tall red haired, smiling young Irishman with the request I make him [Kelly] an assistant city engineer."[78] Kelly used his engineering and political experience to make important friends among Chicago's economic and social elite. His work at the sanitary district put him on friendly terms with *Chicago Tribune* mogul, Colonel Robert McCormick.[79] Kelly's involvement with city sanitation projects made him a longtime acquaintance of the city's leading sewer contractor, Pat Nash. Kelly was also a South Park board member, and though he was tainted by the sanitary district "Whoopee Scandals," most Chicagoans viewed him as an honest engineer and not a politician.

Ed Kelly became mayor because Pat Nash and his advisors believed that Kelly "had always been on the borderline of politics" and thus would not be a threat to the Democratic organization or to Pat Nash. According to Judge Kiley, the actual selection of Kelly took place at the Morrison Hotel the day before the city council meeting. "Nash was in total control," said Kiley. "He informed the assembled Democratic Aldermen that there would be no *Robert's Rules of Order* and that Kelly was his and a select committee's mayoral choice.... He then asked for ayes on Kelly ... he never asked for nays."[80] The next day the city council named Edward J. Kelly as mayor of Chicago by a 47-0 vote.

Mayors Martin Kennelly (left) and Edward Kelly (center), and political strategist Jacob Arvey (right). Irish-American politicians such as Kennelly, Kelly, Daley, and Byrne would dominate mayoral politics in Chicago after Mayor Cermak's assassination in 1933. *Courtesy of the University of Illinois, Chicago.*

The vaunted Chicago Democratic machine was thus born, and Chicago's Irish, after almost a hundred years of effort, were in command of city affairs. The mayor was Irish, the Cook County board president was Irish, the Cook County state's attorney was Irish, the tax assessor would be Irish in 1934, and the head of the Democratic party was Irish. Late a half-century by Tammany Hall standards, they had succeeded at last. It had all come together under a multiethnic coalition, a political organization built by new-breed Democrats eager to professionalize government and willing to share power with those who were willing to work for the party.

The Irish were political winners because with Cermak's leadership they had driven Thompson and the GOP out of City Hall; they had been instrumental cogs in a reborn, ethnically diverse political organization; and under Cermak's guidance they and other ethnic groups had found protection in a hierarchical political structure capable of governing the city and running the party. However, threats and challenges to party unity did not automatically abate with the unifying of the Democratic party under Irish control, because personal ambition and individual antagonisms remained part of the city scene. As in the past, most of these revolts were not based on ethnic cleavages; the main motives for party fights remained individual desire for power, patronage, prestige, and revenge.

From the days of John Comiskey, Irish pols in Chicago had fought for their political place in the sun. They had seen other cities develop political organizations, machines, and structures capable of placing the Irish in powerful government positions. Chicago's Irish politicians lagged behind for many reasons: the city's extremely diverse population, the Harrison family, William Hale Thompson, and their own inability to find a common leader. Finally, after a brief flirtation with city Republicans, Chicago's Irish recognized their vehicle for success was the local Democratic party. And after some bitter factional fighting and feuding, new-breed Irish Democrats found a leader in Bohemian Anton Cermak, who was shrewd enough to put together a unified party structure.

Unlike other political organizations, the late-arriving Chicago Democratic "machine" would not fight professional competence in government; rather, it would incorporate many administrative techniques usually associated with reform and reformers. However, the bottom line remained political control, and that now rested with the Democratic organization. Pat Nash's final remarks to the Democratic aldermen and city leaders attending the Morrison Hotel meeting reaffirmed the role of the organization in post-Cermak Chicago politics. "Before Mr. Kelly was definitely selected," said Nash, "he promised that all jobs would be filled through the ward committeemen. We all want jobs. But I know that no ward committeeman wants a job at the expense of another ward committeeman or the taxpayers. For that reason there will be no one chasing Mr. Kelly around. All applications will come through the ward committeemen."[81]

Pat Nash's efforts to make the organization greater than any individual met with general success, despite periodic political adjustments. Cermak's hard-fought battle to unify the party and take over city government brought power and glory to Chicago Democrats. The Irish were in the vanguard of Cermak's original onslaught, and with their own political infrastructure, based on their long standing in the party, they had several leaders in a position to inherit Cermak's dream. In the subsequent fifty years, Irish Democrats have remained in charge of Chicago government and the local Democracy. The parade of Irish Democrats who have led the city and the party since Cermak has only slightly altered the framework of political control set up by the West Side Bohemian and his Irish allies.[82]

Summary and Epilogue

Anton Cermak put together an organization that followed an old political adage: "you win elections by addition." He included Carter Harrison's old Irish levee supporters; he won over Edward Dunne's reform types in Hyde Park and Oakland on the city's near South Side; and aided by Roger Sullivan's son Boetius, he took in many of the old chief's lieutenants in working-class Irish neighborhoods. However, Cermak's greatest coup was his use of his personal and political friendship with Sullivan's former next-door neighbor, Pat Nash. Nash gave Cermak access to experienced ward leaders and gave the Bohemian greater credibility with other new-breed Irish politicians.

Cermak merged these political alliances with his strong West Side support among Eastern European ethnics. In effect, he allowed his political adversaries little room to mount an anti-Cermak movement. His perennial challenger, Michael Igoe, was left spouting blarney to Irish committeemen; the only Irish committeemen sympathetic to Igoe's pleas were those unable to deliver sizable Democratic votes. John Clark, a far more credible threat than Igoe, was never an intimate of other Democratic leaders. Like Cermak, Clark was a first-rate administrator; but unlike his fellow West Sider, Clark was more of a political loner than an ethnic mingler. Meanwhile, old-school Democratic leaders like T. J. Crowe and Martin J. O'Brien were crushed and then resurrected just enough to become organization team members. Thus

Chicago's Democratic organization was a multi-ethnic coalition, and Mayor Martin Kennelly captures that spirit at a labor-management nationality day at the Western Electric Company's Hawthorne plant in 1948. *Courtesy of the University of Illinois, Chicago.*

Cermak formed a political machine that consumed the meat and potatoes of the Democratic vote while leaving only leftovers to party dissenters.

Cermak did not push out the Irish in order to gain power; instead, he won them over by persuasion, political muscle, and their own belief that he was a winner who could do what no other Democrat had ever done— unify the party. If the Irish ward committeemen as a bloc could have held firm against Cermak in a kind of "ethnic Armageddon," they might have prevented his party takeover. However, in so doing they would have pushed the party back to its dark ages of factional feuding. They also would have reelected Thompson mayor of Chicago in 1931, which would have meant the loss of countless new city jobs and many positions already in Democratic hands. New-breed Irish Democrats recognized the foolishness of divisive enthocentrism, and though some undoubtedly swallowed a little ethnic pride, they latched onto Cermak's fast-moving coattails.

It took Cermak nearly four years to systematize his political control of the Democratic party. He never completely won over Irish leaders like John Clark, Mike Igoe, Martin J. O'Brien, and Jimmy Whalen, but he did incorporate the city's other main Irish spokesmen into the party's ruling circle. Following his death, his closest allies, led by Pat Nash, cleverly replaced the martyred mayor with Ed Kelly, a peripheral politician not associated with political infighting. Nowhere was there evidence of an ethnic showdown on Kelly's selection or Pat Nash's taking control of the organization. According to Otto Kerner, "My father [Otto Kerner, Sr., was Illinois Attorney General] and other Bohemian leaders did not engage in any activities to challenge the organization's selection of Kelly."[83]

Thus Ed Kelly, an engineer and not an Irish politician from the neighborhood, shared power with the venerable Pat Nash, and together they led the nationally famous "Kelly-Nash machine." However, Kelly grew less popular as he acquired more political power, especially following Nash's death in 1943; in 1947, after fourteen years in City Hall, he was dumped for another Irishman, Martin J. Kennelly, a successful businessman.

Jacob Arvey, the former West Side alderman, took command of the machine, and in a series of slick political moves kept the party together and thus the Irish in power. During the early 1950s, Joseph Gill, George Brennan's brother-in-law, succeeded Arvey but was more of a caretaker than a political mover. Finally, in the 1953–1955 period, it all came together for Chicago's Irish inside the Democratic party. After six generations of political activity, the Irish found a man from the neighborhoods who not only took over the party but the city as well. Richard J. Daley, the only Irish mayor of Chicago ever to have been a ward committeeman, became party chairman in 1953. Two years later he was elected mayor, a position he held until his death in 1976.

Richard Daley, like Cermak, saw where the bulk of the Democratic votes came from in the city, and in true Cermak style he proceeded to negotiate directly for that support. In Daley's case it was a deal with South Side leader Bill Dawson for the burgeoning black vote, which gave Daley the strength to tip a hotly contested 1955 mayoral primary in his favor. After securing his black base, Daley continued to use Cermak's model by tying up the vote-rich and nationality-diverse West Side. John Clark, by this time an elder statesman after twenty years as county assessor, and his relative Al Horan, Twenty-ninth Ward leader, supported Daley. Jacob Arvey and the still-significant Twenty-fourth Ward Jewish voters also fell in step behind the party chairman. When all of this city-wide support was added to his Bridgeport stockyards home area, the fifty-three-year-old Daley had enough vote power to become mayor of Chicago.

For over twenty years Daley ran the Democratic party and the city of Chicago. He gained nationwide recognition as the ultimate political "boss" while he exercised enormous control over party and city. However, Daley did not operate as a chief of some ancient Irish clan or as a nationality leader from a narrowly based ethnic community; rather, he ran a multiethnic organization where politics and government became inseparable. Daley was not afraid of blue-ribbon commissions, innovative methods to improve administration, or bright young men eager to impress him with their knowledge of municipal affairs. Like Cermak, Daley mastered administrative detail and was willing to allow debate—as long as it was internal and not detrimental to the Democratic party. Daley never hid his Irishness, and he used so many Irish in his daily dealings because, in the words of one associate, "when he needed someone to help or hire, he dealt with someone he knew and trusted . . . and most often that person was Irish."[84] However, it would be a mistake to label Daley's rule an Irish regime because, like Cermak, Daley read precinct returns and demographics better than anyone else, and he knew which groups delivered the goods. Finally, Daley was not blind to potential adversaries, even if they were Irish; and he played them off against each other and against other ethnic groups, following the first political commandment in Chicago politics: "Don't make anyone who can unmake you."

Unlike every other big-city political machine, Chicago's Irish did not use their numbers to take over the city. Instead, the Irish politicians were the beneficiaries of the efforts and vote tallies of other ethnic groups. A unified Democratic organization or machine came later to Chicago than to any other big city in the northeast and north-central states. Chicago's Irish had established the political framework; they had worked longer in the precincts than any other group; but it took them too long to put the organization together. Machine politics Chicago style, as epitomized by the city's Democratic organization, evolved into an army that had the Irish controlling the officers but not the privates. The foot soldiers were Poles, Jews, Bohemians, Italians, and eventually black Chicagoans; they accepted Irish leadership from Cermak's death to the end of the Daley years.

Today a revolt against Chicago's Irish leadership would find Irish politicians hard-pressed to maintain their control. Their city numbers have been reduced far below the totals of 1930, when Irish pols had enough manpower to team up with Cermak and unify the party. Now, fifty years later, the Irish must cloak their political efforts in the guise of party unity or else make deals based on personal appeal, political trade-offs, issues, or political revenge. The Irish no longer possess enough numbers to trade in the urban political marketplace, and thus they can no longer make appeals to ethnic pride.

In a sense, current Irish politicians are the ultimate new-breeders: they have to avoid nationality—unless they express it in terms of general ethnicity—when attempting to garner white support in an increasingly black city. Thus Irish political leadership in Chicago is somewhat of an anachronism; the huge numbers are gone, and the building blocks, the neighborhoods, have all but disappeared. Economics and the search for the good life find Irishmen filling up suburban shopping centers, not ward meetings.

Chapter XIII

MELVIN G. HOLLI
The Great War Sinks Chicago's German *Kultur*

What have the Russians, Poles, Bulgarians, and Serbs ever done for civilization? They have never made an invention, they have developed no political system, nor given us any new ideas. . . . This is the ignorant, half-civilized, barbarous and sinister race which has declared war against the civilized races of the European order. . . . A victory for the Slav means death to education, constitutionalism, liberalism and free thought. A Slav victory means the obliteration of four centuries of European culture.

—Chicago Abendpost, August 14, 1914

The days of wholesale slander and aspersion cast upon the Slav . . . are over.

—Chicago Free Poland, April 1, 1917

We have long suffered the preachment "you Germans must allow yourself to be assimilated, you must merge in the American people"; but no

one will find us prepared to step down to a lesser
KULTUR.

—President, Natioal German-American
Alliance, November 22, 1915

Death to the Germans . . . avenge wrongs Ger-
many has done to Poland . . . death to the Prus-
sian viper. . . . Be 100 percent loyal.

— Chicago Dziennik Zwiazkowy, 1917-1918

I am a Four Minute Man
I am the mouthpiece of Democracy

. . . .

I am a stoker of the Great Melting Pot.
In four minutes I breathe the flame of true Amer-
ican Patriotism to people of all kinds and
creeds.
I am a soldier. I fight German propaganda, in-
trigue, falsehoods, treachery.

— Chicago Four Minute Men, 1918

Chicago: August 1914

THE SUMMER OF 1914 IN CHICAGO BE-
gan with the kinds of paradoxes that seemed to plague the history of
Germans wherever they were found. On June 13 the cream of Chicago's German-American society gathered to glorify German-America
with the dedication of a Goethe statue. It was rainy and dreary, and
although the day was not an entire washout, it was punctuated by more
disappointments when President Woodrow Wilson and other dignitar-
ies failed to appear. At just about the same time, a well-known University of Illinois literary scholar's lifework, *Kampf um Deutsche Kultur
in Amerika*, was going to press in Germany. Dr. Julius Goebel's pon-
derous series of essays that recorded the German-American struggle for
a place in the American cultural sun, "The Struggle for German Culture
in America," was an ominous augury of things to come. Little did Goebel then realize that the whirlwind of war would soon shatter his pipe
dream for a Periclean age for German culture in America. (An obituarist
would later note that the "World War was the major catastrophe of
Julius Goebel's life.") Goebel had advised the use of the German language to "prevent the superficial process of Americanization." His view
of his host's culture was not very flattering, for he had once warned
Germans of the dangers of slipping into "the slop kitchen of a national
Melting Pot."[1]

The outbreak of World War I in August 1914 did not send the same
seismic shock of horror through Americans as did World War II. Frenzied excitement and the thrill of nationalism ran up the spines of Chicago's multiethnic, foreign-born population. Of Chicago's 2,437,526
people, only 752,111 were classified as native-born Americans in the
school census of 1914. The largest ethnic groups were directly and
nominally derived from England's enemies, the Central Powers. Chicago's Germans were the largest foreign stock (first- and second-generation) group, comprising 399,977, joined by 58,843 Austrians and
some 146,560 Anglophobic Irish. This potential coalition of 600,000
was composed of the city's most gifted and economically comfortable
immigrants (Germans, German-Jews, and Austrians) and the most politically and religiously powerful (Irish). These Central Powers sym-
pathizers would do much twisting of the British lion's tail, as events

would show. The Allies would gain little comfort from the city's 166,134 Russians (more than 90 percent Jews), who were strongly anti-Czarist and pleased to see Kaiser Wilhelm's peak-helmeted warriors tearing up the fabric of Russian society. Chicago's 231,346 first- and second-generation Poles were initially divided, although two years later they would slowly coalesce into an anti-German position. The city's 102,000 Bohemians moved powerfully in the Allied direction, rooting for the Triple Entente to thrash the Central Powers and the tyranny of the Austro-Hungarian Empire. The small Hungarian colony saw things the other way, for continued subjugation of the Slavs seemed to follow the logic of their history and Hungarian self-interest. The Scandinavians, comprising 118,000 Swedish ethnics and 47,496 Norwegians, were generally correctly neutral, but were pro-German in their basic sympathies. Chicago's small Finnish colony was vehemently anti-Russian and saw in Lutheran Germany deliverance from Czarist bondage. The Serbs, Croats, Slovenes, Albanians, Montenegrans, and other Slavic groups, including the Lithuanians, were often divided over the war, depending upon whose imperial heel oppressed them the most. Chicago's small English ethnic population (only 45,714) and tiny French colony of 5,649 were demographic dwarves whose weak voices hardly counted in the war for the hearts and minds of Chicagoans in the long months that followed 1914 and eventually led to American involvement in 1917. Most native-born Americans, reflecting the geopolitical realities of splendid isolation, were solidly neutral and emotionally disengaged.[2]

The Allied powers in 1914 lacked the built-in sympathy and support enjoyed by the Central Powers in Chicago. Later, of course, the residual ties of language, culture, and political ideology would assert themselves and lead to an Anglo-American entente. But in August 1914 that was far from clear, and a betting man who read the newspapers and watched the street action in the city would make the Germans a better than odds-on favorite to win not only the war but the hearts and minds of Chicagoans. Max Annenberg, *Chicago Tribune* circulation manager and Jewish success story, had just returned from a tour of Europe and predicted an easy victory for Germany. Germany has "loyalty, ammunition, guns, and brains," he said. "Inside of a week the Germans will march through Belgium and France as a giant would stride through a kindergarten." Annenberg declared that "France is a corrupt and immoral nation. A few years more, and France would have extinguished itself. Belgium is not much better. But Germany is in the full bloom of health and power." "Here and now I forecast," continued Annenberg, "that a week from Sunday will find France and Belgium conquered by Germany, England suing for peace, and Russia not even in the fight." Other evidence also surfaced that showed support for Germany. A "cigarstore plebiscite," if held over the nation on August 1, according to respected journalist and observer Mark Sullivan, would have come out on Germany's side.[3] The American admiration of Germany's well-ordered, efficient, and technologically and scientifically advanced society was well established, although it would be shaken by the German violation of Belgium's neutrality.

To have lived in Chicago, New York, or any other large city populated by emigres from the nations at war during that boisterous first week of August, as Clifton Child noted, was to have lived vicariously the excitement of nearly every European capital. The war news burst on Chicago like a Roman candle illuminating the August sky. The frenzy among Chicago's Germans almost defies reconstruction. German-language newspapers issued calls for the colors, German reservists appeared at "monster" meetings held to cheer the fatherland on to victory. Chicago's *nordseite* (North Side) was filled with German flags and bands playing German patriotic and martial airs on the street corners and in cafes. Clusters of Northsiders sang *Die Wacht am Rhein* (The Watch on the Rhine). A flush of national chauvinism swept some 2,000 German-Americans into Sieben's Hall, where they swore allegiance to Kaiser Wilhelm and enlisted in a "voluntary regiment" to fight for the fatherland. Chicago's Charles Schoepfer, who in an un-Teutonic lapse of democracy was "elected" colonel of the "regiment," announced that $2,000 had already been subscribed the first night of the war news to transport his unit to Germany.[4]

It was a feverish weekend: the war news reached Chicago on Saturday, August 1, and the mobilization of aid, men, money, and emotions rushed through Sunday and into the next week. Chicago's German consul, Baron Kurt von Reiswitz, announced that more than 1,000 Chicagoans under the age of thirty-nine were liable for military service and that those who refused to comply faced arrest in Germany. The consul's fears were unnecessary, for both young and old responded: one disappointed would-be inductee, Carl Gallauer, lamented, "I am 53. If I were 30 years younger I would fight." He salved the pain of his disappointment with a prediction that Germany would handily defeat her enemies. Chicago's Austrian subjects were also called to the colors by Emperor Francis Joseph: 400 Austrian reservists wearing the imperial red, white, and green were enrolled at the Austrian consulate and told to hold themselves in readiness for transport to Vienna. The Austrian mobilization order not only included all reservists and former militiamen but also offered amnesty to all deserters who returned to bear arms.[5]

Sunday, August 2, saw Chicago's North Side observing its usual continental Sunday with taverns open, but with a patriotic frenzy that outdid the first day of war. In the heart of the German settlement, where North Avenue intersects Clybourn, reporters recorded that excited German could be heard on every wagging tongue. West North Avenue resembled a street in Germany, with red, white, and black flags streaming from every building and German patriotism running high. German beer gardens and cafes swarmed with men and women— Saxons, Plattdeutschers, and Swabians—who huzzahed and broke out in "tremendous applause" whenever an orchestra played the "Watch on the Rhine" or other German patriotic songs. Street-corner bands reaped a harvest of nickels from appreciative burghers. The Germania Club promised cooperation with the Austrian societies in the war effort, and the *Illinois Staats-Zeitung* (a German-language daily) called for a rally at Turner Hall on Clark Street to raise war relief funds for the dependents of Wilhelm's fallen warriors. The German-American National Alliance called for a mass meeting at the auditorium to show support for Germany and to chide some of the American press for its alleged partisan reporting of the war.

On Monday, August 3, the German consulate experienced the "rush to arms" that the Austrians had had on Saturday. Baron von Reiswitz's warning to laggards seemed needless, for some 700 German reservists clogged the ninth floor of the People's Gas Building ready to go "home" to fight. Many were "nattily attired" officers with "upward curling moustaches," although some mechanics and artisans could also be seen in the crowded corridors. A Franco-Prussian veteran of fifty wept when told he was too old to serve the fatherland. Tuesday saw another mass rally, whose watchword was "Mit Herz und Hand für Vaterland," and the next day some 300 German reservists marched smartly through Chicago in a "patriotische Demonstration."[6]

The first great wave of Teutonic patriotism crested on Wednesday night, August 5, in and around the city's lakefront parks and centrally located Auditorium Theater. Led by the German-American National Alliance and a quartet of prominent Chicago Germans—physician Dr. Otto L. Schmidt, businessman and civic leader Charles Wacker, Bismarck Hotel owner Karl Eitel, and H. O. Lange, president of the Germanian Club—a "monster rally" was planned to express mass sympathy for the Central Powers and to right the wrongs allegedly perpetrated upon Germany by the Anglo-American press barons who ridiculed the Kaiser.

At the auditorium, where every seat was taken and an overflow crowd thronged outside, resolutions and rhetoric evoked thunderous applause, and the "white hot temper of Teutonic patriotism" flowed like angry lava. Several hundred German reservists who had reported to the German consul marched into the hall with banners flying and "stirred the crowd to a frenzy of enthusiasm for the Fatherland." A resolution criticizing the American press and expressing the "deepest sympathy with the people of Germany and Austria-Hungary to whom we are bound with everlasting ties of blood and thought," and "for whom we feel as one of them," passed with acclamation through the wildly cheering assembly. Another sent individually to both Emperor Francis Joseph and Kaiser Wilhelm enthusiastically proclaimed: "The German-American citizens of Chicago, assembled in as great a mass meeting as this world city has ever seen, assure your majesty in the name of 2,000,000 Germans in Illinois of our unchangeable love of home and fatherland." The resolutions met with cheers, bravos, and excited applause not only inside but outside as well, where they were transmitted to several thousand Germanophiles unable to get in and standing in the adjacent streets. Inside, Rev. Alfred Meyer, an Elgin pastor, blamed British commercial jealousy and irrational French hatred for the war and praised Kaiser Wilhelm as a man of peaceful instincts. Meyer's comments provoked "wild applause" and drew the crowd, much of which was then composed of Franco-Prussian war veterans, to its feet; "choking with emotion," they shouted themselves hoarse. Women stood up on chairs waving handerchiefs and gloves in frenzied appreciation of the good pastor's words. The meeting drew to a climax with the Radetzki March, made memorable by the past military victories, and the auditorium "roared with cheers" and shook with patriotic appreciation.

Sizable sums of money were committed for war relief, as the Eitel brothers and the *Abendpost* set the ball rolling with pledges of $1,000 each. One more speaker, William Rothman, defended German "weltpolitik," the only speaker of the night to use the "forked tongue" of "perfidious Albion." The meeting closed as 4,000 rose to their feet in a mass singing of "Deutschland über Alles" and, almost as an afterthought, "America." The throng then poured out of the building and joined thousands of Germans who paraded through the Loop waving flags and singing patriotic German songs. Some 5,000 marched to the offices of Chicago's largest English-language dailies and gave what appeared to be a mock serenade with "Die Wacht am Rhein." The crowd gathered for a late-night grand finale at Grant Park on the lakefront. There the Elgin spellbinder and Chicago Judge M. F. Girten aroused more enthusiasm for Deutschland.[7]

This awesome display and mass outpouring of sympathy and patriotism for a foreign land by such a large bloc of newcomers left Chicago reporters uneasy if not shaken, as their observations showed. They had difficulty reporting these Teutonic night rallies and parades in the same way they would have reported Yankee Chautauquas or Rotarians out on a 4th of July toot. No nationality group in Chicago's history had ever unleashed such a spectacular display of patriotism as had Chicago's *Deutschtum*, nor mounted such a vigorous and well-orchestrated campaign on behalf of its ancestral homeland. No greenhorns fresh off the boat, these Germans were a uniquely accomplished group—without peer in the city's immigrant population.

The Germania Club called together a blue-ribbon committee of sixty to raise ten million marks for the German Red Cross. The same committee, led by civic leader Charles H. Wacker and sausage king Oscar F. Mayer, sent a self-serving and rudely patronizing telegram of condolence to President Wilson: "The committee representing citizens of German and Austro-Hungarian birth and extraction here, assembled to devise ways and means of alleviating the stress of war which now lies heavily upon their brethren across the waters [and then as an afterthought] have learned with deep sorrow of the loss sustained by you in the death of your beloved wife."[8]

German-Americans appeared to have their own von Schlieffen Plan. They disputed any alleged or real slur on Germany's honor, and some of them even found themselves defending the very antidemocratic and authoritarian political systems they had rebelled against a half-century earlier. But blood is thicker than water, and time has a way of healing old wounds. German rhetorical preemptive strikes were viewed by their authors as reasonable defensive actions. In the war of words, Chicago's Germania Club president fixed on race, insisting that this is a "war of the Teutonic race against the Slavic . . . whether the civilization of western Europe or the barbarism of Russia is to prevail." The lowly position of the Slav was lowered even more by Germanophiles, who seemed to take perverse and self-righteous delight in ridiculing the "natural serf races of Europe" and referring to their enemies as "Tartars, Mongols, half-Asiatic barbarians" and backward "hordes of the Moscovite." The German press of the Midwest trumpeted forth the charge that "the War was a battle to the bitter end between German civilization and the pan-Slavic, half-Asiatic, and thinly veneered barbarism of Russia."

Both Germany and German-Jewish papers, such as New York's Jewish *Die Tageblatt* and Chicago's *Abendpost* joined in the general assault, inquiring in editorials widely circulated in the Midwest and Chicago:

> What have the Russians, Poles, Bulgarians, and Serbs ever done for civilization? They have never made an invention, they have developed no political system, nor given us any new ideas. All that this race possess has been adopted from others. Their specialties

are massacres, crucifixion of the helpless. . . . This is the ignorant, half-civilized, barbarous and sinister race which has declared war against the civilized races of the European order to dominate in their place. . . . No greater calamity can overtake the world—not only Europe but the whole civilized world—than that this race should come out of this war victoriously. A victory for the Slav means death to education, constitutionalism, liberalism and free thought. A Slav victory means the obliteration of four centuries of European culture. . . .[9]

Ethnic slurs of this kind and the scratch-a-Slav-and-you-find-a-Tartar insults cut Slavic pride to the quick. (Later, of course, German-Americans would pay dearly for their contempt and scorn for the "natural serf races of Europe.") But in the weeks and months immediately following August 1914 there were few Slavs who were sufficiently bilingual or had the forums to counterattack. It was the Bohemians, the oldest and best positioned of Chicago's Slavs, who first lashed back in English. Asking for "fair play" for the Slavs, the president and secretary of the Bohemian American Press Association noted with bitter irony that, although the Germans asked America for "fair play . . . day by day in the German press the name Slav or Slavic rarely has been mentioned without the adjective barbaric, Asiatic, or at least semi-Asiatic." Stop calling the Slavs "ingrate" and "traitor," protested the Bohemian-American spokesman. They also reminded Germans that Prague had a university long before the Germans discovered formal learning and were still gamboling in the forests dressed in animal skins. Another Bohemian reminded his ethnic antagonists that Chicago's 600,000 Slavs (Bohemians, Poles, Russians, Slovaks, Slovenes, Serbs, Croatians) were fed up with insults.

Into the Teutonic din joined the Hungarians, who arraigned the Slavs with charges of "disloyalty and treason." In a heated meeting at Weiss Hall in the German district, Rev. Eugene A. Vecsey charged that "the attacks of the [Chicago] Slavs on their native land are not only false but traitorous." Slavs were grimly reminded that they were still citizens of Hungary, even though in Chicago, and that "charges of treason and blackmail against the Slavs" would not be dealt with lightly in their homeland.[10]

Although Chicago was far removed from the Western front, the city got some taste of wartime mobilization. Seventy-five German reservists, stranded while waiting for transport to Germany, were performing military exercises on the suburban campus of Elmhurst College (founded by German evangelicals). With the students away on summer leave, the reservists were living in the dormitories and using the campus green as a parade ground and drilling area. Chicago Consul Baron von

Reiswitz had made arrangements for the temporary bivouac there, explaining that an additional 1,000 reservists were stranded up the line in New York waiting for transport ships. The following day, the assistant district attorney informed the Baron that forming military companies to serve a foreign power was a contravention of American law.[11]

The city's Irish were also eager to move into the thick of the fight and punch at John Bull from a safe distance in Chicago. Only slightly chastened by such comic-opera fiascos as the "Fenian invasion" of Canada and other serio-comic attempts to create an international incident to win Irish freedom, Chicago's Irish set off a noisy clatter in behalf of a free Ireland and the Central Powers. The Irish were the single most important ethnic and religious power bloc in Chicago—and a formidable force in politics. The schism that had split the Chicago Irish into firebrands and lace-curtain moderates since 1890 was suddenly healed. The Clan-na-Gael Guards, the United Irish Societies, the Ancient Order of Hibernians, and the Associated Gaelic Clubs worked in harmony at Emmet Hall on Sunday, August 2, recruiting 1,000 men and raising $10,000 to equip them with arms and send them to Ireland to fight for home rule. Emmet Hall on Taylor and Ogden rang with the martial air of an induction center. Rifles were stacked in front and recruiting stations set up outside to accommodate the overflow crowd of 5,000 men, where "impromptu patriots" and sidewalk orators addressed them. Irish flags, pennants, badges, and ribbons snapped smartly in the breeze, bands played, and the "volunteers" with their white caps milled through the crowds. Their goal was to recruit two regiments of fighting men and a corps of physicians and nurses ready and waiting for a "call of help" from Dublin.

Later, on Sunday, August 9, some 5,000 Irish would "volunteer" to fight the good fight should Ireland's John Redmond call. At another scene at the Taylor Street hall, Fran Comerford gave a "rousing" speech that set off a nonstop two-minute clatter of applause when he declared that the "green fields of Ireland would turn red with blood rather than orange in surrender." He continued: "Now is the time to strike. With the nations of the earth embroiled in this continental war we have an opportunity. . . . Now is the time for Ireland to clutch the throat of the British empire and make it vomit out the freedom that belongs by right to the Irish people." Talk of an American Gaelic-Germanic alliance materialized, and in mid-August a German-Irish picnic saw nationalistic speakers "lambasting" England and twisting the lion's tail.[12] In Chicago's multiethnic mosaic, the combination of these two ethnic superpowers, Celt and Teuton, was enough to make any Anglophile quail with trepidation.

The Serbians (then called Servians), who began it all with the assassination of an Austrian archduke, also waded into a Chicago version of the Great War. Although a modest-sized group in numbers, they were vocal. Already on July 27, when Austria was moving to crush Serbia, the ardor of Chicago Serbs reached a flash point. "Back to Servia," shouted a group of young men who started for a downtown steamship office. At Best Hall on July 29, 1,500 Serbs cheered patriotic speeches, shouting "Down with Austria. Long live Servia. To Hell with Austria." A small and poor congregation of Orthodox Serbians who had been meeting in inadequate and cramped quarters and had been "saving pennies" from their meager resources for years to build a new, fitting, and "stately edifice" now faced a crisis. Their homeland was under attack. Their pastor explained that, "although the church will mean a lot to us," they were willing to donate the effort of thirty years (some $40,000) as well as melt down the gold and silver from the holy and sacred church vessels to send to their beleaguered homeland. One Chicago paper captured the essence of a successful Serbian sortie on August 5, 1914 with the headline: "Servians Win Skirmish. Austrian Tavern Demolished." According to Mike Sisel, three Serbians entered his saloon and began noisily mapping out a military campaign against Austria. "Not so much noise," commanded Sisel. "You Austrian dog, we might just as well kill you now before we go to war," the Serbians replied. With that they began to wreck the saloon, smashing mirrors, fixtures, and glass doors. Sisel avoided flying beer bottles by hiding under the bar. When he ran for the police, the Serbians briefly enjoyed the liquid spoils of war and beat a hasty retreat before the police could apprehend them. In nearby Gary, Indiana, fights between Serbs and Austrians became so frequent and troublesome that Gary police had to increase their numbers and ban demonstrations and parades by different nationalities after August 6th to maintain public order.[13]

> *Seigneur, donnez-nous la guerre*
> *universelle qui délivera Pologne,*

wrote Adam Mickiewicz in 1832 after the failure of the abortive Polish revolution. In trying to buoy up sagging Polish spirits, Mickiewicz called for a universal war in the form of a prayer:

> *For a universal war . . .*
> *We beseech Thee, O Lord. . . .*

Chicago's Poles were keenly alert to the historic possibilities that war held out for them. Poland had been wiped off the European landscape by a three-way partition in the eighteenth century by the triple "scourge" of Germany, Austria, and Russia. Poland existed only in the imaginations of Poles, a political fantasy of the past. Chicago Poles felt they were the "saving remnant" and had a very special historic responsibility. If Zionism connotes an irrepressible fervor for a nonexistent homeland, then the Poles were Roman Catholicism's Zionists. They were the "Fourth Part," the American Poles, or rather Poles-in-exile, who had carefully and tenderly looked after the weakly flickering flame of Polish nationalism during the long dark night of oppression. Now the conquerors were fighting among themselves. What an exquisite opportunity. Would the "crucified Christ of nations" be resurrected? The Poles were beside themselves. That August, during a purely religious consecration of a new church, St. Mary of the Angels on North Hermitage and Courtland, 20,000 Poles turned a religious celebration into a massive patriotic demonstration. They and their twenty-three marching bands played and sang over and over again the Polish patriotic hymn "God Save Poland," as an astonished Archbishop Quigley laid and blessed the church cornerstone.[14]

At the center of the "Polish downtown" on Milwaukee Avenue and Division, thousands of Poles gathered under the auspices of the Polish national defense committee to hear about the war, express "sympathy for Servia," and go through a ritual of denouncing her occupiers. In mid-August the Polish National Council advised young Polish males not to answer the Russian worldwide calls for military mobilization and said that Poles should wish a pox on the major warring powers. The Chicago president of the Polish National Alliance, Casimir Zychlinski, condemned the "rapacious vultures" who had torn Poland apart and were now at war with one another. Whom shall we support, he asked, the Muscovite or the "brutal audacious Prussian," who deprived Polish children of their culture and religion and who during the "Kulturkampf" brutally punished Polish children for speaking their mother tongue? The president hoped the "robbers" would bleed themselves to death. He warned: "Soon the hour of retribution will strike on history's clock. . . . Woe to you annexers-executioners, woe!" The Alliance's editor John Przypraws blasted the "rape" and "audacity" of Prussian soldiers in Poland.[15]

By the end of August 1914, the Chicago Symphony Orchestra had had a row, the Pope had died, a shortage of imported beer and cordials appeared imminent, and several of Chicago's best waiters had been inducted into the German Army. Numerous recorded and unrecorded encounters had taken place between warring ethnics, including an ex-German officer who had been bludgeoned into insensibility by five bottle-wielding Russians. Chicago's tiny French community had mustered seventy-five volunteers to fight for the tricolor, and the fighting had spilled over not only into the streets but onto the public school playgrounds. On September 3, Mrs. Ella Flagg, the Chicago school superintendent, had to issue an order to quell fighting by the children of different nationalities on the school playgrounds.

By the end of August, the Chicago Opera Company had cancelled its forthcoming season because most of the soloists were abroad and the Italian Army had inducted almost all of the male section of the chorus. Even the bonds of holy matrimony and conjugal bliss could not withstand the combative national loyalties let loose by the guns of August. A Chicago Frenchman named Gustave Bour got into a spat with his Berlin-born wife, Emma, over the rightful ownership of Alsace-Lorraine. Unable to resolve the conflict, Gustave packed his bags, announced to his wife of three months that he was off to fight for France, and deserted her; distraught Emma appeared in domestic relations court on August 5 to file for a divorce.

No cultural or religious institution seemed exempt from the fevers of war. Clergymen with congregations drawn from ethnics from the Central Powers prayed for German victory, and clergymen with congregations drawn from the Allied Powers prayed for the Allies—or at least for the defeat of the Central Powers. A century of peace and industrial progress that was unmarked by any eventful world wars had dulled men's memories about the horrors of war and had brought about an unhealthy worship of militarism. The Darwinian discovery of the survival of the fittest and flaming nationalism also contributed to the new tolerance of war. The Reverend A. J. Loeppert, pastor of Chicago's Second German Methodist Church, summed up a widespread attitude with his remarks that, although he opposed war generally, "nevertheless, good has providentially come to the race out of the evils of war. Wars have been like devastating storms that purify the atmosphere and drive away the still more deadly pestilence."[16]

Even purely cultural agencies such as Chicago's Symphony Orchestra got deeply ensnarled in the web of wartime politics. The symphony's summer concerts at the sylvan glades of Ravinia rang with discord. Although more than three-fourths of the orchestra was composed of Germans, the French, Belgians, and Russians also made themselves heard. In a mistaken gesture of cosmopolitanism, the conductor scheduled several national songs for a mid-August concert. When the orchestra struck up the stirring martial strains of Tchaikovsky's *1812 Overture*, which musically describes Napoleon's painful retreat from Moscow, the Russian musicians enthusiastically commented on the "glorious significance" of the piece. The only Belgian member of the orchestra winced and gritted his teeth when they swept through the Germanic "Die Wacht am Rhein." Several German musicians played sour notes that produced less than a stirring French "La Marseillaise." Arguments erupted. The French musicians were angered by the Russians' gloating over *1812*: "We are with the Russians in the present war, but why should they gloat over the defeat of the great Napoleon?" According to reporters, the air was "blue" with disharmonious "mon dieus," "Gott in Himmels," and unprintable Russian expletives. "Guttural Germans," "roaring Russians," and "temperamental Frenchmen" quarreled almost to the point of a free-for-all. Internal strife threatened to disrupt the future effectiveness of the orchestra. However, a peace conference was held later, in which members agreed to eliminate all patriotic music of the belligerent nations for the duration of the war.[17] For a while it appeared that Ravinia might possibly become the ethnic Sarajevo and Chicago the Balkan tinderbox of mid-America.

German-American War Effort

The German government had realized the value of propaganda before other nations had and, as University of Chicago's Professor Robert Park pointed out, had conducted systematic and careful studies before the war of their potential belligerents to determine which propaganda techniques and strategies would work best. Both German-American leaders and specialists sent from the fatherland agreed that the whole English political tradition that had taken root in American soil must be attacked on a broad front and, if possible, uprooted. Kaiser Wilhelm's government was fully prepared to carry out such a campaign. Less than two weeks after the war had begun, it sent to the United States (on August 15, 1914) an entourage of thirty-one specialists (in addition to the embassy and consulate personnel already in place), led by Dr. Heinrich Albert and Dr. Bernard Dernburg, with bags bulging with $150,000,000 in German treasury notes to bankroll the campaign.[18]

German-Americans were ideally positioned to aid the pro-German movement. They were the single best-organized nationality group in the nation, with upwards of ten million people with ties to the Central Powers (Harvard's Hugo Munsterberg claimed "German blood" for twenty-five million), and the largest, best-organized, and economically most successful of Chicago's ethnic groups. More than 500 German-language papers were published in the nation, a number that almost equalled the combined total of all other foreign-language papers. German-language newspapers and periodicals sold nearly one million and doubtless reached several times more readers. George Sylvester Viereck's *Fatherland*, which made its debut in mid-August trumpeting Teutonic victories, skyrocketed to 100,000 subscribers before the first month of the war ended. The *Fatherland* was secretly on the German government's payroll (a fact not known in the United States at the time) and for all practical purposes was the North American mouthpiece for the official Berlin line on critical issues of the war. The German-American press generally took its cue from the *Fatherland*, whose editorials were treated as unvarnished truth. Viereck's journal was also published in English to maximize its impact on the non-German element, a clever tactic whose wisdom Chicago Poles and Czechs would recognize and follow three years later.

Some eight million copies of pamphlets and books in support of Germany were turned out during American neutrality under the sub-

The *Fatherland*, the leading pro-German publication in the United States, was secretly subsidized by Berlin and attained a wide readership and influence among German-Americans. *Courtesy of Holime.*

sidy of such groups as Chicago's Germanistic Society. Dozens of distinguished personalities and scholars, such as Harvard's Hugo Munsterberg and Edmund von Mach, Columbia's John Burgess, University of Chicago's Ferdinand Schevill, University of Illinois's Julius Goebel, and Chicago Armour Institute's history professor George W. Scherger (just to name a few) wrote and spoke with vigor on behalf of the German cause. "The first war book to appear, not only in America but the whole western world," rolled off the presses on September 15: *The War and America*, an emotional but eloquent defense of German aggression, written by world-renowned psychologist Munsterberg. Viereck, the Byron of American *Deutschtum* and self-proclaimed "wunderkind," later confided that "the cuckoo of [German] propaganda laid its eggs in every nest."[19]

During the two and one-half years of American neutrality, the German government spent an estimated $35 million to advance the German cause, and the German-Americans must have added millions in manpower, lung power, newspaper publications, embargo rallies, Kaiser festivals, and lobbying and letter writing to Washington. The German movement was not without its measurable effects, for a *Literary Digest* national poll revealed that, despite Germany's brazen violation of Belgian neutrality, 242 of 367 editors queried remained solidly neutral, 20 were favorable to the Central Powers, and only 105 sympathized with the victims of aggression and the Allied powers.[20]

Pacifism, both the genuine nonentangling-alliance-isolationist type and the more openly pro-German or Anglophobic type, were also formidable forces on the American scene (doubly so in Chicago with its large Central Powers and Irish populations), and it proved to be a powerful friend of the overseas German cause. Pacifism was also a deeply rooted belief among American clergymen. Even after the sinking of the passenger liner *Lusitania* in May 1915 by a German submarine and the resulting loss of 128 American lives, a poll of 10,000 clergymen of all denominations revealed that an astounding 95 percent were opposed to even "preparedness" for self-defense or to increasing armaments of the poorly armed and small defense force of the nation.[21] In addition, Stanford President David Starr Jordan, Chicago's Jane Addams, socialist Eugene Debs, and a galaxy of other national spellbinders—for a variety of reasons—opposed war. Even President Woodrow Wilson could not ignore the powerful neutralist sentiment in the nation and was forced to campaign on a platform of "He kept us out of war" to win reelection in 1916.

In short, the struggle for control of American foreign policy pitted a number of powerful and formidable forces against each other, not the least of which was the German-American community. It was a hard-fought, no-holds-barred struggle that dragged on into 1917 with no apparent victor, until a series of colossal German affronts, including the Zimmermann telegram, sank German hopes for neutrality and forced America to take action to defend her interests.

Much of what appeared to be brazen, ruthless, and sometimes even a bizarre effort by German-Americans to undermine and subvert American political and social values and to push the United States in the direction of aiding military autocracies instead of democracies derived from a profound Germanic conviction about the weakness or absence of anything that might seriously be called "American culture." In addition, German-America made it eminently clear by word and behavior that the barefoot, babushka-clad peasant cultures of the "huddled masses" and "wretched refuse" (or what Munsterberg called Balkan "half Kultur") were not serious candidates for transplanting in the New World. German-American National Alliance President Charles Hexamer had belligerently informed his hosts: "We have long suffered the preachment 'you Germans must allow yourself to be assimilated, you must merge more in the American people'; but no one will find us prepared to step down to a lesser culture."[22]

It was, however, at the unveiling in 1914 of the Goethe statue in Chicago that Dr. Hugo Munsterberg enunciated the central proposition that undergirded the entire pro-Germany movement. The famous Harvard professor told Chicagoans what many of them already believed: "We who came from Germany to America are not in a foreign country, because the land was not inherited or guaranteed to a single race of ancient origin. If that had been the case, then we Germans should seek no special liberties. But that is not the case. It was, is yet, the right of the strong to decide which of the immigrated races should exercise the greatest influence here." He added: "America is now our country and Germans must take root here."[23] Munsterberg's formal statement reflected a view widely shared by German-Americans that the United States was simply an "open nation," another Polish Ostmark, Bohemian Sudetenland, or alternately a cultural wasteland to be colonized and culturally conquered.

Two months later, at another statue unveiling in northern New York state, Prof. Munsterberg on August 3 (the eve of the German offensive on Belgium) repeated the "open nation" doctrine even more forcefully. He emphasized that the General von Steuben statue "showed that Germans in America were finally conscious of their position, of their rights in this country, and of their duties to it. Too long they had lived under the illusion that America was an Anglo-Saxon country and that all the other racial stocks were only tolerated as more or less welcome guests. This idea had imposed on them the duty of throwing off their German traits and of imitating the English characteristics. This arbitrary construction has finally been shattered. The German-Americans at last became aware that there are no hosts and guests in this land and that not England but all Europe is the mother country of the American nation." Munsterberg rose to the mountaintops praising "Deutschtum" and the fatherland, but above all rang his prescription "there are no hosts or guests in this land." He assured his German-American auditors that their powerful National Alliance, with its legions of intellectual leaders, its "captains of industry," its farmers and workmen, its young and old would "punish" those who spoke out against Germany in America. Munsterberg drew up his oration to a climactic exclamation: "Since I heard the Watch on the Rhine thundering in the Mohawk Valley I know that twenty-five millions [German-Americans] will take care . . . this powerful American influence cannot back the Allies of Russia. . . ."[24]

Early in 1915, German-American Congressman Richard Bartholdt of Missouri reflected those same views in what was called his "last great speech." Speaking of the nation's paternity, he expounded that "not England alone, but all Europe is its mother, and contributions to the blood which now circulates through the Nation's veins have been made by practically all countries, the largest share next to Great Britain having been contributed by Germany or the States now constituting the German Empire." Bartholdt concluded that "ours was not a readymade nation," but a "nation to be."[25]

The rest of the sometimes bizarre picture puzzle of German-American behavior falls into place once this central premise on which the leaders operated is understood. Without that kind of central assumption, German-American behavior seems impudent, disloyal, and contemptuous of the host culture. With it, German-American behavior, which has no parallel by any other national group, makes more sense.

Munsterberg and the German-American leadership were not alone in their notion that America was a virgin land, a cultural tabula rasa upon which the various nationalities and "races" would write large the cultures of the old world. Although reacting to a different set of arguments, Horace M. Kallen, generally accepted as the nation's chief theoretician of "cultural pluralism," propounded a view that fit hand-in-glove with Munsterberg's German "open society" proposition. Kallen, agitated by arguments of E. A. Ross and H. P. Fairchild that southern and eastern European immigrants were not assimilable, agreed with them but turned their proposition into the basic formulation of "cultural pluralism." Kallen argued in *Nation* magazine (February 25, 1915) that America need not be held to a monolingual standard, for English was to the nation what Latin was to the Roman Empire, the "language of the upper and dominant class, not necessarily the masses or the provinces." Each nationality would have its own emotional life, its own language, and its intellectual forms in a "true federal state . . . a federation or commonwealth of nationalities." Kallen asserted that nationality and ethnicity were an "inalienable right" and that Switzerland with its multiple languages and cultures was the model for the United States to emulate.[26] Kallen's doctrine was not original and was probably part of the general intellectual atmosphere and free-floating thought fragments of the time. Professor Munsterberg has simply anticipated Kallen by six months, and although the Munsterberg line envisioned a double-barreled and fractured cultural pluralism where Teuton and Anglo-Saxon held sway, the basic assumption was the same: no single ethno-linguistic stock could lay clear cultural claim to America; it was an "open society" up for grabs.

Chicago's German-Americans began to broadcast the Munsterberg doctrine and continued their agitation for compulsory German language in the public schools, but with a new twist added by the war. The *Abendpost* warned German parents to put their children into German-language elementary classes in the Chicago schools,

> because the German language is destined to become the world language, and that he who does not master it to some degree, will suffer economic disadvantage. . . . If not yet today, the German language surely is bound to become the second language of the land and the world language in the near future . . . it would be advisable to start with German in the first grade, to make this instruction general in all Chicago schools and to put it on equal footing with English![27]

The publication of Illinois Professor Goebel's book *Kampf um Deutsche Kultur in Amerika* also won favor with German-American cultural leaders because it stated the same basic proposition that "German culture and the German spirit are competing in the United States with the culture and ideology of other nations," and to make the influence of the former powerful was the duty of every German-American. A German "working girl" in Chicago who confessed in print that "I have read nothing but German newspapers, although I have been in this country thirty-four years," asserted: "We have reason to be proud of Germany—a country that will soon be the first in the world." With the tide of military victory running in Germany's direction, her delusions of grandeur did not seem unreasonable. By December 1914, German Chicago was bathing in the frothy and heady emotion of successes on the battlefield, and Chicago Germans were more convinced than ever of "a final victory of German arms, which will usher in the German era."[28]

During the closing days of 1914, Professor Eugen Kuehnemann of the University of Breslau said: "The Germans in Chicago must also do their share of the fighting during this great World War. . . . This war is not only being fought with guns and cannon but is even more a clash of the minds and ideologies of people, with the civilization of mankind as the prize." Two years later, during a large Chicago celebration of Emperor Wilhelm's birthday, Professor Kuehnemann sketched the basis of a "German World Power," stretching from the Baltic Sea to the Red Sea to India and boasted that "the German soldier has shown that he is the carrier of true civilization and culture."[29]

The increasing linkage of German culture to German military victory proved to be costly and dangerous for German-Americans. The *Abendpost* had on occasion chortled: "It is a wonderful thing that the war . . . has revived the loyalty and patriotism of German-Americans of the second and third generation." On December 10, 1914, Chicago's Rabbi Emil G. Hirsch was greeted with enthusiastic applause when in a Chicago hall he declaimed: "Our hopes are with those German and Austro-Hungarian soldiers in the trenches over there. . . . If you win, the best there is in the human race will have also won, and with you, the German element of America." Hirsch blasted the Russians for the alleged "raping of Jewish girls, the murder of the little babe at the mother's breast, those were the blessings of the House of Romanov." Hirsch then defended the German political system and elevated the humble foot soldier to lofty heights with his comment that the "German Army is the incarnation of loyal fulfillment of duty, and therefore upholds Kant's philosophy." Dr. Bernard Dernburg then spoke in defense of German violation of Belgium's neutrality, and the hall was filled with three cheers for Germany, Austria, and Hungary, "Hurrah, Hurrah, Hurrah," and the "cheering reverberated throughout the huge auditorium like thunder."[30]

German foot soldiers who exemplified Immanuel Kant's philosophy and Russian brutes who raped civilized women—that was the stuff German-American editors in Chicago reveled in telling. The leaders pointed out again and again that the influence of German "Kultur" rode on the outcome of the war in Europe. Gustav Ohlinger correctly perceived the intimate linkage: "With Germany's victory the prestige of that element would be augmented; with her defeat Germanism in the United States would inevitably succumb."[31] Indeed, German victory would be their triumph and would bring honor and public esteem long overdue the fatherland and German-America.

German-Americans failed to draw a distinction between intrinsic

German culture and the German Empire of Wilhelm II. Perhaps there was no distinction to be drawn. "Kultur" had different German and American meanings. Professor Munsterberg, in a long essay published in 1915, puzzled about the nature and character of German "Kultur." What is German culture? he asked. "Was the burning of Louvain and the cannonading of Rheims cathedral" German culture? His answer was yes. "Kultur" was not the culture of a gentleman or merely the learned arts. "Kultur" was the sum total of all national life forms, including scientific, political, economic, social, artistic, and even military. He concluded that "the German army is the strongest expression of the moral national will to fulfill the ethnical mission of Germany, and in this sense is indeed an embodiment of German Kultur." The German destruction of the cultural treasures of Louvain, Munsterberg concluded, was not a contradiction of German "Kultur." Most Midwesterners thought culture meant the arts and humanities and high literary and musical expression. They had particular difficulty understanding the meaning of German culture and were often perplexed because German-American remarks on culture usually started and ended with a reference to German military efficiency. Consequently, noted a Hoosier writer wryly, "when a German talked of Kultur he first cocked his pistol."[32]

Clearly, something had gone wrong in the German-American process of assimilation. Perhaps it was a failure of leadership, as one scholar suspected; but the problem also seemed more profound. German history had exerted a peculiar twist on modern German character, and that made itself felt upon German-America as well. "Sleepy Michael," the age-old self-parody of the Germanies, was replaced both in cartoon and popular thought by the Iron Chancellor Bismarck and the "blood and iron" of militarism, enhanced by spectacular military victories in the 1860s and 1870s. War had been the midwife of German nationalism, and that had unfortunately influenced its Chicago counterpart. The coming of age of Chicago's Germania had coincided with that key, fatal period. German music, science, philosophy, and technology now had to make way for the fourth horseman of Prussian militarism, adding the spike-helmeted warriors of imperial Germany to the pantheon of German "Kultur." Consequently, German-Americans took increasing pride in the growth of Germany into a world power. Even "Forty-eighters," who had fled the kind of autocracy that Bismarck and Wilhelm fostered, mellowed and basked in the reflected glory of the new German Empire.[33] Some of the tragedy of German history would be played out in America—and Chicago.

Triumphant German militarism, when combined with the widespread Teutonic view that America lacked a culture worthy of the name and was an open society upon which was to be writ large the superior Teutonic culture, was a combustible mix that sometimes led to bizarre, contradictory, and contemptuous actions by elements of the German-American community. Although many of the most rabid German chauvinists realized by 1917 that they had gone too far in expressing their contempt for their host culture and nation, it was then too late. Not only would Americanizers raise the standard of cultural war, but they would be aided by the fierce determination of the Chicago Slavs, who were more than ready to even up old scores and right the wrongs of their own histories.

When the British passenger liner *Lusitania* was sunk by a German submarine in May 1915, killing 128 Americans, the German-American press faithfully defended the fatherland's actions. Chicago's *Abendpost* warned that the sinking should teach Americans a "lesson"—that when Germany spoke, she meant business. When President Wilson protested the loss of American lives and the acts of war against a passenger ship, Chicago's German-American press lacerated and reprimanded the American government for what it called an "unfriendly" and "insulting" attitude toward Germany. Wilson's diplomatic notes on behalf of the American victims against the German aggressors somehow struck German-American editors as "unsportsmanlike" and "unfair"; after all, the victims had not heeded German warnings, got their just deserts, and "now sleep in their eternal sleep in a watery grave."[34] The tendency to blame the victims and not the aggressors had, since the Belgian neutrality violations, hardened into standard editorial policy by Chicago's Teutonic press.

Other events also occurred, and, though they cannot be laid completely at the feet of German-American chauvinists, it is not likely that they could have happened without the public encouragement of a vitriolic and often rabidly intemperate (sometimes anti-American) German-American press. The botched attempt by a German-born, self-styled anarchist to poison Cardinal Mundelein in 1916 shocked not only Chicago but the entire nation. (It was an awesome reminder of an event that occurred in New York only a year earlier, when a bomb-throwing, pistol-firing, deranged Germanophile and former Harvard professor tried to kill J. P. Morgan on the fourth of July, reportedly to try to stop loans to the British.) Although the evidence in the Mundelein poisoning is incomplete, it appears that there may be some connection to German-American hopes for another spokesman that came to naught when Mundelein, a third-generation German-American, nicknamed "old Dutch cleanser," became archbishop of Chicago in 1916. Pressured to speak to his ancestral kinfolk, Mundelein curtly replied: "I shall not speak to

A SILENT COMPANY—Yet its voice is heara above the roar of Cannon.

The sinking of the British passenger liner *Lusitania* in 1915 with the loss of 128 Americans was shrilly defended by the German-American press—especially Chicago's *Abendpost*, which warned that the sinking should teach Americans that when Germany spoke she meant business. *Courtesy of* AMERICA'S BLACK AND WHITE BOOK, 1917.

the Germans as Germans. I have no separate message for any particular nationality."[35] Mundelein refused to support purely German and Austrian relief efforts, and on one occasion reprimanded a group of fatherland zealots for listing the archbishop as a sponsor without his permission. Mundelein made it crystal clear to German-Americans such as Dr. Otto L. Schmidt that he would not support "milk funds" and children's relief that benefited only the Central Powers; he insisted that the other victims of war, such as Polish and Bohemian children, had to be helped also. Needless to say, Chicago's German relief leaders were not about to help the enemy, and such efforts to include Mundelein fizzled. Whether Chicago's crazed anarchist was reacting to Mundelein's cold shoulder or some other slight is not known. In any event, at a dinner held at the University of Chicago for the archbishop, he dumped arsenic into the soup, felling more than one hundred, all of whom were rushed to the hospital and saved. According to *Chamberlin's*, the whole party was saved only because the "crazy cook," in his overzealousness, put in so much poison that the soup turned grey, warning his intended victims by its vile color and taste.[36] What were Chicagoans to think, with German-born assassins in the headlines trying to shoot or poison leading Americans?

German-American aggressiveness was not confined to editors, policy-makers, or saboteurs; it also made its impact felt on the lives of ordinary workaday Chicagoans on the street. In 1915, U.S. Congressman Bartholdt had told German-Americans to stop "creeping around in gum-shoes" and to "put on jack-boots instead" and make themselves heard; and indeed they had. Karol Wachtel, reviewing German-American behavior in a Chicago movie house, was shocked by the applause when newsreels showed zeppelin attacks on civilians or other displays of German military might, or made references to submarine sinkings such as that of the *Lusitania*. Wachtel told the readers of Chicago's *Free Poland* that he could not understand the "bullying insolence of German-Americans in their furious ill-will toward Washington," solely because the United States refused to direct its foreign policy toward Germany's self-interest. He warned that "Germans have developed a gigantic campaign hostile to the government of the United States," and that no other nationality had succeeded in organizing such an effort on behalf of a belligerent overseas power. Wachtel deplored how German-American audiences

> applauded the dreadful and sorrowful pictures of war; when the film showed the fallen enemy, or when the German soldiers derisively led throngs of harassed prisoners of war. We heard them laugh when the film showed a group of Germans in the act of stealing the only cow of a poor Polish family, the woman surrounded by her children, tearfully mourning her loss. . . . But the soldiers laughing and having milked the cow, they lap this precious fluid to the accompaniment of the weeping of the mother and her children. And the German-Americans, evidently considering this act a huge stroke of humor, burst out with laughter until their hands are well-nigh swollen with repeated clapping. They continued their thunderous applause at the sight of a tragic procession of fugitives from Warsaw—where on one hay-wagon was shown the cold corpse of a child in its mother's arms, where there were seen barefooted, tattered and hungry boys, standing in the nasty weather of autumn and gazing at German armored automobiles. There you see looming up the spectre of terror, tears, famine, death; and here they almost shout applause.

And then on the screen appeared the "Prince of Peace, Wilhelm II": "Germans are no more German-Americans, no more fellow citizens, rise from their seats and do homage in acclamations, guttural vociferations, and deafening applause, and this happening in this country. . . ." Wachtel closed his review and then closed his eyes asking: "We listen, we rub our eyes, then clench our fists. Is this Berlin or Chicago?"[37]

Throughout the tension-filled winter of 1917, the German-American press continued its strong pro-fatherland line. When the German government announced unrestricted submarine warfare in February 1917, it was met with a war whoop of joy. "The iron ring around British rascality and brutality is closed," Chicago's *Staats-Zeitung* announced. "Deprived of the munitions and raw materials coming from over the sea, cut off from the bread-furnishing countries . . . the population of England will have to die in six months" or surrender. A few days later the same paper warned Americans to stay out of the "European holocaust," otherwise a war of the races might break out here in America.[38] The release of the famous Zimmermann telegram on March 1, 1917, provoked widespread denunciation of the message as a "British forgery" by the German-American press, including Chicago's feisty *Staats-Zeitung*. The German foreign minister, Count Arthur Zimmermann, had proposed, in the event of war, an alliance with Mexico in which Germany would finance Mexico's efforts to take the "lost territories" of the Southwest. Mexico was also to urge Japan to switch to the German side. German-Americans doubted that the fatherland would plot with Mexico to stir up trouble in America's backyard; but when Zimmermann, a few days later, admitted to having sent the telegram, the German-American press fell into apoplectic silence. The telegram sank any remaining hope that the United States could continue to remain neutral, for as the expert on that question, Barbara Tuchman, put it: "The Prussian invasion plot . . . was as clear as a knife in the back and as near as next door. Everybody understood it in an instant. . . . It was the Prussian boot planted upon our border." The telegram not only "killed" the American illusion of neutrality but cut short the cacophony of conflicting views on how America should react to the crisis: the *Literary Digest*, in its summary of the nation's press for March 17, entitled its story "How Zimmermann United the United States."[39]

But Zimmermann had not united one powerful element, for German-Americans were still ready to fight a last-ditch battle to prevent war with their ancestral homeland. Even as the clock was running down on peace in late March, the fiery *Staats-Zeitung* continued its virulent attack on those opposed to the Central Powers, calling them "crooks," "pseudo-patriots, pharisees, and hypocrites," and "war-like adventurers," and defending the German position. On the eve of war,

April 1, 1917, Chicago's Germans sent a delegation of twenty-five on a "protest special" to Washington to fight against the declaration of war. Even though numerous German-American congressman, including six from Illinois, argued and voted no, the declaration for war against Germany passed. Chicago Congressman and Germanophile Fred Britten predicted that with that declaration a "war of races would break out in our midst."[40] None did.

There was no great groundswell of German-Americans lining up for a chance to kill their kinfolk in the old country. It had been an article of faith with German-Americans that war with the fatherland was "unthinkable" and impossible. Yet suddenly it happened. The emotional cross pressures that surged through German hearts and minds must have been volcanic and explosive; Germans must have been torn to pieces emotionally. We do have the record of one talented German-American for whom the war was too much to bear, that of Dr. Ernest Kunwald, conductor of the Cincinnati Symphony Orchestra. On the evening that Wilson sent his war message to Congress, the Cincinnati Orchestra decided to proceed with its scheduled concert and bowed to a special request from Washington to open the evening with "The Star-Spangled Banner." Kunwald led the orchestra through the national anthem and then turned to the audience with tears streaming down his cheeks and defiantly announced: "But my heart is on the other side."[41] Thousands must have wept with Kunwald that night in the German-American communities across the land.

Chicago's symphony orchestra conductor read the riot act to his German members, sternly warning them that if they stepped out of line on the loyalty issue or made thoughtless "subversive" remarks, he would personally turn them in to the authorities. Later in 1918, German-born conductor Frederick Stock took a leave from the orchestra to obtain his naturalization papers.[42]

The German Missouri Synod Lutheran Church, with its large Chicago and Illinois membership, adjusted very poorly to the war. Missouri Lutherans, who regarded themselves as the "highest cultured people" and a cut above the American crowd, had been vocal Anglophobes and fierce defenders of "Deutschtum" and the war acts of the fatherland. War against the "land of Luther" stunned Missourians, and they displayed a painful ambivalence toward the American war effort. They refused, for example, to permit Liberty loan literature to circulate in the Synod's churches. One prominent Lutheran observer lamented that the "air was pregnant with disaster. And some of our blind people are still dreaming of the day to come when the Germans of our country will come out on top and tell the Yankees what fools they were for entering the war. . . ." Finally, out of fear that their pro-German views might endanger the whole church, synod leaders relented, and on Christmas Day, 1917, they issued a statement of support for the American war effort. Still, that was not enough to satisfy the Americanizers, and the church came under vitriolic attack and painful denunciation for its widespread use of the German language and alleged disloyalty. Outward signs of rejection by the larger American community and the already seething contempt the Slavs expressed toward what hitherto had been regarded one of the most favored and highly regarded immigrant nationalities in America was a soul-searing experience for Missourians, an experience from which they never fully recovered. For Chicago's first-generation Missourians, the war was "Gotterdammerung," and, as Dean Kolhoff so poignantly put it, they withdrew into a "siege and fortress mentality."[43]

Early into the war, German-Americans worked hard to exempt their brethren from military conscription for combat service. Congressman Fred A. "Pop Gun" Britten, from Chicago's German North Side, was one of the leading spokesmen. A former lightweight boxing champ, Pop Gun was known to be "quick on his feet," had a "fast jab," and a flair for publicity, which he had enhanced by demanding that ocean liner menus be printed in English instead of French and by attacking France's use of African troops against Germany. Although an Irishman, he palmed himself off as a German to Chicago voters, opposed the sale of munitions to the Allies, tried to delay the war resolution with amendments, and voted against the final declaration. He then proposed amendments to the draft act to exempt men of German descent from military conscription for overseas duty. "Those Americans who still have fresh warm blood ties applying to their relatives in Germany, Austria, or Hungary" should not be asked to bear arms against the enemy Central Powers, he argued.[44] Britten's amendment to exempt German-Americans from combat duty struck native-born Americans as well as many naturalized citizens as a flagrant evasion of responsibility by newcomers. Others saw it as evidence that the German side of the German-American hyphen was more important than the American.

Equally troublesome and adding to the sources of misunderstanding and distrust was a defective Selective Service Law, which placed a disproportionately heavy burden on the native-born and naturalized for fighting the war. The act based apportionment of quotas on the total population yet drew its conscripts from citizens and declarants-to-be-citizens. In some districts, where the alien population exceeded 30 or even 40 percent of men who were exempt, native-born families had to shoulder an extra heavy burden in providing sons and fathers for the Army. Although this unfair law was amended in December 1917 to apportion quotas more equally, it still did not get to the problem of draft-exempt enemy aliens or "allied with the enemy" aliens. The draft-exempt class in Illinois alone reached an astonishing 252,000, or 26 percent of the state's total registration of 1,574,000. In some districts, where enemy alien males comprised the overwhelming work force on the home front, serious questions were raised by superpatriots—as well as sensible ones—who worried about the security of defense-related installations.[45] By the end of the war it became clear, however, that the overwhelming majority of Germans posed no threat to their adopted land. But by that time it was too late to undo some of the damage wrought by wartime hysteria.

Adding to the fears of some Americans was the indiscreet, arrogant, and garrulous German foreign minister, Arthur Zimmermann, who during the *Lusitania* crisis berated the American ambassador, pounded the table in a rage, and threatened that 500,000 German-American males of draft age (who were technically considered to be reservists in the German Army) "will rise in arms against your government if your gov-

A widely circulated cartoon during World War I shows how terrifying the German submarines were to Americans. *Courtesy of* AMERICA'S BLACK AND WHITE BOOK, 1917.

A good recruiting sergeant for Uncle Sam.

ernment should dare take action against Germany." Ambassador James Gerard, thoroughly annoyed by the overbearing and pompous Zimmermann, snapped back that the United States had 501,000 lampposts and that is where German reservists would find themselves dangling if they tried an uprising. More level-headed Germans later saw the errors of such policies. The German ambassador in Washington, Count Johann von Bernstorff, admitted after the war that the "question of the German-American was never dealt with tactfully in Germany. Our greatest mistake was to expect too much from them."[46] Indeed, having "expected too much from them" in shaping American policy toward Germany had helped to mislead hundreds of German chauvinists into perilous positions where their loyalty was questioned.

Much additional damage was done to the German-American reputation by a harebrained sabotage campaign got underway in 1915 which landed dozens of German-Americans and German nationals in jail and resulted in the expulsion of the Austrian ambassador, Constantin Dumba, the German military and naval attachés, and several civilian commercial representatives. Dumba set up an intrigue to foment strikes and labor turmoil in American munitions factories by threatening both German and Slavic subjects of the Austrian Empire with the charge of "high treason" if they worked in factories that sold to the Allies. President Wilson had Dumba recalled to Austria in 1915. A quartet of others working out of the German consulate office in New York, and with a Hamburg steamship line, planted firebombs in the holds of Allied vessels, triggered and subsidized strikes by longshoremen to hamper Allied shipping, and attempted to corner critical strategic supplies in the United States. They were all expelled.[47]

The harum-scarum and fumbling efforts to blow up railroad bridges connecting the United States and Canada, the Welland Canal, and in other ways to commit acts of war on neutral soil intended to hurt the Allies filled newspaper headlines and spread the fear of German intrigue and subversion. The mysterious explosions in many newly started munitions factories, many of which could have been accidental, added to the widespread general concern about the German contempt for American neutrality. Chicago was shaken by the so-called "Hindu Conspiracy" during the summer of 1917, which resulted in the imprisonment of the publicly visible German-American leader Gustav Jacobsen and three others for conspiring against the neutrality of the United States by clandestinely shipping arms to trigger an uprising in India against the British.[48] The German government's complicity in most of these cases was established after the war. The military value of such campaigns was dubious at best and only served to cast even more suspicion on German-Americans.

When seen from the distance of a half-century, German sabotage efforts seem to be bumbling, ineffectual, and even comic in their incompetence. (The key German operative, Dr. Heinrich Albert, for example, fell asleep on an elevated train in New York City and left behind his briefcase filled with vital information identifying plots, plotters, and payoffs, which was found by the British secret service and released with great sensation to the American press.) It is hard to fathom why the same minds that created such a superior science and war technology for Germany were capable of such incompetence when it came to subversion and espionage.

One unfortunate side effect of this has been the fashion among some historians to dismiss American fears of German and Austrian intrigue as pure, unalloyed war hysteria and patriotic poppycock with little or no substance. However, anyone who looks carefully at the record can see that that was not the case. There was indeed a great

Some solid evidence and even more false rumors of German and Austrian sabotage contributed to the wartime concern about the loyalty of enemy aliens. *Courtesy of* AMERICA'S BLACK AND WHITE BOOK, 1917.

Just whose pet snake is this?

deal of real substance and evidence of large-scale German intervention in the American war economy. What was discovered was believed by Americans to be only the tip of the iceberg and, although later evidence would show they had overestimated the threat, it helps to account for some of the anti-Hun fears, the "keystone cops" attempts at spy-catching, and widespread war hysteria that swept the nation.

Slavic Response

Champing at the bit and waiting for the "hour of retribution" to strike "on history's clock" were Chicago's Slavs and other subject races. On that fateful April 1, 1917, Chicago's *Free Poland* boldly informed Teutonia that "the days of wholesale slander and aspersion cast upon the Slavs . . . are over." Three years earlier, the Polish editor of *Dziennik Zwiazkowy* had warned his German antagonists: "Woe to you annexers-executioners woe!" And woe it would be to the German-American defenders of the fatherland.

Poles and Czechs and other members of the "natural serf races" and their descendants in Chicago were latecomers to the propaganda battle; but once they began, they conducted a successful and sometimes even sophisticated campaign to liberate their homelands and to smear the Kaiser and his backers. That the Czechs and Poles would lead the "subject nationalities" seemed natural. For Chicago was the second largest Polish city in the world, the home of the Polish Roman Catholic Union and the Polish National Alliance. American Poles also viewed Chicago's *Polonia* as the "metropolis" that led and set the style for the "provinces," like Milwaukee, Buffalo, Detroit, and the outer settlements. Chicago was also the second most populous Bohemian city (only Prague being ahead of it) and the home of the Bohemian National Alliance, the Czech Rationalist movement, a center of Czech publishing, and the social and intellectual center around which the social life of Czechs in America was organized.[49]

Stung by the verbal assault, racial defamation, and insult unleashed by Germans since 1914 (e.g., "half-Asiatic barbarian," "half Tartar, ingrate, half-Kultured peasant"), Chicago Slavs were ready to strike back measure for measure. Slavs were not only trying to settle scores for the abuse in Chicago and America but also for the oppression they had put up with as the "hewers of wood and drawers of water"—the *untermenschen* folk of Europe. Like thousands of others, they would work out their anxieties and past frustrations in an American setting in Chicago.

Chicago's Poles and Czechs were initially under German influence, and during the beginning of the war they frequently followed the German pattern in their publications of using "fatherland" to describe the ethnolinguistic areas from which they originated. The Germans, however, put in an early claim on *Fatherland*, copyrighting the title for one of the most successful propaganda journals, begun in mid-August 1914. The use of the term "motherland" to describe their ancestral home practically disappeared from German-American publications. Indeed, "fatherland" increasingly described the realm of the peak-helmeted, jack-booted warriors of Kaiser Wilhelm both in Germany and America. "Fatherland" also became surrounded by a cluster of unpleasant connotations—"nurse killer, despoiler of Louvain, pillager and violator of Belgium, and ruthless executioner of civilian hostages." As the war ground on, Chicago Slavs began consciously to avoid the word "fatherland" and to rely increasingly on the less bellicose and more pacific symbol "motherland." In addition, the feminine symbolization of the homeland by "mother" seemed a better fit for the victim states such as Belgium, France, Poland, and Bohemia. "Mother Russia" also resonated well in pan-Slavic ears. Finally, Anglophile Americans referred to England as the "mother country," never the "fatherland." Chicago's Slavic editors appeared to shrewdly discern these important differences and added "motherland" to the arsenal of symbols used to fight the "Boche" and win American support for freedom for their homelands.[50] (Perhaps George Creel took lessons from the Chicago Slavs.)

They also conspicuously drew away from describing themselves in a manner that might label them "hyphenated Americans." Hyphenated Americans came under growing public criticism from Theodore Roosevelt and others on the national scene for their alleged divided loyalties. It is a mistake, however, to assume, as some historians have, that hyphenated Americans included all those of European ancestry, because they did not. Even the most rabid Americanizer, Teddy Roosevelt, exempted Greek-Americans because of their illustrious history. In the national context, as Professor John Higham has so clearly observed, "behind the hyphenated American was the German-Americans' perceived disloyalty." No one was overly concerned about hyphenated Lithuanian-Americans or Bohemian-Americans and their hoped-for small, inoffensive republics in eastern Europe; but they were concerned about German-Americans as representatives of an autocratic superpower. In Chicago, "hyphenated American" increasingly meant German-American. Chicago's Poles and Bohemians wanted no mistakes in the matter and were determined to set the record straight. "Bang! Goes The Hyphen!" claimed a Chicago Bohemian position paper published in English in 1914. "There are no Bohemian-Americans," only "Americans of Bohemian extraction . . . we owe no divided allegiance." In an exposition entitled "The Polish Hyphen," Chicago's *Free Poland* explained flatly that there was none, and that if Polish-sounding names turned up in disloyal activities, they were probably German or "Moscovite."[51]

The embargo question and neutrality were heated issues that involved all belligerent nationals and ethnics in Chicago. Central Powers rooters raucously supported an embargo on munitions sales to the British and French, and Slavic ethnics and pro-Allied nationals vehemently opposed it. With secret financing from the German government, Chicago's Germans organized and prosecuted a vigorous national embargo movement from 1915 to 1917. Three major conferences were convened, and each year numerous peace rallies were held, relief to Central Powers fund raisers, Kaiser Bill birthday celebrations, Franz Joseph and Bismarck festivals, German Day conclaves, antipreparedness rallies, and in the end antidraft meetings. The embargo on the U.S. sale of war materiel and strategic supplies was, however, the key effort. Chicago's Germans were less interested in keeping their adopted land neutral than in helping their ancestral homeland. When it became clear that Britannia ruled the waves—or as Chicago Teutons put it, "Britannia waives the rules"—and could interdict high-seas surface commerce to Germany, German-Americans then rallied strongly to halt sales to the Allies. In a gala German-Irish rally at Chicago's Bush Temple in December 1914, German-American Congressman Henry Vollmer made crystal clear the motivation behind support of the embargo. "If we refrain from helping the Allies, Germany will defeat this motley gang within three months," he told a wildly applauding crowd that rocked the rafters with its thunderous mass choruses of "Mother Machree" and "Die Wacht am Rhein."[52]

In April 1915 the German government achieved a major propaganda coup, with a large secret payoff of $205,000 to buy up news copy of the American Foreign Language Press Association to push the German embargo line. The message to stop munitions sales to the Allies was broadcast in editorials, features, news items, and other "canned" news to 800 newspapers in thirty languages with an estimated readership of eighteen million. During the summer of 1915 in Chicago, the American Embargo Conference opened a well-financed national office and unleashed a flood of petitions and communications to halt munitions sales. In April of the following year the Chicago office blitzed Congress with 250,000 telegrams and would ultimately be responsible for five million messages sent to Washington, for which the German government paid most of the tolls. Evidence that came to light after the war would show that the embargo groups, the Chicago Friends of Peace, the League of Women for Strict Neutrality, and several other "peace" groups had been generously subsidized by the German government.[53]

The Friends of Peace staged their first big event September 5–7, 1915, in Chicago. Mysteriously, many public personalities received offers of free transportation to the conference. Responding to a widespread suspicion of the time—that the conference was intended to serve the purposes of the Central Powers—several of the proposed resolutions to be acted on were toned down. Still, the strong embargo message came through. William Jennings Bryan, formerly the "bumbling nemesis" of German-America, Anglophobe and professional Irishman Jeremiah O'Leary, and a squad of German-Americans appeared as guest speakers. Samuel Gompers, social gospeler Washington Gladden, the Chicago Peace Society, and the socialists stayed away. Gompers and organized labor suspected that the Chicago group had motives other than simon-pure American neutrality. And their suspicions were confirmed when during the conference the announcement that a Central Powers submarine had torpedoed an Allan Line steamer was met with applause and cheers—and then with cries of "shame!"[54] The spontaneous audience reaction was unsettling to the conference sponsors, who had hoped to mask the partisan purpose of the meeting. Bryan was embarrassed by the spectacle, for he may have been one of the few conferees who supported an embargo for purely American considerations.

Picking up the gauntlet of "false neutrality," Chicago's Bohemians boldly announced in 1915 that they were "utterly and absolutely opposed" to any embargo on the shipment of arms and ammunition. They argued that such action was "highly unneutral" and tantamount to "hostility" against the victim nations fighting the "aggression of the German and Austrian government," who had a "record of unparalleled and unequalled oppression" against the Slavs. An embargo would reward the aggressors, such as the Hapsburg Empire, which "was dripping with the blood of Bohemian martyrs." A munitions embargo would directly help the Central Powers, since they had prepared for war and the Allies had not. The Chicago-Bohemian position paper boiled with indignation: "We condemn severely this hypocritical agitation because it is plainly intended to secure to Germany and Austria permanently the advantage of their long continued preparation for war and thus handicap" the Allies and victims who had not. As "loyal American citizens . . . we endorse the principle of free export of all our products, agricultural and industrial, including the munitions of war, a principle long recognized by international law . . ." and denounce "false neutrality."[55]

Chicago's Polonia joined the Bohemians in blasting the embargo agitation and drew itself into a towering rage, hurling Old Testament fire and brimstone at the peace movement and the "peace at any price" people. Chicago's leading Polish Catholic daily, *Dziennik Zwiazkowy*, deplored the "pacifistic orgy" and the "effeminate doctrinaires" who served "Teutonic propaganda"; the editor poured vials of wrath on the "mad antics" of such "apostles of national cowardice" as William Jennings Bryan and "simple minded little women of the type of . . . Jane Addams." The Chicago Polish Women's Alliance joined the Polish National Council in condemning "peace at any price" in a long and passionate defense of letting the war run its course. "Peace without reparations of wrongs . . . peace without doing justice . . . peace regardless of oceans of blood and tortures . . .—such a peace would be a new crime of nations and an everlasting shame on civilization. . . . Poland to-day is like Lazarus thrown on the bed of blood, fire, and embers—murdering her own children by order of her enemies. . . . We the daughters of this downtrodden, blood bespattered unhappy country do raise our mighty voice of mothers, daughters, sisters, and wives . . . against all peace action."[56] The moral outrage of Chicago's Polonia was repeated day after day, week after week through 1915, 1916, and into 1917, when it sent up a war cry of jubilation when America moved to smite the "Beast of Berlin" and thereby "liberate" the Slavs from Teutonic thralldom.

When Americans began their national debate on "preparedness" in 1916, Chicago's Poles were already ahead of them and eager to jump in and share the bitter lessons of their history with their adopted land. *Chicago Daily News* reporter and Polish-American spokesman Anthony Czarnecki told the Association of Commerce that Poland had lost her independence because she was insufficiently prepared to fight. The moral lesson was that "preparedness would have saved Poland," added Czarnecki, and that the United States should be prepared to defend itself. "We repeat," added Chicago's *Free Poland*, "the defenseless Republic of Poland was conquered by its neighbors armed to the teeth. Poland became the first of the great victims of pacifism in history." Ignace Paderewski, the talented impresario and musician, delivered one of his many eloquent and passionate speeches in behalf of the deliverance of Poland, in which he warned of the dire consequences for those who did not gird their loins to fight. In a powerful and evocative speech in the Chicago Auditorium, the maestro attributed Poland's downfall to a lack of preparedness. "Poland fell because her enemies were numerous, greedy, and unscrupulous! Poland fell because she was generous, trustful, and weak! Poland fell because she had no permanent army to defend her possessions!" His Chicago audience was deeply moved as Paderewski shouted out his climaxes in a voice that shook with emotion. "What is Poland now?" he asked. "It is a vast desert, an immense ruin, a colossal cemetery. It is dead, fallen." That was the price of unpreparedness, warned the great pianist. Chicago Poles bubbled with advice, and *Free Poland* beseeched Americans to heed the lessons of history: "Preparedness, then, is an old issue. America will do well to study the history of Poland, an object lesson in preparedness or rather the lack thereof."[57]

As American entry into the war approached, the *Bohemian Review*, in a statement entitled "Where We Stand To-day," quoted the "fire-eater" abolitionist Wendell Phillips and stormed: "The bloodiest war ever waged is infinitely better than the happiest slavery." And the *Review* made it eminently clear that Czech subordination under the German heel was not the "happiest." Chicago's Poles, in the process of rewriting, reworking, and polishing a position in two languages, arrived at a formulation that fit the occasion perfectly. "America's cause is the cause of freedom and freedom is the cause of Poland," blurted *Free Poland*. That formula helped to hammer an inseparable link between Polonia and America. In addition, the collapse of Czarist Russia in March 1917 removed any last obstacle from Polonia's wholehearted support of the Allied war effort. When the United States declared war, Polonia hummed with excitement and then exploded with "jubilation," for as Dr. Stanley Pliska observed, "If Poland was unable to ride high to victory herself, she at least could come in on the baggage trains of victorious Allied armies"—as she once did in the days of Napoleon. Out of Chicago's newsstands poured "extras" and "specials" in a multiplicity of languages that were greedily snatched up and sold out. The city's "fierce anti-German" Polish daily, *Dziennik Zwiazkowy*, poured fuel on the igniting flames of anti-German "hysteria." With a biblical sense of retribution, the editor called for a "holy war" against the Hun and also against the "degenerate outcasts," the "Prussophiles," and pro-German apologists on the home front. The day after Wilson sent his war message to Congress, Chicago's Czech spokesmen were vying with each other for the best prescription for the destruction of Austria: some said it should be "partitioned," others that it should be cauterized off the face of the earth like a poisonous abscess, but all agreed that "Austria must perish." Later in December, when the United States declared war on the Czech oppressor, the Austro-Hungarian Empire, Chicago Bohemians welcomed the act with "boundless enthusiasm."[58]

A flurry of loyalty and disloyalty testimonials followed, with Chicago Slavs publicly professing fealty to their adopted land while discerning sinister influences among Central Powers ethnics. Chicago's

Chicago's Bohemians, who opposed neutrality, welcomed the war as an opportunity not only to demonstrate their complete loyalty to their adopted land, the United States, but also to strike out against the Germans and Austrians and to win freedom for their homeland. *Courtesy of Holime.*

Polish press had been warning since 1915 that Germans everywhere put loyalty to the "Vaterland" first and thus never assimilated. So deep were the "divided allegiances" that German civilians in Russia, France, England, and elsewhere acted as "spies for Germany," and clandestinely built submarine pens and wireless stations, warned *Free Poland*. Reporter Anthony Czarnecki alerted Chicago's Association of Commerce of the "alien influences . . . working from within." *Free Poland* declared flatly on April 15 that the German-American press was disloyal. The *Bohemian Review*'s peppery editor Jaroslav F. Smetanka asked during that fateful April, "Will Immigrants Be Loyal?" His answer was yes, except for many born in Austria and Germany, who "look upon themselves as a . . . Herrenfolk—a chosen people destined to the rule the world and . . . the weaker races." There will be found "many among the German and Magyar elements," concluded Smetanka, "who will commit treason."[59]

As for Americans of Bohemian descent, that was a different story. The Bohemian press agreed with University of Chicago President Harry Pratt Judson that no more loyal Americans were to be found anywhere. As one of the city's Bohemians explained: "Now it happens I have a chance to be patriotic for the United States and for Bohemia—both at once." We can help our homeland and still help "the good old stars and stripes." "The eager Bohemians," as Chicago's *Chamberlin's* magazine called them, were already enlisting in the British and Canadian armies before the American entry into the war. Although they were the "most loyal of Americans, it is not love of America but hate of the Teuton that sends them into the trenches ahead of the American legions," noted the editor. Chafing under German control for centuries "is why Chicago's Bohemians are so eager for another crack at the Teuton." *Chamberlin's* concluded that the "rabidly anti-Teutonic" Bohemians wanted to have a "hand in the final big smash at Teuton world power."[60]

Chicago's Poles were a part of every aspect of the war effort before, during, and after the American entry. They had been privately raising funds and secretly recruiting and training men for a Polish Legion, which eventually drew into it 3,000 Chicagoans. With Wilson's permission and British support, this unit was trained at Niagara, furnished with Polish officers, and sent to France to fight as a national army of a nation that did not exist. One of the most dramatic events in Poland's rebirth, however, had come earlier, in Wilson's "Peace Without Victory" speech, which he delivered on January 22, 1917. Ignace Paderewski and Colonel Edward House had worked on Wilson for weeks, trying to convince him of the justice of Poland's case for independence. Just before the speech, Colonel House told the pianist, "The bomb

Polish pianist and statesman Ignace Paderewski convinced President Woodrow Wilson that an independent Poland should be created. He also rallied Chicago's *Polonia* to the American war effort. *Courtesy of the Chicago Historical Society.*

will go off in a few days. It will take your breath away." And it did. "Statesman everywhere," intoned Wilson, "are agreed that there should be a united, independent, and autonomous Poland." The news hit Polonia like a runaway freight train at full throttle. (Even ten years later those words still reverberated in the ears of Poles.)[61] The "bleeding Jesus" and "crucified Christ of nations" would be resurrected from America.

The results were predictable. There was nothing that America could have done thereafter that would have antagonized Poles, and everything that the Poles did seemed to contribute to the American war effort. Twenty years after the event, Miecislaus Haiman proudly recalled that, although Poles represented only 4 percent of the United States population, they absorbed 12 percent of the war casualties, indicating that Poles were doing "more than their share, that they were not one-hundred but three-hundred percent American." The first Chicago boy killed in the war was a Polish-American from St. Adalebert's parish, Peter Wojtalewicz. Haiman added that the first German prisoner of war taken by the American Army in France was captured by two Polish boys, one from Milwaukee and one from Chicago.[62]

The Americanization campaigns proved no problem for the Poles—in fact, they acted as a tonic. When the campaigns began, Dr. Joseph Parot pointed out that the Poles attempted to "out Americanize the Americanizers" and at the same time preserve Polonia's culture. According to Parot, this dual process propelled Poles to "rendering more to America than the Americans and rendering more to Poland than the Poles. . . ." The Poles had "The Star-Spangled Banner" translated into Polish, cheered Wilson as a "world statesman" and "one of the greatest lovers of mankind,"[63] and supported with great vigor Liberty loan campaigns, military recruiting, and rooting out subversion at home. The Polish press pursued Americanization Polish style, swatting the German hyphen, supporting the war effort, and celebrating freedom. The resilience, resourcefulness, and toughness of Polonia must have shaken Chicago's Teutonia.

Trapped in a cul-de-sac of their own making, a few thoughtful Germans shuddered at the pending consequences of their past actions. The *Staats-Zeitung*'s fiery Horace Brand admitted in March 1917 that German-Americans had not always been wise in their utterances or moderate in their mastery of emotions, and had often gone to "extremes in denouncing policies, tendencies, and utterances" of the United States. Yet he asked forbearance and "friendship" for those "whose hearts are wrung by war with Germany." (Brand was later dumped as editor, and the *Staats-Zeitung*, which never recovered from its wartime excesses, would collapse in the early 1920s.) In those troubled days of 1917, German-Americans everywhere were in the process of shifting their allegiances. Otto C. Hottinger told a leading Chicago publisher: "I was for my father's fatherland when this country was neutral. When this country got into the fight I was and am for this country."[64] Yet the late shift seemed to many to be expedient shuffling, a disingenuous genuflecting to an inescapable reality. And it was too late to take back the bad words. The years of calumny, contempt, and vituperation, the years of *Herrenvolken* superiority over the "lesser nationalities," and the contempt for America could not be recalled.

Americanization

History sometimes has a cruel and awesome way of righting wrongs, or at least so it seemed to some Chicagoans. Like a downward-moving glacier, it sweeps all before it—the good and the bad indiscriminately. Not only were the haughty *Herrenvolken* attitudes to be swept away but also the transplanted German high culture. Many innocent and unoffending Germans were to be harassed, just as many Slavs had in

FREE POLAND

A SEMI-MONTHLY

The Truth About Poland and Her People

"Entered as second-class matter January 15, 1915, at the post office at Chicago, Illinois, under the Act of March 3, 1879."

Vol. III.—No. 19   JUNE 15, 1917   5 Cents a Copy

DO YOUR BIT

How?

I.
Join the Army or Navy

II.
Join the Red Cross

III.
Buy a Liberty Bond

Now

NATIONAL AMERICAN COMMITTEE
Polish Victims' Relief Fund
IGNACE J. PADEREWSKI, FOUNDER
Honorable WILLIAM H. TAFT,
Honorary President.
IGNACE J. PADEREWSKI,   FRANK A. VANDERLIP,
Chairman Executive Committee.   Honorary Treasurer.
R. S. MONGER.

These words of President Wilson inspire every American of Polish descent:

"Statesmen everywhere are agreed that there should be a united, independent and autonomous Poland."

Chicago's Poles were ecstatic over Woodrow Wilson's support for a free Poland and, as "300 percent Americans," were loyal to the war effort. *Courtesy of Holime.*

the past. Like a violent act of nature, a broad, unbroken, popular front of newcomers and native Americans united to bulldoze and expurge a perceived evil from their cultural landscape. This campaign was not a "wartime hysteria" but a "crusade," a fact that only a few scholars, such as John Higham and Edward G. Hartmann, have understood.[65] A long-suffering host nation's patience had snapped, but without the zealous and eager aid of Slavs and later other newcomers, the campaign to Americanize Chicago's Germans might not have succeeded.

Education and the public schools had been a long-festering sore with Chicago ethnics—many of whom thought Germans had a superior and privileged position in the schools at taxpayer expense. The so-called Kaiserized speller, an eighth-grade spelling book with a one-page encomium to Kaiser Wilhelm, had long raised a stench in the nostrils of Poles and Czechs, and they launched a campaign to remove it. Chicago's Slavic press had been hammering away since 1915 on that issue, and in 1917 they heightened the publicity, with the result that Slavic and other students began spontaneously to tear out the offending page. "Thousands of torn out leaves containing the objectionable article" were left by school children at the Bohemian National Alliance. Chicago newspapers experienced the same phenomenon, reporting that "every mail brings mutilated pages torn from the speller," some accompanied by notes such as this: "My brother is a first-class yeoman in the Navy, so you can see how I feel about the speller."[66] Belatedly, Chicago's school board moved in June 1917 to expunge the offensive material.

The Bismarck School also drew fire, with demands that its name be dropped or changed. Three separate petitions were advanced, the first by Casimir Zychlinski, President of the Polish National Alliance, and a second by V. Geringer, editor of Chicago's Czech daily, *Svornost*; but both were tabled. Polish school board member Anthony Czarnecki put forth a third petition, arguing that Bismarck was a despot like Nero or Attila, and that he had stood for the "autocracy" that had crushed Polish national life so badly that thousands had fled to Chicago—ironically to become taxpayers for a school system that supported the "hated" name Bismarck. Finally, in March 1918 students at the Bismarck School joined in the demand for a name change, and their school became Frederick Funston School.[67]

German-language instruction was also cast into a negative light and came under increasing criticism. On the cutting edge of the language issue during the spring of 1917 were the Poles and other ethnics. A widely circulated and widely read charge that "the teaching of German in our schools is propaganda first and education second," and that it was purely "insidious German propaganda" was made by Milwaukee

Pole Casimir Gonski and reached a large audience through Chicago's *Free Poland*. Chicago's Emily Napieralski, secretary of the Polish Women's Alliance, Anthony Czarnecki, and the *Dziennik Zwiazkowy* editor had been hitting the German education issue hard, complaining of a "Prussianized school board." Native-born Chicagoans and patriots joined them, and public and parental pressures began to take their toll. In September 1917 the school board dropped German-language instruction at the elementary level because of a precipitous drop in the number of students electing the subject. Some writers have described the dropping of German-language instruction as "banned," but that is too strong a word and technically incorrect for Chicago. During 1917 and 1918, students at the secondary level fell out of German-language classes in droves and to a point where German-language instruction in several schools simply collapsed for a lack of students. Thus the decline of German-language instruction in many (but not all) Chicago schools was a popular response by parents, students, and active pressure groups to wartime superpatriotism and was not simply an arbitrary action of "banning" by school board policy-makers. German private schools also came under increasing attack, and many believed, as did the *Czecho-slovak Review*'s Professor B. Simek, that the "German parochial schools were hotbeds of disloyalty."[68] A later generation correctly saw these actions as misguided wartime patriotism, but, of course, a later generation had the luxury of knowing the outcome of the war, unlike those who fought it.

To promote loyalty, Chicagoan Donald Ryerson originated a public speaker campaign called the "Four-Minute Men" in April 1917. The idea, which soon spread across the nation, was adopted in June by the federal government's George Creel and the Committee on Public Information. Nationally, some 75,000 speakers delivered 750,000 speeches during the war period to an estimated 315 million persons. In Chicago nearly 500 speakers delivered about 50,000 speeches, mostly during intermission in 319 cooperating movie theaters, to an estimated audience of 25 million. They all delivered a "canned" speech, which declaimed:

> *I am a Four Minute Man,*
> *I am the mouthpiece of Democracy....*
> *I am a stoker of the Great Melting Pot.*
> *In four minutes I breathe the flame of*
> *   true American Patriotism to people of all kinds and creeds.*
> *I am a soldier. I fight German propaganda, intrigue, falsehoods,*
> *   treachery....*
> *I am a salesman. I sell Liberty Bonds and Thrift Stamps....*
> *I am a Lover. I love the Stars and Stripes.*[69]

Among the multilingual "Four-Minute Men" was Bohemian-born Anton J. Cermak, a rising ethnic star on Chicago's political scene. The future Chicago mayor took his "Four-Minute" patriotism into his political campaign for county sheriff in 1918 and ran one of the most virulent anti-Hun campaigns on record. His aides cautioned him that his wrapping himself in the flag and German-baiting had gone too far, but the undaunted Cermak plowed on with a "vicious anti-German campaign." So exacerbated were interethnic relations that the German community denounced Cermak in meeting after meeting and concocted counter-slurs and horror stories, such as one that claimed Cermak wore a belt made from the skin of a dead German soldier. It was a hard-fought campaign that ended in defeat and emotional depression for Cermak, who for the first time in nineteen years was rejected by the voters.[70] But the Germans had at best won a Pyrrhic and painful victory.

The Czechs, whom the *Abendpost* had called "fanatical hotheads" already in 1915, participated in everything from espionage in enemy consulates and business offices to Liberty loan drives, the "Four-Minute Men" movement, and raising money and men for the Czech Army abroad and a newly formed American Army at home. Czechs who spoke German had infiltrated the Austrian and German consulates and embassies as mail clerks, maids, and service people, and they provided a ready flow of vital information to the American Secret Service of the kind that resulted in the expulsion of Austrian Ambassador Constantin Dumba in 1915. According to George Creel, "Bohemians defeated plot after plot against America." In the standard history of the Czechs in America, Thomas Capek took pride in the fact that many a German "evildoer" was "apprehended and sent to prison on evidence furnished to the Government by loyal Czechoslovaks."[71]

The frenetic activity of the Czechs was also captured in an "incident true as gospel" related by George Creel of a Chicago Bohemian housewife facing visitation from Americanization representatives:

"We are here," the spokesman announced impressively, "in the interests of Americanization."

"I'm sorry," faltered the woman of the house, "but you'll have to come back next week." "What!" the cry was a choice compound of protest and reproach. "You mean that you have no time for our message! That you want to put off your entrance into American life!"

"No, no!" The poor Bohemian woman fell straightway into panic. . . . "We're perfectly willing to be Americanized. Why, we never turn any of them away. But there's nobody home but me. All the boys volunteered, my man's working on munitions, and all the rest are out selling Liberty Bonds. I don't want you to get mad, but can't you come back next week?"[72]

Hun-catching sometimes had its amusing aspects, as seen in a Southwest Side occurrence. In an effort to get evidence on draft resisters, a volunteer American Protective League was formed in Chicago and was credited with 75 percent of the wartime investigations for sedition and espionage. Foreign-speaking operatives were especially vital, and during the summer of 1918 several of them (probably Czechs) were taken along by a motor caravan of APLers to listen in on a meeting of immigrants. When they arrived at the hall where "foul deeds" were suspected, they found it crowded with foreigners listening to a shabbily dressed and bewhiskered speaker demonstrating something on a blackboard. After listening for a while, one of the foreign operatives who had been taken along to interpret burst into laughter: "Let's go home, fellows," he said, "We've got the old bird wrong. He ain't talking anarchy; he's giving a lecture on sex control."[73]

Serious wartime efforts by Germans and German-Americans to rally people behind the cause also drew Czechs to heroic efforts of mockery. In Berlin the Germans had erected a massive wooden carving of General Paul von Hindenburg to rally the public to the war effort and to raise money. Germans who made sizable donations could then drive spikes or large nails into this wooden titan. The stunt attracted so much international attention that Chicago Germans began to imitate the fatherland with their own wooden Hindenburg in Chicago. For a price, the Swabian Ladies Association allowed donors to drive nails into their "Wooden Knight" and thus collected nearly $2,000 for German prisoners of war in Russia and Canada. Chicago Czechs, with their puckish irreverence and adeptness at poking fun of Germans, staged a mock Hindenburg ceremony in Chicago during the spring of 1918. On May 13 the Czechs at a West Side bazaar first sang "The Star-Spangled Banner" and then "Hej Slovane" (Ho Slav), and then began the fun. The next act caused great mirth, because a larger-than-life Hindenburg statue cut out of the trunk of a willow tree with a spiked helmet on top of a misshapen head and body was unveiled. Then followed a kind of mock liturgy, with R. V. Psenka as cantor calling an invocation and the audience responding:[74]

> Program chairman Psenka called:
> Which is the most beautiful quadruped of the world?
> The audience answers: "Hindenburg."
> Who ordered dinner to be eaten in Paris and has not yet arrived?
> Audience responds: "Hindenburg."
> Who is winning battles and losing the war for the Kaiser?
> Response: "Hindenburg."

*Into whose body would everyone of us gleefully stick a fifteen-
inch-long shingle nail?*
Response: "Hindenburg."
*And who is going to help us to make dollars for the liberation of
our motherland and for the defeat of Prussian militarism?*
Response: "Hindenburg."

John Cervenka, the auctioneer, paid thirty dollars twice to drive in the
first two shingle nails into Hindenburg, to the merriment and amusement of an appreciative Czech audience.

Yet the fun was no fun for German-Americans, as the symbolic and
real shingle nails began to hit home from all sides. Other nationalities
joined the prowar, anti-Hun crusade. The Chicago Swedes, who hitherto had been pro-German in sympathy—even to the point that Swedish clergymen had joined the German antiwar remonstrance to Congress
in April—now quickly switched sides. "To wipe out their earlier pro-
German attitude," an historian of Chicago's Swedes wrote, "these
Swedes were more zealous and intolerant in their objections than those
who from the first had been pro-Ally." The conversion was foursquare
and wholehearted. They organized Swedish Liberty Loan drives,
Swedish "Four Minute Men," and formed 100 Liberty Bond savings
clubs in Chicago alone. To maximize Swedish participation, many of
their lodges bought bonds and pressured all members to buy, feeling
that every Chicago Swede should have at least one Liberty Bond. The
Swedish press turned strongly pro-American and solidly anti-German.[75]

Also swept up by the Germanophobia was the city's most fashionable and famous Jewish congregation, Sinai Temple, composed of successful German-Jewish bankers, lawyers, and merchants. Members got
into a fracas with their brillant and dynamic Reform rabbi, Dr. Emil G.
Hirsch. Hirsch, German as much as he was Jewish, had sung the high
praises of Germany, her political system, and her army before American
entry into the war. Statements such as "Our hopes are with those German and Austro-Hungarian soldiers in the trenches over there," "The
German Army ... upholds Kant's philosophy," "We know Germany
will be victorious," and Hirsch's obvious pride in the fact that about
"4,000 Jewish soldiers were awarded the Iron Cross of the second class
and nineteen Jews earned the Iron Cross of the first class"—statements
made between 1914 and 1917—came back to haunt him. As an anti-
Zionist, Hirsch had also questioned the American patriotism of Chicago
Zionists, who in 1918 took some pleasure in the fact that Hirsch's own
temple had mounted a petition campaign to push him out because of
his alleged "disloyalty to the United States." Forced to recant in a kind
of public confessional, Hirsch admitted that many of the young people
at his temple disapproved of "my limited activities in behalf of the

Government." But he explained: "I was reared in Germany," and have nine blood-relatives in the German Army but also some in the British and French forces. Hirsch asserted that he was a pacifist (which seems to be at variance with his public rhetoric), but added that since the Romanov dynasty had been overthrown, he could support the Allies.[76] Although Hirsch felt the painful sting of rejection by some of his own congregation for his philo-Germanism, he survived the storm. No more did he publicly profess to see Immanuel Kant's philosophy marching off to war with German foot soldiers.

With a brilliant German-Jewish leader silenced, the Swedes gone, and the Anglophobic Irish neutralized, the Germans stood alone and bereft of allies. Chicago's Germans had taken some high political risks and lost. During the 1916 presidential campaign their motto was "gegen Roosevelt und Wilson" (against Roosevelt and Wilson), they had in a publicly visible way pinned their hopes on the GOP nominee, Charles Evans Hughes, and lost.[77] Although they still had an ally in "Kaiser Bill" Thompson in the mayor's seat, even he could not buck the patriotic tide and hope to survive politically. A gloomy and foreboding future seemed to face Germans wherever they looked. Even a few of the most bloodthirsty *hunnenfresser* (Hun-eaters) were sons of German immigrants.

The American and Slavic press was pounding away furiously, hitting at every aspect of Germanism and the brutality of the German Army. Chicago's *Dziennik Zwiazkowy, Denni Hlasatel, Free Poland,* the *Bohemian Review,* and *Narod Polski* had set off a withering barrage of savage fire, ridicule, and invective in three languages, Polish, Czech, and English. In addition, many of the best bon mots were reprinted in the English-language publications and also other foreign-language papers. They frequently "swore hatred of Germans" and wished the "complete annihilation" of Russia and Austria, called for boycotts of German-made goods, and insisted that many Germans in America could not be trusted. The Czech *Denni Hlasatel* complained of the "malodorous and criminal practices" of German-Americans. Other endearments included: "fight Germany, our eternal enemy"; "death to the Germans"; "avenge wrongs Germany has done to Poland"; and death to the "Prussian viper." Poles were told that they "must guard American industry" and "beat the Germans" at home and abroad. *Narod Polski* advised: "Box the Kaiser in the ear—that nightmare that has murdered our Polish people for years." Madame Paderewski warned of the "lustful" German soldiers who took Polish girls as "white slaves" into Germany for the officers. Another decried the "bestial soldiers who ravished our women, murdered our children," but now we can "avenge all wrongs." Anthony Czarnecki told a story of how a Polish priest in

Chicago's "False" Armistice Day, November 7, 1918, celebrating victory over Germany and Austria-Hungary. *Courtesy of the Chicago Historical Society.*

Warsaw was shot by the Germans because he had counseled his female parishioners about the lust of the German soldiery.

The "father of the Czechoslovak Republic," Professor Thomas Masaryk, warned a University of Chicago audience that Germans everywhere held other nationalities in contempt and asserted that the "Austrian government represents nothing but organized crime." At St. Hedwig's parish a group of recruits going off to the railroad station were reminded that the Germans were "vicious and savage" and the "worst criminals committing terrible crimes against mothers, sisters, fathers, and brothers in Poland." Another group of recruits going to join the Polish Legion vowed to "cut off Prussia's hydra head." At a big war rally at St. Casimir's, Polish recruits were told to "avenge the crimes committed by Germans, the modern Huns, and return covered with glory." One group of volunteers preparing to enlist in the Polish Legion, then training in Canada, was told to "avenge themselves on the Germans." Amid the hubbub a reporter saw a Polish woman crying as she bid her son adieu on the departing troop train. The woman explained that she was "not weeping for sorrow but for joy that I raised such a son who will go off to fight the Germans."[78]

The actions and thunder of the Slavs caused Chicago Judge John Steck to note in a talk he gave in the German language in August 1918 at Wicker Park Hall that the "hate resentment" against German-Americans did not reflect the sentiments of old stock Yankees and native-born Americans as much as "those of Czechs and Poles and other nationalities which are in conflict with the Germans over there."[79]

By 1918 all stops were pulled and the Americanization crusade steamrollered forward, running down all forms of Germanism whenever or wherever found. The Schiller statue got a coat of coward's yellow paint, and the Goethe monument was threatened with destruction and removed into storage for safety during the war period. Amid charges of a lack of patriotism, the Chicago Symphony Orchestra's German-born conductor, Frederick A. Stock, stepped down from the podium to complete the naturalization process for citizenship. The designated choral director of the Illinois Bicentennial pageant, William Boeppler, was pressured into resigning in 1918 because of his German antecedents. The Chicago Athletic Club began firing its alien German employees in May, and employers in vital war industries began to scrutinize their payrolls with an eye to extirpating potential subversives. German-Americans began to protest the violation of their civil liberties by the Americanization campaign. But very little protest was heard from Chicago's Slavs. In fact, the illustrious Czech Masaryk, speaking in Chicago in May 1918, saw no great problem and explained that "Americanization . . . is equivalent to social equality of all people, which will mean the end of monarchy."[80]

The campaign pressures also resulted in much "voluntary" compliance by German-Americans. Chicago's Germania Club became the Lincoln Club on May 9, 1918, and days later the Bismarck Hotel was rechristened Hotel Randolph, and the Hotel Kaiserhof was renamed the Hotel Atlantic. The imperial-sounding Kaiser Friedrich Mutual Aid Society became the George Washington Benevolent and Aid Society, and the city's German Hospital was redubbed with the American-sounding Grant Hospital. Even private citizens found it prudent to change their names. According to the *Abendpost*, on August 20, 1918, a Harry H. Feilchenfeld became H. H. Field, Hans Kaiser became John Kern, Guttmann became Goodman, Griescheimer became Gresham— just a partial sample of one day's parade of name changes. More than 1,000 Chicago Poles petitioned the city council to abolish German street names in their district, such as Berlin, Hamburg, Frankfurt, Coblentz, Lubeck, and Rhine, and the council complied. Smitten by the new patriotism, old-stock Gold Coast citizens joined the crusade in

Shown here (left) in his later years is the illustrious founder of the Czechoslovak Republic, Thomas G. Masaryk, who in Chicago in 1918 equated the Americanization movement with democracy. Czech-American Anton J. Cermak (right) was a vigorous American patriot and Four Minute Man who conducted a vehement anti-German campaign in the 1918 election of a Chicago sheriff. *Courtesy of Holime.*

December 1918, requesting that Goethe Street be renamed. They denied any anti-German animus and merely said they could not pronounce the name "Goethe" properly and wanted instead the name Boxwood Street. In jest, Alderman "Bathhouse" John Coughlin suggested it be renamed "Busse Place," after the city's only German-American mayor; and two German-American aldermen then suggested it be called "Nutwood Street" to properly characterize the petitioners. German clubs and many civic-minded citizens protested, and Goethe Street remained Goethe Street. An occasional small victory could not, however, conceal the generalized and widespread collapse of Germanism in Chicago and the nation. Already in April 1918, for example, the most powerful and influential ethnic and fraternal lodges the nation had seen, the National German-American Alliance and its Chicago chapter, disbanded voluntarily in the face of fierce congressional pressure.[81]

It had not been a pure and simple nativism or dislike of the foreign-born that had done in Chicago's *Deutschtum*, but a specifically directed anti-Hun campaign fueled and inflamed by ethnic Slavs and other foreign-born Chicagoans with their native-born allies. The Americanization campaign was not a "Know-Nothing" movement, as one writer claimed, but rather a Know-Something movement.[82] Both in Chicago and the nation at large, the Americanizers had been drawn from among the nation's brightest scholars and best-informed citizens and their foreign-born compatriots. This was no pure and simple xenophobia, for if it had been, Chicago's Bohemians, Poles, Slovenes, Serbs, and a variety of others of foreign birth would not have participated under any circumstances. The Americanization campaign was aimed at German-Americans. Chicago's Americanizers appeared to exempt Slavic and southern and eastern European comrades in arms and focused primarily on the potentially subversive Central Powers nationals. Even Theodore Roosevelt, the most thoroughgoing Americanizer, was willing to make exemptions; and in his case it was Chicago's illustrious Greeks whose heritage should not be pushed into the melting pot.

The German-American had, of course, done great damage to his own cultural cause by his openly expressed contempt for and ridicule of the "babushka-clad, barefooted Slavs," who were looked upon by German public spokesmen such as Hugo Munsterberg as "half-kultured" and by others as the "natural serf races" of the German marchlands. German-American behavior and rhetoric toward Slavs had been based on beliefs in the racial inferiority of these Slavic stocks. Finally, German-American cultural spokesmen had become infatuated with German militarism and the autocracy of Wilhelmine Germany, a fatal mix from the point of view of the democratic host nation.

No continental foreign-born group had been so widely and favorably received in the United States or won such high marks from their hosts as had the Germans before World War I. Some public opinion surveys conducted before the war showed that German-Americans were even more highly regarded than were immigrants from the mother culture, England.[83] And after the Great War, it became clear that no ethnic group was so de-ethnicized by a single historic event as were the German-Americans. When Polish-Americans, Lithuanian-Americans, and other subject nationalities underwent a great consciousness-raising, German ethnicity fell into a protracted and permanent slump.

Indexes of *Deutschtum*'s demise in Chicago and the nation abound. A leading German-language daily, *Staats-Zeitung*, lost subscribers and was on the road to extinction. German-language instruction in the public schools collapsed for a lack of student electors and never recovered its prewar position in Chicago. In 1917 the Missouri Synod's Delegates Synod minutes appeared in English for the first time; the synod's new constitution dropped a monolingual insistence on using the language of Luther and instead suggested bilingualism. Dozens of parochial schools also dropped German-language instruction. English-language services also intruded into parishes where German had been the *lingua franca*. Whereas only 471 congregations held English services in 1910, the number preaching in the "perfidious tongue of Albion" in the synod skyrocketed to 2,492 by 1919. The German Evangelical Synod of Missouri, Ohio, and Other States also anglicized its name by dropping "German" from its title. A key indicator of the decline of *Deutschtum* in Chicago was the census, where the number of people identifying themselves as German-born plummeted from 191,000 in 1914 to 112,000 in 1920.[84] Self-identifiers had found it convenient to claim some other than German nationality.

The war damaged German ethnic, linguistic, and cultural institutions beyond repair. As Professor John A. Hawgood saw it, the war "so enhanced the distance between the German and the American that no hyphen could stretch from one end to the other." What little survived came under a final blight, the "shadow of the Swastika" in the 1930s, which extinguished the few smouldering embers of German ethnicity.[85] Even today in Chicago, *Deutschtum* has never experienced a third-generation revival. No phoenix-like resurrection seems to be in the offing. Whereas Chicago has museums and cultural exhibit halls for Lithuanians, Ukrainians, Poles, Swedes, Jews, blacks, and others, no museum or permanent public exhibit of German-America is anywhere to be found. Chicago's Germans had bet on the militarism and autocracy of Kaiser Wilhelm and Marshall von Hindenburg, and they almost lost the heritage of Goethe and Schiller. Ironically, the Schiller and Goethe statues are not *Deutschtum*'s best-known Chicago symbols, but rather the U-505 German submarine captured by the Allies during World War II that is on display in the Museum of Science and Industry. That remains for thousands of Chicagoans the most recognizable German artifact and cultural symbol—fitting epitaph for sunken Germanic aspirations for transplanting the German heritage in Chicago and America.

The best-known German "cultural artifact" in Chicago is this captured submarine, on display at the Museum of Science and Industry. *Courtesy of the Museum of Science and Industry.*

Chapter XIV

MASAKO M. OSAKO

Japanese-Americans:
Melting into the All-American Pot?

I do not know any group in the history of our country who has suffered so much without justification and has come out of it to make such a great contribution with never a scar of resentment or faltering in their love of and loyalty to country.

— Illinois Congressman Barrat O'Hara,
June 11, 1963

"JAPANESE-AMERICANS ARE THE 'MODEL minority': they are law-abiding, polite, clean, hard-working, and assimilate readily to dominant American values." For years this has been the accepted wisdom regarding Japanese as an ethnic group, and perhaps such traits remain characteristic of many Japanese-Americans, whether living in Hawaii, on the West Coast, or in the Midwest. Yet today the community is more restive; some Japanese-Americans are uncomfortable with the "quiet American" image and are reluctant to be typified too easily as "the model minority which has successfully integrated." Like other American ethnics, Japanese-Americans are increasingly concerned with problems of group survival in a mass society, and they seek to preserve ethnic traditions, to identify social problems, and to rectify the injustices of discrimination. But the young are abandoning endogamy—they are marrying outside the Japanese community—at a rapid rate.

How did Japanese-Americans earn their image? How did they achieve success despite the severities of past discrimination? The answer lies partly in the strength of their traditions, particularly family and community structures, as well as in the harsh reality of racial oppression. In the dynamic interaction between the ethnic group and the host society, certain consequences of assimilation follow. The Japanese-American family and community changed significantly in the crucible of assimilation.

Chicago's Japanese-Americans underwent strikingly different experiences from those of their sister communities in Hawaii and on the West Coast: they were forced to relocate three times in alien milieus—to the West Coast, to the internment camps during World War II, and finally to the Midwestern metropolis—in a matter of only one generation. Moreover, the community in Chicago has been little affected by any recent influx of immigrants from Japan.

Large-scale Japanese-American migration to Chicago began after World War II, as the relocation centers in the West closed. As late as 1940, there were only 390 persons of Japanese origin in the city of Chicago. But the figure boomed to 10,829 by the 1950 census. Today there are 15,732 in the greater Chicago area. Until the mid-1950s, the

South Side (the Hyde Park-Kenwood area) and the near North Side along Clark Street were the major centers for Japanese. Today their residences are spread out all over the city, with more than one-third, especially the younger generation, living in suburbs such as Skokie, Evanston, and Des Plaines. The group's migration to predominantly white, middle-class suburbs suggests their social mobility and successful assimilation into American society.

Social Origin and Immigration

Japanese-Americans began to immigrate to the United States around 1880, and eventually slightly more than 190,000—excluding migrants from Hawaii after its annexation—arrived on American shores.[1] It was during the years 1900 to 1924 that a large majority arrived in America— an estimated 89 percent of total Japanese immigrants entered in this twenty-four-year period.[2] At first, most of the immigrants were young, unmarried male sojourners who intended to return home after making their fortunes. In contrast, after the ratification of the final form of the Gentlemen's Agreement in 1908, by which the Japanese government voluntarily limited its immigrants to America, young brides dominated the ranks of new arrivals from Japan. Following the traditional Japanese custom of arranged marriage, a young man residing in the United States could marry a girl in Japan by exchanging photos and being assisted by a go-between. The influx of women ended in 1924 with the ratification of the Omnibus Act, which denied admission to aliens ineligible for citizenship, including most people from Asia and Africa. Fortunately, by this time a large majority of Japanese immigrants were married. By 1924 the basic unit of the Japanese-American community had been transformed from a single male to a family.

A great majority of Japanese immigrants to America were from the farming class, which comprised 90 percent of Japan's population in the nineteenth century.[3] Like many traditional peasants, Japanese farmers generally lived close to subsistence level, though there were class distinctions even among them based on wealth, especially land ownership.[4] Typically, a Japanese village was composed of a handful of landlords, a sizable number of land-owning independent farmers, and a majority of full- or part-tenants. The part-tenant owned his own plot, but since it was too small to provide for his family, he leased an additional piece of land from his wealthier neighbors. The full-tenant, with no or little land of his own, was sometimes called a "water-drinking peasant" (Mizunomi byakushō) because he filled his stomach with water when food was scarce. Many immigrants were from middle or lower socioeconomic groups, but they were respectable people whose parents enjoyed enough trust from fellow villagers and relatives that they could borrow money to finance the son's travel expenses to the United States. Unlike the early Japanese immigrants to Hawaii, who were plantation workers, few of those who landed on the West Coast were so poor as to be indentured laborers.[5]

Life in the Japanese village was taxing and precarious. With limited arable land and dense population, farming was both labor-intensive and capital-intensive. Farm labor was also strictly regulated by a seasonal schedule, such as rice transplantation in June, weeding during the summer months, harvesting in mid-October, and planting of winter wheat in late October. The list of work to be performed was endless: gathering grasses to make compost, bargaining with fertilizer merchants, cleaning ditches, tending cows, feeding silk worms, and so forth. In addition, each task required skill, experience, and perseverance. A common saying, "The peasant is anxious to use the helping hand of even a cat," illustrates this demanding work. Furthermore, floods, drought, pestilence, and rising taxes and fertilizer prices were familiar perils.

Understandably, all the farm family members were required to work, and their contribution to household productivity was an important determinant of their status and power. For example, despite the widespread myth of subjugated Japanese women, many centers of the silk industry, where women were the principal weavers, were known for petticoat government.[6] Similarly, even though Confucianism, Japan's official doctrine during the Tokugawa period (1600–1868), preached the importance of respect for aged parents, the old farmer's status declined as he became feeble and unproductive. Beardsley states:

> A grandfather merits respect, but in addition his ties with other household members become warmer as his exercise of authority diminishes. Skilled handicrafts, menial tasks, and some babytending become his main economic functions.[7]

In Japan the younger sons were almost invariably less fortunate than their eldest brother, for to prevent the subdivision of already small plots, the Japanese practiced primogeniture.[8] The sons other than the heir were encouraged to leave home to find opportunities to earn a livelihood elsewhere, such as industrial employment or as a son-in-law in a family without a male heir. Thus it was no coincidence that many of the male immigrants were younger sons. This was probably a favorable factor in Japanese immigration to the United States, for they were accustomed to hard work and determined to establish themselves in nonfamilial employment.

Rural Japan in the late nineteenth century, where the *Issei** were raised, was undergoing social change from being a largely self-sufficient economy under a feudal system to becoming an expanding commercial economy with growing industrialization.[9] During nearly 300 years of the Tokugawa regime, the village was basically an economically and socially self-contained unit, with peasants bound to the land, caught up by intricate networks of obligatory social relations. But the restoration of imperial rule in 1868 abolished the hereditary caste system of four rigid classes, and with it peasants gained the right of occupational and geographical mobility. In addition, during the second half of the nineteenth century, various modernizing measures were introduced, such as compulsory elementary education, a nationwide postal system, a banking system, and universal military conscription. These changes inevitably touched the lives of the emigrating Issei. Therefore, despite their rural and relatively low-class origin, the majority of the Issei had the equivalent of an eighth-grade education[10] and were familiar with the demands and disciplines of a commercialized economy. They were also sensitive to national pride, since they had experienced military victories over China (1895) and Russia (1905).

Adjustment

Most Japanese immigrants to the West Coast of the United States found jobs in farming and in service industries: prior to World War II, approximately two-thirds of the Japanese urban dwellers were in service industries;[11] the farming Issei started out as hired laborers at farms producing vegetables and fruits.[12] Gradually the latter began to work on their own land, either as tenants or owners. Despite the anti-Japanese sentiment, some Caucasian landowners were willing to lease plots to Japanese farmers once they realized that the leasing was safe and profitable. At times a Japanese immigrant, eager to cultivate his own land, proposed to lease even previously barren land. By 1930, twenty years after the peak immigration period, few of California's Japanese farm work force were still hired laborers.[13]

Past experience of intensive work habits and farming techniques in Japan and the solidarity of the ethnic group contributed much to their advancement. Japanese farmers, living in clusters in such places as Fresno, San Joaquin, and Sacramento, not only exchanged informa-

---

*The first-generation Japanese immigrants are called *Issei* (literally, number one generation). Their children are *Nisei* (second generation), and their grandchildren *Sansei* (third generation).

tion about land availability, lease opportunity, and market conditions, but also pooled money to purchase land and farm equipment. Eventually, Issei farmers developed a business structure that could handle all aspects of agricultural operations, such as seed and fertilizer purchase, farming, harvesting, retailing, and wholesaling. This cooperative network coupled with the Issei's specialization in certain products, like strawberries and cantaloupes, contributed to the farmers' survival in the face of persistent anti-Japanese measures, for example, anti-alien land acts and the boycotts of Japanese farm products. The number of Japanese farmers decreased from 5,152 in 1920 to 3,956 in ten years, and Japanese-owned acreage decreased in that decade from 361,276 to nearly half that figure. And yet by 1941, Japanese farmers raised 42 percent of California's truck crops.[14]

The Issei farmer's survival was achieved by the extremely hard and long labor of every family member, including the wives and children. The Japanese were charged with possessing an unfair superior advantage in economic competition because of their "thrift, industry, low standards of living, willingness to work long hours and the women working as men. . . ."[15] But for their effort they had to pay a penalty. When consumers complained about the rising price of farm products and white farmers became alarmed about their declining share in the market, the success and visibility of Japanese farmers made them an easy target of racial discrimination.

Japanese immigrants, however, were not exclusively farmers. In the pre–World War II days nearly one-third of the Issei lived in urban centers, such as Los Angeles, Seattle, Tacoma, and Portland. Anti-Japanese sentiment and the Issei's lack of English-language skills narrowly limited the kinds of jobs they could obtain. Generally, factory jobs were unavailable to them except for low-paying, menial, and non-unionized ones like canning and slaughtering, which few whites would want. A large majority of urban Japanese opted for small business operations, such as fruit-stands, restaurants, laundries, and barbershops. Domestic service positions for young people and gardening for former peasants were also common occupations. Little skill and capital needed to enter the business are the common characteristics for these trades. Miyamoto reports:

> . . . the restaurant cooking of that day was relatively simple; all one had to know was how to fry an egg, toast bread, and fry a steak. It was known as a "fry cook."[16]

As in the case of Japanese farmers, the Issei in cities progressed from hired hands and apprentices to business owners in urban occupations. For instance, among the Japanese-Americans in Seattle in 1935,

46 percent of income earners operated small businesses. Moreover, another 25 percent were in white-collar occupations, such as clerks, teachers, and stenographers. Less than 19 percent were service or manual workers.[17]

What contributed to the Issei's social mobility? Seattle and other western cities were still expanding in pre–World War II days, and this aided the Issei's business expansion. But more important, historians and sociologists argue, community solidarity and cooperation contributed much to the success.[18] For commercial establishments, the ethnic community was the major source of both customers and suppliers. For example, Japanese restaurants used Japanese laundries, food suppliers, cooks, and waitresses, and catered to Japanese customers. *Kenjinkai*, prefectural associations, were particularly helpful in starting a business. For instance, Miyamoto reports:

> People from the same prefecture often cooperated in particular trades. For example, the first Japanese barber in Seattle was from Yamaguchi-ken. After he became established he helped his friends from the same ken with training and money, so that eventually most of the Japanese barbers in Seattle were from Yamaguchi-ken. Other businesses followed similar patterns.[19]

The traditional financial practice of Japan, *tanomoshiko*, helped to finance many of the new business ventures in the absence of bank loans and government assistance. Tanomoshiko is a combination of an investment fund and credit service. Each member contributes a certain amount of money at designated intervals and receives a lump sum when his turn comes up. Its purpose and scale varied from several women forming a group to purchase wrist watches to a large tanomoshiko capable of financing the purchase of a sizable real estate holding. The system was clearly built on absolute trust, for nothing bound a person to pay his or her share except honor. The prevalence of tanomoshiko in the pre–World War II Japanese community in America is clearly indicative of ethnic solidarity.

For several decades Japanese descendants continued to live in a largely self-sufficient and self-contained "Japanese ghetto," relatively isolated from the dominant society. They built language schools, movie houses, churches, and temples. Although—unlike Japanese farmers—city Issei were not in competition with other Americans, their isolation did not help dispel the dominant society's suspicion and apprehension about Japanese. This was so even though crime and juvenile delinquency rates were extremely low among Japanese descendants.

Discrimination

For some time racial discrimination against Orientals had been an established practice in California. At first, it was the anti-Chinese movement. During the 1860s and 1870s thousands of Chinese laborers were brought in to build railroads and work in mines. But with the completion of the railroads and the economic recessions in the 1880s, Californians began to regard the Chinese as unwanted competitors for jobs. The exclusion act of 1882—suspended for ten years, renewed in 1892, and made indefinite in 1902—officially banned the entry of Chinese immigrants into this country. In the late nineteenth century Japanese laborers were brought in to fill the room vacated by the declining Chinese population. But as early as the turn of the century, Japanese farmers succeeded in their enterprise and, with the help of recessions, eased the labor shortage. This time public opinion turned against the Japanese, who inherited the anti-Oriental fears previously directed at the now-excluded Chinese.

Californians' anti-Japanese feelings were expressed in numerous incidents.[20] On February 5, 1905, the *San Francisco Chronicle*, an influential paper on the Pacific Coast, carried a front-page article charging the threat of "Yellow Peril." For months similar stories appeared almost daily. The Japanese victory over a major European power in the Russo-Japanese war of 1905 also stimulated fears of a war between the United States and Japan. During the same year the Japanese and Korean Exclusion League was formed in San Francisco, the first of many West Coast anti-Japanese groups. The league was financed mostly by the Building Trade Council, and of the 231 organizations affiliated with it in 1908, 195 were labor unions. In the following year the "School Crisis" in San Francisco attracted international attention. The city board of education ordered that Chinese, Japanese, and Korean children be sent to a segregated Oriental public school in the Chinese quarter. The alleged reason was overcrowding in white schools, because many schools were destroyed in the great earthquake and fire of April 1906. The city's attempt at racial segregation was prevented, however, when the U.S. attorney general threatened suit against the school board on constitutional grounds. But a considerable sector of California public opinion denounced the whole affair as an unwarranted intrusion of the federal government into state and municipal matters. In truth, San Francisco politicians had deliberately exploited the race issue to divert public attention from an investigation of municipal graft. The issue was settled at a White House meeting in February 1907. President Theodore Roosevelt persuaded the San Francisco authorities to abandon school segregation, and in return he promised to negotiate with Japan for further limitations on Japanese immigration to the United States. The outcome was the so-called Gentlemen's Agreement of 1907–1908, under which Japan refused exit visas to its nationals going directly to the United States seeking work.

In California, the Gentlemen's Agreement did not slake the thirst of anti-Japanese extremists. Violence against Japanese was common, and in 1913 California passed an Alien Land Bill, which prohibited "aliens ineligible for citizenship" from purchasing land. Aliens could lease agricultural land for a maximum of three years only; lands already owned by or leased to aliens could not be bequeathed. Even though the Japanese effectively undermined this bill by purchasing land under the names of their American-born children or friends, they were acutely aware of possible law suits as well as confiscation of their land.

The persecution was intensified further. In 1920, California tried to plug the loopholes that had made the 1913 land law more or less ineffective. This time the Japanese lost the right even to lease agricultural land, and they were forbidden to act as guardians of native-born minors with respect to property that they themselves could not legally own. Historian Iwata reports that the Japanese share of California's farm product dropped from 12.3 percent in 1921 to 9.3 percent in 1925.[21] To survive, Japanese farmers, despite their reputation for being law-abiding, had no choice but subtly to circumvent the tightening laws.

Throughout the 1920s and 1930s the insecurity resulting from clandestine use and ownership of land, as well as the boycotts of Japanese farm products, deeply troubled Issei farmers. Many living Issei can still recall confrontations with agitated white farmers and their supporters when they drove to the market with a truckload of fresh vegetables. The Issei would return home with a truckload of spoiled produce, having lost several hundred dollars, and fearful for their safety.

The persecution of Japanese descendants on the West Coast entered a new stage when on December 7, 1941 the Japanese Empire executed a surprise attack on Pearl Harbor. The Issei were now regarded as enemy aliens. Anti-Japanese sentiment became nationally acceptable. A Hearst columnist wrote on January 29, 1942:

> I am for the immediate removal of every Japanese on the West Coast to a point deep in the interior . . . let 'em be pinched, hurt, hungry. Personally, I hate Japanese. And that goes for all of them.[22]

The range of those attacking the Japanese descendants was remarkably wide, including trade unions, civic organizations, and religious groups. Only some Quaker groups and the American Civil Liberties Union provided visible support to protect Japanese civil rights.

Internment

On January 29, 1942, the first of a series of orders by U.S. Attorney General Francis Biddle established security areas along the Pacific Coast that required the removal of all enemy aliens from these areas. On February 19, 1942, President Roosevelt signed the infamous Executive Order 9066 which (1) designated military areas where military commanders could exclude persons, and (2) authorized the building of "relocation" camps to house excluded persons. On March 2, 1942, General John DeWitt, then commander in charge of the Western Defense Area, issued an order to evacuate all persons of Japanese ancestry from the western half of the three Pacific Coast states and the southern third of Arizona. "Persons of Japanese ancestry" were defined as all those with as little as one-eighth Japanese blood. More than 111,000 of the 126,000 Japanese in the United States were affected by the order. Of this group, Kitano reports that two-thirds were United States citizens.[23]

On March 2, 1942, the United States Commander in charge of the Western Defense Area ordered an evacuation of all persons of Japanese ancestry from the Pacific coastal states for relocation into the interior of the nation. *Courtesy of the War Relocation Authority.*

At the internment camps, located in remote and barren areas of Arizona, California, Arkansas, Utah, Wyoming, and Idaho, the evacuees began a life in a state of physical and emotional shock. They were kept behind barbed wire and guarded by armed soldiers. The fruit of their thirty years of hard labor was gone. Many had completely lost faith in America, once a promised land, and had to survive the confinement with no knowledge about when and if ever they would return to their home and community. After a period of initial adjustment and shock, the camp life settled down into a dismaying but on the surface orderly routine.[24] Both men and women worked at the camp workshops doing menial tasks for a few dollars a week. There was plenty of time to till. Men and women took up hobbies, classes, and community work. But the sense of powerlessness, boredom, and constriction was pervasive.

In addition to the inconvenience, hardship, and frustration, the internment experience involved varied elements that undermined the traditional fabric of the Japanese community and family. For instance, in the camp, age suddenly lost much of its significance as a sign of status and privilege, essentially because the War Relocation Authority regarded individuals as equals in employment and in the supply of provisions. In addition, Japan and its culture were summarily dismissed as the enemy and undemocratic. The tradition of community autonomy ceased to exist; and its cultural emphasis on hard work and achievement had little meaning in the federal relocation center.

The impact of these changes was most severe on Issei men. Since the camp authority made all the major political and economic decisions for the residents, the household head's status declined sharply: he was no longer a principal wage earner; he could not set a respectable model for his children; he himself was visibly powerless toward the external authority; and above all, he lost confidence in his old cultural heritage and in himself. On the other hand, the younger Nisei could cope with the situation better than his father could. He had American citizenship, a command of English, and less attachment to Japanese culture. Added to this changing status of the two generations, the WRA's policy of appointing only American citizens to administrative positions resulted in the Nisei's ascendance and eventual assumption of leadership in the community and, to a limited extent, at home. This fast and drastic shift in power and status induced considerable frustration and stress among the Issei:

> The men looked as if they had suddenly aged ten years. They lost the capacity to plan for their own futures, let alone those of their sons and daughters. . . . In one sense, it was more a matter of morale than morals.[25]

At the internment camps, located in remote and barren areas of the interior, the evacuees began life again in a state of physical and emotional shock. Most severely affected were Issei men, whose status as heads of households declined sharply because the War Relocation Authority made the major economic and political decisions for residents. *Courtesy of the War Relocation Authority.*

Significantly, however, as Kitagawa points out, the Issei father did not lose affection and concern for his loved ones, and "no immorality to speak of, say, in terms of irregular sex relations, existed."[26] Furthermore, after leaving the relocation center, even though the Issei were more dependent on their own children than before, most of them resumed life as responsible citizens and family men.[27]

Why did not the abrupt and drastic status change of the Issei lead to apathy or antisocial behavior, as it often did in the case of other ethnic minorities such as blacks and Indians? We have already seen that in the traditional Japanese village older people were expected to render their authority to the younger generation at a culturally prescribed time. What happened to the Issei in the camp, then, is in principle consistent with the course of events in traditional rural Japan, even though the transfer in the camp was carried out more brutally. Thus the basic cultural continuity between traditional practice and camp experience eased the possibly harmful impact of the new environment upon family solidarity.

Of course, cultural continuity by itself was not a sufficient condition to maintain family cohesion. The strong Japanese emphasis on the importance of kinship solidarity must have prevented some households from breaking up.[28] Similarly, the cultural definition of the woman's role helped to ease the adverse impact of the internment on the family. Since the Japanese mother has traditionally played a major role in managing domestic tension when there was strife between husband and son, she mediated between them and comforted the one who was defeated. She managed to play this role effectively because the internment affected her life and status more benignly than that of her spouse. Moreover, for the first time in her life she had time for taking hobby classes and socializing with friends in the camp.[29]

Even though a large majority of families kept themselves together, the level of family solidarity varied from one household to another. In their study of family life in and after the relocation camp, Bloom and Kitsuse do recognize such variations and observe that families controlled by authoritarian fathers were more vulnerable than those whose

Two weary but proud Issei mothers hold flags signifying that each has four sons serving in the United States armed forces. *Courtesy of the War Relocation Authority.*

members were tied together primarily by affection.[30] The presence of families and individuals who could not successfully cope with the pressures of the internment does not contradict our interpretation, for families incorporated the cultural traits discussed above with variations.

In many ways, the relocation camp had the characteristics of a prison; but in other important ways it did not. For example, the relocation authority kept the family as the basic unity and eventually took an initiative in relocating its residents. As early as 1942, when it became clear that there were no real grounds for the fear of Japanese-Americans as a threat to national security, the WRA authority began to plan moving its residents to regions other than the Pacific Coast. The first group of camp inmates who left the center were students: they went to attend colleges in the Midwest and East. Other Nisei followed, aided by YMCA and Quaker groups in finding employment and housing. Finally, the Issei parents followed their children. One by one, they moved to cities like Pittsburgh, Milwaukee, New York, and Chicago.

Settling in Chicago

There was a small Japanese population in Chicago prior to World War II. The first-known Japanese national was Kamenosuke Nishi, who moved to this city from San Francisco in 1893 to open a gift shop at the time of the Columbian Exposition.[31] He is said to have amassed $700,000 from the successful management of a store at the corner of Cottage Grove and 27th Street. Handfuls of other Japanese managed small shops or worked at restaurants. The size of the ethnic group increased slowly. As late as 1927, there were only 300 Japanese nationals in the city. They worked mostly in small shops and restaurants, with the exception of Japanese firms such as Mikimoto Pearls and Nippon Shipping Company. Partly because the group was small, unlike their counterparts on the West Coast, they continued to conduct their daily lives in Chicago without public persecution, even during World War II.

The first arrival of internment camp residents in Chicago is recorded on June 12, 1942. The substantial migration occurred from March of the following year through 1950; of 110,000 nationally interned, nearly 30,000 Japanese-Americans moved to Chicago. Many stayed in this city permanently, but almost half returned to the West Coast when the region was freed from the classification of a military sensitive zone. The westward exodus ended by 1960, stabilizing the ethnic population at around 15,000.

There were important reasons why Chicago seemed inviting. Most important, there were jobs in this city. Unlike Detroit or Pittsburgh, Chicago was never dominated by a single industry; it had various light manufacturing and service industries. Clothing, printing, and furniture and cabinet factories existed in large numbers here.[32] Even though the Issei were largely farmers or small storekeepers with little industrial skill or English-language proficiency, they had the proverbial manual dexterity. They were valuable to craft factories such as clothing and furniture makers. Since all Japanese women took sewing lessons as young girls, they were highly skilled seamstresses. Furthermore, hotels and restaurants were abundant in Chicago, and their jobs required neither prior training nor English-language ability.

Compared to the West Coast, Chicago appeared to be more open to Asian immigrants. Even during World War II, the Japanese experienced little overt discrimination, such as physical attacks. Moreover, a number of employers, among them Stevens Hotel, Edgewater Beach Hotel, McGraw-Hill Publishing Company, and Curtiss Candy, were willing to hire Japanese. The relative lack of anti-Japanese feeling was clearly seen in local newspapers. In contrast to the Hearst papers, which spearheaded anti-Japanese sentiments in California, four of the five major Chicago dailies supported the Japanese settlement.[33] From 1943 to 1945, several favorable articles appeared in local papers. For example, on August 12, 1943, Elmer E. Shirrell, Midwest regional director of the War Relocation Authority, was quoted as saying, "Employers are pleased with the quickness and adaptability of their Japanese help."[34] And on September 5, 1945, a headline in the *Chicago Tribune* read: "Jap-Americans sent to Chicago making good: 10,000 prove they are good citizens."

The appearance of ample opportunity and the relative absence of discrimination encouraged many Japanese to migrate to Chicago. But there were problems. The problem of adjustment was serious for many Issei. In the West they spent most of their lives as farmers and shopkeepers in segregated Japanese communities. Now, in their old age, they were forced to begin a new life in the city; now they had to work with non-Japanese workers and live next door to non-Japanese neighbors. Misunderstandings resulting from language deficiency were common. Many Issei were obliged to work in unskilled jobs which failed to use their occupational skills. To ease the frustration, some took to drinking and gambling. Not surprisingly, however, a large majority held steady jobs and kept the family intact.

Another problem was the hesitation of many Chicagoans to offer jobs and apartments to Japanese applicants.[35] The mass media were generally favorable to the Japanese-Americans' arrival, but because of the negative, propaganda stereotypes fostered during the war, many

A mural at the Japanese-American Services Committee building, North Clark Street. The
Noh-like masks express the shock and grief of Japanese-Americans in the face of racial
oppression; the rows of houses on the left represent relocation camp buildings. *Courtesy
of Masako Osako.*

managers were reluctant to hire Japanese. Similar attitudes existed
among landlords and apartment owners. Community leaders visited
prospective employers to explain that their apprehension was ground-
less. And, pressured by the relative labor shortage during the war, they
hired a few Japanese—reluctantly at first. As the workers proved to be
reliable and hardworking, they gradually opened up more positions to
other Japanese-Americans. A similar pattern can be observed in apartment leasing. It was no accident that the resettlers first congregated in
the Hyde Park-Kenwood and North Side areas: the former was a racially transitional area (today almost exclusively black, except for the
University of Chicago area) and the latter was a mixture of commercial
and industrial areas with low residential values. There was initial resistance on the part of apartment owners, but when they realized that
Japanese families were clean, quiet, and punctual in paying the rent,
their reluctance disappeared. A Caucasian neighbor is said to have
mentioned, "Simply by looking at the sidewalk you can tell where the
Japanese live, because they keep not only the front yard, but also the
sidewalk, clean."

The inability of the Japanese to purchase burial sites was still another crucial problem.[36] In 1942, for example, a Japanese nurse was killed in an automobile accident. Since no cemetery would accept her body, it was kept in a funeral home for an entire week. Finally she was buried in Montrose Cemetery, in a small communal plot that had been purchased by the Japanese Mutual Aid Society. In a separate incident, another cemetery discovered the Japanese background of an individual already buried there, and threatened his family with exhumation of the body. The Montrose communal burial plot was small, since it was purchased when the Japanese population in the city was a few thousand, and the problem of burial sites became acute as the Japanese population mushroomed over 20,000 and many of the Issei became old.

In 1947 the Japanese Mutual Aid Society queried twenty-six cemeteries in the city about their policy on accepting the burial of Japanese.[37] Only three of them replied, and only one positively. Realizing the seriousness of the matter, the society appealed to the City Human Rights Commission, which subsequently organized a meeting between the representatives of cemeteries and the leaders of the Japanese community. But the managers, using constitutionally guaranteed freedom of enterprise as their sacred right, would not change their discriminatory stand. An unexpected break came when "Washington Merry-Go-Round" journalist Drew Pearson did a broadcast about the plight of Japanese Chicagoans who had no funeral plots in which to bury their deceased. Soon the *Chicago Daily News* took up this issue. To avoid the reputation of racial bias, the municipal offices pressured the cemetery owners to cooperate. Finally, a few cemeteries agreed to sell plots to Japanese. Today Japanese tombs are concentrated in three of the ten graveyards in the city of Chicago, with only a few in the suburbs.

To overcome the discrimination and adjustment problems of such bizarre experiences, Japanese-Americans initially found the support of community groups critically important. But the eventual success was gained basically through the hard work and determination of each individual Japanese person. In the very beginning of the postinternment period, a few Japanese groups were organized by former community leaders on the West Coast and camps, as well as old residents in Chicago. In cooperation with Christian organizations, notably Quakers and the YWCA, they aided newcomers in settling. Finding jobs and living quarters was their main function. In addition, community leaders contacted government offices, cemetery managements, apartment owners, and employers to counteract anti-Japanese sentiment. They were successful in breaking trends, but their effort bore fruit because Japanese quickly gained their colleagues' and neighbors' acceptance through hard work and honesty.

That these social service functions to fellow Japanese-Americans were soon lessened indicates the success of these community groups. As early as 1946, the Japanese Mutual Aid Society organized a campaign to send relief materials to war-torn Japan, diverting their attention from service to fellow Japanese-Americans. Ryōichi Fujii, local historian of Chicago Japanese-Americans, reports that in November 1947 the Japanese community in Chicago donated 5,500 pounds of clothing and $7,000 in cash to be shipped to Japan.[38] Similar efforts were repeated several times during the following years when the Asian homeland was devastated by floods, earthquakes, and other natural calamities. Reflecting the successful adjustment of the Japanese-Americans in Chicago, only two organizations today continue to render social services to the community members. The Japanese American Service Committee offers a wide range of services to the Japanese-American community, including counseling, educational and cultural programs, social events, hot meals for the aged, and Issei sheltered-workshops. The Chicago Mutual Aid Society offers a limited number of small loans to its members.

The reduced activities of social service organizations is understandable given the income profile of Japanese-Americans provided by the Census Bureau. Gradually, the proportion of households under the poverty level had declined to 6 percent by 1970. At the same time, the censuses of 1950, 1960, and 1970 suggest an expanding middle-class segment among Japanese-Americans.

Current Social Attainment

Most of the Issei are now retired or deceased, and a large portion of the Sansei are still in school. Therefore, the Nisei still constitute the bulk of the Japanese-American labor force. There are several indications that many Japanese-American males in Chicago have attained comfortable middle-class status. According to the 1970 Census, 28.7 percent were professionals, and 58.4 percent were in white-collar occupations. Similarly, 20.8 percent were college graduates and 78.4 percent had high school diplomas. These 1970 Census figures for adults closely approximate the more recent research findings. Sixty-one percent of heads of households are in white-collar occupations, according to Osako's research on Nisei households conducted in 1978–1979. Regarding educational attainment, this study shows that 93 percent of the sampled Nisei males have high school diplomas, and 44 percent have college degrees.

These occupational and educational accomplishments, when contrasted with the past data, indicate a remarkable intergenerational mo-

TABLE I
SHIFT IN OCCUPATIONS OF EMPLOYED JAPANESE MALES IN CALIFORNIA (1940, 1950, 1960) AND IN ILLINOIS (1970, 14 YEARS OLD OR OLDER BY PERCENT

Industry	Japanese Males (by percent)			
	1940	1950	1960	1970
Farm Laborers and Foremen	4.6	19.4	9.2	.5
Service Workers, Except Private Household	8.3	5.4	3.5	4.3
Operatives and Kindred Workers	6.2	6.5	9.1	14.4
Farmers and Farm Managers	4.3	17.1	21.4	0
Laborers, Except Farm and Mine	26.4	17.9	5.9	1.6
Craftsmen, Foremen, and Kindred Workers	2.9	5.2	10.4	21.0
Clerical, Sales, and Kindred Workers	21.1	8.8	12.7	14.3
Managers, Officials, and Proprietors, Except Farm	19.8	8.6	7.9	14.1
Private Household Workers	2.3	3.2	1.1	0
Professional, Technical, and Kindred Workers	3.8	4.4	15.0	29.8
Other and Not Reported (change of classification)	.3	3.5	3.8	0
Total:	100.0	100.0	100.0	100.0

Source: U.S. Census

bility. According to the 1950 Census, of Japanese male descendants aged forty-five years and over, who were mostly Issei, only 3.4 percent were professionals and 17.9 percent white collar. Similarly, the group's schooling was limited. In 1950, 4.8 percent were college graduates and 31.7 percent had high school diplomas.

This achievement, however, does not mean that Japanese-Americans are today completely free from the influence of racial discrimination and prejudice. Patricia Roos has found that the Japanese-Americans' average earnings and status are less than those of Caucasians. She argues that "wage discrimination, structural unemployment, and minimal upward mobility within work organizations" plague Japanese and other Asian-Americans. She attributes these signs of underachievement in part to the lack of verbal skill and the nonassertiveness of Japanese-Americans.[39]

For the leaders of the Japanese American Citizens' League (JACL),

this is not a surprise, for they have counseled many cases of job discrimination, although it was only in 1978 that they formed an affirmative action subcommittee. The subcommittee has taken up several cases
for investigation, but lack of funding is preventing the processing of
more cases. The typical complaint is concerned with promotion. For
instance, an engineer is on the verge of quitting his job after ten years
of service in a Chicago camera company, because, despite his fine technical performance, the management has promoted all the others in the
department except him. The JACL complains that the employers are
pressured by both white and black groups, but since Asians are generally neither assertive nor organized, they are the last ones to be promoted. A JACL member observed:

> A typical Nisei professional is a graduate of a local state university
> with a B.A. degree in engineering or science. He works for an
> organization of varying size as a technical staff member, but his
> career history does not indicate an orderly promotion pattern. He
> is likely to remain as a technical staff member with little managerial
> or supervisory responsibility. In short, the Nisei's occupational at-
> tainments often fail to be commensurate with academic credentials.[40]

Having properly qualified the so-called success story of Japanese-
Americans, we are now ready to ask: Why did Japanese-Americans,
despite race and past persecution, attain substantial upward mobility
in the United States? The significance of this accomplishment is particularly evident in view of their agrarian and relatively lower-class
origins and the severity of racial discrimination, which culminated in
their wartime internment. Historians and sociologists find a common
explanation in two strains in the Japanese tradition: its normative stress
on discipline, hard work, achievement, and education on the one hand,
and the solidarity of family and community on the other. For example,
Harry Kitano observes: ". . . appeals to obligation, duty, and responsibility . . . and ethnic identification" account for the Japanese-American's
achievement.[41] The Issei exerted pressure on the Nisei to conform to
the cultural norms through cultivating the feeling of shame and guilt,
a traditional socializing technique. Underachievers were made to feel
guilty and ashamed by remarks like, "With these poor grades on your
report cards, I wouldn't dare to face your teacher at the next school
conference." Another equally effective means of reinforcing desired
behavior was an appeal to ethnic identity. Many Nisei recall the Issei's
admonition, "Japanese boys don't cry like that" or "Good Japanese
don't think about things like that."

The emphasis on hard work and ethnic pride are effective in inducing desired behavior when the parents themselves live by these

norms and provide secure, loving homes. Most Issei presented a reasonably close model, working hard and keeping the family intact, despite adverse circumstances. Of course, there were some Issei fathers who drank, gambled, and even beat their wives. Some Nisei still have harsh words about their fathers, but virtually all of them recall their mothers as hardworking, loving, and strong—protecting the children from society's harassment as well as from the father's anger and despair. A Nisei woman reminisces about her mother:

> My mother helped father in their produce shop. In the morning while he went to the market, she cooked breakfast, cleaned the house and prepared the store. After father returned, she unloaded with him, arranged and sold vegetables and fruits. While doing all these, somehow she found time to do our laundry, sew our clothes, and supervise our homework. I remember my exhausted mother, ironing our dresses late at night so that we would look neat at school.

Clearly, the stable and close family was instrumental in raising Nisei into responsible adults.

The Japanese-American family could maintain its effective role because the ethnic community supported its efforts. The support was rendered in two ways. First, by maintaining the ethnic culture intact, the community legitimized the traditional emphasis on discipline and education. Second, the community aided the Issei in counteracting racial discrimination and economic pressure. It is plausible that without such support many Japanese-American families could have succumbed to the stress, failing to raise children into respectable, well-adjusted adults.

Suburbanization and Interracial Marriage

Family and community played a vital role in the assimilation and ascendancy of Japanese-Americans. But today there are signs of changes in these institutions. During the last fifteen years Japanese-Americans have begun moving to the Chicago suburbs. Most upper-middle-class suburbs, except Kenilworth and Lake Forest, are now completely open to Asian residents. The loosening of racial barriers in the suburbs and the Japanese-Americans' attainment of middle-class status occurred at about the same time. Presently, one out of four Chicago Japanese-American households is in the suburbs. The suburbanites are younger, better educated, and have higher incomes. They are predominantly white-collar or professional workers, and their decision for the move

Spanning the generations: Issei, Nisei, Sansei. A grandfather (Issei) and granddaughter (Sansei) enjoy each other's company at a Kenjinkai picnic in Montrose Park, June 1979. *Courtesy of Masako Osako.*

is like that of other Americans—largely influenced by the desire for better schools for their children.

What happens to their ties with family and ethnic community after the move? Generally, their participation in the organized activities of the ethnic community in the city becomes less frequent, even though some maintain contact as members of church and temple. When the children are in school, the suburban Nisei parents are involved in local groups such as PTA and Boy Scouts.[42] As the children reach their teens, the wives generally obtain jobs and thus lose considerable time for and interest in community activities, either those of Japanese-Americans or white Americans. The contact with Japanese-American friends in the city also becomes less frequent and more formal, as the Nisei leave the city for the suburbs. City-dwelling and suburban Nisei share fewer common issues and have greater traveling distances for visits.

At the Japanese-American Services Committee center, an Issei man keeps his culture alive by practicing brush painting. *Courtesy of Masako Osako.*

A sizable minority of suburban Nisei are now arriving at a state in the life cycle where their children have left them for college or jobs. Now many of them have both time and money. Are these people returning to the Japanese-American community? Their personal friendships with fellow Japanese-Americans sometimes revive in late middle age. They may join group tours organized by ethnic travel agents. But because they are employed by non-Japanese enterprises, they are largely independent of the ethnic community in the city. Furthermore, even though some suburbs have a sizable Japanese-American population, there have been few instances of Japanese clubs or groups in these places.

Admittedly, the move to the suburbs generally diminishes the frequency of contact with fellow Japanese-Americans, but kinship ties remain strong. This author's recent study indicates that suburban and

city-dwelling Japanese-Americans feel equally committed to a child's
filial responsibility to parents. As expected, however, intergenerational
contact is less frequent between suburban-living children and their
parents in the city. The children now visit their parents perhaps once
a week to share a meal and some chore.

Whether or not the Japanese-Americans continue to maintain close
ties with relatives in the future depends in part on a new development
in Japanese-American mating patterns. While only 15 percent of the
Nisei have married non-Japanese, as many as one-half of the *Sansei*
(the third generation) are choosing spouses from other ethnic groups.[43]
Most Sansei children in the Chicago area grow up among non-Japanese
people. Given the dispersion of Japanese at schools and the increasing
acceptance of marriage with non-Japanese among the Nisei parents,
the trend is likely to continue. Eventually, Japanese-Americans may
become the first nonwhites to merge biologically into the dominant
American society.

What happens to kinship interaction when Japanese-Americans
marry outside their ethnic group? Beyond the point that the total preservation of cultural patterns would be slim, it is impossible to gener-
alize; there is a wide variation from one case to another. In one instance,
an only daughter married a Caucasian boyfriend against the family's
wishes; her family severed ties with her. Adding to her plight, the
marriage soon failed. Rumor has it that the young woman, a semifinalist
in the National Merit Scholar competition, has dropped out of college
and become a bar waitress. In another case, a Sansei boy married an
Irish-American girl, the third child among nine, whom he met while
both had part-time jobs at a grocery store. Now he is in business school
and she is a teacher trainee. The couple lives next door to his parents,
and his grandparents, who live on the same block, delight in the smaller
siblings of their new Irish daughter-in-law.

Variation on the Theme: Comparison between Japanese- and Chinese-Americans

For many Americans, Japanese and Chinese are simply Orientals.
They do not feel much need to differentiate between them. Certainly
it is difficult to distinguish between the two groups by appearance. In
addition, their backgrounds do indicate considerable similarities. For
instance, both groups originally immigrated to the United States as
laborers. They both suffered from racial persecution in the West, which
culminated in the final Chinese Exclusion Act in 1902 and the internment of Japanese in 1942. And the members of the two ethnic groups

are increasingly attaining middle-class status. In the greater Chicago area, 31.2 percent of Chinese and 28.7 percent of Japanese male descendants are professionals.[44] The percentage of white-collar workers in the two groups is 52 percent and 58 percent respectively. The median number of school years completed is 12.3 years among the Chinese and 12.7 years among the Japanese.

Going beyond the aggregate level, however, there are some major differences between the two Asian groups. Most important, while Japanese-Americans are largely homogeneous in terms of social and cultural origins and immigration history, the Chinese are polarized into two divergent groups.[45] As we have seen, most Issei were of rural origin and immigrated to America between 1880 and 1908 (except women) as laborers. Subsequent anti-Japanese sentiments and the internment during World War II heightened the sense among them of sharing a common fate. On the other hand, Chinese-Americans are composed of two different groups: descendants of Chinese laborers and more recent immigrants. The first group represents the offspring of laborers who immigrated to the West Coast before the Exclusion Acts. Three and four generations later, many of these Chinese still remain as service workers and laborers. Recent Chinese immigrants, on the other hand, fled China at the time of the Communist Revolution, which was successfully concluded in 1949. Since they are Mandarins, they cannot even communicate easily with the Cantonese-speaking Chinatown residents. With the exception of the relatives of Chinatown residents, most post-Revolution immigrants are professionally trained. This group includes many well-known scholars, like Francis L. K. Hsu, the president of the American Anthropological Association, I. M. Pei, the famous architect, and two Nobel Prize winners, Zheng-dao Li and Zhen-ning Yang. Some of the newer immigrants may have been obliged to take jobs far below their qualifications because of their deficiency in language, but almost invariably their children go to college and become professionals.

Given such heterogeneity, it is unrealistic to expect a unified Chinese community. There are, in fact, two Chinese-American subcultures. In Chinatown, relative poverty, lack of education, and employment within the Chinese establishment have made many residents continue to depend on the ethnic community. The steady influx of recent immigrants from Hong Kong and Taiwan further encourages the perpetuation of the ethnic culture. A Chinatown youth with poor English facilities may drop out of high school, but he can still obtain a menial job or find a niche in a youth gang.[46] Recently, the younger generation of Cantonese Chinese have attained professional degrees in increasing number; but the mutual aloofness with which the Cantonese-raised and Mandarin-raised students and professionals regard each other still persists.

Chinese-American professionals, on the other hand, are geographically dispersed, many living in suburbs, and more often than not they are employed by non-Chinese organizations.[47] Despite geographical and occupational dispersion, they share common cultural bonds strong enough to form lively social networks. For example, a Midwest group sponsors regular sports tournaments for youth and summer camps for families. In the summer, about one hundred elite Chinese families get together for one week at a forest campsite near Cleveland. The camp offers social, cultural, and athletic activities for all, ranging from the English-speaking preschoolers to the Mandarin-speaking elderly. Motives for joining such a group vary. A few participate in the event because they support its cause (that is, the continuation of the Chinese-American heritage), but most participate for more personal reasons.

The Chinatown Gate at the corner of South Wentworth and Cermak. The attached plaque reads:

CHINA TOWN GATEWAY
ERECTED BY THE CHINESE COMMUNITY OF CHICAGO
WITH DEEP APPRECIATION
FOR THE GENEROSITY AND COOPERATION FROM:
CITY OF CHICAGO. . . .

Courtesy of Masako Osako.

Older Chinese may simply enjoy the spirited conversation in their native language, and others may join the group for the sake of the children. One parent confided to this author that he does not really care for this kind of socializing, but it is the best way to find Chinese boyfriends for his daughters. So he and his wife decided to join the circle when their oldest daughter entered college.

There is a clear difference between successful Chinese- and Japanese-Americans' attitudes toward their ethnic culture. Japanese, when they become successful enough to be fully accepted by white colleagues and neighbors in the suburbs, tend to lose interest in their city-bound ethnic community. On the other hand, Chinese-Americans still maintain an active interest in membership in the Chinese community. The difference is clearly indicated by where they desire to live: successful Japanese pride themselves on moving into a previously all-white neighborhood; in contrast, prosperous Chinese seek a town already inhabited by a sizable number of elite Chinese families. Why is there this difference? Perhaps it is because the immigration of Chinese professionals is more recent. Or perhaps the assimilated Japanese do not wish to be reminded of their past racial oppression. Or perhaps the Chinese maintain some sociocultural mechanism by which they preserve cultural integrity in foreign lands. After all, for several centuries in Southeast Asia, the Chinese have preserved their own expatriate communities without being absorbed into the host societies. On the other hand, all the Japanese colonies in Indonesia and Thailand in premodern times disappeared within a few generations. The speculations about these differences are interesting, but at this point the research reveals no firm and reliable answers to this intriguing question.

The contrast between the Chinese and Japanese experience also throws some light on the seemingly comparable upward mobility of the two groups. Today, in contrast to a few decades ago, both groups have a substantial white-collar population. An important difference exists, however, in that this change represents a significant intergenerational mobility for the Japanese-Americans, while for the Chinese it does so only to a limited extent. The increased professional segment among Chinese-Americans is accounted for significantly by the post–World War II immigration of professional Chinese.[48] Meanwhile, large numbers of middle-aged descendants of Chinese laborers have remained manual workers and lower-level white-collar employees. Large-scale attainment of college education is only a recent phenomenon among Chinese-Americans with Cantonese backgrounds.

For the student of ethnic relations, therefore, the relevant groups to be compared are Japanese-Americans in general and the descendants of Chinese laborers who immigrated prior to 1886. They are both from villages, came as laborers, and went through racial oppression. But while the second-generation Japanese-Americans rapidly attained social mobility and assimilation, the Chinatown Chinese have lagged behind. A close examination of their historical circumstances suggests a few keys to understanding the different course of events.

One major difference in the Japanese and Chinese experience is that the former started families shortly after their immigration, whereas that privilege was denied the Chinese until the 1940s. Because of the Chinese Exclusion Acts, few Chinese were able to bring wives to America. Their sex ratio reached its greatest disparity in 1890, at twenty-seven males to one female, and improved to two to one only by the 1950s. Prolonged bachelorhood increased the men's dependence on ethnic facilities and social networks in Chinatown, aiding the perpetuation of its culture by means of prostitution, gambling, and paternalistic control over employees.[49] In addition, it delayed the arrival of the second generation. In contrast, the Japanese male-female balance was already close to normal by the 1920s.[50] With the help of wives, Japanese immigrants managed to become more independent of the ethnic community. Even though they were assisted by Japanese community cooperation, they had a family as an alternate source of support. The intact family did much to help the Japanese-Americans withstand difficulties.

The different social conditions of late nineteenth-century China and Japan may be another historical factor. After the Opium War (1840–1842) and the Tai Ping Rebellion (1850–1864), China was devastated by the incompetent Ch'in Imperial Rule.[51] On the other hand, Japan initiated a successful social modernization effort beginning with the Meiji Restoration of 1868.[52] Thus many modern systems, such as schools, banking, public service, military institutions, and factories, were familiar institutions to the Issei. Moreover, through the Meiji educational system they were taught the importance of education, success, and loyalty. Reflecting this difference—even though Chinese and Japanese immigrants came from comparable social strata in their respective countries—virtually all the Japanese immigrants were literate, whereas slightly less than half the Chinese were.

A third historical difference was generated by the Japanese-American experience of the United States relocation camps. The war with Japan and the resulting internment deprived many Japanese descendants of pride in their traditional culture. In the internment center their reaction to the international conflict varied. Some opted to return to Japan, but a large majority remained in the United States, feeling that only assimilation and loyalty to American society would bring a brighter future for them. Consequently, they wholeheartedly supported

POPULATION AND SEX RATIO OF CHINESE-AMERICANS, COTERMINOUS UNITED STATES, 1860–1970

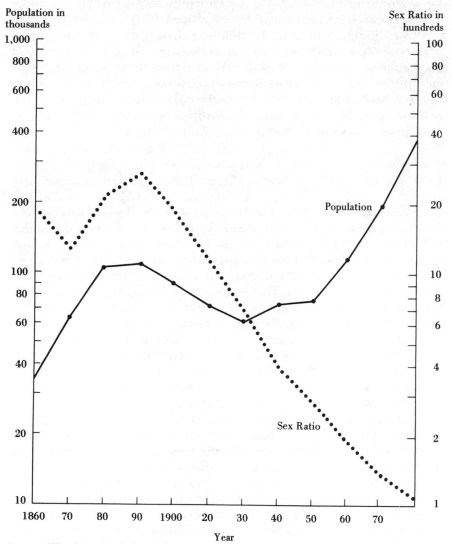

Source: Wen Lang Li, "Chinese Americans," in Anthony Dworkin and Rosalind Dworkin, eds., *The Minority Report* (New York, 1976), p. 303.

Americanization of the Nisei. In contrast, many Cantonese parents, with their traditional background and oppressive, segregated, but shielded life in Chinatown, did not regard Americanization or schooling as a desirable alternative for their offspring.[53]

When the War Relocation Authority was settling the camp residents, its guiding policy was dispersion. The agency—as well as the Japanese themselves—felt that a large concentration would be undesirable because it might cause a recurrence of racial antagonism. In a city like Chicago, whose population was already dense, it was impossible to form a Japanese ghetto in a short period of time. Resulting geographical dispersion, combined with employment in non-Japanese enterprises, reduced the interdependence among Japanese-Americans. Their relative independence is contrasted to the continued dependence of a significant portion of the Cantonese Chinese community on the Chinatown social system.

Conclusion

Many Japanese-Americans today do not wish to be characterized as "the model minority," because the label implies the assumption that to be like "idealized" whites (i.e., hardworking, law-abiding, and middle-class) should be the goal for minorities. And yet it cannot be denied that the Nisei and Sansei in Chicago have pursued largely middle-class occupations and lifestyles. The assets that Japanese-Americans brought to this land—respect for hard work and education, familiarity with modern commercial and employment systems, and cohesive family and community—all contributed to their remarkable social mobility. An irony is that their very success in social mobility and assimilation appears to be inducing rapid changes, if not reduced importance, in their ethnic institutions. Nearly one out of four Japanese-Americans has moved to Chicago suburbs, and a large majority of them work for non-Japanese enterprises. The Nisei family tie is still very strong, measured in terms of interaction, exchange of services and goods, and sense of filial obligation. But the Sansei, many of whom are now reaching young adulthood, are different. They are politically more aware, they take their middle-class status for granted, and above all, they are marrying non-Japanese in large numbers. Whether or not the Japanese-American family will continue to retain distinctively Japanese elements, such as a sharp division of labor between sexes, a strong sense of family loyalty, and an emphasis on discipline and success, is not at all certain.

Such an emerging trend appears to be more pronounced in Chicago than it does in regions like Hawaii and the West Coast, which have larger Japanese populations. The ethnic community in these centers is more persistent in part because of the large size. In contrast to 15,732 Japanese descendants in metropolitan Chicago, there are 104,994 in the Los Angeles area and 169,025 in Honolulu. The residents of larger ethnic concentrations have more opportunity to work with, live with, and marry fellow Japanese-Americans. Moreover, ethnicity is a politically recognizable force in Hawaii and on the West Coast, but in Chicago the Japanese-American population is too small to gain sizable political influence or clout. The Chicago political situation does not encourage Japanese ethnic group members to maintain a keen interest in the community as a whole.

Another major difference between Chicago and the cities with larger Japanese-American populations can be found in the ethnic group's relationship with Japanese *nationals*. Students from Japan and employees of Japanese trading firms and their families predominate among Japanese nationals in Chicago, and there is little interaction between these Japanese nationals and the descendants of immigrants from Japan. The former keep to themselves, and the latter say that they are "aloof" or "condescending." The West Coast and Honolulu situations differ from Chicago. For instance, the Japanese-American population is so large in these regions that even prestigious Japanese banks and businesses, for instance, find it profitable to establish branches to serve the American ethnic community. There the descendants of immigrants are not to be ignored or looked down upon but to be regarded as coveted clients.

It must also be pointed out that, in contrast to the Midwest, the Japanese-American communities in Hawaii and California rapidly absorb new arrivals from Japan who intend to become American citizens. Even though the exact figure of new arrivals is not known, nursing homes for Issei aged are primarily staffed by Japanese nationals, and *Kenjinkai* (prefectural association) parties commonly employ Japan-born music groups. This new blood serves to perpetuate and update Japanese-American culture. Such an infusion is absent in Chicago. On the contrary, some Japanese-Americans, feeling resentful of the Japanese nationals' alleged condescension, make it a policy to disassociate them from ethnic Japanese organizations. For example, a few years ago the Midwest chapter of the Japanese American Citizens' League (JACL) did not participate in the protest against a radio station that broadcast anti-Japanese campaign messages claiming that Japan's aggressive business practices in the auto and steel industries were depriving Illinois residents of jobs. The civic group did not wish to be identified with Japanese national affairs.

Among various developments in the Japanese-American community, potentially the most significant is the rapidly increasing rate of Sansei interracial marriage.[54] If the present high rate continues, assuming little geographical mobility and zero population growth for the ethnic group, in two generations three quarters of the new Japanese-

American children will be of mixed blood. Since interracial marriage is expected to increase, and younger Japanese-American generations are known for having small families, there is a good chance that in a few generations the full members of the Chicago Japanese-American population will have dwindled, and this ethnic group will biologically melt into the dominant white society.[55]

Our next research task seems to be to identify the social, demographic, and political contexts in which a racial minority biologically melts into a majority white population. Is such melting due to the small size of the ethnic population, its middle-class status, or the prestige of its mother nation as a superpower? Speculations are interesting, but this is certainly a profound issue that deserves a more systematic inquiry by future scholars of American ethnicity.

Contributors

MELVIN G. HOLLI, a specialist in urban and ethnic history, is the author of two books on Detroit and with Peter d'A. Jones co-editor and author of *The Ethnic Frontier* and *A Biographical Dictionary of American Mayors, 1820-1980*. He is a director of the Urban Historical Collection and Professor of History at the University of Illinois, Chicago.

PETER d'A. JONES is Professor of History at the University of Illinois at Chicago and the author of several books, including *Since Columbus: Pluralism and Poverty in the History of the Americas* and *The USA: A History of Its People and Society* (two volumes).

CHARLES BRANHAM is Assistant Professor of History at the University of Illinois at Chicago. He was a writer and coproducer of the television series "The Black Experience," which won an Emmy from the Chicago chapter of the National Academy of Arts and Sciences. He completed his Ph.D., a study of Chicago's black politics, at the University of Chicago.

DOMINIC CANDELORO received his Ph.D. at the University of Illinois, Urbana-Champaign. He was Executive Director of the Italians in Chicago NEH Project based at the University of Illinois at Chicago. Funded by the Italian American Executives of Transportation, he has taught Italian American Studies at UICC since 1977. He is a native and current resident of Chicago Heights.

IRVING CUTLER is Professor of Geography and Chairman of the Department of Geography at Chicago State University. He is the author of numerous articles and several books on urban affairs, including *Chicago: Metropolis of the Mid-Continent*, *The Chicago-Milwaukee Corridor*, and *Urban Geography*. He is a founding member of the Chicago Jewish Historical Society and serves on its Board of Directors.

MICHAEL F. FUNCHION is Associate Professor of History at South Dakota State University and the author of *Chicago's Irish Nationalists, 1881-1890*. He is currently serving as editor of a reference volume on

Irish-American organizations which will be published in the Greenwood Press series on ethnic American voluntary organizations.

PAUL M. GREEN is Director of the Institute for Public Policy and Administration and Chairman of the Division of Public Administration in the College of Business and Public Administration at Governors State University. He has written extensively on current and past Illinois and Chicago politics. His articles have appeared in *Illinois Issues*, in a book he co-authored with Peter Colby and David Everson entitled *Illinois Elections*, and in *Illinois: Political Processes and Governmental Performance*.

ARNOLD HIRSCH is an Assistant Professor of History, University of Louisiana at New Orleans. He completed his Ph.D., a study of racial and housing problems, at the University of Illinois, Chicago.

EDWARD R. KANTOWICZ is Associate Professor of History at Carleton University and the author of *Polish-American Politics in Chicago*.

LOUISE AÑO NUEVO KERR is Associate Professor of History at Loyola University and the author of several papers and articles on Mexican-Americans in Chicago and the Mid-west. She is completing a volume on the twentieth-century experience of Chicanos in the United States.

ANDREW T. KOPAN is Professor of Education and Director of Educational Policy Studies and Services in the School of Education at De Paul Unviersity in Chicago. He is an active facilitator in the field of education and ethnicity, serving in a variety of capacities on the national level, and has published articles and books on the subject, including *Rethinking Urban Education, Rethinking Educational Equality*, and *Cultural Pluralism*.

MYRON B. KUROPAS is National Vice-President of the Ukrainian National Association. Born and raised in Chicago, his doctoral dissertation, "The Making of the Ukrainian American, 1884-1939: A Study in Ethnonational Education," was completed at the University of Chicago. During the Ford Administration he served as Special Assistant to the President for Ethnic Affairs.

EDWARD H. MAZUR is Associate Professor of Social Sciences and Urban Studies in the Citywide Institute of the City Colleges of Chicago. His doctoral dissertation, "Minyans For A Prairie City: the Politics of Chicago Jewry, 1850-1940," was completed at the University of Chicago.

MASAKO OSAKO is adjunct Assistant Professor of Sociology at the University of Illinois, Chicago, and has conducted extensive research on the subject of Japanese-Americans and on the questions of gerontology. She is a member of the White House Conference on Aging and is and is associated with the Center for Far Eastern Studies at the University of Chicago.

JACQUELINE PETERSON is an Assistant Professor of History at the University of Minnesota. She completed her Ph.D., a study of eighteenth and nineteenth century Indian and *métis* groups of the Great Lakes region, at the University of Illinois, Chicago.

Appendix

NATIVITY, LANGUAGE, AND SOCIO-ECONOMIC STATUS OF SELECTED CHICAGO ETHNIC GROUPS

FOREIGN-BORN, WHITE FOREIGN STOCK, AND MINORITY POPULATION OF THE CITY OF CHICAGO, 1890

Country of Origin	Foreign Born	White Foreign Stock	Native Born	Total Population
Total	450,666	855,523	649,184	1,099,850
Germany	161,039	325,662		
Ireland	70,028	176,358		
Sweden	43,032	62,235		
England	28,337	55,319		
Bohemia	25,105	42,164		
Canada	24,297	30,821		
Poland	24,086	N. A.		
Norway	21,835	32,612		
Scotland	9,217	20,121		
Russia	7,683	12,063		
Denmark	7,087	10,938		
Austria	6,043	N. A.		
Italy	5,685	8,405		
Netherlands	5,420	N. A.		
France	2,502	6,128		
Switzerland	2,262	N. A.		

Hungary	1,818	1,841		
Wales	1,613	3,447		
Belgium	801	N. A.		
Europe (not spec.)	628	N. A.		
China	584	N. A.		
Greece	245	N. A.		
Cuba and the West Indies	167	N. A.		
Spain	120	N. A.		
Asia (no spec.)	117	N. A.		
South America (not spec.)	78	N. A.		
Mexico	64	N. A.		
Africa (not spec.)	33	N. A.		
Japan	7	N. A.		
Others or not specified	733	67,409		
Negro			14,271	
American Indians			14	
Chinese				567

The population of Chicago had increased from 503,185 in 1880 to 1,099,850 in 1890. The area of the city had grown from approximately 35 square miles to approximately 178 square miles.

FOREIGN-BORN, WHITE FOREIGN STOCK, AND MINORITY POPULATION OF THE CITY OF CHICAGO, 1920

Country of Origin	Foreign Born	White Foreign Stock	Native Born	Total Population
Total	808,558	1,946,298	1,893,147	2,701,705
Poland	137,611	N. A.		
Germany	112,288	421,443		
Russia	102,095	319,566		
Italy	59,215	124,184		
Sweden	58,563	121,326		
Ireland	56,786	199,956		
Czechoslovakia	50,392	N. A.		
Austria	30,491	316,295		
England	26,438	60,998		
Canada	26,392	52,703		
Newfoundland	194	359		
Hungary	26,106	70,209		

Norway	20,481	44,961		
Lithuania	18,923	N. A.		
Greece	11,546	15,539		
Denmark	11,268	22,615		
Scotland	9,910	25,173		
Yugoslavia	9,693	N. A.		
Netherlands	8,843	22,136		
Romania	5,137	7,420		
France	4,569	9,142		
Switzerland	3,452	7,766		
Belgium	3,079	4,975		
Luxemburg	1,967	5,080		
China	1,647	N. A.		
Wales	1,584	4,354		
Finland	1,577	2,301		
Mexico	1,224	1,310		
Armenia	1,028	N. A.		
Others or not specified	5,831	86,487		
Born at sea	228			
Negro			109,458	
American Indians			94	
Chinese				2,353
Japanese				417
Filipino				154

The population of Chicago had increased from 2,185,283 in 1910 to 2,701,705 in 1920. The area of the city had increased from approximately 190 square miles to approximately 198 square miles.

FOREIGN-BORN, WHITE FOREIGN STOCK, AND MINORITY POPULATION OF THE CITY OF CHICAGO, 1970

Country of Origin	Foreign Born	White Foreign Stock	Native Born	Total Population
Total	373,919	1,000,982	2,989,028	3,362,947
Poland	55,711	191,955		
Mexico	38,771	82,097		
Italy	32,539	97,642		
Germany	31,430	99,413		
U.S.S.R.	22,640	64,179		
Greece	15,816	27,990		
Yugoslavia	14,978	28,738		

Ireland	14,709	59,218
Lithuania	12,130	31,629
Cuba	11,920	14,117
Austria	9,559	28,524
Czechoslovakia	8,329	30,492
Philippine Islands	7,841	10,343
Sweden	7,005	26,988
Canada	7,005	22,128
England	6,887	18,508
Hungary	6,651	16,143
Asia (not specified)	4,498	6,664
China	4,403	7,160
Romania	3,547	8,244
Norway	3,094	11,429
Columbia	2,822	3,507
Scotland	2,761	7,879
Japan	2,658	7,370
India	2,392	3,018
Latvia	2,391	3,995
Ecuador	2,084	2,492
France	1,960	5,416
Denmark	1,708	5,887
Guatemala	1,657	1,892
Netherlands	1,479	5,718
Israel	1,398	2,275
Belgium	1,345	3,399
Korea	1,333	1,923
Turkey	1,314	2,240
Jamaica	1,107	1,887
Haiti	1,050	1,358
Argentina	1,039	1,382
Spain	834	1,585
Switzerland	787	2,726
Peru	759	1,026
Brazil	734	981
United Arab Rep. (Egypt)	651	724
Dominican Rep.	550	749
Africa (not spec.)	543	934
Honduras	529	852
Finland	500	2,311
Others or not (specified)	18,071	43,855

Negro	1,102,620	
American Indians	6,575	
Puerto Ricans	78,963	
Chinese		9,357
Japanese		10,833
Filipino		9,497

The population of Chicago had decreased from 3,550,404 in 1960 to 3,362,947 in 1970. The area of the city increased from approximately 224½ square miles to approximately 228 square miles.

ANCESTRY OF POPULATION CITY OF CHICAGO 1980

By Race	
Whites	1,512,411
Negro	1,197,174
By Ethnicity	
Mexico	254,656
Poland	206,208
Germany	113,952
Puerto Rico	113,888
Ireland	105,430
Italy	86,412
England	52,304
Russia[1]	28,054
Greece	23,395
Philippines	22,537
Cuba	11,948
Asian Indians	11,947
Ukraine	11,452
Korea	10,107
Hungary	9,199
Japan	7,705
France	7,644
Norway	6,589
Other Asians & Pacific Islanders	4,096
Scotland	4,053
Netherlands	3,095
Total, All Races	3,005,072

The ancestry data is based upon U.S. Census Bureau sample in northeastern Illinois.

1. This category is probably composed mostly of Jews whose ancestors came from Russia.

MOTHER TONGUE
CITY OF CHICAGO—1920

Mother Tongue	White Foreign Born	White Foreign Stock
Total	805,482	1,946,298
1. German	146,848	431,430
2. Polish	139,360	318,338
3. English & Celtic	116,937	357,370
4. Italian	59,775	124,457
5. Swedish	58,904	121,386
6. Czech	43,676	106,428
7. Lithuanian & Lettish	26,987	44,065
8. Norwegian	20,388	45,029
9. Russian	15,849	28,199
10. Slovak	13,537	25,720
11. Magyar	11,727	19,405
12. Greek	11,520	15,755
13. Danish	11,296	22,561
14. Dutch & Frisian	8,853	21,896
15. Serbo-Croatian	8,456	13,316
16. French	7,237	20,075
17. Slovenian	3,967	7,417
18. Flemish	2,308	3,649
19. Romanian	2,228	3,229
20. Spanish/Portuguese	1,956	2,703
21. Ruthenian	1,249	2,051
22. Finnish	1,217	1,849
23. Syrian & Arabic	1,164	1,672
24. Armenian	1,048	1,310
All Other	1,197	1,861
Of mixed mother tongue	-0-	45,699

Mother tongue was defined as "the language of customary speech in the homes of immigrants prior to immigration."

MOTHER TONGUE
CITY OF CHICAGO—1970

Mother Tongue	Foreign Born	Foreign Stock	Native Born of Native Parentage
Total	373,919	1,000,982	2,361,965
1. Spanish	64,575	112,378	102,541
2. Polish	52,053	170,233	42,207

3. German	49,990	112,144	25,133
4. Italian	32,734	83,477	10,798
5. English	30,709	227,190	1,937,825
6. Yiddish	18,073	47,800	4,394
7. Greek	16,861	27,285	2,132
8. Lithuanian	13,116	27,058	2,165
9. Serbo-Croatian	9,239	16,189	894
10. Ukrainian	8,258	12,860	378
11. Swedish	7,061	18,929	1,814
12. Russian	6,103	9,324	401
13. French	5,253	10,001	7,082
14. Chinese	4,838	7,081	286
15. Hungarian	4,822	8,529	441
16. Czech	3,985	14,727	2,760
17. Slovak	3,841	13,096	1,200
18. Arabic	3,212	4,842	297
19. Norwegian	2,905	7,071	832
20. Japanese	2,627	6,383	1,149
21. Dutch	1,543	3,387	440
22. Danish	1,527	3,000	224
23. Romanian	870	1,548	157
24. Slovenian	802	1,965	116
25. Portuguese	563	836	70
26. Finnish	437	1,767	457
27. American Indian languages	223	358	1,234
All other	24,814	40,678	6,867
Not Reported	2,885	10,846	207,671

Mother Tongue was defined as "the principal language spoken in the home of the person when he was a child." Mother tongue data are useful in identifying ethnic, cultural, and language heritage but do not necessarily indicate language skills or inability to speak English: U.S. Census, 1970.

1970
CHICAGO SMSA
EDUCATION
OF SELECTED ETHNIC GROUPS

Native born of foreign born or mixed parentage	Males Aged 25 and Over		
	High School Graduates	College Graduates	Median Years of Education
USSR	24. %	30.6%	13.1
Japan	38.7	28.8	13.0
Greece	32.0	22.5	12.7

England	30.8	19.4	12.5
Cuba	49.7	13.8	12.5
Ireland	30.	16.8	12.4
Sweden	31.2	14.7	12.3
China	22.1	19.	12.3
Yugoslavia	33.4	8.7	12.1
Czechoslovakia	28.1	10.1	11.9
Poland	24.4	9.	11.2
Germany	23.	9.5	10.9
Negro (native born of native parents)	25.4	4.1	10.7

1970
CHICAGO SMSA
OCCUPATION
OF MALES AGE 16 AND OVER

Native born of foreign born parents or mixed parentage	White Collar	Blue Collar	Service	Farm Workers
USSR	75.2	21.6	3.	.1
Greece	58.1	31.9	9.7	.2
England	57.7	35.6	6.5	.3
Sweden	55.3	38.1	6.1	.6
Ireland	52.2	34.1	13.6	.1
China	50.6	29.8	17.5	2.1
Lithuania	47.3	46.4	6.3	0
Germany	46.2	44.4	8.3	1.
Italy	42.5	47.8	9.5	.1
Czech	42.0	51.4	6.5	0
Poland	38.2	54.6	7.1	0
Yugoslavia	36.5	55.6	7.8	0
Negro (native born of native parentage)	23.9	60.0	15.8	.3

White Collar includes professional, technical, managers and administrators (except farm), sales and clerical workers.
Blue Collar includes craftsmen and kindred workers, operatives, transportation workers and laborers except farm.
Service workers includes private household, and Farm Workers includes managers, foremen and laborers.

1970
CHICAGO SMSA
AGE
(DEPENDENCY)

Native born of foreign or mixed parentage	Males Under Age 18	Males Over Age 65
Sweden	3.9%	25.2%
Czechoslovakia	5.3%	14.9%
USSR	6.8%	9.4%
Poland	9.2%	7.5%
Italy	13.2%	5.2%
Germany	15.5%	29.9%
Ireland	17.1%	18.7%
England	19.2%	14.7%
Yugoslavia	25.3%	2.1%
Greece	31. %	1.0%
Japan	32.1%	.9%
Negro (native born of native born)	45.3%	5.1%
Mexico	55.5%	.8%
Cuba	87.9%	.3%

*Dependency ages are those below 18 and over 65 indicating the percent of population not likely to be in the workforce and dependent upon those in the workforce. This table is organized upon the basis of those groups least to those most dependent.

The number of Cubans, Chinese and Japanese is relatively small compared to the other groups.

The designation USSR probably represents a 70% plus Russian-Jewish ethnocultural group with the rest made up of Ukrainians and other nationalities originating from Russia.

1970
CHICAGO SMSA
INCOME
MEDIAN FAMILY INCOME

Native born of foreign born or mixed parentage		Foreign Born	
USSR	$17,048	England	$12,268
Japan	15,578	Germany	11,916
Greece	13,860	Ireland	11,643
Lithuania	13,876	USSR	11,220
England	13,854	Yugoslavia	11,214

Ireland	13,694	Poland	11,015
Yugoslavia	13,448	Lithuania	11,014
Sweden	13,261	Cuba	10,736
Italy	13,198	China	10,592
Czech	13,106	Japan	10,047
Poland	13,087	Greece	9,960
Cuba	12,440	Italy	9,743
Germany	11,966	Czech	9,144
Mexico	10,029	Sweden	8,571
Negro	8,011		

Notes

INTRODUCTION: THE ETHNIC ODYSSEY

1 Philip Gleason, "Confusion Compounded: The Melting Pot in the 1960s and 1970s," *Ethnicity* 6 (Mar. 1979): 10–20.
2 Quoted in "The Melting Pot and Afterward," in R. J. Meister, ed., *Race and Ethnicity in Modern America* (Lexington, Mass., 1974), p. 23; on the question of identity see Arthur Mann's thoughtful *The One and the Many: Reflections on the American Identity* (Chicago, 1979).

CHAPTER I: IRISH CHICAGO

1 Unless otherwise stated, the word "Irish" in this essay refers to Irish Catholics. Although no exact statistics are available, it appears that the number of Irish Protestants in Chicago was very small.
2 George J. Fleming, "Canal at Chicago" (Ph.D. diss., Catholic University of America, 1950); Bessie Louise Pierce, *A History of Chicago*, 3 vols. (New York, 1937–1957), 1: 179–181, 226, 418; 2: 13, 151, 482; Ruth M. Piper, "The Irish in Chicago, 1848–1871" (M.A. thesis, University of Chicago, 1936); George Potter, *To the Golden Door: The Story of the Irish in Ireland and America* (Boston, 1960), pp. 173, 184, 318, 320; Frederick F. Cook, *Bygone Days in Chicago: Recollections of the "Garden City" of the Sixties* (Chicago, 1910), pp. 179–180; William J. Onahan, "Irish Settlement in Illinois," *Catholic World* 33 (1881): 158–159; Joseph Hamzik, "Gleanings of Archer Road" (MSS, Chicago Historical Society), pp. 37–41; Charles S. Winslow, "Historic Goose Island" (MSS, Chicago Historical Society), pp. 1–13; Local Community Research Committee, "Chicago Communities" (MSS, Chicago Historical Society), Vol. III, Doc. No. 23, Vol. VI, Doc. Nos. 1–3; *Chicago Tribune*, Apr. 19, 1874.
3 Although the vast majority of these had both parents born in Ireland, the figures also include those with only one Irish-born parent. It should be noted that since these figures are based on parentage and not on nativity, they include a small number of persons born in a foreign country (mainly Britain and Canada) other than Ireland, and exclude the minuscule number of Irish immigrants both of whose parents were not born in Ireland.
4 In 1900 there were 72,591 adult males in Chicago who had either both parents born in Ireland or one Irish-born and one native-born parent.

Of these, 34,250 or 47.2 percent were immigrants. See U.S., *Twelfth Census, 1900*, Vol. I, "Population," Part I, pp. 940, 954–955. Although such statistics are unavailable for the years before 1900, it seems reasonable, considering the ratio in 1900, to conclude that the Irish-born outnumbered the American-born until sometime in the 1890s.

5   I also chose 1870 as the point to begin this study because of certain changes that occurred in the church and the Irish nationalist movement around that time. The arrival of Bishop Thomas Foley in 1870 helped to bring greater stability to the Chicago diocese, which had suffered some disruption during the administration of the mentally unstable Bishop James Duggan (1859–1869). And it was in the early 1870s that the Clan-na-Gael replaced the Fenians as the premier Irish nationalist organization in Chicago.

6   U.S., *Eleventh Census, 1890*, "Population," Part I, pp. 670–673, 708, 714, 720, 726, 728. Although its total Irish population was smaller than Chicago's, Boston had more Irish immigrants.

7   U.S., *Eleventh Census, 1890*, "Population," Part I, pp. 670–673, 704, 708, 714, 720, 726, 728; U.S., *Twelfth Census, 1900*, Vol. I, "Population," Part I, pp. 796–799, 866, 874–875, 882–883, 890–891, 898–899, 902–903.

8   City of Chicago, Board of Education, *School Census of the City of Chicago, Taken May, 1884. Total Population of the City Over 21 Years and under 21 Years of Age. By Ward and Division of the City* (Chicago, 1884), pp. 20–31.

9   Edward R. Kantowicz, "Polish Chicago: Survival through Solidarity," in Melvin G. Holli and Peter d'A. Jones, eds., *The Ethnic Frontier: Essays in the History of Group Survival in Chicago and the Midwest* (Grand Rapids, 1977), p. 183.

10 Emmet Larkin, "The Devotional Revolution in Ireland, 1850–75," *The American Historical Review* 77 (1972): 625–652.

11 Although throughout most of the century there were more Germans than Irish in Chicago, only about a quarter or a third of them were Catholics. See Charles H. Shanabruch, "The Catholic Church's Role in the Americanization of Chicago's Immigrants, 1833–1928" (Ph.D. diss., University of Chicago, 1975), pp. 87–88. For a discussion of the problems with Catholic statistics, see John Patrick Walsh, "The Catholic Church in Chicago and Problems of an Urban Society, 1893–1915" (Ph.D. diss., University of Chicago, 1948), pp. 8–12.

12 For the history of Catholicism in nineteenth-century Chicago, see Shanabruch, pp. 1–258; Gilbert J. Garraghan, *The Catholic Church in Chicago 1673–1871* (Chicago, 1921): James J. McGovern, ed., *Souvenir of the Silver Jubilee in the Episcopacy of His Grace, the Most Rev. Patrick Augustine Feehan, Archbishop of Chicago* (Chicago, 1891). For short histories of the various parishes, see Joseph J. Thompson, ed., *The Archdiocese of Chicago* (Des Plaines, 1920). For Feehan, see Cornelius Kirkfleet, *The Life of Patrick Augustine Feehan, Bishop of Nashville, First Archbishop of Chicago, 1829–1902* (Chicago, 1922). For a discussion of the ethnic tensions in the church, see James W. Sanders, *The Education of an Urban Minority: Catholics in Chicago, 1833–1965* (New York, 1977), pp. 40–71.

13 *The Review*, Aug. 15, 1895, cited in Walsh, "The Catholic Church in Chicago," p. 20.

14 Cited in Sanders, *The Education of an Urban Minority*, p. 54.
15 Charles Ffrench, ed., *Biographical History of the American Irish in Chicago* (Chicago, 1897), pp. 796–801; "The Untold Story of Catholic Chicago," *Chicago Daily News*, Special Supplement, Dec. 1966; Local Community Research Committee, "Chicago Communities," Vol. VI, Doc. Nos. 1a, 1b, 7; *Chicago Inter Ocean*, Mar. 16, 17, 19, 1914; Charles J. Bushnell, *The Social Problem at the Chicago Stock Yards* (Chicago, 1902), p. 44; Thompson, *Archdiocese of Chicago*, p. 477.
16 Walsh, "The Catholic Church in Chicago," pp. 5–6, 62–73, 79–81, 332–335; Ffrench, *American Irish in Chicago*, pp. 175, 297, 372; Kirkfleet, *Feehan*, pp. 245–257.
17 Sanders, *The Education of an Urban Minority*, pp. 12–14.
18 *Ibid.*, pp. 18–24, 29.
19 *Western Tablet*, April 3, 1852, cited in Sanders, p. 21.
20 *Ibid.*, pp. 24–30.
21 *Ibid.*, p. 5.
22 William D'Arcy, *The Fenian Movement in the United States, 1858–1886* (Washington, 1947); Piper, "The Irish in Chicago, 1848–1871," pp. 18–27; *Chicago Times-Herald*, Oct. 20, 1895; Mary Onahan Gallery, ed., "The Diaries of William J. Onahan," *Mid-America* 14 (1931): 163.
23 *Gaelic-American*, Nov. 29, 1924; "Constitution of the United Brotherhood [Clan-na-Gael], 1877," reprinted in *Special Commission Act, 1888. Reprint of the Shorthand Notes of the Speeches, Proceedings, and Evidence Taken before the Commissioners*, 12 vols. (London, 1890), 4: 493.
24 Clan-na-Gael Notebook, Devoy Papers, MS 9824, Natiional Library of Ireland.
25 For a list of prominent Clansmen, see *Chicago Inter Ocean*, July 14, 1889. More detailed biographies of some of these can be found in Ffrench, *American Irish in Chicago*. For Sullivan's background, see Michael F. Funchion, *Chicago's Irish Nationalists, 1881–1890* (New York, 1976), pp. 45–46.
26 A list of the officials of these groups and others was usually printed each week in Finerty's *Chicago Citizen*, which began publication in 1882.
27 Founded by Isaac Butt in the 1870s, the Irish Parliamentary party was led by Charles Stewart Parnell during the 1880s. After the Parnell-O'Shea divorce scandal in 1890, the party split into Parnellite and anti-Parnellite factions, but it was reunited in 1900 under the leadership of John Redmond. See Lawrence J. McCaffrey, *Irish Federalism in the 1870's: A Study in Conservative Nationalism* (Philadelphia, 1962); Conor Cruise O'Brien, *Parnell and His Party, 1880–90* (London, 1957); and F.S.L. Lyons, *The Irish Parliamentary Party, 1890–1910* (London, 1951).
28 These speeches were usually reprinted in the *Chicago Citizen*.
29 For the dynamite campaign see Funchion, *Chicago's Irish Nationalists*, pp. 82–86.
30 Thomas N. Brown, *Irish-American Nationalism, 1870–1890* (Philadelphia, 1966), pp. 21–24.
31 *Chicago Citizen*, July 11, 1885; see also *Citizen*, Oct. 26, 1895.
32 For the traditional attitude of the church toward secret societies, see Fergus MacDonald, *The Catholic Church and the Secret Societies in the United States* (New York, 1946), pp. 1–62.
33 For relations between the Clan-na-Gael and the constitutionalists, see

Brown, *Irish-American Nationalism,* pp. 104–106, 109, 112, 121–124, 155–156, 168–171, 176; and Funchion, *Chicago's Irish Nationalists,* pp. 62–64, 73–74, 77–79, 92–93, 95, 98–100, 119–120.

34 McQuaid to Corrigan, Mar. 15, 25, 1886; Feb. 1, 1887; May 6, 1890; Nov. 29, 1891, Archives of the Archdiocese of New York, photostat copies in the University of Notre Dame Archives; Frederick J. Zwierlein, *The Life and Letters of Bishop McQuaid,* 3 vols. (Rochester, 1925–1927),2: 336, 378–379, 383–385, 436, 462; MacDonald, *Secret Societies,* pp. 63–184; Kirkfleet, *Feehan,* pp. 234, 238–240; Robert D. Cross, *The Emergence of Liberal Catholicism in America* (Cambridge, Mass., 1958), pp. 170–171.

35 Feehan was born and reared in Killenaule in the western part of County Tipperary, where the abortive Young Ireland Uprising of 1848 took place. Furthermore, Feehan had a relatively liberal seminary education. Although he completed part of his seminary training at Maynooth, he left there for St. Louis in 1848, a year before Archbishop Cullen arrived in Ireland determined to spread the rigid, ultramontane views of the reactionary Pope Pius IX. Archbishop Corrigan, on the other hand, was one of the first graduates of the North American College in Rome, a bastion of ultramontanism. For Feehan's early life, see Kirkfleet, *Feehan,* pp. 1–23. For Cullen and the Irish church, see Larkin, "Devotional Revolution," pp. 625–652.

36 Diary of John Devoy, Devoy Papers, MS 9820, National Library of Ireland; McQuaid to Corrigan, Feb. 1, 1887, Archives of the Archdiocese of New York, photostat copy in the University of Notre Dame Archives; *Chicago Citizen,* Jan. 3, 1885; Mar. 19, Oct. 15, 1887; *Chicago Inter Ocean,* May 20, 1889; *New World,* Oct. 7, 1893; Kirkfleet, *Feehan,* pp. 123, 129, 134–135, 143–146, 277, 280–282, 294–295; Thompson, *Archdiocese of Chicago,* p. 397; Francis E. Croarkin, *Ninety Years: The Autobiography of Francis E. Croarkin* (Chicago, 1952), p. 47.

37 Ffrench, *American Irish in Chicago,* pp. 796–801; John F. Finerty, *The People's History of Ireland,* 2 vols. (New York, 1904), 2: 928–929; T. P. O'Connor, *Memoirs of an Old Parliamentarian,* 2 vols. (London, 1929), 2: 194–195; "The Untold Story of Catholic Chicago," *Gaelic-American,* Sept. 15, 29, 1923; *Chicago Citizen,* Jan. 3, Dec. 5, 1885; *New World,* Sept. 9, 16, Nov. 25, Dec. 9, 1893; Jan. 13, Mar. 10, 17, April 14, 21, 1894; Mar. 9, 1895; *Chicago Tribune,* Oct. 28, 1889; Mar. 5, 1895; Sept. 25, 1896; *Chicago Inter Ocean,* Mar. 5, 1895.

38 The following are helpful for an understanding of late nineteenth-century Chicago politics: Joel Arthur Tarr, *A Study in Boss Politics: William Lorimer of Chicago* (Urbana, 1971); Lloyd Wendt and Herman Kogan, *Lords of the Levee: The Story of Bathhouse John and Hinky Dink* (New York, 1944); C. O. Johnson, *Carter Henry Harrison I* (Chicago, 1928); Willis J. Abbot, *Carter Henry Harrison: A Memoir* (New York, 1895); Carter H. Harrison II, *Stormy Years: The Autobiography of Carter H. Harrison, Five Times Mayor of Chicago* (Indianapolis, 1935). Carter H. Harrison II, *Growing Up with Chicago* (Chicago, 1944); F. O. Bennett, *Politics and Politicians of Chicago, Cook County, and Illinois, Memorial Volume, 1787–1887* (Chicago, 1886); Perry R. Duis, "The Saloon and the Public City: Chicago and Boston, 1880–1920" (Ph.D. diss., University of Chicago, 1975), pp. 707–725, 745–780.

39 *Chicago Daily News Almanac for 1890*, p. 84. Two other aldermen may also have been Irish, but since their names are common to both Ireland and Great Britain, I did not include them.

40 *Chicago Tribune*, Mar. 25, 1885.

41 For a biographical sketch of O'Hara, see Michael L. Ahern, *The Great Revolution: A History of the Rise and Progress of the People's Party in the City of Chicago and County of Cook* (Chicago, 1874), pp. 123–125. Colorful accounts of the others can be found in Wendt and Kogan, *Lords of the Levee.*

42 *Gaelic-American,* Jan. 10, 1925; Ffrench, *American Irish in Chicago,* pp. 10–15, 713–714; Harrison II, *Growing Up with Chicago,* pp. 209–211; Tarr, *Boss Politics,* 34, 43, 55, 58–59, 74–77, 90–91, 98. For a richly detailed, definitive study of Madden, see Thomas R. Bullard, "From Businessman to Congressman: The Careers of Martin B. Madden" (Ph.D. diss., University of Illinois, Chicago Circle, 1973).

43 See Wendt and Kogan, *Lords of the Levee*; Tarr, pp. 10–12, 65–88; Duis, pp. 707–725, 745–780. Reports in the daily press provide some of the best information on the shenanigans of Irish politicians. For example, see *Chicago Tribune,* Mar. 22, 23, 26, April 3, 7, 10, 1885.

44 Edward M. Levine, *The Irish and Irish Politicians* (Notre Dame, 1966), pp. 32–36, 47–48; William V. Shannon, *The American Irish,* 2nd ed. (New York, 1966), p. 11.

45 Levine, *The Irish,* pp. 36–37; Shannon, pp. 15–16, 52, 60; Lawrence J. McCaffrey, *The Irish Diaspora in America* (Bloomington, Ind., 1976), p. 138.

46 U.S., *Twelfth Census, 1900*, "Special Reports: Occupations," pp. 516–520.

47 *Ibid.*

48 For documentation and a more detailed discussion of the Clan in Chicago politics, see Funchion, *Chicago's Irish Nationalists,* pp. 42–55.

49 Based on U.S., *Eleventh Census, 1890*, "Population," Part II, pp. 650–651.

50 Based on a survey of the biographies of 245 Irish Catholic laymen in Ffrench, *American Irish in Chicago.* Included in the book but omitted from the survey were the biographies of priests, Irish Protestants, and deceased Catholic laymen.

51 For example, Finley Peter Dunne's "Mr. Dooley" columns occasionally refer to the differences between the lace-curtain and working-class Irish during the 1890s. See Charles F. Fanning, Jr., "Finley Peter Dunne and Mr. Dooley: The Chicago Years" (Ph.D. diss., University of Pennsylvania, 1972), pp. 130–133.

52 In 1890, 35.8 percent of all Irish-born male workers were unskilled laborers, compared to 19.6 percent of German-born males and 18.4 percent of Swedish- and Norwegian-born males. Based on U.S., *Eleventh Census, 1900*, "Population," Part II, pp. 650–651. If the second generation, which as a whole ranked higher on the occupational ladder than immigrants, had been included, it seems probable that the Irish would have been at least on a par with the Scandinavians. Unlike the Germans and Irish, relatively few Scandinavians came to Chicago before the 1870s; thus the percentage of second-generation Scandinavians in the labor force would have been far smaller than the percentage of second-generation Germans and Irish.

53 Although the Irish had a smaller percentage of manual workers than

did the Scandinavians, a greater percentage of their male labor force was made up of unskilled workers (23.4 percent compared to 16.7 percent for the Scandinavians). In all respects, however, Irish women fared better than their Scandinavian counterparts. Slightly over one-third of Irish female workers were employed as unskilled laborers, compared to about one-half of Scandinavian women. Based on U.S., *Twelfth Census, 1900*, "Special Reports: Occupations," pp. 516–523.

54 *Chicago Citizen*, July 11, 1885.
55 Charles Cleaver, "Extracts from Articles Which Appeared First in the Chicago *Tribune*," in Mable McIllvaine, ed., *Reminiscences of Chicago during the Forties and Fifties* (Chicago, 1913), pp. 55–56; Pierce, *History of Chicago*, 1:232–233, 377–378, 381–383, 398; 2: 211–214, 379–381, 437–439; Fleming, "Canal at Chicago," pp. 131, 152–153; Bennett, *Politicians in Chicago*, pp. 59, 97–100; Charles M. Thompson, *The Illinois Whigs before 1846* (Urbana, 1915), pp. 78–80, 82, 87–88, 128–129; Solomon Wills to James B. Campbell, Aug. 12, 1838, James B. Campbell Papers, Chicago Historical Society; John P. Senning, "The Know-Nothing Movement in Illinois, 1854–56," *Illinois State Historical Society Journal* 7 (1914): 9–33; Thomas M. O'Keefe, "Chicago's Flirtation with Political Nativism, 1854–1856," *Records of the American Catholic Historical Society of Philadelphia* 82 (1971): 131–158; John F. Flinn, *History of the Chicago Police* (Chicago, 1887), pp. 71–74; William Kirkland and John Moses, *History of Chicago*, 2 vols. (Chicago, 1895), 1: 130–131; *Chicago Tribune*, April 19, 1874; Sanders, *The Education of an Urban Minority*, pp. 19–24; Piper, "The Irish in Chicago," pp. 8, 45–46; M. E. Thomas, *Nativism in the Old Northwest, 1850–1860* (Washington, D.C., 1936), p. 163; Shanabruch. "The Catholic Church's Role in the Americanization of Chicago's Immigrants," pp. 35–57.
56 For example, see the sermon of Rev. M. M. Parkhurst, pastor of the Michigan Avenue Methodist Church, in *Chicago Tribune*, Aug. 14, 1876.
57 For example, see editorial in *Chicago Tribune*, April 1, 1886.
58 John Higham, *Strangers in the Land: Patterns of American Nativism, 1860–1925* (New Brunswick, N.J., 1955), pp. 53, 58–60.
59 H. J. Desmond, *The A.P.A. Movement* (Washington, D.C., 1912), pp. 45–46; Higham, pp. 61–62; Rowland T. Berthoff, *British Immigrants in Industrial America, 1790–1950* (Cambridge, Mass., 1953), p. 201; *Chicago Tribune*, Nov. 4, 1888.
60 *Chicago Citizen*, Jan. 5, 1889, Oct. 4, 1890; Higham, p. 61. For the A.P.A., see Donald L. Kinzer, *An Episode in Anti-Catholicism: The American Protective Association* (Seattle, 1964).
61 *America*, May 30, 1889.
62 For example, see *New World*, Dec. 30, 1893; April 21, 1894.
63 Occasionally, generational conflicts did arise among the ranks of the nationalists. For example, in 1883, when Sullivan, who was born either in Maine or Canada, became president of the Irish National League of America, the Irish-born Finerty complained that non-Irish natives were taking over control of the Irish nationalist movement in America. At this time, however, Finerty was at odds with Sullivan over a number of issues; later on, when he was reconciled with Sullivan, such complaints ceased. Diary of John Devoy, Devoy Papers, MS 9820, National Library of Ireland.

64   "The Untold Story of Catholic Chicago"; Shanabruch, "The Catholic Church's Role in the Americanization of Chicago's Immigrants," pp. 245–255; Jeremiah J. Crowley, *Romanism: A Menace to the Nation* (Aurora, Mo., 1912), pp. 29–52.

65   *Chicago Tribune,* April 19, 1874.

66   F. P. Dunne's "Mr. Dooley" columns make reference to county rivalries. Dunne, however, tends to overemphasize the intensity of these rivalries. See the columns reprinted in Fanning, "Mr. Dooley," pp. 70–71, 86–87, 89.

67   Of the 69 born outside of Chicago, only 12 arrived there before the age of eleven. Of the 57 who arrived in Chicago after the age of ten, 51 had spent their pre-Chicago years entirely in the East and/or Midwest.

68   For colorful accounts of the struggles among local politicians, see Wendt and Kogan, *Lords of the Levee.* Reports in the daily press also provide ample evidence of the often bitter nature of these struggles.

69   Funchion, *Chicago's Irish Nationalists,* pp. 47–50.

70   For documentation and a more detailed account of the Clan-na-Gael split and the Cronin murder, see Funchion, pp. 82–123.

71   Pierce, *History of Chicago,* 3: 537.

72   No doubt some of the immigrants from the west of Ireland were fluent in both English and Irish. There may even have been a few who could only speak Irish. It is interesting to note that, although Irish-language classes were held regularly in Chicago from 1884 on, they attracted only a handful of students. Apparently, few Chicago Irish were interested in spending time studying the language of their ancestors. For the Irish language movement in Chicago see *Chicago Citizen,* Nov. 5, 1892; Jan. 5, 26, April 13, 1895; *New World,* June 16, 1894; *Irish World,* April 20, 1895.

73   Ahern, *The Great Revolution*; Pierce, 3: 342–344.

74   Humbert S. Nelli, *Italians in Chicago, 1880–1930: A Study in Ethnic Mobility* (New York, 1970), pp. 92–112.

75   John M. Allswang, *A House for All Peoples: Ethnic Politics in Chicago, 1890–1936* (Lexington, Ky., 1971).

76   Sanders, *The Education of an Urban Minority,* pp. 54, 108; Walsh, "The Catholic Church in Chicago," pp. 278–279; Shanabruch, pp. 124–155. German Lutherans were also strong opponents of the Edwards Law.

77   For Dixon's biography, see Ffrench, *American Irish in Chicago,* pp. 16–22.

78   "Observer," Letter to the Editor, *Chicago Citizen,* Aug. 27, 1887.

79   *Chicago Citizen,* Sept. 17, 1892; April 15, 29, 1893; July 6, Aug. 31, 1895.

80   Sullivan, Letter to the Editor, *Irish World,* Feb. 16, 1884.

81   In 1890, for example, there were only 5,777 Irish-born males in Chicago who were not American citizens. U.S., *Eleventh Census, 1890,* "Population," Part II, pp. 288–289.

82   J. J. McKenna, *Stories by the Original "Jawn" McKenna* (Chicago, 1918), pp. 62–63.

CHAPTER II: JEWISH CHICAGO: DIVERSITY TO COMMUNITY

This chapter partly derives from research undertaken for the Ph.D. degree in History at the University of Chicago, supervised by Prof. Arthur Mann, for whose guiding counsel the author is deeply grateful.

1 *The Occident,* Dec. 21, 1886.
2 Nathan Glazer, *American Judaism* (Chicago, 1957), p. 23; Marshall Sklare, ed., *The Jews: Social Patterns of an American Group* (New York, 1958), p. 11; Walter LaQueur, *A History of Zionism* (New York, 1972), pp. 3–6, 21–25; Eric E. Hirshler, ed., *Jews From Germany in the United States* (New York, 1955), pp. 22, 34–36, 116.
3 Hyman L. Meites, History of the Jews of Chicago (Chicago, 1924), pp. 37–39.
4 *Ibid.,* p. 46.
5 *Ibid.*
6 Louis Wirth, *The Ghetto* (Chicago, 1928), pp. 257–261; Meites, pp. 37–39,41,46.
7 Bernard Felsenthal and Herman Eliassof, *History of Kehillath Anshe Maariv* (Chicago, 1897), p. 12; Jacob J. Weinstein, *A History of K.A.M. Congregation of the Men of the West* (Chicago, 1951), p. 3.
8 Morris A. Gutstein, *A Priceless Heritage* (New York, 1953), pp. 27, 31; Meites, pp. 53, 78–79.
9 Gutstein, pp. 28–29.
10 Meites, pp. 100–107, 149, 155, 407–416; Wirth, p. 174.
11 *Ibid.,* pp. 172–174.
12 Philip L. Bregstone, *Chicago and its Jews: A Cultural History* (Chicago, 1933), pp. 143–144; Erich Rosenthal, "Acculturation Without Assimilation? The Jewish Community of Chicago, Illinois," *American Journal of Sociology,* LXVI (Nov. 1960), 279; Vivien M. Palmer, *History of Chicago Communities* (typescript, Chicago Historical Society, 1930). V, Document 6.
13 Gutstein, p. 283; Meites, pp. 45–46.
14 Sinai Executive Board Minutes, Dec. 28, 1885; Gutstein, pp. 172–173.
15 *The Reform Advocate,* 1 (26 Sep. 1891).
16 *Ibid.,* p. 21; XXI (May 4, 1901), 305; Harold Korey, "The History of Jewish Education in Chicago" (Master's thesis, Univeristy of Chicago, 1922), p. 40.
17 Wirth, p. 170.
18 *Hull House Maps and Papers* (New York, 1895), pp. 17, 93; Wilfred Carsel, *A History of the Chicago Ladies Garment Workers' Union* (Chicago, 1940), p. 237; Wirth, p. 180.
19 Carsel, pp. 5–6.
20 Charles S. Bernheimer, *The Russian Jew in the United States* (Philadelphia, 1905), pp. 136–137, 321–322; Robert Hunter, *Tenement Conditions in Chicago* (Chicago, 1901), pp. 60, 64, 97, 108; Melech Epstein, *Jewish Labor in the United States* (New York, 1942), I, 104; Rosenthal, pp. 278–279.
21 Florence Kelly, *First Special Report of the Factory Inspectors of Illinois on Small-Pox in the Tenement House Sweatshops of Chicago* (Springfield, Ill., 1894), pp. 6, 8–10, 40.
22 Oscar Handlin, *Adventure in Freedom* (New York, 1954), p. 92.
23 Bernheimer, p. 140.
24 *Yiddishe Arbeiter Welt* (Yiddish), May 10, 1910, p. 3; Epstein, I, 94; Kelly, pp. 10–11; *Hull House Maps and Papers,* p. 41.
25 "The Immigrant," *Council of Jewish Women Monthly Bulletin,* IV (Sep. 1912); Joel A. Tarr, *A Study in Boss Politics: William Lorimer of Chicago* (Urbana, Ill., 1971), pp. 13–14; Bernard Horwich, *My First Eighty Years*

(Chicago, 1939), p. 126. Horwich observes that "crime was rampant and no one was safe. Especially Jews, they were constantly the recipients of well aimed missiles being thrown at them and their long beards made welcome targets for youths who delighted in pulling those beards. These men of Israel carried packs on their backs filled with notions and light dry goods. . . . There was hardly a streetcar where there were not to be found some Jewish peddlers with their packs riding to or from their business."

26   *Sentinel History of Chicago Jewry, 1911–1961* (Chicago, 1961), pp. 79–85; Simon Rawidowicz, ed., *The Chicago Pinkas* (Chicago, 1952), pp. 125–126.

27   *The Occident,* Sep. 28, 1889.

28   *Report of the Senate Vice Committee* (Springfield, Ill., 1916), p. 402; Esther Kohn Papers (Jane Addams Hull House Museum, Chicago), III, n.d., "Speeches and Articles"; Bernheimer, pp. 251–254

29   Wirth, p. 205.

30   *The Occident,* Dec. 31, 1886.

31   *Ibid.,* May 29, 1891.

32   Gutstein, p. 37.

33   Erich Rosenthal, "This Was North Lawndale," *Jewish Social Studies.* XXII (1960), 68–69; Wirth, p. 191.

34   Louis Wirth and Eleanor H. Bernert, eds., *Local Community Fact Book of Chicago* (Chicago, 1949), p. 29; Rosenthal, "Acculturation Without Assimilation," pp. 276–282; "The Jewish Community of Albany Park," Sec. II of *Report of Study of the Jewish People's Institute, Chicago, Illinois* (New York, Jewish Welfare Board, 1937), pp. 2–3, 6.

35   *Ibid.,* pp. 32–40; Meites, p. 535; *History of Chicago Communities,* I, Documents 57, 67, 68, 69.

36   Wirth, pp. 257–261; Bregstone, pp. 143–144; Rawidowicz, *Chicago Pinkas,* p. 79; Paul R. Conway, "The Apartment House Dweller: A Study of Social Change in Hyde Park" (M.A. thesis, University of Chicago, 1926), pp. 214–215.

37   *Sentinel History of Chicago Jewry,* p. 27; Ernest W. Burgess Papers, IV, Box 48, University of Chicago.

38   For an extended and comprehensive examination of the politics of Chicago Jewry, see Edward H. Mazur, "Minyans for a Prairie City: The Politics of Chicago Jewry, 1850–1940" (Ph.D. diss., University of Chicago, 1974). See also Joel A. Tarr, *Boss Politics;* Carter H. Harrison II, *Stormy Years* (Indianapolis, 1935); W.J. Abbott, *Carter Henry Harrison: A Memoir* (New York, 1895); Adolf Kraus, *Reminiscences and Comments* (Chicago, 1925).

39   *Reform Advocate,* XXIII, No. 6 (Mar. 15, 1902), 476.

40   In 1914, Horner's victory margin was 32,633 votes: in 1930, his margin was 691,854. Tom Littlewood, *Horner of Illinois* (Evanston, 1969), pp. 29, 33–35, 44.

41   Adolph Sabath, a Bohemian-Jew, was elected U.S. congressman of the 5th District in 1906 and served until his death in 1952. His aide-de-camp and chief liaison with the Jewish community, Harry Fisher, became a municipal court justice in 1912. Michael and Moe Rosenberg were the chieftains of the 24th Ward, the Lawndale Jewish ghetto. Under their tutelage the ward became one of the leading Democratic bastions

in Chicago. Michael was ward committeeman from 1923 until his death in 1928. His brother Moe succeeded him and governed the ward until he died in 1934. The committeemanship was assumed by Alderman Jacob Arvey, who had served in the city council since 1923. Under his leadership, the 24th Ward, the most Jewish election district in Chicago, became known as the number one Democratic precinct in the United States.

42   *Sunday Jewish Courier,* Apr. 10, 1934, p. 10.
43   A survey of twenty-five precincts with at least a 50% German-Jewish majority indicates that Horner received 77.2% of the German-Jewish vote. A similar survey of 111 Eastern European-Jewish precincts with at least a 55% East European-Jewish majority indicates that Horner received 86.2% of the East European vote.
44   Charles E. Merriam Papers, Apr. 7, 1934, University of Chicago, Box 99, Folder 6.
45   Littlewood, p. 182; *New Republic,* CXVI (Mar. 24, 1947), pp. 20–23. Horner averaged 71.8% of the vote in 30 German-Jewish precincts, compared to 51.6% in 114 precincts with at least a 55% East European-Jewish majority.
46   In the general election, Henry Horner's vote in the 30 German-Jewish precincts averaged 68.3%. The slight decline in German-Jewish support from the primary was more than offset by his 81.3% of the vote in the 114 precincts with at least a 55% East European-Jewish majority.

CHAPTER III THE JEWS OF CHICAGO: SHTETL TO SUBURB

1   Morris A. Gutstein, *A Priceless Heritage* (New York, 1953), pp. 25–34.
2   Seymour Jacob Pomrenze, "Aspects of Chicago Russian-Jewish Life, 1893–1915," in Simon Rawidowicz, ed., *The Chicago Pinkas* (Chicago, 1952), pp. 130–131.
3   Hyman L. Meites, ed., *History of the Jews of Chicago* (Chicago, 1924), pp. 150–151.
4   Louis Wirth, *The Ghetto* (Chicago, 1928), pp. 205–206.
5   Charles Bernheimer, *The Russian Jew in the United States: Studies of Social Conditions in New York, Philadelphia, and Chicago, with a Description of Rural Settlements* (Philadelphia, 1905), pp. 173–174.
6   Nathan Glazer, *American Judaism* (Chicago, 1957), p. 66.
7   Ira Berkow, *Maxwell Street* (Garden City, N.Y., 1977), pp. 10–11.
8   Leonard C. Mishkin, "Orthodoxy: Saga of Chicago's Great West Side," *The Sentinel's History of Chicago Jewry,* 1911–1961 (Chicago, 1961), p. 127.
9   For an overall geography of the Chicago region, which pays close attention to social and ethnic changes, see Irving Cutler, *Chicago: Metropolis of the Mid-Continent,* 2nd ed. (Dubuque, Iowa, 1976). [Eds.]
10   Irving Howe, *World of Our Fathers* (New York, 1976), pp. 618–619.

CHAPTER IV: GREEK SURVIVAL IN CHICAGO

1   Some speculation has existed that Columbus himself was a Greek. See Seraphim G. Canoutas, *Christopher Columbus: A Greek Nobleman* (New York, 1943).

2   For an excellent account of this little-known episode in American colonial history, see E. P. Panagopoulos, *New Smyrna: An Eighteenth Century Greek Odyssey* (Gainseville, Fla., 1966). Contemporary testimony of this colonization is to be found in *Virgina Gazette,* Sept. 29, Oct. 6, 1768.

3   For an account of the "Greek fever" that swept America at the time, see Stephan A. Larabee, *Hellas Observed: The American Experience of Greece, 1775–1865* (New York, 1952), Chs. 3–7; William St. Clair, *That Greece Might Still Be Free: the Philhellenes in the War of Independence* (New York, 1972); Edward M. Earle, "American Interest in the Greek Cause, 1821–1827," *American Historical Review* 33 (Oct. 1927): 44–63; and Harris J. Booras, *Hellenic Independence and America's Contribution to the Cause* (Rutland, Vt., 1934).

4   Thomas Burgess, *Greeks in America: An Account of their Coming, Progress, Customs, Living, and Aspirations* (Boston, 1913), pp. 190–196; and Booras, *Hellenic Independence,* pp. 193–197. For a listing of Greek immigrants in the Union Navy, see P. Perros, "Officers of Greek Descent in the Union Navy, 1861–1865," Athene 24 (Autumn 1964): 12–14ff.

5   Seraphim G. Canoutas, *Hellenism in America or the History of the Greeks in America* (New York, 1918), pp. 160–162; Basil T. Zoustis, *O en Ameriki Hellenismos kai e drasis autou* [The Greeks in America and Their Activity] (New York, 1954), pp. 43–51.

6   For a descriptive analysis of this movement, see Theodore Saloutos, *They Remember America: The Story of Repatriated Greek-Americans* (Berkeley, 1956).

7   Compiled from the 1970 *Census: General Social and Economic Characteristics, Illinois* (U.S. Gov't. Printing Office, 1972), Table 40, p. 325.

8   *Greek Star* (Chicago), Apr. 9, 1937. Founded in Chicago in 1904, this Greek ethnic newspaper remains today the oldest of its kind in continuous publication in the United States.

9   *The Chicago Herald,* May 10, 1887; *Chicago Daily Journal,* April 22, 1924; see also *Chicago Herald and Examiner,* May 2, 1938; Canoutas, *Hellenism,* pp. 184–186.

10 *Chicago Tribune,* Feb. 21, 1897.

11 *Chicago Tribune,* Apr. 7, 1895.

12 *Chicago Tribune,* Feb. 15, 1897.

13 Henry Pratt Fairchild, *Greek Immigration to the United States* (New Haven 1911), pp. 123–124. For a colorful description of Chicago's Greektown at Halsted and Harrison streets, see Edward A. Steiner, *On the Trail of the Immigrant* (New York, 1906), pp. 282–291; see also Theano P. Magaris, *Chroniko tou Halsted Street* [Chronicle of Halsted Street] (Athens, Greece, 1962) and her *Etchings of Chicago* (Athens, 1967).

14 This centuries-old excommunication was lifted on December 7, 1965, by Pope Paul VI and Patriarch Athenagoras of Constantinople in simultaneous ceremonies; see Deno John Geanakoplos, *Byzantine East and Latin West: Two Worlds of Christendom in the Middle Ages and Renaissance* (New York, 1966), preface. Witness also the visit of Pope John Paul II to Istanbul on Nov. 30, 1979, to meet with Patriarch Demetrius in the continuation of the policy of reconciliation, see *Time,* Dec. 10, 1979, p. 91.

15   See Steven Runciman, *The Great Church in Captivity* (Cambridge, Eng., 1968); and Timothy Ware, *Eustratios Argenti: A Study of the Greek Church under Turkish Rule* (Oxford, 1964).

16   Information about the religious affairs of Greek people has been secured from standard sources, which, unless otherwise noted, are in agreement with matters cited: Ernst Benz, *The Eastern Orthodox Church: Its Thought and Life* (New York, 1963); Thomas J. Lacey, *A Study of the Eastern Orthodox Church*, 2nd. rev. ed. (New York, 1912); John Meyendorff, *The Orthodox Church: Its Past and Its Role in the World Today* (New York, 1962); Basil K. Stephanides, *Ecclesiastiki historia* [Ecclesiastical History] (Athens, 1948); Frank Gavin, *Some Aspects of Contemporary Greek Orthodox Thought* (Milwaukee, 1923); Timothy Ware, *The Orthodox Church* (Baltimore, 1963); and Panagiotis Bratsiotis, *The Greek Orthodox Church*, trans. Joseph Blenkinsop (Notre Dame, Ind., 1968).

17   Paul Tillich, "The Interpretation of History," *Chicago Tribune*, July 5, 1970.

18   The distinction is made by Canoutas in *Hellenism*, pp. 162–163 (fn.), and in Burgess, pp. 52–53.

19   Holy Trinity Church, *Forty Years of Greek Life in Chicago, 1897–1937* (Chicago, 1937), pp. 19–22.

20   See Theodore Saloutos, *The Greeks in the United States* (Cambridge, Mass., 1964), pp. 118–120.

21   On September 24, 1794, eight Russian Orthodox monks landed on Kodiak Island. In succeeding years, thousands of Aleuts were baptized, and in 1824 the mission was run by John Veniaminov, who translated the gospel into Aleutian, created schools, and constructed an Aleutian grammar. When, in 1867, Alaska was sold to the United States, a separate diocese was created with the episcopal residence in San Francisco and later in New York. A detailed missionary account appears in the *Encyclopedia Britannica*, 1955 ed., s.v. "Orthodox Eastern Church," by Matthew Spinka.

22   Burgess, p. 54; *Saloniki Greek Press* (Chicago), Dec. 12, 1931.

23   A list of "canonical" and "uncanonical" clergymen based on the political division engendered by the Royalist-Liberal controversy is to be found in the *Monthly Illustrated National Herald* 11 (Apr. 1925):299–301. In Chicago three of the four Greek churches were Royalist. In 1924 a national meeting was called by the Royalist churches to force the Greek government to rescind the Patriarchal Tome of 1922 and again place the American churches under Greece. See *E en eti 1924 en Sikago laiko-kleriko syneleusis* [The Chicago Laity-Clergy Conference in the Year 1924] (printed minutes of proceedings in possession of this writer), pp. 8–11.

24   *Orthodoxy 1964* (Athens, 1964), pp. 350–354.

25   The *symboulion* of the Association of the Community of Holy Trinity Church, the first Chicago *koinotis*, was often at odds with the parish. On several occasions it became involved in court litigations. See Gregory A. Papailiou v. Demetrios Manousos et al., 108 Illinois Appellate Court 272 (1903).

26   For a description of the democratic organization of the Greek church as a *koinotis*, see W. Lloyd Warner and Leo Srole, *The Social System of American Ethnic Groups* (New Haven, 1945), pp. 176–192.

27 *Ibid.*
28 Canoutas, *Hellenism,* pp. 228, 330, 326; Mary S. Economidou, *E Hellenes tis Amerikis opos tous eida* [The Greeks in America as I Saw Them] (New York, 1916), pp. 151–163.
29 Burgess, p. 108.
30 *Greek Star* (Chicago), Oct. 21, 1904 (Chicago Foreign Language Press Survey, WPA Project, 1942).
31 *Greek Star* (Chicago), Feb. 26, 1909; *Saloniki* (Chicago), June 19, July 17, 1915.
32 *Greek Star* (Chicago), Mar. 5, 1909; *Saloniki* (Chicago), July 10, 15, 17, 1916.
33 Theodore N. Constant, "The Religion of the Hellenes," *Athene* 6 (Mar. 1945): 12; *Atlantis* (New York), July 12, Dec. 17, 1908.
34 *Saloniki* (Chicago), Feb. 18, 1914; Nov. 13, 1915.
35 *Saloniki* (Chicago), Dec. 4, 1915; Dec. 15, 1917; *Loxias* (Chicago), March 4, 1911.
36 *Saloniki* (Chicago), Dec. 4, 1915.
37 *Saloniki* (Chicago), Oct. 16, 1915.
38 Two communities, Annunciation and Saint Demetrios, managed to unite into a consolidated community in 1942.
39 For detailed accounts of the role of the church in the Greek community, see Warner and Srole, pp. 156–219; Saloutos, *Greeks in the United States,* pp. 118–137; Burgess, pp. 87–122; Thomas James Lacey, *A Study in Social Heredity as Illustrated by the Greek People* (New York, 1916), pp. 37–39; J. Mayonne Stycos, "Community Cohesion Among the Greeks of Bridgetown," in Arnold Caroline Rose, ed., *Minority Problems* (New York, 1964), pp. 255–256.
40 For an insightful look into the role of the Greek Orthodox Church in ethnic identity and the encroachment of assimilation, see Theodore Saloutos, "The Greek Orthodox Church in the United States and Assimilation," *International Migration Review* 7 (Winter 1973): 395–407.
41 *Saloniki* (Chicago), Sept. 7, 1918.
42 *Greek Star* (Chicago), Jan. 19, 1906.
43 Lacey, *Social Heredity,* p. 27.
44 *Chicago Tribune,* Apr. 7, 1895.
45 *Chicago Tribune,* Feb. 21, 1897.
46 *Greek Star* (Chicago), Apr. 1, 22, 1904.
47 *Greek Star* (Chicago), Sept. 25, 1908; interviews with Pericles Orphanos, George Damolaris, et al., May 21, 1968.
48 See Grace Abbott, "A Study of the Greeks of Chicago," *American Journal of Sociology* 15 (Nov. 1909): 382–384.
49 *Loxias* (Chicago), Feb. 12, June 4, 1910.
50 *Chicago Herald and Examiner,* Nov. 6, 1927.
51 *Loxias* (Chicago), May 21, Oct. 15, 1910.
52 Fairchild, p. 171. At one time Chicago had as many as one thousand Greek-owned candy stores. It still remains the Greek-American center of the candy industry. In 1947 an estimated 350 to 400 shops and eight to ten candy manufacturers were located in the city. See *Greek Star* (Chicago), June 15, 1906.
53 *Chicago Herald and Examiner,* Nov. 6, 1927.

54 *Greek Star* (Chicago), June 8, 1907. For the Horatio Alger stories, see *Monthly Illustrated National Herald* 11 (Apr. 1925): 333–353.
55 *Greek Star* (Chicago), Nov. 14, 1919.
56 Other ethnic groups contributed per capita as follows: Germans, $4.05; English and Irish, $7.14; Italians, $30; Slavs, $28.10; Russians, $14.80. As quoted in Fairchild, pp. 191–192.
57 Eliot Grinnell Mears, *Greece Today: The Aftermath of the Refugee Impact* (Stanford, 1929), pp. 195–197.
58 This was due to the resurgence of Greek immigration following the Displaced Persons Act of 1948. See E. N. Botsas, "Emigration and Capital Formation: The Case of Greece," *Balkan Studies* 10 (1969): 127–134.
59 Florence J. Chaney, "The Social and Educational Protection of the Immigrant Girl in Chicago" (M.A. thesis, University of Chicago), p. 31.
60 G. Abbott, "Study of the Greeks," p. 388.
61 U.S., Congress, House of Representatives, *Hearings before the President's Commission on Immigration and Naturalization*, 82nd Cong., 2nd sess., 1952, pp. 216–218, 431–433, 536–537.
62 Bernard C. Rosen, "Race, Ethnicity and the Achievement Syndrome," *American Sociological Review* 24 (Feb. 1959): 47–60.
63 Leonard Broom, Cora A. Martin, and Betty Maynard, "Status Profiles of Racial and Ethnic Populations," *Social Science Quarterly* 12 (Sept. 1971): 379–388.
64 U.S. Bureau of the Census, *Census of the Population: 1970*, Subject Reports, National Origin and Language, Final Report PC(2)–1a.
65 Rosen, "Race, Ethnicity and the Achievement Syndrome," pp. 47–60.
66 In addition to the Lycurgus Society, there were the Spartan, Tegea, Arcadia, Laconia, and Greek Benevolent societies. *Chicago Tribune*, Feb. 16, 1897.
67 For an analysis of Greeks as joiners of formal organizations, see Constantine A. Yeracaris, "A Study of the Voluntary Associations of the Greek Immigrants of Chicago from 1890 to 1948, with Special Emphasis on World War II and Post War Period" (M.A. thesis, University of Chicago, Sept. 1950).
68 Robert E. Park and E. W. Burgess, *The City* (Chicago, 1925), pp. 120–121.
69 *Kathemerini* (Chicago), Apr. 18, 1929.
70 Supra, pp. 104–105.
71 See *Saloniki* (Chicago), Dec. 5, 26, 1914.
72 Yeracaris, pp. 47–49, 97–99.
73 Robert E. Park and Herbert A. Miller, *Old World Traits Transplanted* (New York, 1921), p. 121.
74 *Chicago Record*, Dec. 13, 1899.
75 *Hull House Bulletin* 6 (1903–1904): 18.
76 S.N. Soter, "Jane Addams, the Hull House, and the Early Greek Immigrant," *Greek Star* (Chicago), Nov. 25, 1964, p. 3.
77 *Hull House Yearbook*, Jan. 1, 1916, p. 33.
78 G. Abbott, "Study of the Greeks," p. 385.
79 Jane Addams, *Twenty Years at Hull House* (New York, 1910, 1961), pp. 268–269; see also *Hull House Yearbook*, Jan. 1, 1913, pp. 23, 26–27; Jan. 1, 1921, pp. 9–10.
80 Addams, *Twenty Years*, pp. 304–305; *Hull House Yearbook*, Jan. 1, 1913, p. 23; and *Forty Years of Greek Life*, p. 57.

81   *Hull House Bulletin* 5 (Autumn 1904): 23–24.
82   A detailed description of social conditions on Halsted Street is to be found in Addams, *Twenty Years*, pp. 80–83.
83   *Hull House Bulletin* 6 (Autumn 1904): 23–24.
84   *Ibid.*
85   Addams, *Twenty Years*, p. 184.
86   Demetrios Michalaros, "1960: Jane Addams Centennial," *Athene 21* (Autumn 1960): 3.
87   *Greek Star* (Chicago), May 23, 1930; Nov. 25, 1964.
88   *Forty Years of Greek Life*, pp. 55–56; Malafouris, p. 141.
89   Constantine D. Orphan, "Goodbye Greektown," *Inland: The Magazine of the Middle West* (Spring 1963): 20.
90   As quoted in James Weber Linn, *Jane Addams: A Biography* (New York, 1935), p. 111.
91   This was also true of AHEPA during its early history. Clippings from American and Greek newspapers in the scrapbooks of Mrs. Bessie Spirides indicate that the Hellas chapter of the Daughters of Penelope (an auxiliary of AHEPA) raised thousands of dollars for Greek schools by holding a series of cultural events in the 1930s and early 1940s. For an up-to-date version of how the AHEPA "family" of organizations operates in Chicago, see *Chicago Tribune*, Nov. 16, 1969. For a definitive account, see George J. Leber, *The History of the Order of AHEPA, 1922–1972* (Washington, D.C., 1972), on the occasion of its fiftieth anniversary.
92   *The Ahepan* 2 (Sept. 1929): 3; Kimon A. Doukas, "The Story of Ahepa." *Athene* 11 (Summer 1950): 39–43.
93   See *American Hellenic World* (Chicago), July 13, 1928.
94   *The Ahepan* 1 (1928): 12.
95   *Chicago Daily Journal*, Dec. 31, 1925.
96   Leber, p. 194.
97   *Greek Press* (Chicago), Feb. 10, 1932; *Greek Star* (Chicago), Apr. 2, 1929; *The Ahepan* 22 (Jan.–Feb. 1948): 15.
98   Leber, p. 241.
99   *The AHEPA Magazine* 6 (Mar. 1932): 28.
100 *The Ahepan* 22 (May–June 1948): 4.
101 *Orthodox Observer*, Sept. 13, 1936, p. 11.
102 *American Hellenic World* (Chicago), Apr. 2, 1927.
103 *Athene* 27 (Autumn 1955): 44.
104 *Greek Press* (Chicago), Jan. 29, 1963; Dec. 8, 1967.
105 See *Greek Star* (Chicago), July 19, 1973.
106 Information concerning educational development in Greece has been secured from the following sources, which, unless otherwise noted, are in agreement with matters cited, Kalliniki Dendrinou Antonakaki, *Greek Education* (New York, 1955); Lazarus Belelis, *Kapodistrias os idritis laikis paideias en Helladi* [Capodistrias as Founder of Popular Education in Greece] (Athens: John N. Sederis, 1908); Kenneth J. Freeman, *Schools of Hellas: An Essay on the Practice and Theory of Ancient Greek Education from 600 to 300 B.C.* (London, 1907); Christos P. Economos, *Koraes os ethnikos paidagogos* [Koraes as National Educator] (Athens, 1904), 2nd ed.; Cornelius C. Felton, *The Schools of Modern Greece* (n.p., 1861): H. I. Marrou, *A History of Education in Antiquity* (New

York, 1956), passim; U.S., Office of Education, *Report of the Commissioner of Education for the Year 1896–97*, "Education in Greece," by Daniel Quinn, vol. 1 (Washington, D.C.) pp. 267–346; and George Milo Wilcox, *Education in Greece* (n.p., 1933).

107   For an in-depth treatment of this development, see the monumental study of Werner Jaeger, *Paideia: The Ideals of Greek Culture*, 3 vols. 2nd ed., trans. Gilbert Highet (New York, 1960).

108   Philipos Johannis, "Public Instruction in Modern Greece," *American Journal of Education* 12 (1862): 571–572. However, higher education was allowed to continue because Mohammed II, conqueror of Constantinople, permitted Patriarch Gennadius Scholarius to reestablish the patriarchal school. See G. Chassiotis, *L'Instruction publique chez les Grecs depuis la prise de Constantinople par les Turcs, jusqu'a nos jours* (Paris, 1881), pp. 4, 34–42.

109   Terrence Spencer, *Fair Greece Sad Relic* (London, 1954), p. 98. Compare the leadership of Archbishop Makarios in the independence struggle in Cyprus with the role of the clergy in the Greek Revolution.

110   Quinn, pp. 296–297.

111   U.S. Department of Labor, Bureau of Immigration, *Annual Report of the Commissioner-General of Immigration, 1910* (Washington, D.C., 1910), table 8, pp. 20–21; *Annual Report of the Commissioner-General of Immigration, 1920*, table 7, pp. 95–97.

112   A sociological study of three generations of Greeks residing in San Antonio, Texas revealed that 100 percent of the families interviewed spoke Greek. See Helen Capanidou, Lauquier, "Culture Among Three Generations of Greeks," *American Catholic Sociological Review* 22 (1961): 224. See also *Encyclopaedia Britannica*, 1955 ed., s.v. "Orthodox Eastern Church," by Matthew Spinka.

113   When the Dillingham Commission made its investigation in Chicago in 1908, it found 193 Greek children (and five Turkish children) enrolled in the public schools of Chicago and 34 Greek children attending a Greek parochial school. See *Abstract of Report on Children of Immigrants in Schools* (Washington, D.C., 1911), pp. 66–67.

114   See Immigrants' Protective League, *Seventh Annual Report for Year Ending January 1, 1916*, p. 5. See also Grace Abbott, *The Immigrant and Community* (New York, 1917), p. 39.

115   G. Abbott, "Study of Greeks," p. 104.

116   Data compiled from a review of the Annual Reports of the Chicago Board of Education for a period 1902 to 1922.

117   See Ernest W. Burgess and Charles Newcomb, *Census Data of the City of Chicago, 1920* (Chicago, 1931), p. 26.

118   C. Orphan, "Goodbye Greektown," p. 23.

119   Cited in Andrew T. Kopan, "Education and Greek Immigrants in Chicago, 1892–1973: A Study in Ethnic Survival" (Ph.D. diss. University of Chicago, 1974), p. 209.

120   For the erosion of Hellenic sentiment among Greek immigrants, see Saloutos, *Greeks in the United States*, pp. 310–325.

121   Hannah B. Clark, *The Public Schools of Chicago* (Chicago, 1897), p. 74; the Greek text of the petition is to be found in the *Greek Star*, Jan. 24, 1936.

122   Interview with Paul Demos, a founder of the league, July 19, 1970.

123 Interview with George Drossos, veteran Greek-language educator of Chicago, Nov. 17, 1967.
124 Chicago Public Schools, "A Comprehensive Design for Bilingual Education" (Chicago Board of Education, 1972), mimeographed, p. 3.
125 *Greek Star* (Chicago), Dec. 23, 1971.
126 Letter of Superintendent James F. Redmond to Hellenic Council on Education, Sept. 5, 1972.
127 See *Greek Press* (Chicago), Apr. 27, 1973; *Chicago Tribune*, July 8, 1973; and *Hellenic Chronicle* (Boston), Oct. 10, 1973.
128 See *Ethnic Studies Process* (Chicago, 1972), pp. 1–46.
129 *Ibid.*
130 Cited in Charles E. Silberman, *Crisis in the Classroom* (New York, 1970), p. 58. See also Colin Greer, "Public Schools: The Myth of the Melting Pot," *Saturday Review* 52 (Nov. 15, 1969): 84–85; and especially his later work, *The Great School Legend. A Revisionist Interpretation of American Public Education* (New York, 1972).
131 For an explanation of this phenomenon, see Bernard C. Rosen, "Race, Ethnicity and the Achievement Syndrome," *American Sociological Review* 24 (Feb. 1959): 47–60.
132 See *Forty Years of Greek Life*, pp. 52–53; *Greek Star* (Chicago), Mar. 8, 1904.
133 *Greek Star* (Chicago), Feb. 9, 1906.
134 *Greek Star* (Chicago), Feb. 16, 1906.
135 *Greek Star* (Chicago), June 15, 1906.
136 *Greek Star* (Chicago), July 3, 1908. Full details of the controversy are to be found in *Forty Years of Greek Life*, pp. 61–62.
137 *Greek Star* (Chicago), Oct. 25, 1907.
138 *Forty Years of Greek Life*, pp. 61–62.
139 *Orthodox Observer* 1:14 (June 9, 1935):5; *Athene* 12:1 (Spring 1951): 34.
140 Addams, *Twenty Years at Hull-House*, p. 305.
141 *Chicago Tribune*, Feb. 21, 22, 1911.
142 Interview with Aristotle Collias, an original member of the group, July 24, 1969.
143 *Chicago Tribune*, Oct. 10, 1912 (with photograph).
144 See *Hull House Yearbook*, Jan. 1, 1913, p. 23; *Forty Years of Greek Life*, p. 57; also Addams, *Twenty Years at Hull-House*, pp. 304–305.
145 *Chicago Tribune*, Sept. 27, 1913.
146 Saloutos, *Greeks in the United States*, p. 114.
147 *Hull House Yearbook*, Jan. 1, 1913, pp. 23, 26–27; Jan. 1, 1927, pp. 9–10.
148 Interview with Dr. S. N. Soter, an original member of the association, Oct. 12, 1967.
149 Interview with Mrs. Bessie Spirides, a longtime observer and archivist of the Chicago Greek scene, Sept. 21, 1970.
150 James Steve Counelis, "Ethnicity: Science, Being, and Educational Opportunity," paper read at the annual meeting of the American Educational Research Association, New Orleans, Feb. 26, 1973, pp. 8–9.
151 Increasingly, Greek ethnicity is being defined by Greek Orthodoxy rather than the Greek language, especially by native-born generations; see Kopan, "Education and Greek Immigrants," pp. 415–420.
152 A rather complete list of Greek achievers in business, politics, education, etc., is to be found in Charles C. Moskos, Jr.'s excellent study

Greek Americans: Struggle and Success (Englewood Cliffs, N.J., 1980), pp. 111–122. It is interesting to note that in the area of education the two highest ranking officers in Illinois have been Michael J. Bakalis, who served as State Superintendent of Public Instruction from 1970 to 1975, and Angeline P. Caruso, currently Superintendent of Chicago Public Schools, both products of the Chicago Greek community and its communal school system.

153   Milton Gordon, *Assimilation in American Life: The Role of Race, Religion and National Origins* (New York, 1964).

CHAPTER V: UKRAINIAN CHICAGO

1   Oscar Halecki, *From Florence to Brest, 1493–1596* (Rome, 1958), pp. 290–293.
2   Ivan Ardan, "The Ruthenians in America," *Charities* 13 (1904–1905): 246ff.
3   Julian Bachynsky, *Ukrayinska Immigratsiya v Syednenych Dershavach Ameryky [The Ukrainian Immigration in the United States of America]* (Livw, 1914), pp. 103–114.
4   Isidore Sohocky, "The Ukrainian Catholic Church of the Byzantine Slavonic Rite in the U.S.A.," condensed and freely translated by Constantine Berder from Ukrainian Catholic Metropolitan See. Byzantine Rite: U.S.A. (Philadelphia, 1958), pp. 249–270; Ivan Volansky, "Pamyaty, Pershoho Ukrayinskoho Katolytskoho Svyashchenyka v Ametydhi" [Memoirs of the First Ukrainian Catholic Priest in America], *Jubilees Almanac of the Ukrainian Greek Catholic Church in the United States, 1884–1934* (Philadelphia, 1934), p. 12.
5   Alex Simirenko, *Pilgrims, Colonists and Frontiersmen: An Ethnic Community in Transition* (New York, 1964), pp. 40–53.
6   Bachynsky, p. 259.
7   *Ibid.*, pp. 292–293.
8   Stephen Kuropas, "Shikago" (Chicago), *Propamyatna Knhla Vidina z Nahody Soroklithnoho Yuvileyu Ukrayinskoho Narodnoho Soyuzu [Jubilee Book of the Ukrainian National Association in Commemoration of the Fortieth Anniversary of its Existence]*, Luka Myshyha, ed. (Jersey City, N.J., 1936), p. 541.
9   *Svoboda*, Dec. 12, 1895.
10   Theodore Turak, "A Celt Among Slavs: Louis Sullivan's Holy Trinity Church," *The Prairie School Review* (4th Qtr., 1972): 7.
11   *Ibid.*, pp. 19–20.
12   *St. Mary's Greek Rite Catholic Church Golden Jubilee Book*, October 2, 1955.
13   Volodymyr Simenovych, "Z Moho Zhyttya" [From My Life], *Kalendar of the Ukrainian National Association for 1931* (Jersey City, N.J., 1931), pp. 69–71. See also Bachynsky, pp. 360, 375, 443.
14   Stephen Kuropas, *op. cit.*; *Svoboda*, Sept. 5, 1900.
15   *Sitch*, Dec. 1, 1931; interview with May Olenec, June 23, 1979.
16   St. Nicholas Church Council Minutes, Dec. 31, 1905.
17   St. Nicholas Church Council Minutes, Feb. 11, 1906.
18   *Sitch*, Dec. 1, 1931.

19 St. Nicholas Church Council Minutes, Nov. 17, 1907.
20 Interview with Rev. John Hundiak, February 16, 1969. Now Bishop Mark of the Ukrainian Orthodox Church of America, Hundiak was once a Ukrainian Catholic priest who served for a brief period as Strutinsky's assistant at St. Nicholas.
21 Interview with Helen Hentisz, Feb. 25, 1969. Mrs. Hentisz is Fr. Strutinsky's granddaughter.
22 Bachynsky, pp. 383–384.
23 Ibid.
24 Svoboda, Aug. 28, 1902 through Oct. 9, 1902.
25 Alexander Lushnycky, "Ukrainians in Pennsylvania," Ukrainians in Pennsylvania (Philadelphia, 1976), p. 21.
26 Stephen Kuropas, p. 547.
27 Svoboda, Oct. 26, 1899.
28 "The History of Sts. Peter and Paul Ukrainian Orthodox Church, 1909–1959," Fifty Years of Service to God and Country, A Jubilee Book, 1959.
29 St. Nicholas Church Council Minutes, Jan. 30, 1910.
30 Mary Troc, Nativity of the Blessed Virgin Mary Church School, Dedication Book, 1956.
31 St. Nicholas Church Minutes, Mar. 9, 1911.
32 Ibid., May 28, 1911.
33 Sitch, Dec. 1, 1931.
34 St. Nicholas Church Council Minutes, Feb. 11, 1906.
35 Semen Kochy, "Pochatke i Rozvyto Tserkvy i Shkole Sv. O. Mykolaya v Shikago" [The Founding and Development of St. Nicholas Church and School in Chicago], Ukrayinske Zyttya [Ukrainian Life], Mar. 7, 1960.
36 St. Nicholas Church Council Minutes, Jan. 3, 1909.
37 Svoboda, Sept. 21, 1905.
38 See St. Nicholas Church Minutes, 1907–1922.
39 Kochy, op. cit.
40 Luka Myshuha, "Yak Formuvavsya Svitohlyad Ukrayinskoho Imigranta ve Amerychi" [The Development of the Ukrainian American Outlook,], Jubilee Book of the Ukrainian National Association, pp. 136–137.
41 "Where We Aim," Ranna Zorya, Jan.–Feb. 1918; "A Call," Ranna Zorya, Mar.–Apr. 1918, pp. 60–62.
42 "Do Istoriyi Ukrayinskoho Pravoslavnoho Rukhu v Shikago, Ill." [Concerning the History of the Ukrainian Orthodox Movement in Chicago, Ill.], Dnipro, May 1946, p. 5.
43 Ibid., p. 7.
44 St. Nicholas Church Council Minutes, Mar. 6, 1921. The author's research, as well as interviews with various persons who knew Fr. Strutinsky well, suggests that his fiscal problems were due more to poor business acumen than to any effort to defraud his community.
45 St. Nicholas Church Council Minutes, Jan. 28, 1923.
46 Antin Dragan, The Ukrainian National Association: Its Past and Present, 1894–1964 (Jersey City, N.J., 1964), pp. 59–60.
47 Bachynsky, p. 332.
48 Svoboda, Feb. 26, 1903.

49   See commentary by Michael Lozynsky in *Svoboda*, May 26, 1904; *Svoboda*, May 10, 1906.
50   *Svoboda*, May 24, 1906.
51   *Svoboda*, Sept. 15, 1914.
52   "Hetman" is a kozak title meaning commander-in-chief. Since Ukrainians had no royal blood line, those who supported Hetman rule in Ukraine came the closest to being monarchist in political orientation within the Ukrainian stream.
53   *Svoboda*, Aug. 20, 1914.
54   Matthew Stachiw, "Nova Ukrayina v Amerytsi" [New Ukraine in America], *Jubilee Book of the Ukrainian Workingman's Association, 1910–1960* (Scranton, Pa., 1960), pp. 96–102; see also *Svoboda*, Dec. 9, 1915.
55   "Ukrayinska Rada v Amerytsi" [The Ukrainian Council in America], *Calendar of the Ukrainian National Association for 1919* (Jersey City, N.J., 1918), pp. 38–44.
56   Osyp Nazaruk, "Po Rokakh Prachi v Amerytsi" [After Years of Work in America], *Sich*, Mar. 26, 1926; Toma Laphychak, "D-r Stepan Hrynevetsky" [Dr. Stephen Hrynevetsky], *Medical Almanac, op. cit.*, pp. 42–44; interview with Philip Wasylowsky, Sept. 26, 1968.
57   Interview with Philip Wasylowsky, Sept. 26, 1968; Toma Lapychak, "D-r Kyrylo Bilyk" [Dr. Cyril Bilyk], *Medical Almanac, op. cit.*, p. 51; Stachiw, pp. 102–107.
58   A photostat copy of the resolution can be found in *Shisdesyat Lit Organizatsinoho Zhittya Ukrayintsiw v Filadelfiyi* [Sixty Years of the Ukrainian Community in Philadelphia], *A Jubilee Book*, p. 67.
59   *Svoboda*, Sept. 22, 1917; Stachiw, p. 103.
60   V. Simenovych, "Nova Ukrayinska Hazeta" [A New Ukrainian Newspaper], *Ukrayina*, May 19, 1917.
61   *Ibid.*, May 19, 1917.
62   A brother of Emily Strutinsky, Miroslav Sichynsky, had assassinated the anti-Ukrainian Polish governor or Galicia, Count Andrew Potocki, in 1908. Sentenced to a long prison term for his crime, Sichynsky soon became a national martyr, a living symbol of Ukrainian independence. The UNA organized a legal fund on his behalf in 1909 and began efforts to obtain—or engineer—his release. With the help of Ukrainian supporters in Galicia, who succeeded in bribing his Polish guards with money sent from America, Sichynsky escaped from prison on November 3, 1911. After living for a time in Scandinavian countries, he arrived to a hero's welcome in America on October 21, 1914. A radical socialist for his entire life (he died in Michigan in 1979 on the eve of the arrival of another Ukrainian symbol of freedom, Valentyn Moroz), he was active with the Federation, Defense of Ukraine, a socialist organization, and the UWA; Stachiw, pp. 102–107. See also Volodymyr Lototcky, "Yak Osvobodv Sya Myroslav Sichynsky" [How Miroslav Sichynsky Freed Himself], *Calendar of the Ukrainian National Association for 1916* (Jersey City, N.J., 1915), pp. 36–43.
63   See "Slavs Combine to Fight German Agents in Russia," *Chicago Tribune*, May 31, 1918.
64   *Ukrayina*, June 6, 1918.
65   *Svoboda*, Nov. 26, 1918.
66   *Svoboda*, Mar. 19, 1919.

67   *Svoboda,* June 3, 1920.
68   On November 12, 1918, at a meeting of the American Carpatho-Rusin Council in Scranton, Pennsylvania, a Rusin-American plebiscite was organized to determine the future of Carpatho-Ukraine. Each religious, fraternal-benefit, and civic society in the Rusin stream was entitled to one vote. Ballots were mailed, returned, and tabulated on December 24 with the following results: union with Czecho-Slovakia (735); union with Ukraine (310); total independence (27); union with Galicia-Bukovina (13); union with Russia (10); union with Hungary (9); union with Galicia (1). Peter Stercho, *Diplomacy of Double Morality: Europe's Crossroads in Carpatho-Ukraine, 1919–1939.*
69   Peter Poniatyshyn, "Ukrayinska Sprava v Amertysi Pid Chas Pershoyi Svitovoyi Viny" [The Ukrainian Situation in America During the First World War], *Jubilee Almanac of Svoboda, 1893–1953* (Jersey City, N.J., 1953), p. 74.
70   M. Nastasiwsky (Michael Tkach), *Ukrayinska Imigratsiya v Spoluchenykh Derzavakh* [The Ukrainian Immigration in the United States] (New York, 1934), pp. 85–89.
71   *Ibid.,* pp. 174–175.
72   *Robitnyk,* Sept. 13, 1919; cited in *ibid.,* p. 176.
73   Cited in Robert E. Park, *The Immigrant Press and Its Control* (New York, 1922), pp. 235–236.
74   Sydney Lens, *Radicalism in America* (New York, 1969), p. 271.
75   Nastasiwsky, pp. 179–182; Stachiw, pp. 110–115; Yaroslaw Chyz, "The Ukrainian Immigrants in the United States," *Calendar of the Ukrainian Workingman's Association for 1940* (Scranton, Pa., 1939); interview with Stephen Kuropas, Aug. 2, 1970.
76   Nastasiwsky, pp. 225–228. Neither *Svoboda* nor *Ukrayina* were dailies at this time.
77   Nastasiwsky, pp. 229–239; Leon Tolopko, "Sorok Rokiv Na Shlyakhu Postopu" [Forty Years on the Road of Progress], *Ukrayinski Visti,* Apr. 14, 1966.
78   Interview with Philip Wasylowsky, Nov. 20, 1968.
79   F. Ichynsky, "Pochatky i Rozvytok Ukrayinskoyi Sektsyi Mishnarodnoho Robitnychoho Ordenu" [The Genesis and Development of the Ukrainian Section of the International Worker's Order], *Narodni Kalendar na rik 1939* [National Calendar for 1939] (New York, 1939), pp. 37–41.
80   Interview with Nicholas Kalishinski (n.d.). WPA Ethnic Press Project #30275, Chicago Public Library.
81   See "Shcho Take Suverennist" [What is Sovereignty?], *Narodni Kalendar na rik 1939,* p. 106.
82   Leon Tolopko, "Na Shklakhu Nevpynoyi Borotby" [In the Unfinished Struggle], *Ukrayinski Visti,* Jan. 29, 1970, pp. 6, 7. See also Frank A. Warren, III, *Liberals and Communism: The "Red Decade" Revisited* (Bloomington, Ind., 1966).
83   See Memorandum for Colonel Conrad from the Military Intelligence Division of the War Department, Sept. 11, 1918; photostat copy in Peter Zadoretsky, "Korotki Narys Istoriyi Sichovoyi Organizatsiyi v Z.D.A." [A Short History of the Sich Organization in the U.S.A.], *Hei Tam Na Hori, Sich Ide* [Hey, On the Hill, Sich is Coming] (Edmonton, 1965), p. 361.

84 Zadoretsky, p. 363; Stephen Musiychuk, "Prychyny Opadku Sichovoyi Organizatsiyi v Z.D.A." [Reasons Behind the Decline of the Sich Organization in the U.S.A.], *Hei Tam Na Hori, Sich Ide*, pp. 373–374; *Sich*, Dec. 10, 1932.

85 *Sichovy Visti*, Apr. 14, 1921.

86 *Sichovy Visti*, June 15, 1922.

87 Nazaruk, *op. cit.*; see also Stephen Hrynevetsky, "Shcho Musit Bute" [What Must Be], *Sich*, Mar. 15, 1916.

88 Musiychuk, pp. 375–376; interview with Philip Wasylowsky, Aug. 6, 1970.

89 *Sichovy Visti*, June 10, 1924.

90 *Sich*, Dec. 5, 1924; Musiychuk, p. 376; interview with Philip Wasylowsky, Aug. 6, 1970.

91 *Sich*, Mar. 15, 1926.

92 *Sich*, June 1, 1926; Jan. 15, 1928; July 1, 1928.

93 *Sich*, Jan. 1, 1928; Feb. 1, 1928; Jan. 1, 1932.

94 *Sich*, Oct. 20, 1926; Oct. 1, 1929; July 15, 1930; Mar. 1, 1930.

95 *Sich*, Jan. 1, 1930.

96 Interview with Nicholas Olek, Aug. 8, 1970.

97 *Sich*, Sept. 1, 1931; Mar. 15, 1930; Jan. 15, Feb. 1, 1930; Aug. 15, 1930.

98 See *Za Ukrayinu* [For the Ukraine: The Tour of His Highness Hetmanych Danylo Skoropadsky Through the United States of America and Canada] (Chicago, 1938), pp. 54–57.

99 *Sich*, Apr. 21, 1934; *Nash Styakh*, Sept. 15, 1934; interview with Nicholas Olek, Aug. 8, 1970.

100 *Sich*, Mar. 31, 1934; June 2, 1934.

101 *Chicago Tribune*, Dec. 18, 1933.

102 *Sich*, Dec. 23, 1933.

103 Volodymyr Riznyk, "Pochatky ODWU i Rozbudov Yi Merezhi: Nashi Uspixy i Trudnosohi" [The Beginnings of ODSU and the Development of Its Affiliates: Our Successes and Problems], *Samostiyna Ukrayina* (Oct.–Nov. 1968), pp. 6–7,8.

104 Interview with Stephen Kuropas, Aug. 2, 1970.

105 Zenovy Knysh, *Pry Dsherelach Ukrayinskoho Organizovanoho Nationalizmu* [Among the Sources of Organized Ukrainian Nationalism] (Toronto, 1970), pp. 30–32.

106 Interview with Ivan Popovych, Aug. 28, 1971.

107 Interview with Stephen Kuropas, June 30, 1979.

108 "The Ninth ODWU Convention," *The Trident*, July–Aug. 1939, pp. 58, 60.

109 *Chicago Herald and Examiner*, May 31, 1937.

110 U.S. Congress, House of Representatives, *Investigation of Un-American Propaganda Activities in the United States: Hearings Before a Special Committee on Un-American Activities*, 76th Cong., 1st Sess., 1939, pp. 5259–5322.

111 *Chicago Daily News*, Sept. 28, 1939.

112 Interview with Stephen Kuropas, June 5, 1970.

113 Stephen W. Mamchur, "Nationalism, Religion and the Problem of Assimilation Among Ukrainians in the United States," unpublished Ph.D. dissertation, Yale University (1942), pp. 101–111.

114 Sohocky, p. 275; Walter E. Warzeski, "Religion and National Conscious-

ness in the History of the Rusins," unpublished Ph.D. dissertation, University of Pittsburgh (1964), pp. 246–248.
115 Mamchur, *op. cit.*, pp. 68–72.
116 *Svoboda* (December 31, 1926).
117 *Svoboda* (January 3, 1927).
118 *Svoboda* (June 24, 1927).
119 Mamchur, *op. cit.*, pp. 126–131.
120 *Ibid.*
121 *Ibid.*, pp. 105–106.
122 *Sich* (December 15, 1931). See also *Fifty Years of Service to God and Community, op. cit.*
123 Anatol Hornysky, "Ukrayinska Baptyska Tserkva v Shikago" (The Ukrainian Baptist Church in Chicago), *The Evangelical Kalendar, "Good Friend" for 1956* (Toronto, 1956), pp. 59–65.
124 Interview with Dmytro Atamanec (February 6, 1969).
125 St. Nicholas Church Council Minutes (June 1, 1923).
126 "Nasha Shkola v Shikago" (Our School in Chicago), *Sich* (January 1, 1926).
127 Ann Czuba, *History of the Ukrainian Catholic Parochial Schools in the United States: A Thesis* (Chicago, 1956), pp. 36–37.
128 Voldymyr Simenovych, "Chomu Vashi Molodi Nedbayut" (Why Your Youth Don't Care), *Ukrayina* (December 4, 1931).
129 See *Narodni Kalendar Na Rik 1939, op. cit.*
130 *Sich* (July 15, 1931).
131 See *Siege Youth*, March, 1931.
132 Mamchur, *op. cit.*, pp. 304–305.
133 Oleh Riznyk, "The History of MUN," *The Senior MUN Manual: A Guide to Action for the Ukrainian National Youth Federation of America* (Chicago, 1961), pp. 5–9.
134 Antin Dragan, *op. cit.*
135 Mary Kozyra and Theodore Luciw, "Minutes of the First Ukrainian Youth's Congress," *Zinochy Svit*, August–September, 1933, p. 31. Jennie H. Kohut, "The UYLNA Story," *The Ukrainian Trend*, Autumn, 1958.
136 "Organization and Work of the Ukrainian Catholic Youth League," *Ukrainian Youth*, May, 1934, p. 17.
137 *Ibid.*, p. 1.
138 John Zadrozny, "The Differences of Opinion Among Ukrainians in Regard to the Soviet Union: A Study of Opinions, Attitudes and Beliefs of a National Minority in the United States," unpublished M.A. thesis, University of Chicago (1946), p. 68.
139 Stephen Kuropas, *op. cit.*, p. 543.
140 *Ukrayina* (August 8, 1930).
141 *Ukrayina* (October 16, 1931).
142 Program Book (October 14, 1934).
143 *Ukrayina* (November 14, 1930).
144 *Ukrayina* (July 11, 1930).
145 *Sich* (March 31, 1934).
146 *Ukrayina* (August 8, 1930).
147 *Sich* (November 15, 1932).
148 *Ukrayina* (November 28, 1930).
149 *Ukrayina* (August 28, 1931).

150 *Sich* (May 1, 1932).
151 *Ukrayina* (August 29, 1930); *Sich* (September 1, 1931); Newspaper clippings in scrapbook of Katherine Domanchuk-Baran; also seee *Ukrainians in the United States* (Chicago, 1937), pp. 136–138.
152 *Chicago Daily News* (May 9, 1932).
153 Newspaper clipping from scrapbook of Katherine Domanchuk-Baran.
154 *U.O.Y.A. Weekly* (August 19, 1934).
155 Luka Myshuha, "Ukrayinska Uchast v Dvokh Svitovykh Vystavakh" (Ukrainian Participation in Two World Fairs), *Golden Jubilee Almanac of the Ukrainian National Association, 1894–1944* (Jersey City, N.J., 1944), pp. 215–216.
156 Wasyl Halich, *Ukrainians in the United States* (Chicago, 1937), p. 142.
157 Stephen Kuropas, *op. cit.*, p. 545.

CHAPTER VI: POLISH CHICAGO

1 Two recent books deal with Poles in Chicago: Victor Green, *For God and Country: The Rise of Polish and Lithuanian Ethnic Consciousness in America* (Madison, 1975), and Edward R. Kantowicz, *Polish-American Politics in Chicago, 1888–1940* (Chicago, 1975). In addition, three unpublished doctoral dissertations document the relations of Polish Catholics with the Church authorities in Chicago: Joseph John Parot, "The American Faith and the Persistence of Chicago Polonia, 1870–1920" (Ph.D. diss., University of Northern Illinois, 1971); James W. Sanders, "The Education of Chicago Catholics: An Urban History" (Ph.D. diss., University of Chicago, 1970); Charles H. Shanabruch, "The Catholic Church's Role in the Americanization of Chicago's Immigrants, 1833–1928" (Ph.D. diss., University of Chicago, 1975). Recent work on Polish-Americans in other parts of the country includes: Victor Greene, *The Slavic Community on Strike* (Notre Dame, 1968); Frank Renkiewicz, "The Polish Settlement of St. Joseph County, Indiana, 1855–1935" (Ph.D. diss., University of Notre Dame, 1967); Carol Ann Golab, "The Polish Communities of Philadelphia, 1870–1920" (Ph.D. diss., University of Pennsylvania, 1971); William Galush, "The Polish National Catholic Church," *Records of the American Catholic Historical Society of Philadelphia*, LXXXIII (Sept.–Dec. 1972), 131–149, and "American Poles and the New Poland," *Ethnicity*, I (Oct. 1974), 209–221. Victor Greene provides a bibliographic survey of the literature on Polish, Czech, and Slovak immigrants in *The Immigration History Newsletter*, VII (Nov. 1975), 6–11.
2 See, for instance, Joseph Wytrwal, *Poles in American History and Tradition* (Detroit, 1969), pp. 75–79.
3 No one should take too seriously any population estimates for Polish-Americans, including my own. Censuses probably underestimate the numbers of Poles and other immigrant and racial minorities; Polish sources overcompensate by giving inflated estimates. My own figures are on the conservative side and are drawn from the following sources: 1890, U.S. and Chicago—extrapolations from U.S. census totals of foreign-born; 1910, U.S.—census totals for "foreign stock"; Chicago—ex-

trapolations from the population of minors in the 1910 school census; 1930, U.S. and Chicago—census totals of foreign stock.

4 Golab, "Polish Communities of Philadelphia," pp. 52–59.

5 See Kantowicz, *Polish-American Politics*, pp. 12–22, for details on these five settlements. Greene, *For God and Country*, pp. 31–33, stresses the mediating effect of established German and Bohemian communities in lessening the culture shock for incoming Poles.

6 Population data for this table was obtained from the Chicago Board of Education School Census, 1898. The data for calculating the 1930 index came from Ernest W. Burgess and Charles Newcomb, eds., *Census Data of the City of Chicago, 1930* (Chicago, 1933). Burgess and Newcomb used "community areas" as a base; these were generally about the same size as a city ward. The index of dissimilarity is explained most fully in Karl and Alma Taeuber, *Negroes in Cities* (Chicago, 1965), pp. 28–31, 195–245.

7 Kantowicz, *Polish-American Politics*, pp. 23–24; Kantowicz, "The Ghetto Experience: Poles in Chicago as a Case Study" (paper delivered at the National Archives Conference on State and Local History, May 1975).

8 Golab emphasizes this pattern of segregation and decentralization for Philadelphia's Poles, "Polish Communities of Philadelphia, pp. 5–7.

9 Kantowicz, "The Ghetto Experience"; statistics were calculated from the 1898 school census.

10 Historians like Humbert Nelli and Howard Chudacoff, who have argued that the ethnic neighborhood was not so common an experience as supposed, fail to take sufficient account of the social and cultural aspects of the ghetto. See Nelli, *The Italians of Chicago* (New York, 1970), p. 45; Chudacoff, "A New Look at Ethnic Neighborhoods," *Journal of American History*, LX (June 1973), 77; Kantowicz, "The Ghetto Experience."

11 Raymond Breton, "Institutional Completeness of Ethnic Communities and the Personal Relations of Immigrants," *American Journal of Sociology*, LXX (1964), 193–205.

12 Jakub Horak, "Assimilation of Czechs in Chicago" (Ph.D., diss., University of Chicago, 1924), pp. 74–75; Greene, *For God and Country*, pp. 54–56.

13 *Ibid.*, pp. 58–63; Kantowicz, *Polish-American Politics*, pp. 14–22, 165–168.

14 Sanders, "Education of Chicago Catholics," pp. 52–59, 114, 183; Parot, "Persistence of Chicago Polonia," pp. 225–226; Francis Bolek, *The Polish American School System* (New York, 1948), p. 5.

15 These figures were obtained from the annual reports submitted by the pastor of each parish to the Archbishop, Archives of the Archdiocese of Chicago (AAD). The proportions of other ethnic groups in ethnic parishes in 1930 were: Lithuanians, 38%; Italians, 36%; Yugoslavs, 33%; Czechoslovaks, 19%.

16 All the financial information in these paragraphs was calculated from the parish annual reports, AAD. See Philip Taylor, *The Distant Magnet* (New York, 1971), pp. 167–209, for estimates of immigrant wages and expenditures during various periods. In the early twentieth century several American dioceses set quotas anywhere from 4% to 10% of annual income as the Church's share. The average Polish contribution of $17.55 would be about 3% or 4% of an unskilled laborer's wage. See Michael N.

Kremer, "Church Support in the United States" (Ph.D. diss., Catholic University of America, 1930).

17 The parish I attended in Chicago in 1975–76 set an official goal of $5.00 per family per week. This total of $260 yearly was about equal to one month's apartment rent. For the wage differences, see "Immigrants in Cities," *Reports of the Immigration Commission,* II, 147.

18 One important exception is the Bohemians. After 1916 their financial support equaled, and sometimes exceeded, the level of the Poles, Lithuanians, and Slovaks. Over the period 1908–1947, the Italians slowly raised their level of financial support, but at all times they remained at the bottom of the list.

19 Joseph Wytrwal, *America's Polish Heritage* (Detroit, 1961), pp. 148–259, contains the best description of the PNA and the PRCU in English.

20 Greene, *For God and Country,* pp. 61–68; Kantowicz, *Polish-American Politics,* pp. 26, 94. Among the Poles, a small socialist leadership group also existed. From 1907 to 1924 the Polish Section of the Socialist party of America published a Polish daily paper in Chicago which heaped scorn on both the Polish priests and the bourgeois nationalists. Other East European groups also had small socialist, and sometimes also communist, contingents. The role of socialism among East European Catholic immigrants cries out for historical study.

21 *Panorama: A Historical Review of Czechs and Slovaks in the USA* (Cicero, Ill., 1976), pp. 31–32; Horak, "Assimilation of Czechs," p. 84; Eugene R. McCarthy, "The Bohemians in Chicago and Their Benevolent Societies" (M.A. thesis, University of Chicago, 1950), pp. 35–38.

22 Joseph Krisciunas, "Lithuanians in Chicago" (M.A. thesis, DePaul University, 1935), pp. 42–44, 50–51, 56–62; Marion Mark Stolarik, "Immigration and Urbanization: The Slovak Experience, 1870–1918" (Ph.D. diss., University of Minnesota, 1974), pp. 228–229.

23 Patrick J. Dignan, "A History of Legal Incorporation of Catholic Property in the United States, 1784–1932" (Ph.D. diss., Catholic University of America, 1933).

24 Greene, *For God and Country,* pp. 70–71; Galush, "Polish National Catholic Church," pp. 132–133; Mark Stolarik, "Lay Initiative in American Slovak Parishes, 1880–1930," *Records of the American Catholic Historical Society of Philadelphia,* LXXXIII (Sept.–Dec. 1972), 151–158.

25 The exact nature of the Resurrectionist-episcopal agreement is uncertain. The only surviving record of it is in the memoirs of the Resurrectionists' Superior-General, Jerome Kajsziewicz, *Pisma: Rosprawy, Listy z Podrozy, Pamietnik o Zgromadzenia* (Berlin, 1872), III, 350. Joseph Parot mounted a search for some firmer evidence of the agreement, but was unsuccessful: see Parot, "Persistence of Polonia," p. 39, n. 55. For the Holy Trinity controversy, see Greene, *For God and Country,* pp. 74–82; Parot, pp. 40–64; John Iwicki, *The First Hundred Years, 1866–1966* (Rome, 1966), pp. 10–64.

26 Greene, *For God and Country,* pp. 103–108; Parot, "Persistence of Polonia," pp. 74–75; Galush, "Polish National Catholic Church," pp. 133–134.

27 Greene, *For God and Country,* p. 109.

28 Galush, "Polish National Catholic Church," pp. 134–145; John P. Gallagher, *A Century of History: The Diocese of Scranton, 1868–1968*

(Scranton, Pa., 1968), pp. 154–223; Theodore Andrews, *The Polish National Catholic Church in America and Poland* (London, 1953), pp. 18–25; Paul Fox, *The Polish National Catholic Church* (Scranton, n.d.), pp. 139–140.

29   Parot, "Persistence of Polonia," pp. 127–154.

30   Bohdan P. Prosko, "Soter Ortynksy: First Ruthenian Bishop in the United States, 1907–1916," *Catholic Historical Review*, LXIII (Jan. 1973), 513–533; Gerald R. Fogarty, "The American Hierarchy and Oriental Rite Catholics, 1890–1907," *Records of the American Catholic Historical Society of Philadelphia*, LXXXV (Mar.–June 1974), 17–28.

31   Parot, "Persistence of Polonia," p. 156; Greene, *For God and Country*, pp. 141–142. The Polish auxiliary in Milwaukee was Edward Kozlowski, no relation to the schismatic Anthony Kozlowski.

32   Greene, *For God and Country*, p. 142, misconstrues the significance of Rhode's appointment, picturing it as a successful conclusion of the Polish recognition drive and ending his book at that point. He implies that Rhode, as auxiliary bishop, shared in the archbishop's corporate, financial authority, which is erroneous. For a good example of how unimportant an auxiliary bishop can be, consult Ch. 7 of Robert I. Gannon, *The Cardinal Spellman Story* (Garden City, N.Y., 1962).

33   Shanabruch, "Church's Role in Americanization," pp. 557–569; Parot, "Persistence of Polonia," pp. 302–303, 311–340.

34   Kruszka to Pius XI, June 9, 1923 (AAD: 7–1923-P–21).

35   The rest of this section is largely derived from my uncompleted research for a forthcoming study of Cardinal Mundelein. It is based mainly on chancery records at the Archdiocesan Archives; the files of *The New World*, Chicago's archdiocesan newspaper; and a collective biography of the Chicago clergy which I have compiled. Some pertinent references to Mundelein's early years can be found in Shanabruch, "Church's Role in Americanization," pp. 554–557; Sanders, "Education of Chicago Catholics," pp. 157–164, 215–236; and Parot, "Persistence of Polonia," pp. 311–322.

36   Polish Clergy Association to George Mundelein, July 9, 1917 (Polish Roman Catholic Union Archives).

37   These figures were obtained by tracing the "cohort" of priests ordained in 1926 and 1927 through their entire careers by means of the official announcements of appointments in *The New World* and the yearly listings in *The Catholic Directory*. The 1916–1917 cohort showed a similar disparity: 22 years waiting time for Polish priests, 15.4 for Irish. However, the cohorts of 1936–37 and thereafter show a different pattern. By this time, Mundelein's seminary was producing such a supply of clerics that all priests of the archdiocese, Polish and non-Polish alike, had to wait between twenty-five and thirty years for a pastorate.

38   See Kantowicz, *Polish-American Politics*, for all references in this section.

39   *Dziennik Chicagoski*, Mar. 14, 1933, p. 4.

40   Sr. Lucille Wargin, C.R., "The Polish Immigrant in the American Community, 1880–1930" (M.A. thesis, De Paul University, 1948), pp. 54–55.

41   Russell Barta, "The Representation of Poles, Italians, Latins and Blacks in the Executive Suites of Chicago's Largest Corporations," *Minority Report* (National Center for Urban Ethnic Affairs, Washington, D.C.).

See also the NORC study by Andrew Greeley and William McCready (Beverly Hills, Cal., 1977).

CHAPTER VII: SUBURBAN ITALIANS

1   For example, see Humbert Nelli, *The Italians in Chicago* (New York, 1970); Rudolph Vecoli, "Chicago's Italians Prior to World War I" (Ph.D. diss., University of Wisconsin, 1963); Thomas Kessner, *The Golden Door* (New York, 1977); George Pozzetta, "The Italians of New York, 1890–1914" (Ph.D. diss., University of North Carolina, 1971); Richard Juliani, "The Social Organization of Immigration: The Italians in Philadelphia" (Ph.D. diss., Pennsylvania State University, 1971): Herbert Gans, *The Urban Villagers* (New York, 1962); William F. Whyte, *Street Corner Society* (Chicago, 1943).

2   Interview with Charles Donovan, Sept. 1979.

3   Pierre De Vise, *Chicago Tribune*, Sept. 28, 1977, sect. 1, p. 3. Chicago Heights has been slipping from 140 in 1970 to 176 in 1975 to 186 in 1977 in De Vise's computation of economic status.

4   Bureau of the Census, 1970 *Census of Population: General Social and Economic Characteristics. Illinois Table 102* (Apr. 1972), p. 574.

5   Most of the statistics in this work are derived from the 1900 manuscript census for Chicago Heights and a study of 1448 petitions for citizenship made by Italians in Chicago Heights between 1907 and 1954. The formal petitions required the following information: name, address, occupation, birth date and birthplace, date of migration, ports of departure and arrival, name of ship, date of first papers, marital status, spouse's birthplace and present residence, date of marriage (after 1928), the names, birth dates, birthplaces, and present residences of all children, the endorsement of two citizen sponsors, their addresses and occupations. The petition also included a renunciation of former citizenship and an affirmation that the petitioner was neither a polygamist nor an anarchist. Though the naturalization papers give us no information on the income and educational level of the petitioners, these documents provide fascinating detail. Elementary quantitative methods, using the computer, produced the figures cited in this work. The study includes only those who applied for citizenship; it excludes those who died, returned to Italy, did not apply for citizenship, or were second generation.

6   *Ibid.*

7   *Ibid.*

8   John Briggs, *An Italian Passage* (New Haven, 1978), p. 85. In his discussion of mate choices in less concentrated Italian neighborhoods, Briggs de-emphasizes the importance of *campanilismo*.

9   Some claim that the name derives from the fact that the Otto house, the first boardinghouse in the area in the 1890s, was very parsimonious in the portions of food it provided, thus rendering its residents perpetually "hungry."

10 Gans, *The Urban Villagers*, p. 230. Gans concludes that the outstanding factor in the Italian-American subculture was the working-class ethos rather than ethnic cultural differences with the middle-class American culture.

11   Oral history interview, Oct. 9, 1979 (source prefers to remain anonymous).
12   Mentioned in a meeting with the Silver Tavern group, Jan. 10, 1980. See note 50.
13   Albert La Morticella to Nino La Morticella, Oct. 11, 1977 (in the possession of the author).
14   *Ibid.*
15   *The Chicago Heights Star,* Jan. 15, 1914, p. 6 (hereafter cited as *The Star*).
16   1900 manuscript census and *Chicago Heights, Illinois* (Chicago, 1914), p. 53 (hereafter cited as *Ad Book*).
17   Note from Bill D'Amico to the author, Oct. 1979.
18   Interview with Dominic Pandolfi, Nick Zaranti, and others, Oct. 9, 1979.
19   Vecoli, "Chicago's Italians Prior to World War I," pp. 203–209.
20   *The Star,* Sept. 7, 1906, p. 1; Dec. 13, 1906, p. 1.
21   *The Star,* Aug. 1, 1918, p. 1; Nov. 7, 1918, p. 1.
22   *Golden Jubilee Souvenir Book: Mt. Carmel School,* Chicago Heights, 1962.
23   Interview with Alphonse Leone, July 1979.
24   *Ibid.* Corroborated by interview with the Silver Tavern group, Jan. 10, 1980.
25   Edward Banfield, *The Moral Basis of a Backward Society* (New York, 1958), p. 10.
26   Obviously, families could have had additional children after they had attained citizenship.
27   *Statuto e Regolamento della Societa Operaia di M.S. Amaseno* (Chicago, 1906), p. 5.
28   *The Star,* June 20, 1918, p. 1.
29   Albert La Morticella to Nino La Morticella, Oct. 11, 1977.
30   See Mormile's naturalization petition, May 20, 1926, Chicago Heights Public Library.
31   *Ad Book,* compiled by Palma Beandette (Chicago, 1914), p. 19.
32   *The Star,* July 2, 1967, pp. 2, 5.
33   Nelli, p. 87.
34   Briggs, p. 273.
35   *The Star,* May 10, 1929, p. 1. This typical headline read "Dante Club Is Active Power For City Good."
36   *Ibid.*
37   *The Star,* Dec. 23, 1941, p. 1.
38   Interview with Mario Bruno, Oct. 1979.
39   Gans, p. 265.
40   Whyte, Chapter II.
41   *The Star,* Apr. 30, 1925, p. 1.
42   Albert La Morticella to Nino La Morticella, Oct. 11, 1977.
43   Interview with Angelo Ciambrone, Nov. 5, 1979.
44   *The Star,* Apr. 9, 1925, p. 1; June 4, 1925, p. 1.
45   *The Star,* Feb. 3, 1933, p. 6.
46   *The Star,* Feb. 17, 1933, p. 1.
47   *The Star,* Apr. 18, 1933, p. 1.
48   *The Star,* May 26, 1933, p. 1.
49   Gans, p. 265.
50   The Silver Tavern group consists of Italian-American male senior citi-

zens who meet every morning for coffee. The Dozenettes is a continuing group of a dozen "girl friends" now in their mid-sixties.

51 Interview with Bruno, Oct. 1979.
52 Interview with Pandolfi, Oct. 9, 1979.
53 *The Star*, Apr. 30, 1925, pp. 1, 4.
54 See Anthony Sorrentino, *Organizing Against Crime* (New York, 1977).
55 *The Star*, July 24, 1924, p. 1. This is the same year that the Klan ran a "Go To Church On Sundays" advertisement in *The Star*, Feb. 15, 1924.
56 *The Star*, June 26, 1924, p. 1.
57 *The Star*, May 15, 1924, p. 1.
58 *The Star*, Apr. 17, 1924, p. 4.
59 *The Star*, Apr. 24, 1924, p. 1.
60 Marian Lanfranchi, "A Political History of Chicago Heights" (Honors paper, Governor's State University, 1976, copy on file in the Chicago Heights Public Library), p. 29.
61 A half-dozen interviewees independently related this same Capone story to the author.
62 Anonymous interviewee, 1979.
63 *Ibid.*
64 Nelli, *Crime Society*, p. 196.
65 Interview with Albert La Morticella, Summer 1978.
66 *The Star*, Feb. 22, 1935, p. 1.
67 *The Star*, Mar. 3, 1942, p. 1.
68 *The Star*, Jan. 20, 1942, p. 1.
69 *The Star*, Dec. 8, 1944, p. 1; Jan. 9, 1945, p. 1; Feb. 13, 1945, p. 1.
70 *The Star*, Nov. 6, 1924; Nov. 9, 1928; Nov. 11, 1932; Nov. 6, 1936; Nov. 8, 1940; Nov. 10, 1944; Nov. 5, 1948.
71 Interview with Richton, Dec. 1979.
72 Lanfranchi, p. 39.

CHAPTER VIII: MEXICAN CHICAGO

1 See especially Paul S. Taylor, *Mexican Labor in the United States: Chicago and the Calumet Region*, University of California Publications in Economics, VII, No. 2 (Berkeley, 1932); Anita Edgar Jones, *Conditions Surrounding Mexicans in Chicago* (San Francisco, 1971); Mark Reisler, "The Mexican Immigrant in the Chicago Area During the 1920's," *Journal of the Illinois State Historical Society*, LXVI (Summer 1973), pp. 144–157.
2 See Edward Jackson Baur, "Delinquency among Mexican Boys in South Chicago" (M.A. thesis, University of Chicago, 1938), and "Mexican Migration to Chicago," WPA Research Library, Records of the Works Progress Administration, Record Group 69, National Archives. See also Louise Año Neuvo Kerr, "The Chicano Experience in Chicago: 1920–1970" (Ph.D. diss., University of Illinois at Chicago Circle, 1976). For further information about population and changes in the Chicano population of Chicago, see Louis Wirth and Eleanor H. Bernert, ed., *Local Community Fact Book of Chicago* (Chicago, 1949).
3 Arthur Corwin, "Causes of Mexican Emigration to the United States: A

Summary View," in Donald Fleming and Bernard Bailyn, eds., *Perspectives in American History* (Cambridge, Mass., 1973), VII, 567–568.

4   For a reliable account of the riots, see Carey McWilliams, *North from Mexico: The Spanish-Speaking People of the United States* (1949; reprint ed., New York, 1968), pp. 244–258.

5   Frank Tannenbaum, *Mexico: The Struggle for Peace and Bread* (New York, 1950), pp. 277–281.

6   Howard F. Cline, *The United States and Mexico* (Cambridge, Mass., rev. ed., 1962), p. 268.

7   Robert C. Jones, *Mexican War Workers in the United States: The Mexico-United States Manpower Recruiting Program and Operation, 1942 to 1944 Inclusive* (Washington, 1945), p. 1.

8   See, for example, George Messersmith to Secretary of State, Aug. 20, 1943 (two telegrams), Records of the War Manpower Commission, Record Group 211, National Archives, Washington, D.C.

9   Manuel Gamio, *Mexican Immigration to the United States: A Study of Human Migration and Adjustment* (1930; reprint ed., New York, 1971), pp. 170–196. See also "Agreement for the Temporary Migration of Mexican Workers" (Aug. 4, 1942), p. 1, Railroad Retirement Board Papers, Chicago. The second point listed under "General Principles" is instructive: "In accordance with the principles enunciated in executive order no. 8802, issued at the White House on June 25, 1941, *Mexican Nationals* [italics mine] who enter the United States as a result of any understanding between the two governments shall not suffer discriminatory acts of any kind."

10   Robert C. Jones, *Mexican War Workers*, p. 2.

11   Messersmith to Secretary of State, Nov. 6, 1942, Records of the War Manpower Commission, Record Group 211.

12   Claude Wickard to Harold D. Smith, Nov. 5, 1942, Records of the Secretary of Agriculture, Record Group 16, National Archives, Washington, D.C. Speaking of the August 4 agreement, Secretary of Agriculture Wickard reported that "the Mexican government . . . insisted upon the asking by the United States of certain minimum guarantees to its nationals who would be so transported" [*sic*].

13   Conference on Mexico's Role in International Intellectual Cooperation, Albuquerque, 1945, *Mexico's Role in International Intellectual Cooperation*, University of New Mexico, School of Inter-American Affairs, Inter-Americana Series, Short Papers, no. 6 (Albuquerque, 1945), p. 43.

14   Churchill Murray to John D. Coates, Jan. 4, 1945, Records of the War Manpower Commission, Record Group 211. Murray wrote of the projected need for 1,000 Mexican nationals in heavy industry. In John D. Coates to Churchill Murray, Dec. 1, 1944, Coates had announced the need for an additional 25,000 Mexican nationals in the forge, foundry, tire, and other industries.

15   "Employment Situation in Important Labor Market Areas" [1943], p. 8, Records of the War Manpower Commission, Record Group 211.

16   "Estimate of Percentage by Which Unfilled Openings Could Be Reduced at Wage Rates Indicated," Railroad Retirement Board Papers, n.d.

17   "Mexican Placements, May 1, 1943 Thru September 30, 1945," Oct. 1945, Records of the War Manpower Commission, Record Group 211.

18   *Ibid.*
19   "Mexican Program—Status Tabulation," Aug. 18, 1945, Railroad Retirement Board Papers.
20   "Relations with Immigration and Naturalization Service," Nov. 13, 1944, Railroad Retirement Board Papers.
21   "Unfilled Openings, Referrals and Placements from Oct. 1 to Oct. 25, 1945," Railroad Retirement Board Papers, n.d.
22   W. H. Spencer to Executive Director, War Manpower Commission, Sept. 7, 1945, Records of the War Manpower Commission, Record Group 211.
23   E. J. Brock to Director of the United States Employment Service, Jan. 30, 1946, Records of the War Manpower Commission, Record Group 211.
24   H. B. Lautz to Mario Lasso, Consulate General of Mexico, Chicago, Dec. 11, 1944, Records of the War Manpower Commission, Record Group 211.
25   F. M. Wilson to Operating Officers of Member Roads, Mar. 16, 1944, with six-page attachment, "Hints on the Employment of Imported Mexican Laborers," Railroad Retirement Board Papers.
26   Director of Employment and Claims to Washington Representative of the War Manpower Commission, Sept. 2, 1943, Records of the War Manpower Commission, Record Group 211.
27   *Chicago Tribune*, Aug. 17, 1945; Mar. 21, 1945. The program was initiated by Mexico for all interested teachers in the United States and Canada. Courses were to be taken at the National Autonomous University of Mexico. The language program was designed to teach the teachers a non-Castilian way of speaking Spanish. For details, see Conference on Mexico's Role in International Intellectual Cooperation, *Mexico's Role in International Intellectual Cooperation.*
28   *New York Times*, June 10, 1943.
29   Messersmith to Laurence Duggan, June 21, 1943, Records of the State Department, Record Group 84, State Department, Washington, D.C. Messersmith, Ambassador to Mexico, outlined the extensive coverage given to the zoot-suit riots by the Mexican press. Included in Messersmith's files is a bound volume of clippings from Mexican newspapers referring to the riots. See also *Business Week*, Jan. 1, 1944, p. 82; *New York Times*, June 11, 1943; June 16, 1943; June 17, 1943.
30   Frank X. Pax to the Mexican Patriotic Committee, Aug. 20, 1943, Chicago Area Project Papers, Chicago Historical Society (hereafter CHS).
31   David J. Saposs, "Report on Rapid Survey of Resident Latin American Problems and Recommended Program," Apr. 3, 1942, Chicago Area Project Papers, CHS.
32   "Request to Coordinator of Inter-American Affairs for Grant to Aid Latin Americans in Chicago," n.d., Chicago Area Project Papers, CHS.
33   *Ibid.*
34   *Chicago Tribune*, Aug. 12, 1945.
35   See Corwin, "Causes of Mexican Emigration," p. 570. In 1946, 91,456 illegals were returned to Mexico; 45,215 in 1950; 1,075,168 in 1954.
36   U.S. Bureau of the Census, *U.S. Census of the Population: 1950*, IV, *Special Reports*, Part 3, Chapter C, Persons of Spanish Surname (Washington, D.C., 1953), 3C–16.

37   U.S. Immigration and Naturalization Service, *Annual Reports, 1946–50* (Washington, D.C., 1946–50).

38   *Chicago Tribune*, Sept. 16, 1947.

39   Anita Edgar Jones, *Mexicans in Chicago* (San Francisco, 1971), p. 25.

40   U.S. Immigration and Naturalization Service, *Annual Reports, 1950–70* (Washington, D.C., 1950–70).

41   U.S. Bureau of the Census, *U.S. Census of Population: 1950*, IV, *Special Reports*, Part 3, Chapter A, Nativity and Parentage (Washington, D.C., 1954), 3A–265.

42   *Ibid.*

43   *Ibid.*

44   U.S. Bureau of the Census, *U.S. Census of Population: 1950*, IV, *Special Reports*, Part 4, Chapter B, Population Mobility—States and State Economic Areas (Washington, D.C., 1956), 4B–32.

45   U.S. Bureau of the Census, *U.S. Census of Population: 1950*, IV, *Special Reports*, Part 3, Chapter A, Nativity and Parentage, 3A–265.

46   *Ibid.*

47   Herman P. Miller, *Income of the American People* (New York, 1955), p. 99.

48   *Chicago Sun-Times*, Oct. 19, 1953.

49   James W. Wilkie, *The Mexican Revolution: Federal Expenditure and Social Change since 1910*, 2nd ed. (Berkeley, 1970), pp. 218–219.

50   Pan American Council, "Mexicans in Industry in Chicago" (1942), p. 85, Immigrants' Protective League Papers, Urban Collection, University of Illinois at Chicago Circle.

51   Adena Miller Rich to Nelson Rockefeller, July 15, 1944, Immigrants' Protective League Papers, Urban Collection, University of Illinois at Chicago Circle.

52   "Loyal South America," *Chicago Tribune*, Feb. 11, 1942.

53   Clifford Shaw, Frederick M. Zorbaugh, Henry D. McKay, and Leonard S. Cottrell, *Delinquency Areas: A Study of the Geographical Distribution of School Truants, Juvenile Delinquents, and Adult Defenders in Chicago* (Chicago, 1929), pp. 204–206.

54   Shaw and McKay, "Rejoinder," *American Sociological Review*, XIV (Oct. 1949), 617.

55   "Mexicans in Chicago Industry: A Survey of Leading Employers of Mexicans in Chicago," Apr. 1, 1944, pp. 4, 6, 9, 17, Immigrants' Protective League Papers, Urban Collection, University of Illinois at Chicago Circle.

56   Adena Miller Rich, "Educational Requirements for Naturalization—Do They Need Revision?" *Social Service Review*, XVIII (Oct. 1944), 382–385.

57   *Ibid.*, p. 385.

58   Interview with Encarnacion Chico, Jan. 5, 1974, taken by James Garvey as part of his research on Mexicans in Back of the Yards for a Loyola University class in Chicano history. See also F. M. Wilson to Operating Officers of Member Roads, Mar. 16, 1944, Railroad Retirement Board Papers.

59   Pan American Council, "Mexicans in Industry in Chicago," p. 3.

60   Rich to Rockefeller, July 15, 1944.

61   "Summary of the Development, Activities, and Future Plans of the

Mexican Civic Committee of the West Side," n.d., Chicago Area Project Papers, CHS.
62 *Chicago Tribune*, Aug. 12, 1945.
63 See copies of "Broadcast" and "A B C" in Chicago Area Project Papers, CHS.
64 Frank X. Pax to Most Reverend Samuel A. Stritch, July 14, 1943, Chicago Area Project Papers, CHS.
65 Pax to Mexican Patriotic Committee, Aug. 20, 1943, Chicago Area Project Papers, CHS.
66 Victor Borella to Ernest Burgess, n.d., Chicago Area Project Papers, CHS.
67 *Chicago Tribune*, June 16, 1946. See also "Mexican Welfare Council Brochure" (Oct. 27, 1945), Chicago Area Project Papers, CHS.
68 "Broadcast" 1 (n.d.), Chicago Area Project Papers, CHS.
69 Pax, "Mexican Americans in Chicago—A General Survey" (Jan. 1948), Metropolitan Welfare Council Papers, CHS.
70 *Ibid.*, pp. 22–24.
71 *Ibid.*, p. 16.
72 *Ibid.*, p. 19.
73 *Ibid.* See also *The Railway Conductor*, Mar. 3, 1930, and Director of Publicity, NAACP, to Editor, Apr. 9, 1930, both in NAACP Papers, Library of Congress, Washington, D.C.
74 Pax, "Mexican Americans in Chicago," p. 10.
75 "Illinois Federation of Mexican Americans Report—1950," Mexican Community Committee Papers, Special Collections, University of Illinois at Chicago Circle.
76 *Chicago Tribune*, June 13, 1948.
77 Committee on Division III, "Contract Laborers/Social Service" (1947), Metropolitan Welfare Council Papers, CHS.
78 Pax, "Mexican Americans in Chicago," p. 21. See also *Chicago Tribune*, May 1, 1947.
79 "Data Book for 1950–51" (Aug. 1, 1951), Chicago Area Project Papers, CHS.
80 *Christian Science Monitor*, Oct. 13, 1951.
81 *Ibid.* See also "Monthly Report of the Director" (Aug. 1951), Chicago Area Project Papers, CHS.
82 *Chicago Sun-Times*, Oct. 19, 1953.
83 Salvador Herrerra to Martin Ortiz, n.d., Chicago Area Project Papers, CHS. Herrerra's undated letter makes specific reference to the *Chicago Sun-Times* story of Oct. 19, 1953.
84 Martin Ortiz to Clinton White, n.d., Chicago Area Project papers, CHS. Reference is made to a *Chicago Sun-Times* story of Mar. 8, 1954, which cited Ortiz as a "representative" of the Mexican-American community. Jose Chapa had subsequently condemned Ortiz and the Mexican-American Council on radio station WCRW. Ortiz wrote to White, WCRW's president, to complain.
85 Milton R. Konvitz, *Civil Rights in Immigration* (Ithaca, N.Y., 1953), pp. 147–148.
86 "Broadcast" 1 (n.d.), Chicago Area Project Papers, CHS; "Bulletin of the Midwest Committee for the Foreign-Born" (Sept. 27, 1953), Chicago Area Project papers, CHS.

87   Mexican American Council to Dear Friend, n.d., Chicago Area Project Papers, CHS. Reference is made to a report of Dec. 5, 1955, evidently intended to be sent with the letter.

CHAPTER IX: FRENCH-INDIAN CHICAGO

This chapter derives from research initially begun under the supervision of the late Professor Gilbert Osofsky at the University of Illinois at Chicago Circle. It owes much to his inspiration and is written in his honor.

1   Earliest descriptions of the Chicago portage, with its frozen marshes and floods, are those of Marquette, Joliet, and LaSalle, 1674-1682. See A. T. Andreas, *History of Chicago, From the Earliest Period to the Present Time* (Chicago, 1884), I, 44–45. Later descriptions can be found in Henry Rowe Schoolcraft, "A Journey up the Illinois River in 1821," in Milo M. Quaife, ed., *Pictures of Illinois One Hundred Years Ago* (Chicago, 1918), pp. 120–121; Gurdon Hubbard, "Recollections of First Year," Gurdon Hubbard Papers, Chicago Historical Society; Charles Cleaver, *Early Chicago Reminiscences* (Chicago, 1882), pp. 28, 30, 46; Edwin O. Gale, *Early Chicago and Vicinity* (Chicago, 1902), p. 105; Colbee C. Benton, in Paul Angle, ed., *Prairie State: Impressions of Illinois* (Chicago, 1968), p. 114; Bessie Louise Pierce, *A History of Chicago, 1673-1848* (New York, 1937), pp. 6–12.

2   Cleaver, pp. 28–29; Andreas, p. 192; "Remarks of Hon. George Bates," *Michigan Historical Collections*, 40 vols. (Lansing, 1877-1929), II, 180–181.

3   William H. Keating was one of the more outspoken critics of Chicago as a site for future settlement. See his *Narrative of an Expedition to the Source of St. Peter's River, Lake Winnepeek, Lake of the Woods, etc. Performed in the Year 1823. . . .* (London, 1825), I, 162–163, 165–166. For more favorable comments, see James Herrington to Jacob Herrington, Chicago, January 27, 1831, in Alphabetical File: James Herrington, Chicago Historical Society; "Recollections of First Year," p. 20; Charles Butler Journal, Friday, August 2, 1833, in Letter File: Charles Butler, Chicago Historical Society; Benton, *A Visitor to Chicago In Indian Days*, Paul M. Angle and James R. Getz, eds. (Chicago, 1957), p. 76; Andreas, p. 129. Charlotte Erickson's "The British Immigration in the Old Northwest, 1815-1860," in David M. Ellis, ed., *The Frontier in American Development* (Ithaca, N.Y., 1969) is an interesting study of the British exception to the American farmer's aversion to prairie living during this period.

4   Gale, pp. 105–106; Cleaver, p. 28; Andreas, p. 207. Wolves were numerous on Chicago's north side as late as 1834.

5   See Cleaver, p. 30 for description of street drainage and building raising. Population estimates for the years 1833-1837 vary somewhat: Andreas claimed that the town grew from 200 in 1833 to 4,000 in 1837 (p. 142); a visitor's estimate in 1833 was 350, as cited in Angle, p. 64. Pierce (p. 14) lists 3,989 whites and 77 blacks in 1837.

6   See the Augustus Dilg Collection and the Albert Scharf Papers, Chicago Historical Society. See also Andreas, Ch. 1, and Louis Deliette, "Memoir Concerning the Illinois Country," Theodore C. Pease and Ray-

mond C. Werner, eds., *Collections of the Illinois State Historical Library*, XXIII, French Series 1 (1934) (a copy signed "DeGannes" is in the Edward Everett Ayer Collection, Newberry Library, Chicago); Hiram Beckwith, *The Illinois and Indiana Indians* (Chicago, 1884), pp. 99–117; Raymond E. Hauser, "An Ethnohistory of the Illinois Indian Tribe, 1673-1832" (Ph.D. diss., Northern Illinois University, 1973).

7   For geographic movement and settlement patterns of the Great Lakes tribes, see George Quimby, *Indians in the Upper Great Lakes Region, 11,000 B.C. to A.D. 1800* (Chicago, 1960) and James E. Fitting and Charles Cleland, "Late Prehistoric Settlement Patterns in the Upper Great Lakes," *Ethnohistory*, XVI (1969), 289–302. For cultural variations, see W. Vernon Kinietz, *The Indians of the Western Great Lakes, 1615-1760* (Occasional Contributions from the Museum of Anthropology of the University of Michigan, No. 10, 1940; reprinted by University of Michigan Press, 1965).

8   Quimby, p. 110.

9   *Ibid.*, pp. 109–115. The 1600-1760 estimated population density of the Great Lakes tribes of one per square mile assumes that Great Lakes peoples were subsistence farmers as well as hunters during this period. A growing literature concerns the impact of the fur trade upon Indian society: see, most recently, Calvin Martin, "The European Impact on the Culture of a Northeastern Algonquian Tribe: An Ecological Interpretation," *William and Mary Quarterly*, XXXI, Ser. 1 (1974), 3–26.

10 Quimby, pp. 147–151. See also Quimby, *Indian Culture and European Trade Goods* (Madison, Wis., 1966); Harold Hickerson, *The Chippewa and Their Neighbors: A Study in Ethnohistory* (New York, 1970); Felix M. Keesing, "The Menomini Indians of Wisconsin," *Memoirs of the American Philosophical Society*, X (1939); and Arthur J. Ray, *Indians in the Fur Trade: Their Role as Trappers, Hunters, and Middlemen in the Lands Southwest of Hudson Bay 1660-1870* (Toronto, 1974).

11 Quimby, *Indians in the Upper Great Lakes*, pp. 151 and *passim*. That traditional authority was threatened is indicated by the tribal attempt to integrate British and American fathers into the patrilineal clan structure. Britishers were made members of a new clan, "the Lion," and Americans, "the Eagle."

12 Andreas, pp. 34–45; James A. Clifton, *The Prairie People: Continuity and Change in Potawatomi Indian Culture, 1665-1965* (Lawrence, Kan., 1977); Erminie Wheeler-Voegelin and David B. Stone, *Indians of Illinois and Northwestern Indiana* (New York, 1974).

13 Quimby, pp. 147–151; John Kinzie Papers and Accounts, Chicago Historical Society; the Chicago Historical Society's collection of material artifacts, particularly the Fort Dearborn display; Arthur Woodward, *The Denominators of the Fur Trade* (Pasadena, Cal., 1970), pp. 22–23, and *passim*.

14 Madore Beaubien Papers, Beaubien Family Papers (including information on Chief Alexander Robinson) and Billy Caldwell Papers, Chicago Historical Society. See also Jacqueline Peterson, "Ethnogenesis: Métis Development and Influence in the Great Lakes Region, 1690-1836" (Ph.D. diss., University of Illinois, Chicago Circle, 1977).

15 Juliette Kinzie, *Wau-bun, The Early Days in the Northwest* (Chicago, 1932), pp. 193–194; Beaubien Family Papers, Chicago Historical Society.

16   John Kinzie Papers and Accounts, Chicago Historical Society; "Recollections of First Year," Gurdon S. Hubbard Papers; American Fur Company Papers, Letter Books, Chicago Historical Society; John Jacob Astor to Ramsay Crooks, New York, Mar. 17, 1817, in *Collections of the State Historical Society of Wisconsin* (Madison, 1854-1931), XIX, 451. See also Gordon Charles Davidson, *The Northwest Company* (New York, 1918); David Lavender, *The Fist in the Wilderness* (Garden City, N.Y., 1964); John D. Haeger, "The American Fur Company and the Chicago of 1812-1835," *Journal of the Illinois State Historical Society* (Summer 1968), 117–139.

17   Account Books, American Fur Company Papers, Chicago Historical Society. Details of the estates of the American Fur Company's competition at Chicago, William Wallace and John Crafts, are given in Ernest B. East's "Contributions to Chicago History from Peoria County Records," Part I, *Journal of the Illinois State Historical Society* (Mar.-Dec. 1938), 197–207. See especially Robert Stuart to John Crafts, Aug. 20, 1824; Mar. 2, 1825; Aug. 26, 1824, American Fur Company Papers, Chicago Historical Society.

18   John Kinzie Papers and Accounts, Chicago Historical Society; Robert Stuart to Astor, Sep. 12, 1825, American Fur Company Papers, Chicago Historical Society.

19   Quimby, pp. 1–20. In 1800, most of the land at Chicago was free of water at least half of the year. The lake continues to recede.

20   Cleaver, pp. 15–16; Juliette Kinzie, pp. 205–211; Keating, pp. 165–166.

21   Juliette Kinzie, pp. 209–211; Benton in Paul Angle, *Prairie State*, pp. 112–114; Surgeon John Cooper's description in James Grant Wilson Papers, Chicago Historical Society; Captain John Whistler, 1808, Fort Dearborn Paper, Chicago Historical Society.

22   Robert Stuart to John Kinzie, Oct. 22, 1825, American Fur Company Papers, Chicago Historical Society; Juliette Kinzie, p. 215; testimony of Mary Galloway, wife of Archibald Clybourne, in Andreas, *History of Chicago*, p. 103; Ernest B. East, "The Inhabitants of Chicago, 1825-1831," *Journal of the Illinois State Historical Society* (1944), 155.

23   Keating, in Angle, p. 84; Marshall Smelser, "Material Customs in the Territory of Illinois," *Journal of the Illinois State Historical Society* (Apr. 1936), 17; Andreas, p. 134; Beaubien Family Papers, Chicago Historical Society; "Beaubiens of Chicago," MS in Frank Gordon Beaubien Papers, Chicago Historical Society.

24   Information concerning Jean Baptiste Point du Sable is elusive. For a brief sketch, see Lyman Draper interview with Robert Forsyth in Lyman S. Draper Manuscripts, S, XXII (1868), 104, Wisconsin Historical Society, Madison, Wisconsin. See also Milo M. Quaife, *Checagou* (Chicago, 1933), p. 90; Pierce, *A History of Chicago*, p. 13; William C. Smith to James May, Fort Dearborn, Dec. 9, 1803, William C. Smith Papers, Chicago Historical Society; "Beaubiens of Chicago," Frank Gordon Beaubien Papers, Chicago Historical Society. The Wayne County records at Detroit, Michigan show the sale of du Sable's house to Lalime, as well as several Indian grants of land to Kinzie at Detroit. Pierre Menard claimed to have purchased a tract of land on the north bank of the Chicago River from an "Indian" named Bonhomme and later sold it to the Kinzies for $50. No houses are mentioned in these transactions.

25 Juliette Kinzie, p. 210. There is a drawing in the Augustus Dilg Collection, Chicago Historical Society, of the old Kinzie house which fairly matches Mrs. Kinzie's description. See also John Wentworth, *Early Chicago* (Chicago, 1876), p. 23, and Elizabeth Therese Baird, "Reminiscence of Early Days on Mackinac Island," *Collections of the State Historical Society of Wisconsin*, XIV, 25. For a description of the "poteaux en terre" of the lower Illinois country, see John Reynolds, *The Pioneer History of Illinois* (Belleville, Ill., 1852), pp. 30–31.

26 Smelser, pp. 18–19; John McDermott, ed., *The French in the Mississippi Valley* (Urbana, Ill., 1965), pp. 26–40. For a description of "half-breed" housing, see John H. Fonda in *Collections of the State Historical Society of Wisconsin*, V, 232; Peterson, *op. cit.*, Ch. 5.

27 Jane F. Babson, "The Architecture of Early Illinois Forts," *Journal of the Illinois State Historical Society* (Spring 1968), 9–40; Fred Kniffer, "Folk Housing: Key to Diffusion," *Annals of the Association of American Geographers* (Dec. 1965); Interview by Milo M. Quaife of Emily (Beaubien) LeBeau, Aug. 3, 1911, in Emily LeBeau Papers, Chicago Historical Society.

28 "The water lay 6 inches to 9 inches deep the year round," according to Cleaver, p. 30. See also "William B. Ogden," *Fergus Historical Series*, No. 17 (Chicago, 1882), 45; Benton in Angle, p. 114; Quaife, *Checagou*, p. 78.

29 John Kinzie Papers and Accounts, Chicago Historical Society; F. Clever Bald, *Detroit's First American Decade, 1796-1805* (Ann Arbor, 1948), p. 12. See also Eleanor Lytle Kinzie Gordon, *John Kinzie, the Father of Chicago: A Sketch* (1910). This inflated family history suggests that Kinzie lived in New York City and ran off to Quebec to learn a silversmith's trade, a plausible though unsubstantiated story.

30 John Kinzie Papers and Accounts; Quaife, p. 95; Pierce, p. 21; Lyman S. Draper Manuscripts, S, XXII (1868), 102, Wisconsin Historical Society, Madison, Wisconsin; Clifton, "Captain Billy Caldwell."

31 Surgeon John Cooper of the first garrison at Fort Dearborn said that Kinzie was a man of "ungovernable temper," who had bitter quarrels with people; Cooper also charged Kinzie with Lalime's murder. See the James Grant Wilson Papers, Chicago Historical Society. See also *Hyde Park-Kenwood Voices*, III, No. 8 (1960), in John Kinzie Papers; Matthew Irwin to William Eustis, Chicago, July 3, 1812, in Lewis Cass Papers, II, Clements Library, Ann Arbor, Michigan.

32 Blad, p. 76; John Kinzie Papers and Accounts.

33 John Kinzie Papers and Accounts; Andreas, pp. 90–91; Lewis Cass to John Calhoun, Jan. 9, 1819, Lewis Cass Papers, Burton Historical Collection, Detroit Public Library.

34 John Kinzie Papers and Accounts; Robert Stuart to Astor, Sept. 12, 1825, American Fur Company Papers; Robert Stuart to J. B. Beaubien, Sept. 11, 1825, American Fur Company Papers; Gurdon Hubbard, Jan. 2, 1828, Gurdon S. Hubbard Papers.

35 Conway, p. 405 and *passim*; Charles J. Kappler, ed., *Indian Affairs. Law and Treaties* (Washington, D.C., 1904), II, 402–404; James R. Clifton, "Captain Billy Caldwell: The Reconstruction of an Abused Identity," paper read at the American Historical Association meetings, Dec. 1976, Washington, D.C.

36 Eleanor L. K. Gordon, *John Kinzie, Father of Chicago*, p. 28; John Kinzie Papers and Accounts; Ramsay Crooks to John Kinzie, Oct. 29, 1819 and Aug. 11, 1819 and Robert Stuart to Kinzie, 1826-1827, in American Fur Company Papers.

37 Between 1829 and 1830 alone, prominent Chicagoans Archibald Clybourne, Samuel Miller, Archibald Caldwell, Mark Beaubien, Alexander Robinson, and Russell Heacock were licensed to keep tavern. See Ernest East, "Contributions to Chicago History From Peoria County Records," Part II, *Journal of the Illinois State Historical Society* (1938), 328–329; "Beaubiens of Chicago," Frank Gordon Beaubien Papers, Chicago Historical Society.

38 Kinzie Family Papers; Gale, p. 125.

39 Juliette Kinzie, p. 209.

40 *Ibid.*, p. 205.

41 See Keating in Angle, *Prairie State*, pp. 84–86. Mrs. Kinzie's *Wau-bun*, while an important historical document, is unfortunately skewed to favor the family's social aspirations.

42 Juliette Kinzie Papers, Chicago Historical Society; Eleanor L. K. Gordon, pp. 6–7. Trader Clark's first name is listed variously as John and Alexander. Mrs. Kinzie omitted this branch of the Kinzie family in her *Wau-Bun*.

43 Gordon, *loc. cit.*; Andreas, pp. 101–102.

44 Andreas, p. 100; John Kinzie Papers; Robert Stuart to John Crafts, Mar. 2, 1825, American Fur Company Papers.

45 Andreas, pp. 100–102; Wentworth, *Early Chicago*, Supplemental Notes, pp. 34–35.

46 East, "Contributions," Part II, 329–331, 336–339; East, "The Inhabitants of Chicago, 1825-1831," *passim*.

47 The canal section, platted and sold in 1831, held the only lots on the market when the Eastern speculators began to arrive in 1833. Its location, the central loop, gave it a speculative advantage over areas further away from the new harbor. The Kinzie family did not pre-empt the Point, and it went to southerners who did not have a flair for exciting the Eastern interest. See Andreas, pp. 111, 130–132; also Gale, p. 54.

48 Mark Beaubien Papers, Chicago Historical Society; Andreas, pp. 106, 288–289.

49 For the *habitant* dancing tradition, see John Reynolds, *The Pioneer History of Illinois*, pp. 52–53. Cleaver, *Early Chicago Reminiscences*, pp. 5–12; John H. Kinzie Papers; "John Dean Caton Recollections," *Reception to the Settlers of Chicago Prior to 1840, by the Calumet Club of Chicago, Tuesday evening, May 27, 1879* (Chicago, 1879), 36–37. For a discussion of the liquor problem, see Marshall Smelser, pp. 11–13; Thomas Forsyth to General William Clark, Peoria, Apr. 9, 1824, Thomas Forsyth Papers, Folder 2, Missouri Historical Society, St. Louis, Missouri.

50 Juliette Kinzie, p. 205; Beaubien Family Papers.

51 "John Wentworth's Recollections," Calumet Club, pp. 42, 48; Cleaver, p. 13. Beaubien's tavern was only 16 by 24 feet, yet in 1833-34, forty people were being boarded in shifts. No one knows how many people actually slept there in a given evening.

52 "John Wentworth's Recollections," Calumet Club, pp. 49, 71. In the winter of 1835-36, prominent Easterners and the Kinzies built the Lake

House on the North Side. Gale said "they ain't going to call it no tavern," and Cleaver said there was a joke circulating that no one worth less than $10,000 would be allowed to stay there. Weekly dancing parties were held there by invitation only. At least some of the French Creoles were being included; there is an 1843 dance ticket in the Beaubien Family Papers requesting the company of the "misses Beaubien." See also "Beaubiens of Chicago," Frank Gordon Beaubien Papers; Gale, p. 118.

53   On the Beaubien farm at Grosse Pointe, see Bald, p. 35. Beaubien was early Chicago's most colorful character, according to most Easterners' recollections. He is mentioned in nearly every old settler's reminiscences, especially in Gale, Cleaver, the John Wentworth Papers, Chicago Historical Society, and "Sketch of Hon. J. Young Scammon," *Chicago Magazine*, Mar. 1857, reprinted in *Fergus Historical Series*, No. 5 (Chicago, 1876). See "Beaubiens of Chicago," Frank Gordon Beaubien Papers and Beaubien Family Papers, for particulars, and Andreas (p. 107) for a physical description. "His favorite dress on 'great occasions' was a swallow-tail coat with brass buttons. . . . He was in his glory at a horse-race."

54   Andreas, pp. 85, 174; East, "Contributions," Part I, pp. 191–197.

55   East, "Contributions," Part I, pp. 191–197; Wentworth, *Early Chicago*, p. 41.

56   *Ibid.*

57   See Jean Baptiste Beaubien Papers for original voting lists; "Beaubiens of Chicago," Frank Gordon Beaubien Papers; Andreas, pp. 600–602.

58   Andreas, p. 602; East, "The Inhabitants of Chicago," *passim.*

59   Regarding the first Board of Trustees, see Andreas, pp. 174–175; *Chicago Democrat* (Dec. 10, 1833).

60   John Kinzie Papers, Madore Beaubien Papers, and Beaubien Family Papers; for a vivid description of Reverend See, see Juliette Kinzie, p. 216.

61   For a description of private schools in Detroit, see Bald, pp. 88–91; Beaubien Family Papers.

62   "The Beaubiens of Chicago," Frank Gordon Beaubien Papers; Madore Beaubien and Billy Caldwell Papers; Clifton, "Captain Billy Caldwell."

63   John Kinzie Papers; Madore Beaubien 1881 and 1882 letters, Madore Beaubien Papers; Andreas, pp. 204–209.

64   Andreas, p. 205; Mary Ann Hubbard, *Family Memories* (printed for private circulation, 1912), p. 68.

65   Andreas, p. 205; letter from John Watkins in Calumet Club, pp. 73–74.

66   Andreas, pp. 299–301; Reverend Jeremiah Porter, *Early Chicago's Religious History* (Chicago, 1881), pp. 54–58.

67   Andreas, pp. 288–289; Gale, p. 60.

68   Andreas, p. 289; Porter, pp. 56–57.

69   Gale, p. 60; Andreas, p. 289.

70   Andreas, pp. 174, 111–124; Beaubien Family Papers.

71   Andreas, pp. 132–133; *Chicago Democrat*, Nov. 26, 1833; Wentworth, *Early Chicago*, pp. 39–40.

72   John Wentworth to Lydia Wentworth, Nov. 10, 1836, John Wentworth Papers, Chicago Historical Society; Madore Beaubien Papers; Harriet

Martineau, in *Reminiscences of Early Chicago* (Chicago, 1912), p. 30; Cleaver, p. 27.

73   Charles Fenno Hoffman, in *Reminiscences of Early Chicago*, pp. 21–22; Beaubien Family Papers; Porter, p. 78; Cleaver, pp. 5, 12. According to Cleaver, large hunts of over 100 men were still being held in 1834. He describes improvised sleighs built by setting crockery crates filled with hay on two young saplings shaved at the end to create runners. See Reynolds, p. 229, for the French Creole habit of cardplaying on Sunday.

74   Cleaver, p. 12. For descriptions of the Guignolée and other French customs transplanted in the Illinois country, see Natalia Maree Belting, *Kaskaskia Under the French Regime*, Illinois Studies in the Social Sciences, XXIX, No. 3 (Urbana, 1948), J. M. Carriere, *Life and Customs in the French Villages of the Old Illinois Country* (Report of the Canadian Historical Association, 1939).

75   See Andreas, pp. 267–271, for a treatment of Chicago's role in the Black Hawk War; interview with Madore Beaubien, *Chicago Times*, May 16, 1882, in "Beaubiens of Chicago," p. 39, Frank Gordon Beaubien Papers.

76   Andreas, pp. 122–128, 174–175; Kappler, ed., pp. 402–403; Charles Royce, *Indian Land Cessions in the United States*, 18th Annual Report of the Bureau of American Ethnology (Washington, 1899), pp. 750–751; Anselm J. Gerwing, "The Chicago Indian Treaty of 1833," *Journal of the Illinois State Historical Society* (1964); Wentworth, *Early Chicago*, pp. 39–40.

77   Andreas, pp. 120–121; "Biography of Thomas Church," *Fergus Historical Series*, No. 5 (Chicago, 1876), p. 42.

78   Andreas, pp. 131–133. See Daniel Elazar, *Cities of the Prairie* (New York, 1970), pp. 153–180, for Illinois migration streams; "List of Settlers of Chicago Who Came Between January, 1831, and December, 1836," in Rufus Blanchard, *Discovery and Conquest of the Northwest, With the History of Chicago* (Wheaton, 1879), pp. 424–433.

79   See Madore Beaubien Papers. For affinity of French Creoles for the Potawatomi and Potawatomi culture, Mark Beaubien spoke of this on his deathbed in "Beaubiens of Chicago," Frank Gordon Beaubien Papers.

80   Andreas, pp. 130–131; Kinzie Family Papers; "William B. Ogden," *Fergus Historical Series*, No. 17 (Chicago, 1882); "John Dean Caton Recollections," Calumet Club, p. 35; John Wentworth to Lydia Wentworth, Nov. 10, 1836, John Wentworth Papers.

81   Beaubien Family Papers; "Beaubiens of Chicago," Frank Gordon Beaubien Papers.

82   Beaubien Family Papers; store inventory, Madore Beaubien Papers.

83   Andreas, p. 103.

84   Juliette Kinzie, pp. 227–229.

85   John Harris Kinzie Papers, 1833-1837, Chicago Historical Society; Harriet Martineau, *Reminiscenes of Early Chicago*, p. 32; Martineau, "Strange Early Days," *Annals of Chicago*, IX (Chicago, 1876).

86   Cleaver, pp. 13, 24; Gale, p. 122; John Wentworth to Lydia Wentworth, Nov. 10, 1836, in John Wentworth Papers.

87   Cleaver, p. 27.

88   Andreas, pp. 122–125.

89   *Ibid.*, p. 123; Charles Latrobe, *A Rambler in North America* (London, 1836), pp. 201, 207, 210–211.

90   Andreas, p. 124; Latrobe, pp. 213–214. For the influence of mixed-bloods in Potawatomi politics and the treaty of 1833, see miscellaneous fragment, n.d., Alphabetical File: James Herrington, Chicago Historical Society; Frank R. Grover, *Antoine Ouilmette* (Evanston, 1908), pp. 12–16; Conway, pp. 410–418; Clifton, "Captain Billy Caldwell."
91   Andreas, pp. 126–128; Porter, pp. 71–73; *Chicago Democrat* (Dec. 10, 1833).
92   Andreas, pp. 126–128; Kappler, ed., pp. 402–410.
93   Porter, pp. 73–74.
94   *Ibid.*
95   Gale, p. 154; Madore Beaubien Papers.
96   In his old age Madore Beaubien said that he wanted his children to honor his name and lamented the fact that Chicago had not remembered him. See interview in *Chicago Times*, May 16, 1882, in "Beaubiens of Chicago," Frank Gordon Beaubien Papers. See also John Dean Caton, *The Last of the Illinois and a Sketch of the Pottawatomie* (Chicago, 1876), pp. 26–30; Wentworth, *Early Chicago*, pp. 35–36.
97   Pierce, pp. 57–69. See also John D. Haeger, *Men and Money: The Urban Frontier at Green Bay, 1815–1840* (Mt. Pleasant, Mich.: Clarke Historical Library, Central Michigan University, 1970) for a comparable takeover by Eastern speculators of another fur-trading town.

CHAPTER X: BLACK CHICAGO

1   Edward H. Wright, the "Iron Master" of Chicago politics, came to the city in 1884 (*Chicago Inter-Ocean*, June 14, 1900); Dan Jackson came in 1892 (Works Progress Administration, "The Negro in Illinois," Hirsh Collection, Carter G. Woodson Regional Center, Chicago Public Library [hereafter cited as WPA papers]); Louis B. Anderson came in about 1894 (Thomas Yenser, ed., *Who's Who in Colored America* [Brooklyn, 1942], p. 29); DePriest came to Chicago in 1889 (*Broad Ax*, Apr. 18, 1903); Archibald Carey came in 1898 (Joseph A. Logsdon, "The Rev. Archibald Carey and the Negro in Chicago Politics" [M.A. thesis, University of Chicago, 1961], p. 9).
2   Bessie Louise Pierce, *A History of Chicago*, 3 vols. (New York, 1937 [I], 1940 [II], 1957 [III]), is the most comprehensive study of the city yet produced; unfortunately, it only goes up to 1893. The best general studies of black Chicago are: St. Clair Drake and Horace Clayton, *Black Metropolis* (New York, 1945), and the more limited study by Allan H. Spear, *Black Chicago* (Chicago, 1967), which covers the period from 1890 to 1920. The best general study of black politics is still Harold Gosnell's *Negro Politicans* (Chicago, 1935), which can be supplemented with James Q. Wilson's interpretive discussion of more contemporary politics in Chicago and other cities, *Negro Politics* (New York, 1961).
3   Mason Fishback, "Illinois Legislation on Slavery and Free Negroes, 1818-1865," *Transactions of the Illinois State Historical Society*, IX (Springfield, Ill., 1904), 414–432; *Public Laws of the State of Illinois passed by the . . . General Assembly* (1853); *Illinois Revised Statutes* (1845).
4   *Weekly Chicago Democrat*, Nov. 3, 1846.

5   Estelle Hill Scott, *Occupational Changes Among Negroes in Chicago* (Chicago, WPA, 1939, mimeographed), p. 18. The servant class claimed 53.7% of all Negro workers: 47.3% of the males and 77.1% of the females.

6   *Ibid.*, p. 49.

7   *Ibid.*, p. 20.

8   Alma Herbst, *The Negro in the Slaughtering and Meat Packing Industry in Chicago* (New York, 1932), pp. 19–29.

9   The sewer riot received extensive coverage in the *Chicago Tribune*, Nov. 30, 1899; *Chicago Times-Herald*, Nov. 29, 1899; *Chicago Inter-Ocean*, Nov. 15, 1899; *Chicago Record-Herald*, Nov. 29, 1899 (the *Record-Herald's* headline states that the riot took place on 29th Street, but its text states that it occurred on 39th Street); *Daily Inter-Ocean*, Nov. 29, 1899; *Chicago Journal*, Nov. 29, 1899. On the teamster's strike see *Chicago Tribune*, Apr. 7-May 3, 1905; *Broad Ax*, Oct. 15, 1904; May 6, 13, 20, 27, 1905; Spear, *Black Chicago*, p. 40.

10 *Chicago Tribune*, Feb. 10, 1890. In 1888 a black man was charged $3.55 for a 35¢ order of roast beef and a 5¢ cup of coffee at the Brevort House. He sued and was awarded $15. In another case, filed by Josephine M. Curry against the People's Theatre, the judge declared that placing Negroes in a special part of the theatre on the basis of race was as discriminatory as denying a person admittance to the theatre altogether. The proprietor was fined $100 (*Chicago Tribune*, Mar. 16 and 17, 1866). These and similar cases of racial discrimination cited in Pierce, pp. 49–50.

11 Thomas Philpott, "The House and the Neighborhood: Housing Reform and Neighborhood Work in Chicago, 1880-1930" (Ph.D. diss., University of Chicago, 1974), p. 184. For a general discussion of the emergence of the "color line" in Chicago, see Ch. 4, pp. 149–184.

12 Rayford Logan, *The Betrayal of the Negro: From Rutherford B. Hayes to Woodrow Wilson* (New York, 1954), p. 9.

13 Ann Lane, "The Negro's Response: A Study in Desperation," in Frederic Cople Jaher, *The Age of Industrialism in America* (New York, 1968), p. 111; Richard Hofstadter, *Social Darwinism in American Thought* (Philadelphia, 1944), p. 148.

14 Spear, p. 61.

15 Fannie Barrier Williams, "Social Bonds in the 'Black Belt' of Chicago," *Charities*, XV, No. 1 (Oct. 7, 1905), 40.

16 Early national Negro political debates centered on assertion of Negro "manhood" rights and the explosive questions of black emigration from the United States. By the 1850s, however, the implications of national passage of the Fugitive Slave Law of 1850 became the major political question facing Northern blacks. Pre-Civil War debate is explored in Howard Holman Bell, *A Survey of the Negro Convention Movement, 1830-1861* (New York, 1969, a reprint of Bell's Ph.D. diss., Northwestern University, 1953).

17 See V. Jacque Voegeli, *Free But Not Equal* (Chicago, 1967), p. 2. Democratic and Republican jockeying over the race issue is recorded in *Chicago Tribune*, March 6, 1862; July 15, 1862; Aug. 10, 1862; Jan. 16, 1863; Feb. 12 and 13, 1863; *Chicago Times*, Feb. 13, 1863. See also Frank L. Klement, *The Copperheads in the Middle West* (Chicago, 1960),

and Norman Dwight Harris, *The Study of Negro Servitude in Illinois, and of the Slavery Agitation in that State, 1719-1864* (Chicago, 1904).

18 Drake and Cayton, pp. 44–50.

19 Certificate of Freedom, Nov. 28, 1844, William Tyler Brown, Clerk of Circuit Court of Madison County, Illinois, John Jones Collection, Chicago Historical Society (hereafter CHS); *Chicago Tribune*, May 22, 1879.

20 *Chicago Tribune*, Jan. 2, 1874.

21 Mrs. Lavinia Jones Lee to Caroline McIlvaine, Apr. 21, 1905, John Jones Collection, CHS; Genna Rae McNeil, "The Price of Redemption: The Repeal of the Illinois Black Laws, 1864-1865" (unpublished paper in possession of author), ms. p. 37.

22 *Chicago Times*, Nov. 23, 1864; *Journal of the House of Representatives, Proceedings*, Feb. 4, 1865, p. 551, cited in McNeil, p. 57.

23 *Chicago Tribune*, Dec. 9, 1864; John Jones, *The Black Laws of Illinois and a Few Reasons Why They Should be Repealed* (Chicago, 1864), in John Jones Collection, CHS.

24 The interrelationship between the repeal campaign, white abolitionism, and partisan political concerns emerged from a reading of the McNeil paper, but responsibility for the interpretation is entirely my own.

25 *Chicago Tribune*, May 22, 1879.

26 Spear, pp. 51–89.

27 Gosnell, pp. 65–66. Thomas received 11,532 votes in 1876, although the total black population was less than 7,000. See also *Conservator*, Dec. 23, 1882.

28 Thomas introduced House Bill No. 45, "An Act to protect all citizens in their civil and legal rights," *Journal of the House of Representatives of the Thirty-Fourth General Assembly of the State of Illinois* (Springfield, 1885), p. 113; *Laws of the State of Illinois enacted by the 34th General Assembly*, Jan. 7-June 26, 1885 (Springfield, 1885), pp. 64–65; Edward E. Wilson, "The Chicago Negro in Politics," *The Voice*, Mar. 1907, pp. 98–103.

29 *Journal of the House of Representatives . . .*, 1889, pp. 181, 424.

30 Joseph J. Boris, ed., *Who's Who in Colored America: A Biographical Dictionary of Notable Living Persons of Negro Descent in America* (New York, 1927), p. 145; The Washington Intercollegiate Club of Chicago, *Intercollegian Wonder Book, or The Negro in Chicago, 1779-1927* (Chicago, 1927), p. 112 [hereafter *Intercollegian*]; *Inter-Ocean*, Jan. 14, 1900; August Meier, *Negro Thought in America, 1880-1915* (Ann Arbor, 1963), p. 178; Spear, pp. 61–63. Apparently not everyone thought so highly of Atty. Morris. A *Broad Ax* headline on March 27, 1909 read: "COL. E. H. MORRIS AT ONE TIME CHIEF ATTORNEY FOR THE 'GAMBLER TRUST' "; Morris was charged with defending several notorious gamblers in court. See also *Broad Ax*, July 2, 1910; May 18, 1918.

31 *Defender*, June 21, 1924.

32 *Journal of the House . . .*, HB 239, HB 23, p. 1509; *Journal of the House . . .*, 1905, pp. 80, 664, 665, 730, 744, 777.

33 *Broad Ax*, May 18, 1918; *Defender*, Feb. 3, 1933; *Journal of the House . . .*, 1905, HB 155, pp. 638, 645.

34 *Defender*, June 21, 1924; WPA Papers; Gosnell, pp. 111–112; Ira Katznelson, *Black Men, White Cities* (New York, 1973), p. 91.

35 *Broad Ax*, Dec. 25, 1909.

36 *Defender*, Feb. 4, 1933; *Journal of the House . . .* , 1895, pp. 133, 104; *ibid.*, 1897, pp. 133, 104, 183, 282; W. G. Sea, "The Eighth Illinois," *Negro History Bulletin*, VII, No. 7 (Apr. 1944), 149–150; William B. Gatewood, "An Experiment in Color: The Eighth Illinois Volunteers, 1898-1899," *Journal of the Illinois State Historical Society*, LXV, No. 3 (Autumn 1972), 293–305.

37 *Defender*, Oct. 24, 1932; Thomas Bullard, "From Businessman to Congressman: The Careers of Martin B. Madden" (Ph.D. diss., University of Illinois at Chicago Circle, 1973), p. 80.

38 *Journal of the House . . .* , 1897, HB 50, pp. 83, 420, 502; HB 263, pp. 182, 183; HB 395, p. 244. See also pp. 152, 667, 714, 907.

39 *Defender*, July 2, 1927; *Inter-Ocean*, Aug. 14, 1895; William M. Tuttle, Jr., *Race Riot: Chicago in the Red Summer of 1919* (New York, 1970), p. 113; Arna Bontemps and Jack Conroy, *Anyplace But Here* (New York, 1966), pp. 142–144.

40 James A. Roe, ed., *Blue Book of the State of Illinois, 1899* (Springfield, 1899), p. 297; *Journal of the House . . .* , HB 462, HB 463, and HB 686, pp. 275, 301. Martin also introduced HB 810, which would permit children of school age to attend public schools nearest their homes. The bill may have been intended as an anti-discriminatory piece of legislation—a safeguard against school segregation through district gerrymandering. *Journal*, p. 676; *Defender*, Feb. 4, 1933.

41 *Journal*, 1899, HB 577, p. 277; HB 715 and 716, p. 338.

42 *Ibid.*, HB 561, p. 275; HB 562, p. 275; HB 578, p. 277; HB 689, p. 301.

43 Spear, pp. 62–63.

44 *Journal*, 1901, HB 6, p. 46; HB 278, p. 151.

45 *Ibid.*, HB 235, p. 151; HB 400, p. 191; HB 41, p. 66; HB 482, p. 66; HB 564, p. 263.

46 *Ibid.*, HB 553, p. 208; HB 682, p. 362; *Gideon v. Wainright*, 372 U.S. 335 (1963): 1030, 1032; *Douglas v. California*, 372 U.S. 352 (1963): 1031; *Escobedo v. Illinois*, 378 U.S. 478 (1964): 1032.

47 Mae Felts Herringshaw, ed., "Chicago Men of 1913," *Clark J. Herringshaw's City Blue Book of Current Biography* (Chicago, 1913), p. 159; *Broad Ax*, Apr. 20, 1901; *Chicago Tribune*, Dec. 9, 1900; Mar. 2, 1901; Mar. 3 and 14, 1901; *Inter-Ocean*, Nov. 21, 1900; Mar. 25, 1901.

48 *Inter-Ocean*, Jan. 4, 1891; *Chicago Tribune*, May 6, 1897; Gosnell, p. 112; *Broad Ax*, Dec. 25, 1909.

49 Buckner died in 1913, two years before DePriest became the city's first black alderman. The Buckner funeral cortège was one mile long; DePriest was in charge, and Madden delivered the eulogy. A John Buckner Memorial Association was incorporated in 1925, with DePriest as president. See *Defender*, Nov. 12, 1932; Dec. 26, 1913; May 30, 1925; Sept. 15, 1928; Apr. 3, 1926.

50 *Broad Ax*, Dec. 30, 1905; Aug. 15, 1908; Drake, pp. 361–362.

51 *Defender*, Feb. 5, 1938.

52 Members of the assistant corporations council were Franklin A. Denison and Earl B. Dickerson; State Representatives Buckner, Bish, R. R. Jackson, William Warfield, George W. Blackwell and Charles Jenkins; State Senator Jackson; Aldermen Jackson, Earl B. Dickerson, and William L. Dawson; and Congressman Dawson.

53 Gosnell, pp. 216–217.

54 Logsdon, "The Rev. Archibald Carey and the Negro in Chicago Politics," pp. 36–39.
55 *Ibid.*, pp. 24–25.
56 Mark Miles Fisher, *The Master's Slave: Elijah John Fisher* (Philadelphia, 1922), pp. 75, 145.
57 Deneen to Fisher, April 9, 1904; "A Word to Colored Voters, Endorsing Charles S. Deneen for Governor of the State of Illinois, in the primary of May 6, 1904," Dunne to Fisher, June 14, 1905; Deneen to Fisher, Aug. 17, 1908 (thanks for endorsement); letter, National Taft Bureau, 1908, in Fisher, pp. 75, 76, 93, 107, 145–146. In 1905, Fisher needed $20,000 to complete his church in time for a Chicago meeting of the National Baptist Convention. He got financial help from Frank O. Lowden, later Governor of Illinois, and George Dixon of Borden Milk Company, and from Republican judges McEwn, Hanecy, and Fisher, pp. 95–96.
58 Albert L. Kreiling, "The Making of Racial Identities in the Black Press: A Cultural Analysis of Race Journalism in Chicago, 1878-1929" (Ph.D. diss., University of Illinois, Urbana-Champaign, 1973).
59 Ralph Nelson Davis, "The Negro Newspaper in Chicago" (M.A. thesis, University of Chicago, 1939), p. 30; Kreiling, p. 165.
60 *Defender*, Apr. 3, 1926; Davis, pp. 42–43; I. Garland Penn, *The Afro-American Press* (Springfield, 1891), pp. 256–258.
61 Davis, pp. 31–32.
62 *Broad Ax*, July 15, 1899; Jan. 6, 1900.
63 Taylor's economic radicalism can be found in *Broad Ax*, July 15, 1899 and Jan. 6, 1900. His Democratic allegiance was, however, not unswerving. On occasion he would commend or even endorse a Republican, usually a black Republican, for elective office. He was particularly partial to Ed Wright (*Broad Ax*, Feb. 10, 1900) and Oscar DePriest (*Broad Ax*, Dec. 27, 1904).
64 The paper's political views are revealed in *Conservator*, Dec. 23, 1882; Davis, p. 16.
65 Wilson, p. 100.
66 *Inter-Ocean*, Oct. 28, 1892; Nov. 13, 1893.
67 *Ibid.*, June 10, 1894.
68 *Defender*, July 5, 1930; *Intercollegian*, p. 103; Gosnell, p. 154.
69 *Defender*, Nov. 5, 1932; *Intercollegian*, p. 135; *Defender*, Jan. 4, 1913.
70 Gosnell, p. 154; *Defender*, Nov. 5, 1932.
71 *Defender*, Nov. 5, 1932.
72 *Defender*, July 5, 1930; Gosnell, p. 155; *Intercollegian*, p. 135.
73 Gosnell, p. 154.
74 Ellen Josephine Beckman, "The Relationship of the Government of the City of Chicago to Cook County from 1893 to 1916" (M.A. thesis, University of Chicago, 1940), p. 608; *Chicago Daily News*, Aug. 20, 1900.
75 *Chicago Tribune*, Mar. 1, 1895; Jan. 5, 1896; Apr. 8, 1896; *Chicago Daily News*, Apr. 2, 1910; Beckman, p. 14.
76 The Republican nominee in 1900 was Daniel M. Jackson, a Southside funeral director with gambling interests, who was defeated, in part, by the use of the race issue in the white press. *Broad Ax*, Feb. 9, 1901; May 4, 1907; Gosnell, pp. 83, 131, 156.
77 *Defender*, Apr. 20, 1929; Drake, p. 361; Gosnell, p. 164.

78   *Broad Ax*, Dec. 30, 1905; Gosnell, p. 168.

79   *Broad Ax*, Apr. 18, 1903; Dec. 30, 1905.

80   *Broad Ax*, Dec. 30, 1905; Gosnell, p. 169.

81   *Inter-Ocean*, "The Rise of the Sumner Club," Jan. 14, 1900. Both Harding and Madden were members of the Hamilton Club. *Blue Book, 1911*, pp. 68, 72.

82   *Defender*, Feb. 12, 1910; June 6, 1929; *Chicago Whip*, May 10, 1929; July 6, 1929; Gosnell, pp. 111, 316, 318; Spear, p. 781.

83   *Defender*, Mar. 4, 1910.

84   *Defender*, Feb. 5, 1910.

85   *Defender*, Feb. 3, 1912; *Broad Ax*, Nov. 28, 1914.

86   The extent of Wright's concern for the independence of political organizations representing black Chicagoans is perhaps over-emphasized in eulogies and articles written by Wright partisans after his death. Yet his activities between 1900 and 1915 seem to bear out this general interpretation. See *Defender*, Dec. 24, 1932; Dec. 31, 1932; *Chicago Whip*, Aug. 16, 1930. Wright is credited with having Anderson appointed assistant county attorney, with getting Dr. Daniel Hale Williams appointed to the Cook County Hospital Staff and F. L. Barnett as the first assistant states attorney while Wright was County Commissioner. *Intercollegian*, p. 103.

87   *Inter-Ocean*, Jan. 23, 1895; Alfreda M. Duster, ed., *Crusade for Justice; The Autobiography of Ida B. Wells* (Chicago, 1970), xxix, 352.

88   *Broad Ax*, Nov. 2, 1907; Nov. 9, 1908; May 21, 1910.

89   Merriam Papers, University of Chicago, Box LXXIV, Folder 4; *Interim Report*, Municipal Voters League, Thirteenth Year, 1926, p. 1. Criticisms of Anderson and Jackson can be found in *Twenty-Sixth Annual Preliminary Report*, MVL, 1912, 1919, 1920, 1925, and 1927.

90   Author's interview with Mae C. Barnett, Jan. 2, 1972.

91   Heinz Eulau and Kenneth Prewitt, *Labyrinths of Democracy: Adaptations, Linkages, Representation, and Policies in Urban Politics* (Indianapolis, 1973), p. 262.

92   It was the geography of Chicago ward politics that allowed blacks to advance so rapidly. Chicago used the ward system with relatively small, ethnically homogenous political units, which, coupled with residential segregation, enabled blacks to maximize their numbers. On the other hand, New York blacks had to contend with large political units gerrymandered to protect Italian and Jewish political power.

93   Katznelson, pp. 102–103.

94   *Ibid.*, pp. 196–197.

95   Wilson, pp. 169–185.

96   Martin Kilson, "Political Change in the Negro Ghetto, 1900-1940's," in Nathan I. Huggins, Martin Kilson, and Daniel M. Fox, eds., *Key Issues in the Afro-American Experience* (New York, 1971), pp. 167–174.

97   *Ibid.*, pp. 174–182.

98   *Ibid.*, pp. 182–183.

99   "Diary," John Jones Collection, CHS, no pagination.

100   *Ibid.*

101   *Broad Ax*, Nov. 2, 1907.

102   *Defender*, Sept. 7, 1912.

103   In 1938, Democrat Edward M. Sneed, the first black Democratic ward committeeman, was elected to the county commission.

104 A fuller understanding of the interrelationship between black economic nationalism, laissez-faire capitalism, and black political conservatism can be found in Meier, *Negro Thought in America*, and Louis Harlan, *Booker T. Washington: The Making of a Black Leader, 1856-1902* (New York, 1972).

105 *Chicago Chronicle*, Nov. 8, 1906.

106 *Chicago Tribune*, Jan. 2, 1874.

107 *Ibid.*, Mar. 12, 1875. The article, which described a party given by Jones for his daughter Lavinia, was headlined "Chicago's Favoite Colored Citizen."

108 *Chicago Whip*, Mar. 29, 1924.

109 Henry McGhee, "The Negro in the Chicago Post Office" (M.A. thesis, University of Chicago, 1961), pp. 7-8, cited in Katznelson, pp. 96-97.

110 Robert L. Factor, *The Black Response to America* (Menlo Park, Cal., 1970), pp. 48-58.

111 *The Appeal*, Aug. 28, 1888, cited in Spear, p. 125.

112 *Chicago Daily News*, Apr. 6, 1895; *Inter-Ocean*, Apr. 6, 1885.

113 *Broad Ax*, Oct. 1, 1898; Aug. 12, 1899. The Colored Democratic League established its permanent headquarters on Oct. 1, 1898.

114 *Broad Ax*, Aug. 12, 1899. Newby edited the *Indianapolis Courier* from 1892 to 1893, and when he came to Chicago he also served as editor and owner of two short-lived papers, the *Chicago Leader* (1896-1897) and the *Chicago Plaindealer* (1916-1918). *Who's Who in Colored America*, 6th ed., 1941-1944, p. 384.

115 *Broad Ax*, Oct. 1, 1898; May 26, 1900; Apr. 20, 1901; Spear, p. 125.

116 *Broad Ax*, Apr. 6, 1900; Apr. 20, 1901; May 18, 1901.

117 Harrison's popularity with blacks gave rise to the overly optimistic prediction that "the social ostracism that made in former days the life of a 'nigger democrat' as he was termed, a burden, has been obliterated." *Broad Ax*, Oct. 1, 1898. See also *Broad Ax*, Apr. 6, 1911; Gosnell, p. 252. The *Conservator* endorsed Carter Harrison II in 1878 and 1880. Nelson, p. 14.

118 Wilson, p. 101.

119 Spear, p. 125; Meier, p. 274. The traditional anti-Democratic argument is presented in Henry Rucker, "Why Colored Men Cannot be Democrats," *Voice of the Negro*, I, No. 9 (Sept. 1904), 386-390. The article makes a special reference to the treatment of blacks at Democratic political conventions and cites Southern demagogues like Tillman and Vardaman.

120 I am particularly impressed with Kilson's analysis of the "modernization" of black politics. The experience is similar in many important ways to those of a West African political elite. See his *Political Change in a West African State: A Study of the Modernization Process in Sierra Leone* (Cambridge, Mass., 1966), especially the sub-chapters "A Note on the 'Mass Factor' in Political Change," pp. 117-122, and "The 'Mass Factor' in Political Change," pp. 284-286.

121 Wilson, pp. 102-103.

CHAPTER XI: BLACKS AND HOUSING

1 Pauline Maier, "Popular Uprisings and Civil Authority in Eighteenth-Century America," *William and Mary Quarterly*, XXVII, Ser. 3 (1970),

3–35; Maier, *From Resistance to Revolution* (New York, 1972); Gordon S. Wood, "A Note on Mobs in the American Revolution," *William and Mary Quarterly,* XXIII, Ser. 3 (1966), 635–642; Leonard Richards, *Gentlemen of Property and Standing: Anti-Abolition Mobs in Jacksonian America* (New York, 1970); Michael Feldberg, "Urbanization as a Cause of Violence: Philadelphia as a Test Case," in Allen F. Davis and Mark Haller, eds., *The Peoples of Philadelphia* (Philadelphia, 1973), pp. 53–70.

2   National Advisory Commission on Civil Disorders, *Report* (New York, 1968); Stanley Lieberson and Arnold R. Silverman, "The Precipitants and Underlying Conditions of Race Riots," *American Sociological Review,* XXX (Dec. 1965), 887–898; or any of the studies produced by the Lemberg Center for the Study of Violence at Brandeis University, to cite just a few of the better-known examples.

3   In 1940 the white population of the city was 3,114,564; by 1960 it had declined to 2,712,748. The black population, meanwhile, had risen from 277,731 to 812,637.

4   *Chicago Daily News,* July 12, 1951; *Chicago Sun-Times,* July 13, 1951; *New York Times,* July 14, 1951 and Oct. 21, 1951.

5   *New York Times,* Aug. 1, 1951; *Chicago Defender,* Aug. 11, 1951 and Sept. 15, 1951.

6   *Chicago Daily News,* July 17, 1951.

7   The Fernwood riot occurred in Aug. 1947 at a veterans' emergency housing project bordered by 104th Place, 106th Street, Halsted, and Fernwood Park. The Englewood disorder took place in November 1949 and was centered around the intersection of 56th and Peoria. For the effect of the press's silence, see William Peters, "The Race War in Chicago," *New Republic,* CXXII, No. 2 (Jan. 9, 1950), 12.

8   *New York Times,* July 14, 1951; Homer Jack, "Chicago Has One More Chance," *The Nation,* CLXV, No. 11 (Sept. 13, 1947), 252; Chicago Commission on Human Relations (hereafter cited as CHR), "Memorandum on Fernwood Park Homes" (mimeographed, n.d.); "Peoria Street Incident" (mimeographed, n.d.).

9   CHR, "Memorandum on Airport Homes" (mimeographed, n.d.); "Documentary Report of the Anti-Racial Demonstrations and Violence Against the Home and Persons of Mr. and Mrs. Roscoe Johnson, 7153 St. Lawrence Ave., July 25, 1949" (mimeographed, n.d.); "Tuley Park Incident" (mimeographed, n.d.); *The Trumbull Park Homes Disturbances* (Chicago, n.d.); CHR, "A Preliminary Report on Racial Disturbances for the Period July 21 to August 4, 1957" (mimeographed, n.d.).

10   For the period 1917-1921, see Chicago Commission on Race Relations, *The Negro in Chicago* (Chicago, 1922), p. 122; for the period 1944-1946, see Chicago Council Against Religious and Racial Discrimination, "Arson-Bombings and Other Terrorism Against Negro Households in Chicago, Documented Memorandum No. VII" (Aug. 3, 1946; mimeographed).

11   Counting only the largest disturbances, at least eight separate major racial disorders have been documented for Chicago (including Cicero) from 1946 to 1957. The incidents were: Airport Homes, 1946; Fernwood Homes, 1947; Park Manor, two separate incidents in 1949 and 1950; Tuley Park, 1950; Cicero, 1951; Trumbull Park beginning in 1953; and Calumet Park, 1957. None of the disputes over the use of community

facilities occurred before 1950. The analysis that follows is based on an examination of all these incidents as well as several lesser disorders.

12   *Chicago Sun-Times,* July 14, 1951; Charles Abrams, *Forbidden Neighbors* (New York, 1955), p. 105.

13   See, for example, *Chicago Daily News,* December 3, 1946, or *Chicago Tribune,* August 15–17, 1947; although these stories are limited, their coverage is extensive compared to that given later riots. One can search the press in vain to find any significant mention of the troubles in Park Manor during the last week of July 1949 or of the Peoria Street incident of November 8–12, 1949. For the attitudes of race relations officials and the press, as well as for details of their cooperation, see CHR, *The People of Chicago* (Chicago, n.d.), p. 3; *Fourth Chicago Conference on Civic Unity* (Chicago, 1952), pp. 77–78; "Memorandum on Airport Homes," p. 15; "Memorandum on Fernwood Park Homes," pp. 5, 8; "Peoria Street Incident," pp. 22, 28; "Documentary Report of the Violence . . . ," p. 20.

14   Allen Day Grimshaw, "A Study in Social Violence: Urban Race Riots in the United States" (Ph.D. diss., University of Pennsylvania, 1959), pp. 207–208.

15   CHR research memoranda and the daily press were used to compile arrest lists for the Fernwood riot of 1947, the Park Manor disorder of 1949, the Peoria Street incident in Englewood in 1949, the Trumbull Park disturbances of the mid-1950s, and the Calumet Park uprising of 1957. The lists for the first three episodes appear to be comprehensive, or nearly so. The Trumbull Park outbreaks, however, lasted for years, and the list compiled for that disorder covers arrests made from Aug. 1953 through Aug. 1954; though the CHR reported 120 persons arrested in the Calumet Park rioting, no list of arrestees was found. The 51 names obtained for this riot were gleaned from press reports and represent, apparently, 42.5% of all Calumet Park arrestees.

16   CHR, "Peoria Street Incident," pp. 32, 35; "Notes on Special Meeting of the Board of Directors," Dec. 5, 1949, Chicago Urban League Papers, Manuscript Collection, The Library, University of Illinois at Chicago Circle.

17   CHR, "Documentary Memorandum, The White Circle League" (mimeographed, n.d.), *passim.*

18   George Rudé warns against treating violent crowds as "militant minorit[ies] to be sharply marked off from the larger number of citizens . . ." and notes that a "bond of sympathy and common interest" may link "the active few with the inactive many." See his *The Crowd in History: A Study of Popular Disturbances in France and England, 1730-1848* (New York, 1964), pp. 211–212.

19   CHR, "Documentary Report on Recurrence of Anti-Racial Disturbances in the 7100 and 7200 Blocks on St. Lawrence Avenue" (mimeographed, n.d.), pp. 15–16, 22.

20   William Gremley, "Social Control in Cicero, Illinois" (mimeographed, n.d.), p. 8, in the Catholic Interracial Council Papers, Box 2, Chicago Historical Society (hereafter CHS); ACLU Observers' Report for July 13, 1951, American Civil Liberties Union—Illinois Division Papers, Addenda, Box 13, Folder: Cicero Riot—1951, Joseph Regenstein Library, University of Chicago; CHR, "Memorandum on Airport Homes," p. 4.

21   Thomas Rook, Report, Nov. 17, 1949, 1 in Catholic Interracial Council Papers, Box 1, CHS; ACLU Observers' Report, July 13, 1951.

22   CHR, "Memorandum on Airport Homes," p. 14; Homer Jack, "Documented Memorandum VIII, The Racial Factor in the Veterans' Airport Housing Project" (mimeographed, n.d.), pp. 2, 4; *Chicago Tribune*, Dec. 12, 1946.

23   CHR, *The Trumbull Park Homes Disturbances*, pp. 12, 19, 23, 30, 32, and 49.

24   Joseph Parot, "Ethnic vs. Black Metropolis: The Origins of Polish-Black Housing Tensions in Chicago," *Polish American Studies*, XXIX (Spring-Autumn 1972), 5–33; Pierre de Vise, *Chicago's Widening Color Gap* (Chicago, 1967), pp. 71–73. De Vise shows that Poles and Italians were the "whites" found in the greatest numbers in areas adjacent to the expanding Black Belt.

25   *Chicago Defender*, July 28, 1951.

26   CHR, "Report on Press, Radio, and Television Coverage of Racial Disturbances in Chicago from July 28 to August 15, 1957" (mimeographed, n.d.), pp. 5–6.

27   *Chicago Defender*, Apr. 18, 1957.

28   Chandler Owen, "A Program for the Solution of the Trumbull Housing Conflict" (1954?), p. 13, in the Robert E. Merriam Papers, Box 23, Folder 2, Joseph Regenstein Library, University of Chicago.

29   It is understood that such a method is imprecise at best and it is not intended to reduce each ethnic group to exact percentages of rioters. It was simply deemed appropriate to go beyond the *assumption* that the local residents arrested during a riot were ethnically representative of the community involved; and the attempt to establish, in broad terms, the general ethnic composition of the various mobs was thus desirable. The arrest lists were surveyed independently by the author (a Jew) and two colleagues (a Polish-American and a scholar of French-Irish extraction) who are specialists in urban history. The results, which were highly corroborative in almost every case, were then combined to minimize possible error. The percentages in tables III, IV, and V represent the averages produced by that collaboration.

30   *Chicago Defender*, Apr. 18, 1957.

31   Evelyn M. Kitagawa and Karl E. Taeuber, eds., *Local Community Fact Book: Chicago Metropolitan Area, 1960* (Chicago, 1963), pp. 112, 116, 118, and 150.

32   CHR, "Memorandum on Airport Homes," pp. 13–14.

33   CHR, "Memorandum on Fernwood Park Homes," pp. 2–5; The Community Relations Service, "Housing and Race Relations in Chicago," (Sept. 22, 1948), pp. 50–51, in the Archibald J. Carey, Jr. Papers, Box 5, Folder 34, CHS.

34   CHR, "Documentary Report of the Anti-Racial Demonstrations . . . ," p. 1 and Appendix A.

35   CHR, "Peoria Street Incident," *passim*.

36   CHR, "A Preliminary Report . . . ," p. 6.

37   CHR, *The Trumbull Park Homes Disturbances*, pp. 10–11; *Chicago Daily News*, Apr. 10, 1954.

38   CHR, "Memorandum on Airport Homes," p. 14.

39   Homer Jack, "Chicago Has One More Chance," p. 251.

40   CHR, "Documentary Report of the Anti-Racial Demonstrations. . . . ,"
      pp. 1, 30. For Cicero, see Homer Jack, "Cicero Nightmare," *Nation,*
      CLXXIII, No. 4 (July 28, 1951), 64–65; Mary Yedinak, "Cicero: Why it
      Rioted" (B.A. thesis, University of Illinois—Champaign, 1967), p. 13.
41   Despite the proximity of the Black Belt and the apparent availability of
      black targets, there were only reports of three cars being stoned by
      white teens and only a single injury was recorded. CHR, "Documentary
      Report of the Anti-Racial Demonstrations . . . ," pp. 11–12.
42   CHR, "Emerald Street Incident" (mimeographed, n.d.), pp. 19–20.
43   American Civil Liberties Union, Chicago Division, "Report" (mimeo-
      graphed, n.d.), Chicago Urban League Papers, University of Illinois at
      Chicago Circle. The ACLU report on the Englewood disorder noted
      that the neighborhood around 56th and Peoria "has been known for
      some years as one of the most dangerous spots" in the city insofar as
      race relations were concerned. The black enclaves of Morgan Park, Lily-
      dale, and the wartime developments in Princeton Park and West Ches-
      terfield surrounded and worried white Roseland residents. See the
      Minutes of the Regular Meeting of the Board of Directors of the Met-
      ropolitan Housing Council, April 1, 1943 and August 3, 1943, in the
      Metropolitan Housing and Planning Council Papers (hereafter MHPC),
      Manuscript Collection, The Library, University of Illinois at Chicago
      Circle.
44   "White drivers without white flags were warned by white bystanders
      to keep their dome lights on to avoid damage to their automobiles."
      CHR, "A Preliminary Report . . . ," p. 11; Richards, *Gentlemen of Prop-
      erty and Standing,* p. 120.
45   CHR, "Peoria Street Incident," p. 31.
46   *Chicago Bee,* Feb. 23, 1947; CHR, *The People of Chicago,* p. 7; Com-
      munity Relations Service, "Housing and Race Relations in Chicago,"
      p. 37.
47   CHR, "Memorandum on Fernwood Park Homes," pp. 19–20.
48   Edward H. Palmer served as Director of Tenant and Community Re-
      lations at the Trumbull Park Homes from 1960 to 1962; during that time
      he had "direct personal knowledge" of CHA placement procedures at
      the project and swore that he received "oral instructions" to permit no
      more than 25 black families to reside in Trumbull Park Homes at any
      one time. His affidavit of June 7, 1968 is in the Business and Profes-
      sional People in the Public Interest Papers (hereafter BPPPI), Box 3,
      CHS. For reports of the original "deal," see CHR, *The Trumbull Park
      Homes Disturbances,* p. 50.
49   Holman D. Pettibone, president of the Chicago Title and Trust Com-
      pany and a key figure in the city's redevelopment program, felt that all
      plans "rise and fall on public housing for relocation." Holman D. Pet-
      tibone to Martin Kennelly, Sept. 18, 1952, Holman D. Pettibone Papers,
      Box 8, CHS. See also Martin Meyerson and Edward C. Banfield, *Poli-
      tics, Planning, and the Public Interest* (New York, 1955), p. 19.
50   Meyerson and Banfield, p. 124.
51   CHR, "Memorandum on Airport Homes," p. 9; "Memorandum on Fern-
      wood Park Homes," p. 31; Chicago City Council, *Journal of the Pro-
      ceedings* (Oct. 15, 1947), p. 1032.
52   Chicago Housing Authority, untitled typewritten statement, Oct. 24, 1947

in the MHPC Papers; *Chicago Defender,* Dec. 6, 1947; Minutes of the
Board of Governors Meeting, Nov. 5, 1947, MHPC Papers.

53 Chicago City Council, *Journal of the Proceedings* (Mar. 15, 1948), p. 2040.

54 Meyerson and Banfield, pp. 83–87; "Memorandum of Record" of an
interview with Robert R. Taylor, June 27, 1956, in the BPPPI Papers,
Box 1, CHS.

55 Meyerson and Banfield, *passim.*

56 After a second group of project sites had been selected, Ferd Kramer,
president of the MHPC, met with Mayor Richard J. Daley and informed
him that it was bad planning to "relegate all low rent projects to the
South Side." Daley "took note of the argument, but made no commit-
ments." Later, the MHPC Board was warned that "if Alderman (Emil V.)
Pacini (10th) appraises the local temper correctly, the mayor cannot
help very much to reverse the situation": "Memorandum of Conclusions of the Special Board Meeting on Public Housing in Chicago"
(n.d.), MHPC Paper, UICC.

57 Meyerson and Banfield, pp. 122–136, 135n.; Meyerson and Banfield
emphasize the decision made to open all projects to nonnwhites, "as
soon as consistent with the maintenance of law and order," after rioting
broke out at Trumbull Park; it should be noted, however, that no time
constraint was placed on the CHA, and the reference to "law and order"
opened the door to indefinite delay. As of June 1959 there were still no
blacks in the Bridgeport Homes and only two black families in Lawndale Gardens; twenty-one black families occupied the 925-unit Lathrop
Homes and twenty of Trumbull Park's 462 units were occupied by blacks.
At that time CHA Chairman Alvin Rose spoke of non-discrimination as
a "goal" rather than a policy and stated that he would not take any
"further steps in integration . . . until he was sure it could be done
without violence": *Chicago Defender,* May 2, 1953; Memorandum from
Judy Miller and Kale Williams to Bill Berry, et al., June 16, 1959, and
Kale Williams to Ken Douty, June 26, 1959, in the ACLU Papers, Box 11,
Folder 8, Joseph Regenstein Library, University of Chicago.

58 The aldermen, closely attuned to developments within their wards, thus
knew that the violent opposition to the CHA was rooted in the local
residents and not a roving band of agitators; the latter could have been
safely ignored—the former could not.

59 Meyerson and Banfield, 199.

60 Francis W. McPeek, "Human Relations: Imperatives for Public Action"
(speech delivered at the Chicago Commission of Human Relations
Twelfth Annual Awards in Human Relations Luncheon, Dec. 10, 1957).

CHAPTER XII IRISH CHICAGO: MULTI-ETHNIC MACHINE

1 Quin O'Brien addressing the Irish Fellowship Club of Chicago, Dec. 9,
1916.

2 Thomas N. Brown, *Irish American Nationalism* (Philadelphia, 1966),
p. 17.

3 Ruth Margaret Piper, "The Irish in Chicago" (M.A. thesis, University
of Chicago, 1936), p. 8.

4 *Chicago Tribune,* Apr. 19, 1874.

5   Andrew Townsend, "The Germans of Chicago" (Ph.D. Diss., University of Chicago, 1927), p. 11.
6   B. L. Pierce, *A History of Chicago: From Town to City 1848-1871* (New York, 1940), p. 151.
7   Piper, p. 7.
8   *Skandanavien,* Sept. 27, 1890; Piper, p. 7.
9   William B. Ogden Letter Books II, Chicago Historical Society; B. L. Pierce, *A History of Chicago: The Beginning of a City 1673-1848* (New York, 1937), p. 383; *Chicago Tribune,* Apr. 19, 1874.
10 Letter from Solomon Wills to James B. Campbell, Aug. 12, 1838, James B. Campbell papers, Chicago Historical Society, Chicago, Illinois.
11 Sister M. Sevina Pahorezki, *The Social and Political Activities of William James Onahan* (Washington, D.C., 1942). William James Onahan claims Douglas converted to Catholicism on his deathbed.
12 Piper, p. 39.
13 *Chicago Tribune,* Apr. 19, 1874.
14 Frederick Francis Cook, *Bygone Days in Chicago* (Chicago, 1910), p. 13.
15 Lawrence J. McCaffrey, *The Irish Diaspora in America* (Bloomington, Ind., 1976), p. 118.
16 *Chicago Tribune,* July 27, 1868.
17 *Ibid.*
18 *Chicago Evening Post,* Sept. 9, 1868.
19 *Chicago Tribune,* Apr. 19, 1874.
20 *Svornost,* Mar. 17, 1892.
21 *Illinois Staats-Zeitung,* Apr. 21, 1892.
22 *Svenska-Tribunen Nyheter,* Jan. 26, 1915; Oct. 6, 1906.
23 William V. Shannon, *The American Irish* (New York, 1963), p. 16.
24 Thomas N. Brown, "Nationalism and the Irish Peasant," *The Review of Politics* 15 (Oct. 1953): 407.
25 *Chicago Tribune,* Apr. 19, 1874.
26 Piper, p. 47.
27 Herbert Wiltsee, "Religious Developments in Chicago 1893-1915" (M.A. thesis, University of Chicago, 1953), p. 11.
28 Piper, p. 12.
29 Carter H. Harrison, *Growing Up with Chicago* (Chicago, 1944), p. 24.
30 John Paul Bocock, "Irish Conquest of Our Cities," *Forum* (Apr. 1894), p. 186.
31 *Chicago Tribune,* Mar. 27, 1883.
32 See Len O'Connor, *Clout* (Chicago, 1975), pp. 9–10; Virgil W. Peterson, *Barbarians in Our Midst* (Boston, 1952), pp. 45–55.
33 *Chicago Herald and Examiner,* June 5, 1924.
34 Harold Mayer and Richard Wade, *Chicago: Growth of a Metropolis* (Chicago, 1969), p. 176.
35 *Chicago Tribune,* Apr. 15, 1920; Edward F. Dunne, *Illinois: The Heart of the Nation* (Chicago, 1933), 2:477; Charles H. Hermann, *Recollections of Life and Doings in Chicago: From the Haymarket Riot to the End of World War I by an Oldtimer* (Chicago, 1945), p. 123.
36 *Chicago Times,* Nov. 3, 1890. It was the Irish saloonkeeper-politicians and the other nationality groups who would keep the Hopkins-Sullivan, Irish-dominated faction from taking party control until the 1914-1915 period.

37 Dunne, *Illinois: The Heart of the Nation*, 2:188; Sophie Eisenstein, "The Elections of 1912 in Chicago" (M.A. thesis, University of Chicago, 1947), p. 10.
38 *Chicago Daily News*, Apr. 1, 1911. Merriam was using a number of Democratic aldermanic candidates as examples of boss politics and corrupt influence in the city.
39 *Ibid.*
40 Interview with Judge Ulysses S. Schwartz, Chicago, Illinois, Jan 15, 1971.
41 Lloyd Wendt and Herman Kogan, *Big Bill of Chicago* (Indianapolis, 1953), p. 95.
42 See Andrew M. Greeley, *That Most Distressful Nation* (Chicago, 1972).
43 *Chicago Tribune*, Sept. 4, 1929.
44 Interview with former Cook County Democratic Chairman Jacob Arvey, Chicago, 1972.
45 *Chicago Tribune*, Aug. 1, 1929.
46 Edward Kelly (a future mayor of Chicago), the other Democrat on the South Park Board, was caught in the political switches because he served the sanitary district as its chief engineer while personally being very close to Pat Nash—a strong Crowe-O'Brien foe.
47 *Chicago American*, June 25, 1912.
48 See Alex Gottfried, *Boss Cermak of Chicago: A Study of Political Leadership* (Seattle, 1962); John M. Allswang, *A House for All People: Ethnic Politics in Chicago* (Lexington, Ky., 1971); Mike Royko, *Boss: Richard J. Daley of Chicago* (New York, 1971); Andrew Greeley, *Distressful Nation*; Len O'Connor, *Clout*.
49 Gottfried, p. 184.
50 *Denni Hlasatel*, Apr. 2, 1917.
51 Kostner's political ability, his wise spectrum of friends, and his rivalry with Cermak are illustrated in the following two stories. 1) Before ward residents paid their property taxes, Kostner invited them to give him their bills if they thought their taxes were too high. Invariably, Kostner reduced the property owners' taxes, and to remind a resident of his efforts he stamped the reduced tax forms "compliments of Alderman Kostner." 2) Kostner had a regular pinochle game at his home, and among the players were Judges Henry Horner and Hugo Pam (Jewish), his cousin John Toman (Bohemian), William Dever (Mrs. Kostner's Irish 2nd cousin) prior to his election as mayor, and Cermak's leading protégé and personal secretary, Henry Sonnenschein (Bohemian-Jew). One night an enraged Cermak stormed into Kostner's house looking for Sonnenschein. The heavyset Cermak nearly lifted Sonnenschein bodily out of his chair, screaming, "You know who you work for—me—not him." The "him" was of course the bemused Kostner, who never put his cards down as Cermak led Sonnenschein out of the house (personal interview).
52 Personal interview with Jacob Arvey.
53 See Carroll H. Wooddy, *The Case of Frank L. Smith* (Chicago, 1931).
54 In 1928 a special sanitary district election was held in conjunction with the regular contest. Democrat Ross Woodhull, another Cermak ally, easily beat Republican Edward Moore in this race.
55 *Chicago Herald and Examiner*, Apr. 25, 1929.
56 *Ibid.*

57 Personal interview.
58 *Chicago Tribune*, Feb. 2, 1939.
59 Clayton Smith was an Episcopalian and a Mason. Thus his Irishness was not that much of a factor in an analysis of the alleged Irish vs. non-Irish controversy inside the party.
60 Cermak, with the assistance of 24th Ward committeeman Moe Rosenberg, picked up Pat Nash, a 28th Ward committeeman, and paid off the campaign debt of over $75,000.
61 In 1914, 69 percent of Chicago's Democratic committeemen were Irish; in 1978 that figure had dropped slightly to 66 percent.
62 See *Public Service Leader*, Nov. 1932. The *Leader* was the local Democratic newspaper.
63 *Chicago American*, Mar. 18, 1931; Gottfried, *Boss Cermak*, p. 226.
64 *Chicago Herald and Examiner*, Mar. 22, 1931.
65 *Chicago Tribune*, Mar. 28, 1931.
66 *Chicago Herald and Examiner*, Mar. 28, 1931.
67 Personal interview with Judge Roger Kiley.
68 *Chicago Tribune*, Mar. 24, 1931.
69 The only exception to this trend was Hinky Dink's 1st Ward, where Democratic mayoral percentages dropped slightly due to the efforts of Republican ward committeeman Daniel Serritella—a Capone lieutenant and a Thompson buddy. Still, Cermak carried the ward with 71 percent of the vote.
70 Personal interview.
71 *Chicago Tribune*, Apr. 19, 1932.
72 No incident in Chicago political folklore has more interpretations or has generated juicier gossip than Zangara's assassination of Cermak. Many knowledgeable people believe Zangara was aiming at the mayor and not the president-elect. They argue that Zangara was a hired killer employed by Chicago mobster Frank Nitti; that Cermak was killed because of his involvement with Chicago hoodlums who thought the mayor wanted to control the soon-to-be-profitable brewery business in the city; and that Nitti hit Cermak because the mayor had a few months previous tried to assassinate him.
73 *Chicago American*, Mar. 6, 1933.
74 Personal interview with Jacob Arvey.
75 Personal interview.
76 Bowler, a former professional bicycle rider, had succeeded notorious "boodle" alderman John Powers in the near West Side 25th Ward.
77 Clark's 16 votes broke down as follows: 11 of the 19 GOP aldermen; 5 of the 30 Democratic aldermen.
78 Carter H. Harrison, *Growing Up with Chicago*, p. 321.
79 McCormick served a term as sanitary district trustee from 1907 to 1910 and throughout his life he kept a strong interest in district affairs. His friendship with Kelly stemmed from their mutual sanitary district experience.
80 Personal interview with Judge Roger Kiley.
81 *Chicago Tribune*, Apr. 14, 1933. The ward committeemen were members of the Cook County Democratic central committee headed by Nash.
82 Only two non-Irishmen have served as either mayor or party chairman since Cermak's death. In the late 1940s, Jacob Arvey (Jewish) was se-

lected party chairman; and in 1976, Michael Bilandic (Croatian) was named to replace the deceased Mayor Richard J. Daley.

83 Interview with former governor and United States Appellate Judge Otto Kerner.

84 Personal interview. For a full treatment of the Irish chieftain theme, see Eugene Kennedy, *Himself: The Life and Times of Richard J. Daley* (New York, 1978). For the best insider's study of the machine, see Milton Rakove, *Don't Make No Waves: Don't Back No Losers* (Bloomington, Ind., 1975).

CHAPTER XIII: THE GREAT WAR SINKS CHICAGO'S GERMAN *KULTUR*

1 Woodrow Wilson to Otto L. Schmidt, May 4, 1917, and "Goethe Monument Association," file in Otto L. Schmidt papers, Vol. III, Chicago Historical Society; *Jahrbuch, Deutsch-Amerikanischen Historischen Gesellschaft von Illinois* (Chicago, 1932), 32: 544, 550–551; Goebel quoted in U.S., Congress, Senate, Subcommittee of the Judiciary, *Hearings, National German-American Alliance*, 65th Cong., 2nd sess., 1918, p. 695 (see also p. 597); Rudolf A. Hofmeister, *The Germans of Chicago* (Champaign, Ill., 1976), p. 60.

2 *Fatherland*, Sept. 30, 1914, pp. 14, 15; population figures from Frank D. Loomis, *Americanization in Chicago* (Chicago, 1920).

3 *Chicago Tribune*, Aug. 15, 1914; Wayne A. Nichols, "Crossroads Oratory: A Study of the Four-Minute Men" (Ph.D. diss., Columbia University, 1953); Mark Sullivan, *Our Times* (New York, 1953), 5: 53.

4 Clifton J. Child, *The German-Americans in Politics, 1914-1917* (Madison, 1939), p. 22; *Chicago Tribune*, Aug. 2, 3, 1914.

5 *Chicago Tribune*, Aug. 2, 3, 1914.

6 *Chicago Tribune*, Aug. 2, 3, 4, 1914; Child, *German-Americans in Politics*, p. 25.

7 *Chicago Tribune*, Aug. 6, 8, 1914; Andrew Jackie Townsend, "The Germans of Chicago," *Jahrbuch, Deutsch-Amerikanischen Historischen Gesellschaft . . .* , 32:70–71; Carl Wittke, *German-Americans and the World War* (Columbus, Ohio, 1936), p. 27.

8 *Chicago Tribune*, Aug. 6, 8, 1914; Thomas R. Bullard, "Chicago's German Businessmen, 1871-1914" (M.A. seminar paper, University of Illinois, Chicago Circle, 1969).

9 Wittke, p. 7; *Die Tageblatt*, reprinted in *Fatherland*, Aug. 10, 1914, p. 13, and in *Chicago Abendpost*, Aug. 14, 1914 (Foreign Language Press Survey microfilm).

10 *Chicago Tribune*, Aug. 3, 10, 1914.

11 *Chicago Tribune*, Aug. 12, 18, 1914.

12 *Chicago Tribune*, Aug. 2, 3, 11, 16, 1914; Charles Fanning, *Finley Peter Dunne and Mr. Dooley: The Chicago Years* (Lexington, Ky., 1978), pp. 156, 169; *Abendpost*, Aug. 16, 1914.

13 *Chicago Tribune*, Aug. 4, 5, 1914; Paul M. Angle, "Chicago and the First World War," *Chicago History* 7 (Fall 1964): 136–137; Cedric C. Cummings, *Indiana Public Opinion and the World War* (Indianapolis, 1945), p. 61.

14 Louis Gerson, *Woodrow Wilson and the Rebirth of Poland, 1914-1920*
    (New Haven, 1953), p. viii; *Chicago Tribune*, Aug. 3, 4, 15, 1914; Ther-
    esita Polzin, *The Polish Americans: Whence and Wither* (Pulaski, Wis.,
    1973), pp. 19, 20; Helena Znaniecki Lopata, *Polish-Americans: Status
    Competition in an Ethnic Community* (Englewood Cliffs, N.J., 1976),
    pp. 16–24.
15 *Dziennik Zwiazkowy*, Aug. 1, 10, 1914 (Foreign Language Press Survey
    microfilm).
16 *Chicago Tribune*, Aug. 6, 10, 20, 1914; Angle, "Chicago and the First
    World War," p. 141; Hofmeister, *Germans of Chicago*, p. 62.
17 *Chicago Tribune*, August 17, 1914; Angle, "Chicago and the First World
    War," pp. 138–139. For the national scene, Frederick C. Luebke's *Bonds
    of Loyalty: German-Americans and World War I* (Dekalb, Ill., 1974) is
    the best modern book-length study of the question. Luebke correctly
    takes issue with an older generation of historians and sociologists who
    argued that rampant nativism hindered the assimilation of Germans into
    American life. The Americanization campaign in both Chicago and the
    nation accelerated the movement of Germans into the melting pot.
18 Robert Park, *The Immigrant Press and Its Control* (Chicago, 1922),
    pp. 413–423; *Hearings, Brewing and Liquor Interests*, Subcommittee of
    Judiciary, United States Senate (Washington, 1919), 1:ix, x.
19 F. Luebke, *Bonds of Loyalty*, p. 45; Neil M. Johnson, *George Sylvester
    Viereck* (Urbana, Ill., 1972), pp. 5, 7, 22; Margaret Munsterberg, *Hugo
    Munsterberg: His Life and Work* (New York, 1922), p. 262; *Illinois Staats-
    Zeitung*, Sept. 24, 1914; George S. Viereck, *Spreading Germs of Hate*
    (New York, 1930), p. 86; Phyllis Keller, *States of Belonging: German-
    American Intellectuals and the First World War* (Cambridge, 1979), p. 188.
20 *Literary Digest* 41 (Nov. 14, 1914): 939.
21 Nichols, "Crossroads Oratory: A Study of the Four-Minute Men of World
    War I," pp. 7, 8, 9, 12; *Hearings, Brewing and Liquor Interests*, p. x;
    A. W. Thurner, "The Mayor . . . ," *Journal* of the Illinois State Historical
    Society 66 (Summer 1973): 132.
22 *Hearings, National German-American Alliance*, p. 24; Hugo Munster-
    berg, *The Peace and America* (New York, 1915), p. 123.
23 Munsterberg paraphrased from *Illinois Staats-Zeitung*, July 5, 1914.
24 Munsterberg, *The War and America* (New York, 1914), pp. 50, 55, 56.
25 *German Achievements in America* (New York, 1916), pp. 88, 89.
26 "Democracy Versus the Melting Pot," *Nation* 100 (Feb. 15, 1915):
    217–219.
27 *Abendpost*, Sept. 9, 1914.
28 *Abendpost*, Dec. 11, 1914.
29 *Abendpost*, Feb. 28, 1916.
30 *Abendpost*, Aug. 22, Dec. 11, 1914; Townsend, "Germans of Chicago,"
    p. 59.
31 Gustav Ohlinger, *Their Faith and Allegiance* (New York, 1916), p. 66.
32 Munsterberg, *The Peace and America*, pp. 120–122, 132, 137, 146, 150;
    Cedric C. Cummings, *Indiana Public Opinion and World War, 1914–17*
    (Indianapolis, 1945), p. 48; Park, *Immigrant Press*, p. 417.
33 Guido A. Dobert, "The Disintegration of the Immigrant Community:
    The Cincinnati Germans, 1870-1920" (Ph.D. diss., University of Chi-
    cago, 1965), p. 3; Child, *German-Americans in Politics*, p. 22; Eugen

Seeger, *Wonder City* (Chicago, 1890), pp. 108, 344; Townsend, "Germans of Chicago," pp. 37, 59.

34 *Abendpost,* May 8, 11, 1915; *Illinois Staats-Zeitung,* July 13, 21, 24, 1915.
35 *Abendpost,* Feb. 9, 1916; *Chicago Tribune,* Feb. 9, 1916.
36 *Chamberlin's* 13 (Mar. 1916): 26; Luebke, *Bonds of Loyalty,* pp. 115–116; Otto L. Schmidt to Gustav H. Jacobsen, May 25, 1916, Schmidt Papers, I, Chicago Historical Society.
37 Child, *German-Americans in Politics,* p. 112; "Furor Teutonicus," in *Free Poland* 2 (Feb. 1, 1916): 11.
38 *Illinois Staats-Zeitung,* Feb. 1, 4, 1917; *Chicago Tribune,* Feb. 1, 4. The *Tribune* often reprinted the most bellicose editorials of Chicago's German-American press.
39 Barbara Tuchman, *The Zimmermann Telegram* (New York, 1958), pp. 185–186, 199, 200.
40 *Illinois Staats-Zeitung,* Mar. 26, 1917; Fred Britten, Biographical File. Chicago Historical Society; Paul Holbo, "They Voted Against War: A Study of Motivations" (Ph.D. diss., University of Chicago, 1961), p. 264; Andrew Jackie Townsend, "The Germans of Chicago" (Ph.D. diss., University of Chicago, 1927), p. 96.
41 Richard O'Connor, *The German-Americans: An Informal History* (Boston, 1968), p. 406.
42 Townsend, "Germans of Chicago," p. 107.
43 Dean W. Kolhoff, "Missouri Synod Lutherans and the Image of Germany, 1914-1945" (Ph.D. diss., University of Chicago, 1973), pp. 1, 43, 74, 76, 93, 102, 104.
44 Holbo, "They Voted Against War," pp. 85, 88, 89, 284; *Viereck's American Weekly* 6 (May 16, 1917): 250.
45 "The Immigrants and the War: Ninth Annual Report of the Immigrants' Protective League, Dec. 31, 1917," p. 8; Immigrants' Protective League Papers, MSS Division, University of Illinois, Chicago Circle; Marguerite E. Jenison, *The War-time Organization of Illinois* (Springfield, Ill., 1923), pp. 100, 102–103; U.S., Congress, House, *Hearings Before Committee on Immigration and Naturalization,* 66th Cong., 1st sess., Oct. 1919, 1:8–11, 13–15, 23, 40–42.
46 James W. Gerard, *My Four Years in Germany* (New York, 1917), p. 237; J. Bernstorff, *My Three Years in America* (New York, 1920), p. 23.
47 U.S., Congress, Senate, Subcommittee of the U.S. Judiciary, *Hearings: Brewing and Liquor Interests and Bolshevik Propaganda,* 65th Cong., 1st sess., pp. x, xv; Franz Rintelen von Kleist, *The Dark Invaders: Wartime Reminiscences of a German Naval Officer* (New York, 1933), pp. 83–133, 166–181. Although Count Johann Bernstorff denied complicity of the German Embassy, the weight of the evidence suggests the contrary. *My Three Years in America,* pp. 112–126.
48 Townsend, "Germans in Chicago," p. 100.
49 Stanley R. Pliska, "Polish Independence and Polish-Americans" (Ph.D. diss., Columbia University, 1955), p. 266; Jacub Horak, "The Assimilation of Czechs in Chicago" (Ph.D. diss., University of Chicago, 1940), pp. 15, 32, 52, 53.
50 *Fatherland,* Aug. 15, 1915; *Dziennik Zwiazkowy,* Dec. 15, 1916; Mar. 15, 1918; *Denni Hlasatel,* Mar. 29, 1918; May 13, 30, 1918.
51 John Higham, *Strangers in the Land: Patterns of American Nativism,*

1860-1925 (New York, 1963), p. 198; Edward G. Hartmann, *The Movement to Americanize the Immigrant* (New York, 1948), p. 107; *The Position of the Bohemians in the European War* (Chicago, 1915), pp. 38, 39; *Free Poland,* Feb. 1, 1916. For Greek-Americans, see the chapter in this volume by Andrew Kopan.

52 *Abendpost,* Dec. 2, 1914; Townsend, "Germans of Chicago," pp. 88–92.

53 W. R. MacDonald to O. L. Schmidt, Nov. 3, 1915, Otto L. Schmidt papers, IV; *Hearings, Brewing and Liquor Interests,* pp. xx, xxv; Townsend, p. 91; Viereck, *Spreading the Germs of Hate,* pp. 99–101.

54 *Chicago Tribune,* Sept. 8, 11, 1915; Townsend, p. 80; F. Luebke, *Bonds of Loyalty,* pp. 137–138; Samuel Gompers, *Seventy Years of Life and Labor* (New York, 1925), p. 341.

55 *The Position of the Bohemians in the European War* (Chicago, 1915), pp. 15, 16, 24.

56 *Free Poland,* Oct. 1, 1915, pp. 4, 5; Feb. 1, 1917, p. 2; *Dziennik Zwiazkowy,* Feb. 22, Mar. 2, 1917; Charles Pergler, "Where We stand To-Day," *Bohemian Review* 1 (Mar. 1917): 9.

57 *Free Poland,* Feb. 16, June 16, July 16, 1916; Oct. 16, 1917.

58 Pergler, "Where We Stand To-Day," p. 9; see also *Bohemian Review,* Dec. 1917; *Free Poland,* Mar. 1, 1917, p. 5; Plisha, "Polish Independence and the Polish Americans," p. 189; *Dziennik Zwiazkowy,* Mar. 3, 1917; *Denni Hlasatel,* Apr. 3, 1917; Edward R. Kantowicz, *Polish-American Politics in Chicago* (Chicago, 1975), p. 112.

59 *Free Poland,* Dec. 1, 1915, p. 10; *ibid.,* Jan. 1, 1916, p. 30; *ibid.,* Jan. 16, 1916, p. 3; *ibid.,* Apr. 15, 1917; "Will Immigrants Be Loyal?" *Bohemian Review* 1 (Apr. 1917): 8, 9.

60 "The Eager Bohemians," *Chamberlin's* 15 (Sept. 1917): 7; (Oct. 1917): 30; *Bohemian Review* 1 (Aug. 1917): 16.

61 Louis L. Gerson, *Woodrow Wilson and the Rebirth of Poland, 1914-1920* (New Haven, 1953), pp. 66–70; Kantowicz, *Polish-American Politics,* p. 111; Eugene Kusielewicz, "Woodrow Wilson and the Rebirth of Poland," *Polish-American Studies* 12 (Jan.-June 1955): 1, 2.

62 Miecislaus Haiman, *The Poles of Chicago, 1837-1937* (Chicago, 1937), p. 7.

63 Joseph J. Parot, "The American Faith and the Persistence of Chicago Polonia, 1870-1920" (Ph.D. diss., Northern Illinois University, 1917), pp. 273–275, 277–278, 284; *Free Poland,* Feb. 1, 1917, p. 1. Louis J. Zake asserted that American Poles "faced little or no social pressure to force denationalization. Thus no real· nationality problem ever arose with regard to the Polish American communities." L. Zake, "The Development of the National Department as Representative of the Polish-American Community in the United States, 1916-1923" (Ph.D. diss., University of Chicago, 1979), p. 18.

64 *Illinois Staats-Zeitung,* Mar. 11, 1917; *Chicago Tribune,* Mar. 11, 1917; *Chamberlin's* 15 (Oct. 1917): 17.

65 Higham, *Strangers in the Land,* pp. 129, 162, 199, 207, 216–217; Hartmann, *The Movement to Americanize the Immigrant,* pp. 105, 107, 272–273.

66 *Chicago Tribune,* June 5, 1915; *Bohemian Review* 1 (June 1917): 14; *Free Poland,* Apr. 1, 1917; *Literary Digest,* Aug. 25, 1917.

67 *Narod Polski,* July 25, 1917; *Dziennik Zwiazkowy,* Apr. 26, 1918; Hofmeister, *The Germans of Chicago,* p. 75.
68 *Free Poland,* July 1, 1917, p. 6; *Dziennik Zwiazkowy,* Apr. 26, 1918; *Narod Polski,* July 25, 1917; Hofmeister, pp. 73–74; *Czechoslovak Review* 3 (Aug. 1919): 231.
69 History Committee of the Four Minute Men of Chicago, *Four Minute Men of Chicago* (Chicago, 1919), pp. 9, 20, 24.
70 Gottfried, *Boss Cermak,* pp. 93, 94.
71 *Abendpost,* Jan. 14, 1915; Thomas Capek, *The Czechs in America* (Boston, 1920), pp. 270, 276; George Creel, *How We Advertised America: The First Telling of the Amazing Story of the Committee on Public Information that Carried the Gospel of Americanism to Every Corner of the Globe* (New York, 1920), p. 175; Viereck, *Spreading the Germs of Hate,* p. 136.
72 George Creel, "Our Aliens—Were They Loyal or Disloyal?" *Everybody's Magazine* 40 (Mar. 1919): 36.
73 J. Seymour Currey, *Illinois Activities in the World War, 1914-1920* (Chicago, 1921), 1:227, 242.
74 *Abendpost,* Feb. 5, 1916; *Denni Hlasatel,* May 13, 1918.
75 Gustav E. Johnson, "The Swedes of Chicago" (Ph.D. diss., University of Chicago, 1940), pp. 55, 56; *Svenska Kuriren,* Apr. 18, Aug. 8, Oct. 17, 1918.
76 *Abendpost,* Dec. 11, 1914; Jan. 28, 1916; *Daily Jewish Courier,* Apr. 12, 14, 1918; Bessie L. Pierce, *A History of Chicago* (Chicago, 1957), 3:447–448.
77 Townsend, "Germans of Chicago," p. 90.
78 *Dziennik Zwiazkowy,* Oct. 29, 1914; June 11, 1917; Oct. 22, 23, 1917; Apr. 26, 1918; Mar. 28, 1918; June 11, 1918; May 27, 1918; July 6,1918; June 24, 1918; June 19, 1918; July 16, 1918; *Polonia,* Dec. 13, 1917; Jan. 31, 1918; *Narod Polski,* Apr. 10, 1918; *Denni Hlasatel,* June 13, 1915; May 28, 1918; Apr. 3, May 27, 1917; *Bohemian Review* 1 (Apr. 1917); *Free Poland* (see 1917, 1918 issues).
79 *Abendpost,* Aug. 15, 1918.
80 Townsend, p. 107; Hofmeister, pp. 69, 72; Wittke, *German-Americans and the World War,* p. 184; *Denni Hlasatel,* May 29, 1918.
81 Hofmeister, pp. 75–76; *Chicago Tribune,* Apr. 12, 28, 1918.
82 Hofmeister, pp. 68ff.
83 See, for example, public opinion surveys cited in Higham, *Strangers in the Land,* p. 196.
84 Paul T. Dietz, "The Transition from German to English in the Missouri Synod from 1910 to 1947," *Concordia Historical Institute Quarterly* 12 (Oct. 1949): 102–103; Kolhof, "Missouri Synod Lutherans," p. 93; Hofmeister, p. 12.
85 John A. Hawgood, *The Tragedy of German-America* (New York, 1940), pp. 297, 302.

CHAPTER XIV: JAPANESE-AMERICANS

1 The immigration statistics of Japanese-Americans suffer from various inconsistencies and inaccuracies. For details, see William Petersen,*Japanese Americans* (New York, 1971), pp. 14–19.

2   Roger Daniels, "The Issei Generation," in Akemi Tachiki et al., *Roots: An Asian American Reader* (Los Angeles, 1971), pp. 138–149.

3   See Harry Kitano, *Japanese Americans* (Englewood Cliffs, N.J., 1969), p. 15; Leonard Bloom and Ruth Reimer, *Removal and Return: The Socio-economic Effects of the War on the Japanese Americans* (Los Angeles, 1949), Ch. 1.

4   See John Embree, *A Japanese Village: Suyemura* (Chicago, 1939); Edward Norbeck, *Changing Japan* (New York, 1962); Tadashi Fukutake, *Japanese Rural Society* (London, 1972).

5   See Petersen, *Japanese Americans*, pp. 9–37; Ichikawa Tomonori, "Hiroshima-wangen Jigozen-son Keiyaku Imin no Shakai-Chirigakuteki Kosatsu" [A Social Geographical Study of Japanese Indentured Emigrants to Hawaii from Kuchida Village in Southern Hiroshima Prefecture], *Shigaku Kenkyu (Historical Journal)*, 99:33–52.

6   William Goode, *World Revolution and Family Patterns* (Englewood Cliffs, N.J., 1966), p. 346.

7   Richard Beardsley et al., *Village in Japan* (Chicago, 1959), p. 220.

8   See Marion J. Levy, Jr., "Contrasting Factors in the Modernization of China and Japan," *Economic Development and Cultural Changes* 2 (Oct. 1953): 161–197.

9   Edwin Reischauer, *Japan: The Story of a Nation* (New York, 1974), pp. 99–145.

10 See Petersen, *Japanese Americans*, pp. 9–14.

11 Kitano, *Japanese Americans*, pp. 15–22; Ichibashi, *Japanese in the United States*, Chs. 8–10.

12 See Masakuau Iwata, "The Japanese Immigrants in California Agriculture," *Agricultural History* 36 (1962): 33–52.

13 For the decline of Japanese agriculture in California, see Thomas Bailey, "California, Japan and the Alien Land Legislation of 1913," *Pacific Historical Review* 1 (1932): 36–59; Iwata, *op. cit.*; John Modell, "The Japanese of Los Angeles: A Study in Growth and Accommodation, 1900–1946" (Ph.D. diss., Columbia University, 1969).

14 There is a controversy concerning the extent to which the Alien Land acts impeded Japanese agriculture in California. On one hand, Nisei scholars like Masakuzu Iwata and Harry Kitano emphasize their dire emotional and economic impact on the Japanese farmers. On the other hand, non-Japanese scholars like Roger Daniels, Carey McWilliams, and John Modell interpret the land acts as less potent. For instance, Daniels termed the 1920 law "an empty gesture, an ineffective irritant; it caused much litigation, but in no way significantly affected land tenure in the state." *Politics of Prejudice* (Berkeley, 1962), p. 88. See Petersen, *Japanese Americans*, for further discussion.

15 This charge was made in 1920 by V. S. McClatchy, vocal advocate of the Japanese Exclusion Act of California, quoted in Iwata, "The Japanese Immigrants in California Agriculture," p. 30.

16 Shotora Frank Miyamoto, *Social Solidarity among the Japanese in Seattle* (Seattle, 1939), p. 74.

17 *Ibid.*, p. 70.

18 For community solidarity see Ichibashi, *Japanese in the United States*; Kitano, *Japanese Americans*, pp. 14–18; Kenji Ima, "Japanese Ameri-

cans: Making of Good People," in Gary and Rosalind Dworkin, eds., *The Minority Report* (New York, 1976), pp. 254–296.

19   Miyamoto, pp. 74–75.
20   Numerous scholarly works have been published on the subject of discrimination against Japanese. For example, Roger Daniels, *The Politics of Prejudice* (Berkeley, 1962); Sidney L. Gulick, *The Japanese American Problem: A Study of the Racial Relations of the East and the West* (New York, 1914); Dorothy S. Thomas and Richard Nishimoto, *The Spoilage* (Berkeley, 1946).
21   Iwata, p. 7.
22   Quoted in Kitano, p. 32.
23   Kitano, p. 33; see also Allan R. Bosworth, *America's Concentration Camps* (New York, 1967); Leonard Broom and John Kitsuse, *The Managed Casualty* (Berkeley, 1956).
24   Several Nisei scholars have written revealing personal accounts of life in the relocation camp. For example, Raisuke Kitagawa, *Issei and Nisei: The Internment Years* (New York, 1967); Bill Hosokawa, *Nisei: The Quiet Americans* (New York, 1969). See also Masako Osako, "Aging and Family among Japanese Americans: The Role of Ethnic Tradition in the Adjustment to Old Age," *The Gerontologist* 19 (No. 5, 1979): 448–455.
25   Kitagawa, *Issei and Nisei*, p. 91.
26   *Ibid.*, p. 92.
27   Petersen, pp. 131–143; Kitano, pp. 44–46.
28   See Beardsley et al., *Village in Japan*; Robert Bellah, *Tokugawa Religion* (New York, 1957); Ezra Vogel, *Japan's New Middle Class* (Berkeley, 1964).
29   Kitagawa, pp. 91–92.
30   Bloom and Kitsuse, *The Managed Casualty*, p. 40.
31   Ryoichi Fujii, *Shikago Nikkeijinshi* [History of Japanese Americans in Chicago] (Chicago, 1968), p. 85. This section draws heavily from Mr. Fukii's work.
32   U.S. Government Census Bureau, *Japanese, Chinese, and Filipinos in America* (Washington, D.C., 1973). During World War II, labor shortages were a problem in the city. Elmer E. Shirrell, Midwest Regional Director of the WRA, tried to recruit Japanese-Americans from the relocation camps. "Employers in Chicago are clamouring for American Japanese workers because 3,500 job offers are going begging. . . . Chicago must find 375,000 new workers by December 1 [1943], if the city is to carry its allotted load of the war contract" (*Chicago Tribune*, Oct. 1, 1943).
33   Fujii, *Shikago Nikkeijinshi*, p. 95.
34   *Ibid.*, p. 98.
35   *Ibid.*, pp. 104–111.
36   *Ibid.*, pp. 146–149; See also Japanese American Mutual Aid Society of Chicago, "History of Japanese American Mutual Aid Society" (undated brochure).
37   Fujii, p. 148.
38   *Ibid.*, pp. 141–146.
39   See Masako Osako, "Aging and Family among Japanese Americans."
40   Although quantitative evidence is not yet available for Japanese-Americans, several articles argue similar points regarding Chinese-Ameri-

cans. For example, Wen Lan Li, "Chinese Americans: Exclusion from the Melting Pot," in Gary and Rosalind Dworkin, eds., *The Minority Report*; John T. Ma, "The Professional Chinese Americans" in Yuan-Li Wu, ed., *Economic Conditions of Chinese Americans* (Chicago, 1980).

41 Kitano, p. 68.

42 The information about the effect of suburbanization is primarily drawn from the present author's recent study of 250 Japanese-American families in Chicago.

43 See Darrel Montero and Gene Levine, "Socioeconomic Mobility Among Three Generations of Japanese Americans," *Journal of Social Issues* 29 (No. 2): 33–48.

44 U.S. Government Census Bureau, *Japanese, Chinese, and Filipinos in America.*

45 For the history of Chinese-Americans, see Rose Hum Lee, *The Chinese in the U.S.* (Hong Kong, 1960); S. W. Kung, *Chinese in American Life* (Seattle, 1962); Francis L. K. Hsu, *The Challenge of the American Dream: The Chinese in the U.S.* (Belmont, Cal., 1971); Melford S. Weiss, *Valley City: A Chinese Community in America* (Cambridge, Mass., 1974).

46 See Leslie Mairland, "Five Hurt in Chinatown Gang Fight: Flare-up Follows Month's Truce," *New York Times*, Sept. 10, 1976; Berkeley Rice, "The New Gangs of Chinatown," *Psychology Today* 10 (May, 1977): 60–69; Betty Lee Sung, *Gangs in New York's Chinatown* (New York, 1977).

47 See Ma, "The Professional Chinese Americans."

48 *Ibid.*; see also Wen Lang Li, "Chinese Americans: Exclusion from the Melting Pot."

49 Stanford Lyman, "Marriage and the Family among Chinese Immigrants to America, 1850–1960," *Phylon* 29 (No. 4, 1968): 321–330.

50 John Modell, "The Japanese American Family: Perspective for Future Investigation," *Pacific Historical Review* 37 (1968): 67–81.

51 See John Fairbank et al., *China: Tradition and Transformation* (Boston, 1978).

52 Reischauer, *Japan: The Story of a Nation*, Chs. 8, 9.

53 See D. Y. Yuan, "Voluntary Segregation: A Study of New York Chinatown," in Minako Kurokawa, ed., *Minority Responses* (New York, 1970).

54 More than 40 percent of Japanese-American men now marry women who are not Japanese-Americans. The interracial marriage rate is higher for the younger generations. See Martin Kilson, "Whether Integration?" *American Scholar* 45 (No. 3, 1970): 365–367.

55 See Milton M. Gordon, *Assimilation in American Life* (New York, 1964); Thomas Sewell, "Ethnicity in a Changing America," *Daedalus* 107 (Winter 1978): 213–237.

Index

Addams, Jane, 133, 139, 141, 142, 143, 161, 163, 181, 475; pacifism condemned by Poles, 494
Albert, Heinrich, 473; loses espionage information to British, 489
Allswang, John, cited, 42
American Fur Company, 314ff.
Anderson, Louis B., 368
Ardan, Ivan, 171
Arvey, Jacob, 63, 64, 67, 87, 457; quoted, 443

Bakalis, Dr. Michael, 157
Balaban, Barney, 87
Barnett, Ferdinand L., 361, 365, 374
Barnett, Ida Wells, 369
Bartholdt, Richard, 477, 483
Barzynski, Rev. Joseph B., 226
Barzynski, Rev. Wincenty, 226ff.
Beaubien, Jean Baptiste, 310, 314
Beaubien, Madore, 328, 333, 335, 336
Beaubien, Mark, 312, 320, 321, 328, 333, 332; wife Monique, 322; and Sauganash Tavern, 320, 327
Bellow, Saul, 90, 92
Bentley, Charles, 350
Bernstorff, Count Johann von, on German-Americans, 488
Bilyk, Dr. Cyril, 187, 191
Bish, James E., 350, 362
Blacks: Appomatox Club, 367, 368; black codes in Illinois, 329, 340, 345; in Chicago, 339-379; in Chicago baseball, 369; in politics, 346ff.; population in Chicago, 339-341ff.; riot of 1899, 342; riots over housing, 381ff.
Bohemians (Czechs), 217; on false neutrality, 493; hyphenated issue, 491-492; "Kaiserized speller," 501; rabidly anti-Teutonic, 497; ridicule Hindenburg, 504-505; war effort, 503-505; welcome war, 495-496; population, 468

Brennan, George, 431, 433; and "new breed" politics, 435ff.
Brewster, William, and fur trade, 308
Britten, Congressman Fred A., warns against war, 485; sponsors draft exempt law, 486
Brown, Thomas N., 25
Bryan, William J., at Chicago Peace Conference, 493-494
Buckner, James C., 351-352, 356
Busse, Fred, 428

Caldwell, Chief Billy, 314, 319
Carey, Rev. Archibald, 357, 358, 359
Caruso, Angeline P., 157
Cermak, Anton J., 65, 66, 431, 434, 441; assassinated, 541; campaign for sheriff, 503; mayor, 434ff., 449-450; U.S. Senate campaign, 446; and multi-ethnic coalition, 454-456
Chakonas, Christ, 114, 115
Checagou, 302
Chicago, ethnic population, 462; nativism, 35, 36; public schools, 21, 22; symphony, 471-473
Chicano, *see* Mexican-Americans
Chinese-Americans, assimilation, 540; Chinatown, 537-538; education, 537; immigration, 540; Mandarin and Cantonese, 537ff.
Cicero Housing Riot, 383-386
Clan-na-Gael, 23, 24
Clybourne, Archibald, 311
Combiths, Thomas, 114
Conant and Mack fur traders, 308
Corkery, Daniel, 30
Corr, Frank, acting mayor, 1933, 452
Corrigan, Archbishop Michael, 27
Coughlin, John A. "Bathtub," 28, 423, 429
Cronin, Patrick H., murder of, 24, 25, 40
Crowe, Timothy, 439, 440, 441, 446, 447, 455